MINNESOTA STUDIES IN THE PHILOSOPHY OF SCIENCE

Minnesota Studies in the
PHILOSOPHY OF SCIENCE

VOLUME II
Concepts, Theories, and the Mind-Body Problem

EDITED BY

HERBERT FEIGL, MICHAEL SCRIVEN
AND GROVER MAXWELL

FOR THE MINNESOTA CENTER FOR PHILOSOPHY OF SCIENCE

UNIVERSITY OF MINNESOTA PRESS, MINNEAPOLIS

PRINTED IN THE UNITED STATES OF AMERICA

Fourth printing 1972

Library of Congress Catalog Card Number: 57-12861

ISBN 0-8166-0158-5

PUBLISHED IN GREAT BRITAIN, INDIA, AND PAKISTAN BY THE
OXFORD UNIVERSITY PRESS, LONDON, BOMBAY, AND KARACHI

Preface

This second volume of *Minnesota Studies in the Philosophy of Science* presents further results of the collaborative research of the Minnesota Center for the Philosophy of Science in the area of the philosophical and methodological problems of science in general, psychology in particular. Again, some of the essays concern the broader philosophical foundations while others concentrate on more circumscribed logical or methodological issues.

In the course of the Center's work in recent years it has become increasingly clear that our publications will continue to reflect the sustained efforts of the research staff and some of its collaborators toward an analysis and clarification of a number of difficult and controversial topics. We expect to return to some of these in future volumes. For example, while it is expected that most of the material which will appear in the next volume will grow out of our current research in the philosophy of physics, some of it will undoubtedly still be concerned with the general foundations of science and the philosophy of psychology. Although none of the following essays presuppose knowledge of the contents of any of the others, there are a number of common themes which provide a large measure of integration. Some of these common concerns are suggested in the Synopsis which follows this preface and which also contains brief abstracts of all the papers which appear in the volume.

Despite a certain common basic orientation in logical analysis and the methodology of science among the staff and its collaborators, there remain divergencies which even very extensive and intensive discussion did not remove. But, this is hardly surprising in philosophy. Even in the philosophy of science, individual differences in background, training, and predilections manifest themselves in the finished product, no matter how thoroughly the ideas are thrashed out before their embodi-

Preface

ment in written and printed form. We are confident that this will prove advantageous to the reader who will, after all, have to decide for himself which ideas he finds most valid and fruitful.

As stated in the preface to the first volume, the core staff of the Center during the first three years of operation was drawn from the University of Minnesota's faculty and consisted of Paul E. Meehl (Chairman, Psychology Department), Wilfrid S. Sellars (Chairman, Philosophy Department), Michael Scriven (Philosophy Department; Center Research Associate; currently at Swarthmore College), and Herbert Feigl (Philosophy Department; Director of the Center). Additional research staff members since the summer or autumn of 1956 were H. Gavin Alexander (M.A., Oxford, Lecturer in Philosophy, University of Manchester), Dr. Grover Maxwell, Dr. William R. Rozeboom (Ph.D., Psychology, University of Chicago), and Professor Adolf Grünbaum (Lehigh University; visiting professor at the Center, autumn semester 1956–1957). Three conferences (1954, 1955, and 1956) were held at Princeton University where we profited from the collaboration, later greatly extended by correspondence, with Professors C. G. Hempel, Henry Mehlberg, Hilary Putnam, and Dr. Paul Oppenheim. Some of the results are incorporated in the essays of the present volume. Again, we wish to acknowledge with deep appreciation our indebtedness to the Louis W. and Maud Hill Family Foundation, to the administration of the University of Minnesota, and to its Graduate School, which generously provided a stipend for one of its research assistants, and to the visitors and collaborators named in the preface to the first volume of this series. We have received invaluable assistance from our secretary, Betty Jacobsen; from William H. Capitan, who prepared the index; from Alvin H. Miller, who helped compile some of the bibliographies; and from the staff of the University of Minnesota Press.

Herbert Feigl, *Director*
Michael Scriven, *Research Associate*
Grover Maxwell, *Research Assistant*
MINNESOTA CENTER FOR PHILOSOPHY OF SCIENCE

June 1957

Synopsis

The following brief summaries are to provide a first orientation regarding the issues discussed in the essays contained in the present volume. The first essay deals with the very fundamental and controversial question concerning the possibility of attaining a unified conceptual system and a unity of laws which will be necessary and sufficient for all fields of scientific explanation.

1. *Unity of Science as a Working Hypothesis*: PAUL OPPENHEIM and HILARY PUTNAM. The aim of the paper is to formulate a precise concept of Unity of Science and to determine to what extent that unity can be attained. On the basis of precise definitions of the crucial concepts involved, it is argued in detail that tentative acceptance of a working hypothesis is justified, according to which full empirical Unity of Science can be attained. This justification is given, partly on methodological grounds, partly because there is a large mass of direct and indirect evidence in its favor.

A portion of the third paper presents a view which differs on several points from that of the first in the analysis of reduction of one science to another. This essay and the one preceding it reflect partly divergent views on a number of specific issues which arise in connection with scientific explanation and the concepts which it employs.

2. *The Theoretician's Dilemma*: CARL G. HEMPEL. This essay examines the significance, for scientific theorizing, of terms which purport to refer to non-observable, or "hypothetical" things or events; it discusses ways in which such terms may be interpreted by reference to an observational vocabulary, and it then deals with the question whether, and in what sense, theoretical terms might be altogether avoided in the formulation of effective scientific theories.

3. *Definitions, Explanations, and Theories*: MICHAEL SCRIVEN. In an attempt to deal with such problems as the analysis of laws and disposi-

tions, and the relation of theoretical concepts to the observation language, the author undertakes a rather extensive study of definitions. This approach to the *formulation* of the meaning of terms brings out the limitations there are on any brief summary of meaning such as a definition, and consequently the limitations on the programs of 'reducing' one language to another, for example, that of chemistry to that of physics, that of meaning to that of descriptions of linguistic usage, mental states to behavior, laws to event descriptions, and in general, theory to observations. Some interesting consequences appear for the usual analyses of scientific explanations, theories, and concepts, and also for analyses of names, rules, analyticity, and stipulative definitions.

The next three essays examine in detail some of the topics discussed in the preceding ones. It is interesting to note the important points of agreement and disagreement. For example, although there is some divergence on the analysis of generalizations and scientific laws, most of the writers agree that any purely extensional analysis of disposition terms is inadequate.

4. *Disposition Concepts and Extensional Logic:* ARTHUR PAP. The major attempts to analyze disposition concepts and counterfactual conditionals within the framework of extensional logic are critically examined. By an "extensional logic" is meant a logic that treats all compound statements as truth-functional, in particular implications as so-called material implications. Analytical philosophers and logicians who have approached the problem more or less within this framework include Bergmann, Hempel and Oppenheim, Carnap (reduction sentences), Kaila, Storer, Popper, and Braithwaite. But all such analyses are found inadequate for one reason or another. Instead it is proposed that the analysis of disposition concepts be built upon a primitive and nonextensional concept of "natural" implication (corresponding to A. W. Burks' "causal implication" and Reichenbach's "(synthetic) nomological implication"). With the help of this primitive concept an apparently adequate schema of explicit definition of disposition concepts is constructed. It is emphasized, however, that the abandonment of extensional logic as a tool of analysis of causal language does not involve a breach with any essential tenet of empiricism, such as the Humean theory of the logical contingency of laws of nature.

5. *Counterfactuals, Dispositions, and the Causal Modalities:* WILFRID SELLARS. This paper consists of an introductory section describing the

over-all structure of the argument, and four parts: I. Counterfactuals, II. Thing-Kinds and Causal Properties, III. Causal Connection: The Dialectic of the Controversy, and IV. Toward a Theory of the Causal Modalities. Readers primarily interested in logical problems relating to scientific inference and in the controversy between the 'regularity' and 'entailment' analyses of lawlike statements should note that the discussion of these topics in Parts III and IV does not presuppose familiarity with the arguments of the first two parts. Again, the discussion of thing-kinds and causal properties in Part II is reasonably independent of the analysis and resolution of Goodman's puzzle about counterfactuals, which is the burden of Part I.

6. *General Statements as Rules of Inference?*: H. GAVIN ALEXANDER. The view that general statements should be regarded as rules of inference or inference licenses has been supported in four ways. (1) We often infer directly from particular to particular with no major premise (Ryle). (2) The basis of induction must be a principle of inference rather than a statement of the uniformity of nature (Black, Braithwaite). (3) Laws in science are inference licenses not statements (Toulmin). (4) Counterfactual conditionals can only be derived from general truths which are expressed in the form of material rules of inference (Sellars). These four lines of argument are each examined carefully, and it is shown that none of them is at all conclusive.

The remaining papers are more directly relevant to the philosophy of psychology, specifically to the mind-body problem. The importance of the phenomenal field, emphasized in the Zener paper, is a theme which reappears in the detailed analysis of the traditional mind-body problem contained in the essay by Feigl.

7. *Persons*: P. F. STRAWSON. The author argues that certain traditional philosophical problems ('the unity of the self,' 'knowledge of other minds,' 'union of mind and body') are interdependent and can be finally resolved only by full recognition of the logical primacy of the concept of a person. This involves a complete repudiation both of the Cartesian tradition and its 'empiricist' variants. The argument pivots on the logical notions of individual and predicate, and on the requirement that individuals should be distinguishable and identifiable.

8. *The Significance of Experience of the Individual for the Science of Psychology*: KARL ZENER. This paper consists of a critique of current behavioristic methodology from the point of view of Gestalt theory

and of suggestions for changes in outlook and emphasis in the general methodology of psychology. It is argued that conscious experiences—direct awareness in the phenomenal field, including more rarely occurring experiences—are themselves (as opposed to mere verbal reports about them) not only legitimate as data but are of crucial importance for the science of psychology. It is contended that a too narrowly conceived principle of intersubjective testability has narrowed the range of experience accessible to scientific treatment, and a more liberal criterion is proposed and developed. Such changes "would involve clearer recognition of the peculiar necessity for the full development of psychology as a *science* that a sufficient number of its scientific observers and experimenters themselves be highly developed in those characteristics which may be thought of as most essentially and significantly 'human.'"

9. *The "Mental" and the "Physical"*: HERBERT FEIGL. The subject matter and the methods of psychology can be successfully clarified only through a comprehensive logical analysis of the relations of the mental and the physical. This problem, perhaps because of its extreme complexity and its central place in the disputes between various "Weltanschauungen" is nowadays frequently ignored (or repressed?) by psychologists and even by many philosophers. It is contended that the philosophies of phenomenalism, neutral monism, as well as behaviorism (American or recent British) cannot do justice to the problem because of their (respective) reductionistic tendencies. Nevertheless, there is the possibility and plausibility of a monistic view based on a realistic, logical-empiricist analysis of the factual problems and the logical perplexities of the mind-body puzzle. Through such an analysis, utilizing some basic principles of logical syntax, semantics, and pragmatics, an identity or double-language view of the relation of the mental and the physical (anticipated in various metaphysical and epistemological versions by A. Riehl, M. Schlick, B. Russell and some American critical realists) can be more securely established. This requires, however, several fairly radical revisions of the traditional conceptions of acquaintance, description, subjectivity, objectivity, spatiality, qualitative and quantitative knowledge, teleology, and reference (intentionality). By allocating the various difficulties to their proper domains and by resolving them through logical analysis, the plausibility of dualistic doctrines (old and new) is greatly diminished. In the light of these clarifications a more

Synopsis

adequate understanding of the various approaches in current psychological theory can be achieved.

The last article and the appendix, by treating themes which appeared in Volume I, exemplify an important feature of this series—the opportunity for sustained research and for the continuation of fruitful controversy on specific problems. Meehl's article supplements his own paper "Problems in the Actuarial Characterization of a Person" and some of the other papers of Volume I which were concerned with methodological issues of psychology and psychoanalysis. The Appendix contributed by Sellars and Chisholm concentrates on the problem of intentionality, which is an important part of the mind-problem, and thus connects with a corresponding section in Feigl's essay.

10. *When Shall We Use Our Heads Instead of the Formula?*: P. E. MEEHL.. In making his decision about an individual case the clinician may possess special information which, combined with psychological theory and plausible, "accepted" (but unverified) empirical generalizations, would lead to a prediction differing from that yielded by a tested statistical function which provides no place for insertion of the special information. It is argued that some circumstances justify a counter-actuarial prediction. However, the present primitive state of theoretical knowledge in psychology does not justify "countermanding the formula" except in extremely clearcut cases.

Appendix: *Intentionality and the Mental*: RODERICK M. CHISHOLM and WILFRID SELLARS. The core of the Appendix is an exchange of correspondence between Wilfrid Sellars and Professor Roderick Chisholm of Brown University concerning the account of the logical character of statements about mental episodes and dispositions (thoughts, beliefs, desires, attitudes, etc.), which was sketched by the former in his essay, "Empiricism and the Philosophy of Mind," printed in Volume I of this series. The correspondence is preceded by an introduction defining the problem in general terms, and by a reprinting, with additions and omissions, of Professor Chisholm's recent paper, "Sentences about Believing," in *Proceedings of the Aristotelian Society*, 56:125–148 (1955–1956).

Contents

Contents

Contents

MINNESOTA STUDIES IN THE PHILOSOPHY OF SCIENCE

Unity of Science as a Working Hypothesis

1. Introduction

1.1. The expression "Unity of Science" is often encountered, but its precise content is difficult to specify in a satisfactory manner. It is the aim of this paper to formulate a precise concept of Unity of Science; and to examine to what extent that unity can be attained.

A concern with Unity of Science hardly needs justification. We are guided especially by the conviction that Science of Science, i.e., the meta-scientific study of major aspects of science, is the natural means for counterbalancing specialization by promoting the integration of scientific knowledge. The desirability of this goal is widely recognized; for example, many universities have programs with this end in view; but it is often pursued by means different from the one just mentioned, and the conception of the Unity of Science might be especially suited as an organizing principle for an enterprise of this kind.

1.2. As a preliminary, we will distinguish, in order of increasing strength, three broad concepts of Unity of Science:

First, Unity of Science in the weakest sense is attained to the extent to which all the terms of science [1] are reduced to the terms of some one discipline (e.g., physics, or psychology). This concept of Unity of Language (12) may be replaced by a number of sub-concepts depending on the manner in which one specifies the notion of "reduction" involved. Certain authors, for example, construe reduction as the definition of the terms of science by means of those in the selected basic discipline (reduction by means of biconditionals (47)); and some of these require the definitions in question to be analytic, or "true in virtue of the meanings of the terms involved" (epistemological reduction);

AUTHORS' NOTE: We wish to express our thanks to C. G. Hempel for constructive criticism. The responsibility for any shortcomings is, however, exclusively ours.

others impose no such restriction upon the biconditionals effecting reduction. The notion of reduction we shall employ is a wider one, and is designed to include reduction by means of biconditionals as a special case.

Second, Unity of Science in a stronger sense (because it implies Unity of Language, whereas the reverse is not the case) is represented by *Unity of Laws* (12). It is attained to the extent to which the laws of science become reduced to the laws of some one discipline. If the ideal of such an all-comprehensive explanatory system were realized, one could call it *Unitary Science* (18, 19, 20, 80). The exact meaning of 'Unity of Laws' depends, again, on the concept of "reduction" employed.

Third, Unity of Science in the strongest sense is realized if the laws of science are not only reduced to the laws of some one discipline, but the laws of that discipline are in some intuitive sense "unified" or "connected." It is difficult to see how this last requirement can be made precise; and it will not be imposed here. Nevertheless, trivial realizations of "Unity of Science" will be excluded, for example, the simple conjunction of several branches of science does not reduce the particular branches in the sense we shall specify.

1.3. In the present paper, the term 'Unity of Science' will be used in two senses, to refer, first, to an ideal *state* of science, and, second, to a pervasive *trend* within science, seeking the attainment of that ideal.

In the first sense, 'Unity of Science' means the state of unitary science. It involves the two constituents mentioned above: unity of vocabulary, or "Unity of Language"; and unity of explanatory principles, or "Unity of Laws." That Unity of Science, in this sense, can be fully realized constitutes an over-arching meta-scientific hypothesis which enables one to see a unity in scientific activities that might otherwise appear disconnected or unrelated, and which encourages the construction of a unified body of knowledge.

In the second sense, Unity of Science exists as a trend within scientific inquiry, whether or not unitary science is ever attained, and notwithstanding the simultaneous existence, (and, of course, legitimacy) of other, even *incompatible*, trends.

1.4. The expression 'Unity of Science' is employed in various other senses, of which two will be briefly mentioned in order to distinguish them from the sense with which we are concerned. In the first place, what is sometimes referred to is something that we may call the *Unity of Method* in science. This might be represented by the thesis that all the empirical sciences employ the same standards of explanation, of significance, of evidence, etc.

In the second place, a radical reductionist thesis (of an alleged "logical," not an empirical kind) is sometimes referred to as the thesis of the Unity of Science. Sometimes the "reduction" asserted is the definability of all the terms of science in terms of *sensationalistic predicates* (10); sometimes the notion of "reduction" is wider (11) and predicates referring to *observable qualities of physical things* are taken as basic (12). These theses are epistemological ones, and ones which today appear doubtful. The epistemological uses of the terms 'reduction', 'physicalism', 'Unity of Science', etc., should be carefully distinguished from the use of these terms in the present paper.

2. Unity of Science and Micro-Reduction

2.1. In this paper we shall employ a concept of reduction introduced by Kemeny and Oppenheim in their paper on the subject (47), to which the reader is referred for a more detailed exposition. The principal requirements may be summarized as follows: given two theories T_1 and T_2, T_2 is said to be *reduced* to T_1 if and only if:

(1) The vocabulary of T_2 contains terms not in the vocabulary of T_1.

(2) Any observational data explainable by T_2 are explainable by T_1.

(3) T_1 is at least as well systematized as T_2. (T_1 is normally more complicated than T_2; but this is allowable, because the reducing theory normally explains more than the reduced theory. However, the "ratio," so to speak, of simplicity to explanatory power should be at least as great in the case of the reducing theory as in the case of the reduced theory.) [2]

Kemeny and Oppenheim also define the reduction of a branch of science B_2 by another branch B_1 (e.g., the reduction of chemistry to physics). Their procedure is as follows: take the accepted theories of B_2 at a given time t as T_2. Then B_2 is reduced to B_1 at time t if and only if there is some theory T_1 in B_1 at t such that T_1 reduces T_2 (47). Analogously, if *some* of the theories of B_2 are reduced by some T_1 belonging to branch B_1 at t, we shall speak of a *partial reduction* of B_2 to B_1 at t. This approach presupposes (1) the familiar assumption that some division of the total vocabulary of both branches into theoretical

5

and observational terms is given, and (2) that the two branches have the same observational vocabulary.

2.2. The essential feature of a micro-reduction is that the branch B_1 deals with the parts of the objects dealt with by B_2. We must suppose that corresponding to each branch we have a specific universe of discourse U_{Bi}; [3] and that we have a part-whole relation, Pt (75; 76, especially p. 91). Under the following conditions we shall say that the reduction of B_2 to B_1 [4] is a micro-reduction: B_2 is reduced to B_1; and the objects in the universe of discourse of B_2 are wholes which possess a decomposition (75; 76, especially p. 91) into proper parts all of which belong to the universe of discourse of B_1. For example, let us suppose B_2 is a branch of science which has multicellular living things as its universe of discourse. Let B_1 be a branch with cells as its universe of discourse. Then the things in the universe of discourse of B_2 can be decomposed into proper parts belonging to the universe of discourse of B_1. If, in addition, it is the case that B_1 reduces B_2 at the time t, we shall say that B_1 micro-reduces B_2 at time t.

We shall also say that a branch B_1 is a potential micro-reducer of a branch B_2 if the objects in the universe of discourse of B_2 are wholes which possess a decomposition into proper parts all of which belong to the universe of discourse of B_1. The definition is the same as the definition of 'micro-reduces' except for the omission of the clause 'B_2 is reduced to B_1.'

Any micro-reduction constitutes a step in the direction of Unity of Language in science. For, if B_1 reduces B_2, it explains everything that B_2 does (and normally, more besides). Then, even if we cannot define in B_1 analogues for some of the theoretical terms of B_2, we can use B_1 in place of B_2. Thus any reduction, in the sense explained, permits a "reduction" of the total vocabulary of science by making it possible to dispense with some terms.[5] Not every reduction moves in the direction of Unity of Science; for instance reductions within a branch lead to a simplification of the vocabulary of science, but they do not necessarily lead in the direction of Unity of Science as we have characterized it (although they may at times fit into that trend). However, micro-reductions, and even partial micro-reductions, insofar as they permit us to replace some of the terms of one branch of science by terms of another, do move in this direction.

Likewise, the micro-reduction of B_2 to B_1 moves in the direction of

Unity of Laws; for it "reduces" the total number of scientific laws by making it possible, in principle, to dispense with the laws of B_2 and explain the relevant observations by using B_1.

The relations 'micro-reduces' and 'potential micro-reducer' have very simple properties: (1) they are transitive (this follows from the transitivity of the relations 'reduces' and 'Pt'); (2) they are irreflexive (no branch can micro-reduce itself); (3) they are asymmetric (if B_1 microreduces B_2, B_2 never micro-reduces B_1). The two latter properties are not purely formal; however, they require for their derivation only the (certainly true) empirical assumption that there does not exist an infinite descending chain of proper parts, i.e., a series of things $x_1, x_2, x_3 \ldots$ such that x_2 is a proper part of x_1, x_3 is a proper part of x_2, etc.

The just-mentioned formal property of the relation 'micro-reduces'—its transitivity—is of great importance for the program of Unity of Science. It means that micro-reductions have a cumulative character. That is, if a branch B_3 is micro-reduced to B_2, and B_2 is in turn microreduced to B_1, then B_3 is automatically micro-reduced to B_1. This simple fact is sometimes overlooked in objections [6] to the theoretical possibility of attaining unitary science by means of micro-reduction. Thus it has been contended that one manifestly cannot explain human behavior by reference to the laws of atomic physics. It would indeed be fantastic to suppose that the simplest regularity in the field of psychology could be explained directly—i.e., "skipping" intervening branches of science—by employing subatomic theories. But one may believe in the attainability of unitary science without thereby committing oneself to this absurdity. It is not absurd to suppose that psychological laws may eventually be explained in terms of the behavior of individual neurons in the brain; that the behavior of individual cells—including neurons—may eventually be explained in terms of their biochemical constitution; and that the behavior of molecules—including the macro-molecules that make up living cells—may eventually be explained in terms of atomic physics. If this is achieved, then psychological laws will have, in principle, been reduced to laws of atomic physics, although it would nevertheless be hopelessly impractical to try to derive the behavior of a single human being directly from his constitution in terms of elementary particles.

2.3. Unitary science certainly does not exist today. But will it ever be attained? It is useful to divide this question into two subquestions:

(1) If unitary science can be attained at all, how can it be attained? (2) Can it be attained at all?

First of all, there are various abstractly possible ways in which unitary science might be attained. However, it seems very doubtful, to say the least, that a branch B_2 could be reduced to a branch B_1, if the things in the universe of discourse of B_2 are not themselves in the universe of discourse of B_1 and also do not possess a decomposition into parts in the universe of discourse of B_1. ("They don't speak about the same things.")

It does not follow that B_1 must be a potential micro-reducer of B_2, i.e., that all reductions are micro-reductions.

There are many cases in which the reducing theory and the reduced theory belong to the same branch, or to branches with the same universe of discourse. When we come, however, to branches with different universes—say, physics and psychology—it seems clear that the possibility of reduction depends on the existence of a structural connection between the universes via the 'Pt' relation. Thus one cannot plausibly suppose—for the present at least—that the behavior of inorganic matter is explainable by reference to psychological laws; for inorganic materials do not consist of living parts. One supposes that psychology may be reducible to physics, but not that physics may be reducible to psychology!

Thus, the only method of attaining unitary science that appears to be seriously available at present is micro-reduction.

To turn now to our second question, can unitary science be attained? We certainly do not wish to maintain that it has been established that this is the case. But it does not follow, as some philosophers seem to think, that a tentative acceptance of the hypothesis that unitary science can be attained is therefore a mere "act of faith." We believe that this hypothesis is credible;[7] and we shall attempt to support this in the latter part of this paper, by providing empirical, methodological, and pragmatic reasons in its support. We therefore think the assumption that unitary science can be attained through cumulative micro-reduction recommends itself as a working hypothesis.[8] That is, we believe that it is in accord with the standards of reasonable scientific judgment to tentatively accept this hypothesis and to work on the assumption that further progress can be made in this direction, without claiming that its truth has been established, or denying that success may finally elude us.

8

3. Reductive Levels

3.1. As a basis for our further discussion, we wish to consider now the possibility of ordering branches in such a way as to indicate the major potential micro-reductions standing between the present situation and the state of unitary science. The most natural way to do this is by their universes of discourse. We offer, therefore, a system of *reductive levels* so chosen that a branch with the things of a given level as its universe of discourse will always be a potential micro-reducer of any branch with things of the next higher level (if there is one) as its universe of discourse.

Certain conditions of adequacy follow immediately from our aim. Thus:

(1) There must be several levels.

(2) The number of levels must be finite.

(3) There must be a unique lowest level (i.e., a unique "beginner" under the relation 'potential micro-reducer'); this means that success at transforming all the *potential* micro-reductions connecting these branches into *actual* micro-reductions must, *ipso facto*, mean reduction to a single branch.

(4) Any thing of any level except the lowest must possess a decomposition into things belonging to the next lower level. In this sense each level, will be as it were a "common denominator" for the level immediately above it.

(5) Nothing on any level should have a part on any higher level.

(6) The levels must be selected in a way which is "natural" [9] and justifiable from the standpoint of present-day empirical science. In particular, the step from any one of our reductive levels to the next lower level must correspond to what is, scientifically speaking, a crucial step in the trend toward over-all physicalistic reduction.

The accompanying list gives the levels we shall employ; [10] the reader may verify that the six conditions we have listed are all satisfied.

6	Social groups
5	(Multicellular) living things
4	Cells
3	Molecules
2	Atoms
1	Elementary particles

Any whole which possesses a decomposition into parts all of which

Paul Oppenheim and Hilary Putnam

are on a given level, will be counted as also belonging to that level. Thus each level includes all higher levels. However, the highest level to which a thing belongs will be considered the "proper" level of that thing.

This inclusion relation among our levels reflects the fact that scientific laws which apply to the things of a given level and to all combinations of those things also apply to all things of higher level. Thus a physicist, when he speaks about "all physical objects," is also speaking about living things—but not qua living things.

We maintain that each of our levels is *necessary* in the sense that it would be utopian to suppose that one might reduce all of the major theories or a whole branch concerned with any one of our six levels to a theory concerned with a lower level, *skipping* entirely the *immediately* lower level; and we maintain that our levels are *sufficient* in the sense that it would *not* be utopian to suppose that a major theory on any one of our levels *might* be directly reduced to the next lower level. (Although this is *not* to deny that it may be convenient, in special cases, to introduce intervening steps.)

However, this contention is significant only if we suppose some set of *predicates* to be associated with each of these levels. Otherwise, as has been pointed out,[11] *trivial* micro-reductions would be possible; e.g., we might introduce the property "Tran" (namely, the property of being an atom of a transparent substance) and then "explain the transparency of water in terms of properties on the atomic level," namely, by the hypothesis that all atoms of water have the property Tran. More explicitly, the explanation would consist of the statements

   (a) $(x)(x$ is transparent $\equiv (y)(y$ is an atom of $x \supset Tran(y))$
   (b) $(x)(x$ is water $\supset (y)(y$ is an atom of $x \supset Tran(y))$

To exclude such trivial "micro-reductions," we shall suppose that with each level there is associated a list of the theoretical predicates normally employed to characterize things on that level at present (e.g., with level 1, there would be associated the predicates used to specify spatio-temporal coordinates, mass-energy, and electric charge). And when we speak of a theory concerning a given level, we will mean not only a theory whose universe of discourse is that level, but one whose predicates belong to the appropriate list. Unless the hypothesis that theories concerning level $n + 1$ can be reduced by a theory concerning level n is restricted in this way, it lacks any clear empirical significance.

10

3.2. If the "part-whole" ('Pt') relation is understood in the wide sense, that x Pt y holds if x is spatially or temporally contained in y, then everything, continuous or discontinuous, belongs to one or another reductive level; in particular to level 1 (at least), since it is a whole consisting of elementary particles. However, one may wish to understand 'whole' in a narrower sense (as "structured organization of elements" [12]). Such a specialization involves two essential steps: (1) the construction of a calculus with such a narrower notion as its primitive concept, and (2) the definition of a particular 'Pt' relation satisfying the axioms of the calculus.

Then the problem will arise that some things do not belong to any level. Hence a theory dealing with such things might not be micro-reduced even if all the micro-reductions indicated by our system of levels were accomplished; and for this reason, unitary science might not be attained.

For a trivial example, "a man in a phone booth" is an aggregate of things on different levels which we would not regard as a whole in such a narrower sense. Thus, such an "object" does not belong to any reductive level; although the "phone booth" belongs to level 3 and the man belongs to level 5.

The problem posed by such aggregates is not serious, however. We may safely make the assumption that the behavior of "man in phone booths" (to be carefully distinguished from "men in phone booths") could be completely explained given (a) a complete physicochemical theory (i.e., a theory of levels up to 3, including "phone booths"), and (b) a complete individual psychology (or more generally, a theory of levels up to 5). With this assumption in force, we are able to say: If we can construct a theory that explains the behavior of all the objects in our system of levels, then it will also handle the aggregates of such objects.

4. The Credibility of Our Working Hypothesis

4.1. John Stuart Mill asserts (55, Book VI, Chapter 7) that since (in our wording) human social groups are wholes whose parts are individual persons, the "laws of the phenomena of society" are "derived from and may be resolved into the laws of the nature of individual man." In our terminology, this is to suggest that it is a logical truth that theories concerning social groups (level 6) can be micro-reduced by theories concerning individual living things (level 5); and, *mutatis mutandis*, it would have to be a logical truth that theories concerning any other level can be micro-reduced by theories concerning the next lower level. As a consequence, what we have called the "working hypothesis" that unitary science can be attained would likewise be a logical truth.

Mill's contention is, however, not so much wrong as it is vague. What is one to count as "the nature of individual man"? As pointed out above (section 3.1) the question whether theories concerning a given reductive level can be reduced by a theory concerning the next lower level has empirical content only if the theoretical vocabularies are specified; that is, only if one associates with each level, as we have supposed to be done, a particular set of theoretical concepts. Given, e.g., a sociological theory T_2, the question whether there exists a true psychological theory T_1 *in a particular vocabulary* which reduces T_2 is an empirical question. Thus our "working hypothesis" is one that can only be justified on empirical grounds.

Among the factors on which the degree of credibility of any empirical hypothesis depends are (45, p. 307) the *simplicity* of the hypothesis, the *variety* of the evidence, its *reliability*, and, last but not least, the *factual support* afforded by the evidence. We proceed to discuss each of these factors.

4.2. As for the *simplicity* [13] of the hypothesis that unitary science can be attained, it suffices to consider the traditional alternatives mentioned by those who oppose it. "Hypotheses" such as Psychism and Neo-Vitalism assert that the various objects studied by contemporary science have special parts or attributes, unknown to present-day science, in addition to those indicated in our system of reductive levels. For example, men are said to have not only cells as parts; there is also an immaterial "psyche"; living things are animated by "entelechies" or "vital forces"; social groups are moved by "group minds." But, in none of these cases are we provided *at present* with postulates or coordinating definitions which would permit the derivation of testable predictions. Hence, the claims made for the hypothetical entities just mentioned lack any clear scientific meaning; and as a consequence, the question of supporting evidence cannot even be raised.

On the other hand, if the effort at micro-reduction should seem to fail, we cannot preclude the introduction of theories postulating presently unknown relevant parts or presently unknown relevant attributes

12

for some or all of the objects studied by science. Such theories are perfectly admissible, provided they have genuine explanatory value. For example, Dalton's chemical theory of molecules might not be reducible to the best available theory of atoms at a given time if the latter theory ignores the existence of the electrical properties of atoms. Thus the hypothesis of micro-reducibility,[14] as the meaning is specified at a particular time, may be false because of the insufficiency of the theoretical apparatus of the reducing branch.

Of course, a new working hypothesis of micro-reducibility, obtained by enlarging the list of attributes associated with the lowest level, might then be correct. However, if there are presently unknown attributes of a more radical kind (e.g., attributes which are relevant for explaining the behavior of living, but not of non-living things), then no such simple "repair" would seem possible. In this sense, Unity of Science is an alternative to the view that it will eventually be necessary to *bifurcate* the conceptual system of science, by the postulation of new entities or new attributes unrelated to those needed for the study of inanimate phenomena.

4.3. The requirement that there be *variety* of evidence assumes a simple form in our present case. If all the past successes referred to a single pair of levels, then this would be poor evidence indeed that theories concerning each level can be reduced by theories concerning a lower level. For example, if all the past successes were on the atomic level, we should hardly regard as justified the inference that laws concerning social groups can be explained by reference to the "individual psychology" of the members of those groups. Thus, the first requirement is that one should be able to provide examples of successful micro-reductions between several pairs of levels, preferably between all pairs.

Second, within a given level what is required is, preferably, examples of different kinds, rather than a repetition of essentially the same example many times. In short, one wants good evidence that *all* the phenomena of the given level can be micro-reduced.

We shall present below a survey of the past successes in each level. This survey is, of course, only a sketch; the successful micro-reductions and projected micro-reductions in biochemistry alone would fill a large book. But even from this sketch it will be apparent, we believe, how great the variety of these successful micro-reductions is in both the respects discussed.

13

4.4. Moreover, we shall, of course, present only evidence from authorities regarded as *reliable* in the particular area from which the theory or experiment involved is drawn.

4.5. The important factor *factual support* is discussed only briefly now, because we shall devote to it many of the following pages and would otherwise interrupt our presentation.

The first question raised in connection with any hypothesis is, of course, what *factual support* it possesses; that is, what confirmatory or disconfirmatory evidence is available. The evidence supporting a hypothesis is conveniently subdivided into that providing *direct* and that providing *indirect* factual support. By the direct factual support for a hypothesis we mean, roughly,[15] the proportion of confirmatory as opposed to disconfirmatory instances. By the indirect factual support, we mean the inductive support obtained from other well-confirmed hypotheses that lend credibility to the given hypothesis. While intuitively adequate quantitative measures of direct factual support have been worked out by Kemeny and Oppenheim,[16] no such measures exist for indirect factual support. The present paper will rely only on intuitive judgments of these magnitudes, and will not assume that quantitative explicata will be worked out.

As our hypothesis is that theories of each reductive level can be micro-reduced by theories of the next lower level, a "confirming instance" is simply any successful micro-reduction between any two of our levels. The *direct* factual support for our hypothesis is thus provided by the *past successes* at reducing laws about the things on each level by means of laws referring to the parts on lower (usually, the next lower) levels. In the sequel, we shall survey the past successes with respect to each pair of levels.

As *indirect* factual support, we shall cite evidence supporting the hypothesis that each reductive level is, in evolution and ontogenesis (in a wide sense presently to be specified) prior to the one above it. The hypothesis of *evolution* means here that (for $n = 1 \ldots 5$) there was a time when there were things of level n, but no things of any higher level. This hypothesis is highly speculative on levels 1 and 2; fortunately the micro-reducibility of the molecular to the atomic level and of the atomic level to the elementary particle level is relatively well established on other grounds.

Similarly, the hypothesis of ontogenesis is that, in certain cases, for

14

any particular object on level n, there was a time when it did not exist, but when some of its parts on the next lower level existed; and that it developed or was causally produced out of these parts.[17]

The reason for our regarding evolution and ontogenesis as providing indirect factual support for the Unity of Science hypothesis may be formulated as follows:

Let us, as is customary in science, assume causal determination as a guiding principle; i.e., let us assume that things that appear later in time can be accounted for in terms of things and processes at earlier times. Then, if we find that there was a time when a certain whole did not exist, and that things on a lower level came together to form that whole, it is very natural to suppose that the characteristics of the whole can be causally explained by reference to these earlier events and parts; and that the theory of these characteristics can be micro-reduced by a theory involving only characteristics of the parts.

For the same reason, we may cite as further indirect factual support for the hypothesis of empirical Unity of Science the various successes at synthesizing things of each level out of things on the next lower level. Synthesis strongly increases the evidence that the characteristics of the whole in question are causally determined by the characteristics, including spatio-temporal arrangement, of its parts by showing that the object is produced, under controlled laboratory conditions, whenever parts with those characteristics are arranged in that way.

The consideration just outlined seems to us to constitute an argument against the view that, as objects of a given level combine to form wholes belonging to a higher level, there appear certain new phenomena which are "emergent" (35, p. 151; 76, p. 93) in the sense of being forever irreducible to laws governing the phenomena on the level of the parts. What our argument opposes is not, of course, the obviously true statement that there are many phenomena which are not reducible by currently available theories pertaining to lower levels; our working hypothesis rejects merely the claim of absolute irreducibility, unless such a claim is supported by a theory which has a sufficiently high degree of credibility; thus far we are not aware of any such theory. It is not sufficient, for example, simply to advance the claim that certain phenomena considered to be specifically human, such as the use of verbal language, in an abstract and generalized way, can never be explained on the basis of neurophysiological theories, or to make the claim that this conceptual

15

capacity distinguishes man in principle and not only in degree from non-human animals.

4.6. Let us mention in passing certain pragmatic and methodological points of view which speak in favor of our working hypothesis:

(1) It is of practical value, because it provides a good synopsis of scientific activity and of the relations among the several scientific disciplines.

(2) It is, as has often been remarked, fruitful in the sense of stimulating many different kinds of scientific research. By way of contrast, belief in the irreducibility of various phenomena has yet to yield a single accepted scientific theory.

(3) It corresponds methodologically to what might be called the "Democritean tendency" in science; that is, the pervasive methodological tendency [18] to try, insofar as is possible, to explain apparently dissimilar phenomena in terms of qualitatively identical parts and their spatio-temporal relations.

5. Past Successes at Each Level

5.1. By comparison with what we shall find on lower levels, the micro-reduction of level 6 to lower ones has not yet advanced very far, especially in regard to human societies. This may have at least two reasons: First of all, the body of well established theoretical knowledge on level 6 is still rather rudimentary, so that there is not much to be micro-reduced. Second, while various precise theories concerning certain special types of phenomena on level 5 have been developed, it seems as if a good deal of further theoretical knowledge concerning other areas on the same level will be needed before reductive success on a larger scale can be expected.[19] However, in the case of certain very primitive groups of organisms, astonishing successes have been achieved. For instance, the differentiation into social castes among certain kinds of insects has been tentatively explained in terms of the secretion of so-called social hormones (3).

Many writers [20] believe that there are some laws common to all forms of animal association, including that of humans. Of greater potential relevance to such laws are experiments dealing with "pecking order" among domestic fowl (29). In particular, experiments showing that the social structure can be influenced by the amount of male hormone in individual birds suggest possible parallels farther up the evolutionary scale.

With respect to the problems of human social organization, as will be seen presently, two things are striking: (1) the most developed body of theory is undoubtedly in the field of *economics*, and this is at present entirely micro-reductionistic in character; (2) the main approaches to *social* theory are *all* likewise of this character. (The technical term 'micro-reduction' is not, of course, employed by writers in these fields. However, many writers have discussed "the Principle of Methodological Individualism"; [21] and this is nothing more than the special form our working hypothesis takes in application to human social groups.)

In economics, if very weak assumptions are satisfied, it is possible to represent the way in which an individual orders his choices by means of an individual preference function. In terms of these functions, the economist attempts to explain group phenomena, such as the market, to account for collective consumer behavior, to solve the problems of welfare economics, etc. As theories for which a micro-reductionistic derivation is accepted in economics we could cite all the standard macro-theories; e.g., the theories of the business cycle, theories of currency fluctuation (Gresham's law to the effect that bad money drives out good is a familiar example), the principle of marginal utility, the law of demand, laws connecting change in interest rate with changes in inventory, plans, equipment, etc. The relevant point is while the economist is no longer dependent on the oversimplified assumption of "economic man," the explanation of economic phenomena is still in terms of the preferences, choices, and actions available to *individuals*.

In the realm of *sociology*, one can hardly speak of any major theory as "accepted." But it is of interest to survey some of the major theoretical approaches from the standpoint of micro-reduction.

On the one hand, there is the *economic determinism* represented by Marx and Veblen. In the case of Marx the assumptions of classical economics are openly made: Individuals are supposed—at least on the average, and in the long run—to act in accordance with their material interests. From this assumption, together with a theory of the business cycle which, for all its undoubted originality, Marx based on the classical laws of the market, Marx derives his major laws and predictions. Thus Marxist sociology is micro-reductionistic in the same sense as classical economics, and shares the same basic weakness (the assumption of "economic man").

Veblen, although stressing class interests and class divisions as did

17

Marx, introduces some non-economic factors in his sociology. His account is ultimately in terms of individual psychology; his hypothesis of "conspicuous consumption" is a brilliant—and characteristic—example.

Max Weber produced a sociology strongly antithetical to Marx's. Yet each of his explanations of group phenomena is ultimately in terms of individual psychology; e.g., in his discussion of political parties, he argues that people enjoy working under a "charismatic" leader, etc.

Indeed the psychological (and hence micro-reductionistic) character of the major sociologies (including those of Mannheim, Simmel, etc., as well as the ones mentioned above (54, 86, 94, 103)) is often recognized. Thus one may safely say, that while there is no one accepted sociological theory, all of these theoretical approaches represent attempted micro-reductions.

5.2. Since Schleiden and Schwann (1838/9), it is known that all living things consist of cells. Consequently, explaining the laws valid on level 5 by those on the cell level means micro-reducing all phenomena of plants and animals to level 4.

As instances of past successes in connection with level 5 we have chosen to cite, in preference to other types of example, micro-reductions and projected micro-reductions dealing with central nervous systems as wholes and nerve cells as parts. Our selection of these examples has not been determined by anthropocentrism. First of all, substantially similar problems arise in the case of multicellular animals, as nearly all of them possess a nervous system; and, second, the question of micro-reducing those aspects of behavior that are controlled by the central nervous system in man and the higher animals is easily the most significative (85, p. 1) one at this level, and therefore most worth discussing.

Very great activity is, in fact, apparent in the direction of micro-reducing the phenomena of the central nervous system. Much of this activity is very recent; and most of it falls under two main headings: neurology, and the logical design of nerve nets. (Once again, the technical term 'micro-reduction' is not actually employed by workers in these fields. Instead, one finds widespread and lasting discussion concerning the advantages of "molecular" versus "molar" [22] explanations, and concerning "reductionism." [23])

Theories constructed by neurologists are the product of highly detailed experimental work in neuroanatomy, neurochemistry, and neurophysiology, including the study of electric activity of the nervous system, e.g., electroencephalography.[24]

As a result of these efforts, it has proved possible to advance more or less hypothetical explanations on the cellular level for such phenomena as association, memory, motivation, emotional disturbance, and some of the phenomena connected with learning, intelligence, and perception. For example, a theory of the brain has been advanced by Hebb (32) which accounts for all of the above-mentioned phenomena. A classical psychological law, the Weber-Fechner law (insofar as it seems to apply), has likewise been micro-reduced, as a result of the work of Hoagland (36).

We turn now to the *logical design* of nerve nets: The logician Turing [25] proposed (and solved) the problem of giving a characterization of *computing machines* in the widest sense—mechanisms for solving problems by effective series of logical operations. This naturally suggests the idea of seeing whether a "Turing machine" could consist of the elements used in neurological theories of the brain; that is, whether it could consist of a network of neurons. Such a nerve network could then serve as a hypothetical model for the brain.

Such a network was first constructed by McCulloch and Pitts.[26] The basic element is the neuron, which, at any instant, is either *firing* or *not firing* (quiescent). On account of the "all or none" character of the activity of this basic element, the nerve net designed by McCulloch and Pitts constitutes, as it were, a digital computer. The various relations of propositional logic can be represented by instituting suitable connections between neurons; and in this way the hypothetical net can be "programmed" to solve any problem that will yield to a predetermined sequence of logical or mathematical operations. McCulloch and Pitts employ approximately 10^4 elements in their net; in this respect they are well below the upper limit set by neurological investigation, since the number of neurons in the brain is estimated to be of the order of magnitude of 10^{10}. In other respects, their model was, however, unrealistic: no allowance is made for time delay, or for random error, both of which are important features of all biological processes.

Nerve nets incorporating both of these features have been designed by von Neumann. Von Neumann's model employs bundles of nerves rather than single nerves to form a network; this permits the simultaneous performance of each operation as many as 20,000 times as a check against error. This technique of constructing a computer is impractical at the level of present-day technology, von Neumann admits, "but quite practical for a perfectly conceivable, more advanced technology, and for the natural relay-organs (neurons). I.e., it merely calls for micro-componentry which is not at all unnatural as a concept on this level" (97, p. 87). Still further advances in the direction of adapting these models to neurological data are anticipated. In terms of such nerve nets it is possible to give hypothetical micro-reductions for memory, exact thinking, distinguishing similarity or dissimilarity of stimulus patterns, abstracting of "essential" components of a stimulus pattern, recognition of shape regardless of form and of chord regardless of pitch (phenomena of great importance in Gestalt psychology (5, pp. 128, 129, 152)), purposeful behavior as controlled by negative feedback, adaptive behavior, and mental disorders.

It is the task of the neurophysiologist to test these models by investigating the existence of such nets, scanning units, reverberating networks, and pathways of feedback, and to provide physiological evidence of their functioning. Promising studies have been made in this respect.

5.3. As past successes in connection with level 4 (i.e. as cases in which phenomena involving whole cells [27] have been explained by theories concerning the molecular level) we shall cite micro-reductions dealing with three phenomena that have a fundamental character for all of biological science: the *decoding, duplication,* and *mutation* of the genetic information that is ultimately responsible for the development and maintenance of order in the cell. Our objective will be to show that at least one well-worked-out micro-reducing theory has been advanced for each phenomenon.[28] (The special form taken by our working hypothesis on this level is "methodological mechanism.")

Biologists have long had good evidence indicating that the genetic information in the cell's nucleus—acting as an "inherited message"—exerts its control over cell biochemistry through the production of specific protein catalysts (enzymes) that mediate particular steps (reactions) in the chemical order that is the cell's life. The problem of "decoding" the control information in the nucleus thus reduces to how the specific molecules that comprise it serve to specify the construction of specific protein catalysts. The problem of *duplication* (one aspect of the over-all problem of inheritance) reduces to how the molecules of genetic material can be copied—like so many "blueprints."

And the problem of *mutation* (elementary step in the evolution of new inheritable messages) reduces to how "new" forms of the genetic molecules can arise.

In the last twenty years evidence has accumulated implicating *desoxyribose nucleic acid* (DNA) as the principal "message-carrying" molecule and constituting the genetic material of the chromosomes. Crick and Watson's [29] brilliant analysis of DNA structure leads to powerful microreducing theories that explain the decoding and duplication of DNA. It is known that the giant molecules that make up the nucleic acids have, like proteins (49, 66, 67), the structure of a backbone with side groups attached. But, whereas the proteins are polypeptides, or chains of amino-acid residues (slightly over 20 kinds of amino acids are known); the nucleic acids have a phosphate-sugar backbone, and there are only 4 kinds of side groups all of which are nitrogen bases (purines and pyrimidines). Crick and Watson's model contains a pair of DNA chains wound around a common axis in the form of two interlocking helices. The two helices are held together (forming a helical "ladder") by hydrogen bonds between pairs of the nitrogen bases, one belonging to each helix. Although 4 bases occur as side groups only 2 of 16 conceivable pairings are possible, for steric reasons. These 2 pairs of bases recur along the length of the DNA molecule and thus invite a picturesque analogy with the dots and dashes of the Morse code. They can be arranged in any sequence: there is enough DNA in a single cell of the human body to encode in this way 1000 large textbooks. The model can be said to imply that the genetic "language" of the inherited control message is a "language of surfaces": the information in DNA structure is decoded as a sequence of amino acids in the proteins which are synthesized under ultimate DNA control. The surface structure of the DNA helix, dictated by the sequence of base pairs, specifies like a template [30] the sequence of amino acids laid down end to end in the fabrication of polypeptides.

Watson and Crick's model immediately suggests how the DNA might produce an exact copy of itself—for transmission as an inherited message to the succeeding generation of cells. The DNA molecule, as noted above, consists of two interwoven helices, each of which is the complement of the other. Thus each chain may act as a mold on which a complementary chain can be synthesized. The two chains of a DNA molecule need only unwind and separate. Each begins to build a new

21

complement onto itself, as loose units, floating in the cell, attach themselves to the bases in the single DNA chain. When the process is completed, there are two pairs of chains where before there was only one! [31]

Mutation of the genetic information has been explained in a molecular (micro-reduction) theory advanced some years ago by Delbrück.[32] Delbrück's theory was conceived long before the newer knowledge of DNA was available; but it is a very general model in no way vitiated by Crick and Watson's model of the particular molecule constituting the genetic material. Delbrück, like many others, assumed that the gene is a single large "nucleo-protein" molecule. (This term is used for macromolecules, such as viruses and the hypothetical "genes," which consist of protein and nucleic acid. Some recent theories even assume that an entire chromosome is a single such molecule.) According to Delbrück's theory, different quantum levels within the atoms of the molecule correspond to different hereditary characteristics. A mutation is simply a quantum jump of a rare type (i.e., one with a high activation energy). The observed variation of the spontaneous mutation rate with temperature is in good quantitative agreement with the theory.

Such hypotheses and models as those of Crick and Watson, and of Delbrück, are at present far from sufficient for a complete micro-reduction of the major biological generalization, e.g., evolution and general genetic theory (including the problem of the control of development). But they constitute an encouraging start towards this ultimate goal and, to this extent, an indirect support for our working hypothesis.

5.4. Only in the twentieth century has it been possible to micro-reduce to the atomic and in some cases directly to the subatomic level most of the *macro-physical* aspects of matter (e.g., the high fluidity of water, the elasticity of rubber, and the hardness of diamond) as well as the *chemical* phenomena of the elements, i.e. those changes of the peripheral electrons which leave the nucleus unaffected. In particular, electronic theories explain, e.g., the laws governing valence, the various types of bonds, and the "resonance" of molecules between several equivalent electronic structures. A complete explanation of these phenomena and those of the Periodic Table is possible only with the help of Pauli's exclusion principle which states in one form that no two electrons of the same atom can be alike in all of 4 "quantum numbers." While some molecular laws are not yet micro-reduced, there is every hope that further successes will be obtained in these respects. Thus Pauling (63, 64) writes:

There are still problems to be solved, and some of them are great problems—an example is the problem of the detailed nature of catalytic activity. We can feel sure, however, that this problem will in the course of time be solved in terms of quantum theory as it now exists: there seems little reason to believe that some fundamental new principle remains to be discovered in order that catalysis be explained (64).

5.5. Micro-reduction of level 2 to level 1 has been mentioned in the preceding section because many molecular phenomena are at present (skipping the atomic level) explained with reference to laws of elementary particles.[33] Bohr's basic (and now somewhat outdated) model of the atom as a kind of "solar system" of elementary particles is today part of everyone's conceptual apparatus; while the mathematical development of theory in its present form is formidable indeed! Thus we shall not attempt to give any details of this success. But the high rate of progress in this field certainly gives reason to hope that the unsolved problems, especially as to the forces that hold the nucleus together, will likewise be explained in terms of an elementary particle theory.

6. Evolution, Ontogenesis, and Synthesis

6.1. As pointed out in section 4.5, *evolution* provides *indirect* factual support for the working hypothesis that unitary science is attainable. Evolution (in the present sense) is an over-all phenomenon involving all levels, from 1 through 6; the mechanisms of chance variation and "selection" operate throughout in ways characteristic for the evolutionary level involved.[34] Time scales have, indeed, been worked out by various scientists showing the times when the first things of each level first appeared.[35] (These times are, of course, the less hypothetical the higher the level involved.) But even if the hypothesis of evolution should fail to hold in the case of certain levels, it is important to note that whenever it does hold—whenever it can be shown that things of a given level existed before things of the next higher level came into existence—some degree of indirect support is provided to the particular special case of our working hypothesis that concerns those two levels.

The hypothesis of "evolution" is most speculative insofar as it concerns levels 1 to 3. Various cosmological hypotheses are at present undergoing lively discussion.[36] According to one of these, strongly urged by Gamow (24, 25, 26), the first nuclei did not form out of elementary particles until five to thirty minutes after the start of the universe's

23

expansion; molecules may not have been able to exist until considerably later. Most present-day cosmologists still subscribe to such evolutionary views of the universe; i.e., there was a "zero point" from which the evolution of matter began, with diminishing density through expansion. However, H. Bondi, T. Gold, and F. Hoyle have advanced a conflicting idea, the "steady state" theory, according to which there is no "zero point" from which the evolution of matter began; but matter is continuously created, so that its density remains constant in spite of expansion. There seems to be hope that these rival hypotheses will be submitted to specific empirical tests in the near future. But, fortunately, we do not have to depend on hypotheses that are still so highly controversial: as we have seen, the micro-reducibility of molecular and atomic phenomena is today not open to serious doubt.

Less speculative are theories concerning the origin of life (transition from level 3 to level 4). Calvin (9; Fox, 22) points out that four mechanisms have been discovered which lead to the formation of amino acids and other organic materials in a mixture of gases duplicating the composition of the primitive terrestrial atmosphere.[37] These have, in fact, been tested experimentally with positive results. Many biologists today accept with Oparin (61) the view that the evolution of life as such was not a single chance event but a long process possibly requiring as many as two billion years, until precellular living organisms first appeared.

According to such views, "chemical evolution" gradually leads in an appropriate environment to evolution in the familiar Darwinian sense. In such a process, it hardly has meaning to speak of a point at which "life appeared." To this day controversies exist concerning the "dividing line" between living and non-living things. In particular, viruses are classified by some biologists as *living*, because they exhibit *self-duplication* and *mutability*; but most biologists refuse to apply the term to them, because viruses exhibit these characteristic phenomena of life only due to activities of a living cell with which they are in contact. But, wherever one draws the line,[38] non-living molecules preceded primordial living substance, and the latter evolved gradually into highly organized living units, the unicellular ancestors of all living things. The "first complex molecules endowed with the faculty of reproducing their own kind" must have been synthesized—and with them the beginning of evolution in the Darwinian sense—a few billion years ago, Goldschmidt

(27, p. 84) asserts: "all the facts of biology, geology, paleontology, biochemistry, and radiology not only agree with this statement but actually prove it."

Evolution at the next two levels (from level 4 to level 5, and from 5 to 6) is not speculative at all, but forms part of the broad line of Darwinian evolution, so well marked out by the various kinds of evidence referred to in the statement just quoted. The line of development is again a continuous one; [39] and it is to some extent arbitrary (as in the case of "living" versus "non-living") to give a "point" at which true multicellulars first appeared, or at which an animal is "social" rather than "solitary." But in spite of this arbitrariness, it is safe to say that:

(a) Multicellulars evolved from what were originally competing single cells; the "selection" by the environment was in this case determined by the superior survival value of the cooperative structure.[40]

(b) Social animals evolved from solitary ones for similar reasons; and, indeed, there were millions of years during which there were *only* solitary animals on earth, and not yet their organizations into social structures.[41]

6.2. To illustrate *ontogenesis*, we must show that particular things of a particular level have arisen out of particular things of the next lower level. For example, it is a consequence of most contemporary cosmological theories—whether of the evolutionary or of the "steady state" type—that each existent atom must have originally been formed by a union of elementary particles. (Of course an atom of an element may subsequently undergo "transmutation.") However, such theories are extremely speculative. On the other hand, the chemical union of atoms to form molecules is commonplace in nature.

Coming to the higher levels of the reductive hierarchy, we have unfortunately a hiatus at the level of cells. Individual cells do *not*, as far as our observations go, ever develop out of individual molecules; on the contrary, "cells come only from cells," as Virchow stated about one hundred years ago. However, a characteristic example of ontogenesis of things of one level out of things of the next lower level is afforded by the development of multicellular organisms through the process of mitosis and cell division. All the hereditary characteristics of the organism are specified in the "genetic information" carried in the chromosomes of each individual cell, and are transmitted to the resultant organism through cell division and mitosis.

A more startling example of ontogenesis at this level is provided by the *slime molds* studied by Bonner (3). These are isolated amoebae; but, at a certain stage, they "clump" together chemotactically and form a simple multicellular organism, a sausage-like "slug"! This "slug" crawls with comparative rapidity and good coordination. It even has senses of a sort, for it is attracted by light.

As to the level of social groups, we have some ontogenetic data, however slight; for children, according to the well-known studies of Piaget (70, 71) (and other authorities on child behavior), acquire the capacity to cooperate with one another, to be concerned with each other's welfare, and to form groups in which they treat one another as peers, only after a number of years (not before seven years of age, in Piaget's studies). Here one has in a rudimentary form what we are looking for: the ontogenetic development of progressively more social behavior (level 6) by what begin as relatively "egocentric" and unsocialized individuals (level 5).

6.3. *Synthesis* affords factual support for micro-reduction much as ontogenesis does; however, the evidence is better because synthesis usually takes place under *controlled* conditions. Thus it enables one to show that one can obtain an object of the kind under investigation *invariably* by instituting the appropriate causal relations among the parts that go to make it up. For this reason, we may say that success in synthesizing is as strong evidence as one can have for the possibility of micro-reduction, short of actually finding the micro-reducing theory.

To begin on the lowest level of the reductive hierarchy, that one can obtain an atom by bringing together the appropriate elementary particles is a basic consequence of elementary nuclear physics. A common example from the operation of atomic piles is the synthesis of deuterium. This proceeds as one bombards protons (in, e.g., hydrogen gas) with neutrons.

The synthesis of a molecule by chemically uniting atoms is an elementary laboratory demonstration. One familiar example is the union of oxygen and hydrogen gas. Under the influence of an electric spark one obtains the appearance of H_2O molecules.

The next level is that of life. "On the borderline" are the viruses. Thus success at synthesizing a virus out of non-living macro-molecules would count as a first step to the synthesis of cells (which at present seems to be an achievement for the far distant future).

While success at synthesizing a virus out of atoms is not yet in sight, synthesis out of *non-living* highly complex macro-molecules has been accomplished. At the University of California Virus Laboratory (23), protein obtained from viruses has been mixed with nucleic acid to obtain active virus. The protein does not behave like a virus—it is completely non-infectious. However, the reconstituted virus has the same structure as "natural" virus, and will produce the tobacco mosaic disease when applied to plants. Also new "artificial" viruses have been produced by combining the nucleic acid from one kind of virus with the protein from a different kind. Impressive results in synthesizing proteins have been accomplished: e.g., R. B. Woodward and C. H. Schramm (107; see also Nogushi and Hayakawa, 60; and Oparin, 61) have synthesized "protein analogues"—giant polymers containing at least 10,000 amino-acid residues.

At the next level, no one has of course synthesized a whole multicellular organism out of individual cells; but here too there is an impressive partial success to report. Recent experiments have provided detailed descriptions of the manner in which cells organize themselves into whole multicellular tissues. These studies show that even isolated whole cells, when brought together in random groups, could effectuate the characteristic construction of such tissues.[42] Similar phenomena are well known in the case of sponges and fresh-water polyps.

Lastly, the "synthesis" of a new social group by bringing together previously separated individuals is extremely familiar; e.g., the organization of new clubs, trade unions, professional associations, etc. One has even the deliberate formation of whole new societies, e.g., the formation of the Oneida community of utopians, in the nineteenth century, or of the state of Israel by Zionists in the twentieth.

There have been experimental studies in this field; among them, the pioneer work of Kurt Lewin and his school is especially well known.[43]

7. Concluding Remarks

The possibility that all science may one day be reduced to microphysics (in the sense in which chemistry seems today to be reduced to it), and the presence of a unifying trend toward micro-reduction running through much of scientific activity, have often been noticed both by specialists in the various sciences and by meta-scientists. But these opinions have, in general, been expressed in a more or less vague manner and without very deep-going justification. It has been our aim, first, to provide precise definitions for the crucial concepts involved, and, second, to reply to the frequently made accusations that belief in the attainability of unitary science is "a mere act of faith." We hope to have shown that, on the contrary, a tentative acceptance of this belief, an acceptance of it as a working hypothesis, is *justified*, and that the hypothesis is *credible*, partly on methodological grounds (e.g., the simplicity of the hypothesis, as opposed to the bifurcation that rival suppositions create in the conceptual system of science), and partly because there is really a large mass of direct and indirect evidence in its favor.

The idea of reductive levels employed in our discussion suggests what may plausibly be regarded as a *natural order of sciences*. For this purpose, it suffices to take as "fundamental disciplines" the branches corresponding to our levels. It is understandable that many of the well-known orderings of things [44] have a rough similarity to our reductive levels, and that corresponding orderings of sciences are more or less similar to our order of 6 "fundamental disciplines." Again, several successive levels may be grouped together (e.g. physics today conventionally deals at least with levels 1, 2, and 3; just as biology deals with at least levels 4 and 5). Thus we often encounter a division into simply physics, biology, and social sciences. But these other efforts to solve a problem which goes back to ancient times [45] have apparently been made on more or less intuitive grounds; it does not seem to have been realized that these orderings are "natural" in a deeper sense, of being based on the relation of *potential micro-reducer* obtaining between the branches of science.

It should be emphasized that these six "fundamental disciplines" are, largely, fictitious ones (e.g., there is no actual branch whose universe of discourse is *strictly* molecules and combinations thereof). If one wishes a less idealized approach, one may utilize a concept in semantical information theory which has been defined by one of us (3). This is the semantical functor: 'the amount of information the statement S contains about the class C' (or, in symbols: $inf(S, C)$). Then one can characterize any theory S (or any branch, if we are willing to identify a branch with a conjunction of theories) by a sextuple: namely, $inf(S,$ level 1), $inf(S,$ level 2) . . . $inf(S,$ level 6). This sextuple can be regarded as the "locus" of the branch S in a six-dimensional space. The axes are the loci of the imaginary "fundamental disciplines" just referred to; any real branch (e.g., present-day biology) will probably have a position not quite on any axis, but nearer to one than to the others.

Whereas the orderings to which we referred above generally begin with the historically given branches, the procedure just described reverses this tendency. First a continuous order is defined in which any imaginable branch can be located; then one investigates the relations among the actually existing branches. These positions may be expected to change with time; e.g., as micro-reduction proceeds, "biology" will occupy a position closer to the "level 1" axis, and so will all the other branches. The continuous order may be described as "Darwinian" rather than "Linnean"; it derives its naturalness, not from agreement with intuitive or customary classifications, but from its high systematic import in the light of the hypothesis that Unity of Science is attainable.

NOTES

[1] Science, in the wider sense, may be understood as including the formal disciplines, mathematics, and logic, as well as the empirical ones. In this paper, we shall be concerned with science only in the sense of empirical disciplines, including the sociohumanistic ones.

[2] By a "theory" (in the widest sense) we mean any hypothesis, generalization, or law (whether deterministic or statistical), or any conjunction of these; likewise by "phenomena" (in the widest sense) we shall mean either particular occurrences or theoretically formulated general patterns. Throughout this paper, "explanation" ("explainable" etc.) is used as defined in Hempel and Oppenheim (35). As to "explanatory power," there is a definite connection with "systematic power." See Kemeny and Oppenheim (46, 47).

[3] If we are willing to adopt a "Taxonomic System" for classifying all the things dealt with by science, then the various classes and subclasses in such a system could represent the possible "universes of discourse." In this case, the U_{Bi} of any branch would be associated with the extension of a taxonomic term in the sense of Oppenheim (62).

[4] Henceforth, we shall as a rule omit the clause 'at time t'.

[5] Oppenheim (62, section 3) has a method for measuring such a reduction.

[6] Of course, in some cases, such "skipping" does occur in the process of micro-reduction, as shall be illustrated later on.

[7] As to degree of credibility, see Kemeny and Oppenheim (45, especially p. 307).

[8] The "acceptance, as an overall fundamental working hypothesis, of the reduction theory, with physical science as most general, to which all others are reducible; with biological science less general; and with social science least general of all," has been emphasized by Hockett (37, especially p. 571).

[9] As to natural, see Hempel (33, p. 52), and Hempel and Oppenheim (34, pp. 107, 110).

[10] Many well known hierarchical orders of the same kind (including some compatible with ours) can be found in modern writings. It suffices to give the following quotation from an article by L. von Bertalanffy (95, p. 164): "Reality, in the modern conception, appears as a tremendous hierarchical order of organized entities, leading, in a superposition of many levels, from physical and chemical to biological and sociological systems. Unity of Science is granted, not by an utopian reduction of all

sciences to physics and chemistry, but by the structural uniformities of the different levels of reality." As to the last sentence, we refer in the last paragraph of section 2.2 to the problem noted. Von Bertalanffy has done pioneer work in developing a General System Theory which, in spite of some differences of emphasis, is an interesting contribution to our problem.

[11] The following example is a slight modification of the one given in Hempel and Oppenheim (35, p. 148). See also Rescher and Oppenheim (76, pp. 93, 94).

[12] See Rescher and Oppenheim (76, p. 100), and Rescher (75). Of course, nothing is intrinsically a "true" whole; the characterization of certain things as "wholes" is always a function of the point of view, i.e. of the particular 'Pt' relation selected. For instance, if a taxonomic system is given, it is very natural to define 'Pt' so that the "wholes" will correspond to the things of the system. Similarly for *aggregate* see Rescher and Oppenheim (76, p. 90, n. 1).

[13] See Kemeny and Oppenheim (47, n. 6). A suggestive characterization of *simplicity* in terms of the "entropy" of a theory has been put forward by Rothstein (78). Using Rothstein's terms, we may say that any micro-reduction moves in the direction of lower entropy (greater organization).

[14] The statement that B_2 is *micro-reducible* to B_1 means (according to the analysis we adopt here) that some true theory belonging to B_1—i.e., some true theory with the appropriate vocabulary and universe of discourse, whether accepted or not, and whether it is ever even written down or not—micro-reduces every true theory of B_2. This seems to be what people have in mind when they assert that a given B_2 may not be reduced to a given B_1 at a certain time, but may nonetheless be reducible (microreducible) to it.

[15] See Kemeny and Oppenheim (45, p. 307); also for "related concepts," like Carnap's "degree of confirmation" see Carnap (13).

[16] As to degree of credibility see Kemeny and Oppenheim (45, especially p. 307).

[17] Using a term introduced by Kurt Lewin (48), we can also say in such a case: any particular object on level n is *genidentical* with these parts.

[18] Though we cannot accept Sir Arthur Eddington's idealistic implications, we quote from his *Philosophy of Physical Science* (17, p. 125): "I conclude therefore that our engrained form of thought is such that we shall not rest satisfied until we are able to represent all physical phenomena as an interplay of a vast number of structural units intrinsically alike. All the diversity of phenomena will be then seen to correspond to different forms of relatedness of these units or, as we should usually say, different configurations."

[19] M. Scriven has set forth some suggestive considerations on this subject in his essay, "A Possible Distinction between Traditional Scientific Disciplines and the Study of Human Behavior" (79).

[20] See e.g. Kartman (43), with many quotations, references, and notes, some of them micro-reductionistic.

[21] This term has been introduced by F. A. Hayek (31). See also Watkins (98, especially pp. 729–732) and Watkins (99). We owe valuable information in economics to W. J. Baumol, Princeton University.

[22] This distinction, first made by C. D. Broad (6, p. 616), adopted by E. C. Tolman (90), C. L. Hull (39), and others, is still in use, in spite of objections against this terminology.

[23] This is the form our working hypothesis takes on this level in this field. See in this connection the often quoted paper by K. MacCorquodale and P. E. Meehl, "On a Distinction between Hypothetical Constructs and Intervening Variables" (52), and some of the discussions in the "Symposium on the Probability Approach in Psychology" (73), as well as references therein, to H. Feigl, W. Koehler, D. Krech, and C. C. Pratt.

[24] As to neuroanatomy, see e.g. W. Penfield (69); as to neurochemistry, see e.g.

Rosenblueth (77, especially Chapter 26 for acetylcholine and the summaries on pp. 134–135, 274–275); as to The Electric Activity of the Nervous System, see the book of this title by Brazier (5). See this last book also for neuroanatomy, neurophysiology, neurochemistry. See Brazier (5, pp. 128, 129, 152) for micro-reduction of Gestalt phenomena mentioned below.

[25] Turing (91, 92). For an excellent popular presentation, see Kemeny (44).

[26] See the often quoted paper by McCulloch and Pitts (53), and later publications by these authors, as well as other papers in this field in the same Bulletin of Mathematical Biophysics, e.g. by N. Rashevsky. See also Platt (72) for a "complementary approach which might be called amplifier theory." For more up to date details, see Shannon and McCarthy's (82) Automata Studies, including von Neumann's model, discussed by him (82, pp. 43–98).

[27] Throughout this paper, "cell" is used in a wide sense, i.e., "Unicellular" organism or single cell in a multicellular organism.

[28] For more details and much of the following, see Simpson, Pittendrigh and Tiffany (87), Goldschmidt (28), and Horowitz (38). For valuable suggestions we are indebted to C. S. Pittendrigh who also coined the terms "message carrying molecule" and "languages of surface" used in our text.

[29] See in reference to the following discussion Watson and Crick (100), also (101), and (102), and Crick (15).

[30] Pauling and Delbrück (68). A micro-reducing theory has been proposed for these activities using the "lock-key" model. See Pauling, Campbell and Pressman (65), and Burnet (8).

[31] For a mechanical model, see von Neumann (96) and Jacobson (40).

[32] See Timoféeff-Ressovsky (89, especially pp. 108–138). It should, however, be noted that since Delbrück's theory was put forward, his model has proved inadequate for explaining genetic facts concerning mutation. And it is reproduced here only as a historical case of a micro-reducing theory that, in its day, served valuable functions.

[33] We think that, throughout this paper, our usage of thing language also on this level is admissible in spite of well-known difficulties and refer e.g. to Born (4), and Johnson (42).

[34] See e.g. Broad (6, especially p. 93), as to "a general tendency of one order to combine with each other under suitable conditions to form complexes of the next order." See also Blum (1, and 2, especially p. 608); Needham (59, especially pp. 184–185); and Dodd (16).

[35] This wording takes care of "regression," a reversal of trend, illustrated e.g. by parasitism.

[36] For a clear survey of cosmological hypotheses see the 12 articles published in the issue of Scientific American cited under Gamow (26).

[37] Perhaps the most sensational method is an experiment suggested by H. C. Urey and made by S. L. Miller (56, 57), according to which amino acids are formed when an electric discharge passes through a mixture of methane, hydrogen, ammonia, and water.

[38] "Actually life has many attributes, almost any one of which we can reproduce in a nonliving system. It is only when they all appear to a greater or lesser degree in the same system simultaneously that we call it living" (Calvin, 9, p. 252). Thus the dividing line between "living" and "non-living" is obtained by transforming an underlying "multidimensional concept of order" (see Hempel and Oppenheim, 34, pp. 65–77), in a more or less arbitrary way, into a dichotomy. See also Stanley (88, especially pp. 15 and 16 of the reprint of this article).

[39] See note 38 above.

[40] For details, see Lindsey (50, especially pp. 136–139, 152–153, 342–344). See also Burkholder (7).

[41] See e.g. the publications (104, 105, 106) by Wheeler. See also Haskins (30,

31

Paul Oppenheim and Hilary Putnam

especially pp. 30–36). Since we are considering evolution on level 6 as a whole, we can refrain from discussing the great difference between, on the one hand, chance mutations, natural selection, and "instinctive" choices and, on the other hand, the specific faculty of man of consciously and willfully directing social evolution in time stretches of specifically small orders of magnitude (see Zilsel, 108).

[42] See Moscana (58) and his references, especially to work by the same author and by Paul Weiss.

[43] See Lippitt (51). For recent experiments, see Sherif and Sherif (84, Chapters 6 and 9), and Sherif (83).

[44] See note 10 above.

[45] For details, see Flint (21), and Vannerus (93). Auguste Comte in his Cours de Philosophie Positive, Première et Deuxième Leçons (14), has given a hierarchical order of 6 "fundamental disciplines" which, independently from its philosophical background, is amazingly modern in many respects, as several contemporary authors recognize.

REFERENCES

1. Blum, H. F. Time's Arrow and Evolution. Princeton: Princeton Univ. Press, 1951.
2. Blum, H. F. "Perspectives in Evolution," American Scientist, 43:595–610 (1955).
3. Bonner, J. T. Morphogenesis. Princeton: Princeton Univ. Press, 1952.
4. Born, M. "The Interpretation of Quantum Mechanics," British Journal for the Philosophy of Science, 3:95–106 (1953).
5. Brazier, M. A. B. The Electric Activity of the Nervous System. London: Sir Isaac Pitman & Sons, Ltd., 1951.
6. Broad, C. D. The Mind and its Place in Nature. New York: Harcourt, Brace, 1925.
7. Burkholder, P. R. "Cooperation and Conflict among Primitive Organisms," American Scientist, 40:601–631 (1952).
8. Burnet, M. "How Antibodies are Made," Scientific American, 191:74–78 (November 1954).
9. Calvin, M. "Chemical Evolution and the Origin of Life," American Scientist, 44:248–263 (1956).
10. Carnap, R. Der logische Aufbau der Welt. Berlin-Schlachtensee: Im Weltkreis-Verlag, 1928. Summary in N. Goodman, The Structure of Appearances, pp. 114–146. Cambridge: Harvard Univ. Press, 1951.
11. Carnap, R. "Testability and Meaning," Philosophy of Science, 3:419–471 (1936), and 4:2–40 (1937). Reprinted by Graduate Philosophy Club, Yale University, New Haven, 1950.
12. Carnap, R. Logical Foundations of the Unity of Science, International Encyclopedia of Unified Science. Vol. I, pp. 42–62. Chicago: Univ. of Chicago Press, 1938.
13. Carnap, R. Logical Foundations of Probability. Chicago: Univ. of Chicago Press, 1950.
14. Comte, Auguste. Cours de Philosophie Positive. 6 Vols. Paris: Bachelier, 1830–42.
15. Crick, F. H. C. "The Structure of Hereditary Material," Scientific American, 191: 54–61 (October 1954).
16. Dodd, S. C. "A Mass-Time Triangle," Philosophy of Science, 11:233–244 (1944).
17. Eddington, Sir Arthur. The Philosophy of Physical Science. Cambridge: Cambridge University Press, 1949.
18. Feigl, H. "Logical Empiricism," in D. D. Runes (ed.), Twentieth Century

Philosophy, pp. 371–416. New York: Philosophical Library, 1943. Reprinted in H. Feigl and W. Sellars (eds.), *Readings in Philosophical Analysis*. New York: Appleton-Century-Crofts, 1949.

19. Feigl, H. "Unity of Science and Unitary Science," in H. Feigl and M. Brodbeck (eds.), *Readings in the Philosophy of Science*, pp. 382–384. New York: Appleton-Century-Crofts, 1953.

20. Feigl, H. "Functionalism, Psychological Theory and the Uniting Sciences: Some Discussion Remarks," *Psychological Review*, 62:232–235 (1955).

21. Flint, R. *Philosophy as Scientia Scientiarum and the History of the Sciences*. New York: Scribner, 1904.

22. Fox, S. W. "The Evolution of Protein Molecules and Thermal Synthesis of Biochemical Substances," *American Scientist*, 44:347–359 (1956).

23. Fraenkel-Conrat, H. "Rebuilding a Virus," *Scientific American*, 194:42–47 (June 1956).

24. Gamow, G. "The Origin and Evolution of the Universe," *American Scientist*, 39:393–406 (1951).

25. Gamow, G. *The Creation of the Universe*. New York: Viking Press, 1952.

26. Gamow, G. "The Evolutionary Universe," *Scientific American*, 195:136–154 (September 1956).

27. Goldschmidt, R. B. "Evolution, as Viewed by One Geneticist," *American Scientist*, 40:84–98 (1952).

28. Goldschmidt, R. B. *Theoretical Genetics*. Berkeley and Los Angeles: Univ. of California Press, 1955.

29. Guhl, A. M. "The Social Order of Chickens," *Scientific American*, 194:42–46 (February 1956).

30. Haskins, C. P. *Of Societies and Man*. New York: Norton & Co., 1951.

31. Hayek, F. A. *Individualism and the Economic Order*. Chicago: Univ. of Chicago Press, 1948.

32. Hebb, D. O. *The Organization of Behavior*. New York: Wiley, 1949.

33. Hempel, C. G. *Fundamentals of Concept Formation in the Empirical Sciences*, Vol. II, No. 7 of *International Encyclopedia of Unified Science*. Chicago: Univ. of Chicago Press, 1952.

34. Hempel, C. G., and P. Oppenheim. *Der Typusbegriff im Lichte der neuen Logik; wissenschaftstheoretische Untersuchungen zur Konstitutionsforschung und Psychologie*. Leiden: A. W. Sythoff, 1936.

35. Hempel, C. G., and P. Oppenheim. "Studies in the Logic of Explanation," *Philosophy of Science*, 15:135–175 (1948).

36. Hoagland, H. "The Weber-Fechner Law and the All-or-None Theory," *Journal of General Psychology*, 3:351–373 (1930).

37. Hockett, C. H. "Biophysics, Linguistics, and the Unity of Science," *American Scientist*, 36:558–572 (1948).

38. Horowitz, N. H. "The Gene," *Scientific American*, 195:78–90 (October 1956).

39. Hull, C. L. *Principles of Animal Behavior*. New York: D. Appleton-Century, Inc., 1943.

40. Jacobson, H. "Information, Reproduction, and the Origin of Life," *American Scientist*, 43:119–127 (1955).

41. Jeffress, L. A. *Cerebral Mechanisms in Behavior; the Hixon Symposium*. New York: Wiley, 1951.

42. Johnson, M. "The Meaning of Time and Space in Philosophies of Science," *American Scientist*, 39:412–431 (1951).

43. Kartman, L. "Metaphorical Appeals in Biological Thought," *American Scientist*, 44:296–301 (1956).

44. Kemeny, J. G. "Man Viewed as a Machine," *Scientific American*, 192:58–66 (April 1955).

45. Kemeny, J. G., and P. Oppenheim. "Degree of Factual Support," *Philosophy of Science*, 19:307–324 (1952).
46. Kemeny, J. G., and P. Oppenheim. "Systematic Power," *Philosophy of Science*, 22:27–33 (1955).
47. Kemeny, J. G., and P. Oppenheim. "On Reduction," *Philosophical Studies*, 7:6–19 (1956).
48. Lewin, Kurt. *Der Begriff der Genese*. Berlin: Verlag von Julius Springer, 1922.
49. Linderstrom-Lang, K. U. "How is a Protein Made?" *American Scientist*, 41:100–106 (1953).
50. Lindsey, A. W. *Organic Evolution*. St. Louis: C. V. Mosbey Company, 1952.
51. Lippitt, R. "Field Theory and Experiment in Social Psychology," *American Journal of Sociology*, 45:26–79 (1939).
52. MacCorquodale, K., and P. E. Meehl. "On a Distinction Between Hypothetical Constructs and Intervening Variables," *Psychological Review*, 55:95–105 (1948).
53. McCulloch, W. S., and W. Pitts. "A Logical Calculus of the Ideas Immanent in Nervous Activity," *Bulletin of Mathematical Biophysics*, 5:115–133 (1943).
54. Mannheim, K. *Ideology and Utopia*. New York: Harcourt, Brace, 1936.
55. Mill, John Stuart. *System of Logic*. New York: Harper, 1848 (1st ed. London, 1843).
56. Miller, S. L. "A Production of Amino Acids Under Possible Primitive Earth Conditions," *Science*, 117:528–529 (1953).
57. Miller, S. L. "Production of Some Organic Compounds Under Possible Primitive Earth Conditions," *Journal of the American Chemical Society*, 77:2351–2361 (1955).
58. Moscana, A. "Development of Heterotypic Combinations of Dissociated Embryonic Chick Cells," *Proceedings of the Society for Experimental Biology and Medicine*, 92:410–416 (1956).
59. Needham, J. *Time*. New York: Macmillan, 1943.
60. Nogushi, J., and T. Hayakawa. Letter to the Editor, *Journal of the American Chemical Society*, 76:2846–2848 (1954).
61. Oparin, A. I. *The Origin of Life*. New York: Macmillan, 1938 (Dover Publications, Inc. edition, 1953).
62. Oppenheim, P. "Dimensions of Knowledge," *Revue Internationale de Philosophie*, Fascicule 40, Section 7 (1957).
63. Pauling, L. "Chemical Achievement and Hope for the Future," *American Scientist*, 36:51–58 (1948).
64. Pauling, L. "Quantum Theory and Chemistry," *Science*, 113:92–94 (1951).
65. Pauling, L., D. H. Campbell, and D. Pressmann. "The Nature of Forces between Antigen and Antibody and of the Precipitation Reaction," *Physical Review*, 63:203–219 (1943).
66. Pauling, L., and R. B. Corey. "Two Hydrogen-Bonded Spiral Configurations of the Polypeptide Chain," *Journal of the American Chemical Society*, 72:5349 (1950).
67. Pauling, L., and R. B. Corey. "Atomic Coordination and Structure Factors for Two Helical Configurations," *Proceedings of the National Academy of Science* (U.S.), 37:235 (1951).
68. Pauling, L., and M. Delbrück. "The Nature of Intermolecular Forces Operative in Biological Processes," *Science*, 92:585–586 (1940).
69. Penfield, W. "The Cerebral Cortex and the Mind of Man," in P. Laslett (ed.), *The Physical Basis of Mind*, pp. 56–64. Oxford: Blackwell, 1950.
70. Piaget, J. *The Moral Judgment of the Child*. London: Kegan Paul, Trench, Trubner and Company, Ltd., 1932.
71. Piaget, J. *The Language and Thought of the Child*. London: Kegan Paul, Trench, Trubner and Company; New York: Harcourt, Brace, 1926.

72. Platt, J. R. "Amplification Aspects of Biological Response and Mental Activity," American Scientist, 44:180–197 (1956).
73. Probability Approach in Psychology (Symposium), Psychological Review, 62: 193–242 (1955).
74. Rashevsky, N. Papers in general of Rashevsky, published in the Bulletin of Mathematical Biophysics, 5 (1943).
75. Rescher, N. "Axioms of the Part Relation," Philosophical Studies, 6:8–11 (1955).
76. Rescher, N. and P. Oppenheim. "Logical Analysis of Gestalt Concepts," British Journal for the Philosophy of Science, 6:89–106 (1955).
77. Rosenblueth, A. The Transmission of Nerve Impulses at Neuroeffector Junctions and Peripheral Synapses. New York: Technological Press of MIT and Wiley, 1950.
78. Rothstein, J. Communication, Organization, and Science. Indian Hills, Colorado: Falcon's Wing Press, 1957.
79. Scriven, M. "A Possible Distinction between Traditional Scientific Disciplines and the Study of Human Behavior," in H. Feigl and M. Scriven (eds.), Vol. I, Minnesota Studies in the Philosophy of Science, pp. 330–339. Minneapolis: Univ. of Minnesota Press, 1956.
80. Sellars, W. "A Semantical Solution of the Mind-Body Problem," Methodos, 5:45–84 (1953).
81. Sellars, W. "Empiricism and the Philosophy of Mind," in H. Feigl and M. Scriven (eds.), Minnesota Studies in the Philosophy of Science, Vol. I, pp. 253–329. Minneapolis: Univ. of Minnesota Press, 1956.
82. Shannon, C. E., and J. McCarthy (eds.), Automata Studies. Princeton: Princeton Univ. Press, 1956.
83. Sherif, M. "Experiments in Group Conflict," Scientific American, 195:54–58 (November 1956).
84. Sherif, M., and C. W. Sherif. An Outline of Social Psychology. New York: Harper, 1956.
85. Sherrington, Charles. The Integrative Action of the Nervous System. New Haven: Yale Univ. Press, 1948.
86. Simmel, G. Sociologie. Leipzig: Juncker und Humblot, 1908.
87. Simpson, G. G., C. S. Pittendrigh, and C. H. Tiffany. Life. New York: Harcourt, Brace, 1957.
88. Stanley, W. M. "The Structure of Viruses," reprinted from publication No. 14 of the American Association for the Advancement of Science, The Cell and Protoplasm, pp. 120–135 (reprint consulted) (1940).
89. Timoféeff-Ressovsky, N. W. Experimentelle Mutationsforschung in der Vererbungslehre. Dresden und Leipzig: Verlag von Theodor Steinkopff, 1937.
90. Tolman, E. C. Purposive Behavior in Animals and Men. New York: The Century Company, 1932.
91. Turing, A. M. "On Computable Numbers, With an Application to the Entscheidungsproblem," Proceedings of the London Mathematical Society, Ser. 2, 42:230–265 (1936).
92. Turing, A. M. "A Correction," Proceedings of the London Mathematcial Society, Ser. 2, 43:544–546 (1937).
93. Vannerus, A. Vetenskapssystematik. Stockholm: Aktiebolaget Ljus, 1907.
94. Veblen, T. The Theory of the Leisure Class. London: Macmillan, 1899.
95. Von Bertalanffy, L. "An Outline of General System Theory," The British Journal for the Philosophy of Science, 1:134–165 (1950).
96. Von Neumann, John. "The General and Logical Theory of Automata," in L. A. Jeffress (ed.), Cerebral Mechanisms in Behavior; The Hixon Symposium, pp. 20–41. New York: John Wiley and Sons, Inc., 1951.

Paul Oppenheim and Hilary Putnam

97. Von Neumann, John. "Probabilistic Logics and the Synthesis of Reliable Organisms from Unreliable Components," in C. E. Shannon and J. McCarthy (eds.), *Automata Studies*. Princeton: Princeton Univ. Press, 1956.
98. Watkins, J. W. N. "Ideal Types and Historical Explanation," in H. Feigl and M. Brodbeck (eds.), *Readings in the Philosophy of Science*, pp. 723–743. New York: Appleton-Century-Crofts, 1953.
99. Watkins, J. W. N. "A Reply," *Philosophy of Science*, 22:58–62 (1955).
100. Watson, J. D., and F. H. C. Crick. "The Structure of DNA," *Cold Spring Harbor Symposium on Quantitative Biology*, 18:123–131 (1953).
101. Watson, J. D., and F. H. C. Crick. "Molecular Structure of Nucleic Acids—A Structure for Desoxyribosenucleic Acid," *Nature*, 171:737–738 (1953).
102. Watson, J. D., and F. H. C. Crick. "Genetical Implications of the Structure of Desoxyribosenucleic Acid," *Nature*, 171:964–967 (1953).
103. Weber, M. *The Theory of Social and Economic Organization*, translated by A. M. Henderson and T. Persons. New York: Oxford Univ. Press, 1947.
104. Wheeler, W. M. *Social Life Among the Insects*. New York: Harcourt, Brace, 1923.
105. Wheeler, W. M. *Emergent Evolution and the Development of Societies*. New York: Norton & Co., 1928.
106. Wheeler, W. M. "Animal Societies," *Scientific Monthly*, 39:289–301 (1934).
107. Woodward, R. B., and C. H. Schramm. Letter to the Editor, *Journal of the American Chemical Society*, 69:1551 (1947).
108. Zilsel, E. "History and Biological Evolution," *Philosophy of Science*, 7:121–128 (1940).

The Theoretician's Dilemma
A STUDY IN THE LOGIC OF THEORY CONSTRUCTION

1. Deductive and Inductive Systematization

Scientific research in its various branches seeks not merely to record particular occurrences in the world of our experience: it tries to discover regularities in the flux of events and thus to establish general laws which may be used for prediction, postdiction,[1] and explanation.

The principles of Newtonian mechanics, for example, make it possible, given the present positions and momenta of the celestial objects that make up the solar system, to predict their positions and momenta for a specified future time or to postdict them for a specified time in the past; similarly, those principles permit an explanation of the present positions and momenta by reference to those at some earlier time. In addition to thus accounting for particular facts such as those just mentioned, the principles of Newtonian mechanics also explain certain "general facts," i.e., empirical uniformities such as Kepler's laws of planetary motion; for the latter can be deduced from the former.[2]

Scientific explanation, prediction, and postdiction all have the same logical character: they show that the fact under consideration can be inferred from certain other facts by means of specified general laws. In the simplest case, this type of argument may be schematized as a deductive inference of the following form:

$$(1.1) \qquad \frac{C_1, C_2 \ldots C_k}{L_1, L_2 \ldots L_r}$$

$$E$$

AUTHOR'S NOTE: I am indebted to the Council of the Humanities at Princeton University for the award of a Senior Fellowship for the academic year 1956–57, which, by reducing my teaching load, gave me additional time for research. The present study is part of the work done during my tenure as a Senior Fellow.

Here, C_1, C_2, C_k are statements of particular occurrences (e.g., of the position and momenta of certain celestial bodies at a specified time), and L_1, L_2 . . . L_r are general laws (e.g., those of Newtonian mechanics); finally, E is a sentence stating whatever is being explained, predicted, or postdicted. And the argument has its intended force only if its conclusion, E, follows deductively from the premises.[3]

While explanation, prediction, and postdiction are alike in their logical structure, they differ in certain other respects. For example, an argument of the form (1.1) will qualify as a prediction only if E refers to an occurrence at a time later than that at which the argument is offered; in the case of a postdiction, the event must occur before the presentation of the argument. These differences, however, require no fuller study here, for the purpose of the preceding discussion was simply to point out the role of general laws in scientific explanation, prediction, and postdiction.

For these three types of scientific procedure, we will use the common term '*(deductive) systematization*'. More precisely, that term will be used to refer, first, to any argument of the form (1.1) that meets the requirements indicated above, no matter whether it serves as an explanation, a prediction, a postdiction, or in still some other capacity; second, to the procedure of establishing arguments of the kind just characterized.

So far, we have considered only those cases of explanation, prediction, and related procedures which can be construed as deductive arguments. There are many instances of scientific explanation and prediction, however, which do not fall into a strictly deductive pattern. For example, when Johnny comes down with the measles, this might be explained by pointing out that he caught the disease from his sister, who is just recovering from it. The particular antecedent facts here invoked are that of Johnny's exposure and, let us assume, the further fact that Johnny had not had the measles previously. But to connect these with the event to be explained, we cannot adduce a general law to the effect that under the specified circumstances, the measles is invariably transmitted to the exposed person: what can be asserted is only a high probability (in the sense of statistical frequency) of transmission. The same type of argument can be used also for predicting or postdicting the occurrence of a case of the measles.

Similarly, in a psychoanalytic explanation of the neurotic behavior of an adult by reference to certain childhood experiences, the generalizations which might be invoked to connect the antecedent events with those to be explained can be construed at best as establishing more or less high probabilities for the connections at hand, but surely not as expressions of unexceptional uniformities.

Explanations, predictions, and postdictions of the kind here illustrated differ from those previously discussed in two important respects: The laws invoked are of a different form, and the statement to be established does not follow deductively from the explanatory statements adduced. We will now consider these differences somewhat more closely.

The laws referred to in connection with the schema (1.1), such as the laws of Newtonian mechanics, are what we will call *statements of strictly universal form, or strictly universal statements.* A statement of this kind is an assertion—which may be true or false—to the effect that all cases which meet certain specified conditions will unexceptionally have such and such further characteristics. For example, the statement 'All crows are black' is a sentence of strictly universal form; and so is Newton's first law of motion, that any material body which is not acted upon by an external force persists in its state of rest or of rectilinear motion at constant speed.

The laws invoked in the second type of explanatory and related arguments, on the other hand, are, as we will say, of *statistical form;* they are *statistical probability statements.* A statement of this kind is an assertion—which may be true or false—to the effect that for cases which meet conditions of a specified kind, the probability of having such and such further characteristics is so-and-so much.[4]

To put the distinction in a nutshell: A strictly universal statement of the simplest kind has the form 'All cases of P are cases of Q'; a statistical probability statement of the simplest kind has the form 'The probability for a case of P to be a case of Q is r.' While the former implies an assertion about any particular instance of P—namely, that it is also an instance of Q—the latter implies no similar assertion concerning any particular instance of P or even concerning any finite set of such instances.[5] This circumstance gives rise to the second distinctive characteristic mentioned above: the statement E describing the occurrence under explanation or prediction or postdiction (for example, Johnny's catching the measles) is not logically deducible from the explanatory statements adduced (for example, (C_1) Johnny was exposed to the

39

measles; (C_2) Johnny had not previously had the measles; (L) For persons who have not previously had the measles and are exposed to it, the probability is .92 that they will contract the disease); rather, on the assumption that the explanatory statements adduced are true, it is very likely, though not certain, that E is true as well. This kind of argument, therefore, is inductive rather than strictly deductive in character: it calls for the acceptance of E on the basis of other statements which constitute only partial, if strongly supporting, grounds for it. An argument of this kind—no matter whether it is used for explanation, prediction, or postdiction, or for yet another purpose—will be called an *inductive systematization*. In particular, we will assume of an inductive systematization that the conclusion is not logically implied by the premises.[6] Again, the procedure of establishing an argument of the kind just described will also be called inductive systematization.

By way of further illustration, let us note here two explanatory arguments which are of the inductive kind just characterized. They are adduced by von Mises in a statement to the effect that the everyday notion of causal explanation will eventually adjust itself to changes in the logical form of scientific theories (especially to the use of statistical probability statements as explanatory principles): "We think," von Mises says, that "people will gradually come to be satisfied by causal statements of this kind: It is *because* the die was loaded that the 'six' shows more frequently (but we do not know what the next number will be); or: *Because* the vacuum was heightened and the voltage increased, the radiation became more intense (but we do not know the precise number of scintillations that will occur in the next minute)."[7] Clearly, both of these statements can be construed as inductive explanations of certain physical phenomena.

All the cases of scientific systematization we have considered share this characteristic: they make use of general laws or general principles either of strictly universal or of statistical form. These general laws have the function of establishing systematic connections among empirical facts in such a way that with their help some empirical occurrences may be inferred, by way of explanation, prediction, or postdiction, from other such occurrences. When, in an explanation, we say that the event described by E occurred "because" of the circumstances detailed in C_1, C_2 . . . C_k, that phrase has significance if it can be construed as referring to general laws which render C_1, C_2 . . . C_k relevant to E in the sense that, granted the truth of the former, they make the truth of the latter either certain (as in a deductive systematization) or inductively probable (as in an inductive systematization). It is for this reason that the establishment of general laws is of crucial importance in the empirical sciences.

2. Observables and Theoretical Entities

Scientific systematization is ultimately aimed at establishing explanatory and predictive order among the bewilderingly complex "data" of our experience, the phenomena that can be directly "observed" by us. It is a remarkable fact, therefore, that the greatest advances in scientific systematization have not been accomplished by means of laws referring explicitly to *observables*, i.e., to things and events which are ascertainable by direct observation, but rather by means of laws that speak of various *hypothetical*, or *theoretical*, *entities*, i.e., presumptive objects, events, and attributes which cannot be perceived or otherwise directly observed by us.

For a fuller discussion of this point, it will be helpful to refer to the familiar distinction between two levels of scientific systematization: the level of *empirical generalization*, and the level of *theory formation*.[8] The early stages in the development of a scientific discipline usually belong to the former level, which is characterized by the search for laws (of universal or statistical form) which establish connections among the directly observable aspects of the subject matter under study. The more advanced stages belong to the second level, where research is aimed at comprehensive laws, in terms of hypothetical entities, which will account for the uniformities established on the first level. On the first level, we find everyday physical generalizations such as 'Where there is light there is heat,' 'Iron rusts in damp air,' 'Wood floats on water, iron sinks in it'; but we might assign to it also such more precise quantitative laws as Galileo's, Kepler's, Hooke's, and Snell's laws, as well as botanical and zoological generalizations about the concomitance of certain observable anatomical, physical, functional, and other characteristics in the members of a given species; generalizations in psychology that assert correlations among diverse observable aspects of learning, of perception, and so forth; and various descriptive generalizations in economics, sociology, and anthropology. All these generalizations, whether of strictly universal or of statistical form, purport to express regular connections among

41

directly observable phenomena, and they lend themselves, therefore, to explanatory, predictive, and postdictive use.

On the second level, we encounter general statements that refer to electric, magnetic, and gravitational fields, to molecules, atoms, and a variety of subatomic particles; or to ego, id, superego, libido, sublimation, fixation, and transference; or to various not directly observable entities invoked in recent learning theories.

In accordance with the distinction here made, we will assume that the (extra-logical) vocabulary of empirical science, or of any of its branches, is divided into two classes: *observational terms* and *theoretical terms*. In regard to an observational term it is possible, under suitable circumstances, to decide by means of direct observation whether the term does or does not apply to a given situation.

Observation may here be construed so broadly as to include not only perception, but also sensation and introspection; or it may be limited to the perception of what in principle is publicly ascertainable, i.e., perceivable also by others. The subsequent discussion will be independent of how narrowly or how liberally the notion of observation is construed; it may be worth noting, however, that empirical science aims for a system of publicly testable statements, and that, accordingly, the observational data whose correct prediction is the hallmark of a successful theory are at least thought of as couched in terms on whose applicability in a given situation different individuals can decide, with high agreement, by means of direct observation. Statements which purport to describe readings of measuring instruments, changes in color or odor accompanying a chemical reaction, utterances made, or other kinds of overt behavior shown by a given subject under specified observable conditions—these all illustrate the use of *intersubjectively applicable* observational terms.[9]

Theoretical terms, on the other hand, usually purport to refer to not directly observable entities and their characteristics; they function, in a manner soon to be examined more closely, in scientific theories intended to explain empirical generalizations.

The preceding characterization of the two vocabularies is obviously vague; it offers no precise criterion by means of which any scientific term may be unequivocally classified as an observational term or as a theoretical one. But no such precise criterion is needed here; the questions to be examined in this essay are independent of precisely where the dividing line between the terms of the observational and the theoretical vocabularies is drawn.

3. Why Theoretical Terms?

The use of theoretical terms in science gives rise to a perplexing problem: Why should science resort to the assumption of hypothetical entities when it is interested in establishing predictive and explanatory connections among observables? Would it not be sufficient for the purpose, and much less extravagant at that, to search for a system of general laws mentioning only observables, and thus expressed in terms of the observational vocabulary alone?

Many general statements in terms of observables have indeed been formulated; they constitute the empirical generalizations mentioned in the preceding section. But, vexingly, many, if not all, of them suffer from definite shortcomings: they usually have a rather limited range of application; and even within that range, they have exceptions, so that actually they are not true general statements. Take, for example, one of our earlier illustrations of an empirical generalization:

(3.1)   Wood floats on water; iron sinks in it.

This statement has a narrow range of application in the sense that it refers only to wooden and iron objects and concerns their floating behavior only in regard to water.[10] And, what is even more important, it has exceptions: certain kinds of wood will sink in water, and a hollow iron sphere of suitable dimensions will float on it.

As the history of science shows, flaws of this kind can often be remedied by attributing to the phenomena under study certain further constituents or characteristics which, though not open to direct observation, are connected in specified ways with the observable aspects of the subject matter under investigation, and which make it possible to establish systematic connections among the latter. By way of illustration—though it is admittedly an oversimplified one—consider the sentence (3.1). A much more satisfactory generalization is obtained by means of the concept of the specific gravity of a body x, which is definable as the quotient of its weight and its volume:

(3.2)   Def.: $s(x) = w(x)/v(x)$

Let us assume that w and v have been characterized operationally, i.e., in terms of the directly observable outcomes of specified measuring procedures, and that therefore they are counted among the observables. Then s, as determined by (3.1), might be viewed as a characteristic that is less directly observable; and, just for the sake of obtaining a simple illustration, we will classify s as a hypothetical entity. For s, we may now state the following generalization, which is a corollary of the principle of Archimedes:

(3.3)   A solid body floats on a liquid if its specific gravity is less than that of the liquid.

This statement avoids, first of all, the exceptions we noted above as refuting (3.1): it predicts correctly the behavior of a piece of heavy wood and of a hollow iron sphere. Moreover, it has a much wider scope: it refers to any kind of solid object and concerns its floating behavior in regard to any liquid. Even the new generalization has certain limitations, of course, and thus invites further improvement. But instead of pursuing this process, let us now examine more closely the way in which a systematic connection among observables is achieved, in our illustration, by the law (3.3), which involves a detour through the domain of unobservables.

Suppose that we wish to predict whether a certain solid object b will float on a given body l of liquid. We will then first have to ascertain, by appropriate operational procedure, the weight and the volume of b and l. Let the results of these measurements be expressed by the following four statements O_1, O_2, O_3, O_4:

(3.4) (O_1) $w(b) = w_1$; (O_2) $v(b) = v_1$;
        (O_3) $w(l) = w_2$; (O_4) $v(l) = v_2$

where w_1, w_2, v_1, v_2, are certain positive real numbers. By means of the definition (3.2), we can infer, from (3.4), the specific gravities of b and l:

(3.5) $s(b) = w_1/v_1$; $s(l) = w_2/v_2$

Suppose now that the first of these values is less than the second; then (3.4), via (3.5) implies that

(3.6) $s(b) < s(l)$

By means of the law (3.3), we can now infer that

(3.7)   b floats on l

This sentence will also be called O_5. The sentences O_1, O_2, O_3, O_4, O_5 then share the characteristic that they are expressed entirely in terms of

44

the observational vocabulary; for on our assumption, 'w' and 'v' are observational terms, and so are 'b' and 'l', which name certain observable
bodies; finally, 'floats on' is an observational term because under suitable circumstances, direct observation will show whether a given observable object floats on a given observable liquid. On the other hand,
the sentences (3.2), (3.3), (3.5), and (3.6) lack that characteristic, for
they all contain the term 's', which, in our illustration, belongs to the
theoretical vocabulary.

The systematic transition from the "observational data" listed in (3.4)
to the prediction (3.7) of an observable phenomenon is schematized in
the accompanying diagram. Here, an arrow represents a deductive in-

$$(3.8) \quad \left. \begin{array}{l} \left. \begin{array}{l} O_1 \\ O_2 \end{array} \right\} \xrightarrow{(3.2)} s(b) = v_1/w_1 \\[2mm] \left. \begin{array}{l} O_3 \\ O_4 \end{array} \right\} \xrightarrow{(3.2)} s(l) = v_2/w_2 \end{array} \right\} \xrightarrow{} s(b) < s(l) \xrightarrow{(3.9)} O_5$$

Data described in terms of observables	Systematic connection effected by statements making reference to non-observables	Prediction in terms of observables

ference; mention, above an arrow, of a further sentence indicates that
the deduction is effected by means of that sentence, i.e., that the conclusion stated at the right end follows logically from the premises listed
at the left, taken in conjunction with the sentence mentioned above the
arrow. Note that the argument just considered illustrates the schema
(1.1), with O_1, O_2, O_3, O_4 constituting the statements of particular facts,
the sentences (3.2) and (3.3) taking the place of the general laws, and
O_5 that of E.[11]

Thus, the assumption of non-observable entities serves the purposes
of systematization: it provides connections among observables in the
form of laws containing theoretical terms, and this detour via the
domain of hypothetical entities offers certain advantages, some of which
were indicated above.

In the case of our illustration, however, brief reflection will show that
the advantages obtained by the "theoretical detour" could just as well
have been obtained without ever resorting to the use of a theoretical

term. Indeed, by virtue of the definition (3.2), the law (3.3) can be restated as follows:

(3.3′) A solid body floats on a liquid if the quotient of its weight and its volume is less than the corresponding quotient for the liquid.

This alternative version clearly shares the advantages we found (3.3) to have over the crude generalization (3.1); and, of course, it permits the deductive transition from O_1, O_2, O_3, O_4 to O_5 just as well as does (3.3) in conjunction with (3.2).

The question arises therefore whether the systematization achieved by general principles containing theoretical terms can always be duplicated by means of general statements couched exclusively in observational terms. To prepare for an examination of this important problem, we must first consider more closely the form and function of a scientific theory.

4. Structure and Interpretation of a Theory

Formally, a scientific theory may be considered as a set of sentences expressed in terms of a specific vocabulary. The vocabulary, V_T, of a theory T will be understood to consist of the extralogical terms of T, i.e., those which do not belong to the vocabulary of pure logic. Usually, some of the terms of V are defined by means of others; but, on pain of a circle or an infinite regress, not all the terms of V can be so defined. Hence, V may be assumed to be divided into two subsets: *primitive terms*—those for which no definition is specified—and *defined terms*. Analogously, many of the sentences of a theory are derivable from others by means of the principles of deductive logic (and of the definitions of the defined terms); but, on pain of a vicious circle or an infinite regress in the deduction, not all of the theoretical sentences can be thus established. Hence, the set of sentences asserted by T falls into two subsets: *primitive sentences*, or *postulates* (also called *axioms*), and *derivative sentences*, or *theorems*. Henceforth, we will assume that theories are given in the form of axiomatized systems as here described; i.e., by listing, first, the primitive and the derivative terms and the definitions for the latter, second, the postulates. In addition, the theory will always be thought of as formulated within a linguistic framework of a clearly specified logical structure, which determines, in particular, the rules of deductive inference.

The classical paradigms of deductive systems of this kind are the axiomatizations of various mathematical theories, such as Euclidean, and various forms of non-Euclidean geometry, and the theory of groups and other branches of abstract algebra; [12] but by now, a number of theories in empirical science have likewise been put into axiomatic form, or approximations thereof; among them, parts of classical and relativistic mechanics,[13] certain segments of biological theory [14] and some theoretical systems in psychology, especially in the field of learning; [15] in economic theory, the concept of utility, among others, has received axiomatic treatment.[16]

If the primitive terms and the postulates of an axiomatized system have been specified, then the proof of theorems, i.e., the derivation of further sentences from the primitive ones—can be carried out by means of the purely formal canons of deductive logic, and thus, without any reference to the meanings of the terms and sentences at hand; indeed, for the deductive development of an axiomatized system, no meanings need be assigned at all to its expressions, primitive or derived.

However, a deductive system can function as a theory in empirical science only if it has been given an *interpretation* by reference to empirical phenomena. We may think of such interpretation as being effected by the specification of a set of *interpretative sentences*, which connect certain terms of the theoretical vocabulary with observational terms.[17] The character of these sentences will be examined in considerable detail in subsequent sections; at present may be mentioned, merely as an example, that interpretative sentences might take the form of so-called operational definitions, i.e., of statements specifying the meanings of theoretical terms with the help of observational ones; of special importance among these are rules for the measurement of theoretical quantities by reference to observable responses of measuring instruments or other indicators.

The manner in which a theory establishes explanatory and predictive connections among statements couched in observational terms can now be illustrated in outline by the following example. Suppose that the Newtonian theory of mechanics is used to study the motions, under the exclusive influence of their mutual gravitational attraction, of two bodies, such as the components of a double-star system, or the moon and a rocket coasting freely 100 miles above the moon's surface. On the basis of appropriate observational data, each of the two bodies may be assigned a certain mass, and, at a given instant t_0, a certain position

47

and velocity in some specified frame of reference. Thus, a first step is taken which leads, via interpretative sentences in the form of rules of measurement, from certain statements $O_1, O_2 \ldots O_k$ which describe observable instrument readings, to certain theoretical statements, say $H_1, H_2 \ldots H_6$ which assign to each of the two bodies a specific numerical value of the theoretical quantities mass, position, and velocity. From these statements, the law of gravitation, which is couched entirely in theoretical terms, leads to a further theoretical statement, H_7, which specifies the force of the gravitational attraction the two bodies exert upon each other at t_0; and H_7 in conjunction with the preceding theoretical statements and the laws of Newtonian mechanics implies, via a deductive argument involving the principles of the calculus, certain statements H_8, H_9, H_{10}, H_{11}, which give the positions and velocities of the two objects at a specified later time, say t_1. Finally, use in reverse of the interpretative sentences leads, from the last four theoretical statements, to a set of sentences $O'_1, O'_2 \ldots O'_m$, which describe observable phenomena, namely, instrument readings that are indicative of the predicted positions and velocities.

By means of a schema analogous to (3.8), the procedure may be represented as follows:

$$(4.1) \quad \{O_1, O_2 \ldots O_k\} \xrightarrow{R} \{H_1, H_2 \ldots H_6\} \xrightarrow{G} \{H_1, H_2 \ldots H_6, H_7\}$$
$$\xrightarrow{LM} \{H_8, H_9, H_{10}, H_{11}\} \xrightarrow{R} \{O'_1, O'_2 \ldots O'_m\}$$

Here, R is the set of the rules of measurement for mass, position, and velocity; these rules constitute the interpretative sentences; G is Newton's law of gravitation, and LM are the Newtonian laws of motion.

In reference to psychology, similar schematic analyses of the function of theories or of hypotheses involving "intervening variables" have repeatedly been presented in the methodological literature.[18] Here, the observational data with which the procedure starts usually concern certain observable aspects of an initial state of a given subject, plus certain observable stimuli acting upon the latter; and the final observational statements describe a response made by the subject. The theoretical statements mediating the transition from the former to the latter refer to various hypothetical entities, such as drives, reserves, inhibitions, or whatever other not directly observable characteristics, qualities, or psychological states are postulated by the theory at hand.

5. The Theoretician's Dilemma

The preceding account of the function of theories raises anew the problem encountered in section 3, namely, whether the theoretical detour, through a domain of not directly observable things, events, or characteristics cannot be entirely avoided. Assume, for example, that—as will often be the case—the interpretative sentences as well as the laws asserted by the theory have the form of equations which connect certain expressions in terms of theoretical quantities either with other such expressions, or with expressions in terms of observable quantities. Then the problem can be stated in Hull's succinct formulation: "If you have a secure equational linkage extending from the antecedent observable conditions through to the consequent observable conditions, why, even though to do so might not be positively pernicious, use several equations where one would do?" [19] Skinner makes the same point in more general form when he criticizes the construction, in psychological theories, of causal chains in which a first link consisting of an observable and controllable event is connected with a final ("third") one of the same kind by an intermediate link which usually is not open to observation and control. Skinner argues: "Unless there is a weak spot in our causal chain so that the second link is not lawfully determined by the first, or the third by the second, then the first and third links must be lawfully related. If we must always go back beyond the second link for prediction and control, we may avoid many tiresome and exhausting digressions by examining the third link as a function of the first." [20]

The conclusion suggested by these arguments might be called *the paradox of theorizing*. It asserts that if the terms and the general principles of a scientific theory serve their purpose, i.e., if they establish definite connections among observable phenomena, then they can be dispensed with since any chain of laws and interpretative statements establishing such a connection should then be replaceable by a law which directly links observational antecedents to observational consequents.

By adding to this crucial thesis two further statements which are obviously true, we obtain the premises for an argument in the classical form of a dilemma:

(5.1.) If the terms and principles of a theory serve their purpose they are unnecessary, as just pointed out, and if they don't serve their purpose they are surely unnecessary. But given any theory, its terms and principles either serve their purpose or they don't. Hence, the terms and principles of any theory are unnecessary.

This argument, whose conclusion accords well with the views of extreme methodological behaviorists in psychology, will be called the *theoretician's dilemma.*

However, before yielding to glee or to gloom over the outcome of this argument, it will be well to remember that the considerations adduced so far in support of the crucial first premise were formulated rather sketchily. In order to form a more careful judgment on the issue, it will therefore be necessary to inquire whether the sketch can be filled in so as to yield a cogent argument. To this task we now turn.

6. Operational Definitions and Reduction Sentences

It will be well to begin by considering more closely the character of interpretative sentences. In the simplest case, such a sentence could be an *explicit definition* of a theoretical expression in terms of observational ones, as illustrated by (3.2). In this case, the theoretical term is unnecessary in the strong sense that it can always be avoided in favor of an observational expression, its definiens. If all the primitives of a theory T are thus defined, then clearly T can be stated entirely in observational terms, and all its general principles will indeed be laws that directly connect observables with observables.

This would be true, in particular, of any theory that meets the standards of operationism in the narrow sense that each of its terms is introduced by an explicit definition which states an observable response whose occurrence is necessary and sufficient, under specified observable test conditions, for the applicability of the term in question. Suppose, for example, that the theoretical term is a one-place predicate, or property term, 'Q'. Then an operational definition of the kind just mentioned would take the form

(6.1)   Def. $Qx \equiv (Cx \supset Ex)$

i.e., an object x has (by definition) the property Q if and only if it is such that if it is under test conditions of kind C, then it exhibits an effect, or response of kind E. Tolman's definition of expectancy of food provides an illustration: "When we assert that a rat expects food at L, what we assert is that *if* (1) he is deprived of food, (2) he has been trained on path P, (3) he is now put on path P, (4) path P is now blocked, and (5) there are other paths which lead away from path P, one of which points directly to location L, *then* he will run down the path which points directly to location L." [21] We can obtain this formulation by replacing, in (6.1), 'Qx' by 'rat x expects food at location L,' 'Cx' by the conjunction of the conditions (1), (2), (3), (4), (5) for rat x, and 'Ex' by 'x runs down the path which points directly to location L.'

However, as has been shown by Carnap in a now classical argument,[22] this manner of defining scientific terms, no matter how natural it may seem, encounters a serious difficulty. For on the standard extensional interpretation, a conditional sentence, such as the definiens in (6.1), is false only if its antecedent is true and its consequent false. Hence, for any object which does not satisfy the test conditions C, and for which therefore the antecedent of the definiens is false, the definiens as a whole is true; consequently, such an object will be assigned the property Q. In terms of our illustration: of any rat not exposed to the conditions (1)–(5) just stated, we would have to say that he expected food at L—no matter what kind of behavior the rat might exhibit.

One way out of this difficulty is suggested by the following consideration. In saying that a given rat expects food at L, we intend to attribute to the animal a state or a disposition which, under circumstances (1)–(5), will cause the rat to run down the path pointing directly to L; hence, in a proper operational definition, E must be tied to C nomologically, i.e., by virtue of general laws of the kind expressing causal connections. The extensional 'if . . . then . . .'—which requires neither logical nor nomological necessity of connection—would therefore have to be replaced in (6.1) by a stricter, nomological counterpart that might be worded perhaps as 'if . . . then, with causal necessity, . . .' However, the ideas of law and of causal or nomological necessity as here invoked are not clear enough at present to make this approach seem promising.[23]

Carnap [24] has proposed an alternative way of meeting the difficulty encountered by definitions of the form (6.1); it consists in providing a partial rather than a complete specification of meaning for 'Q'. This is done by means of so-called reduction sentences; in the simplest case, (6.1) would be replaced by the following *bilateral reduction sentence*:

(6.2) $Cx \supset (Qx \equiv Ex)$

i.e., if an object is under test conditions of kind C, then it has the property Q if and only if it exhibits a response of kind E. Here, the use of extensional connectives no longer has the undesirable aspects it exhibited in (6.1); if an object is not under test conditions C, then the entire formula (6.2) is true of it, but this implies nothing as to whether the object does, or does not, have the property Q. On the other hand, while (6.1) offers a full explicit definition of 'Q', (6.2) specifies the meaning of 'Q' only partly, namely, for just those objects that meet condition C; for those which don't, the meaning of 'Q' is left unspecified. In our illustration, for example, (6.3) would specify the meaning of 'x expects food at L' only for rats that meet conditions (1)–(5); for them, running down the path which pointed to L would be a necessary and sufficient condition of food expectancy. In reference to rats that don't meet the test conditions (1)–(5), the meaning of 'x expects food at L' would be left open; it could be further specified subsequently by means of additional reduction sentences.

In fact, it is this interpretation which is required for Tolman's concept of food expectancy. For while the passage quoted above seems to have exactly the form (6.1), this construal is ruled out by the following sentence which immediately follows the one quoted earlier: "When we assert that he does *not* expect food at location L, what we assert is that, under the same conditions, he will *not* run down the path which points directly to location L." The total interpretation thus given to 'rat x expects food at L' is most satisfactorily formulated in terms of a sentence of the form (6.2), in the manner outlined in the preceding paragraph.[25]

As this example vividly illustrates, reduction sentences offer an excellent way of formulating precisely the intent of operational definitions. By construing the latter as merely partial specifications of meaning, this approach treats theoretical concepts as "open"; and the provision for a set of different, and mutually supplementary, reduction sentences for a given term reflects the availability, for most theoretical terms, of different operational criteria of application, pertaining to different contexts.[26]

It should be noted, however, that while an analysis in terms of reduction sentences construes theoretical terms as not fully defined by reference to observables, it does not prove that a full explicit definition in observational, terms *cannot* be achieved for theoretical expressions.

And indeed, it seems questionable whether a proof to this effect could even be significantly asked for. The next section deals with this issue in some detail.

7. On the Definability of Theoretical Terms by Means of an Observational Vocabulary

The first, quite general, point to be made here is this: the definition of any term, say 'v', by means of a set V of other terms, say 'v₁', 'v₂' . . . 'vₙ', will have to state, in its definiens, a necessary and sufficient condition for the applicability of 'v' expressed in terms of some or all of the members of V. And in order to be able to judge whether this can be done in a given case, we will have to know how the terms under consideration are to be understood. For example, the vocabulary consisting of the terms 'male' and 'offspring of' permits the formulation of a necessary and sufficient condition of application for the term 'son of' in its biological, but not in its legal sense. How the given terms are to be understood can be indicated by specifying a set U of sentences which are to be considered as true, and which connect the given terms with each other and perhaps with other terms. Thus, U will be a set of sentences containing 'v', 'v₁' . . . 'vₙ' and possibly also other extralogical constants. For example, in the case of the biological use of the terms 'son', 'male', and 'offspring', in reference to humans, the following set of sentences—let us call it U_1—might be given: 'Every son is male,' 'No daughter is male,' 'x is an offspring of y if and only if x is a son or a daughter of y.'

Generally, the sentences of U specify just what assumptions are to be made, in the search for a definition, concerning the concepts under consideration; and the problem of definability now turns into the question whether it is possible to formulate, in terms of $v_1, v_2 \ldots v_n$, a condition which, *in virtue of the assumptions included in U*, will be both necessary and sufficient for v. Thus, using an idea set forth and developed technically by Tarski,[27] we see that the concept of definability of 'v' by means of 'v₁', 'v₂' . . . 'vₙ' acquires a precise meaning only if it is explicitly relativized by reference to a set U of specifying assumptions. That precise meaning may now be stated as follows:

(7.1) 'v' is definable by means of the vocabulary $V = \{$'v₁', 'v₂' . . .'vₙ'$\}$

relative to a finite set U of statements containing, at least, 'v' and all the

Carl G. Hempel

elements of V if from U there is deducible at least one sentence stating a necessary and sufficient condition for v in terms of no other extralogical constants than the members of V.

If all the terms under study are one-place predicates of the first order, for example, then a sentence of the required kind could most simply be stated in the form

(7.2) $v(x) \equiv D(x, v_1, v_2 \ldots v_n)$,

where the expression on the right-hand side stands for a sentential function whose only free variable is 'x', and which contains no extralogical constants other than those included in V.

Similarly, in the case of our illustration, the set U_1 specified above implies the statement:

x is a son of $y \equiv$ (x is male and x is an offspring of y),

so that, relatively to U_1, 'son' is definable as 'male offspring'.

We should add here an amplifying remark. A definition, when it is not simply a convention introducing an abbreviatory notation (such as the convention to let 'x^5' be short for '$x \cdot x \cdot x \cdot x \cdot x$') is usually considered as stating the synonymy of two expressions, or, as it is often put, the *identity of their meanings*. Now the question of the definability of a given term 'v' by means of a set V of other terms surely is not simply one of notational fiat; and indeed it will normally be construed as concerning the possibility of expressing the meaning which the term 'v' possesses with the help of the meanings of the members of V. If this conception is adopted, then naturally the information needed to answer the question of definability will concern the *meanings* of 'v' and of the members of V; accordingly, the statements in U, which provide this information, will then be required not simply to be true, but to be analytic, i.e., true by virtue of the intended meanings of the constituent terms. In this case, the statements in U would have the character of meaning postulates in the sense of Kemeny and Carnap.[28]

But in a study of the definability of theoretical expressions by means of observational terms, it is neither necessary nor even advisable to construe definition in this intensional manner. For, first of all, the idea of meaning, and related notions such as those of analyticity and synonymy, are by no means as clear as they have long been considered to be,[29] and it will be better, therefore, to avoid them when this is possible.

Secondly, even if those concepts are accepted as clearly intelligible,

54

the definability of a theoretical term still cannot be construed exclusively as the existence of a synonymous expression containing only observational terms: it would be quite sufficient if a coextensive (rather than a strictly cointensive, or synonymous) expression in terms of observables were forthcoming. For such an expression would state an empirically necessary and sufficient observational condition of applicability for the theoretical term; and this is all that is required for our purposes. In fact, the sentence stating the condition—which might have the form (7.2), for example—can then be given the status of a truth-by-definition, by a suitable reformalization of the theory at hand.

It is of interest to note here that a necessary and sufficient observational condition for a theoretical term, say 'Q', might be inductively discovered even if only a partial specification of the meaning of 'Q' in terms of observables were available. Suppose, for example, that a set of alternative conditions of application for 'Q' has been specified by means of bilateral reduction sentences:

(7.3) $C_1x \supset (Qx \equiv E_1x)$
       $C_2x \supset (Qx \equiv E_2x)$
       . . . .
       $C_nx \supset (Qx \equiv E_nx)$

where all predicates except 'Q' are observational. Suppose further that suitable investigations lead to the following empirical generalizations:

(7.4) $C_1x \supset (Ox \equiv E_1x)$
       $C_2x \supset (Ox \equiv E_2x)$
       . . . .
       $C_nx \supset (Ox \equiv E_nx)$

where 'Ox' stands for a sentential function in 'x' which contains no non-observational extralogical terms. These findings, in combination with (7.3), would inductively support the hypothesis

(7.5) $Qx \equiv Ox$

which presents a necessary and sufficient observational condition for Q. However, (7.5) even if true (its acceptance involves the usual "inductive risk") clearly does not express a synonymy; if it did, no empirical investigations would be needed in the first place to establish it. Rather, it states that, as a matter of empirical fact, 'Q' is coextensive with 'O', or, that O is an empirically necessary and sufficient condition for Q.[30]

And if we wish, we may then imagine the theory-plus-interpretation at hand to be thrown into the form of a deductive system in which (7.5) becomes a definitional truth, and (7.3) assumes the character of a set of empirical statements equivalent to those listed in (7.4).

It might be mentioned here in passing that a similarly broad extensional interpretation of definability is called for also in the context of the problem whether a given scientific discipline, such as psychology, can be "reduced" to another, such as biology or even physics and chemistry. For one component of this problem is the question whether the terms of the first discipline can be defined by means of those of the latter; and what is wanted for this purpose is again a set of empirical hypotheses providing, for each psychological term, a necessary and sufficient condition of application expressed in the vocabulary of biology, or of physics and chemistry.

When we say, for example, that the concepts of the various chemical elements are definable in physical terms by a characterization of the specific ways in which their molecules are composed of elementary physical particles, we are clearly referring to results of experimental research rather than of a mere analysis of what is *meant* by the terms naming the various elements. If the latter were the case, it would indeed be quite incomprehensible why the problems pertaining to the definability of scientific terms should present any difficulty, and why they should be the objects of much conjecture and controversy.

The preceding considerations have important implications for our question whether all theoretical terms in empirical science can be defined in terms of observables. First of all, they show that the question as stated is elliptical: to complete it, we have to specify some set U of statements as referred to in (7.1). What set could reasonably be chosen for this purpose? One natural choice would be the set of all statements, in theoretical or observational terms, that are accepted as presumably true by contemporary science. Now, this pragmatic-historical characterization is by no means precise and unambiguous; there is a wide border area containing statements for which it cannot be clearly determined whether they are accepted by contemporary science. But no matter how the claims of these border-area statements are adjudicated, and no matter where—within reason—the borderline between observational and theoretical terms is drawn, it is at least an open question whether the set of presently accepted scientific statements implies for every theoretical term a necessary and sufficient condition of applicability in terms of observables. Certainly those who have asserted such definability have not supported their claim by actually deducing such conditions, or by presenting cogent general reasons for the possibility of doing so.

There is another way in which the claim of definability may be construed, namely as the assertion that as our scientific knowledge becomes more comprehensive, it will eventually be possible to deduce from it necessary and sufficient conditions of the required kind. (This is the sense in which definability is usually understood by those who claim the eventual definability of the concepts of psychology in terms of those of biology or of physics and chemistry; for that all the requisite definition statements—even in an extensional, empirical sense—cannot be deduced from current psychological, biological, physical, and chemical principles seems clear.[31]) But to assert definability of a theoretical term in this sense is to make a twofold claim: first, that the term in question will not be abandoned in the further development of scientific theorizing; and second, that general laws will be discovered which establish certain necessary and sufficient conditions, expressible in observational terms, for the applicability of the theoretical term at hand. Clearly, the truth of these claims cannot be established by philosophic arguments, but at best by the results of further scientific research.

Despite the precariousness of the problem, various claims and counterclaims have been advanced by philosophers of science and by methodologically interested scientists concerning the possibility of defining theoretical terms by reference to observables.

Some among the philosophers have simply urged that nothing short of explicit definition in terms of a vocabulary that is clearly understood can provide an acceptable method of introducing new terms into the language of science; and the argument supporting this view is to the effect that otherwise the new terms are not intelligible.[32] To this question we will return later. The protagonists of this view do not make an assertion, then, about the actual definability of the theoretical terms used in contemporary empirical science; rather, they stress the importance of clarifying the ideas of science by restating them, as far as possible, in a language with a clear and simple logical structure, and in such a way as to introduce all theoretical terms by means of suitable definitions.

Other writers, however, have argued, in effect, that scientific theories and the way in which they function have certain pervasive logical or methodological characteristics which presumably are not affected by changes in scientific knowledge, and which provide a basis on which the question as to the definability of theoretical terms can be settled without the need either to examine all the statements accepted by contemporary science or to wait for the results of further research.

An illuminating example of a careful use of this type of procedure is provided by Carnap's argument, referred to in the beginning of section 6 above, which shows that definitions of the form (6.1) cannot serve to introduce scientific concepts of the kind they were meant to specify. The argument is limited, however, in the sense that it does not show (and does not claim to show) that an explicit definition of theoretical terms by means of observational ones is generally impossible.

Recently,[33] Carnap has extended his examination of the problem in the following direction. Suppose that a given object, b, exhibits this kind of lawful behavior: whenever b is under conditions of a certain observable kind C, then it shows a response of a specified observable kind E. We then say that b has the disposition to react to C by E; let us call this dispositional property Q for short. Clearly, our earlier discussion in section 6 concerns the problem of precisely defining 'Q' in terms of 'C' and 'E'; we noted there, following Carnap, that we will either have to resign ourselves to a partial specification of meaning for 'Q' by means of the bilateral reduction sentence (6.2); or, if we insist on an explicit complete definition, we will have to use causal modalities in the definiens.

But no matter which of these alternative courses is chosen, the resulting disposition term 'Q' has this characteristic: if a given object b is under condition C and fails to show response E, or briefly, if Cb but ∼Eb, then this establishes conclusively that b lacks the property Q, or briefly that ∼Qb. This characteristic, Carnap argues, distinguishes "pure disposition terms," such as 'Q', from the theoretical terms used in science; for though the latter are connected with the observational vocabulary by certain interpretative sentences—Carnap calls them C-rules—those rules will not, in general, permit a set of observational data (such as 'Cb' and '∼Eb' above) to constitute conclusive evidence for or against the applicability of the theoretical term in a given situation. There are two reasons for this assertion. First, the interpretative sentences for a given theoretical term provide an observational interpretation only within a certain limited range; thus, for example, in the case of the theoretical term 'mass', no C-rule is directly applicable to a sentence S_m ascribing a certain value of mass to a given body, if the value is either so small that the body is not directly observable or so large that the observer cannot "manipulate the body." [34]

And second, a direct observational interpretation for a theoretical term always involves the tacit understanding that the occurrence or absence of the requisite observable response in the specified test situation is to serve as a criterion only if there are no disturbing factors, or, provided that "the environment is in a normal state." [35] Thus, for example, a rule of correspondence might specify the deflection of a magnetic needle as an observable symptom of an electric current in a nearby wire, but with the tacit understanding that the response of the needle is to count only if there are no disturbing factors, such as, say, a sudden magnetic storm.

Generally, then, Carnap holds that "if a scientist has decided to use a certain term 'M' in such a way, that for certain sentences about M, any possible observational results can never be absolutely conclusive evidence but at best evidence yielding a high probability," then the appropriate place for 'M' is in the theoretical vocabulary.[36]

Now we should note, first of all, that if Carnap's arguments are sound, they establish that the theoretical terms of science cannot be construed as pure disposition terms, and thus even if, by the use of causal modalities, explicit definitions of the latter should be achieved, this method would be unavailing for theoretical terms. But the arguments do not show—and are not claimed to show—that theoretical terms can in no way be explicitly defined in terms of observables. In fact, if Carnap's statement quoted in the preceding paragraph is accepted, then many terms that can be explicitly defined by means of the observational vocabulary must be qualified as theoretical. For example, let 'R' be a two-place observational predicate, and let a one-place predicate 'M_1' be defined as follows:

(7.6)   Def. $M_1 x \equiv (\exists y)\, Rxy$

i.e., an object x has the property M_1 just in case it stands in relation R to at least one object y. If, for example, 'Rxy' stands for 'x is less heavy than y', then M_1 is the property of being exceeded in weight by at least one object, or, of not being the heaviest of all objects.

Carl G. Hempel

Let us assume, as customary, that the domain of objects under study is infinite or at least has not been assigned any definite maximum number of elements. Consider now the possibility of conclusive observational evidence for or against the sentence 'M_1a', which attributes M_1 to a certain object a. Obviously, a single observational finding, to the effect that a bears R to a certain object b, or that Rab, would suffice to verify 'M_1a' completely. But no finite set of observational data—'Raa', 'Rab', 'Rac', and so forth—would suffice for a conclusive refutation of 'M_1a'. According to Carnap's criterion, therefore, 'M_1', though defined in terms of the observational predicate 'R', might have to be classified as a theoretical term.

But possibly, in the passage quoted above, Carnap meant to require of a theoretical term 'M' that for certain sentences about M no observational results can be conclusively verificatory or falsificatory evidence. Yet even terms meeting this requirement can be explicitly defined in terms of observables. Let 'S' be a three-place observational predicate; for example, 'Sxyz' might stand for 'x is farther away from y than from z.' And let 'M_2' be defined as follows:

(7.7)   Def. $M_2x \equiv (\exists y)(z)(\sim(z = y) \supset Sxyz)$.

In our example, an object x has M_2 just in case there is an object y from which it is farther away than from any other object z. Consider now the sentence 'M_2a'. As is readily seen, no finite set of observational findings (all the relevant ones would have the form 'Sabc' or '$\sim$Sabc') can be conclusive evidence, either verificatory or falsificatory, concerning 'M_2a'. Hence, though explicitly defined in terms of the observational predicate 'S', the term 'M_2' is theoretical according to the criterion suggested by Carnap.

The preceding discussion illustrates an elementary but important point: when a term, say a one-place predicate 'Q', is defined in terms of observables, its definiens must state a necessary and sufficient condition for the applicability of 'Q', i.e., for the truth of sentences of the form 'Qb'. But even though that condition is then stated completely in observational terms, it still may not enable us to decide, on the basis of a finite number of observational findings, whether 'Q' applies to a given object b; for the truth condition for 'Qb' as provided by the definiens may not be equivalent to a finite set of sentences each of which expresses a potential observational finding.

To add one more example to those given before: suppose that the property term 'iron object' and the relation terms 'attracts' and 'in the vicinity of' are included in the observational vocabulary. Then the definition

(7.8)   Def. x is a magnet $\equiv$ x attracts every iron object in its vicinity

is in terms of observables; but the criterion it provides for an object b being a magnet cannot be expressed in terms of any finite number of observational findings; for to establish that b is a magnet, we would have to show that any piece of iron which, at any time whatever, is brought into the vicinity of b, will be attracted by b; and this is an assertion about an infinity of cases.

To express the idea more formally, let us assume that our observational vocabulary contains, in addition to individual names for observable objects, just first-order predicates of any degree, representing attributes (i.e., properties or relations) which are observable in the sense that a small number of direct observations will suffice, under suitable conditions, to ascertain whether a given object or group of objects exhibits the attribute in question.

Now let us adopt the following definitions: An *atomic sentence* is a sentence, such as 'Pa', 'Rcd', 'Sadg', which ascribes an observable attribute to a specified object or group of objects. A *basic sentence* is an atomic sentence or the negation of an atomic sentence. A *molecular sentence* is a sentence formed from a finite number of atomic sentences by means of truth-functional connectives. Basic sentences will be considered as included among the molecular sentences.

Basic sentences can be considered as the simplest statements describing potential results of direct observation: they assert that some specified set of (one or more) objects has, or lacks, such and such an observable attribute.

Now by virtue of a theorem of truth-functional logic, there exist for every molecular statement S certain finite classes of basic statements which imply S, and certain other such classes which imply the negation of S. Thus, the molecular sentence 'Pa v ($\sim$Pa · Rab)' is implied by {'Pa'} and also by {'$\sim$Pa', 'Rab'}, for example; whereas its negation is implied by the set {'$\sim$Pa', '$\sim$Rab'}. This shows that for each molecular sentence S, it is possible to specify a set of basic sentences whose truth would conclusively verify S, and also a set of basic sentences whose truth would verify the negation of S, and would thus conclusively refute S. Thus, a molecular sentence is capable both of conclusive observational verification and of conclusive observational falsification "in principle," i.e., in the sense that potential data can be described whose occurrence would verify the sentence, and others whose occurrence would falsify it; but not of course in the sense that the two kinds of data might occur jointly—indeed, they are incompatible with each other.

But molecular sentences are the only ones which have this characteristic. A sentence which contains quantifiers non-vacuously is not both verifiable and falsifiable in the sense just indicated.

Returning now to the definition of scientific terms, we may accordingly distinguish two kinds of explicit definitions, those with molecular and those with non-molecular definiens. In both cases, all the extralogical terms in the definiens belong to the observational vocabulary; but in the former, the definiens contains truth-functional connectives as the only logical terms; in the latter, it also contains quantifiers. The definitions (7.6), (7.7), and (7.8) above are of the non-molecular type; the molecular type is illustrated by

(7.9)   Son xy $\equiv$ (Male x $\cdot$ Offspring xy).

We may say now that all and only definitions with molecular definiens provide finite *observational criteria* of application for the terms they define: in the case of a non-molecular definiens, the ascription of the defined attribute to a given case cannot be conclusively based on a finite set of observational findings.

Definition by means of a molecular observational definiens does not suffice to introduce all non-observational terms of science. That this is so might seem to be clear from the preceding discussion, for surely terms of the kind defined in (7.6) and (7.7) will be permissible and indeed needed in science. This reason is not conclusive, however. For the circumstance that a term, say 'M', is originally introduced by a definition with non-molecular definiens does not preclude the possibility that 'M' is in fact coextensive with a certain observational predicate, or some molecular compound of such predicates, say 'O_M'. And if this is the case, it might be discovered by further research, and 'M' could then be (re-)defined by 'O_M'.

There is another argument, however, which shows that, granting certain plausible general assumptions concerning the observational vocabulary, not all non-observational scientific terms can be defined by means of molecular observational expressions. We will now briefly consider this argument.[37] The observational vocabulary will be assumed to be finite. It may contain individual names designating certain observable objects; first-order predicate terms with any finite number of places, representing properties and relations of observable objects; and also functors, i.e., terms expressing quantitative aspects—such as weight in grams, volume in cubic centimeters, age in days—of the observable objects. However, in accordance with our assumption of observability, we will suppose that each of the functors can take on only a finite number of different values; this corresponds to the fact that only a finite number of different weights, for example, can be ascertained and distinguished by direct observation.

In contrast to these functors in the observational vocabulary, the theoretical vocabulary of physics, for example, contains a large number of functors whose permissible values range over all real numbers or over all real numbers within a certain interval.

Thus, for example, the distance between two points may theoretically have any non-negative value whatever. Now a definition of the required kind for a theoretical functor would have to specify, for each of its permissible values, a finite observational criterion of application. For example, in the case of the theoretical functor 'length', a necessary and sufficient condition, in the form of a finite observational criterion, would have to be forthcoming for each of the infinitely many statements of the form 'The distance, in centimeters, between points x and y is r' or briefly, '$l(x,y) = r$', where r is some real number.

Hence, we would have to specify, for each value of 'r', a corresponding finitely ascertainable configuration of observables. But this is impossible because in view of the limits of discrimination in direct observation, only a finite, though very large, number of finitely observable configurations can altogether be ascertained and distinguished.

However, if we drop the requirement of a *molecular* equivalent, in observational terms, for each permissible value of a theoretical functor, then an infinity of different values may become available.[38] Consider, for example, the functor 'the number of cells contained in organism y'. If 'x is a cell', 'y is an organism', and 'x is contained in y' are admitted as observational expressions, then it is possible to give a separate criterion of applicability, in terms of observables, for each of the infinitely many values 1, 2, 3 . . . which that functor may theoretically assume.[39] This can be done by means of the Frege-Russell analysis of cardinal numbers. For n = 1, for example, the necessary and sufficient condition is the following:

(7.10) $(\exists \mu)\ (v)\ (y$ is an organism $\cdot\ ((v$ is a cell $\cdot\ v$ is contained in $y) \supset (v = \mu)))$.

All extralogical constants occurring in this definiens are, on our assumption, observation terms; but the expression contains two quantifiers and thus is clearly non-molecular. Generally, the definiens for any value n will require $n + 1$ quantifiers.

Thus, the reach of explicit definition in terms of observables, even in the first-order functional calculus, is greatly extended if quantification is permitted in the definiens. And if stronger logical means are countenanced, vast further extensions may be obtained. For example, the functor 'the number of cells contained in y' can be explicitly defined by the single expression

(7.11) $\hat{\alpha}\ (\alpha$ sim $\hat{x}\ (x$ is a cell $\cdot\ x$ is contained in $y))$.

Here, the circumflex accent is the symbol of class abstraction, and 'sim' the symbol for similarity of classes (in the sense of one-to-one matchability of their elements); both of these symbols belong to the vocabulary of pure logic (more specifically, of the logic of classes).

So far, we have examined only functors whose values are integers. Can functors with rational and even irrational values be similarly defined in terms of observables? Consider, for example, the theoretical functor 'length in centimeters'. Is it possible to express, in observational terms, a necessary and sufficient condition for

(7.12) $l(x,y) = r$

for every non-negative value of r? We might try to develop a suitable definition which would correspond to the fundamental method of measuring length by means of rigid rods. And indeed, if our observational vocabulary contains a name for the standard meter bar, and furthermore the (purely qualitative) terms required to describe the fundamental measuring procedure, it is possible to state, for any specified rational or irrational value of r, a necessary and sufficient condition for (7.12). However, the definiens will in most cases be far from molecular in form: it will be teeming with symbols of quantification over individuals and over classes and relations of various types.[40] We will indicate, in brief outline, the way in which such definitions may be obtained. Expressions assumed to belong to the observational vocabulary will be italicized.

First, *the segment determined by points* x,y will be said to have a length of 100 centimeters if it is *congruent with* (i.e., can be made to coincide with) *the segment marked off on the standard meter bar*. This definiens is even of molecular form. But consider next the observational criterion for $l(x,y) = .25$. It may be stated in the following form, which begins with a quantificational phrase: there are four *segments*, each *marked off on a rigid body*, such that (i) all four are *congruent with* each other; (ii) their *sum* (i.e., the segment obtained by placing them end to end along a straight line) is *congruent with the segment marked off on the standard meter bar*; (iii) any of the four *segments* is *congruent with the segment determined by points* x,y. Analogously, an explicit observational definiens can be formulated for any other value of n that is a rational multiple of 100, and hence, for any rational value of n.

Next, the consideration that an irrational number can be construed as the limit of a sequence of rational numbers yields the following necessary and sufficient condition for $l(x,y) = r$, where r is irrational: the *segment determined by points* x,y contains an infinite sequence of *points* $x_1, x_2, x_3 \ldots$ such that (i) x_1 is *between* x and y, x_2 *between* x_1 and y, and so forth; (ii) given any *segment* S of rational length, there is a *point*, say x_n, in the sequence such that the *segments determined by* x_n and y, $x_n + 1$ and y, and so forth are all *shorter than* S, (iii) the lengths of the *segments determined by* x and x_1, x and x_2, and so forth, form a sequence of rational numbers with the limit r.

Finally, the idea underlying the preceding definition can be used to formulate an explicit definiens for the expression 'l(x,y)' in such a way that its range of values is the set of all non-negative numbers.

Definitions of the kind here outlined are attainable only at the cost of using a strong logical apparatus, namely, a logic of sets adequate for the development of the theory of real numbers.[41] This price will be considered too high by nominalists, who hold that many of the logical concepts and principles here required, beginning with the general concept of set, are intrinsically obscure and should not, therefore, be used in a purported explication of the meanings of scientific terms. This is not the place to discuss the nominalistic strictures, however; and besides, it would no doubt be generally considered a worthwhile advance in clarification if for a set of theoretical scientific expressions explicit definitions in terms of observables can be constructed at all.

Another objection that might be raised against the definitional procedure here outlined is that it takes a schematic and oversimplified view of the fundamental measurement of length, and that it is rather liberal in construing as observational certain terms needed in the definiens, such as 'rigid body' and 'point'. This is quite true. By including the term 'point' in the observational vocabulary, for example, we construed points as directly observable physical objects; but our observational criterion for two points x,y determining a segment of irrational length required that there should be an infinite sequence of other points between x and y. This condition is never satisfied by the observable "points" in the form of small physical objects, or marks on rigid bodies, which are used in the fundamental measurement of length. As a consequence, the actual performance of fundamental measurement as represented in the above definition will never yield an irrational value for the length of a segment. But this does not show that no meaning has been assigned to irrational lengths; on the contrary, our outline of the definition shows that a meaning can indeed be formulated in observational terms for the assignment of any specified irrational value to the length of a physical line segment, as well as for the functor 'length in cm' in general.

However, the concept of length thus defined is not adequate for a physical theory which incorporates geometry, say in its Euclidean form. For the latter requires that certain segments which are well accessible to direct measurement—such as the diagonal of a square whose sides have a length of 100 centimeters—have an irrational length value; and statements to this effect will always turn out to be false if the criterion just discussed is made strictly definitory of length; for that procedure, as we noted, will always yield a rational value for the length of a given segment.

What the preceding argument about quantitative terms (represented by functors) shows, then, is this: the fact that the set of permissible values of a theoretical functor term is denumerably infinite or even has the cardinality of the continuum does not exclude the possibility of an explicit definition for it by means of a finite vocabulary containing only qualitative terms which are, by reasonably liberal standards, observational in character. The argument does not show, however, that such a definition is available for every functor term required by science (even our illustrative definition of 'length' turned out not to meet the needs of theoretical physics); and indeed, as was pointed out early in this section, a general proof to this effect cannot be expected.

A number of writers have taken the position that even if in principle theoretical terms could be avoided in favor of observational ones, it would be practically impossible or—what is more serious—methodologically disadvantageous or even stultifying to do so.

There is, for example, the answer given by Tolman and by Spence to the problem considered by Hull, which was mentioned in section 5 above: if intervening theoretical variables can establish a secure linkage between antecedent and consequent observable conditions, why should we not use just one functional connection that directly links antecedents and consequents? Spence adduces as one reason, also suggested by Tolman,[42] the following consideration: the mathematical function required to express the connection will be so complex that it is humanly impossible to conceive of it all at once; we can arrive at it only by breaking it down into a sequence of simpler functional connections, mediated by intervening variables. This argument, then, attributes to the introduction of unobservable theoretical entities an important practical role in the context of discovering interdependencies among observables, and presumably also in the context of actually performing the calculations required for the explanation or prediction of specific occurrences on the basis of those interdependencies.

An important methodological function is attributed to hypothetical entities in an interesting passage of Hull's essay on intervening variables in molar behavior theory.[43] The crucial point of Hull's argument is this: Suppose that in order to explain or predict the response of a subject in a given situation, we attribute to the subject, at the time t_1 of his response, a certain habit strength, which has the status of a hypothetical entity. That strength is, in Hull's theory, "merely a quantitative representation of the perseverative after-effects" of certain earlier observable events, such as observable stimuli received in temporally remote learning situations. Consequently, if reference to the hypothetical entity, habit strength, were avoided by linking the subject's observable response at t_1 directly to the observable stimuli received earlier then we would be invoking, as causal determinants for the response, certain observable events which at the time of the response, have long ceased to exist. And Hull rejects this notion, apparently inevitable when intervening hypothetical entities are eschewed, of causal action over a temporal distance: "it is hard to believe that an event such as stimulation in a remote learning situation can be causally active long after it has ceased to act on the receptors. I fully agree with Lewin that all the factors alleged to be causally influential in the determination of any other event must be in existence at the time of such causal action." [44] The hypothetical factor represented by the habit strength of the subject at the time t_1 of his response permits an explanation that accords with this principle.

Though the concluding part of the passage just quoted sounds quite metaphysical, the basic import of Hull's argument is methodological. It credits the assumption of explanatory hypothetical entities with an accomplishment that is well described by Feigl in another context: "the discontinuous and historical character (action at a spatial and/or temporal distance) of the phenomenalistically restricted account vanishes and is replaced by a spatio-temporally continuous (contiguous) and nomologically coherent formulation on the level of hypothetical construction." [45] Such spatio-temporally continuous theories appear to recommend themselves for at least two reasons: first, they possess a certain formal simplicity, which at present can hardly be characterized in precise terms, but which is reflected, for example, in the possibility of using the powerful and elegant mathematical machinery of the calculus for the deduction, from the postulates of the theory, of explanatory and predictive connections among particular occurrences. And second, as was mentioned in section 3, the past development of empirical science seems to show that explanatory and predictive principles asserting discontinuous connections among (spatio-temporally separated) observable events are likely to be found to have limited scope and various kinds of exceptions. The use of theories in terms of hypothetical entities frequently makes it possible to account for such exceptions by means of suitable assumptions concerning the hypothetical entities involved.

Another, more general, argument that must be considered here has been developed in a lucid and precise manner by Braithwaite,[46] who gives credit to Ramsey for the basic principle.[47] Braithwaite's main contention is that "theoretical terms can only be defined by means of observable properties on condition that the theory cannot be adapted properly to apply to new situations." [48] He elaborates this idea by reference to a simple, precisely formulated, miniature model of an interpreted theory. Without going into the details of that model—which would require too long a digression here—Braithwaite's claim can be adequately illustrated, it seems, by the following example: suppose that the term 'temperature' is interpreted, at a certain stage of scientific research, only by reference to the readings of a mercury thermometer. If this observational criterion is taken as just a partial interpretation (namely as a sufficient but not necessary condition), then the possibility is left open of adding further partial interpretations, by reference to other thermometrical substances which are usable above the boiling point or below the freezing point of mercury; and this permits a vast increase in the range of application of such laws as those connecting the temperature of a metal rod with its length or with its electric resistance, or the temperature of a gas with its pressure or its volume. If, however, the original criterion is given the status of a complete definiens, then the theory is not capable of such expansion; rather, the original definition has to be abandoned in favor of another one, which is incompatible with the first.[49]

The concept of intelligence lends itself to a similar argument: if test criteria which presuppose, on the part of the subject, the ability to read or at least to use language extensively are accorded the status of full definitions, then difficulties of the sort just indicated arise when the concept and the corresponding theory are to be extended to very young children or to animals.

However, the argument here outlined can hardly be said to establish what is claimed, namely that "A theory which it is hoped may be expanded in the future to explain more generalizations than it was originally designed to explain must allow more freedom to its theoretical terms than would be given them were they to be logical constructions out of observable entities" [50] (and thus defined in terms of the latter). For clearly, the procedure of expanding a theory at the cost of changing the definitions of some theoretical terms is not logically faulty; nor can it even be said to be difficult or inconvenient for the scientist, for the problem at hand is rather one for the methodologist or the logician, who seeks to give a clear "explication" or "logical reconstruction" of the changes occurring in an expansion of a given theory. And in the type of case discussed by Braithwaite, for example, this can be done in alternative ways—either in terms of additions to the original partial interpretation, or in terms of a total change of definition for some theoretical expressions. And if it is held that this latter method constitutes, not an expansion of the original theory, but a transition to a new one, this would raise more a terminological question than a methodological objection.

But though the above argument against definition does not have the intended systematic weight, it throws into relief an important heuristic aspect of scientific theorizing: when a scientist introduces theoretical entities such as electric currents, magnetic fields, chemical valences, or subconscious mechanisms, he intends them to serve as explanatory factors which have an existence independent of the observable symptoms by which they manifest themselves; or, to put it in more sober terms: whatever observational criteria of application the scientist may provide are intended by him to describe just symptoms or indications of the presence of the entity in question, but not to give an exhaustive characterization of it. The scientist does indeed wish to leave open the possibility of adding to his theory further statements involving his theoretical terms—statements which may yield new interpretative connections between theoretical and observational terms; and yet he will regard these as additional assumptions about the same hypothetical entities to which the theoretical terms referred before the expansion. This way of looking at theoretical terms appears to have definite heuristic value. It stimulates the invention and use of powerfully explanatory concepts for which only some links with experience can be indicated at the time, but which are fruitful in suggesting further lines of research that may lead to additional connections with the data of direct observation.[51]

The survey made in the present section has yielded no conclusive argument for or against the possibility of explicitly defining all theoretical terms of empirical science by means of a purely observational vocabulary; and in fact we have found strong reasons to doubt that any argument can settle the question once and for all.

As for the theoretical terms currently in use, we are quite unable at present to formulate observational definientia for all of them, and thus to make them, in principle, unnecessary. In effect, therefore, most theoretical terms are presently used in science on the basis of only a partial experiential interpretation; and this use, as we noted, appears to offer distinct heuristic advantages.

In view of the importance that thus attaches to the idea of partial interpretation, we will now consider somewhat more closely what kind of formal account might be given of it, and we will then turn to the question whether, or in what sense, the verdict of dispensability as proclaimed by the "theoretician's dilemma," applies also to theoretical terms which have been only partially interpreted, and which, therefore, cannot be dispensed with simply by virtue of definition.

8. Interpretative Systems

Carnap's theory of reduction sentences is the first systematic study of the logic of partial definition. The introduction of a term by means of a chain of reduction sentences differs in two significant respects from the use of a chain of definitions. First, it specifies the meaning of the term only partially and thus does not provide a way of eliminating the term from all contexts in which it may occur. Second, as a rule, it does not amount just to a notational convention, but involves empirical assertions. If, for example, the term 'Q' is introduced by the two reduction sentences

(8.1) $C_1x \supset (Qx \equiv E_1x)$
(8.2) $C_2x \supset (Qx \equiv E_2x)$

then the following empirical law is asserted by implication:

(8.3) $(x) ((C_1x \cdot E_1x) \supset (C_2x \supset E_2x))$

i.e., roughly speaking: any object that shows a positive response under the first test condition will, when put into the second test condition, show a positive response as well. Thus, a chain of reduction sentences for a given term normally combines two functions of language that are often considered as sharply distinct: the stipulative assignment of meaning, and the assertion or description of empirical fact.

Reduction sentences, as we saw earlier, are very well suited for the formulation of operational criteria of application as partial definitions. But they are subject to rather severe limitations as to logical form and thus do not seem sufficient to provide a satisfactory general schema for the partial interpretation of theoretical terms.[52] A broader view of interpretation is suggested by Campbell's conception of a physical theory as consisting of a "hypothesis," represented by a set of sentences in theoretical terms, and a "dictionary," which relates the latter to concepts of experimental physics (which must be interconnected by empirical laws).[53] In contrast to the standard conception of a dictionary, Campbell's dictionary is assumed to contain, not definitions for the theoretical terms, but statements to the effect that a theoretical sentence of a certain kind is true if and only if a corresponding empirical sentence of a specified kind is true.[54] Thus, rather than definitions, the dictionary provides rules of translation; and partial rules at that, for no claim is made that a translation must be specified for each theoretical statement or for each empirical statement.

This latter feature accords well, for example, with the consideration that a particular observable macro-state of a given physical system may correspond to a large number of theoretically distinguishable micro-states; so that, for a theoretical sentence describing just one of those micro-states, the sentence describing the corresponding macro-state does not express a necessary and sufficient condition, and hence provides no translation.[55]

The statements in Campbell's dictionary evidently do not have the character of reduction sentences; they might be formulated, however, as biconditionals in which a sentence in theoretical terms is connected, by an "if and only if" clause, with a sentence in observational terms.

In other contexts, neither reduction sentences nor such biconditionals seem to be adequate. For as a rule, the presence of a hypothetical entity H, such as a certain kind of electric field, will have observable symptoms only if certain observational conditions, O_1, are satisfied, such as the presence of suitable detecting devices, which will then have to show observable responses, O_2. A sentence stating this kind of criterion would have the character of a generalized reduction sentence; it might be put into the form

$$(8.4) \quad O_1 \supset (H \supset O_2)$$

where 'O_1' and 'O_2' are sentences—possibly quite complex ones—in terms of observables, and 'H' is a sentence which is expressed in theoretical terms.

But there is no good reason to limit interpretative statements to just the three types here considered. In order to obtain a general concept of partial interpretation, we will now admit as interpretative statements any sentences, of whatever logical form, which contain theoretical and observational terms. On the assumption that the theoretical and observational statements of empirical science are formulated within a specified logical framework, this idea can be stated more precisely and explicitly as follows:

(8.5) Let T be a theory *characterized by* a set of postulates in terms of a finite *theoretical vocabulary* V_T, and let V_B be a second set of extra-logical terms, to be called the *basic vocabulary*, which shares no term with V_T. By an *interpretative system* for T with the basis V_B we will then understand a set J of sentences which (i) is finite, (ii) is logically compatible with T, (iii) contains no extra-logical term that is not contained in V_T or V_B, (iv) contains every element of V_T and V_B essentially, i.e., it is not logically equivalent to some set of sentences in which some term of V_T or V_B does not occur at all.[56]

In applying the concept here defined to the analysis of scientific theories, we will have to assume, of course, that V_B consists of terms which are antecedently understood. They might be observational terms, in the somewhat vague sense explained earlier; but we need not insist on this. One might well take the view, for example, that certain disposition terms such as 'malleable', 'elastic', 'hungry', and 'tired' are not strictly observation terms, and are not known to be explicitly definable by means of observation terms; and yet, such terms might be taken to be well understood in the sense that they are used with a high degree of agreement by different competent observers. In this case, it would be quite reasonable to use these terms in interpreting a given theory, i.e., to admit them into V_B.

Campbell's conception of the function of his "dictionary" illustrates this possibility very well and shows that it comes closer to actual scientific procedure. Campbell specifies that the interpretation provided by the dictionary must be in terms of what he calls "concepts," such as the terms 'temperature', 'electrical resistance', 'silver', and 'iron' as used in experimental physics and chemistry. These are hardly observational in the narrow sense, for they are specifically conceived as representing clusters of empirical laws: "Thus, if we say anything about electrical resistance we assume that Ohm's Law is true; bodies for which Ohm's Law is not true, gases for example, have no electrical resistance." [57] And when we qualify a given body as silver, we attribute to it certain kinds of lawful behavior concerning solubility in various liquids, melting point, and so forth. But even though one might not wish to qualify these terms as observational, one may still consider them as well understood, and as used with high intersubjective agreement, by scientific experimenters; and thus, they might be admitted into V_B.

Interpretative systems as just defined include as special cases all the types of interpretation we considered earlier, namely, interpretation by explicit definitions for all theoretical terms, by chains of reduction sentences, by biconditional translation statements in the sense of Campbell's dictionary, and by generalized reduction sentences of the form (8.4); but of course they also allow for interpretative statements in a large variety of other forms.

Interpretative systems have the same two characteristics which distinguish chains of reduction sentences from chains of definitions: First, an interpretative system normally effects only a partial interpretation of the terms in V_T; i.e., it does not lay down (by explicit statement or by logical implication), for every term in V_T, a necessary and sufficient condition of application in terms of V_B. Second, like a chain of reduction sentences for a given theoretical term, an interpretative system will normally not be purely stipulative in character, but will imply certain statements in terms of V_B alone which are not logical truths, and which, on the conception of V_B as consisting of antecedently understood empirical terms, may be viewed as expressing empirical assertions. Thus, here again, we find a combination of the stipulative and the descriptive use of language.

But, to turn to a third point of comparison, an interpretative system need not provide an interpretation—complete or incomplete—for each term in V_T individually. In this respect it differs from a set of definitions, which specifies for each term a necessary and sufficient condition, and from a set of reduction sentences, which provides for each term a necessary and a—usually different—sufficient condition. It is quite possible that an interpretative system provides, for some or even all of the terms in V_T, no necessary or no sufficient condition in terms of V_B, or indeed neither of the two; instead, it might specify, by explicit statement or by logical implication, sufficient or necessary conditions in terms of V_B only for certain expressions containing several terms of V_T—for example, in the manner of Campbell's dictionary.

As a rule, therefore, when a theory T is interpreted by an interpretative system J, the theoretical terms are not dispensable in the narrow sense of eliminability from all contexts, in favor of defining expressions in terms of V_B. Nor are they generally dispensable in the sense that J provides, for every sentence H that can be formed by means of V_T, a "translation" into terms of V_B, i.e., a sentence O in terms of V_B such the the biconditional $H \equiv O$ [58] is logically deducible from J.

Are theoretical terms, then, altogether indispensable on this broad conception of interpretation so that the "paradox of theorizing" formulated in section 5 no longer applies to them? We consider this question in the next section.

9. Functional Replaceability of Theoretical Terms

The systematizing function of a theory T, as interpreted by an interpretative system J will consist in permitting inferences from given "data" in terms of V_B to certain other (e.g., predictive) statements in terms of V_B. If O_1 is the statement expressing the data, O_2 the inferred statement, then the connection may be symbolized thus:

(9.1) $(O_1 \cdot T \cdot J) \longrightarrow O_2$

Here, as in similar contexts below, 'T' stands for the set of postulates of the theory at hand; the arrow represents deductive implication.

Now, (9.1) holds if and only if $T \cdot J$ implies the sentence $O_1 \supset O_2$; so that (9.1) is tantamount to

(9.2) $(T \cdot J) \longrightarrow (O_1 \supset O_2)$

Whatever systematization is achieved among the V_B-sentences is clearly accomplished by T in conjunction with J. It will be convenient therefore to consider the postulates of T together with the sentences of J as the postulates of a deductive system T', which will be called an *interpreted theory*. Its vocabulary $V_{T'}$ will be the sum of V_T and V_B.

What was noted in connection with (9.1) and (9.2) may now be restated thus: If an interpreted theory T' establishes a deductive transition from O_1 to O_2, i.e., if

(9.3) $(O_1 \cdot T') \longrightarrow O_2$

then

(9.4) $T' \longrightarrow (O_1 \supset O_2)$

and conversely, where T' is the set of postulates of the interpreted theory.

Now it can readily be shown that an interpreted theory T' establishes exactly the same deductive connections among V_B-sentences as does the set of all those theorems of T' which are expressible in terms of

Carl G. Hempel

V_B alone; we will call this the set of V_B-theorems, or V_B-consequences, of T', and will designate it by '$O_{T'}$'. This means, that for all purposes of deductive systematization, T' is, as we will say, functionally equivalent to the set $O_{T'}$, which contains not a single theoretical term.

The proof is as follows: The deductive transition, represented in (9.3), from O_1 to O_2 can be achieved just as well by using, instead of T', simply the sentence $O_1 \supset O_2$, which by virtue of (9.4) belongs to $O_{T'}$; for we have, by *modus ponens*,

$$(9.5) \quad (O_1 \cdot (O_1 \supset O_2)) \longrightarrow O_2$$

And since $O_{T'}$ surely contains all the V_B-sentences of the form $O_1 \supset O_2$ that are implied by T', the set $O_{T'}$ suffices to effect all the deductive systematizations achievable by means of T'. On the other hand, $O_{T'}$ is no stronger in this respect than T'; for $O_{T'}$ permits the deductive transition from O_1 to O_2 only if it implies $O_1 \supset O_2$; but in this case, T' also implies $O_1 \supset O_2$, which means, in view of the equivalence of (9.4) with (9.3), that T' will permit the deductive transition from O_1 to O_2.

Thus, *the deductive systematization that an interpreted theory T' achieves among sentences expressed in terms of a basic vocabulary V_B is exactly the same as that accomplished by the set $O_{T'}$ of those statements (theorems) of T' which can be expressed in terms of V_B alone*. In this sense, the theoretical terms used in T can be dispensed with.

But $O_{T'}$ is normally an unwieldy infinite set of statements, and the question arises therefore whether there is some generally applicable method of making it more manageable and perspicuous by putting it into the form of an axiomatized theoretical system T'_B, which would be formulated in terms of V_B alone. A theorem in formal logic which was recently proved by Craig shows that this is indeed the case, provided only that T' satisfies certain extremely liberal and unconfining conditions.[59]

Thus Craig's theorem has a definite bearing upon the problems raised by the "paradox of theorizing," which was stated in section 5 in somewhat vague terms. The theorem at hand points out one way in which the "paradox" can be given a clear and precise interpretation and a rigorous proof: It shows that for any theory T' using both theoretical terms and non-theoretical, previously understood ones, there exists, under certain very widely satisfied conditions, an axiomatized theoretical system T'_B which uses only the non-theoretical terms of T' and yet is functionally equivalent with T' in the sense of effecting, among the sentences expressible in the non-theoretical vocabulary, exactly the same deductive connections as T'.

Should empirical science then avail itself of this method and replace all its theories involving assumptions about hypothetical entities by functionally equivalent theoretical systems couched exclusively in terms which have direct observational reference or which are, at any rate, clearly understood? There are various reasons which make this inadvisable in consideration of the objectives of scientific theorizing.

To begin with, let us consider the general character of Craig's method. Disregarding many subtle points of detail, the procedure may be described as follows: By means of a constructive procedure, Craig arranges all the V_B-theorems of T' in a sequence. This sequence is highly redundant, for it contains, for any sentence occurring in it, also all its logical equivalents (as far as they are expressible in V_B). Craig prescribes a procedure for eliminating many, though not even all, of these duplications. The remaining sequence therefore still contains each V_B-theorem of T' in at least one of its various equivalent formulations. Finally, all the sentences in this remaining sequence are made postulates of T'_B. Thus, the set of V_B-theorems of T' is "axiomatized" in T'_B only in a rather Pickwickian sense, namely by making every sentence of the set, in some of its many equivalent formulations, a postulate of T'_B; whereas normally, the axiomatization of a set of sentences is intended to select as postulates just a small subset from which the rest can then be logically derived as theorems. In this manner, the axiomatization expresses the content of the whole set "in a form which is psychologically or mathematically more perspicuous." [60] And since Craig's method in effect includes all sentences that are to be axiomatized among the postulates of T'_B, the latter, as Craig himself puts it, "fail to simplify or to provide genuine insight." [61]

The loss in simplicity which results from discarding the theoretical terms of T' is reflected in the circumstance that the set of postulates which Craig's method yields for T'_B is always infinite. Even in cases where actually there exists some finite subset of $O_{T'}$ of V_B-theorems of T' from which all the rest can be deduced, Craig's procedure will not yield such a subset: that is the price of the universal applicability of Craig's method.

Carl G. Hempel

Now there are cases where an infinity of postulates may not be excessively unwieldy; notably when the axioms are specified by means of axiom-schemata,[62] i.e., by stipulations to the effect that any sentence that has one of a finite number of specified forms (such as 'x = x', for example) is to count as an axiom. But the manner in which the axioms, or postulates, of T'_B are specified by Craig's method is vastly more intricate, and the resulting system would be practically unmanageable—to say nothing of the loss in heuristic fertility and suggestiveness which results from the elimination of the theoretical concepts and hypotheses. For empirical science, therefore, this method of dispensing with theoretical expressions would be quite unsatisfactory.

So far, we have examined the eliminability of theoretical concepts and assumptions only in the context of deductive systematization: we considered an interpreted theory T' exclusively as a vehicle of establishing deductive transitions among observational sentences. However, such theories may also afford means of inductive systematization (in the sense outlined in section 1); and an analysis of this function will yield a further argument against the elimination of theoretical expressions by means of Craig's method.

By way of illustration, we will refer to the following example, which is deliberately oversimplified in order the more clearly to exhibit the essentials: we will assume that V_T contains the term 'white phosphorus', or 'P' for short, and that the interpretative system incorporated into T' states no sufficient observational conditions of application for it, but several necessary ones. These will be assumed to be independent of each other in the sense that, though in the case of white phosphorus they occur jointly, any one of them will in certain other cases occur in the absence of one or more of the others. Those necessary conditions might be the following: white phosphorus has a garlic-like odor; it is soluble in turpentine, in vegetable oils, and in ether; it produces skin burns. In symbolic notation:

(9.6) $(x)\ (Px \supset Gx)$
(9.7) $(x)\ (Px \supset Tx)$
(9.8) $(x)\ (Px \supset Vx)$
(9.9) $(x)\ (Px \supset Ex)$
(9.10) $(x)\ (Px \supset Sx)$

All predicates other than 'P' that occur in these sentences will belong, then, to V_B.

Now let V_T contain just one term in addition to 'P', namely 'has an ignition temperature of 30° C', or 'I' for short; and let there be exactly one interpretative sentence for 'I', to the effect that if an object has the property I then it will burst into flame if surrounded by air in which a thermometer shows a reading above 30° C. This property will be considered as observable and will be represented by the predicate 'F' in V_B. The interpretative sentence for 'I', then, is

(9.11) $(x) (Ix \supset Fx)$

Finally, we will assume that the theoretical part of T' contains one single postulate, namely,

(9.12) $(x) (Px \supset Ix)$

i.e., white phosphorus has an ignition temperature of 30° C. Let the seven sentences (9.6)–(9.12) represent the total content of T'.

Then, as is readily seen, T' has no consequences in terms of V_B except for purely logical truths; consequently, T' will permit a deductive transition from one V_B-sentence to another only if the latter is logically implied by the former, so that T' is not required to establish the connection. In other words: T' effects no deductive systematization among V_B-sentences at all. Nevertheless, T' may play an essential role in establishing, among the V_B-sentences, certain explanatory or predictive connections of an inductive kind. Suppose, for example, that a certain object, b, has been found to have all the characteristics G, T, V, E, S. In view of the sentences (9.6)–(9.10), according to which these characteristics are symptomatic of P, it might then well be inferred that b is white phosphorus. This inference would be inductive rather than deductive, and part of its strength would derive from the mutual independence which we assumed to exist among those five observable symptoms of white phosphorus. The sentence 'Pb' which has thus been arrived at inductively leads, via (9.12), to the prediction 'Ib', which in turn, in virtue of (9.11), yields the forecast 'Fb'. Thus, T' permits the transition from the observational data 'Gb', 'Tb', 'Vb', 'Eb', 'Sb' to the observational prediction 'Fb'. But the transition requires an inductive step, consisting of the acceptance of 'Pb' on the strength of the five data sentences, which support, but which, of course, do not conclusively establish, 'Pb'.

On the other hand, the system T'_B obtained by Craig's method does not lend itself to this inductive use; in fact, all its sentences are logical truths and thus T'$_B$ makes no empirical assertion at all, for, as was noted above, all the V$_B$-theorems of T' are logically true statements.[63]

Thus, if the systematizing use of an interpreted theory T' is conceived as involving inductive as well as deductive procedures, then the corresponding system T'$_B$ cannot, in general, replace T'.

Another, inductively simpler, method of obtaining a functional equivalent, in observational terms, of a given interpreted theory T' is provided by an idea of Ramsey's. In effect, the method amounts to treating all theoretical terms as existentially quantified variables, so that all the extra-logical constants that occur in Ramsey's manner of formulating a theory belong to the observational vocabulary.[64] Thus, for example, the interpreted theory determined by our formulas (9.6)–(9.12) would be expressed by the following sentence, which we will call the *Ramsey-sentence associated with the given theory.*

(9.13) $(\exists\phi)\,(\exists\psi)\,(x)\,((\,(\phi x \supset \psi x)\cdot(\phi x \supset (Gx\cdot Tx\cdot Vx\cdot Ex\cdot Sx))\cdot(\psi x \supset Fx))$

This sentence is equivalent to the expression obtained by conjoining the sentences (9.6)–(9.12), replacing 'P' and 'I' throughout by the variables 'ϕ' and 'ψ' respectively, and prefixing existential quantifiers with regard to the latter. Thus, (9.13) asserts that there are two properties, ϕ and ψ, otherwise unspecified, such that any object with the property ϕ also has the property ψ, and any object with the property ϕ also has the (observable, fully specified) properties G, T, V, E, S, and any object with the property ψ also has the (observable, fully specified) property F.

An interpreted theory T' as we have been conceiving it is not, of course, logically equivalent with its associated Ramsey-sentence any more than it is logically equivalent with the associated Craig-system T'$_B$; in fact, each of the two is implied by, but does not in turn imply, T'. But though the Ramsey-sentence contains, apart from variables and logical constants, only terms from V$_B$, it can be shown to imply exactly the same V$_B$-sentences as does T'; hence, it establishes exactly the same deductive transitions among V$_B$-sentences as does T'. In this respect then, the Ramsey-sentence associated with T' is on a par with the Craig-system T'$_B$ obtainable from T'. But its logical apparatus is more extravagant than that required by T' or by T'$_B$. In our illustration, (9.6)–(9.12), for example, T' and T'$_B$ contain variables and quantifiers only with respect to individuals (physical objects), whereas the Ramsey-sentence (9.13) contains variables and quantifiers also for properties of individuals; thus, while T' and T'$_B$ require only a first-order functional calculus, the Ramsey-sentence calls for a second-order functional calculus.

But this means that the Ramsey-sentence associated with an interpreted theory T' avoids reference to hypothetical entities only in letter—replacing Latin constants by Greek variables—rather than in spirit. For it still asserts the existence of certain entities of the kind postulated by T', without guaranteeing any more than does T' that those entities are observable or at least fully characterizable in terms of observables. Hence, Ramsey-sentences provide no satisfactory way of avoiding theoretical concepts.

And indeed, Ramsey himself made no such claim. Rather, his construal of theoretical terms as existentially quantified variables appears to have been motivated by considerations of the following kind: If theoretical terms are treated as constants which are not fully defined in terms of antecedently understood observational terms, then the sentences that can formally be constructed out of them do not have the character of assertions with fully specified meanings, which can be significantly held to be either true or false; rather, their status is comparable to that of sentential functions, with the theoretical terms playing the role of variables. But of a theory, we want to be able to predicate truth or falsity, and the construal of theoretical terms as existentially quantified variables yields a formulation which meets this requirement and at the same time retains all the intended empirical implications of the theory.

This consideration raises a further problem concerning the status of partially interpreted theories; that problem will be discussed in the next section.

10. On Meaning and Truth of Scientific Theories

The problem suggested by Ramsey's approach is this: if, in the manner of section 8, we construe the theoretical terms of a theory as extralogical constants for which the system J provides only a partial interpretation in terms of the antecedently understood vocabulary V_B, can the sentences formed by means of the theoretical vocabulary nevertheless be considered as statements which make definite assertions, and which are either true or false?

The question might seem to come under the jurisdiction of semantics, and more specifically, of the semantical theory of truth. But this is not the case. What the semantical theory of truth provides (under certain conditions) is a general definition of truth for the sentences of a given language L. That definition is stated in a suitable metalanguage, M, of L and permits the formulation of a necessary and sufficient condition of truth for any sentence S of L. This condition is represented simply by a translation of S into M.[65] (To be suited for its purpose, M must therefore contain a translation of every sentence of L and must meet certain other conditions which are precisely specified in the semantical theory of truth.) But if the truth criteria thus stated in M are to be intelligible at all, then clearly all the translations of L-statements into M must be assumed to be significant to begin with. Instead of deciding the question of the significance of L-sentences, the semantical definition of truth presupposes that it has been settled antecedently.

For quite analogous reasons, semantics does not enable us to decide whether the theoretical terms in a given system T' do, or do not, have semantical, or factual, or ontological reference—a characteristic which some writers have considered as distinguishing genuinely theoretical constructs from auxiliary or intervening theoretical terms.[66] One difficulty with the claims and counter-claims that have been made in this connection lies in the failure of the discussants to indicate clearly what they wish to assert by attributing ontological reference to a given term. Let us note here that from a purely semantical point of view, it is possible to attribute semantical reference to any term of a language L that is taken to be understood: the referent can be specified in the same manner as the truth condition of a given sentence in L, namely by translation into a suitable metalanguage. For example, using English as a metalanguage, we might say, in reference to Freud's terminology, that 'Verdraengung' designates repression, 'Sublimierung', sublimation, and so on. Plainly, this kind of information is unilluminating for those who wish to use existential reference as a distinctive characteristic of a certain kind of theoretical terms; nor does it help those who want to know whether, or in what sense, the entities designated by theoretical terms can be said actually to exist—a question to which we will return.

Semantics, then, does not answer the question raised at the beginning of this section; we have to look elsewhere for criteria of significance for theoretical terms and sentences.

Generally speaking, we might qualify a theoretical expression as intelligible or significant if it has been adequately explained in terms which we consider as antecedently understood. In our earlier discussion, such terms were represented by the vocabulary V_B (plus the terms of logic). But now the question arises, What constitutes an "adequate" explanation? No generally binding standards can be specified: the answer is ultimately determined by one's philosophical conscience. The logical and epistemological puritan will declare intelligible only what has been explicitly defined in terms of V_B; and he may impose further restrictions, in a nominalistic vein, for example, on the logical apparatus that may be used in formulating the definitions. Others will find terms introduced by reduction sentences quite intelligible, and still others will even countenance an interpretation as tenuous as that afforded by an interpretative system. One of the most important advantages of definition lies in the fact that it ensures the possibility of an equivalent restatement of any theoretical sentence in terms of V_B. Partial interpretation does not guarantee this; consequently it does not provide, for every sentence expressible in theoretical terms, a necessary and sufficient condition of truth that can be stated in terms which are antecedently understood. This, no doubt, is the basic difficulty that critics find with the method of partial interpretation.

In defense of partial interpretation, on the other hand, it can be said that to understand an expression is to know how to use it, and in a formal reconstruction the "how to" is expressed by means of rules. Partial interpretation as we have construed it provides such rules. These show, for example, what sentences in terms of V_B alone may be inferred from sentences containing theoretical terms; and thus they specify, in particular, a set of V_B-sentences that are implied, and hence indirectly asserted, by an interpreted theory T'. (If the set is empty, the theory does not fall within the domain of empirical science.) Conversely, the rules also show that sentences in theoretical terms may be inferred from V_B-sentences. Thus, there are close resemblances between our theoretical sentences and those sentences which are intelligible in the narrower sense of being expressible entirely in terms of V_B—a circumstance which militates in favor of admitting theoretical sentences into the class of significant statements.

It should be mentioned that if this policy is adopted, then we will have to recognize as significant (though not, of course, as interesting or worth investigating) certain interpreted systems which surely would not qualify as potential scientific theories. For example, let L be the conjunction of some finite number of empirical generalizations about learning behavior, formulated in terms of an observational vocabulary V_B, and let P be the conjunction of a finite number of arbitrary sentences formed out of a set V_T of arbitrarily chosen uninterpreted terms (for example, P might be the conjunction of the postulates of some axiomatization of elliptic geometry). Then, by making P the postulates of T and by choosing the sentence $P \supset L$ as the only member of our interpretative system J, we obtain an interpreted theory, which "explains" in a trivial way all the given empirical generalizations, since $T \cdot J$ plainly implies L. Yet, needless to say, T' would not be considered a satisfactory learning theory.[67] The characteristic here illustrated does not vitiate our analysis of partial interpretation, since the latter does not claim that every partially interpreted theoretical system is a potentially interesting theory; and indeed, even the requirement of full definition of all theoretical terms by means of V_B still leaves room for similarly unrewarding "theories." Examples like our mock "learning theory" simply remind us that, in addition to having an empirical interpretation (which is necessary if there are to be any empirically testable consequences) a good scientific theory must satisfy various important further conditions; its V_B-consequences must be empirically well confirmed; it must effect a logically simple systematization of the pertinent V_B-sentences, it must suggest further empirical laws, and so forth.

If the sentences of a partially interpreted theory T' are granted the status of significant statements, they can be said to be either true or false. And then the question, touched upon earlier in this section, as to the factual reference of theoretical terms, can be dealt with in a quite straightforward manner: To assert that the terms of a given theory have factual reference, that the entities they purport to refer to actually exist, is tantamount to asserting that what the theory tells us is true; and this in turn is tantamount to asserting the theory. When we say, for example, that the elementary particles of contemporary physical theory actually exist, we assert that there occur in the universe particles of the various kinds indicated by physical theory, governed by specified physical laws, and showing certain specific kinds of observable symptoms—again indicated by physical theory—of their presence in certain specified circumstances. But this is tantamount to asserting the truth of the (interpreted) physical theory of elementary particles. Similarly, asserting the existence of the drives, reserves, habit strengths, postulated by a given theory of learning amounts to affirming the truth of the system consisting of the statements of the theory and its empirical interpretation.[68]

Thus understood, the existence of hypothetical entities with specified characteristics and interrelations, as assumed by a given theory, can be examined inductively in the same sense in which the truth of the theory itself can be examined, namely, by an empirical investigation of its V_B-consequences.

According to the conception just outlined, we have to attribute factual reference to all the (extra-logical) terms of a theory if that theory is true; hence, this characteristic provides no basis for a semantical dichotomy in the theoretical vocabulary. Also, the factual reference, as here construed, of theoretical terms does not depend on whether those terms are avoidable in favor of expressions couched in terms of V_B alone. Even if all the theoretical terms of a theory T' are explicitly defined in terms of V_B, so that their use affords a convenient shorthand way of saying what could also be said by means of V_B alone, they will still have factual reference if what the theory says is true.

The preceding observations on truth and on factual reference in regard to partially interpreted theories rest on the assumption that the sentences of such theories are accorded the status of statements. For those who find this assumption unacceptable, there are at least two other ways of construing what we have called an interpreted theory. The first of these is Ramsey's method, which was described in the previous section. It has the very attractive feature of representing an interpreted theory in the form of a bona fide statement, which contains no extra-logical constants other than those contained in V_B, and still has exactly the same V_B-consequences as the interpreted theory stated in terms of incompletely interpreted theoretical constants. It is perhaps the most satisfactory way of conceiving the logical character of a scientific theory, and it will be objectionable mainly, or perhaps only, to those who, on philosophical grounds, are opposed to the ontological commitments [69] involved in countenancing all the requisite variables ranging over domains other than that of the individuals of the theory (such as, for example, the set of all quantitative characteristics of physical objects, or the set of all dyadic relations among them, or sets of such sets, and so forth).

Those finally, who, like the contemporary nominalists, reject such strong ontological commitments, may adopt a conception of scientific theories, not as significant statements, but as intricate devices for inferring, from intelligible initial statements, expressed in terms of an antecedently understood vocabulary V_B, certain other, again intelligible, statements in terms of that vocabulary.[70] The theoretical terms are then construed as meaningless auxiliary marks, which serve as convenient symbolic devices in the transition from one set of experiential statements to another. To be sure, the conception of laws and theories as extra-logical principles of inference does not reflect the way in which they are used by theoretical scientists. In publications dealing with problems of theoretical physics, or biology, or psychology, for example, sentences containing theoretical terms are normally treated on a par with those which serve to describe empirical data: together with the latter, they function as premises and as conclusions of deductive and of inductive arguments. And indeed, for the working scientist the actual formulation and use of theoretical principles as complex extra-logical rules of inference would be a hindrance rather than a help. However, the purpose of those who suggest this conception is not, of course, to facilitate the work of the scientist but rather to clarify the import of his formulations; and from the viewpoint of a philosophical analyst with nominalistic inclinations, for example, the proposed view of scientific sentences which by his standards are not intelligible statements, does represent an advance in clarification.

However, the question posed by the theoretician's dilemma can be raised also in regard to the two alternative conceptions of the status of a theory. Concerning Ramsey's formulation, we may ask whether it is not possible to dispense altogether with the existentially quantified variables which represent the theoretical terms, and thus to avoid the ontological commitment they require, without sacrificing any of the deductive connections that the Ramsey-sentence establishes among V_B-sentences. And in regard to theories conceived as inferential devices, we may ask whether they cannot be replaced by a functionally equivalent set of rules—i.e., one establishing exactly the same inferential transitions among V_B-sentences—which uses none of the "meaningless marks."

In both cases, Craig's theorem gives an affirmative answer by describing a general method for constructing the desired kind of equivalent (provided only that the original formulation meets the very weak requirements of that theorem). But again, in both cases, the result has the same shortcomings that were mentioned in section 8: First of all, the method would replace the Ramsey-sentence by an infinite set of postulates, or the body of inferential rules by an infinite set of rules, in terms of V_B, and would thus lead to a loss of economy. Second, the resulting system of postulates or of inferential rules would not lend itself to inductive prediction and explanation. And third, it would have the pragmatic defect, partly reflected already in the second point, of being less fruitful heuristically than the system using theoretical terms.

When scientists or methodologists claim that the theoretical terms of a given theory refer to entities which have an existence of their own, which are essential constituents or aspects of the world we live in, then, no matter what individual connotations they may connect with this assertion, the reasons they could adduce in support of it seem clearly to lie in the fact that those terms function in a well-confirmed theory which effects an economical systematization, both deductive and inductive, of a large class of particular facts and empirical generalizations, and which is heuristically fertile in suggesting further questions and new hypotheses. And as far as suitability for inductive systematization, along with economy and heuristic fertility, are considered essential characteristics of a scientific theory, theoretical terms cannot be replaced without serious loss by formulations in terms of observables only: the theoretician's dilemma, whose conclusion asserts the contrary, starts with a false premise.

NOTES

[1] This term was suggested by a passage in Reichenbach's volume (70), where the word 'postdictability' is used to refer to the possibility of determining "past data in terms of given observations" (p. 13). In a similar context, Ryle uses the term 'retrodict' (see, for example, (78, p. 124)), and Walsh speaks of the historians' "business to 'retrodict' the past: to establish, on the basis of present evidence, what the past must have been like" (93, p. 41). According to a remark in Acton's review of Walsh's book (*Mind*, vol. 62 (1953), pp. 564–565), the word 'retrodiction' was used in this sense already by J. M. Robertson in *Buckle and his Critics* (1895).

[2] More accurately: it can be deduced from the principles of Newtonian mechanics that Kepler's laws hold in approximation, namely, on the assumption that the forces exerted upon the planets by celestial objects other than the sun (especially other planets) are negligible.

[3] For a fuller presentation of this deductive schema of scientific explanation and prediction, see Popper (62, section 12, and 63, Chapter 25), and Hempel and Oppenheim (36).

[4] The distinction here made refers, then, exclusively to the form of the statements under consideration, and not to their truth status or to the extent to which they are

supported by empirical evidence. If it were established, for example, that actually only 80 per cent of all crows are black, this would not show that 'all crows are black,' or S_1 for short, was a statistical probability statement, but rather that it was a false statement of strictly universal form, and that 'The probability for a crow to be black is .8,' or S_2 for short, was a true statement of statistical form.

Furthermore, to be sure, neither S_1 nor S_2 can ever be established conclusively: they can only be more or less well supported by available evidence; each of them thus has a more or less high logical, or inductive, probability, relative to that evidence. But this again does not affect at all the fact that S_1 is of strictly universal and S_2 of statistical form.

[5] For a fuller discussion of this point, see, for example, Nagel (55, section 7), Reichenbach (71, sections 63–67), Cramer (18, Chapter 13).

[6] The explanatory and predictive use of statistical laws constitutes perhaps the most important type of inductive systematization; but the occurrence of such laws among the premises is not required by our general concept of inductive systematization. And indeed, as Carnap (11, pp. 574–575) has pointed out, it is sometimes possible to make predictions of an inductive character exclusively on the basis of information about a finite set of particular cases, without the mediation of any laws whatever. For example, information to the effect that a large sample of instances of P has been examined, that all of its elements have the characteristic Q, and that a certain case x, not included in the sample, is an instance of P, will lend high inductive support to the prediction that x, too, has the characteristic Q. Also, it is sometimes possible to base an inductive systematization on a set of premises which include one or more strictly universal statements, but no statistical laws. An example of such a systematization will be found in Section 9, in the prediction based on the formulas (9.6)–(9.12).

[7] Mises (54, p. 188). Whether it is advisable to refer to explanations of this kind as causal is debatable: since the classical conception of causality is intimately bound up with the idea of strictly universal laws connecting cause and effect, it might be better to reserve the term 'causal explanation' for some or all of those explanatory arguments of form (1.1) in which all the laws invoked are of strictly universal form.

[8] Northrop (59, Chapters III and IV), for example, presents this distinction very suggestively; he refers to the two levels as "the natural history stage of inquiry" and "the stage of deductively formulated theory." A very lucid and concise discussion of the idea at hand will be found in Feigl (20).

[9] In his essay on Skinner's analysis of learning (in Estes et al. (19)), Verplanck throws an illuminating sidelight on the importance, for the observational vocabulary (the terms of the data-language, as he calls it), of high uniformity of use among different experimenters. Verplanck argues that while much of Skinner's data-language is sound in this respect, it is "contaminated" by the inclusion, in its vocabulary, of two kinds of terms that are not suited for the description of objective scientific data. The first kind includes terms "that cannot be successfully used by many others"; the second kind includes certain terms that should properly be treated as higher order theoretical expressions.

The non-precise and pragmatic character of the requirement of intersubjective uniformity of use is nicely reflected in Verplanck's conjecture "that if one were to work with Skinner, and read his records with him, he would find himself able to make the same discriminations as does Skinner and hence eventually give some of them at least data-language status" (loc. cit., p. 279n).

[10] It should be mentioned, however, that the idea of the range of application of a generalization is here used in an intuitive sense which it would be difficult to explicate. The range of application of (3.1), for example, might plausibly be held to be narrower than here indicated: it might be construed as consisting only of wooden-objects-placed-in-water, and iron-objects-placed-in-water. On the other hand, (3.1) may be equivalently restated thus: Any object whatever has the two properties of either not

being wood or floating on water, and of either not being iron or sinking in water. In this form, the generalization might be said to have the largest possible range of application, the class of all objects whatever.

[11] Since (3.2) was presented as a definition, it might be considered inappropriate to include it among the general laws effecting the predictive transition from O_1, O_2, O_3, O_4, to O_5. And indeed, it is quite possible to construe the concept of logical deduction as applied to (1.1) in such a way that it includes the use of any definition as an additional premise. In this case, (3.3) is the only law invoked in the prediction here considered. On the other hand, it is also possible to treat sentences such as (3.2), which are usually classified as purely definitional, on a par with other statements of universal form, which are qualified as general laws. This view is favored by the consideration, for example, that when a theory conflicts with pertinent empirical data, it is sometimes the "laws" and sometimes the "definitions" that are modified in order to accommodate the evidence. Our analysis of deductive systematization is neutral with respect to this issue.

[12] A lucid elementary discussion of the nature of axiomatized mathematical systems may be found in Cohen and Nagel (15, Chapter VI; also reprinted in Feigl and Brodbeck (24)). For an analysis in a similar vein, with special emphasis on geometry, see also Hempel (30). An excellent systematic account of the axiomatic method is given in Tarski (84, Chapters VI–X); this presentation, which makes use of some concepts of elementary symbolic logic, as developed in earlier chapters, includes several simple illustrations from mathematics. A careful logical study of deductive systems in empirical science, with special attention to the role of theoretical terms, is carried out in the first three chapters of Braithwaite (4), and a logically more advanced exposition of the axiomatic method, coupled with applications to biological theory, has been given by Woodger, especially in (98) and (99).

[13] See, for example, Hermes (37); Walker (92); McKinsey, Sugar, and Suppes (52); McKinsey and Suppes (53); Rubin and Suppes (75), and the further references given in these publications. An important pioneer work in the field is Reichenbach (68).

[14] See especially Woodger (98) and (99).

[15] See, for example, Hull et al. (39).

[16] For example, in von Neumann and Morgenstern (58, Chapter III and Appendix).

[17] Statements effecting an empirical interpretation of theoretical terms have been discussed in the methodological literature under a variety of names. For example, Reichenbach, who quite early emphasized the importance of the idea with special reference to the relation between pure and physical geometry, speaks of *coordinative definitions* (69, section 4; also 72, Chapter VIII); Campbell (7, Chapter VI; an excerpt from this chapter is reprinted in Feigl and Brodbeck (24)) and Ramsey (67, pp. 212–236) assume a *dictionary* connecting theoretical and empirical terms. (See also Section 8 below). Margenau (48, especially Chapter 4) speaks of *rules of correspondence*, and recently Carnap (14) has likewise used the general term 'correspondence rules'. Northrop's *epistemic correlations* (59, especially Chapter VII) may be viewed as a special kind of interpretative statements. For a discussion of interpretation as a semantical procedure, see Carnap (10, sections 23, 24, 25), and Hutten (40, especially Chapter II). A fuller discussion of interpretative statements is included in sections 6, 7, 8 of the present essay.

[18] A lucid and concise presentation may be found, for example, in Bergmann and Spence (3).

[19] Hull (38, p. 284).

[20] Skinner (80, p. 35).

[21] Tolman, Ritchie, and Kalish (88, p. 15). See also the detailed critical analysis of Tolman's characterization of expectancy in MacCorquodale and Meehl (47, pp. 179–181).

[22] See Carnap (8, section 4).

[23] On this point, and on the general problem of explicating the concept of a law of nature, see Braithwaite (4, Chapter IX); Burks (6); Carnap (14, section 9); Goodman (28); Hempel and Oppenheim (36, Part III); Reichenbach (73).

[24] In his theory of reduction sentences, developed in Carnap (8). There is a question, however, whether certain conditions which Carnap imposes upon reduction sentences do not implicitly invoke causal modalities. On this point, see Hempel (34, section 3).

[25] And in fact, the total specification of meaning effected by the passages quoted is then summarized by the authors in their "definition" DF II, which has exactly the form (6.2) of a bilateral reduction sentence for 'rat x expects food at L.' (Tolman, Ritchie, and Kalish (88, p. 15).)

[26] For a fuller discussion, see Carnap (8, section 7) and Carnap (14, section 10).

[27] See Tarski (83, especially pp. 80–83).

[28] See Kemeny (41) and (42); Carnap (12).

[29] On this point, see especially Quine (65); Goodman (26); White (95) and (96, Part II). The significance of the notion of analyticity in special reference to theoretical statements is critically examined, for example, in Pap (60) and (61) and in Hempel (34). Arguments in defense of concepts such as analyticity and synonymy are advanced in the following articles, among others: Carnap (12, 13); Grice and Strawson (29); Martin (49); Mates (51); Wang (94).

[30] Since the reduction sentences (7.3) determine the meaning of 'Q' for those and only those cases which meet at least one of the conditions $C_1, C_2 \ldots C_n$, it might be argued that (7.4) in conjunction with (7.3) inductively supports, not (7.5), but only the following hypothesis, which limits the assertion of (7.5) to the cases just specified:

$$(7.5') \quad (C_1x \vee C_2x \vee \ldots \vee C_nx) \supset (Qx \equiv Ox)$$

and that what (7.5) asserts beyond this, namely,

$$(7.5'') \quad \sim(C_1x \vee C_2x \vee \ldots \vee C_nx) \supset (Qx \equiv Ox)$$

constitutes a stipulation rather than an empirical hypothesis. But this does not alter the fact that (7.5), since it implies (7.5'), is empirical in character, and that its acceptance requires therefore inductive support.

[31] This point is discussed more fully in Hempel (32). On the problem of "reducing" the concepts of one discipline to those of another, the following publications have important bearing: Nagel (56) and (57); Woodger (100, pp. 271ff); Kemeny and Oppenheim (43).

[32] One writer who is impelled by his "philosophical conscience" to take this view is Goodman (see 27, Chapter I; 28, Chapter II, section 1). A similar position was taken by Russell when he insisted that physical objects should be conceived as "logical constructions" out of sense-data, and thus as definable in terms of the latter (see, for example, 77, Chapter VIII).

[33] See Carnap (14, especially sections 9, 10).

[34] Carnap (14, section 10).

[35] Carnap (14, section 10).

[36] Carnap (14, section 10). An idea which is similar in spirit, but not quite as clear in its content, has been put forward by Pap in (60) and in (61, sections 10–13 and 70), with the claim (not made by Carnap for his argument) that it establishes the "untenability" of the "thesis of explicit definability" (of theoretical terms by means of observational ones). Pap (60, p. 8). On the other hand, Bergmann (especially in 1 and 2) holds that many concepts of theoretical physics, including "even the particle notions of classical physics could, in principle, be introduced by explicit definitions. This, by the way, is also true of all the concepts of scientific psychology." Bergmann (2, section 1). In the same context Bergmann mentions that the method of partial

interpretation seems to be necessary in order to dissolve some of the puzzles concerning quantum theory. However, this strong assertion is supported chiefly by sketches of some sample definitions. Bergmann suggests, for example, that 'This place is in an electric field' can be defined by a sentence of the form 'If R_1 then R_2,' where R_1 stands for a sentence to the effect that there is an electroscope at the place in question, and R_2 stands "for the description of the behavior of the electroscope (in an electric field)." (1, pp. 98–99.) However, this kind of definition may be questioned on the basis of Carnap's arguments, which have just been considered. And in addition, even if unobjectionable, some examples cannot establish the general thesis at issue. Thus, the question remains unsettled.

[37] The basic idea was outlined earlier in Hempel (33, p. 30).

[38] I am grateful to Herbert Bohnert who, in a conversation some years ago, provided the stimulus for the development of the ideas here outlined concerning the definability of functors with infinitely many permissible values. Mr. Bohnert remarked on that occasion that explicit definition of such functors in terms of an observational vocabulary should be possible along lines indicated by the Frege-Russell theory of natural and of real numbers.

[39] If it should be objected that 'cell' and 'organism' are theoretical rather than observational terms, then they may be replaced, without affecting the crux of the argument, by terms whose observational character is less controversial, such as 'marble' and 'bag', for example.

[40] I was mistaken, therefore, when in an earlier essay I asserted that "no sentence expressible in observation terms and logical terms alone can state a sufficient condition (let alone a necessary and sufficient one) for a sentence of the form 'the length of interval i is r centimeters.'" Hempel (35, p. 68.) The consideration that led me to this assertion (loc. cit., pp. 66–68) overlooked the point made above (between (7.7) and (7.8)), namely that a sentence expressed in observational and logical terms alone may represent a necessary and sufficient condition for the truth of a given theoretical sentence without providing finite observational truth criteria for that sentence: it may be non-molecular in form.

[41] The argument can readily be extended to functors taking complex numbers or vectors of any number of components as values. Our reasoning has relied essentially on the Frege-Russell method of defining the various kinds of numbers (integers, rational, irrational, complex numbers, etc.) in terms of the concepts of the logic of sets. For a detailed outline of the procedure, see Russell (76); fuller technical accounts may be found in many works on symbolic logic.

[42] See Tolman (87, as reprinted in Marx, 50, p. 89); and Spence (82, p. 65n).

[43] Hull (38).

[44] Hull (38, p. 285).

[45] Feigl (21, p. 40).

[46] Braithwaite (4, Chapter III).

[47] See the essay "Theories" (1929) in Ramsey (67).

[48] Braithwaite (4, p. 76).

[49] This point is also made in Carnap (8, section 7) in a discussion of the advantages of reduction sentences over definitions in the introduction of scientific terms. And Feigl eloquently argues in the same vein in his essay (23), in which the general principle is illustrated by various suggestive examples taken from physics and psychology.

[50] Braithwaite (4, p. 76).

[51] An excellent concise synopsis of various arguments in favor of invoking "hypothetical constructs" will be found in Feigl (21, pp. 38–41). Some aspects of the "semantic realism" concerning theoretical terms and sentences which Feigl presents in the same article are discussed in section 10 of the present essay.

[52] This has been pointed out by Carnap himself; see, for example, his (14).

Carl G. Hempel

[53] See Campbell (7, Chapter VI). Important parts of this chapter are reprinted in Feigl and Brodbeck (24).

[54] Campbell (7, p. 122).

[55] However, this does not show that there cannot possibly be any necessary and sufficient condition in observational terms for the theoretical sentence: the problem of proving or disproving this latter claim is subject to difficulties analogous to those discussed in section 7 in regard to definability.

[56] The intuitive notion of interpretation, as well as the conception reflected in Campbell's idea of an interpretative dictionary, would seem to call for the following additional condition: (v) Each sentence of J contains essentially terms from V_T as well as terms from V_B. However, this requirement introduces no further restriction of the concept of interpretative system; for any system J that meets conditions (i) to (iv) can be stated in an equivalent form that satisfies (v) as well. To this end, it suffices to replace the member sentences of J by their conjunction; this yields a logically equivalent interpretative system which contains only one sentence, and which satisfies (v) since J satisfies (iv).

[57] Campbell (71, p. 43).

[58] Here, and on some subsequent occasions where there is no danger of misunderstandings, logical connectives are used autonymously; the expression 'H $\equiv$ O', for example, represents the sentence obtained by placing the triple-bar symbol (for 'if and only if') between the sentences of which 'H' and 'O' are names.

[59] Craig's paper (16) contains the first published account of this interesting theorem. A less condensed and less technical presentation, with explicit though brief references to applications such as the one here considered, is given in Craig (17).

In application to the issue we are discussing, the result obtained by Craig may be briefly stated as follows: Let the set V_T' of primitive terms of T' and the set of postulates of T' be specified effectively, i.e., in a manner allowing anyone, given any expression, to decide in a finite number of steps whether the expression is a primitive term (or postulate) of T'. Let V_T' be divided, by an effective criterion that may otherwise be chosen at will, into two mutually exclusive vocabularies, V_T and V_B. Finally, let the rules of the logic used be such that there is an effective method of determining, for any given finite sequence of expressions, whether it is a valid deduction according to those rules.

Then there exists a general method (i.e., a method applicable in all cases meeting the conditions just outlined) of effectively constructing (i.e., characterizing the postulates and the rules of inference of) a new system T'$_B$ whose set of primitives is V_B; and whose theorems are exactly those theorems of T' which contain no extralogical constants other than those contained in V_B.

Note that the theorem permits us to draw the dividing line between V_T and V_B wherever we please, as long as the criterion used to effect the division permits us to decide in a finite number of steps to which of the two sets a given term belongs. This condition as well as the requirement of an effective characterization of V_T' will be trivially satisfied, for example, if V_T' is finite, and its member terms as well as those of V_B and V_T are specified simply by enumerating them individually.

The further requirement of an effective characterization of the postulates and the rules of logic for T' are so liberal that no doubt any scientific theory that has yet been considered can be formalized in a manner that satisfies them—as long as the connections between theoretical and observational expressions can be assumed to be expressible in the form of definite statements. The only important case I am aware of in which this condition would be violated is that of a theory for which no definite rules of interpretation are specified—say, on the ground that the criteria of application for theoretical expressions always have to be left somewhat vague. A conception of this kind may have been intended, for example, by A. Wald's remark "In order to apply [a scientific] theory to real phenomena, we need some rules for establishing the cor-

92

respondence between the idealized objects of the theory and those of the real world. These rules will always be somewhat vague and can never form a part of the theory itself." Wald (91, p. 1).

The conditions of Craig's theorem are satisfiable, however, if the vagueness here referred to is reflected in definite rules. Thus, for example, the interpretative sentences for a given theory might take the form of statistical probability statements (a possibility mentioned in Carnap (14, section 5)), or perhaps of logical probability statements (each specifying the logical probability of some theoretical sentence relative to a specified sentence in observational terms, or vice versa). Either of these procedures would yield an interpretation of a more general kind than that characterized by the definition of an interpretative system given in section 8 of the present essay. Yet even to theories which are interpreted in this wider sense, Craig's theorem can be applied.

[60] Craig (17, p. 49). It may be well to note briefly two further points which were established by Craig, in the studies here referred to: (i) A theory T' may have a set of V_B-consequences that cannot be axiomatized by means of a finite set of postulates expressible in terms of V_B. (ii) There is no general method that permits an effective decision, for every theory T', as to whether its V_B-consequences can, or cannot, be axiomatized by means of a finite set of postulates.

[61] Craig (17, p. 49). This fact does not detract in the least, of course, from the importance and interest of Craig's result as a theorem in logic.

[62] On this method, first used by von Neumann, see Carnap (9, pp. 29–30 and p. 96), where further references to the literature are given.

[63] This does not preclude the possibility of effecting the transition from the five data sentences to 'Fb' in a purely deductive fashion by means of a suitable modification of T'; in fact, just the addition, to T', of the statement '(x) ((Gx · Tx · Vx · Ex · Sx) ⊃ Px)' would have the desired effect. But the modified theory thus obtained is clearly stronger than T'.

[64] Ramsey (67, pp. 212–215, 231).

[65] See Tarski (85, p. 350).

[66] On this point see, for example, MacCorquodale and Meehl (46); Lindzey (45); Feigl (21), (22); Hempel (31); Rozeboom (74).

[67] It is of interest to note here that if in addition to the conditions specified in section 8, an interpreted theory were also required to meet the criteria of significance for theoretical terms and sentences that have recently been proposed by Carnap in (14, sections 6, 7, 8), the terms and the sentences of our mock "learning theory" would be ruled out as nonsignificant.

[68] More precisely, the assertion that there exist entities of the various kinds (such as hypothetical objects and events and their various qualitative and quantitative properties and relations) postulated by an interpreted theory T' is expressed by the Ramsey-sentence associated with T'. It is obtained by replacing all theoretical constants in the conjunction of the postulates of T' by variables and binding all these by existential quantifiers placed before the resulting expression. The sentence thus obtained is a logical consequence of the postulates of T'; but the converse does not hold; hence strictly speaking, the assertion of the existence of the various hypothetical entities assumed in a theory is logically weaker than the theory itself.

For suggestive observations on the question of the reality of theoretical entities, see, for example, Toulmin (89, pp. 134–139) and Smart (81).

[69] The concept is used here in Quine's sense, according to which a theory is ontologically committed to those entities which must be included in the domains over which its bound variables range if the theory is to be true. Quine develops and defends this idea in several of the essays comprising his book (66).

[70] This conception of laws or theories as inferential principles has been suggested, on different grounds, by several authors, such as Schlick (who says that he owes the idea to Wittgenstein; see Schlick, 79, p. 151 and p. 155); Ramsey (see 67, p. 241),

Carl G. Hempel

Ryle (see 78, especially pp. 120–125), and Toulmin (see 89, Chapters III and IV). (Toulmin remarks, however, that to think of laws of nature as rules or licenses "reflects only a part of their nature" (*loc. cit.*, p. 105).) See also Braithwaite's discussion of the issue in (4, pp. 85–87). Finally, Popper's essay (64) contains several critical and constructive comments that bear on this issue and on some of the other questions discussed in the present study.

REFERENCES

1. Bergmann, Gustav. "The Logic of Psychological Concepts," *Philosophy of Science*, 18:93–110 (1951).
2. Bergmann, Gustav. "Comments on Professor Hempel's 'The Concept of Cognitive Significance,'" *Proceedings of the American Academy of Arts and Sciences*, 80(No.1):78–86 (1951). Reprinted in Gustav Bergmann, *The Metaphysics of Logical Positivism*. New York: Longmans, Green and Co., 1954.
3. Bergmann, Gustav, and Kenneth Spence. "Operationism and Theory in Psychology," *Psychological Review*, 48:1–14 (1941). Reprinted in Marx (50).
4. Braithwaite, R. B. *Scientific Explanation*. Cambridge, England: Cambridge Univ. Press, 1953.
5. Bridgman, P. W. *The Logic of Modern Physics*. New York: Macmillan, 1927.
6. Burks, Arthur W. "The Logic of Causal Propositions," *Mind*, 60:363–382 (1951).
7. Campbell, Norman R. *Physics: The Elements*. New York: Dover, 1920.
8. Carnap, Rudolf. "Testability and Meaning," *Philosophy of Science*, 3:420–468 (1936); 4:1–40 (1937). Reprinted as a monograph by Whitlock's Inc., New Haven, Conn., 1950. Excerpts reprinted in Feigl and Brodbeck (24).
9. Carnap, Rudolf. *The Logical Syntax of Language*. New York and London: Humanities, 1937.
10. Carnap, Rudolf. *Foundations of Logic and Mathematics*. Chicago: Univ. of Chicago Press, 1939.
11. Carnap, Rudolf. *Logical Foundations of Probability*. Chicago: Univ. of Chicago Press, 1950.
12. Carnap, Rudolf. "Meaning Postulates," *Philosophical Studies*, 3:65–73 (1952).
13. Carnap, Rudolf. "Meaning and Synonymy in Natural Languages," *Philosophical Studies*, 6:33–47 (1955).
14. Carnap, Rudolf. "The Methodological Character of Theoretical Concepts," in H. Feigl, and M. Scriven (eds.), *The Foundations of Science and the Concepts of Psychology and Psychoanalysis*, pp. 38–76. Minneapolis: Univ. of Minnesota Press, 1956.
15. Cohen, M. R., and E. Nagel. *Introduction to Logic and Scientific Method*. New York: Harcourt, Brace, 1934.
16. Craig, William. "On Axiomatizability within a System," *Journal of Symbolic Logic*, 18:30–32 (1953).
17. Craig, William. "Replacement of Auxiliary Expressions," *Philosophical Review*, 65:38–55 (1956).
18. Cramér, Harald. *Mathematical Methods of Statistics*. Princeton: Princeton Univ. Press, 1946.
19. Estes, W. K., S. Koch, K. MacCorquodale, P. E. Meehl, C. G. Mueller, W. S. Schoenfeld, and W. S. Verplanck. *Modern Learning Theory*. New York: Appleton-Century-Crofts, 1954.
20. Feigl, Herbert. "Some Remarks on the Meaning of Scientific Explanation," (A slightly modified version of comments first published in *Psychological Review*, 52(1948)), in Feigl and Sellars (25, pp. 510–514).
21. Feigl, Herbert. "Existential Hypotheses," *Philosophy of Science*, 17:35–62 (1950).

22. Feigl, Herbert. "Logical Reconstruction, Realism, and Pure Semiotic," *Philosophy of Science*, 17:186–195 (1950).
23. Feigl, Herbert. "Principles and Problems of Theory Construction in Psychology," in W. Dennis (ed.), *Current Trends in Psychological Theory*, pp. 179–213. Pittsburgh: Univ. of Pittsburgh Press, 1951.
24. Feigl, Herbert, and May Brodbeck (eds.). *Readings in the Philosophy of Science.* New York: Appleton-Century-Crofts, 1953.
25. Feigl, Herbert, and Wilfrid Sellars (eds.). *Readings in Philosophical Analysis.* New York: Appleton-Century-Crofts, 1949.
26. Goodman, Nelson. "On Likeness of Meaning," *Analysis*, 10:1–7 (1949). Reprinted in a revised form in Linsky (45).
27. Goodman, Nelson. *The Structure of Appearance.* Cambridge, Mass.: Harvard Univ. Press, 1951.
28. Goodman, Nelson. *Fact, Fiction, and Forecast.* Cambridge, Mass.: Harvard Univ. Press, 1955.
29. Grice, H. P., and P. F. Strawson. "In Defense of a Dogma," *Philosophical Review*, 65:141–158 (1956).
30. Hempel, Carl G. "Geometry and Empirical Science," *American Mathematical Monthly*, 52:7–17 (1945). Reprinted in Feigl and Sellars (25), in Wiener (97), and in James R. Newman (ed.), *The World of Mathematics.* New York: Simon and Schuster, 1956.
31. Hempel, Carl G. "A Note on Semantic Realism," *Philosophy of Science*, 17:169–173 (1950).
32. Hempel, Carl G. "General System Theory and the Unity of Science," *Human Biology*, 23:313–322 (1951).
33. Hempel, Carl D. *Fundamentals of Concept Formation in Empirical Science.* Chicago: Univ. of Chicago Press, 1952.
34. Hempel, Carl G. "Implications of Carnap's Work for the Philosophy of Science," in P. A. Schilpp (ed.), *The Philosophy of Rudolf Carnap.* New York: Tudor (forthcoming).
35. Hempel, Carl G. "The Concept of Cognitive Significance: A Reconsideration," *Proceedings of the American Academy of Arts and Sciences*, 80(No. 1):61–77 (1951).
36. Hempel, Carl G., and Paul Oppenheim. "Studies in the Logic of Explanation," *Philosophy of Science*, 15:135–175 (1948). Reprinted in part in Feigl and Brodbeck (24).
37. Hermes, H. "Eine Axiomatisierung der allgemeinen Mechanik," *Forschungen zur Logik und Grundlegung der exakten Wissenschaften.* Neue Folge, Heft 3. Leipzig, 1938.
38. Hull, C. L. "The Problem of Intervening Variables in Molar Behavior Theory," *Psychological Review*, 50:273–291 (1943). Reprinted in Marx (50).
39. Hull, C. L., C. I. Hovland, R. T. Ross, M. Hall, D. T. Perkins, and F. B. Fitch. *Mathematico-Deductive Theory of Rote Learning.* New Haven: Yale Univ. Press, 1940.
40. Hutten, Ernest H. *The Language of Modern Physics: An Introduction to the Philosophy of Science.* London and New York: Macmillan, 1956.
41. Kemeny, John G. Review of Carnap, *Logical Foundations of Probability. Journal of Symbolic Logic*, 16:205–207 (1951).
42. Kemeny, John G. "Extension of the Methods of Inductive Logic," *Philosophical Studies*, 3:38–42 (1952).
43. Kemeny, John G., and Paul Oppenheim. "On Reduction," *Philosophical Studies*, 7:6–19 (1956).
44. Lindzey, Gardner. "Hypothetical Constructs, Conventional Constructs, and the Use of Physiological Data in Psychological Theory," *Psychiatry*, 16:27–33 (1953).

45. Linsky, Leonard (ed.). *Semantics and the Philosophy of Language*. Urbana, Ill.: Univ. of Illinois Press, 1952.

46. MacCorquodale, K., and P. Meehl. "On a Distinction between Hypothetical Constructs and Intervening Variables," *Psychological Review*, 55:95–107 (1948). Reprinted in Feigl and Brodbeck (24) and, with omissions, in Marx (50).

47. MacCorquodale, K., and P. Meehl. "Edward C. Tolman," in Estes *et al.* (19), pp. 177–266.

48. Margenau, Henry. *The Nature of Physical Reality*. New York: McGraw-Hill Book Co., 1950.

49. Martin, R. M. "On 'Analytic,'" *Philosophical Studies*, 3:42–47 (1952).

50. Marx, Melvin H. (ed.). *Psychological Theory*. New York: Macmillan, 1951.

51. Mates, Benson. "Analytic Sentences," *Philosophical Review*, 60:525–534 (1951).

52. McKinsey, J. C. C., A. C. Sugar, and P. Suppes. "Axiomatic Foundations of Classical Particle Mechanics," *Journal of Rational Mechanics and Analysis*, 2:253–272 (1953).

53. McKinsey, J. C. C., and P. Suppes. "Transformations of Systems of Classical Particle Mechanics," *Journal of Rational Mechanics and Analysis*, 2:273–289 (1953).

54. Mises, R. von. *Positivism: A Study in Human Understanding*. Cambridge, Mass.: Harvard Univ. Press, 1951.

55. Nagel, Ernest. *Principles of the Theory of Probability*. Chicago: Univ. of Chicago Press, 1939.

56. Nagel, Ernest. "The Meaning of Reduction in the Natural Sciences," in Robert C. Stauffer (ed.), *Science and Civilization*. Madison, Wis.: Univ. of Wisconsin Press, 1949. Reprinted in Wiener (97).

57. Nagel, Ernest. "Mechanistic Explanation and Organismic Biology," *Philosophy and Phenomenological Research*. 11:327–338 (1951).

58. Neumann, John von, and Oskar Morgenstern. *Theory of Games and Economic Behavior*, 2d ed. Princeton: Princeton Univ. Press, 1947.

59. Northrop, F. S. C. *The Logic of the Sciences and the Humanities*. New York: Macmillan, 1947.

60. Pap, Arthur. "Reduction Sentences and Open Concepts," *Methodos*, 5:3–28 (1953).

61. Pap, Arthur. *Analytische Erkenntnistheorie*. Wien: J. Springer, 1955.

62. Popper, Karl. *Logik der Forschung*. Wien: J. Springer, 1935.

63. Popper, Karl. *The Open Society and its Enemies*. London: G. Routledge & Sons, 1945.

64. Popper, Karl. "Three Views Concerning Human Knowledge," in H. D. Lewis (ed.), *Contemporary British Philosophy: Personal Statements*. New York: Macmillan, 1956.

65. Quine, W. V. "Two Dogmas of Empiricism," *Philosophical Review*, 60:20–43 (1951). Reprinted in Quine (66).

66. Quine, W. V. *From a Logical Point of View*. Cambridge, Mass.: Harvard Univ. Press, 1953.

67. Ramsey, Frank Plumpton. *The Foundations of Mathematics and other Logical Essays*. London and New York: Humanities, 1931.

68. Reichenbach, Hans. *Axiomatik der relativistischen Raum-Zeit-Lehre*. Braunschweig: F. Vieweg & Sohn, 1924.

69. Reichenbach, Hans. *Philosophie der Raum-Zeit-Lehre*. Berlin: W. de Gruyter & Co., 1928.

70. Reichenbach, Hans. *Philosophic Foundations of Quantum Mechanics*. Berkeley and Los Angeles: Univ. of California Press, 1944.

71. Reichenbach, Hans. *The Theory of Probability*. Berkeley: Univ. of California Press, 1949.

72. Reichenbach, Hans. *The Rise of Scientific Philosophy*. Berkeley and Los Angeles: Univ. of California Press, 1951.
73. Reichenbach, Hans. *Nomological Statements and Admissible Operations*. Amsterdam: North Holland Pub. Co., 1954.
74. Rozeboom, William W. "Mediation Variables in Scientific Theory," *Psychological Review*, 63:249–264 (1956).
75. Rubin, H., and P. Suppes. *Transformations of System of Relativistic Particle Mechanics*. Technical Report No. 2. Prepared under contract for Office of Naval Research. Stanford University, Stanford, 1953.
76. Russell, Bertrand. *Introduction to Mathematical Philosophy*. London and New York: Macmillan, 1919.
77. Russell, Bertrand. *Mysticism and Logic*. New York: W. W. Norton & Co., 1929.
78. Ryle, Gilbert. *The Concept of Mind*. London: Hutchinson's Univ. Libr., 1949.
79. Schlick, M. "Die Kausalitaet in der gegenwaertigen Physik," *Die Naturwissenschaften*, 19:145–162 (1931).
80. Skinner, B. F. *Science and Human Behavior*. New York: Macmillan, 1953.
81. Smart, J. J. C. "The Reality of Theoretical Entities," *Australasian Journal of Philosophy*, 34:1–12 (1956).
82. Spence, Kenneth W. "The Nature of Theory Construction in Contemporary Psychology," *Psychological Review*, 51:47–68 (1944). Reprinted in Marx (50).
83. Tarski, Alfred. "Einge methodologische Untersuchungen über die Definierbarkeit der Begriffe," *Erkenntnis* 5:80–100 (1935). English translation in Tarski (86).
84. Tarski, Alfred. *Introduction to Logic and to the Methodology of Deductive Sciences*. New York: Oxford University Press, 1941.
85. Tarski, Alfred. "The Semantic Conception of Truth," *Philosophy and Phenomenological Research*, 4:341–375 (1944). Reprinted in Feigl and Sellars (25) and in Linsky (45).
86. Tarski, Alfred. *Logic, Semantics, Metamathematics*. Tr. by J. H. Woodger. Oxford: The Clarendon Press, 1956.
87. Tolman, E. C. "Operational Behaviorism and Current Trends in Psychology," *Proceedings of the 25th Anniversary Celebration of the Inauguration of Graduate Study*, Los Angeles, 1936, pp. 89–103. Reprinted in Marx (50).
88. Tolman, E. C., B. F. Ritchie, and D. Kalish. "Studies in Spatial Learning. I. Orientation and the Short-Cut," *Journal of Experimental Psychology*, 36:13–24 (1946).
89. Toulmin, Stephen. *The Philosophy of Science*. London: Hutchinson's Univ. Libr., 1953.
90. Verplanck, W. S. "Burrhus F. Skinner," in Estes *et al.* (19), pp. 267–316.
91. Wald, A. *On the Principles of Statistical Inference*. Notre Dame: Univ. of Notre Dame Press, 1942.
92. Walker, A. G. "Foundations of Relativity: Parts I and II," *Proceedings of the Royal Society of Edinburgh*, 62:319–335 (1943–1949).
93. Walsh, W. H. *An Introduction to Philosophy of History*. London: Hutchinson's Univ. Libr., 1951.
94. Wang, Hao. "Notes on the Analytic-Synthetic Distinction," *Theoria*, 21:158–178 (1955).
95. White, Morton G. "The Analytic and the Synthetic: An Untenable Dualism," in S. Hook (ed.), *John Dewey: Philosopher of Science and of Freedom*. New York: Dial Press, 1950. Reprinted in Linsky (45).
96. White, Morton G. *Toward Reunion in Philosophy*. Cambridge, Mass.: Harvard Univ. Press, 1956.
97. Wiener, Philip P. (ed.). *Readings in Philosophy of Science*. New York: Scribner, 1953.

98. Woodger, J. H. *The Axiomatic Method in Biology*. Cambridge, England: Cambridge Univ. Press, 1937.
99. Woodger, J. H. *The Technique of Theory Construction*. Chicago: Univ. of Chicago Press, 1939.
100. Woodger, J. H. *Biology and Language*. Cambridge, England: Cambridge Univ. Press, 1952.

Definitions, Explanations, and Theories

1. *General Introduction.* The ensuing account is not intended to be a full treatment of the topics referred to in the title. A number of specific points that have concerned recent writers on logic and the philosophy of science and which are related to these topics are discussed and an attempt is made to indicate how these are related. These points include a discussion of translation, rules, dispositions, theoretical concepts, correlational concepts, statistical explanation, incomplete explanations, 'bridge laws,' unobservable entities, implicit definition, etc. But many other points would have to be dealt with, and those mentioned dealt with in more detail, in order to justify a claim of completeness.[1] It is not even supposed that the present topics are the most important or the most controversial in any treatment of definitions, explanations, and theories, nor that the treatment of these topics is of great originality. But it does represent a different approach from those which have been commonly supported. It is different in method from the approach of the positivist symbolic logicians whose work led us to the major reconsideration of these topics which occurred in the earlier part of this century. And it is different in certain of its results from the approach of the Wittgensteinian school of logicians whose method it shares.

2. *Analytic Method.* I shall call my interpretation of this method, the method of *context analysis*, in order to focus attention on its complementarity with traditional and symbolic logic which might be called *content analysis.*

The differences in approach, which in no way amount to incompatibility, arise from the difference in the success with which formaliza-

---

[1] I have discussed many further points that arise in the analysis of one of these topics in "Explanations" (unpublished D. Phil. thesis, Oxford, 1956), especially pp 246–420; but others of equal importance I did not discuss at all.

tion can be employed for these two kinds of analysis. Context analysis is undertaken in the belief that the meaning of terms or concepts or logical problems can only be thoroughly understood if we include a meticulous examination of the circumstances in which they occur, rather than relying on a relatively rapidly extracted formalization of their apparent internal logical features. The context analyst's viewpoint as thus stated has two important corollaries. First, it regards the rigor of symbolic logic as partly spurious; for the problems of analysis with which we are faced concern already existing concepts and problems, and experience makes very clear that these are not governed by rigorous rules and definitions. This is not to deny that within symbolic logic, *taken as a branch of mathematics*, the highest standards of rigor obtain; it is only to assert that this rigor is not the same thing as rigor in the analysis of an ordinary logical problem.

Second, it views the utility of symbolic logic as partly illusory; the chief claim for symbolic logic—that it provides a means of *avoiding* as well as *solving* problems—is held to rest on the mistaken belief that a language can in general be rich enough to perform the tasks required of it without containing the traps which produce the confusion or puzzlement. Nevertheless, context analysis is frequently facilitated by limited formalization and in certain cases, for example, proof theory and dimension theory, regards a highly formal analysis as the best means for success. But it should be noted that the latter cases do not include such common topics as those mentioned in the title or introduction to this paper—or at the most refer to special instances of them. The context analyst employs a different tool; instead of formalization, he uses comparison. The purpose of these comparisons is to elicit the less apparent significance of the concept (etc.) which is under analysis. It is thought that the process of exhaustive comparison with cases where the meaning of the concepts is clear is the best way of discovering the function of the expression(s) being considered. The function is not itself the meaning but is a guide to the meaning just as the manifest form is not itself the meaning but is a guide to the meaning. So the two approaches could alternatively be described as *functional analysis* and *formal analysis*.[2]

[2] The importance of context is a central theme of P. F. Strawson's *Introduction to Logical Theory*, especially pp. 187, 213–217. London: Methuen, 1952. The role of comparison in philosophical method is excellently expressed by F. Waismann in

It is as well to remember that the context analyst's claim about analysis is largely an empirical one; it is the claim that most logical problems [3] can be solved only by reference to detailed and varied examples described with considerable care. If the logical problem is to give an analysis of the concept of a theory, then it will be necessary to examine with some thoroughness various aspects of various theories—their susceptibility to disconfirmation by observation, the extent to which they involve reference to unobservable entities, etc. Now this is a position which can hardly be said to rest on a naive error as to the nature of logic or the infallibility of common sense; in fact it is hard to see how it could be denied at all. The functional analyst, however, sees his position as implicitly rejected by that of a formal analyst who puts up a simple and neat symbolic model of what he takes to be the essential features of a theory and argues for the reform of language so as to use the term "theory" only for things that are represented by this model. In this—the programmatic—aspect of their activities the representative of the formal approach is normally called a *reconstructionist*. For want of a better term, I would describe the context analyst's alternative as that of the *repairist*. The actual continuity of the two positions should now be apparent. The context analyst should indeed be entirely amenable to the formal analyst's solution *if* two points can be substantiated: first, that the model embodies the *essential* features of a theory (i.e., the identifying criteria), and second, that redefining the original term or introducing a new one will produce a *substantial improvement*. His general view will tend to be that if there are very few essential characteristics of a theory, we do not need anything that could be appropriately described as a formal model or a revision of language; while if there are very many, the formal model will not be sufficiently less complex than the original logical structure to make its comprehension and adoption worthwhile.[4] It is obvious that there may be intermediate cases where the gains *will* outweigh the losses; and in such cases the two

"How I See Philosophy," in H. D. Lewis (ed.), *Contemporary British Philosophy*, pp. 445–490. London: Allen & Unwin, 1956.

[3] By which I mean such problems as giving an analysis of meaning, inference, and necessity.

[4] I think the most important argument for context analysis depends on the vast amount of information about the meaning of a term that is implicit in a well-described example of its use over and above that which can be summarized in any manageable form by a definition or set of definitions. The present paper in part endeavors to illustrate the truth of this remark.

analysts will and often do agree. It is therefore essential not to suppose there is an irreconcilable difference between the procedures of the two schools of analysis.

In fact, we can readily see that when their positions are so stated that such a difference exists, one of them is actually at fault. For a formal analyst to propose an analysis of theories which he could not support by showing that it refers to and illuminates important examples of what we usually call "theories" would be as irresponsible as it would be for a context analyst to insist that precisification or enlargement of our logical vocabulary is always superfluous.

Despite the impossibility of defending either position when stated in a way that makes it sharply distinguishable from the other, there is certainly a considerable difference (even visually) between the characteristic results of an investigation by representatives of the two schools.[5] In fact it is nearly as common for context analysts to regard their method as illuminating, precise, and indeed responsible for a new revolution in philosophy, as it is for content analysts and non-analytical philosophers to regard it as an insidious, corrupting, decadent, faddish, sloppy, and pointless perversion of the great traditions. It is worth adding that the Minnesota Center for Philosophy of Science has found the interaction of the two viewpoints a source of great stimulation and hybrid vigor and has until now always had staff members whose primary allegiance is to different schools.

3. Definitions: Introduction. We begin with some very simple points. They will all be necessary. We may start by assuming that a definition gives or is supposed to give the meaning of a term or terms. These terms may have already been in use or they may have been coined for a special purpose by the proposer of the definition. There are many ways in which the meaning of a term can be given, some of them rather strikingly different from others. Let us consider some of the particular types generated by these alternatives.

4. Dictionary Definitions. In a traditionally pre-eminent position there is the explicit linguistic definition of a word in current use, such as the following example from Webster's New Collegiate Dictionary (1953).

exotic. Introduced from a foreign country; extraneous; foreign . . .

$$(4.1)$$

[5] For example, compare this paper or Strawson's paper with the one by Pap in this volume or the one by Carnap in the first volume of *Minnesota Studies in the*

How does this *give the meaning* of a term? We who understand the conventions of the dictionary interpret the line of type as expressing the interchangeability, i.e., sameness of meaning, of the term "exotic" and any of the three words or phrases, separated by the semicolons, which follow it. If we understand some of the latter, then—by virtue of this definition—we understand the term we looked up. Hence this arrangement of words (which is not a sentence) gives us the meaning of the term.

There are some complications, however. Is this still a definition if we do not understand the words separated by semicolons? It can perfectly well still give *the* meaning of "exotic" although we would not understand what that was. But this is so only if these terms, mysterious to us, actually have meaning. If they are meaningless, this would not be a proper definition of the term "exotic", for it would not give it any meaning. So we must distinguish between understanding a definition and deciding whether it is a definition at all; the second requires more investigation.

5. *Erroneous Definitions*. Now could such a definition be in error; or could it never be in error? Although the line of type 4.1 does not make up a sentence, it nevertheless—in the context of the dictionary—expresses a claim. Similarly a string of flags may have meaning. This claim or assertion is about the meaning of "exotic", and, in the case of the dictionary chosen, this claim is in error. "Exotic" does not now mean "foreign" or "extraneous"; in fact the entailment holds in neither direction. Hence dictionary definitions can be in error in so far as they do not correctly represent the meaning of the terms they contain. We can decide whether they err only in cases where we understand both the term *defined*, and the terms *used in* the definition, or have indirect evidence about their meaning.[6] The recognition of error in a definition does not require that we be capable of giving a better definition, any

Philosophy of Science. The paper by Sellars in this volume affords an excellent example of a synthesis of the two approaches.

[6] This does not mean that whenever we understand all the terms involved we can always tell whether a dictionary definition is at fault; for there may be senses of the term given or not given about which we are ignorant. However to understand the term requires at least that we understand one sense of it (usually the main sense, and usually several other senses as is certainly the case with, e.g. "but"), so when we understand all the terms in a definition we can *sometimes* say that it is definitely incorrect, sometimes that it is definitely incomplete, and in the remaining cases that it is correct with respect to the senses it does discuss.

more than the ability to recognize one's dog in a canine lineup depends on one's ability to describe him in terms which would enable another to do so. The ability to use a term correctly is so enormously different from the ability to correctly formulate its use that the context analyst always relies on the first (which we know how to identify if we know how to speak the language) whenever a great deal hinges on the meaning of a word.

It would be unfair to criticize the definition quoted by pointing out that "extraneous" is not (and probably never was) synonymous with the literal meaning of "foreign". For the dictionary conventions, properly understood, do not imply that the alternatives are exactly equivalent, but rather that in certain contexts each will be a near-synonym for the term defined—and these contexts may differ slightly. The perceptive reader picks up some of the flavor of the term—its refinements of meaning—by studying the range of its synonyms. Of course, unless the contexts are specified in which each substitution is permissible, the definition will not be fully adequate; and it is chiefly for this reason that the Oxford English Dictionary runs to eleven volumes—it actually gives contexts for the different uses of the terms by means of quotations, i.e., by giving examples of the proper use.

6. *Dictionaries versus Encyclopedias.* There is clearly a certain vagueness about dictionary definitions, and indeed there are very marked differences between those proposed in one dictionary and those proposed in another dictionary, so one cannot place very much reliance on every definition in every dictionary; a considerable amount of research beyond the dictionaries is often required in order to obtain even a limited understanding of the meaning of a term. Conversely, a good deal of information is contained in a dictionary which is not strictly part of the meaning of terms at all, e.g., the family relationships of biblical figures and the fact that mistletoe is the state emblem of Oklahoma. And there is clearly great difficulty about drawing a line between *information about* a defined class and *the definition of* that class. Is it part of the definition of "Iroquois" that this Indian confederacy was centered in New York State or that it admitted the Tuscarora in 1722? These facts are given in Webster, but such facts can't all be dismissed as irrelevant to a proper definition, because the distinguishing part of definition consists only of such facts. Of course, we might conclude that the term is not definable other than as "an Indian tribe"; yet some-

one who reads the 'definition' in Webster will actually be in nearly as good a position as anyone else to say that he understands the meaning of the term. Moreover, a confederacy with different members, admitted at different times, centered in Oklahoma rather than New York would not be the Iroquois at all, but the so-called Five Civilized Tribes; so such facts are not wholly *independent* of the meaning of the term "Iroquois". One doesn't have to know some Iroquois by sight in order to use their tribe's name properly; and the same is true of any individual's name.

7. *Definitions as Substitution Rules.* Now the usual decision procedure advocated in logic textbooks amounts to taking definitions as giving substitution rules (elimination rules); in deciding whether the property P is part of the definition of the term X, one asks "Could there be any meaning in the description of something as 'an X that isn't P'?" If the answer is "Yes," then P cannot be part of the definition of X since if it is, the description would be self-contradictory. Unfortunately, as the Iroquois example shows, this approach would whittle away virtually every property which could *possibly* be part of the meaning, leaving us with the alternatives of saying the term has no satisfactory definition or that some other criterion for definition must be employed.

It may be thought that proper names could well be said to have no definition in the sense of a substitution rule (i.e., to have no intralinguistic equivalent). But "Iroquois" is not a proper name of the kind for which substitution rules cannot be given, if indeed there are any such; its capitalization is logically as irrelevant as that of nouns in German. To make a decisive point against the decision procedure of the last paragraph, however, we need only show its inapplicability to other important kinds of terms.

The term "lemon" as the name of a fruit is defined by Webster as "The acid fruit of a tree (citrus limonia) related to the orange." Suppose that there is a way of identifying the tree without looking at its fruit. We can now ask whether something could possibly still be a lemon if it grew on a special variety of quince tree in place of the quinces. Supposing that it is exactly the same in every respect—shape, taste, color, etc.—we would indeed be surprised but we would surely not deny that it was a lemon. We might call it a 'quince-grown lemon' but the justification for this kind of description (cf. 'corn-fed beef') usually lies in some difference in quality of the end product which in this case is not present, *ex hypothesi*. It would simply be a lemon with an odd history. Moreover, if we were able to produce them in a hydroponic farm from a chemical pulp itself synthesized from a purely inorganic mixture, they would surely still be lemons, though the fruit of no tree. Again, if by selective crossbreeding of lemon trees we could produce a fruit which was in every respect except taste identical with what we now call a lemon, but had a curious pungent flavor of its own, not sweet but not really acid either, we would surely no more abandon the term "lemon" for it than we abandon the term "grapefruit" for the sweeter, pink-fleshed products of the lower Rio Grande Valley. Then what sort of fruit *is* a lemon? We can clearly divide and conquer any concomitance of physical or genetic characteristics in the same way; and yet the term clearly has no distinct meaning over and above such characteristics. The answer must be that a lemon is something with some or most of these properties, e.g., those given by Webster, but that no one of these properties is individually necessary. Hence, the usual decision procedure fails again.

The formal analyst will about this stage propose that such sloppy terms could well be smartened up by adopting an exact definition; and we could then concentrate on the important work for science, which is research into the nature of the world and prediction and control of its future. The functional analyst will raise his two crucial questions: What 'exact definition' could we adopt, and what advantages would there really be in doing this? The theme of this paper is that no exact definition could be adopted which would exhibit significant advantages over the present 'vague' definitions—not only for commonplace terms like "lemon" but even more certainly for the crucial terms of theoretical and observational science. Yet I still wish to maintain an intensional account of definition; my aim is to retain the notions of synonymy etc., but to recognize their limitations.

The points so far made should lead us to abandon the idea that a good definition contains only terms each of which is necessarily connected with the term being defined. (Of course, I do not at all wish to deny that *some* definitions are like this, e.g., "sibling" = "brother or sister".) I said at the beginning of this section that this idea is equivalent to regarding definitions as substitution rules. For two terms to be intersubstitutable, it is both necessary and sufficient that the decision procedure we have just examined should be applicable. If the rule applies, then all the properties P_i which pass the test must be present when X is present and vice versa. (Using the rule in reverse we ascertain whether the conditions are jointly sufficient as well as severally necessary.) Hence any sentence where either X or the set P_i occurs will be unchanged in meaning if the other is substituted. Conversely, if X and the set P_i can be substituted for each other without loss of meaning, it cannot be the case that one of the P_i, say P_n, fails to pass the decision procedure since such a failure would have made the substitution impossible in any context where the compound description "X but not P_n" occurs (this would be a self-contradiction if the set P_i is substituted for X, but is not a contradiction as it stands, *ex hypothesi*).

In consequence of these considerations, we may wish to restrict the term "definition" to substitution rules at the expense of saying that large numbers of common words are undefinable. Before doing this let us examine a few other examples of dictionary definitions. The price may turn out to be higher than we can pay, to be in fact an error strictly comparable to the idea that good definitions must capture the 'real essence' of a concept from which all other properties could be deduced. In both cases, as we shall see, the only respectable candidates come from mathematics, and mathematics is a poor ideal for a logical analysis of the factual sciences since its truths are mostly analytic and its criteria for existence mostly conceptual.

8. *'Undefinable' Terms.* In the first place it is completely mistaken to suppose that scientific vocabularies do not contain words with the systematic evasiveness of the examples considered above. Not only do the relatively undeveloped sciences such as meteorology and psychology contain innumerable words with the same logical properties, but even the highly developed sciences such as physics exhibit them, though often in a disguised form. The commonest indication of their real nature is a history of change in the operational criteria. Such terms as "acid" and "temperature" have certainly changed their operational meaning over the last few centuries, and this indicates—what careful study clearly reveals—that no complete analysis of their meaning can be given in terms of a set P_i, each necessarily connected with their application in the sense explained above. However, it is quite unnecessary for us to complicate our task by dealing with such concepts over whose definitions a good many disputes have raged and still arise. We shall find it

easier to deal with everyday terms and easy to justify the application of our conclusions to scientific terms. The very few special properties of the latter will be dealt with specifically, e.g. the reference to un-observed entities.

Before coming to that stage of the argument, however, I want to lay the foundations for a constructive account of definition by examination of some other logical types of dictionary definition, for the moment continuing to use the term 'definition' in the wider sense indicated at the beginning of section 3.

Language is put together with conjunctions, prepositions, and pronouns which for the lexicographer present in part a similar and in part a different problem from that of defining nouns and adjectives. It is clear that they have meaning, and it is fairly clear—as we shall see—that this meaning usually cannot be given by an intra-linguistic equivalent that is satisfactory for all contexts. This raises the problem of selecting the proper interpretation of an ambiguous term, a problem common enough for any grammatical class. In the definition of "but" as a *conjunction connecting coordinate elements* (it is defined in eleven other grammatical categories) there are *still* two alternative meanings given, viz. "with this exception" and "on the contrary; yet; notwithstanding." We are unable to formulate a single substitution rule which takes account of this residual ambiguity; for the rule cannot be a satisfactory substitution rule if it includes both (since they are different in meaning), and it cannot be adequate if it leaves out either. We can only formulate *two* rules and select one rather than the other depending on the *context*. And we cannot do that unless we understand the context so well that we can make some quite subtle discriminations. Not only can no single rule be given here, as is the case with all ambiguous terms, but the actual rule given is not an exact substitution rule. Webster gives as an example of the first use the phrase "whence all *but* he had fled" and one cannot substitute "with this exception" for "but" in this context and retain the grammatical proprieties. (In this context "except" would do, but in others "except" produces nonsense.)

This incompleteness is not accidental or the result of inefficiency but typical of the approximative process of conveying meaning by definitions. The formalist sees what he takes to be the ideal situation where exact rules, unambiguous forms, and necessary connections are the only ones allowed, and hastens to reform language in that direction; the functionalist hesitates pending further consideration, dubious whether such a pervasive feature can be legislated out of existence, suspicious that if the new language was used to do the tasks for which language is required it might immediately acquire these features. If so, there has been no gain in redefining terms and a great loss of time and energy. It may be better to recognize from the beginning that there are certain limits of precision beyond which definitions in an applied language usually cannot go. We shall argue that the same is true of laws and explanations in science.

The reconstructionist might concede the possibility of such a situation but argue that one does not progress by sitting still in the face of the possibility that we are incapable of movement. But the repairist has a reply. Not only has the reconstructionist been trying for many decades to produce definitions and rules which will eliminate our difficulties, without—he argues—any noticeable success (the pragmatic counter-argument), but there are some strong reasons for suspecting that success is impossible and not merely frustrated by apathy (the logical counter-argument). These reasons arise from a consideration of the function of language. We may expect, the functionalist argues, that a noun, X,[7] used to refer to something, P_1, which always in fact occurs together with P_2, will soon come to be applied upon the appearance of P_2 in the expectation that P_1 will also be present. In the course of time we may discover that P_2 is one of a family of predicates which provides a better basis for classifying things like X than does P_1's family. Eventually, we shall adopt P_2 as the primary meaning of X. Or we may never quite decide. In either event there will be a long intermediate stage during which it would be quite incorrect to assert that X meant P_1 alone or that it meant P_2 alone. Yet during that time the term X is no less useful or less comprehensible than before. Hence the substitution type of definition would hardly apply at all to what may be a central scientific term, since it will apply only when we can categorically distinguish the essential from the accidental properties of X.

To this the formalist's standard reply is that we must distinguish the context of discovery from the context of justification and analysis. Imprecise terms may suffice for the rough-and-ready needs of the frontier

[7] The symbols are here and on some other occasions used as names of words as well as words, since there is no danger of confusion.

of research; but when we wish to say what we have discovered as opposed to what we have defined, then we must be able to distinguish definitions from empirical statements. The functionalist counters by saying that it is dubious whether anyone except the historian, i.e., the student of the context of discovery, needs to be able to distinguish discovery from definition to the degree of precision which the formalist is seeking; and for the rest, it is quite easy to say what we know and what evidence we have for it, and also to explain what terms mean ('define' them, in the usual sense) without having to make any but the most elementary distinctions between necessarily-connected P_i's and empirically-connected P_i's. Thus the physicist would not permit one to assert that conservative systems were *discovered* to obey the conservation laws or that canal rays were *defined* as having a positive charge. But he does not have to answer the question whether it's a matter of fact or definition that neon has the atomic weight 20.2; the relative unimportance of this question is a central tenet of this paper. One's logical reflexes make one fight against this conclusion. But if the distinction is an artificial one, why should one suppose that answers are not also artificial, i.e., do not reflect a real difference? I think the answer must be "The distinction does *not* apply here": there are truths by definition and empirical truths and there are also truths that are a compound like "Men are less than 120 feet tall." So the functionalist argues that there is a certain class of examples where a predicate can be said to be part of the meaning of a term and yet can also be said to tell us something empirical when it is applied to the term. And the more one reflects on the difference between knowing how to use a language and knowing how to formulate its rules correctly (or identify correct formulations of its rules), the more odd it would seem to insist that there *must* be a yes-or-no answer to the question "Is 'X is P' true by definition?" Compare "Is it a matter of convention (rather than free choice) that the clan gathers every Easter?" and "Is it by rational consideration (rather than unreasoning acceptance) that a Communist adopts the Moscow 'line'?"

This, then, would be the functionalist position argued on the basis of the noun-adjective type of term. The particular interest of the so-called connectives, i.e., words like "but", "and", "or", and "therefore", lies in their pervasiveness throughout a language; regardless of the boundaries between theory and observation, between scientific terms and the terms of everyday speech. We do not have a scientific definition of "but", as opposed to an ordinary definition of it. Moreover, the structure of assertion and argument depends almost entirely on these terms—the content analyst would say entirely. What we talk about varies from the laboratory to the kitchen, but what follows from what we say is dependent almost solely on the location and meaning of the connectives in our statements. Inference, proof, and argument, then, in science as in common experience depend on these words. This should suggest to us that the limitations we discovered to the precision with which these terms can be defined have little if any practical effect on the precision of descriptions and proofs involving them. It is a misunderstanding of linguistic accuracy and clarity to suppose their attainment depends on the possibility of formulating exact substitution rules for the terms employed. Indeed it is not clear that these goals would even be rendered easier of general attainment were such rules available, because the price of such rules is a loss in the utility of the language (here it would be a loss in the range of applicability of the connective).

Notice that a similar argument does not apply to quantitatively vague terms: one cannot achieve certain kinds of linguistic precision without using non-vague terms such as numerical predicates instead of "many", "large", "heavy", etc. The natural conclusion that all kinds of indeterminateness are handicaps to precise expression of scientific data and hypotheses is that challenged by the functional analyst, because his study discovers the necessity for, and advantages of, certain kinds of 'indeterminacy' of definable meaning.[8] Of course, the terms "many", "large", etc. are immensely useful and are not wholly replaced but are supplemented when we extend the language to include numerical predicates. With respect to certain terms, however, no such useful addition can be made—according to the functional analyst—because their very function is already best served by their indeterminate form. The physicist can't use a definition of "force" which makes Newton's first law of motion [9] simply definitional or simply empirical because it isn't simply one or the other. This doesn't mean that it's a queer mixture, either; any more than the number 0 is a queer mixture of positive and negative. One could say it's positive because it's not negative and vice

---

[8] Not the same as actual vagueness; for the latter is a reflection of indeterminacy of the concept. The general property of non-susceptibility to exact definition is something else, perhaps best regarded as a limitation of the procedures of definition in a given language; it does not follow there is an associated vague concept, e.g., "but".

[9] A body under no forces moves with constant velocity.

versa, but this is needless paradox. It is only a little better to say 0 has a property in common with positive numbers and a property in common with negative numbers. So one could say that the first law is definitional because it could very properly be included in or entailed by an adequate explanation of the meaning of the term "force", and it is empirical because it would be false [10] in a Galilean world (where the motion of particles under no forces is ultimately circular). But "being definitional" and "being empirical" are uneasy bedfellows no less than "positive" and "negative"; one should rather admit they are not true contradictories.

9. *Inter-categorical Definitions.* Now the definitions we have so far solicited from the dictionary exhibit at least one common logical feature. They all provide words that, precisely or imprecisely, necessarily or empirically, tell us about the meaning of a term by providing alternative words that would not be completely out of place if substituted for the term defined—though we might have to do a little grammatical trimming as in the case where "but" was defined as "with this exception". If they have not been exact substitution rules, they were nevertheless *possible* substitution rules, i.e., they offered a translation in the same grammatical category as the original.

I wish now to mention some strikingly different cases. Taking another connective of an even more fundamental nature, we find that "and" is defined by Webster in the following terms: "a particle expressing the general relation of connection or addition, used to conjoin word with word, phrase with phrase, clause with clause." Now this is a grammatical account of the role of the word, not a possible substitute for it. It does not appear to express an equivalence which might have enabled us to first employ the term when we learned the language as a native, it tells us something about the word from the viewpoint of the grammarian. It does this partly because there is no alternative. One can produce synonyms for "but" if one is prepared to separate out enough contexts. "And" is too fundamental. So Webster abandons the search for synonyms completely and instead talks about function. I want to say two things about this definition. First, it seems remotely possible that there are circumstances in which it would give someone complete understanding of the meaning of a term, e.g., a foreigner with an understand-

---

[10] This is something of an oversimplification since there are some possible though unlikely escapes from the mentioned disproof.

ing of the grammatical vocabulary and the terms "with", "of", "or", etc. which occur in the definition. Second, there are clearly better ways of explaining the meaning of the term than this, e.g. in the context of a series of questions and answers about the properties of a single object where one can conjoin the answers into one statement and indicate the equivalence of this statement to the set of separate answers. (This is neither a standard case of ostensive definition nor of contextual definition—if it were the latter, it would certainly occur in the dictionary, which contains many such cases.)

10. *The Definition of "Definition"*. Again we must decide whether to draw the line at calling this a definition or not. Webster would allow it not only in practice but in theory ("a formulation of the meaning or meanings of a word; as, *dictionary definitions*") unless we object to the term "meaning" in the same way. But his product contains many examples which make his own definition too narrow, e.g. definitions of *phrases* such as "definite article" (the adjacent entry to "definition"), and translations of sentences in foreign languages, e.g., "Le roi est mort, vive le roi." The formalists are well behind us by this time, and only Richard Robinson—with an occasional disciple—is out in front.[11] The objections to a restriction of the term "definition" which would exclude the above definition of "and" are, to repeat, that we must then say "and" is indefinable, which makes rather mysterious the fact that it is quite easy to explain what it means, and that no more restrictive analysis appears to hold up under careful scrutiny—perfect synonymy in natural languages being virtually imaginary. The objection to the wider interpretation offered by Robinson is that a flash of (telepathic or other) insight is an odd-looking definition. But there is a way of meeting the objections to a narrower view of definition. We examine with care the difference between indefinability and incomprehensibility, taking "indefinable" to mean simply "such that no explicit definition of it can be formulated" rather than "such that no explanation of its meaning can be given". Then we abandon the ideal of exact synonymy in favor of the realistic, fully satisfactory concept of practical or conditional synonymy (discussed at length later in this paper). (This is perfectly

---

[11] ". . . any process, whether verbal or otherwise, by which any individual, whether God or angel or man or beast, brings any individual, whether himself or another, to know the meaning of any elementary symbol, whether a word or other . . ." *Definition*, p. 27. Oxford: The Clarendon Press, 1950.

compatible with the rejection of some definitions of a given term as inferior to others on the grounds that they are *less* adequate formulations of intralinguistic equivalents, i.e. synonymous terms.)

If we adopt this position, according to which a definition expresses a substitution possibility under certain conditions and with a workable degree of accuracy, it appears that we would still be able to reject the proffered 'definition' of "and". For surely, as I have said above, "a particle expressing the general relation of connection or addition, etc." cannot be used as a substitute for "and", any more than "a noun made up of the three letters 'i' 'n' and 'k' in that order" can be used as a substitute for "ink". The clues in a crossword puzzle are not always synonyms for the missing words though they are usually unambiguous— but obscure—references to them. Similarly there are many ways in which we can unambiguously—and not obscurely—convey the meaning of a term to someone other than by giving a synonymous term or conjunction of terms. We might add to this reason for differentiating Webster's definition of "and" from his definition of most common nouns, the further reason that the latter alone can be regarded as reflecting the meaning the terms originally have for us. The definition of a term, it might be said, is the one which serves correctly to introduce it to the language-user previously unfamiliar with it. Robinson is right in stressing the connection of definition with bringing someone to understand a word, and right in stressing that definition refers only to elementary terms.[12] We do not talk of the definition of a sentence. But it also seems that a definition has a preferred status among possible explanations of meaning which in part depends on its role as the *proper* formulation of the meaning of the term for the language-learner. A particular language has a structure of a particular kind according to which some expressions about the meaning of terms are definitions and some are not, even though almost all could be used for bringing someone to know the meaning of a term. Certainly, in a natural language there are usually several slightly different formulas which are all acceptable as expressing 'the' definition of a given term; but they are distinguishable from the

[12] Robinson's elementary terms are (my interpretation) terms which contain no proper parts such that the meaning of the term as a whole can be inferred by the usual rules from the meaning of the proper parts. Thus, the term "book end" has proper parts with meaning but its own meaning could not be inferred from their meaning by the usual rules (which would give it a meaning analogous to that of "rope end").

many other true and complete statements about the meaning which the sophisticated user of the language can produce, and these other statements are such that the individual learning the language could (virtually) never extend his vocabulary by learning them. They would include such analyses as the grammatically slanted one of "and", as well as others which involve 'circularity' or more difficult terms than the one being defined.

The implied *functional* (or *genetic*) character of definition I have here been proposing is not the same as the *formal* one of requiring substitutability. It is possible for a substitution rule to fail the functional requirement—Dr. Johnson's celebrated 'definition' of "net" is a case in point, as is the definition of "sibling" as "male sibling or female sibling." [13] And conversely, a functionally satisfactory definition may not be a substitution rule—ignoring ostensive 'definition' for the moment —we may by way of an example mention the 'recursive definitions' of number theory.[14]

If this *functional* condition is allowed, we see a further reason for our disquiet about the definition of "and". Even though there are conceivable circumstances in which it might be used to introduce someone to the meaning of the term, they are so queer as almost to evade description: how *could* someone have understood the quite sophisticated grammatical vocabulary and the meaning of "with", "or", "connection", and "addition" without understanding the word "and"? If some doubts are entertained whether the functional condition is allowable, then they may be allayed by asking whether it would be perfectly satisfactory if all definitions were couched in terms more abstract and complicated than that which is being defined? Or again if they were all circular, directly or at first or second remove? It seems clear that part of the function of definitions is the explanation of the meaning of the terms defined, *in the language as it stands*; and this is not possible or is extremely difficult if they are substitution rules of a kind in which the

[13] If one alters the substitution-rule requirement to an elimination-rule requirement (and the distinction is not usually made, though its importance is here apparent) the genetic condition is satisfied more or less adequately. For to require eliminability is to require that none of the defining terms be such that they could only be understood via an understanding of the defined term, i.e. it is almost the genetic condition.

[14] See, e.g. R. L. Wilder, *Introduction to the Foundations of Mathematics*, p. 253. New York: Wiley, 1952. A simpler example than the one he gives would be the definition of the square of a positive integer by the two assertions (a) the square of 1 is 1; (b) the square of $(n + 1)$ is greater than the square of n by $(2n + 1)$.

proffered substitute is harder to understand than, or impossible to understand without understanding, the defined term.

11. The Misleading Analogy with Mathematical Definition; The Actual Limitations on Redefinition. Before exploring the further consequences of this analysis of definition for certain traditional beliefs about definition, it is important to examine one possible objection. It might be said that an elementary understanding of formal systems reveals the possibility of defining terms in a large number of different ways, providing that corresponding changes are made in the status (but not the statement) of other definitions and propositions. To use the example given above we may define the square of an integer in terms of addition and subtraction in the recursive fashion indicated; in which case we will be able to prove that the square is equal to the self-product of the integer. Or, alternatively, we may define the square as the self-product; in which case we can readily prove that the differences between successive squares are the successive odd numbers (the formula on which the recursive definition is based). In either case, it would be argued, there is no change at all in the set of true propositions about numbers, in which we are to believe. Hence the functional condition, which would single out one of these as a correct definition and reject the other, is too restrictive.

But the functional condition would not have this consequence. It only requires that in a given formalization we be consistent about our descriptions of the various formulas. The ones which are used to express theorems are not usable to express definitions in the same system because one can't give proofs for definitions and one has to be able to give them for theorems. Mathematicians are very used to dealing with alternative formalizations and the comment that we can define the function "square of an integer" recursively as indicated does not mean that we can (in the ordinary way) assert that this is the definition of that function. It is not, since the accepted formalization introduces it as the self-product. But, and here is the crucial point, even the degree of arbitrariness which is permissible in the formalization of a deductive system, is not generally possible for a highly interpreted language. Essentially this is because the sentences expressing laws in one formalization—which would be adopted as definitions in another—are empirically true, not necessarily true as are most mathematical propositions. (One must add the qualification "most" in view of the Axiom of Choice, etc.)

In the first place, of course, one cannot 'reformalize' English plus its scientific extensions, hence its present structure places definite limitations on what can be a definition. Second, in spite of the limitations on the program of formalizing Cantorian mathematics imposed by the Skolem paradox, truth-in-*all*-normal-interpretations remains an important criterion for judging the desirability of a mathematical axiom, whereas it counts against an axiom for a formalization of a physical theory (though some with this property are permissible). Hence a switch from one definition to another which was previously a law involves a risk which does not (generally) arise in mathematics, viz. discovery that this world is one in which the assumed interpretation does not give true statements. Since there are many cases (it would be wrong to say all) where the meaning of a term is impervious to new discoveries, this indicates that such a reformalization involves a change in the meaning. For example, the traits 'dominant' and 'autonomous' correlate very highly but to incorporate this correlation into the meaning of the terms by a 'reformalization' would be a plain error, roughly because the terms have other commitments of much greater importance in determining their meaning which require that *this* connection be dispensable by the facts in certain circumstances.

This point is elementary enough, but its significance has been obscured by the long search for extensional analyses (i.e., analyses in which necessity is nothing more than truth without *existing* exceptions) in the positivist logical tradition, since on an extensional analysis the distinction cannot be sustained. Thus Hempel is prone to saying ". . . if we wish, we may then imagine the theory-plus-interpretation at hand to be thrown into the form of a deductive system in which (7.5) becomes a definitional truth, and (7.3) assumes the character of a set of empirical statements . . ." (p. 56, "The Theoretician's Dilemma"). According to what I am now saying, this could be done only at the expense of giving the terms in (7.5) a new meaning. The remark then becomes somewhat unexciting since it then expresses the fact that we can always adopt a new meaning for a given symbol.

Hempel's idea that a law can be adopted as a definition (presumably without change of meaning) is derived from his extensional requirements for a definition, viz. a set of empirically necessary and sufficient conditions for the application of a term. This is unsatisfactory according to both the formal and the functional criteria. It is not a formally satisfactory substitution rule since it makes nonsense out of many perfectly sensible subjunctive statements; and it is not functionally satisfactory because it elevates any accidental but exceptionless concomitants of a given condition or entity to the status of defining characteristics, i.e. characteristics which could be used to introduce and adequately express the *meaning* of the term. The further errors into which it seems to me this leads him in connection with, e.g., the hypotheses of reducibility will be considered below; for the moment, let us spell out the two simple reasons mentioned against the extensional account of definition.

Suppose all faculty members at Harvard live in a special city housing project, the Bainbridge Development. They do this by free choice, because they prefer the company of their colleagues and the rents are paid by the estate of Jonathan Bainbridge ('03); the city gave them first refusal on the space and no one else lives there. Clearly this will continue to be the case! Then this residence characteristic is an empirically necessary and sufficient condition for the application of the term "faculty member at Harvard". If we regard this as a justification for defining it in that way, the conditional statement, "If they increase the size of the faculty by another 850, some faculty members at Harvard will not be living in Bainbridge Development," (S) becomes self-contradictory. Now consider Hempel's suggestion about the possibility of rearranging the deductive system. We adopt the residence predicate as definitory of "Harvard faculty member" and we observe the empirical fact that all Harvard faculty members have jobs on the teaching staff at the largest private university in Massachusetts. The analogy with mathematics appears to hold in the sense that the same two statements about the Harvard faculty are held to be true, although true for different reasons. Is this not a perfectly satisfactory alternative method of defining the term?

It is not, since the meaning of the term "Harvard faculty member" is wholly independent of possible housing shortages in the city of Cambridge, Massachusetts, and the second formulation makes it wholly dependent on this. The corresponding situation cannot arise—empirically or even logically—in mathematics because no future contingency will falsify the theorem which we adopt as a definition in the second formalization. It is an *essential part of the meaning* of "Harvard faculty member" that sentences such as S are sensible rather than nonsensical, that we can use the term to describe changes in the residence of the group to which it refers, just as it is an essential part of the meaning of "resident of the Bainbridge Development" that it be independent of the occupation of those to whom it applies. In fifty years, it may be a radioactive slum where a few dying Martians live; the term will not have altered its meaning in the literal sense, even if the associations may have soured for those who know what has happened. Hence there often *is* a literal meaning for a term, i.e. a shifting boundary beyond which only misuse and metaphor lie.

Similarly, and in this case consequently, we should be doing a poor service to the language-learner were we to suggest that "Harvard faculty member" could be defined as "one who lives in the Bainbridge Development" since he would then suppose, for example, that when the Bainbridge Development is wiped out by a cobalt bomb, the term no longer has any application—which would simply be an error in his understanding of its meaning. An error of a different kind would result when he claimed to have *discovered* the occupational similarity of Harvard faculty members.

It is therefore not possible to reformalize interpreted languages and theories without changing the meaning—in the only useful sense—of certain of the terms, a point to which I shall make further reference in the later parts of this paper. The special features of mathematics make it a dangerous ideal for the logician concerned with the analysis of theoretical language, but we observed that it is even true in mathematics that the functional requirement applies to a given formalization.

12. Definitions of Logical Constants in Symbolic Logic. A nice example of the borderland arises in connection with the definability of the 'logical constants' in terms of each other. There is an understandable sense in which we can say that "and" (as a *statement* connective, only!) is definable in terms of "not" and "or" according to the rule

> p and q: It is not the case that; either p is not the case or q is not the case or neither p nor q are the case.

This almost satisfies the formal requirement (the exceptions make it a poor but not an absurd definition), but one can see the improbability of supposing that it could satisfy the genetic requirement in any ordinary language used for the usual purposes. But let that point go and examine the claimed possibility of defining "not" in terms of the Sheffer stroke function which we introduce according to the rule

p/q: either p or q is not the case.

The suggestion is that we use the definition

p is not the case: p/p.

This clearly violates the functional condition since the notion being defined is not only linguistically prior to that doing the defining in terms of feasible language training, but is directly involved in it and hence could not conceivably be learnt *from* this definition. (At least, not unless it is possible to acquire the apparently compound notion of a disjunction of negations without first acquiring that of a negation. This is not a problem of experimental psychology; for it can be answered by—and only answered by—a logical analysis which provides an account of what it would be like for someone to do this. (In formal terms this amounts to giving a model of a behavior-descriptive system which is (1) adequate for ordinary language-using situations and (2) in which the description in question is true.) If it can be shown to be logically possible, the point I am making would have to be modified, without any necessity for research into what is physically possible for the human organism.) This point is well put by Strawson in the following words: "The stroke-formula has an especial charm in that it illustrates with peculiar clarity the remoteness of the conception of definition within a formal system from the ordinary conception of verbal elucidation of meaning." [15] The actual account of definition that Strawson adopts, however, is equivalent to the straight synonym approach. [16]

It is important not to forget that even the mathematical concept of definition is tied to the functional criterion within the system; if we define $f(x_i)$ as $g(x_i) \cdot h(x_i)$, we cannot also define $g(x_i) \cdot h(x_i)$ as $f(x_i)$. This is because we normally wish our definitions to serve as *elimination* rules, not merely substitution rules, i.e., the substitution has a particular point. The condition which ensures that this point is attainable is the functional condition, the requirement that the series of definitions should be such that the terms used in each definition are comprehensible independently of the term being defined. The special peculiarity of defining the negation of a proposition in terms of the stroke opera-

[15] *Op. cit.*, p. 97.
[16] *Ibid.*, p. 9.

tor is that it violates the functional condition *in interpretation* but not *in the uninterpreted calculus.* How can one be said to understand a term in an uninterpreted calculus? When one can give its permissible equivalences and transformations, etc. Thus, there is nothing at all wrong with using the stroke operator, defined by an uninterpreted truth table to define the uninterpreted "$\sim$p". But one cannot define the logical concept of negation in terms of the logical concept of double negation, in the ordinary sense of definition, because one cannot introduce the latter without using and understanding the former; and if one has to use it and understand it, one is operating according to some kind of a definition already. This might of course be something unformalizable and not a definition in the usual sense; but in the propositional calculus it is in fact formalizable, e.g. in truth table form. Hence, the definition does not serve to *introduce* the concept; and hence, more crucially, it cannot serve to *eliminate* it. So the mathematician's ideal of a definition as an elimination rule is attained only formally (the *sign* "$\sim$p" can be eliminated) but not semantically (the *concept* of monadic negation is not eliminated). This is different from the situation in a calculus where we define "and" in terms of "not" and "or". Apart from the literal weaknesses of the truth-functional formalization,[17] semantic elimination is in this case perfectly possible, since the concept of conjunction does not enter into the concept of negation and disjunction. I think this is a reason for preferring the axiomatization of *Principia Mathematica* or Hilbert and Ackermann to the hyper-formalized performances by, e.g., Church in *Introduction to Mathematical Logic*,[18] unless systemic elegance is regarded as more important than interpretable logical analysis. Of course, after all the connectives have been introduced, there is no difference between the systems; but their means of introducing the connectives makes one of them a reasonable *analysis* of the connectives we use in non-formal logic, while the other is not.

13. *Definitions as Analyses.* To say that a definition of a term already in use should be an analysis is, I think, another way of asserting the functional condition. If we are appraising a formal system supposed to represent the usual connectives, we regard it as a defect if they are represented as defined in terms of concepts which are incomprehensible

[17] Strawson, *op. cit.,* pp. 78–79.
[18] Alonzo Church, *Introduction to Mathematical Logic.* Princeton: Princeton Univ. Press, 1956.

prior to the comprehension of the defined term, partly because they cannot be an analysis of what is meant by the defined term. Certainly Moore had something like this in mind when he said "we cannot define anything except by an analysis," [19] which he later elucidates by saying that a concept has been analysed when "nobody can know that the *analysandum* applies to an object without knowing that the *analysans* applies to it." [20] This would eliminate such definitions as "brother" = "male sibling" and would not eliminate "sibling" = "a brother or sister"; it would eliminate the grammatical definition of "and" and the stroke-operator definition of "not"; but allow the definition of the statement connective "and" in terms of "not" and "or", etc. It is well not to suppose that Moore imagines that someone who knows the *analysandum* can properly be applied in a certain case, thereby knows *what the analysis of it is*. Robinson misinterprets Moore in this way and criticizes him for it, talking of his ". . . peculiar view that analysis is always easy and obvious. . . ." [21] He knows that it *applies*, if someone produces it; but he has not necessarily got it in mind *as the analysis*. In somewhat the same way, the man who knows how to swim an eight-beat crawl knows how to coordinate his arm and leg movements in the ratio of one cycle to eight cycles; but he may not even be aware that this is what he is doing in the sense of being able to produce this fact. However, he can very readily be brought to see that this is what he knows how to do (slow-motion in photography, etc.).

14. Definability and Reducibility. There is a type of putative definition of considerable importance closely related to the Moorean type of analytical definition on the one hand, and to the intercategorical definition, e.g., the grammatical definition of "and", on the other. This is exemplified by the definition of "(visual) light" as "electromagnetic waves from such-and-such a frequency range", and by the definition of "thirst" as "the state of an organism, after such-and-such a period of deprivation, which has a tendency to emit such-and-such response patterns". It is not the case that someone using the defined term must know that the defining terms apply in the same range of cases, hence this is not a Moorean analysis and does not satisfy the functional condition. Nor, on the other hand, would its use as a substitution rule

[19] G. E. Moore, *Principia Ethica*, p. 10. Cambridge: Cambridge Univ. Press, 1903.
[20] P. A. Schilpp (ed.), *The Philosophy of G. E. Moore*, p. 663. New York: Tudor, 1952. Quoted in Robinson.
[21] *Ibid.*, p. 175.

produce a nonsensical result, so it is not an inter-categorical definition.

The reductionists are those who have supported programs which involve 'reducing' optics and chemistry to the physics of waves, fields and particles, or psychology to the study of observable behavior, or biology to chemistry, or history and ethics to psychology, or ethics to decision theory, etc.[22] As Hempel observes, "one component of this problem is the question whether the terms of the first discipline can be defined by means of those of the latter" (this volume, p. 56). The preceding discussion should alert us to the possibility of two different interpretations of this question. Does it mean "can be defined" in this way now, or does it mean "can be defined" in this way in some future reconstructioning of our language? I think most discussions of reduction have been inconclusive due to a failure to specify which of these alternatives is under consideration.[23] If the first, we shall certainly have to abandon the functional condition on definition and even—as we shall see—modify the formal condition, which makes a definition possible only in a peripheral sense. If the second, then the issue becomes either trivial—since one can always introduce a term in any way one likes—or involves a hidden condition to the effect that the meaning of the redefined term must not be too different from the original meaning of the term; in which case the first alternative question must be answered.

I shall assert that the reductionist thesis, in so far as it involves definability is untenable, in so far as it involves redefinability is pointless, and in so far as it involves anything else amounts to the assertion that there's an explanation for everything.

First, then, to answer the question whether one can properly define the term to be reduced in terms of the reduction base, we notice immediately that the functional condition has to be abandoned since with respect to the English language as it now stands (which is all we can consider under the first alternative), we can certainly understand "light" without in any way understanding or recognizing the correctness of an analysis in terms of "electromagnetic". There may well be said to be a technical usage of the term according to which it is *defined in terms of* "electromagnetic"; but to consider that alone is

---

[22] The reduction of mathematics to logic is another instance; but the objections to it are, in important part, different.

[23] An exception must be made of Professor Nagel's excellent paper, "The Meaning of Reduction in the Natural Sciences," reprinted in P. Wiener (ed.), *Readings in Philosophy of Science*, pp. 531–559. New York: Scribner, 1953.

comparable to considering a language in which the term has been re-defined in that way, i.e., amounts to considering the second alternative. Of course, the functional condition, although implicitly accepted by most logicians who actually propose only the formal condition—as we have seen—may be abandoned experimentally in order to see how strong a sense of definition is left for the reductionist.

Unfortunately, the formal condition cannot survive either. For suppose that what we might call a temporal Döppler shift is discovered to be operating, i.e., the wave lengths of visible light are steadily changing, but without any effect on the ordinary phenomena of vision. (It is not only that we find ourselves able to see by what was previously identified as ultraviolet light *according to its wave length* and unable to see what was previously in the wave band of red light; the same objects at the same temperature and under the same conditions still have the same visual appearance, but the measured wave length of what we see as yellow light has increased quite noticeably and gives every appearance of reaching the point where it would have been called red prior to the beginning of the shift.) Suppose also that no biological explanation gives any (independent) support to the claim that our retinal sensitivities have altered, and that the wave length of the sodium lines, etc. also changes. Then we would have the sort of situation which produces fundamental changes in theoretical physics; but it would certainly not produce any change, fundamental or otherwise, in our ordinary use of the term "light". Why should it? The same things have the same colors, the same devices shed light, darkness comes at the same time, etc. Yet the proposed 'definition' of light no longer applies, i.e. the description just given is nonsensical. Hence it cannot be a substitution rule; hence, the formal criterion is violated. "Light" does not mean what the definition asserted it does mean. Nor is this case like the definition of "lemon" where we might be able to say that an approximately correct substitution rule has been proposed (a move which has its own serious difficulties—it will be discussed later); for there is every possibility that the present definition will be as far wrong as we care to specify, given time.

This conclusion leaves as the only possibility for saving the reductionist position the adoption of a weaker sense of definition. The immediate candidate is Hempel's 'set of empirically necessary and sufficient conditions.' But this has the crucial difficulty of failing to distinguish between an empirically well-confirmed correlation and what we would now regard as a definitional connection, as a basis for definition, a point made above in terms of the description "Harvard faculty member". It eliminates forever the question, "Is this true by definition or is it a matter of fact?" a question which it is indeed mistaken to suppose can always be usefully asked or answered (see section 8 above), but equally mistaken to suppose need never be answered. It eliminates as meaningless the consideration of certain hypotheses and conditional statements which are of great importance in the discussions of theoretical physics. It should be clear that if we can only support the definability aspect of reductionism by using such a weak account of definition, then the definability thesis had better be called something else since all it now amounts to is the requirement that the original term be applicable in the same cases as the 'reduction' of it, assuming our beliefs remain the same, and regardless of differences of meaning such as those between "featherless, tailless biped" and "human". To suppose that "human" can be defined in such a way is to suppose that the meaning of the term makes it perfectly applicable to a plucked chicken, and this is simply to display ignorance of its meaning.

It is important to make two extensions of the above remarks. In the first place, it is entirely incidental that the example chosen—the definition of "light"—happens to be of a term in ordinary language. We could have equally well chosen a chemical term such as "aqua regia" or a psychological term such as "drive", and the corresponding reductions in terms of atomic physics and neurophysiology respectively.

In the second place, even in the Hempelian sense of "definable", the thesis does not hold owing to the imprecision of the terms involved. That is, no exact set of necessary and sufficient conditions in the reduction vocabulary could be specified for the important terms from the discipline which is to be reduced. It may seem odd that such a seemingly practical limitation should be thought to really count against an abstract logical thesis. But the limitation is not one of careless practice; it is rather an essential feature of theoretical terms that they are not reducible by definition or empirical correlation to an observation base and a fortiori not reducible to the theoretical terms of another discipline. This point and its effect on the 'deductive ideal' for explanations will be further examined below.

We should now turn to the second alternative, that of interpreting the definability thesis as applying to a possible, not an actual language.

Of this I want to say that it can be done only at the expense of the applicability of the language. The reason is very simple; the fact that a term is introduced by means of a certain definition does not guarantee that the term will always be correctly defined in that way. Thus, if we construct a new language within which the usual terms of chemistry are replaced by their 'reduction' in terms of atomic physics, I am suggesting that the terms will not retain these meanings if the language is used as a language for chemists in chemical laboratories. If it is so used, I am suggesting that the terms would quickly metamorphose in such a way as to reacquire their original unreduced meanings. This has nothing to do with the linguistic *habits* of chemists making them recalcitrant about altering their theoretical vocabulary: it reflects the *logical* point that the observation vocabulary and procedures of chemistry differ from those of atomic physics. Not that theoretical terms are *explicitly definable* in terms of the observational vocabulary; but without doubt their meaning is in part or wholly a function of their relation to the observation language. Chemists use, not bubble chambers and bevatrons, but flame tests and litmus solutions; psychologists use, not neurone probes and electroencephalographs, but T-mazes and Skinner boxes; naturalists use binoculars and counting devices rather than the electron microscope, etc.[24]

Naturally the reductionist believes that even the observation base of chemistry can be described in terms of the reduction base of atomic physics. But the description is one which depends upon the correctness of atomic physics whereas the meaning of chemical terms does not—in general. The example of the definition of "light", discussed at some length above, shows the way in which a redefinition in terms of the reduction base gives new hostages to fortune in a way which greatly reduces the utility of the redefined term and the viability of theories phrased in terms of it. Such a handicap is offset by no apparent gain. The unity of science can be exhibited in other ways; the utility of terms whose meaning is directly related to the observable phenomena is far greater than if some other domain must be consulted before definite

---

[24] Of course, there are physical chemists, neuropsychologists like Hebb, and laboratory biologists. But the existence of shades of grey does not lessen the difference between black and white. I shall in fact argue for the necessity of shades of grey below; here I argue for the necessity of black and white (differences of meaning between the terms used by those whose observational vocabularies are different). Different semantic rules imply different concepts.

proof of their applicability can be obtained. In short, the precision is bought at the expense of the utility.

15. *The Concept of 'Completed Science.'* The formalist at this stage is likely to resuscitate the 'context of discovery vs. context of justification' distinction; to suggest that for 'completed science' the redefinition will be advantageous. To do this is to interpret the definability thesis in a yet more utopian way. The very notion of 'completed science' reflects a misunderstanding of the context of scientific research; it depends on the metaphysical supposition of a determinate list of possible questions within a given field. There is no such list. Not only are there an infinite number of logically distinguishable questions—which would not in itself preclude the possibility of answering them all—but there is an infinite number of possible new types of question, and there is at least one type of question which permits no end to its answers.

These points can even be made at the observation level. There is no such thing as a 'complete description' of the contents of a laboratory. Not because there are an infinite number of *atoms* in the room, but because there is an indefinite number of *things* in the room [25] and an indefinite number of relations between them and always an indefinite number of answers to the question, "What is the *best* description?" Of course, in any given context we can often talk of a complete description, e.g., for the police files, for the public health records, for the bank's inventory, for the interior decorator, for the time-and-motion investigator, and for the biologist. In the same way we can come to the end of a particular type of enquiry in a scientific field; and in certain cases, we can even define the field in terms of a type of enquiry rather than a type of subject matter. But physics, chemistry, astronomy, and psychology are fields which are not restricted by the interests of one type of enquirer, e.g., the man using only optical instruments and only interested in finding linear relations.

So, first, the idea of the 'completed science' is a myth; but second, the redefinability thesis seems to lose most of its little remaining point in such circumstances. If all the questions have been answered, then we already know the relation of the concepts in the sciences at both levels, and this relation is already formalized. What virtue is there in converting these empirical relations into matters of definition? One disadvantage would be the impossibility of teaching the history of science

[25] I owe this point to Stuart Hampshire.

without the most appalling confusion since all the terms used in the contemporary science would have meanings different from that used in history, and every conceptual problem would have to be radically and confusingly reformulated. Another would be a development of my last point: even if the science is complete, it is presumably not completely dead, i.e., it is still applied, if not to 'really new' situations at least to situations new to those who confront them. In that case the criteria of application will rapidly come to supplant the reduction-base criteria, as before, because the theory is still supposed to be an account of the original field for the worker in that field, not for the worker in the reduction-base field. One can redefine the chemical vocabulary in terms of atomic physics, but as long as people are dealing with the kind of practical problems the applied chemist deals with, e.g. making analyses of samples, so long will the terms he uses have their meaning connected with the reactions of his samples to chemical tests, rather than to atomic physics.

Perhaps, however, one should go even further and ask whether the chemist as such might not become superfluous to the atomic physicist armed with a computer and various devices for producing beams of test particles. The answer to this is that one can hardly deny it as a logical possibility though for both theoretical and economic reasons it is highly improbable. But such an event would not save the definability thesis of reductionism. It would merely show that the chemist's problems can be solved by means of atomic physics better than by specifically chemical techniques. Remembering that the chemist's problems are often solvable with the help of a balance, a gas flame and a few dollars worth of reagents and glassware, rather than computers and beam analyzers, one can see the economic improbability of this occurrence. Remembering that the synthesis of organic compounds for specific purposes shows no signs of being a terminable process since, for one reason, the list of purposes comes from fields as diverse as agriculture and zoology and can always include as desiderata previously uncatalogued properties, one can see the theoretical improbability of the occurrence. There is also the sense in which the completeness of one science is impossible before all sciences are complete.

16. The Acceptable Aspects of Reductionism. Finally, there seem to me to be two further insuperable objections to the definability thesis in any form. In the first place it is unnecessary for the reductionist posi-

tion and in the second place it involves an unjustifiable assumption about the logical form of concepts. I shall not elaborate these points here beyond a few paragraphs, since their substance will be expanded in the later parts of this paper.

The reductionist position contains a certain element of truth which, as far as I can see, does not carry over to the definability thesis. This truth is that we are committed to explaining macro-phenomena in terms of micro-phenomena and thus must believe that the truths of the macro-level (whether observations or statements about theoretical entities) can be accounted for in micro-terms.[26] The levels are not independent; they bear the relationship of explaining level to phenomena level, just as within each level there is also a distinction to be made between the observed phenomena and the phenomena postulated to explain them. Chemical reactions per se are not part of the observed phenomena of atomic physics—which would include, e.g., tracks on photographic plates exposed at high altitudes—but they consist in (can be described in terms of) atomic phenomena and hence must be explicable in atomic terms. Why? Because the atomic level is the level to which we turn for an explanation of what we accept as basic data at the chemical level, e.g., the periodic table. If we cannot find an account there, we take that to be a deficiency of the micro-theory; it may be remediable there or we may have to invoke a new micro-theory, or we may have to invoke a micro-micro-level, the nuclear level. This procedure is what the search for explanations chiefly amounts to, in our world, with science as it now stands. It is by no means inconceivable that we shall have to accept limits to this procedure and it is often argued that in quantum mechanics we have already done so. At the moment, outside such areas, we have the very best inductive reasons for persevering in many such cases. In others, such as the reduction of psychology to the behavior level, we need to be very clear in what we consider the subject matter to consist; since only in one interpretation can even this form of the reductionist view be maintained.[27]

[26] As I understand him, Nagel (loc. cit.) does not agree with this. To say that we are committed to the existence of a micro-account is by no means to say that we are not sometimes likely to find, or committed to finding non-micro-accounts. There is nothing very mysterious about the former claim; it is mostly an analytic consequence of the identification of a particular level as the micro-level with respect to another.

[27] See "A Study of Radical Behaviorism" in Volume I of Minnesota Studies in the Philosophy of Science.

But the claim that the macro-facts can be given a micro-explanation does not at all involve the claim that the macro-terms can be defined by micro-terms. In fact, reflection indicates how unlikely this will be in general: the Chinese have a perfectly adequate language for ordinary descriptive purposes, but it is far from being the case that we can give explicit definitions of each Chinese character in terms of the English vocabulary. Certainly we can (a) often give good approximations to an explicit (or simple contextual) definition, and (b) always explain— eventually—what the character means, in English. Even this need not be possible as between macro- and micro-languages; but supposing it is, the definability thesis is not thereby supported except in the sense in which it is indistinguishable from the thesis that a micro-explanation can be given of any macro-phenomena. We have seen that in this sense—a matter of fact, not of meaning—the definability thesis is very misleadingly titled.

As a particular application of the above remarks, it should be noted that an identity thesis on the mind-body problem is a case of reduction. For if it merely asserts extensional coexistence, it is not a solution of the mind-body problem but an assertion about the goings on in the world; whereas if it asserts an intensional identity, it runs onto the logical reefs partially charted above. (But Professor Feigl's noble analysis in this volume suggests, and I think shows, the possibility of a channel through the reefs.)

There remains for many people the intuitive feeling that it must be possible to construct, in the micro-language, a concept which would have the same role as any given macro-concept, if the micro-theory is going to be capable of making the 'same' predictions and giving the 'same' explanations, etc. as the macro-theory. This view I shall call the isomorphism thesis, a name suggested by Paul Meehl. It seems to me to rest upon a very strong assumption about the ways in which terms may be given meaning. It is quite common in certain branches of applied chemistry and zoology for a distinction to be made between substances on the basis of their origin or history even when this does not coincide with any intrinsic physical differences. To take an example from gemmology, the stones known as Cape emeralds (from their origin and color) are physically identical with the hydrated calcium-aluminum silicate usually called "prehnite" and found in the Hautes Alpes region and Connecticut. Now we would not expect *this* distinction to manifest itself at the micro-level, nor would its failure to do so in any way affect the success of predictions about the behavior of the stone under conditions of heating, scratching, illuminating, etc.

The isomorphist might say that gemmology is partly geography or economics and that this part is not reducible. This move is dangerous since it immediately leads to the question why, e.g., variations in the strength of gravity between Cape Province and Connecticut are not also questions of geography. What we undertake to reduce must not be defined in terms of what we can achieve. But it might be said, by the isomorphist, that his language does contain an isomorphic element for each of the terms "Cape emerald" and "prehnite", viz. the physico-chemical description of the mineral, qualified by a geographical description of the origin. That is, he imports the geography into the micro-language. Then what does the isomorphist position amount to? It looks very much like "If you can't beat them, hire them": it does not provide us with a further characteristic of a micro-language over and above its explanatory ability with respect to the macro-phenomena.

Certainly it is a requirement of a micro-theory that it be able to answer the question, "What do X's consist of?" for every name, "X", of a macro-state or macro-entity; and if the X's figure in macro-laws, then their micro-equivalent must figure in formally similar laws or else we cannot be said to have correctly given the micro-equivalent of X. But our example shows that one cannot always give a purely micro-account of some X's, e.g., when they are distinguished from Y's by something which has no micro-reduction. If these examples do not count against isomorphism, then it is no more than a reiteration of the defining condition of any micro-account, that it explain macro-phenomena by analysing macro-concepts.

The question naturally arising from these criticisms of the reductionist program concerns the extent to which similar criticisms can be made of the proposals to reduce theoretical terms to the observation vocabulary. I think very similar criticisms can be made; but it will repay us first to pursue somewhat further our study of the many curious ways of defining which even the limitations of the dictionary encompass. There is a somewhat crude form of the latter program embodied in the operationist criterion of meaning (in its characteristic interpretations), to which the objections can readily be extrapolated from the above account.

131

17. Definitions in Terms of Linguistic Function. The limitations of explicit identification with synonyms as a means of definition were discussed in the earlier part of the paper, and it is now time to examine some of its relatives on the other side of the family from those that abandon the formal requirement of meaning equivalence (intensional equivalence) in favor of the empirical requirement of truth equivalence (extensional equivalence). The cases to be examined retain intensional equivalence but abandon the explicit form; or compromise with both, but in a different way from Hempel's candidates.

It will be recalled that the definition of "but" was given as a set of synonym sets, the major divisions being according to grammatical categories and the minor according to context, this being illustrated by examples. The definition of "and" consisted primarily in a direct reference to its grammatical function, "a particle . . . used to conjoin word with word, etc.", although the context where it could so serve is indicated by reference to the meaning ". . . connection or addition. . . ." This definition thus reverses the methods of context and meaning specification employed in the definition of "but".

It is not hard to find further cases in which some reference to the function of a word is involved in giving its definition. In fact the conventions of the dictionary disguise the fact that every word which is both a noun and an adjective or verb, etc., e.g., "board" and "hand" has its various definitions distinguished by reference to these grammatical criteria. In what sense is this a defect? It is a defect in the sense that it involves abandonment of the formal criterion since one certainly does not find the part-of-speech label in the context of the uncomprehended term.

It may not violate the functional criterion since, even if the labels are not understood, the mere displaying of various alternative definitions may provide enough assistance for the reader to select the appropriate one, given the context in which the term occurs. But to give several definitions is hardly to give *the* definition of a term and the conclusion I want to insist on is that in many cases there is *no* way of giving the definition of a term in a particular context unless some labeling according to function is allowed. What is *the* definition of "board"? Well, it depends on the context. If we know from the context what its *grammatical* function is, we may then be able to give the definition. Again, we may not be able to do this, because the term may still be ambiguous, no matter whether it is a verb, an adjective, or, as in this case, a noun.

The sign 1/4/57 in the top right-hand corner of a business letter will be read by an American as January 4, and by an Englishman as April 1, without either having a suspicion that it is ambiguous. The context that decides will here consist in data about the nationality and residence of the author, the addressee, etc.

In view of such cases, why shouldn't it be allowable to use some other clues in order to identify its relevant sense, such as a reference to the type of situation of those who used the term? Certainly a dictionary does this, with its descriptions "colloquial", "slang", "geometry", "classical", "obsolete", "Old Persian", etc. These are not, as is commonly thought, merely further information of an etymological nature, though indeed for someone who already or otherwise understands the word in question, they serve this purpose. They are also aids to selecting one sense of the word from the others. Yet they could form no part of the "definition" in the sense of "synonymous terms".

And if these devices fail us, as they commonly do, we have to rely on the partial meaning we are able to abstract from the original context to distinguish among the remaining alternatives. So the definition gives us sets of possible translations, but only incomplete rules of selection. Nor should it be thought that these difficulties afflict only ambiguous terms.

For, in the first place, it is a great problem to decide when a term is ambiguous. Is the word "rational" (or "certain") ambiguous because there are important differences between what it takes to be rational/certain in different situations, e.g. observing the standards of deductive versus inductive logic? Is the word "ground" ambiguous to the extent of having 23 different definitions as in Webster, or is the smaller number given in other dictionaries a more accurate analysis? Whereas philosophers often proliferate 'senses' of words the dictionary defines quite simply, e.g., "rational", the reverse is even more common. To some extent, this is because the term "ambiguous" itself involves some context reference; what senses are distinguishable depends upon what is to count as a sense, i.e. what differences are significant for the current discussion.

But there remain many cases where it is possible to argue as strongly for regarding a term as ambiguous as against it; and in such cases, it seems a little absurd always to suppose that one point of view is *really* correct, and the other incorrect. ("Number" is unambiguous because it means "the basic arithmetical concept"; ambiguous because it includes integers, fractions, imaginary numbers, etc.) Hence a real difficulty remains for the lexicographer with respect to terms referring to linguistic function. If he can see a difference in linguistic function he is very inclined to distinguish meanings: how *could* a noun and a verb have the *same* meaning? But couldn't a conjunction connecting co-ordinate elements have the same meaning as a conjunction introducing a subordinate clause? And exactly what *is* the difference in meaning between "board" in "room and board" (noun use) as opposed to "You may board here" (verb use) *except* function? Different synonyms may be relevant *because* of the different function; but could one really understand one meaning and not be able to understand the other? If not, the ambiguity here is unlike that between "board" meaning "plank" and "board" meaning "group of directors". I want to suggest that distinguishing meanings (and hence defining terms) commonly involves, is facilitated by, and sometimes necessitates reference to linguistic function.

In the second place, there are many occasions when any definition of a term *must* involve reference to linguistic function—although we may prefer to say the term is indefinable. I have in mind such cases as "here", "him", "today", "this", as well as more complex cases such as the Oxford English Dictionary (but not the Webster) definition of "good" in terms of its role in the *procedure* of commendation. I do not include for the moment the other standard 'indefinables' such as "red", "itch", "cold", etc. because they are at least further away from the 'ideal' cases of triangles and squares.

Now "here" can be defined, and is by Webster, as "in this place"; but then we find "this" defined as "a demonstrative word referring particularly to what is present or near in place, time. . . ." So the linguistic function comes in at one remove. It could be avoided even then, at the cost of complete circularity; but the dictionary is intended to serve the purpose of explaining meanings not merely providing synonyms, and hence it, like a logical system, adopts the functional criterion as far as it can.

Once more, as with the word "and", we find ourselves in something of a dilemma because, unlike 'definitions' of "red", "cold", etc. these definitions in terms of linguistic function are (a) complete and correct; (b) usable, admittedly in odd circumstances; (c) possibly analytic; and (d) about the meaning of the words. Thus we hesitate about saying the terms are indefinable. I wish to bring out the difficulty of a decision here in order to bring out the continuity of these definitions with 'contextual definitions' and 'implicit definitions' as well as with 'ostensive definitions.' But I think there are considerable dangers in overlooking the differences, so the fact that in this paper I use the term "definition" in all these cases is not to be regarded as evidence that I take them all to be *essentially* the same. Certainly I wish to retain a distinction between "defining a term" and "explaining the meaning of a term" and hence do not agree with Robinson's account. Since (a), (b), and (d) have already been discussed or do not need discussing, I shall add a few comments on (c).

18. *The Analyticity of Definitions and Statements about Linguistic Function.* It would normally be said that the definition of "this" just quoted was a metalinguistic statement, and that the dictionary slips these in among the translation rules because its conventions do not provide for a distinction between use and mention. The term to be defined occurs in heavy type and the definition may say something *about* it or give a synonym *for* it.

There is an alternative interpretation. Since the grammatical classification also occurs, along with various etymological facts, etc., it might be better to say that the material given is always *about* the term and that sometimes it contains other terms which the conventions entitle one to regard as jointly or separately synonymous, while at other times no such terms are given.

These synonyms should be regarded as being asserted to be synonyms by the definition just as the demonstrative properties of "this" are asserted by the definition. Hence it is always the case that dictionary definitions are empirical statements about meaning, linguistic function, origin, etc. This is supported by the extent to which other material is included; Robinson cites as examples judgments on the success of theories (definition of "phlogiston" as "the supposed cause of fire"), on the state of the metal market ("gold" as "the most precious metal" (Oxford English Dictionary)), on proper spelling ("-ize" preferred to "-ise" by the Oxford English Dictionary). Other important non-synonymous material includes pictures (often almost essential, e.g., for "cuneiform," "illusion, optical"), definitions involving the use of the frequent qualifications "*usually*", "*occasionally*", "*excluding*", etc., and 'incomplete' definitions of various kinds as, e.g. of "meson".

Moreover, if we are to be allowed to use our wits to the extent of distinguishing between the various senses offered, there is no reason to suppose us incapable of *deriving synonyms from statements of linguistic function.* Thus we can see from the definition of "this" that in some contexts we can substitute "the country I am now in" for "this country". The lexicographer himself faces the choice of giving a multiplicity of senses or what might be called a generating formula for such senses, i.e. a description of linguistic function (cf. the definitions of "but" and "and"). Surely we should not regard one of these processes as defining and the other as something else (cf. recursive definitions in mathematics).

Finally, it could be added that definitions in terms of linguistic function are analytic just as are definitions in terms of synonyms and unlike etymological remarks, so we should not feel we are opening the floodgates when we admit them as definitions.

About this latter point it is necessary to make some qualifications.[28] Consider the following statements.

"Brother" comes from an Anglo-Saxon word. (18.1)
"Brother" has seven letters. (18.2)
"Brother" means the same as "male sibling". (18.3)
"Brother" means the same as "Brother". (18.4)
Brothers are male siblings. (18.5)

We may consider 18.1 to be a paradigm of an empirical statement (a synthetic statement) about a term in a language. We discover its truth by an investigation quite independent of the procedure of coming to understand the statement itself. 18.5 is a paradigm of a simple definitionally-true statement (analytic statement); we could not be said to understand the statement without knowing it is true. There are some definitionally true statements of great complexity which we could be said to understand without recognizing their truth, so we extend the account of "analytic" to mean "such that its truth follows necessarily from the meaning (i.e. rules of use) of its terms", i.e., requires no independent empirical investigation. Now 18.2, 18.3, and 18.4

---

[28] The ensuing account owes a very great deal to some discussions with Gavin Alexander. Its relevance to the nature of laws is discussed in his paper in the present volume.

present a more serious problem. For in an obvious sense they tell us something about a particular sign,[29] and it is clearly a matter of empirical fact that this particular sign has the properties of composition and equivalence, etc. that it has in a certain language. Yet on the other hand, it also appears that an understanding of the meaning of the terms involved is perfectly adequate grounds for deciding the truth of the statements without recourse to further empirical investigation.

True, we do have to do some *counting* in order to decide about 18.2, even though the capacity to do the counting may be required as part of understanding "seven". If we wrote down a Chinese phrase, put it in quotes, and added the predicate "consists of three characters", we see that in an analogous case we might well understand this *one* Chinese phrase, and understand what a character is in *general* terms, i.e. the sign unit in Chinese script, and what "three" means, without knowing (or being susceptible to a proof involving no further premises) that the statement was true. Let us then accept 18.2 as synthetic. Now, 18.3 is in the same situation, although it is more complicated. The trick of translating it into another language which sometimes clarifies the logical nature of statements, is unhelpful here since the requirement of knowing the meaning of the terms then involves knowing two languages; someone could certainly *make the same statement* without knowing that it's true, but that doesn't show that if he understood the meaning of all the terms involved, he wouldn't know it was true.

This brings out the extent to which the term "involved" needs clarification. Is a term that is mentioned by name in a statement involved in the statement? If it is, 18.3 is analytic; if not, not. I think that the analytic-synthetic distinction originates in 'unmixed' discourse, i.e., discourse in which terms are used, not mentioned. It naturally extends to cases like 18.1 and probably 18.2. But then, with 18.3, one gets a conflation of the criteria: understanding the terms 'involved' and making the empirical investigation required to establish the truth of the statement about them *amount to the same thing*. Some refinement of the analytic-synthetic distinction is required *if* the distinction is to be preserved in such cases. (Or one could call them, unhelpfully, synthetic a priori.) The natural redefinition would be of "analytic" as "true by virtue of the definitions (and rules of use) of the words and conventions

[29] Type, not token, to use Peirce's distinction, or, more precisely, a language-bound type, since translation affects the truth.

used". Thus, 18.3, which does not use the word "brother", is synthetic. But 18.4 is *surely* analytic! The naming convention is merely instantiated, and it is hence directly derivable from that convention (which would presumably be expressed in the meta-metalanguage) in the same way in which "Brothers are brothers" or, more completely, 18.5, is directly derivable from the conventions governing the meaning of its used terms, e.g., 18.3. (Although I use the terms "directly derivable" and "necessarily follows" in the definitions of "analytic" above, these are not to be construed as meaning the converse of entailment, or deducibility; one cannot express rules of use in the object language, hence analytic statements in the object language cannot be deduced from rules of use.)

It is worth noting that certain further difficulties arise in connection with such statements as "This sentence is in English" (18.6) where the *sentence itself* is mentioned as well as used. It would seem most satisfactory in such cases to admit the limitations of the analytic-synthetic distinction when dealing with mixed-level statements. For if we agree that 18.6 is analytic, then

This sentence contains five words   (18.7)

is very similar but is 'more synthetic,' etc. Whereas if we consider taking 18.6 as synthetic, its similarity to 18.4 and thus 18.5 can be enlarged as can also its important differences from

> The first sentence quoted in the sentence after that in which 18.7 was quoted, in the paper by Scriven in the volume . . . is in English.   (18.8)

These qualifications being made, we nevertheless can see the considerable strength of the contention that statements of linguistic function are very similar to definitions by synonym, particularly if the latter are exemplified from a dictionary. 18.3 tells us something about the meaning and use of the term "brother" by telling us it is the same as that of "male sibling". Instead it might have been rephrased in terms of function and context and told us that it should be used in talking of families with children to refer to any of the male children (18.3′).

Once we see that statements expressing the complete meaning of a term in a form usable by the language-learner are not always statements of intra-linguistic equivalence, we are in a position to consider using the term "definition" in the wider sense which would include all such statements. I believe this is a viable alternative to the traditional one, and to Robinson's. While it is naturally extensible to contextual definition, it would not include either ostensive or theory-implicit definition (definition by postulate).

The most important point for our further considerations of the discussion in this subsection, is the possibility of expressing definitions in the metalanguage. In fact definitions can only be expressed in the metalanguage *unless* some special convention is adopted to distinguish those object-language statements which are definitions from the others. Such a convention is the device of putting " = Df." between the defined and defining terms. There is no internal evidence which enables us to recognize definitions, i.e., the content analyst has to accept the radical difference in the logical nature of a sentence which different contexts can make possible. In a simple artificial language, however, definitions are of less importance, the defined terms being characteristically eliminable.[30] It is only when interpretation and explication and analysis of terms whose meaning is subtly shifting or highly complex becomes necessary that we turn to and need to study definition. But Church admits the peculiar difficulty of the present point when he refers to and avoids "such puzzling questions" as the nature of the sign " = Df." [31]

19. Definitions as Rules. The most interesting alternative view of the logical status of definitions amounts to taking them as rules of the language and hence as neither true nor false, but either adopted or ignored, applicable or irrelevant. Thus a rule like "Automobiles must keep to the left of the street" will apply in England, Sweden, and Australia and will not apply in Brazil or the United States. But if someone does not obey it, it will not thereby have been shown to have been *false* but only to have been ignored. In short, although general in form, a rule does not assert general compliance; it is neither true nor false, although the statement *that* it applies to a certain country or game or language is true or false. Definitions are simply linguistic rules of equivalence (or function, if the wider sense of "definition" is adopted) and even such errors as we find in dictionaries are actually formulations of rules which are not observed and so neither true nor false, just as the 'correct' definitions are actually merely those which are observed.

[30] Church, *op. cit.*, Vol. I, p. 76n.
[31] *Ibid.*, p. 77.

The notion of 'error' or 'correctness' derives from the preface or title of the dictionary which itself makes or implies the claim that the attached set of rules does apply to the English-speaking people: this claim is either true or false, but not the definitions themselves.[32]

This position is peculiarly well suited to treatment of so-called stipulative (or legislative or impromptu) definitions. These are to be regarded as rules of the language game which are proposed for future observance; and as everyone appears to agree, whatever their view of dictionary definitions, stipulative definitions are proposals or promises, etc. and hence are definitely not true or false.

The central question in assessing this account of definitions is the relation between the facts about how a language is used and the definitions which are in some way connected with these facts. The usual assertion, contra the rule analysis, is that dictionary definitions are reports of usage and hence true or false. Let us consider this view.

20. Dictionary Definitions as Reports of Usage. I would imagine that an ordinary empirical report of usage would be a statement something like the following:

> The Swahili-speaking peoples use the word "hiranu" to refer to male siblings in 89 per cent of the occasions when the term is employed.   (20.1)
> Of the 11 per cent remaining cases, 10 per cent were cases where the speaker was judged on other grounds to be somewhat illiterate or relatively immature.   (20.2)

While I do not think we normally refer to inter-linguistic translations as definitions, we can in this case waive the point since an intra-linguistic explanation could be readily substituted and consider the following sentence as closely similar to a definition.

> "Hiranu" in Swahili means the same as "brother" in English.   (20.3)

It seems fairly clear that 20.3 is significantly different from statements like 20.1 and 20.2. I would regard it as a hypothesis which is supported by 20.1 and 20.2 but needs a good deal more support. It is of little

---

[32] One of the problems about sentences like 18.3 is whether the implicit restriction to the English language does not make them analytic. Now "English" is defined by the total set of such rules; but it is similar to a word like "Iroquois" in that it clearly doesn't depend on every single rule—English changes, but "English" doesn't change its meaning (cf. "America", "Thames", etc.); yet this does not make every rule contingent.

consequence that 11 per cent of the population do not use "hiranu" as we use "brother"; it is doubtless the case that a similar percentage of our population, e.g. that under the age of four years plus adult immigrants, similarly misuse the term. And anyway it is ambiguous (lay 'brothers' can be single children). These facts in themselves do not count against the usual dictionary definition of "brother". Of course, if 99 per cent of the population used it in another way, we would have a great deal of trouble in sustaining 20.3 or its intra-English analogue. The kind of further information we need in judging whether 20.3 is justified concerns the homogeneity of the usage of the remaining 11 per cent (has the word other senses, i.e., is there a consistent usage around another norm?); the compresence of other relevant properties with male siblinghood, e.g. normal size and pigmentation and their absence in the aberrant cases (Were all dwarfs and albinos among them? i.e., Does "hiranu" involve the property of manliness or normality? etc.). And so on, indefinitely. The trained eye of a language-using creature and particularly that of a multilingual creature picks out these possibilities and discards them with immense speed and efficiency; the analysis of meanings in natural languages to any degree of subtlety is a formidable task to do implicitly but a hundred times more difficult to do *explicitly*. Homo sapiens alone among the species can do the former, but only an expert in linguistics can approach the latter.

Now, should we say 20.3 is a report of usage of a highly complex kind; or should we rather say that it is a statement about the meanings of words which is related to and supported by reports of usage in a highly complex way? Are statements about right and wrong complex statements about what people want, admire, encourage, etc.; or are they rather ethical statements which are related to what people want, etc.; or something else again? Are statements about the validity of arguments complex statements about the truth and falsity of the premises or are they merely related to such statements? and so on. Insofar as my arguments about reducibility in the earlier sections have weight, they support the second alternatives here. For when we introduce and build up a new vocabulary and approach and new treatment and interests in a subject which has been discussed in other ways before, we can virtually never dispense with the new vocabulary in favor of the old one, whether this is scientific analysis, ethics, or logical analysis.

The suggestion that 20.3 is a report of usage prompts the question,

"What does it tell us about usage?" The answer to this question is extremely difficult: one can indicate this, suggest that, rule out something else. But one would have to qualify what one said many times because it is so dependent on the other aspects of the language and the group which uses it; and one could never in any circumstances say that a statement of the precision of 20.1 or 20.2 followed from it. Yet 20.3 is not a sloppy summary about usage; it is a precise statement about meaning. How central is this type of point to the whole enterprise of logical analysis, and how difficult it is for the formalist to deal with it adequately! The virtues of a natural language in science, as in philosophy or literature, lie in the eternal struggle to produce understanding by coining or using terms with irreducible, 'indefinable' dimensions of meaning, not incomprehensible for this reason but instead more comprehensible—so far is the formalist wrong and reconstructionism stultifying.[33]

21. *The Truth of Rules.* Now 20.3 is not a rule as it stands, but an assertion as to the applicability of a rule, as the "definitions are rules" supporter would quickly point out. The rule would presumably be

"hiranu" means "brother" (21.1)

This, it would be suggested, is the appropriate rule for Swahili-English translation, but not for Urdu-English translation. But in neither case is it true or false; it is merely applicable or relevant to the one case and not the other.

The position which I prefer to this one would deal with the situation as follows: I would say that 21.1 as it stands is neither a rule nor a statement of any other kind. It is a sentence of grammatically proper structure. In one context it *could* be a rule. Let us examine the sort of context required by considering the sentence

If a card is faced during the deal, the dealer redeals. (21.2)

This could be an 'accidentally true' statement about a game or it might be a rule. For it to be a rule, violations of it would have to be regarded—when observed—as punishable, inappropriate, or as reprehensible (unsporting); it would have to be *generally* observed, be related in certain ways to the definition of the game and its governing body if any, etc.

[33] See F. Waismann, "Verifiability," in A. Flew (ed.), *Logic and Language*, Vol. 1, Oxford: Blackwell, 1951; "Language Strata," Vol. 2, 1953; J. J. C. Smart, "Theory Construction," Vol. 2, 1953.

These conditions are both weaker and stronger than the conditions for it to be an accidentally true statement about the game. Suppose that a set of such conditions do obtain; then 21.2 is a rule of the relevant game. And, in the context of that game, it can be used to make a *true* statement. Suppose an argument arises as to who redeals after a card is turned up. If a player utters 21.5 with the appropriate intonation, it would then be appropriate for someone to turn to the rulebook, look up the relevant section and then say of the man who uttered 21.5, "He's absolutely right," or "It's perfectly true, the dealer *does* redeal." (The use of the present tense in rule language is somewhat unusual; cf. "If Socrates *is* a man and . . ." uttered *today* about the dead Greek philosopher.)

It might be asked: how could 21.1 ever be *accidentally* true—and if not, is 21.2 analogous to it? It is preferable to consider different examples

The left bower is a higher card than the trump ace.	(21.3)
The penalty for a revoke is two tricks.	(21.4)

These examples have the feature that—so far as I can see—they could not intelligibly be said to be accidentally true. This is roughly because they non-vacuously involve rule-impregnated terms, i.e. they do not admit of a descriptive rather than prescriptive interpretation—whereas 21.2 does. I think that 21.1 is very similar in that "means" ties us straight down to a certain type of verification procedure, just as "higher than" and "penalty" do here, where they are applied to terms whose definition involves them, viz., "bower" and "revoke", while "redeals" does not since it is not so applied. It seems to me very difficult to deny that if 21.4 was uttered at a bridge table in the context of an argument, it would be categorically true. Certainly as it stands it is neither true nor false, in somewhat the same way as "He loves cinnamon ice cream" is neither true nor false. But given the context in which the reference is clear, then the evaluation words are the same in both cases, viz. "true", "correct", etc.

21.3 even has the special interest that the term "left bower" is so defined (in euchre, etc.) that it is analytically true.

Now it is *possible* to say in reply to all this that when I say 21.4 can be true what I am *really* saying is that it is true that 21.4 applies to, e.g., bridge. The person at a bridge table who utters it *should be taken* to be saying, "21.4 is the relevant rule," etc.

This appears to me to be a forced interpretation; but one could compromise in the following way. One might say that 21.4 without context is a rule and is neither true nor false. In a certain context it can be used to make a statement which is true or false and which is equivalent to "21.4 applies here" (although not identical, since it is in the object language). This view has the consequence that one must be able to identify rules without examining the activities which they are said to govern. It is apparently easy to identify 21.3 and 21.4 as rules. But 21.2 is not, by itself, definitely a rule or not a rule. It may be in a different logical category, just as "Automobiles must keep to the left of the street" might well be a piece of advice (cf. "Automobiles must be regularly greased"). Many examples are even less committed to rule status, e.g., "The owner gets his property back immediately the stolen goods have been recovered." How does one tell whether this is an unobserved rule or merely a false statement?

A more satisfactory compromise, then, would involve saying that a rule is an abstraction or legislation about certain aspects of behavior in what is called a "game", (rather than saying it is a sentence which *might* be this) and that it is neither true nor false although a statement can be made with the same words which *is* true or false. The only drawback about this analysis (apart from the fact that it leaves 21.3 in the odd position of being neither true nor false) is its failure to do the required trick for definitions. For we must surely regard the definitions in a particular dictionary as statements made in a certain context rather than as non-true non-false *candidates* for exemplification. When we open a *Swahili-English* dictionary and find opposite the "hiranu" the word "brother", this is like opening a supposed book of *bridge* rules and finding that the list of penalties includes 21.4. *The context is provided* and the translation of "hiranu", as also the listing of penalties, is correct or incorrect, this to be decided according to the complex procedure previously mentioned.[34] It appears to me that the relation between the utterances " '21.4' applies here" and "21.4" is like that between " 'The sky is blue' is true" and "The sky is blue."

There remains to be considered what is perhaps the most powerful argument for the 'definitions are rules' view, viz. the analysis of stipulative definitions.

---

[34] No essential difference arises if we consider a dictionary of the English language; the other kind was employed in order to eliminate the 'translation move.'

22. *Stipulative Definitions.* Just as one might propose a variant of golf in which a player is restricted to two clubs, or plays with a hockey stick, so one may propose variants of English in which an old rule is changed or a new one added. These proposals are in both cases rules and in the second case are referred to as stipulative definitions. A typical example would be the introduction of the term "climatic tolerance factor" or "CTF" for an individual's score on a series of tests done under varying conditions of humidity, air velocity, and temperature. It is surely absurd to debate whether such a definition is true or false. It is a proposed rule. Hence, one might argue, other definitions should be construed as *accepted* rules: still neither true nor false. But we must lay the context and some comparisons out a little more fully before we can judge the merit of this suggestion.

If a man says, "Let's start a fashion for wearing odd socks," he has proposed a pattern of behavior. Certainly his proposal is not true or false per se. But subsequently we can say, "It's fashionable to wear odd socks" and be right or wrong. If a man says, "Let's use the term 'climatic tolerance factor' for the score on these tests," his proposal is not true or false, but in a year or two we can say " 'CTF' means 'score on these tests' " and be right or wrong. For the world is no respector of word inventors, and the more widespread the term's acceptance becomes, the more likely it is that a deviant usage will develop and, perhaps, become dominant.

Now at the time the innovator makes his odd-sock proposal, would it be correct to say immediately that it is fashionable to wear odd socks? Clearly not, unless Beau Brummell himself is the original speaker and even then the statement would be anticipatory even if reliably so. A fashion is a fashion only if it catches on. So, just as it would be an error to suppose that the progenitor of a new pattern of behavior is in a wholly privileged position with respect to its future development, so it is an error to suppose that he can always guarantee even a short period of acceptance. When we consider the special case of inventing a new term, however, we are inclined to say that here at least the innovator's word is law, for a stipulative definition is a fashion which requires only his own acceptance to verify the statement that the term has the meaning he proposed. And in the case of a man introducing a term in the preface to a book which he has already written, he can be fairly certain he is correct about the term's meaning in that book. (It seems this case is more like legislating: the legislature's word is law as soon as it says it is.)

But if he can be correct, what has happened to the idea of the stipulative definition as neither true nor false? The truth seems to be that the exact form of a stipulative definition has never been very clearly specified. According to Copi, they may be proposals (which he expands as commands or invitations), or they may be predictions.[35] Can a *definition* really be all these things? Is it not rather that the definition may *figure in* a proposal or command and be *related to* a prediction? More exactly, the proposal or command is to the effect that a certain sentence be accepted as a meaning rule, the prediction is to the effect that this sentence will be the correct expression of a meaning rule governing the term in a certain context. As we can see from this formulation, which seems to me more accurate, the sense in which the proposal involves a definition is the weak sense in which a proposal of marriage involves a marriage or the proposal of a truce involves a truce. No *actual* definition, marriage or truce is being discussed, but a *contemplated* one is outlined.

But that which is proposed is a definition of the ordinary kind: there is nothing special about it except that it does not yet apply. I suggest, therefore, that we abandon the term "stipulative definition" (or "legislative definition" or "impromptu definition") as a distinct category of *definition*, retaining it—if at all—merely to refer to the circumstances in which a particular formulation of a definition is found. In this way we avoid the embarrassment of explaining what possible difference there is between the statement "In *Modern Elementary Logic*, 'p $\equiv$ q' means 'p and q are inter-deducible'" when made by the author of that (fictitious) book in the introduction and when made by a student of contemporary notations. The legislation passed by Parliament is not itself true or false, but its passage makes true a statement made in the same words; the definition in the introduction is not quite so immune to judgment, because it is *also* a statement about the meaning of the word as used thereafter. Hence it *is* true or false as soon as its employment is created. What we should say of it in that space of time which may exist (or may not, depending on which is written first, the book or the introduction) before its employment is created is discussed below. But here

[35] "Further Remarks on Definition and Analysis," *Philosophical Studies*, 7(Nos. 1–2):20 (January–February, 1956).

we should note the analogy would have to be with a legislature which passes, not a law, but an 'observed law.' There are circumstances in which we would agree their act does create an observed law (e.g., if the practice already exists, cf. a dictionary definition). But even when a law isn't observed at all we can still say it *is* the law, whereas a definition which is totally ignored in the sequel in favor of another usage could hardly be said to be 'the definition of' that term as it occurs in the sequel (and the context makes it clear that it is intended to refer to the sequel).

This is *not* to reduce all stipulative definitions to predictions—the only one of Copi's alternatives which can be true or false. The definitions he has in mind are not predictions—much less so, in fact, than his 'lexical' (dictionary) definitions are 'empirical reports of word usage.' [36] But both, being the same, are true or false—in the same way and for the same reasons—even if not analytically so in the standard sense. It may even be agreed that the sentence which is being proposed for a definition is at that very instant (supposing there to be as yet no other usage of the term in the proposed sense) true, because it 'constitutes its own usage.' But at that very instant it is not in the full sense a definition: a proposed rule is not a rule; the proposed marriage is not, at the moment of proposal, a success or a failure; though it will turn out to be one or the other just as the sentence will turn out to be a correct or an incorrect formulation of the definition when the usage comes into existence. And just as we may have good grounds for pessimism about the proposed marriage so we may have good objections to the proposed definition. We must realize that "a proposed definition" means "a sentence which it is proposed we should take as a definition" and not "a definition which is expressed in a proposal".[37]

I conclude from this discussion that, absurd though it may be to regard proposals as true or false, and mistaken though it may be to regard the definition forms which are the subject of some proposals in certain fleeting contexts as true or false, this can be regarded as due to the fact they are not yet definitions, just as a proposed marriage is not yet a marriage, a contemplated vacation not yet a vacation.

Is it not very dogmatic to say, as I appear to be saying, that the

[36] *Ibid.*

[37] It is really very unfortunate that proposals, i.e. propositions, are not propositions, i.e. not true or false!

mathematician who begins a systematization of a new branch of the calculus with what he calls a set of definitions, is misusing the latter term? But I am no more saying this than I am that one would be unjustified in writing and so naming an 'introduction' to a book before writing the book. Certainly, if one never wrote the book it would be somewhat odd to refer to what one had written as an introduction: it would be a curiosity, an arrow sign without a head. What could it refer to? To the proposed, but nonexistent book, i.e. it would read *as if* there were a book attached to it. Again, one sometimes hears the reply made to an enquiry about the progress of someone's book, "Well, I've completed the table of contents." It isn't a table of existing contents, but an existing table of contemplated contents. Similarly, a 'stipulative definition,' e.g. a proposed abbreviation, is a rule which governs no actual usage—at the moment of its formulation—but can be referred to as a definition simply because it is intended to govern a contemplated usage. And after the usage is created, it is no longer a stipulative definition but just a good or bad definition.

We are here facing another version of the difficulty that the analysis of rules faces over identifying something as a rule without there being any game in existence to which it applies. Independent of all contexts, one could not so identify a rule, unless it contained several terms from rule language used non-vacuously—and we cannot easily decide what a non-vacuous use would be in such a case.[38] But *in a certain context*, say contemplation of a possible new game, we can *consider them* as rules. The mathematician setting out a formalized system shows us how insignificant the stipulative definition's moment of existence commonly is. For he does not pad his presentation of the definitions of the system as proposals or predictions; he merely lists them as definitions. By so doing he commits himself to the claim that they are the correct definitions of the terms he is about to use; but are his definitions lexical or stipulative? The answer I have given, by denying the existence of the separate category, is "Neither: for these are not proposals, predictions, or reports." They are statements about the meaning of certain symbols in a certain context which, when they will be read, already exists (hence

---

[38] Nor indeed can we easily decide whether the terms are from rule language; consider the following sentence: "Only one marriage can be declared at one time." Is it a statement of impossibility, a rule of prudence, or a moral rule? We cannot say; in fact, we can add to the alternatives by pointing out that it is a rule of the card game gaigel (*Hoyle*, 39th edn., p. 148. Cincinnati: U.S. Playing Card Co., 1941).

148

they are not predictions—it would be erroneous to say in writing a preface that Chapter VI *will be* about anthropology, even though it was not yet written, even if the author intended to write it about anthropology; the convention requires the present tense, the timeless present); and they are not reports because strictly speaking this *would* require the existence of their usage prior to their formulation. A man who sets out the rules of a new version of contract bridge in a booklet called "Rules and Strategy in Three-Handed Contract Bridge" is not reporting on a usage even when someone has played the game after he formulated it. (Although we *could* say "He's reporting on future player-behavior," this seems very queer.) Nor is he predicting. But what he does is to make up (define) a game; and that is what the mathematician does; but the latter and not the former (usually) commits himself to defining the game which is played by him in the succeeding pages and hence he may be wrong (not that an *occasional* slip would establish this).

To recapitulate, I have been suggesting that the argument from consideration of stipulative definitions is unsatisfactory for the following reasons: the explanation of the initial incorrigibility of a stipulative definition lies in the convention of supposing-that-it-is-the-definition, not in any intrinsic characteristic; and the explanation of the fact that stipulative definitions are very commonly correct definitions of the use of the term when its usage is also produced lies in the fact that people can very commonly obey the rules they lay down for their own linguistic behavior. When someone actually proceeds to use the term in question in accordance with his stipulations, he continues to make the assertion of the (originally) stipulative definition true.

23. *Final Assessment of Definitions-as-Rules View.* The preceding section has been principally concerned with the attack on the view that definitions are neither true nor false *because* they are like rules. I was arguing that they are only like rules-in-a-stating-context and these can be true. If we have something very abstract in mind when we talk of a definition, such as a complex function for which a mathematician introduces an abbreviation by defining the two as equivalent, then (a) his proposal (if the definition is introduced by a proposal, command, etc.) is neither true nor false but it isn't the definition; (b) the definition he proposes is immediately neither true nor false in the usual way because the proposing convention is not the asserting convention; (c)

but the definition is subsequently either true or false.[39] While I have been talking in much of the above as if definitions were a kind of rule, I want finally to qualify this as a precise formulation by saying that I think the term "rule" *is* commonly used for the non-true, non-false abstraction from rule-governed behavior or contemplated behavior (but cf. 21.3), while I think the term "definition" is more commonly used for statements of the form " 'x' means 'y'," or for the equivalences found in dictionaries of a specific language, and I think these are true or false. One can abstract from these and use the term "definition" for what we would usually call "possible definitions", but I do not think this is usual. Hence it would be misleading to identify definitions as rules, except when this difference is irrelevant or less important than the undoubted similarities.

It should be noticed, however, that the theory of games provides certain meta-rules which may or may not be correctly stated, e.g. "In zero-sum two-player games, for maximum expectation stakes should be less than half the players' capital." Somewhat analogous to these (but I think a little less so than Professor Braithwaite suggests [40]) are moral rules of which it seems to me some are obviously true, e.g. "Murder is wrong" (cf. "The left bower is higher than the ace of trumps"); while others are better construed as too context dependent to be true or false as they stand, e.g. "Polygamy is wrong" (cf. "No player may stake more on a hand than he has on the table before the first bid is made").

24. The Application and Invocation of Rules. A further caution must be added to what has been said in such metaphorical terms about 'abstracting rules from behavior.' Someone might watch poker played every night for a year and have no idea whether the 'royalties' rule is regarded as applying, i.e. whether holders of royal flushes are paid a fixed sum by everyone in the game, whether they are betting or not in the particular hand. Rules which apply are not necessarily regularly invoked.

[39] If a stipulative definition were ever a prediction, which I do not think is so, it would be immediately true or false. I would say that the statement "In the sequel 'cabad' will be used to mean 'without virtue' " is a prediction about future usage but not a definition, my argument being the same as that in connection with the proposal interpretation above.

[40] *The Theory of Games as a Tool for the Moral Philosopher.* Cambridge: Cambridge Univ. Press, 1956. Cf. my review in *Ethics* (forthcoming). There seems to be a pressing need for a companion volume written by some cardsharp mathematician (or perhaps a lifeman) called "The Theory of Games as a Tool for the Immoral Philosopher."

But that they apply can be determined by various means of enquiry, and when we talk of rules as abstractions from behavior we have to include potential behavior. To say that a rule applies is to say that in certain circumstances certain procedures are correct. In the case of definitions a similar problem arises over constantly concomitant 'accidental characteristics.' Despite the cautions already entered against insisting these must be either purely definitory or purely empirical, there are often distinctions to be made which depend upon (manifest themselves as) the answers to questions about *possible* states of affairs and might never show up in natural usage. Hence we must regard definitions as abstractions from actual plus potential language practices. As the term "usage" is often taken to include both, this comment does not necessarily amount to a criticism of the view that definitions are abstractions from, or encapsulations of, usage. This point is of central importance for the discussion of definitions with empirical content, presuppositions, or bearing, to which we now return. (And it is virtually unmanageable within the usual categories of designation, denotation, connotation, etc. as is the succeeding discussion of names.)

25. *Names of Individuals.* Can one define terms such as "Immanuel Kant", "805 Harvard Avenue, Swarthmore"? It should not be supposed that a categorical distinction exists between such terms as these, and "Iroquois" or "Hindu"; nor between the latter and "native" or "lemon". Neither is there any merit, so far as I can see, in regarding one group as epistemologically or psychologically prior to another. To do so would be like regarding one of the following groups as epistemologically primary: motorcycles, automobiles, and buses.

Suppose we were to propound the definition

<blockquote>Immanual Kant: German philosopher, (1724–1804) author of
"Critique of Pure Reason," etc.   (25.1)</blockquote>

This might be an entry in a pocket biographical 'dictionary,' but—we feel—it can hardly be regarded as a respectable definition. The chief reason would presumably be that the 'defining terms' actually provide empirical information rather than defining characteristics. The statement "Kant died in 1804" is not analytic. As it stands, this argument is no different from that which would make a definition of a term such as "lemon" or "copper" impossible. It will be recalled, however, that we produced one remaining type of analytic statement from the usual 'definitions' of those terms, viz. the assertion that the thing has at least one of the properties mentioned in the definition. Does even this residual strand of definatory connection snap in the present case? Is it self-contradictory to say "Immanuel Kant was neither German, a philosopher, born in 1724, died in 1804, nor was he author of 'The Critique of Pure Reason' "?

As it stands, this is definitely not a contradiction. Research could quite well uncover the fact that though a lifelong inhabitant of Germany, Kant was technically a French citizen, that his life span was 1725–1805 and that he successfully passed off as his own the work of an impecunious Russian refugee whom he secretly supported in a neighbouring village.

But then, 25.1 was very brief. If we were to include in it everything that we believe to be true about the man, his whereabouts at a particular time on a particular day, the names of the children whose godfather he was and the food he preferred, his address in Königsberg and what he said in his letters, would it *still* be conceivable that Immanuel Kant might have none of these properties?

It is as though we were to ask if London would still be London were it located in the Sahara, constructed entirely of concrete igloos arranged in concentric circles and inhabited by little green men from the Orion nebula.

Is there a story I can tell in every such case which would make us want to say that we were wrong before in what we said about X, for it is essentially still X and yet it has none of the properties $Y_1, Y_2 \ldots$? It seems to me that *if* there is such a story it can rationally persuade only by pointing out certain properties $y_i, y_{i+1} \ldots$ which we overlooked in the first listing, and that they must also be more important criteria (jointly) than the original set. In the case of a man about whom we know very little or a city of little character, it might appear that such stories are not hard to find. But this is not so unless we leave out of our original listing some y_i which are decisive. Thus we could only tell the story about Kant because we could rely on the indicators "the man called by this name in his neighbourhood", "the man whose parents were . . .", "the man who submitted certain manuscripts under his name", etc. more *strongly than* on the set quoted. In that case they should be included in the total set of indicators. Would it then be a definition of the term?

Let us begin by asking: Would the name be an abbreviation of this list? Certainly it would seem not, for those who referred to the philosopher by this name during his lifetime could hardly be said to be referring to his death date, subsequent fame, etc. (For if one says the name changed its meaning as the man changed, then one can't step into the same river twice). Is the name an abbreviation for the maximum consistent sub-description compounded from these indicators? No, for some of them are immensely more important than others in determining identity. And what sense could it make to speak of giving them weights—for first one would have to settle all the doubtful cases and no unique number could result. Then perhaps a matrix of conditional weights, expressed very approximately? Perhaps, but how could we ever write this all out—for we have listed very few of the indicators so far—and is not what he ate on July 13, 1795 with his two business friends, of considerable importance in possible debates about identity, etc., etc. And is "Immanuel Kant" really an abbreviation for all this?

There is surely something quite wrong about this approach. A symbol can only be said to be an abbreviation if the lengthier symbol series is specifiable in advance; and here we are trying to discover it.

Well, then might it not be an analysis of the term, a making explicit of what is packed into it? Most certainly this cannot be the case if we mean that everyone who used the symbol knew even a significant part of what is involved in the sort of analysis we have just been listing.

There is only one analysis that can be given of the term's meaning and that is by reference to its linguistic function; and it will not provide a general translation rule. The reason we feel that we can't just deny flatly the necessity of the connection of the name with the disjunction of the indicators is because the *function* of this name only exists in all its usual applications if the indicator set *is* consistent. If we have a large number of the facts wrong, then difficulties arise about the use of the term. But unless we do, the name is a label for a man (or baby) of a certain appearance who in fact has a certain history at every moment, and any substantial parts of that appearance or that history are *criteria for the application* of the term but not a *translation* of the term, i.e. not its meaning in the usual sense. This name-symbol has a use in certain contexts; we can describe those contexts and the use, and we can say no more. We can say that the use *presupposes* the existence of a man with a good proportion of the indicator properties.

153

i.e. that the contexts of its use are those in which at least some are known to apply, and there are no good reasons for thinking that others, believed to be relevant, do not apply.

To illustrate, the name would be applied correctly by someone who saw Kant, knew what he looked like, and had no reason to believe that this was not the man born in 1724 of such and such parents (a fact which the watcher knew to be true of Kant). Now if some doubt exists about the applicability of the second criterion to the individual with Kant-like appearance, some doubt exists whether this individual *is* Kant; and it may be resolved by finding that no one with this appearance, etc. was born on the quoted date of those parents but shortly afterwards (belief error) or by finding that this is a younger brother or simply someone with similar looks (observation error). But to apply the name is not to assert the original combination of facts, though it is to commit oneself to (to evince one's belief in) them. The scholar of a subsequent century may apply the name according to a non-overlapping set of criteria (e.g. the philosophical views expounded in certain books) and will generally but not necessarily convey overlapping information, depending on what his reader or listener knows. But it is the peculiar virtue of an individual name that we can distinguish criteria for application from information conveyed, from use, and from the meaning of the term: for the first two are stateable in given cases, the third follows from them, and we have no standard interpretation of the fourth. Herein lies an important difference from the case of common nouns and one which has been commonly enough noted. However, it is the similarities between individual names and common nouns with which we shall be more concerned.

Notice, then, the immense utility of a dictionary entry such as 25.1 in contexts where the capitalizing convention is understood, i.e. in which it is not read as a translating rule but as a locating rule, locating the thing referred to by the name in the system of pigeonholes called Life-span, Occupation, and Nationality—probably quite well enough to satisfy whatever unclarity it was that prompted looking up the reference. In this respect it does just what the average dictionary definition does. The fact that a term may have several different dictionary definitions itself in another way suggests that the function of such definitions is the *location* of a word on a language map not the production of a set of equivalent terms. The paradox of analysis, in one way, and the con-

154

text dependence of the utility of most dictionary definitions, in another, bring out the desperate limitations on such a program.

But, to a greater degree than most dictionary definitions, the utility of the terms defined by such as 25.1 depend on the existence of stabilities in the world to which it refers. It should not surprise us greatly if the useful terms of theoretical physics may prove to be imbued in a similar way with a commitment to a certain state of affairs. It is not merely that if Kant had not existed, the name would not have had any use—for in that respect "father" (= "male parent") is no different. But if people (places, etc.) did not retain some characteristics while changing others in a certain stated way, names would not work as they do; [41] that they have the function ('meaning') they have, therefore entails that these things happen. Yet to use the terms is not to assert these conditions exist.

Might not one talk here of conditional equivalences, of conditional translation rules and hence of conditional definitions? "If and as long as certain conditions obtain, then 25.1 and its relatives can be regarded as definitions." I think this is clearly useful under some circumstances, and the preceding discussion should have reduced our opposition to a non-translation rule, but it has certain drawbacks, perhaps the most important being the abandonment of the functional condition for the term as used by Kant's friends (and it was surely the same term), and the suggestion that other definitions are non-conditional. It is to this latter suggestion that section 28 is devoted. There remains to be discussed first a pair of apparently serious difficulties with the preceding account of names.

26. *The 'Stipulative' Definition of Individual Names.* Is it not perfectly possible that a name could be *introduced* by a definition and hence false to say that names can not be defined? But the difficulty would then be to decide whether the term was indeed an individual name. For we may quite well extend the convention of capitalizing to cover not only class terms (Iroquois, Spaniard, etc.) but also descriptions. Are not such terms as "King-of-the-Roost", "Old Maid", and "He" in the well-known games, and "Emir", and "Vice-Chancellor" actually descriptions which have a formalized significance and *in a particular context* individual reference? It is certainly not the case that these are

---

[41] For another aspect of this problem see Strawson's paper "Persons" in this volume.

the names of individual human beings, since human names persist beyond the ending of a game or a job. Yet sometimes these role terms do so also; think of gangsters, generals, public schoolboys and Indian chiefs who retain the description they earn on a particular occasion as a permanent sobriquet. In these cases, however, a change in the logical nature of the term takes place which is in some respects comparable to that undergone by the name of a chemical complex like "gold" as it is successively shifted from one set of foundations to another with the progress of science. The difference is that in the case of an individual who picks up one of these capitalized descriptive names, there is a shift from one logical category to another, from the descriptive to the referring function. How can we verify this? By the very procedure of section 25 where we brought out the impossibility of giving a translation of a name. The same considerations apply to the suggestion that when a baby is christened, his name is—so to speak—stipulatively defined! The label-attaching procedure is not the translation-offering procedure; and even if it were, the subsequent use of the name would rapidly convert it from a linguistic equivalent of a description to a referring device.[42] As we said before, there is nothing more surprising about the fact that someone's name refers at his christening to a little baby and at his death to an old man than there is about the fact that we can step into the same river twice.

27. *The Names of Fictitious Individuals.* It may be thought that an exception to the above separation of referring and translating procedures would have to be made for the names of individuals in fiction. After all, there *is* no one to whom these names refer, yet they have meaning; hence must they not be equivalent to some descriptive phrase? But no more must this be so than must it be false to say that there are descriptions of sensations and sunsets in fiction. The latter are still descriptions although they do not describe existing things, and the former are names although they have no existing referent. The decisive factor is the role the terms play in the given context, i.e. how they are to be understood there. And they are to be understood not as one under-

[42] Strawson ("On Referring," in A. Flew (ed.), *Essays in Conceptual Analysis.* London: Macmillan, 1956) gives the nice example of "The Great War" which almost changed from description to name but was dragged back into oblivion by its descriptive component when its descriptive reference became ambiguous. See also G. E. M. Anscombe's discussion of the naming paradox in "Report on Analysis Problem No. 10," *Analysis,* 17:49–52, January, 1957.

stands an account of real activities but as one understands fiction, which is by no means easily stated.[43] There is a good deal of similarity, however, and for fiction to be understood at all the names in it must be regarded as having just the same sort of role as names in ordinary descriptive discourse, except that we don't assume they refer to real people. If you like, we don't 'count it against' these names that they have no owners in the real world. It is not at all obvious why we should find, or in what respects we do find, fictional stories of any interest, but we do. Now, if it turned out that what we had read, thinking it to be a novel, was actually a biography, then it is clear we would not have to abandon certain translations of the names in the novel. The names would fit on the shoulders of their rightful owners just as all names do, not as a description does. Their logic would not have changed in this respect, although we might continually be seeing them in an odd light, so to speak shaking ourselves when we address them; for it is only in dreams that we see characters from novels.

Nevertheless, might not some statements about fictional characters become analytic whereas this is never true of real characters: for example, "Hamlet is the Prince of Denmark in Shakespeare's play of the same name," cf. "George VI was King of England throughout the Second World War." We may discover that the monarch crowned George VI died early in the war and had his place taken by a hitherto unknown twin, but this we cannot say of Hamlet. Yet the comparison between these examples is not quite fair. "George VI was an English king" is a little closer analogy and a little more analytic, but this is because the name is a kingly name. "George VI" was probably also the name of several pomeranians, but the one to which the earlier example is supposed to refer had to be a king, just as "The Champ" has to be or have been a boxing champion in certain usages. Hence such names are in a sense disguised descriptions; and we say this partly because they do figure in apparently analytic propositions. The analyticity of such propositions, however, is of a slightly curious kind; it depends upon the existence of a referent for the name term.

"The first member of the house of Windsor was an English monarch" is certainly, it would seem, analytic—since Windsor is an English royal

<hr>

[43] See "The Language of Fiction" symposium in *The Aristotelian Society Proceedings*, Supplementary Volume 28 (1954), consisting of papers by Margaret Macdonald and the present author.

house. But what about "The fifty-third member of the house of Windsor was an English monarch"? One can say it is analytically true or that it is neither true nor false (Strawson) or that it is—àt the moment—false (Russell). I have been arguing for Strawson's position. Hence, if "George VI" is a disguised description, then it can occur in an analytic proposition of the above kind under certain presuppositions. In this sense, could one not argue that "Hamlet" is also a disguised description?

But this is not the relevant sense for our general argument. "Hamlet" may be, for literature, equivalent to a description like "the Prince of Denmark in a great Shakespearian tragedy"; but this is an inter-categorical type of equivalence analogous to those discussed earlier. It does not in the least follow that one could substitute the description mentioned for the name *within the play*. Literary dictionaries and dictionaries of mythology are not wrongly so called, but the definitions they contain are not translation rules for *the original context of use* of the names that occur as entries. Entries in dictionaries of biography provide context-dependent translation rules, but not for the term as used at the baptism of its bearer, and hence not unconditional translation rules.

This discussion should have made a little clearer the multiple functions of terms, including names, and part of the relationships between the presuppositions of descriptions and of names. Ordinary individual names cannot, while unique descriptions can, figure in analytic statements in their primary contexts, even under the appropriate presuppositions.

28. Existence as a Presupposition of Names. Whereas we do not say that statements in the present tense about the ninetieth King of England's poetry preferences are now true or false, if the tense is changed we can regard them as predictions which may be (but are not necessarily) in this category. Such small grammatical points show the Russellian account of descriptions mistaken and similar points make the usual analyses of definitions unsound; nor are these weaknesses to be dismissed because of the apparent unimportance of the grammatical difficulties raised against them. On the contrary, the only possible interest of the Russellian account of descriptions, or the logic texts' account of definitions, lies in their elucidation of (or improvement over) the ordinary grammatical conventions. For if it is *descriptions* and *definitions* we are interested in analyzing, this means descriptions and definitions in the pre-analytic sense or else every first analysis will be correct. And they can't be improvements until we are clear what the original concepts are, or can show they are unclear.

Strawson argues that statements *about* "The x which is y" are true or false only if there *is* an x which is y. It would appear that some modification of this view is called for with respect to descriptive phrases in fiction: "the first man to land on Mars" may be a character in a well-known TV 'space opera' and it may be correct to say about him that he is a member of the United States Air Force, even though he does not in fact exist. But if we simply say this, we are making the same error of confusing contexts as in section 27; it is only correct to say one thing about him and false to say another in the context *in which he is* 'taken to exist' (though only as a character in fiction exists). We can easily see the truth of this in the given case because as a matter of *actual fact*, it is *neither* true nor false at the moment that the first man to land on Mars is or was a member of the United States Air Force, since there neither is nor has been any such man. One day, it may be true, literally. But even today, it may be true of the character. The same applies to statements about individuals referred to by name. So there needs to be an x which is y in real or *conventional* existence.

There remains the apparently distinct case of descriptive phrases such as "The greatest prime number" about which true assertions can apparently be made (e.g., that there are a finite number of primes smaller than it) although no such number could possibly exist. Again, the solution lies in seeing that such descriptions occur only in the context of e.g. reductio ad absurdum proofs where they are *being taken* as referring to something that exists in order to see what conclusions can be inferred. How can one 'take something to exist' which could not possibly exist? The answer is that one can do it in the way mathematicians do it; and that one can do it brings out some of the troubles with the view that mathematical propositions are the negations of self-contradictory statements.

Now, can we extend the presupposition approach to common nouns, names with an avowed multiple reference? Can't statements about centaurs' anatomy be true or false even though there are no centaurs? Only because there is a context (mythology) in which they are treated as existing (i.e., are described). We are thus prevented from drawing any exciting ontological conclusions from the use of a class term. Furthermore, a case which Strawson does consider, many of those cases

159

Michael Scriven

where the name of the class itself forms the subject of a sentence must be regarded as involving a non-presuppositional analysis.[44]

It is true that centaurs have legs and false that they have two heads (except—we may add—for an occasional one) but is it true or false that they have navels? Perhaps no one ever decided; and in that case one can hardly insist that there really is an answer. Even if one day we find what we then call centaurs, and look to see, this does not decide the original question any more than subsequent events can falsify statements about the service affiliations of a TV hero whose serial adventures involve landing on Mars. Herein lies the main difference between the logic of fiction and the logic of fact: there is no need for grammatically sensible questions about fictional characters to have answers. ("What did Hamlet study at Wittenberg?")

I would conclude that the Strawson analysis, for this reason at least, requires modification in the way suggested.[45] The other senses in which sentences in fiction may be said to be true, I have discussed, albeit incompletely, in the reference cited.

Now this discussion may appear to be very distant from the realm of philosophy of science; but it will soon be seen that the connection is quite close—between statements about theoretical entities and fictional entities, between logical presuppositions and the pragmatic presuppositions of a scientific vocabulary.

29. General Names and Scientific Concepts. It is possible to extend the contextual analysis of names and its main corollary, the truth requirement, into the field of class terms such as "moron", "neurotic", "particle", "group", and "number". Apart then, from existence assertions, fictional entities, and consideration contexts [46] we do require certain presuppositions to be fulfilled before we are prepared to say that statements referring to such classes are true or false. If we make statements about the business success of a group of college graduates

---

[44] *Introduction to Logical Theory*, pp. 191–192.

[45] There are other interesting difficulties. For example, "The golden mountain is golden" is analytically true; but on Russell's account it is false, and on Strawson's neither true nor false. But again, the latter account can more easily be modified to deal with the case.

[46] I use this phrase to cover cases where something is *treated as* existing, without judgment being intended as to whether it does exist; the consideration of the greatest prime number's properties is in fact designed to show that it does *not* exist. These cases do not include the fictional cases where judgment of nonexistence is a necessary condition of understanding *what it is* we're reading (though not *what we read*).

in pharmacology who score in the top 2 per cent on the Miller analogy, it is a presupposition of such statements that there is such a group, i.e. that some graduating pharmacologists are in the ninety-eighth percentile. This is, for our purposes, a less important point than its consequences; but even so it has to be slightly qualified in order to be wholly defensible.[47]

A much more important point arises when we ask about terms which are introduced to serve approximately the same function as the description in the last example. Suppose that we look up the term "pistil" in Webster; we find the words "the ovule-bearing organ of a seed plant". Now here is a description beginning with the definite article. If it is really substitutable for "pistil" then by an extension of the previous analysis, we must agree that use of the latter term has certain existential presuppositions, viz. that seed plants have a special structure which carries the megasporangia. The problem is where to locate and how to describe this existential assumption. It is clearly unsatisfactory to put it into the definition of the term, for at least the reasons against the Russellian theory of descriptions; bluntly, because names, descriptions, and descriptive terms do not make statements but are the constituents of statements. Equally clear, it is not a matter of logical necessity that the existential assumption should be true for the term to have meaning. The meaning of descriptions and names of this kind is not that to which they refer but, roughly, their *potential* referring and describing abilities: we might produce a name for the 132nd element, confident of its eventual creation and, in some detail, of its properties, and the name will have meaning before it has reference.[48]

There is a *practical* inference from the existence of the term to the present, or expected future, or past or fictional, etc. satisfaction of its presuppositions; but this is not a logical necessity, for someone might simply make the term up and write a definition for it on the blackboard.[49] The logical necessity only arises when we wish to make up meaningful empirical statements and discourse using the term. Then

---

[47] P. F. Strawson, "A Reply to Mr. Sellars," *Philosophical Review*, 63:227ff (1954).

[48] See further, Strawson, *Introduction to Logical Theory*, pp. 189ff.

[49] One might ask whether this is enough to create a *word*, or whether a word does not have to have a part in some language game, at least a prospective game. Is a 'stipulative definition' that no one ever intends to use and never uses and is never seen by anyone except the definer, which is in fact just a doodle, *really* a definition? If we answer No it seems we bring psychology into logic; but should we answer Yes just to keep it out?

we can certainly say there is a logical necessity for the presuppositions to be true if statements involving the term are to be true or false, the very minor qualifications that arise in cases of deception and indirect reference being unimportant for the usual contexts of scientific and practical empirical exposition and proof.

Now I wish to propose the following thesis. Many of the propositions that are commonly called definitions of scientific terms are not—as we have already seen—definitions by the usual logician's standards, or else they are not definitions by the criterion of the scientist's use. They are in fact *conditional translation rules*, not pure translation rules; this does not mean they *assert* that certain states of affairs exist, but merely that the existence of such conditions is a presupposition of their acceptability as translations. And further, they usually provide translations only in certain contexts.

This possibility was considered earlier with respect to individual names and there heavily qualified because of the logical chasm that divides 'purely' referring expressions from descriptions.[50] But we saw even there that the difference was a difference of function *in certain cases*; while in other cases (historical), a translation was satisfactory.

Now we are considering general names in the sciences, common names, the kind of word we do find defined in technical dictionaries and glossaries. And I want to say of most of them that their equivalence with their usual definitions can never accord to the logician's ideal of an absolute translation rule but is dependent on context and on the continuance of certain empirical conditions.

The exceptions are of two kinds: there are some 'definitions' which are not translation rules at all, and there are some which are unconditional translation rules. The first do not count against my negative thesis about definitions of scientific terms, the second do. We must see how important the exceptions are.

A term like "pistil" exhibits a fairly common pattern. It is coined (from the Latin for a pestle) to apply to a particular structure observed

[50] The difference being somewhat analogous to that between a photograph of a man, and a street map on which his house is marked as devices for conveying his identity. The former tells you nothing *incidentally*, it is simply a picture of the man, useful only if you ever see him in good light; the latter tells you incidentally something about the relationship of certain streets to each other and perhaps to other prominent cartographical features—and it's entirely dependent for its utility on the man's continued residence in the same place. Yet even this analogy underestimates the difference between names and descriptions since a man can change his face as

to be common to seed-bearing flowers. It was defined then more or less as it is now, and in what we would usually call a precise way. But immediately it is coined, possible border-line cases can be conceived and often enough materialize. There are two kinds of such difficulty.[51] On the one hand, there are the spore-bearing plants with their spore-bearing structures, which raise the question whether spores are to count as seeds and hence, e.g. ascocarps as pistils. The difficulty here is the range of the term "seed". These are the so-called intensional vagueness difficulties. Then there are the more profound and disturbing difficulties which arise if circumstances begin to make the application of the term difficult not only near its border but at its very center. Imagine that a certain species of plant no longer continues to have distinct structural elements in the usual way but instead they metamorphose irregularly and discontinuously. For a fraction of a second we see what appears to be a pistil, then it vanishes to reappear in changed form later, then again subsequently, but this time as a petal. This is not a borderline case in the sense of being near the border between one of the stated criteria and its converse domain; instead, this is a situation which is not included in (or excluded by) or nearly included in the definition, a situation which is not even envisaged by the definition. Of course, it is a borderline case in a more general sense.

Its interest lies in the fact it undercuts one of the presuppositions of this category of words, the thing-kind words. The standard 'borderline case' merely undercuts the utility of a particular term as we might attack the introduction of a term for stout baldish middle-aged men if it were to be used in a sociological study.

The effect of such possibilities is to suggest that the definition as it stands is not a translation rule, since we might very well object to referring to seed-bearing structures in such plants in their moments of existence as pistils, on the grounds that this ephemeral character makes them quite unlike what in other plants we call pistils even though it is not prohibited by any feature of the definition. The feature of sus-

well as his address. His name *is* his identity, the trappings of his life might have belonged to another man. (What we refer to as "changing his name", say from X to Y, does not have the consequence of falsifying the statement "That's X" even when made subsequently to the change.)

[51] In the following paragraph I am putting a point due to and very well stated by Max Black in "Definition, Presupposition, and Assertion," *Philosophical Review*, 62: 532–550 (1952). Reprinted in the same author's *Problems in Analysis*. London: Routledge & Kegan Paul, 1954.

tained or slowly changing existence is such a pervasive property of our world that we neglect to specify it in our definitions. But the situation is not so easily saved. There are other equally important requirements, an indefinite list of them such as the absence of little gnomes which stand smiling in the heart of certain flowers, their bodies merging with the stem, bearing in their arms small baskets of seeds. They qualify as pistils on the definition but the botanist would indeed be hard to find who would not consider coining another term for them rather than apply the same. No definitions for such terms could be given within a reasonable space which would exhaust all such possibilities quite apart from the residual problem of intensional vagueness which would arise in each case.

Might one not avoid these problems by saying that in these cases we are in just as much doubt whether to apply the term "structure" as the term "pistil" and that consequently the definition can be saved as a translation rule at the moderate expense of vagueness about its scope within the language? I think this reply is inadequate since the defining terms in such examples are usually much more general than the defined term and hence will be applicable in a wider variety of cases: the word "thing", for example, often occurs and knows almost no bounds whereas the *particular* kind of thing we are defining may be quite closely bound in terms of space-time variations. Furthermore there remains the practical question whether the term cannot be properly applied in *some* such cases, e.g. if the metamorphosis of 'pistil' to 'petal' does not occur, although the vanishing behavior does. Translation rules without application rules are incomplete analyses of meaning; and part of the meaning of such terms as "proton", "nucleus", and "maladjusted" is their potential of application in just such 'central-borderline' cases, of which very little indication is given in their definitions. Nor can much be given, for learning how to use even general names is not just learning how to translate them. Semantic rules cannot all be stated though they can be learned, cf. rules of tact.

30. *Conditional Definitions.* Yet these difficulties might be faced if there were no alternative. The alternative, however, appears to be greatly preferable. It would consist in arguing that certain terms are defined under certain conditions, in the following way:

As long as $C_1, C_2, \ldots C_n$ hold, "X" may be translated as "Y".

$$(30.1)$$

This is, logically, the standard form of most definitions in science.[52] We commonly ignore the antecedent and in ordinary contexts this does little harm, for in ordinary contexts they are fulfilled. And ultimately we must abandon even this form since the context evades complete description. But if we begin to argue that the proper logical analysis of definitions is *unconditional* translation rules, we should reintroduce the conditions. The most important fact to be remembered about 30.1 is that it is not an exhaustive analysis of the meaning of X. It is a statement which *partially* specifies or explains the meaning of X.[53] The idea of the unconditional translation rule as a total specification of meaning derives from mathematics and certain atypical examples beloved of logicians ("father" = "male parent", etc.). So we regard our dictionary definition of "pistil" as presupposing certain standard conditions of the physical world. We cannot list these exhaustively in specific terms but we can do so in a general form by reference to, e.g. "the morphological conditions hitherto encountered." But since the translation given is applicable in a much wider range of cases than this, more would have to be said. We see immediately that an exact listing of the Cs could not be given.

It is in general true that the meaning of scientific terms can be usefully but inadequately summed up in such a form as 30.1, and not in any shorter form. Only when the total role of the term in the language is understood can the user undertake to extend or modify 30.1. In particular, the question whether a term has *changed its meaning* when we use a different Y as translation can be seen to be dependent on whether a different set of Cs is involved. As the situation usually is, we cannot draw any such conclusion: as long as the International Gas Thermometer Scale of temperature correlated well with thermodynamic predictions involving the concept, one could regard the latter concept as linguistically equivalent to the former. When these conditions ceased to obtain, the equivalence ceased to be observed; but it does not follow that the term changed its meaning, only that we use different criteria under

---

[52] It should not be supposed that it is equivalent to the formally similar bilateral reduction sentences of Carnap's *Testability and Meaning* (New Haven: Wittlock's, 1950): the connectives here are not truth-functional, nor do they permit transposition of X into the conditions, etc., etc.

[53] Cf. A. Kaplan, "Definition and Specification of Meaning," *Journal of Philosophy*, 43:281–288 (1946). It should be noticed that my use of the term "indicator" does not correspond to his in this article or in any article of his since; a definition is given below.

different conditions, somewhat as different thermometric instruments were used in different ranges. The operationist analysis overlooks this conditionality of the definitions and hence too readily takes a different Y to show there must be a different X involved (quite apart from the difficulties with what it produces as the Y). The identification of intelligence with score on the Stanford-Binet tests, or anxiety with score on the Taylor scale, etc. is not an absolute identification but one that is conditional on the continuance of certain regularities, such as that between ratings by teachers and score on the Binet. In terms of this analysis we can even see a way of dealing with the very odd identification of colors with electromagnetic waves of a certain frequency: as long as there is a correlation between our visual criteria and the wavelength, and as long as we are only concerned with physical significance not intension, we may take the two as equivalent.[54] Thus contextual conditions as well as empirical ones may be required in the antecedent, corresponding to the various references to scope, function, etc. which we observe in the dictionary.

In fact, most of our difficulties with dictionary definitions can be salvaged with this device—at the expense, indeed, of accepting their incompleteness as analyses of meaning. I have tried to argue that this incompleteness must be accepted, that it is no mere accident that the Oxford English Dictionary, for all its volumes, is still far short of giving a complete analysis of the meaning of many of the terms it contains. The essential point to be made is that 'definitions' are usually mnemonic devices, rough approximations which serve usefully as a first analysis of a term's meaning but require—in any important case—almost unending supplementation via examination of paradigmatic examples of the term's use. It is no accident that, on the one hand, Carnap's school has had to abandon the long search for precise definitions of theoretical terms in science in terms of the observation language [55] and, on the other hand, the contextual analysts have eschewed the great tradition of

[54] A particularly interesting case arises over the supposed 'two senses' of "probability". In fact, I suggest, statistical frequency can be taken as giving a value of a certain probability *only under certain conditions*, e.g., the physical symmetry of the die, the randomness of the throwing, the force of gravity, etc.; it is hence a derivative case of the primary theoretical sense and strictly analogous to the gas thermometer 'definition' of temperature.

[55] Rudolf Carnap, "The Methodological Character of Theoretical Concepts," in *Minnesota Studies in the Philosophy of Science*, Vol. I, p. 48.

systematic philosophy with its deductions and definitions of the important concepts.

Even more significant is the fact that in both cases the successor to the definition has been exemplification. The 'definition by postulate' and the 'correspondence rule' of the semioticians and the 'appeal to ordinary language' of the Oxford analysts are two sides of the same coin. For the postulates of an interpreted theory are the paradigm cases of the use of the theoretical terms just as the standard cases of the use of terms are those which exemplify its meaning *if anything can*. The difference between the formalist and the functionalist resides here in the fact that the latter is sceptical about the applicability of formal logic to (a) ordinary philosophical problems and (b) scientific problems of philosophical interest. He would perhaps suggest that rigor in the sciences can be adequately achieved by the scientist and mathematician (and the symbolic logician falls into this category), but that the philosophically interesting problems will usually not be amenable to solution by reformalization but by *deformalization*, and would perhaps instance the debates over determinism among the quantum mechanicians and those over creation among the cosmologists. This is in no way to suggest that formalizing scientific theories is unimportant or easy; it is neither, and to say that it is of dubious *philosophical* concern is only to express a view about the distinction between scientific and philosophical issues.[56] In fact, if it is agreed that formalization is of *eventual* use for scientific purposes and that the utility of a formalization is dependent upon what can be proved as theorems, then one must see the formalist as getting at the philosophical problem by trying various possible solutions out, while the functionalist is getting at it by taking it to pieces where it stands, this to be followed by a technician's formalization of the best informal solution. For problems deeply imbedded in scientific theory such as the status of Mach's principle, the formalist

[56] This difference, and the consequences of exemplification for philosophical method are most illuminatingly discussed in "How I see Philosophy," F. Waismann, *Contemporary British Philosophy*, pp. 445f. The most fundamental example I can think of to establish the priority of exemplification over definition arises in connection with the attempt to explain what is meant by the notion of 'logical form' which is crucial to any development of logic (and hence to the formalist analysis). It seems to me that Strawson ("Propositions, Concepts, and Logical Truths," *Philosophical Quarterly*, 7:15–25 (January 1957)) has shown Quine's attempt to be dependent on examples which actually disprove Quine's conclusion—that extensional logic is adequate. See also William Kneale, "The Province of Logic," in *Contemporary British Philosophy*, especially pp. 254f.

is better equipped technically; for others, such as the analysis of scientific laws, he may be hampered by the requirements of a formal analysis. Neither approach is a priori inferior.

Before continuing, however, I wish to examine some of the exceptions to the thesis put forward earlier in the last section. I said there were two kinds of exception: some things commonly called definitions are not translation rules at all, and some are unconditional translation rules. There are various kinds under each heading, and I shall only mention a few.

Recursive definition does not provide a translation rule; it only provides a *means* for obtaining one for a specific instance. The distinction is logically rather important,[57] but this device is rarely used in the sciences although common in mathematics. 'Ostensive definitions' are more obviously not translation rules, and less obviously definitions; although they are certainly involved in explaining the meaning of some scientific terms. They involve and depend on the labeling function of terms. Naturally enough, they are beyond the domain of formal analysis, and since most terms involve some labeling function, such terms cannot be fully analyzed formally. Their translation rules, if such can be found for them, merely leave out the labeling problem, which arises again as the defining terms are themselves analyzed. So the logical nature of the simple name is not wholly distinct from that of the abstract scientific term, and the better a definition of the latter is, the less it will say about the application (or correspondence) 'rules': for these if verbalized are *descriptions* not *definitions*. Hence ostensive definitions are related to but to be distinguished from, 'definition by example' where the example is always linguistically specified. The latter is a general case of the 'implicit' ('postulational') or 'contextual' definition, a point which I think has not been stressed before; and both are cases of limited-scope translation rules, i.e., of partial meaning specifications.

Contextual definitions can be treated in the same way as explicit

[57] If it were not a distinction, the formalization of mathematics would be enormously simplified; putting it another way, such definitions provide the basic analysis of transfinite numbers, and a restriction to translation rules would make these inaccessible. It is interesting to read Kronecker and Poincaré insisting upon explicit definability in mathematics for reasons very similar to those advanced by the positivists for the same thesis with respect to scientific vocabularies, viz. the avoidance of metaphysical wastelands. The reason is a good one, but if there's even a little uranium in the wastelands, the issue becomes very much harder to settle.

definitions have been here, and sometimes include unconditional translation rules. But both contextual and implicit definitions involve a special complication of some logical interest. To understand a contextual definition such as that given in "X is to the right of Y when viewed by Z" = "The signed angle XZY is greater than zero", one has to read it in a certain way, viz. read it as embodying a proper (usually the only proper) usage of the terms that are not already defined with respect to those that are. For it would be a mistake to suppose that the use of the variables "X" and "Y" plus a substitution rule is essentially different from the use of individual names plus an understanding that they occur vacuously—and the latter is a case of definition by example (or 'definition by description').

If one correctly understands the meaning of a term which is explained by an example or series of examples, one understands which of the details of the examples are essential and which are dispensable (tautology). That we can do this with considerable precision is perhaps surprising but that we can do it in philosophy is no more surprising than is learning a foreign language without the aid of a dictionary. It would in fact be more unsound to suggest that explaining the meaning of a term by examples must be imprecise than it would to suggest that a traveler in a foreign land can never come to understand precisely what its terms mean. (The latter view has at least the plausibility arising from inter-cultural differences, a weak form of the chemist's versus physicist's meaning differences, which the former lacks.) Finally, there is the so-called implicit definition or definition by postulates which I have already likened to definition by example and which again is on the borderline of what is normally accepted as the extension of "definition", chiefly because it apparently does not provide translation rules for the terms which are to be defined.

It is not to be overlooked, however, that the language contains certain devices which enable us to transform these cases into explicit definition, chief among them being the phrases "that which . . .", "the . . . which . . .", etc. Thus we can define temperature explicitly as "that which satisfies the relations and laws . . .". It is no objection to this to argue that the term for temperature occurs again in the defining phrase, since we may simply place a variable there of which we say that it represents temperature if and only if it simultaneously satisfies all the equations given. There is nothing more improper about this device than that of contextual definition.[58] In this form it is particularly clear that the use of a term with this definition has empirical presuppositions since its phraseology can only be scientifically justified if it is in fact the case that these laws CAN be simultaneously satisfied; so the definition as transformed exhibits the conditional element which must inhere in any definition by example since the latter cannot have application without the existence of the state of affairs described in the example (or in examples which are seen to be essentially similar). This kind of definition is closely allied to definition in terms of linguistic function, where a reference is made to its grammatical role; here the reference is to its epistemological role.

But it appears I am talking here only about the presuppositions of use, not of the definition itself. For, if the scientific concept of temperature could be fully expressed by the postulates listed after the "that which satisfies" phrase, then this definition would be a perfect translation rule.

Here the example of the Iroquois is again useful. The term "Iroquois", like the concept of temperature, that of the pistil of a flower, and other important concepts, is in a strong sense committed to the existence of specifiable conditions in the world; the capitalization of the term "Iroquois" brings out how far in the direction of an individual name that class name goes, but its absence should not lead us to overlook the similar element in the other terms. Immediately we must make the usual amendment to take care of fictional existence and 'consideration' contexts—for the use of the term "Martians" in Ray Bradbury's novels and in this sentence is not meaningless even if there are no Martians, and the same applies to "ectoplasm", "interstellar liner", etc.

The term "pistil" was chosen with some care from the dictionary, for there are relatively few definitions therein which begin with the definite article, and presuppositions are more easily pinned on those that do; we may agree that terms such as "continent" and "king" will retain their meaning whether or not the earth's geography and society change radically. Even if it turned out that we have all been deceived about the world in which we live and that it has never had continents or

---

[58] There is an analogy in symbolic logic; Church's concept of lambda-definability, and its proved equivalents involving recursiveness or Turing-computability (or, if we prefer to treat of an individual rather than a class, the Hilbert epsilon- or Hailperin nu-operator).

kings, it would seem we can perfectly well use those concepts to describe the content of our fantasy. But is this really so? Would not the words which we then use actually be fraternal twins of—rather than identical to—the original notions? The antecedent conditions of the usual definitions not being fulfilled, do we not merely seize upon the nearest approximation? We can see part of the answer by reflecting on the term "phlogiston", defined by Webster as "the hypothetical principle of fire, regarded as a material substance". The term "hypothetical" is out of place if this is supposed to be a translation rule, since, when the theory was current, "phlogiston" meant the (actual) principle of fire. Yet, knowing what we do, we could not so define it today. Webster (and the Oxford dictionary) play their encyclopaedic role when they tell us this, not their translating role; but here they do it perforce. The term "phlogiston" could only have been correctly defined at any time by a conditional definition: "If there is a principle of fire with the properties of a substance, then 'phlogiston' = 'the principle of fire, regarded as a substance'." Since the antecedent is now believed to be false, this 'definition' gives us no standard use for the term; and no other meaning rules were ever given or implicit.[59]

With the term "aether" it is easy to see how the discovery that the exact conditions originally (implicitly) involved could not be met laid the way open to producing a successor with different but still similar conditions in the antecedent. In a way I am saying that the distinction between having application and having meaning, which Strawson has rightly emphasized, is made somewhat less satisfactory by what I take to be the commitment to existence involved in many terms to varying degrees—brought out most clearly in the case of some abstract nouns for which a definite description definition is given but inherent in many others. With respect to a noun like "temperature" I have suggested the following points among others.

1. The usual brief definitions which have been given at various stages in the history of heat physics (e.g. "what the International Gas Thermometer measures", "linear function of mean kinetic energy per unit volume", etc.) are conditional translation rules and the conditions in-

[59] The secondary uses such as that involved in comparing the elusiveness of a proposed concept with the concept of phlogiston are contexts in which no commitment to the truth of the conditions is involved, and so they can be treated as if true for the purposes in hand.

clude the truth of various correlation laws and interpretations. The discovery of the falsehood or rather, the excessive inaccuracy of these, did not mean that the meaning of the term changed, only that this conditional definition ceased to be applicable.

2. Such definitions nevertheless had great utility during the currency of the belief in their conditions; one should not suppose that definitions are no use unless they provide unconditional translation rules.

3. These definitions were also, if one wants to be precise, known to be somewhat inaccurate even when generally accepted; thus in a second way, definitions are not unconditional translation rules.

4. The concept of temperature itself did not and does not lend itself to summary in any brief working definition, i.e. nothing better than those definitions given could be given, cf. the names "Kant" and "Iroquois".

5. Something more precise, but either less like a definition or less readily applicable, could be given by means of (a) listing all the relevant laws and employing the 'that which' device, or (b) defining it in terms of other abstract thermodynamic concepts.

6. The alternative (5a) is still imprecise because of the imprecision of the interpretation procedures for the elementary terms in the formalization, and (5b) is a special case of (5a).

Some of the uses of the 'paradigm case' argument in current philosophy have ignored the above distinction between committed and uncommitted words. It will not quite do to argue that the statement "Everything is an illusion" is analytically false on the grounds that the paradigm cases of the use of the word "real" would be included. For one must also show that the fact these paradigm cases concern actual circumstances is *essential*, a much more difficult task, i.e. show that the term "real" is committed.[60]

I wish now to examine the other class of exceptions to the thesis about the general necessity for conditional definition of scientific—and other—terms, the class of cases where we feel we certainly have an unconditional definition. The first group I have in mind are definitions by correlative terms, well illustrated by "endothermic" = "not exothermic", "psychotic" = "non-neurotic non-normal", "good" = "non-

---

[60] A different approach to the same issue is discussed in the essays by Flew and Urmson in *Essays in Conceptual Analysis*, op. cit., and that by Gellner in *The Rationalist Annual, 1957*. London: Watts, 1957.

evil non-neutral", etc. It is unfortunate that logic texts still act as if such definitions are actually or almost illicit; they must constitute a great majority of all the proper definitions in existence, on the textbook criteria for definitions. Their dubiety is sometimes said to be due to their potential circularity. But every definition is potentially circular, and it is surely less likely that the definer will make the mistake of defining correlative terms by means of each other than that he will make this mistake with other terms, since correlative terms are usually introduced together, the one being defined in terms of previous concepts, the other in terms of the one. An extension of such definitions naturally occurs with the introduction of multiple categories, e.g. colors, forms of argument, etc., but these are usually all defined in terms of a common set of properties, variously modified. Then the usual difficulties arise; but when a rule governing such a set is that it is an exhaustive set, one of its members can be defined as the exclusion of the rest. Indeed, the second definition above refers to a tripartite division.

In my view, there is no question but that many such definitions conform to the traditional ideal of unconditional translation rules, since they are specifically designed to do so. They are indeed notational conveniences to avoid repetitions of negations or overly long predicate chains. Indeed we may simultaneously consider all abbreviatory definitions. But one should consider the possibility that "CT Factor" = "score on such and such tests" is not a 'pure' translation rule, but rather a conditional one, because the defining terms include some with commitments, i.e. a referring function.[61] If, for example, "entropy" could be adequately defined in the way it is often introduced, as the quotient of heat and absolute temperature, then it would be as committed a term as temperature. (In fact, it is as far committed although other meaning rules besides this one apply.) A definition in terms of meaningless terms could not give meaning to the defined term.

As against this one could say that an abbreviatory definition is unconditional even though it involves a committed term, by noting that the abbreviation would have no application if the commitments weren't

---

[61] Although I think Strawson is generally correct in what he says about referring, it appears to me that there is a referring element in many terms that he would take as descriptive. The use of the term "committed" is intended to avoid confusion with his "referring" both with respect to the extension of the terms and also with respect to his restriction to real existence in dealing with the presuppositions of referring terms.

fulfilled, and arguing that it is a perfect translation rule regardless. Now we may certainly say that about such a term as "hippogriff" which we might introduce as an abbreviation for "a centaur with a griffin's trunk and torso replacing the human's". It is wholly uncommitted because its application does not depend on the fulfillment of certain conditions. But an abbreviation for a function of temperature not only depends for its *application* on certain conditions, it might be said; it could have no meaning if they are not fulfilled, because they are conditions of *applicability* not merely conditions for actual application. The latter are already given *within* a definition. If there aren't any half-griffins in fact, fiction or forecast,[62] then the term "hippogriff" has no application; but it has meaning, i.e. is *applicable*, because there *might* be. But if there is no quantity which satisfies the temperature equations, the term "entropy"—being defined in terms of an existence-committed definite description—has no *meaning*.[63]

Abbreviatory and correlative definitions do require us to qualify the view that no definitions are precise and prevent us from accepting the view that no statements are analytic; but they do not seriously affect the view that most definitions of scientific terms are conditional. For, if conditional definitions are those which give no meaning to the terms they define unless certain conditions are fulfilled, abbreviatory definitions do not all escape. Whereas if, on the other hand, we were to say that conditional definitions are those which are only correct under certain conditions, they are excluded; but even so these form a small class in science as compared with mathematics.

---

[62] Capitalization here actually does produce an individual name (cf. baedeker, theory of relativity, nylons) and hence changes the truth value!

[63] Notice the difference between the ease with which we avoid confusing "There are no centaurs" with "The term 'centaur' has no meaning", and the difficulty in distinguishing "There is no phlogiston (aether, etc.)" and "The term 'phlogiston' ("aether", etc.) has no meaning". If it turns out there was no Black Hole of Calcutta, then the term is not abandoned but becomes the name of the fictitious entity; I suggest it is misleading to say its meaning does not change. The meaning of "temperature" does not necessarily change when our beliefs and hence its 'definition' changes; that of "The Black Hole of Calcutta" does when our beliefs change. The difference from Strawson will be apparent. The principal reason, put again, is that a particular and important application rule for the latter expression has been abandoned in the case described, whereas in the former case no rule has been abandoned but one has been rendered inapplicable (by the falsification of its conditions for application). The only escape from this argument, as far as I can see, would consist in saying that "Kant", "Iroquois", "Black Hole of Calcutta", etc. have a meaning which is neutral with respect to the existence of their nominatum, which seems to me to overlook the distinction between such terms and the names of mythological individuals, the

The intra-linguistic specification of meaning can employ various modifications and special kinds of 30.1. The conditions C_1 . . . C_n may include logical as well as empirical requirements, and they may be stated in statistical rather than categorical terms. The form "X" = "Y" may be replaced by a probability relation, and one of the components may involve a conditional. Some of these cases will be examined below. It is worth commenting in passing that the celebrated intervening variable, hypothetical construct distinction of Meehl and McCorquodale becomes in the above terms a distinction between concepts definable by unconditional translation rules and those definable by conditional translation rules; for, as will be argued below, the least suggestion that an abbreviatory definition can represent a state of an organism when the defining terms are stimulus and response variables, is a commitment to a further, non-formalizable dimension of meaning and hence an abandonment of the unconditional for a conditional definition, where the conditions are to the effect that inner states are (a) associated with, and (b) altered in a discernible way by the quoted variables. This is the rejection of action-at-a-time-interval condition and is definitely an empirical assumption (which Skinner, for example, explicitly avoids).

31. Statistical Concepts and Vagueness. In order to deal with apparently imprecise concepts it is useful to examine some weaker forms of pure and conditional definition.

The usual diagnostic categories of psychiatry afford excellent examples of what have been called cluster concepts, correlation concepts, or statistical concepts. Were we to try to analyze such a concept as "schizophrenia", for example, we would notice the following points:

1. There is substantial and sometimes almost complete disagreement between psychiatrists over the classification of patients as schizophrenic even when they have the same data about them.

2. There are some extreme differences in observable symptoms be-

former being epistemologically prior to, as well as ontologically different from, the latter. I want to say that physical concepts, properly understood, have an element of this commitment in their meaning (so that if there was *nothing* that satisfied the total set of equations for temperature we should have to say the term had lost its primary meaning, like "phlogiston"), but that this commitment is not expressed in the usual definitions of it and hence an abandonment of one of these is not a sufficient indication of a change of meaning. The cases like "pistil" are more difficult, but must, I think, be included under the same heading as "temperature" not merely because of the definite description form (cf. "the Court of King Arthur") but because of their incompleteness and hence conditionality.

tween even those patients about whose diagnosis a large number of psychiatrists agree, e.g. the catatonic and the hebephrenic, the one silent and appallingly depressed, perhaps comatose, the other vocal and laughing.

3. Fundamentally different hypotheses about the etiology of the condition are maintained by highly qualified psychiatrists—dietary, traumatic, imprinting, deprivational, hereditary, etc.

In the face of this what can we say about the meaning of the term "schizophrenia"? In particular, do we have to accept the view that several different meanings are being given to the term? The operationist strain in us is certainly inclined to do so. But the conclusion is not unavoidable, and the logician's task here is to sort out—as far as this is possible—the conditions, defining criteria, and 'mere symptoms.' In the first place it may be the case that the clinicians all agree that schizophrenia is to be defined as that psychic disorder which manifests itself in a set of alternative conditions whose *relationships* they more or less agree on, e.g. that the simple schizophrenic exhibits less affect than the paranoid and more than the catatonic, that such and such symptoms distinguish the schizophrenic from the manic-depressive, etc. Their disagreement is over the actual properties of any one class. Now this is by no means an unlikely state of affairs, because the crucial component of the definition is the term "psychic disorder". Those of an environmentalist persuasion will have a totally different concept of the nature of psychic disorders (i.e., the etiology and dynamics, not the phenotype) from the hereditarians, and although both may be persuaded to acknowledge the existence of a family of such disorders which they identify by the term "schizophrenias", their theoretical orientation leads them to emphasize different data in locating the individual schizophrenias—the former laying great stress on parental divorce or delinquency, say, the latter on familial incidence.

Now I do not believe that this possibility is actually adequate to the situation, so widespread is the disagreement; but without doubt it is a most important element in it. It is clear that a sceptic could maintain that no such disease entity in fact exists, which he might put by saying there is no such thing as schizophrenia. This formulation is ambiguous, since it would also be appropriate if we had rid the world of an identifiable condition. Nor would it do to say "The term 'schizophrenia' has no application", since that requires that it have a meaning. The sceptic is suggesting, more radically, that although the term has 'a use' (too many uses, in fact), the presuppositions of its meaningfulness do not obtain; hence, that it cannot have the meaning it is supposed to have. He would be denying, e.g. that a discriminable affectual psychosis with the subdivisions mentioned, exists. And this brings home to us the conditional nature of the original definition. The term has no meaning unless there is such a disease entity; it is a committed term. It would not merely be the case that there isn't now any schizophrenia; it would be the case that we have to discard the idea that we had given a real meaning to "schizophrenia". We see here in outline the ontogenesis of a theory-*directed* word, the early harbinger of a theory and the ancestor of a theory-*impregnated* word.

It may be appropriate here to meet the possible objection that the only cases where 'conditions for a definition' can be justified are those where they express the conditions for the *logical* possibility of satisfaction of the definite descriptions, relations, or equations. But whereas, e.g., the value of the determinant of a set of simultaneous equations certainly figures in a condition for their possession of a unique solution and hence in a condition for the meaningfulness of some definite description which refers to it, and hence in a condition for the soundness of any definition which involves this definite description, other cases are equally important. Amongst them is the usual interpretation where, whatever, e.g., "schizophrenia" means, at least it is a name of some psychoses that have been observed (meaning rule). Hence, the mere possibility that in a different world there could be something which satisfies the other meaning rules is not enough to show that "schizophrenia", *as understood now*, is meaningful. By an extension of the category of meaning rules, one could consider this as a case of logical possibility, of course; but this is to destroy the distinction between logical possibility and actuality. The extreme counterexamples are those where the conditions are entirely empirical, e.g., the existence of a law correlating A and B which makes the definition of A as B *in certain contexts* a useful one. (It is a serious error to suppose that for a given A, any highly correlated B could be so used in some context.)

Supposing that we are in *doubt* whether there is such a disease or not, then we 'play along,' looking for further evidence that will enable us to put meat on the definition outline we have, itself a limb of a skeletal theory. In part, the present situation is that different groups have plumped for different varieties of meat. The rules of successful concept formation are as hard to specify as the rules for good betting in poker, where the relevant individual variables of the other players are so important and so hard to assess that the truisms (mathematical or otherwise) that we can produce in which their values must be substituted are of little use by comparison with the skilled and unemotional judgment by which these values are ascertained, even if then substituted into a less exact formula. (Nevertheless, much can be done in both cases by supervised practice and familiarity with those rules that can be given.) As subsequent material comes in we adjust our conditions, or our definitions, or our symptom list, trying to produce a concept which maximizes predictive success, explanatory utility, theoretical fertility, etc.; and here again statistical analysis is essential (the 'most reliable indicator' procedures).

The process is well illustrated in the case of general paresis, originally isolated on the basis of observable symptoms and finally discovered to be a postsyphilitic condition for which the pathognomic (decisive) indicator is "spirochetes in the brain", available certainly at the post mortem. It looks as if we must say the definition of the term changed because we previously did not include this indicator at all. But this would be so only if we identify the disease entity with the cluster of accepted indicators. This is illicit because the term is a theoretical one, albeit in a fairly vague and low-level theory; and doing it forces us to deny that we discovered paresis to have the pathognomic sign "spirochetes in the brain". It is even perfectly satisfactory to say that we discovered paresis is cerebral syphilis, meaning that it can be correctly defined as such. But the definition is conditional.

Certainly we do have to accept the idea that the term cannot be defined except very vaguely and with many conditions, and it is to avoid this that one's operational tendencies try to persuade one to make it a logical construction out of the symptoms.

On the other hand, we can apparently in extreme cases infer from the weighting one clinician accords to the various indicators that he is using the term in a totally different way from another. Does not this show the indicators form part of the meaning of the term? Not necessarily, for our understanding of the general laws in the field may well be adequate for us to see that it is empirically impossible for him to have the 'same concept in mind.' To illustrate by the converse case, the man who rates delusional material very high and familial incidence very low may be using the term "schizophrenia" with essentially the same meaning as one who reverses these. The 'pay off,' the decision as to who was right (in using their weighting) is not like the pay off for the man who is trying to predict race-winning behavior by horses from their bloodline as opposed to their horoscope; we all know what shows him to be right, or wrong, or wasting his time. In the present case, the pay off is in terms of finally isolating a useful construct, perhaps one that ties in with a particular neurological condition. And one can't sharply draw the line between a useful and a useless concept, nor between striking riches of the kind one sets out to find and discovering something else rather than what is, in the original vague sense, schizophrenia.

It should be clear to what an extent these concepts are connected with the theory, however feeble that may be; and I use the term to include even epistemological bets such as "no action at a distance is possible," or "past circumstances can only affect present behavior if they produced persisting tissue changes." But we introduce the student to these terms by mentioning only a certain set of indicators and their rough weights. He has to 'catch on' to the total game himself; and usually he could be helped considerably by examination of comparable cases such as the wandering fortunes of the useful concepts of "acid" in chemistry, and "gene" and "species" in biology. The legitimacy of the usual textbook account derives from the fact that if the condition does manifest itself in these ways, we may add this stipulation to the antecedents in a conditional definition where we replace the theoretical "Y" by the set of indicators, appropriately weighted.

During the above discussion I have introduced references to 'weighted indicators' and I should repeat that I do not use the term in either of the ways Kaplan—to whom it is due—proposes, and that it variously includes elements of the case history, visible symptoms, the results of laboratory tests, and the effects of various kinds of treatment, whether or not these form part of the meaning, so long as they can be grounds for an inference to the condition. Since all of these will not always be available, the clinician must frequently make a diagnosis from a subset; and this he does with some probability. Now what is it the probability of? The most natural reply (since we wish to say that he is sometimes right!) is that he is attempting to predict the compresence or eventual presence of the rest of the 'indicator cluster.' This fails (a) because it brings us back to the idea that the cluster *is* the condition, which makes it impossible to argue that the condition is *responsible* for the symptoms, and (b) because on some occasions we have, not only lack of information with respect to a key indicator, but information that it is definitely absent; and we nevertheless can and do make correct diagnoses.[64] The point is readily seen from the fact that "being brought up in an orphanage" and "being constantly rejected by his mother" can both be heavily weighted indicators for a certain diagnosis, though they *could not* both be true.

Consequently, the 'probability' of the diagnosis is the probability that the disease entity (*whatever it turns out to be*) is present, i.e., it is the probability of a probability. It is not, e.g., the probability that the verbal response "schizophrenia" will be emitted by a group of clinicians (which depends further on their abilities). Consequently, no numerical assignment (except in the very vaguest terms) is possible and no instance-counting probability assessment based on sets of similar cases is even remotely likely. It should not, incidentally, be thought that psychiatry is much worse off than internal medicine or neurology as far as the *unreliability* of its diagnoses [65] is concerned, nor is it wholly unlike them with respect to the *decidability* of its diagnoses. Deciding whether a certain diagnosis was right is often as complex as deciding whether a certain definition is correct or a certain translation the best, or a certain rule properly formulated, procedures which I have suggested are not remotely like the procedure of verification of a statement in the plain observation language to which it was once thought the more abstract statements of science should be 'reducible.'

32. *Dispositional Concepts, Theory Language, and Observation Language.* When someone believes himself to have identified a *new* disease entity, it is extremely likely that the rules governing his use of the new term, whether explicitly formulated or not, will involve some reference to visible symptoms. This may only be incidental, as in some cases we have already considered; and it is just possible for it to be entirely absent from the formulation, as when a theoretical account of it is im-

---

[64] That is to say, indicators are not severally necessary, though they are jointly sufficient conditions for the disease. Indeed many subsets, some non-overlapping, are typically sufficient sets for positive diagnosis.

[65] See, e.g., T. A. Peppard, "Mistakes in Diagnosis," *Minnesota Medicine*, 1949, Vol. 32, pp. 510f. For this reference and for most of the illustrative material in these sections, I am greatly indebted to Paul Meehl.

mediately seen and adopted. John N. Rosen apparently defines "schizophrenic" as something like "psychotic currently expecting withholding of love—historically produced by operation on him of perverse maternal instinct in preverbal period". The 'inner-state' reference in this definition is impervious to almost any verbal reports from the patient, i.e., the expectation referred to may be detectable only by the analyst; but the definition is clearly a committed one, at least in form. Allied with this definition are a set of empirically related indicators on the basis of which the apparent absence of one of the defining properties can often be ignored. This does not show the indicators to be part of the definition; cf. hereditary color blindness—perfectly predictable on the basis of knowledge about the parent's color blindness, to the extent that apparent success on the tests by the progeny can be ignored unless very highly repeatable.

But there can be terms with a similar analysis where the theoretical element is greatly reduced—although not altogether eliminated, as has been suggested. Suppose we observe a condition analogous to the hereditary phenyl-thio-carbamide sensitivity, the element in this case being a certain preservative agent used in frozen juices and the response being sharp distaste on the part of those who can detect it all and nothing on the part of everyone else. We might call the sensitive people "propiacs". What would be the correct definition of this term? It certainly appears as if we could give an unconditional definition of it.

"x is a propiac" = "x can taste traces of thorium propionate in frozen juice" (32.1)

We notice that there is a difference in the verbs on the two sides of the definition. We here say x is something if he can do something; cf. x is strong if he can lift heavy weights, etc., is intelligent if . . ., is elastic if . . ., is magnetized if . . ., and so on. We are not merely abbreviating, but changing the mode of speech; and we can do this legitimately only for certain reasons. The reasons are that the individual to whom we ascribe the property exhibits considerable constancy of reaction to the substance, or to the necessity for lifting heavy weights, or solving problems, etc. If he did not, we would not locate his success in himself but in some fortuitous or at least independent circumstances. We take care that the taste tests are conducted on individuals separated from each other, to eliminate the use of visual cues; or we randomize the samples; or we give lie-detector tests; or we decrease any incentives for success, etc. The procedures for obtaining the kind of evidence we need are well known, varied, and often complicated. And we would never introduce the term at all, let alone apply it to a particular individual, unless we had grounds for thinking that it is a capacity resident in the individual. (Of course, we might introduce a term meaning "x sometimes responds as if he can taste. . . .") However, having made the step from noticing by careful examination that some people on some occasions taste the stuff to the conclusion that it is the same people on each occasion who do this, and that their success is due to their actually tasting it, we have justified the introduction of a property term. And we have justified, simultaneously, its power to explain—not summarize—the observed behavior. Suppose that someone is not altogether clear how to go about deciding whether someone can really taste this substance. Would it do to say "Give him some to drink and then ask him"? For the many reasons just given, this would not be enough; we have to say a good deal (or assume it) about the conditions of the experiment. So it certainly will not do to say that 32.1 is equivalent to

"x is a propiac" = "If x drinks . . . he will then say . . ." (32.2)

"Propiac" is an ability word, and in a different category of discourse from overt behavior descriptions such as occur in 32.2. All our previous discussions about reducibility, about the differences between rule language and behavior language, validity language and truth language, macro-language and micro-language, etc. come to bear at this point. Equally well, however, it is true that from an ability assertion, properly understood, we may infer that under certain conditions certain results are very likely. And we may also infer from the failure of repeated 'proper' tests that the ability is not present.

Now it may appear that the real difficulty over this case arises only because an inner state is involved in 32.1; perhaps this kind of ability is unusual in not being reducible to simple observational language. If we say that a substance is elastic we are saying it is such that it recovers almost completely from a certain range of deformations. And the deformation and recovery are perfectly observable. But the mere sequence of these conditions does not constitute proof that the substance is elastic; the recovery may have been due, not to the innate elasticity, but to some local expansion due to ultrasonic heating. The property of elasticity, therefore, is not equivalent to any set of truth-functional statements about observable reactions. Here, again, we rapidly learn the procedures of testing, and the relevant alternatives, and hence learn how to move from one type of language to the other—a move which appears to me best described as a move from the observation language to the theoretical language. I use the term "theoretical" here because (a) there is a distinction in this context between what is 'simply observable' and such properties as we are considering; (b) the one is not explicitly definable in terms of the other (cf. "area" which is explicitly definable in terms of observables and is also observable); (c) a 'new conceptual framework' is involved (Conant's criterion for a theory); and (d) certain explanatory and colligatory procedures become possible; and all of these are important (though not individually necessary nor wholly independent) criteria for theories.[66]

If we are prepared to say that terms definable in terms of the observation language plus the causal modality are observational, then the chief obstacle is removed which prevents us from including the present class. But surely to do this is to mistake the essential point of the causal modality; it is an expression of a language shift and the consequent theoretical commitment. When we introduce terms such as "propiac" we are in a way summing up observations; but not in the way in which the generalization "All Xs are Ys" sums up all statements of the form "X_1 is Y." For one cannot deduce the occurrence of the observable consequent from the occurrence of the observable antecedent together with the statement that the subject has the property under consideration; whereas one can deduce "This is a Y" from "All Xs are Ys" and "This is an X."[67]

Developing the very simple example with which we began this section can lead us in several directions. First we should consider whether a conditional translation rule could not be devised to relate the theoretical properties we are considering to the observation language. In a rather sloppy sense, this is so, i.e., if we are prepared to include certain restrictions on the scope of the rule, and certain rather vague references

[66] Skinner's definition of "theory" on which he predicates his attack on them, is a special case of (d); hence it is not surprising that he can engage in a good deal of theoretical activity in the wider and more usual sense given here.

[67] Attempts to make the deduction work in both cases will inevitably involve the introduction of such descriptions as "the proper test conditions," which are surreptitious guarantees of the deductions and hence circular.

to 'proper' test circumstances. It was in this sense, we noted, that one can give a 'definition' of "schizophrenia" in terms of indicator sets. And this sloppiness is common to, though not universal to, conditional definitions; the fact is that language shifts of this kind are not susceptible to precise definition, conditional or otherwise.

Second, we should notice that there is nothing in the least trivial about the explanation of the test-plus-result (T,R) pair by appeal to the theoretical property. For example, one may be able to explain the behavior of a ball of some unknown material which is compressed and then expands by appeal to the fact that it is elastic. This would be an explanation because it selects the actual cause from among the large set of possible causes (such as the ball being ductile, but hollow and made to expand by heating). If being elastic meant no more than recovering after deforming, then we would not be giving an explanation at all. One can't explain the event conjunction $Tx_1 \cdot Rx_1$ by saying "Tx_1 is always followed by Rx_1"; this is clearly a complete trivialization of the idea of explanation, since it is both false and unilluminating. The explanation lies in the fact that x_1 is of such a kind that it will do this under certain more-or-less exactly specifiable conditions. The explanation arises because we pick out x_1's composition as against special circumstantial features of various possible kinds. This kind of explanation is quite different from those in which the whole trick lies in showing how from certain premises we can get the conclusions we are interested in as, e.g., in explaining the laws of refraction in terms of the wave theory of light. Here the trick consists in showing which of certain alternative possible explanations, each of them obviously adequate if applicable, is the appropriate one. I have elsewhere called this a selection explanation,[68] or a discrimination explanation,[69] as opposed to a derivation explanation.

I said that if we admitted causal implication into the observation language, we would have removed—illegitimately—the main obstacle to regarding dispositions as part of the observation language. The other obstacle is the pervasive and irritating 'proper test conditions' clause. This, too, marks the transition into a new level of language and insulates it from the observation language, thereby making it immensely

[68] In "Explanations," unpublished D. Phil. Thesis, Oxford, 1956, e.g., p. 378 and p. 451.
[69] In Vol. I of *Minnesota Studies in the Philosophy of Science*, "A Study of Radical Behaviorism," p. 121.

more useful. This is the case because it saves a regularity at the expense of a mystery, and most such mysteries are eventually dispelled, at least from this level of language. That is, we are prepared to insist that a substance such as salt is water-soluble, even if under apparently standard conditions it fails to dissolve in water; and we can do this only because 'soluble' is a theoretical property which is related to the test-plus-result pairs *via* an escape clause which covers such possibilities as invisible layers of grease on the salt crystals. Having the causal modality involved provides us with safeguards in other situations too, as for example when the substance does dissolve owing, not to its solubility, but to the presence of some ultra-high frequency standing waves which disperse it as it enters the solvent. Even if we lacked the escape clause, we would be able to avoid the conclusion that this substance was soluble by showing that dissolution was not *caused* by the mere immersion into the solvent, as is required by the definition, but by this other agency. But since there are cases where we wish to say the substance is soluble even when it does not in fact dissolve, and hence a fortiori its dissolving was not caused by immersion, we do need the extra insulation of the 'proper test conditions' clause.[70]

The third side of the theoretician's triangle is the probability concept; it is a buffer between states and manifestations, between causal claims and observation claims. To say that X causes Y is to say that under proper conditions, an X will be followed by a Y; and we can usually put enough into the 'proper conditions' clause to produce the proposition that under such and such *specifiable* conditions an X will *probably* be followed by a Y. Actual physical laws, like actual definitions in physics, rarely provide a basis for more than this; for it is almost impossible to think of anything referred to as a law in physics that is literally true when taken to refer to observables. They only provide a good basis for *probable* inferences; we count as laws general statements

---

[70] It will now be clear why I would disagree even with Carnap's revised position about dispositions: he says, "In my view, they occupy an intermediate position between the observational terms of L₀ and the theoretical terms; they are more closely related to the former than to the latter." P. 63, Vol. I, *Minnesota Studies in the Philosophy of Science*, "The Methodological Character of Theoretical Concepts." But it must be noted that his idea of how one could define such terms is much simpler than mine. Since, however, he gives elasticity as an example, I would have to argue that his analysis is too simple, rather than that he is using the term "disposition" to refer to something other than the kind of property I discuss in this section. I have myself avoided the term in the body of this paper because it is heavily involved in disputes which I have tried to circumvent as far as possible.

185

of certain kinds which provide the simplest working approximation. Newton's Laws (all five of them) are not charitably so called today but properly. Thus the requirement of simplicity and the acceptance of approximations enters already at the level of the formulation of laws and definitions as well as—a common observation—when formulating theories. This is one of the basic points of the present paper.

Now the situation in which we found it useful to introduce the term "propiac" was an extremely simple one. It involved only the one response, one test substance, and no hypotheses about the biochemistry. I wish next to consider the complications that ensue when, on the one hand, we introduce or study properties which are dependent on more than one indicator and are hence more like our earlier examples of psychiatric conditions and, on the other, when we wish to connect one of these theoretical properties, whether simple or complex, to other levels of theory or description. But first something more must be said about the distinctions between observation language, theory language, and disposition language—the third being, in my view, a part of the second.

Suppose it were suggested that a property term which one would normally consign to the observation language, such as "red", is really dispositional, on the grounds that it can be analyzed in terms of what a normal observer would see under standard conditions. 'To be red is to have a disposition to produce red sense data in normal observers.'

Here I think we can clearly see that an attempt is being made to abolish one level of language in favor of another by suggesting that a real translation is possible between them. Apart from the infinite regress possibilities which are opened up (since the same analysis can be applied to the terms of the antecedent and the consequent, pace the phenomenalists), the crucial difficulty arises with the 'standard conditions and normal observer' requirement. The exact procedure of deciding whether these are present is the procedure of deciding that the object is really red. It is therefore illicit to suggest that some independent procedure can be established for identifying these, which could then be regarded as prior to, or logically more fundamental than the identification of red.

Nevertheless, although these reasons suggest that "red" can perfectly well be taken as part of the observation vocabulary, there are many circumstances in which it is appropriate to get back to appearances, i.e. to the subjective vocabulary rather than the objective vocabulary which includes the color terms. The mistake is to suppose that such a procedure could be universally applied to render the objective vocabulary abbreviatory, 'technically useful but logically superfluous.' I think it doubtful whether a subjective language of the kind required could be constructed at all; but whether it can or not, I see no real way in which the required reduction could be performed. This is an issue where the promissory note involved in 'standard conditions, etc.' has to be cashed before the view that depends on it can be regarded as any sort of a competitor in the market.

Certainly the very term "observation language" is context dependent. The observation language of observational astronomy is different from that of the psychology of vision or that of cosmology by one level in each direction. But there is an obvious series of contexts in which "red" is part of the observation language. The same points can be made in turn about each level that is taken as the observation language with respect to the next level of the language: that is, almost every term at one level can be expanded in terms of standard conditions, causal and logical modalities, and terms of the next level down. In fact, the procedure for identifying levels in part involves an investigation of this possibility.

Hence, there are no properties which can be regarded as 'pure dispositions' or 'essentially dispositional,' etc. (as opposed to 'pure observable'). Only in a certain context or by reference to their historical introduction could such a claim be given support. Certainly "elastic", "magnetized", and the rest, were introduced via some reference to test conditions and test results, and certainly for ordinary purposes of macrostudy in a simple laboratory they are correctly defined in such terms. But in other contexts they must simply be regarded as observable properties, e.g. when connected very firmly with a certain micro-structure which can be identified by one glance at a meter. It may be this which leads Carnap to assign them an intermediate place. But I think not, to judge from what he takes to be terms of the observation language; certainly they are theoretical with respect to "bending", "thermometer reading, t", etc.

33. *The Micro-Equivalents of Macro-Properties.* It is here appropriate to recall, though not to repeat, a great deal that was said earlier about the relation between properties at different levels of language. For many reasons, among them the necessity to distinguish (some) discoveries from (some) definitions, it is an error to suppose that an analysis of the

meaning of a term such as "elastic" or "propiac" necessarily involves a reference to the micro-structure. Naturally, an analysis of the phenomena of elasticity will lead the solid-state physicist to a micro-equivalent; that is what his job involves. And, for him, the appropriate definition of "elastic" might be in terms of a certain micro-structure. This would be a conditional definition, obviously with context conditions. But the straightforward logical analysis designed to meet the functional requirement for definitions would only provide a one-level reduction, dependent on previously obtained understanding of the procedure of inferring states from behavior. If it was supposed to result in a definition which meets the formal condition, the problems of standard conditions and causal language must be shelved by introducing these undefined terms among the defining terms. No more can be done.[71] I hope that this approach makes a little less puzzling the fact that what may be a dispositional concept at one level may be non-dispositional at another. The answer consists in seeing that (a) something different is involved in each case, not the same thing; and (b) a dispositional analysis is a property not of a given predicate but of a given predicate with respect to a given reduction base; and (c) the observation language vs. theory language distinction will not necessarily place a concept in the same category as its various reduction equivalents at each level, since the range of observation and hence of theory varies at each level.

It is not hard to express the requirement for identifying a micro-equivalent of the dispositional property D: it is a property D' such that together with the micro-equivalent T' of the 'defining' test conditions T it causally produces [72] the micro-condition R' which has the macro-equivalent R. The T-T', R-R' distinctions are just as important as the D-D' distinction and must be available before D' can be defined or discovered. If one ignores them, one soon gets into trouble in trying to explain what laws support the causal assertions, since these laws will usually relate theoretical concepts, not observational concepts.

34. Complicated Conditional Concepts; Psychological Dispositions. The other development of my remarks towards the end of section 31 relates to more complicated 'conditional properties.' It has been cus-

---

[71] For an opposing view see Pap's essay in this volume.

[72] To say C causes E is, as far as I can see, to say that C' plus the laws of the micro-domain plus SC' (where SC are the standing conditions, i.e. the environmental description which is not mentioned in C) entail E'. (Causal talk *essentially* involves the C-SC distinction.)

tomary to distinguish among these, second-order dispositions, capacities, powers, etc. I do not feel that any new points are involved in this that are of interest for our present purposes. It is worth noticing that such distinctions, although they could, of course, be made for an abstract artificial language are scarcely possible in any applied language since the cross connections of the terms at different levels make a single label misleading, even if the context is specified. The idea and its limitations are well exemplified in the following cases. To say a substance is magnetic is to say it is such that a certain range of test conditions will produce the test result of being magnetized, which is in turn to say that a certain range of test conditions will produce such results as the rearrangement of iron filings. So the property of being magnetic is a second-order disposition with respect to the observation language of iron-filing patterns, the motion of compass needles, etc.

The close connection with the micro-indicators for magnetic substances makes it possible to argue that the term is best regarded as a micro-observational term. Our answer would be that to do so is to adopt a new definition for the term, one that would be useful for the physicist but would have the drawback for everyday use that its direct—although two-stage—connection to everyday observations would be weakened into an empirical connection. It is better to suppose that the term has a different meaning for the physicist who adopts this suggestion. The hazards of physical theories provide small danger of shipwreck for ordinary language, which therefore has an advantage as a basis for rebuilding scientific theories. But it, too, undergoes slow modification as physical theory advances into the realm of observation and multiple confirmation.

"Magnetic" thus appears to be a good example of a second-order disposition. But is it not perfectly possible to argue that one can observe whether something is magnetized and that "magnetic" is therefore only first order? Think of a moving magnet and the current it induces in a closed circuit which can be read directly off an ammeter; looking at this situation, when suitable experimental precautions have been taken is surely 'observing that the bar is magnetized.' But, it may be replied, isn't this at least more an inference than observing those events in terms of which we define magnetized, e.g. the ammeter's reading? Yet sometimes, with a highly standardized design, one can be just as sure that the ammeter's displacement means the bar is a magnet as one can be of another indicator, e.g., that the motion of the compass needles is of the appropriate kind is not due to the table being moved, etc. So the distinctions are not only context dependent but far from immutable.

"Magnetized" clearly involves multiple indicators, and hence represents one degree of generality more than "propiac" as defined by us. By the time we come to "narcissitic" and "schizophrenic" and "meson" we have lost most of the point of talking of them as dispositions of a given order. We would not say this of a thing-word such as "meson" anyway; but its logical relation to its components is not essentially different from that of a predicate term.[73] The main difficulty is that some of the indicators are clearly observable, others are themselves inferred, so the terms themselves fall into no one category. It is the possibility of selecting or creating such complex concepts—with respect to a given base—that makes the procedure of theorizing a creative activity, not reducible to rules. Further complications are provided by the existential elements in such terms as "breakable", "valuable", and "psychic", where it is being said that there is, for example, some way in which the object can be broken. The so-called mongrel categoricals such as "migrating" are best analyzed as involving certain dispositions plus certain current behavior; and Hampshire has suggested that the usual psychological dispositions such as "generous", "irritable", "unreliable" should be placed in this category. This is certainly too strong a position to take about all psychological dispositions; Meehl has suggested that a clearly hereditary late-maturing disposition is a good counter-example, where familial incidence plus, e.g., certain types of dream material at age 30 when happily married, make the likelihood of, e.g., regression under certain conditions almost certain, although never previously instanced.

Further complications are involved in the celebrated examples such as "dishonesty", whose various facets such as lying, cheating, and stealing may well not be significantly correlated, with the consequence that knowing someone is dishonest does not enable one to make inferences about their responses to, e.g., a lying opportunity. This leads the theoretician in the field of psychology to the suggestion that scientifically

[73] In general, the role of 'unobservable entities' in theories follows what has been said about 'unobservable (in one context) states.' The difficulties of making electrons measure up to the usual ontological criteria is closely analogous to the corresponding difficulties over the transfinite cardinals. One learns to handle them according to their own rules; and this is not easy nor without danger.

fruitful concepts are those for which the manifest signs are highly correlated. But if one selects traits which have highly correlated behavior manifestations, the suspicion arises that mere verbal proliferation of names for a single type of behavior has produced the apparently multiple correlations. It is not too hard, in specific cases, to solve such difficulties; but one does so only by making distinctions between meaning connections and empirical connections—not sharp distinctions and in many cases no distinctions, but sometimes clear distinctions. The main incidental moral of the dilemma is that predictive efficiency is not the only criterion for the theoretical utility of concepts.

Examination of other cases shows that the kind of evidence which supports ('amounts to') a judgment of, e.g. "generosity" is not susceptible to easy analysis. Meehl, in Minnesota Center for Philosophy of Science communications, has illustrated this well by bringing out that very large numbers of instances of giving money to the church, and to the cancer research institutes, do not alone constitute good grounds for saying someone is generous, if by this we mean likely to give money to heart research, beggars, etc. It is perfectly possible that this person's character structure is such as to make our evidential basis quite irrelevant, e.g. if they are (a) pious, (b) scared of getting cancer, and (c) as mean as Scrooge with respect to all appeals not connected with (a) or (b). The consideration of our reaction to this possibility, I think, makes clear the highly inferential nature of the step from observations to character classifications and, hence, the error involved in the suggestion that some kind of explicit definition could be given. Nor is this a mere shortcoming of a natural language; to show that it is, one must show that the generality of "generous" is a greater disadvantage than advantage for theoretical purposes. To put the difficulty another way: What exactly are the desiderata in a theoretical vocabulary for a behavioral science? One must begin one's answer by attempting to list the aims of such a science, or the characterological part of it, and weighting their importance. But after that, if that is possible, we run out of rules: between the methodological perspectives of Freud and Skinner there is about as wide a range as imagination could allow, and their relative success is far from obviously different.

35. *The Theoretician's Dilemma.* It is important to base any general conclusions upon a detailed study of the extreme attempts, and I will preface mine by mentioning that I attempted to do this for Skinner in

Michael Scriven

Volume I of *Minnesota Studies in the Philosophy of Science*.[74] What seems to me clear is that even the least theoretical approach is absolutely committed to the use of concepts which are quite definitely not abbreviations for observation-language complexes, i.e. no translation rules are available. My response to the 'theoretician's dilemma' [75] is therefore more obdurate than Hempel's. I would say that the very presentation of the data in a form suitable for predictions of any generality usually involves theoretical terms, that attempts at explanation, especially of laws relating observables, even more clearly require them, and that no possible line can be drawn between theory and observation which has significance except in a particular context of research (often space bound as well as time bound); so the use of theoretical terms can immediately be justified by reference to a different branch of or approach to the subject in which they are observational or potentially so. The neutrino affords one example among many; it was at least useful in summarizing results, its particle status (this being its main theoretical element) also offering a chance to tie its behavior in with that of other particles and hence offering great explanatory potential; and it was an hypothesis about the existence of something that might well be and finally was *observed* in the relevant sense. That a neutrino could be observed, although the concept was not precisely definable in terms of the previous observation language, is explained by the impossibility of so defining the term "particle" (cf. "event"); and it illustrates the limitations of an 'observation-language only' approach. (It is perhaps worth adding that the usual argument for 'intervening variables' theories—that they provide a reduction in the number of required relationships—is invalid. If it were not, theory *languages* would be much harder to justify.)

36. *Explanations.* The preceding discussion brings out some interesting points for the analysis of explanation. In particular it repeatedly exemplifies the essentially non-deductive character of typical scientific explanations. If we wish to explain the observed phenomenon P, we can only do this by reference to scientific laws and concepts, if there is some way of establishing a connection between the scientific concepts and the observation terms involved in the description Dp of P. I have argued that in general no translation of the one into the other is

[74] "A Study of Radical Behaviorism," pp. 88–130.
[75] See Hempel's paper in the present volume.

possible and that the ideal of a deduction of Dp from the usual singular statements and law statements is therefore unsound. The deductive model of explanation is set out with singular clarity in a paper by Hempel and Oppenheim,[76] and I have elsewhere illustrated my present contention by arguing that no single one of their four preliminary examples of scientific explanation can in fact be made to accord with the requirements of the deductive model.[77] The trouble always lies in substantiating the idea that by tightening up the description a little, an exact deduction could be achieved. This is never possible because at the one end, the so-called bridge laws (or correspondence rules), i.e. the relations of vocabularies of different levels, are not exact, and at the other the scientific laws are not exact. It is virtually impossible, as previously remarked, to find a single example of something that is normally called a law in science which can be precisely formulated in non-probability terms. Where such an example can be thought of, there will inevitably be other laws required in the explanation of which this will not be true—for the first one will involve highly theoretical terms, needing subsidiary laws for relation to the lower level vocabularies. Mere subsumption under a generalization, the apparent alternative to all these difficulties, is a profoundly atypical kind of explanation ("Why does light obey Snell's Law?" "Because all electromagnetic wave phenomena do.") and also remains inapplicable to the explanation of events or observation-language laws. As a result of these and other considerations, I think it certain that all scientific explanations, with quite negligible exceptions, are 'statistical' or better, probabilistic; and the authors of the deductive model explicitly exclude consideration of such.

A discussion of these explanations discloses the comparative unimportance of the differences between the logical structure of explanation in the physical and in the behavioral sciences. In each case, the creation of colligatory, test-insulated concepts is the crucial step, and these may have explanatory utility either through comparatively precise but limited laws or through less precise but more general correlations; this is the essential remnant of the usually accepted differences, viewed through the glass of explanatory structure. It is important to see the difference

[76] "The Logic of Scientific Explanation," reprinted in Feigl and Brodbeck (eds.), *Readings in the Philosophy of Science*, pp. 319–352. New York: Appleton-Century-Crofts, 1953.
[77] In "Explanations," *loc. cit.*

between the 'sufficient-condition' and the 'proximate-condition' analyses of cause, to which I drew attention in an earlier footnote, because the usual explanations of psychology and history cannot, while those of physics can, be redescribed in terms of the sufficient-condition analysis. Were this the only correct analysis of causal statements, a serious limitation would still remain on explanations in these fields; but in fact no such limitation can be sustained.

This point was implicit in our discussion earlier of the causal modality as a theory-founding device; when one asserts that X causes Y one is certainly committed to the generalization that an identical cause would produce an identical effect, but this in no way commits one to any necessity for producing laws not involving the term "identical", which justify this claim. Producing laws is one way, not necessarily more conclusive, and usually less easy than other ways of supporting the causal statement. In history and psychology there are very well established ways of directly supporting such statements which do not involve stating laws such as those in physics.[78] (The idea of individual causation has, I think, this not inconsiderable basis.) But it is the phrases "identical cause" and "identical effect" which tell us we have shifted linguistic gear; for these are the promissory notes which, could they be filled in, would eliminate the theory language, and which cannot be filled in.[79]

The approach to explanation here endorsed naturally places considerable emphasis upon an adequate treatment of the concept of probability which itself poses a nice question of definition. It is my view, which I hope to develop more fully on another occasion, that the fundamental concept of probability is, like that of cause, an essentially promissory, theory-founding idea. Put very roughly, as above, a consequence of this view is that statistical probability is a special case of the probability of a hypothesis;[80] put more precisely, the former is also a special

[78] A development of this point renders logically untenable any claim that explanations and predictions have a similar logical structure. (There are many other such points; see the thesis mentioned above and Scheffler "Explanation, Prediction and Abstraction," British Journal for the Philosophy of Science, 7:293–309 (February, 1957).)

[79] It would be of considerable interest to expand these remarks in connection with mathematics where they might seem at first not to apply; Wittgenstein's Remarks on the Foundations of Mathematics (Oxford: Blackwell, 1956) contains many comments on this theme which support the possibility of making such an extension.

[80] The specialization is in the constancy of a set of conditions which enables an instance-counting procedure to produce a numerical and reliable estimate of probability.

case—of the probability of a statement on one language level, given statements on another. The complexity of the procedure of identifying the bearer of an individual name in problem cases (transposed brains, etc.) is a good example of the way in which the analysis of verification and definition is tied up with the basic probability concept.

I hope that enough has been said—and I fear too much has been said—to suggest that a re-examination of some very elementary logical notions is remarkably far-reaching in its consequences for the problems of mature philosophy.

Disposition Concepts and Extensional Logic

One of the striking differences between natural languages, both conversational and scientific, and the extensional languages constructed by logicians is that most conditional statements, i.e., statements of the form "if p, then q", of a natural language are not truth-functional. A statement compounded out of simpler statements is truth-functional if its truth-value is uniquely determined by the truth-values of the component statements. The symbolic expression of this idea of truth-functionality, as given in *Principia Mathematica*, is $p \equiv q \supset (f(p) \equiv f(q))$. That is, if "$f(p)$" is any truth-function of "p", and "q" has the same truth-value as "p", however widely it may differ in meaning, then "$f(q)$" has the same truth-value as "$f(p)$". Clearly, if I am given just the truth-values of "p" and "q", not their meanings, I cannot deduce the truth-value of "if p, then q"—with a single exception: if "p" is given as true and "q" as false, it follows that "if p, then q" is false, provided it has a truth-value at all. On the contrary, the knowledge that matters for determination of the truth-value of a "natural" conditional—let us call them henceforth "natural implications", in contrast to those truth-functional statements which logicians call "material conditionals" or "material implications"—is rather knowledge of the *meanings* of the component statements. In the case of simple analytic implications like "if A has a niece, then A is not an only child" such knowledge of meanings is even sufficient for knowledge of the truth of the implication; at any rate knowledge of the truth-value of antecedent and consequent is irrelevant. In the case of those synthetic natural implications which assert causal connections, knowledge of meanings is not, indeed, sufficient, but it is necessary, and knowledge of the truth-values of the component statements is not presupposed by knowledge of the truth-value of the implication.[1] Consider the conditional (which may or may

196

not be "contrary-to-fact"): if I pull the trigger, the gun will fire. It would be sad if belief in such an implication were warranted only by knowledge of the truth of antecedent and consequent separately, for in that case it would be impossible for man to acquire the power of even limited control over the course of events by acquiring warranted beliefs about causal connections. Notice further that frequently presumed knowledge of a causal implication is a means to knowledge of the truth, or at least probability, of the antecedent; if this is an acid then it will turn blue litmus paper red; the reaction occurred; thus the hypothesis is confirmed. Knowledge of the *consequences* of suppositions is independent of knowledge of the truth-values of the suppositions, no matter whether the consequences be logical or causal.

The difference between material implication and natural implication has been widely discussed. The logician's use of "if p, then q" in the truth-functional sense of "not both p and not-q", symbolized by "$p \supset q$", is fully justified by the objective of constructing an adequate theory of deductive inference, since the intensional meaning of "if, then", be it logical or causal connection, is actually irrelevant to the validity of formal deductive inferences involving conditional statements. This is to say that such conditional inference-forms as *modus ponens*, *modus tollens*, and hypothetical syllogism would remain valid in the sense of leading always to true conclusions from true premises if their conditional premises or conditional conclusions were interpreted as material conditionals asserting no "connections" whatever. The so-called, and perhaps misnamed, paradoxes of material implication, viz., that a false statement materially implies any statement and a true statement is materially implied by any statement, are not logical paradoxes. The formal logician need not be disturbed by the fact that the statements "if New York is a small village, then there are sea serpents" and "if New York is a small village, then there are no sea serpents" are, as symbolized in extensional logic, both true; for since this is due to the falsity of their common antecedent, *modus ponens* cannot be applied to deduce the contradiction that there both are and are not sea serpents. No contradiction arises. However, it is in the *application* of extensional logic for the purpose of precise formulation of empirical concepts and propositions that serious difficulties arise. The "paradoxical" feature of material implication that the mere falsehood of the antecedent ensures the truth of the implication leads, not to formal inconsistency, but to grossly *counterintuitive* factual assertions when extensional logic is applied to the language of empirical science. This becomes particularly evident if one tries to formalize so-called *operational definitions* by means of extensional logic. For the definiens of an operational definition is a conditional whose antecedent describes a test operation and whose consequent describes a result which such an operation has if performed upon a certain kind of object under specified conditions. A concept which is operationally defined in this sense may be called a "disposition concept." Suppose, then, that a disposition concept is defined by a material conditional as follows:

$$Dx,t = (Ox,t \supset Rx,t) \ldots \tag{D_1}$$

The question might be raised whether the time-argument could be omitted from the disposition predicate, so that the definition would look as follows: $Dx = (t)(Ox,t \supset Rx,t)$. Which form of definition is suitable depends on inductive considerations. If the disposition is "intrinsic" in the sense that a generalization of the form $(t)(x)[x \epsilon K \supset (Ox,t \supset Rx,t)]$ has been highly confirmed (where K is a natural kind), a time-independent disposition predicate is appropriate. Examples of such intrinsic dispositions are solubility and melting point (the latter is an example of a quantitative disposition whose operational definition accordingly would require the use of functors, not just of qualitative predicates). On the other hand, the symbol "Dx,t" is appropriate if D is such that for some objects y both "$(\exists t)(Oy,t \cdot Ry,t)$" and "$(\exists t)(Oy,t \cdot \sim Ry,t)$" holds; for example, being electrically charged, elasticity, irritability. Now, as Carnap pointed out in *Testability and Meaning*, a definition of the form of D_1 has the counterintuitive consequence that any object has D at any time at which it is not subjected to O, and that any object on which O is never performed has D at all times.[2]

There is a close analogy between the interpretation of the Aristotelian A and E propositions as generalized material implications (or "formal implications," in Russell's terminology) and the extensional interpretation of operational definitions, in that both have the consequences that intuitively incompatible statements are compatible after all. If "all A are B" means "$(x)(Ax \supset Bx)$" and "no A are B" means "$(x)(Ax \supset \sim Bx)$", then both may be true, since both would be true if nothing had the property A, which is logically possible. Thus the student introduced to extensional symbolic logic learns to his amazement that both "all unicorns live in the Bronx zoo" and "no unicorns live in the Bronx zoo" are true statements—for the simple reason that there are no unicorns, from which it follows that there are no unicorns of any kind, neither unicorns that live in the Bronx zoo nor unicorns that don't live in the Bronx zoo. Similarly, suppose a physical functor like "temperature" were operationally defined as follows: $temp(x,t) = y =_{df}$, a thermometer is brought into thermal contact with x at $t \supset$ the top of the thermometric liquid coincides with the mark y at $t + dt$. Then the clearly incompatible statements "$temp(a,t_o) = 50$" and "$temp(a,t_o) = 70$" would both be true, on the basis of this definition, if no thermometer were in contact with a at t_o; indeed a would have all temperatures whatsoever at any time at which its temperature is not measured.[3]

Some philosophers have suggested that the reason why counterintuitive consequences result if material implication is substituted for natural implication is that a material implication is true in cases where the corresponding natural implication has no truth-value. If the antecedent of a natural implication is false, they suggest, then the natural implication is "undetermined"; it is true just in case both antecedent and consequent are true, and false in case the antecedent is true and the consequent is false.[4] Now, the combinations FF and FT do, indeed, leave the truth-value of a natural implication undetermined in the sense that they leave it an open question which its truth-value is. But the same holds for the combination TT. It is not the case that every true statement naturally implies every true statement. If it should be replied that nevertheless the joint truth of antecedent and consequent confirms a natural implication, it must be pointed out that if so, then the joint falsehood of antecedent and consequent likewise confirms it, by the principle that whatever evidence confirms a given statement S also confirms whatever statement is logically equivalent to S:[5] if "p and q" confirms "if p, then q", then "not-q and not-p" confirms "if not-q, then not-p", and therefore confirms "if p, then q". Or, to put it differently but equivalently: if "p and q" confirms "if p, then q" then it also confirms "if not-q, then not-p", but this is to say that a natural implication is confirmable by an FF case. To illustrate: suppose I say to a student "if you study for the course at least one hour every day, then you will pass the course." If this conditional prediction is confirmed by the fact that the advised student put in at least one hour for the course every day and passed the course, then the same fact ought to confirm the equivalent prediction formulated in the future perfect: "if you will not pass the course, then you will not have studied for it at least one hour every day." But further, it just is not the case that no truth-value is ordinarily assigned to a natural implication whose antecedent is false. Everybody distinguishes between true and false contrary-to-fact conditionals. In particular, the belief that an object has a certain disposition may motivate people to subject it, or prevent it from being subjected, to the corresponding test operation; we are, for example, careful not to drop a fragile and valuable object because we believe that it would break if it were dropped. What we believe is a proposition, something that is true or false; to say that it only becomes true when its antecedent and consequent are confirmed, is to confuse truth and confirmation.[6]

Let us see, now, whether perhaps a more complicated kind of explicit definition of disposition concepts within the framework of extensional logic can be constructed which avoids the shortcoming of D_1: that an object upon which test operation O is not performed has any disposition whatsoever that is defined by means of O. Philosophers who follow the precept "to discover the meaning of a factual sentence 'p' reflect on the empirical evidence which would induce you to assert that p" might arrive at such a definition by the following reasoning. What makes one say of a wooden object that it is not soluble in water even before testing it for solubility in water, i.e., before immersing it in water? Obviously its similarity to other objects which have been immersed in water and were found not to dissolve therein. And what makes one say of a piece of sugar that it is soluble before having immersed it? Evidently the fact that other pieces of sugar have been immersed and found to dissolve. In general terms: the evidence "$(x_1 \epsilon K \cdot Ox_1 \cdot Rx_1) \cdot (x_2 \epsilon K \cdot Ox_2 \cdot Rx_2) \ldots (x_n \epsilon K \cdot Ox_n \cdot Rx_n)$" led to the generalization "$(x)(x \epsilon K \supset (Ox \supset Rx))$" from which, together with "$x_o \epsilon K$", we deduce "$Ox_o \supset Rx_o$". The latter conditional is not vacuously asserted, i.e., just on the evidence "$\sim Ox_o$", but it is asserted on the specified inductive evidence. Such indirect confirmability [7] of dispositional statements seems accurately reflected by the definition schema: [8]

$$Dx = (\exists f)[fx \cdot (\exists y)(\exists t)(fy \cdot Oy,t) \cdot (z)(t)(fz \cdot Oz,t \supset Rz,t)] \quad (D_2)$$

If we take as values of "f" alternatively "being wooden" and "being sugar", then it can easily be seen that on the basis of such a definition, involving application of the higher functional calculus to descriptive predicates, wooden objects that are never immersed in a liquid L are not soluble in L, whereas pieces of sugar can with inductive warrant be characterized as soluble in L even if they are not actually immersed in L.

Unfortunately, however, the undesirable consequences of D_1 reappear if certain artificial predicates are constructed and substituted for the predicate variable "f". Thus Carnap pointed out to Kaila that if "$(x = a) \lor (x = b)$", where a is the match that was burned up before ever making contact with water and b an object that was immersed and dissolved, is taken as the value of "f", "Da" is again provable. This seemed to be a trivial objection, since evidently "f" was meant to range over "properties" in the ordinary sense of "property": who would ever say that it is a property of the match to be either identical with itself or with the lump of sugar on the saucer? But if "f" is restricted to general properties, i.e., properties that are not defined in terms of individual constants, the undesirable consequences are still not precluded. As Wedberg pointed out (loc. cit.), vacuous confirmation of dispositional statements would still be possible by taking "$O \supset R$" as value of "f". Nevertheless, I doubt whether the objection from the range of the predicate variable is insurmountable. To be sure, it would lead us to a dead end if we defined the range of "f" as the class of properties that determine natural kinds. For our philosophical objective is to clarify the meaning of "disposition" by showing how disposition concepts are definable in terms of clearer concepts. But I suspect that we need the concept of "disposition" for the explication of "natural kind", in the following way: if a class K is an ultimate natural kind (an infima species, in scholastic terminology), then, if one member of K has a disposition D, all members of K have D. If "ultimate natural kind" could be satisfactorily defined along this line, "natural kind" would be simply definable as "logical sum of ultimate natural kinds". To illustrate: would a physicist admit that two samples of iron might have a different melting point? He would surely suspect impurities if the two samples, heated under the same standard pressure, melted at different temperatures. And after making sure that the surprising result is not due to experimental error, he would invent names for two subspecies of iron—that is, he would cease to regard iron as an "ultimate" kind—and look for differentiating properties other than the difference of melting point in order to "account" for the latter.

But be this as it may, it seems that vacuous truth of dispositional statements could be precluded without dragging in the problematic concept of "natural kind" by the following restriction on the range of "f": we exclude not only properties defined by individual constants, but also general properties that are truth-functional compounds of the observable transient properties O and R.[9] There remains, nevertheless, a serious objection relating to the second conjunct in the scope of the existential quantifier: there is a confusion between the *meaning* of a dispositional statement and the inductive *evidence* for it. To see this, just suppose a universe in which the range of temperature is either so high or so low that liquids are causally impossible in it. If so, nothing can ever be immersed in a liquid, hence, if "Oy,t" means "y is immersed in L at t", "$(\exists y)(\exists t)(fy \cdot Oy,t)$" will be false for all values of "f". But surely the meaning of "soluble" is such that even relative to this imaginary universe "sugar is soluble" would be true: in using the dispositional predicate "soluble" we express in a condensed way the subjunctive conditional "if a sample of sugar were immersed in a liquid, then it would dissolve," and this just does not entail that some sample of sugar, or even anything at all, is ever *actually* immersed in a liquid. True, no mind could have any evidence for believing a proposition of the form "x is soluble" if nothing were ever observed to dissolve; indeed, it is unlikely that a conscious organism living in our imaginary universe (for the sake of argument, let us assume that the causal laws governing that universe are such that conscious life is possible in it in spite of the prevailing extreme temperatures) would even have the concept of solubility. But it does not follow that the proposition could not be true just the same.

The idea underlying D_2 is obviously this: the evidence on which a contrary-to-fact conditional is asserted—if it is a confirmable, and hence cognitively meaningful, statement at all—is some law that has been confirmed to some degree; therefore the conditional is best analyzed as an implicit assertion of the existence and prior confirmation of a law connecting O and R.[10] Now, I agree that the existence of some law in accordance with which the consequent is deducible from the antecedent is implicitly asserted by any singular counterfactual conditional, though the assertor may not be able to say *which* that law is (formally speaking, he may not know which value of "f" yields a universal conditional—the third conjunct of the definiens—which is probably true). To take an extreme example: if I say, "if you had asked your landlord more politely to repaint the kitchen, he would have agreed to do it," I have but the vaguest idea of the complex psychological conditions that must be fulfilled if a landlord is to respond favorably to a tenant's request which he is not legally obligated to satisfy, yet to the extent that I believe in determinism I believe that there is a complex condition which is causally sufficient for a landlord's compliance with such a request.[11] But that there is confirming evidence for the law whose existence is asserted—and more specifically *instantial* evidence—is *causally*, not *logically*, presupposed by the assertion of the dispositional statement. A proposition q is causally presupposed by an assertion of proposition p, if p would not have been asserted unless q had been believed; in other words, if the acceptance of q is one of the causal conditions for the assertion of p;[12] whereas q is logically presupposed by the assertion of p, if p entails q. To add an illustration to the one already given: consider the singular dispositional statement "the melting point of x is 200° F", which means that x would melt at any time at which its temperature were raised to 200° F (provided the atmospheric pressure is standard). Surely this proposition is logically compatible with the proposition that nothing ever reaches the specified temperature. That there should be instantial evidence for a law of the form "any instance of natural kind K would, under standard atmospheric pressure, melt if it reached 200° F" is therefore not logically presupposed by the dispositional statement, though very likely it is causally presupposed by its assertion.

Could our schema of explicit definition, then, be salvaged by extruding the existential clause? Only if "$(z)(Fz \cdot Oz \supset Rz)$" (where "F" is a constant predicate substituted for the variable "f") were an adequate expression of a law. But that it is not follows from the fact that it is entailed by "$\sim(\exists z)(Fz \cdot Oz)$." Thus, if "F" means "is wooden", and it so happens that no wooden thing is ever immersed in a liquid, it would be true to say of a match that it is soluble. It may well be that to ascribe D to x is to ascribe to x some intrinsic property f (however "intrinsic" may be explicated) such that "Rx" is deducible from "$fx \cdot Ox$" by means of a law; but this, as most writers on the contrary-to-fact conditional have recognized, leaves the extensionalist with the tough task of expressing laws in an extensional language. The view that every *singular* counterfactual conditional derives its warrant from a *universal* conditional is sound—though one cannot tell by a mere glance at the predicates of the singular conditional which universal conditional is presupposed [13]—but it should not be overlooked that universal conditionals that are accorded the status of laws by scientists may themselves be counterfactual. There are no finite physical systems that are strictly closed, isolated from external influences, but the law of the conservation of energy says that if there were such a system its total energy would remain constant; there are no gases that are "ideal" in the sense that their molecules do not exert "intermolecular" forces on one another, but the general gas law says that if there were such a gas it would exactly satisfy the equation "PV = RT"; there are no bodies that are not acted on by any external forces (indeed, the existence of such bodies is incompatible with the universal presence of gravitation), but the law of inertia says that if there were such a body it would be in a state of rest or uniform motion relative to the fixed stars.[14] If such laws were formulated extensionally, as negative existential statements, like "there are no ideal gases that do not satisfy the equation: PV = RT", they would be vacuously true; anything whatsoever could be truly asserted to happen under the imagined unrealizable conditions. And it could hardly be maintained that, in analogy to the process of validation of singular contrary-to-fact conditionals, such laws are asserted as consequences of more general laws that have been instantially confirmed. If the general gas law, for example, is asserted as a deductive consequence of anything, then it is of the kinetic theory of gases, whose constituent propositions are surely not the kind of generalizations that could be instantially confirmed.[15]

But further, there is the much-discussed difficulty of distinguishing extensionally laws from universal propositions that are but *accidental*. It may be the case that all the people who ever inhabited a certain house H before H was torn down died before the age of 65. The statement "for any x, if x is an inhabitant of H, then x dies before 65" would then be true, yet nobody would want to say that it expresses a law. As Chisholm and Goodman have pointed out, if it were a law, then it would support a counterfactual conditional like "if Mr. Smith (who is not one of the inhabitants of H) had inhabited H, he would have died before 65." Now, an extensionalist might try the following approach: what distinguishes laws from accidental universals is, not an obscure modality of existential necessity (as contrasted with logical necessity), but their strict universality. That is, a universal statement expresses a law only if either it contains no individual constants or else is deducible as a special case from well-confirmed universal statements that contain no individual constants. The predicates of the fundamental laws, i.e., those that contain no individual constants, should be purely general.

However, a serious criticism must be raised against this approach. Just suppose that H were uniquely characterized by a property P which is purely general in the sense that it *might* be possessed by an unlimited number of objects.[16] P might be the property of having a green roof; that is, it might happen that H and only H has P. In that case the accidental universal could be expressed in terms of purely general predicates: for any x, if x is an inhabitant of a house that has a green roof, then x dies before 65.[17] It may be replied that although the antecedent predicate is purely general it refers, in the above statement, to a finite class that can be exhausted by enumeration of its members, and that it is this feature which marks the statement as accidental. Admittedly, so the reply may continue, it sounds absurd to infer from it "if y were an inhabitant of a house that has a green roof, then y would die before 65," but this is because we tacitly give an intensional interpretation to the antecedent predicate. If instead it were interpreted extensionally, viz., in the sense of "if y were identical with one of the elements of the actual extension of the predicate," the inferred subjunctive conditional would be perfectly reasonable. To cite directly the proponent of this explication of the distinction under discussion, Karl Popper: ". . . the phrase 'If x were an A . . .' can be interpreted (1) if 'A' is a term in a strictly universal law, to mean 'If x has the property A . . .' (but it can also be interpreted in the way described under (2)); and (2), if 'A' is a term in an 'accidental' or numerically universal statement, it *must* be interpreted 'If x is identical with one of the elements of A.' " [18]

But this just won't do. For "x is one of the elements of A" would, in the sense intended by Popper, be expressed in the symbolism of *Principia Mathematica* as follows: $x = a \vee x = b \vee \ldots \vee x = n$, where $a, b \ldots n$ are all the actual members of A.[19] But if Popper were right, then, if "all A are B" is accidental, it could be analytically deduced from it that such and such objects are members of B, which is surely not the case. To prove this formally for the case where the actual extension of "A" consists of just two individuals a and b: $(x)(x = a \vee x = b \supset x \,\epsilon\, B)$

Arthur Pap

is equivalent to $(x)[(x = a \supset x \in B) \cdot (x = b \supset x \in B)]$, which is equivalent to the simple conjunction: $a \in B \cdot b \in B$. But surely it can be supposed without self-contradiction that, as a matter of accident, all the inhabitants of houses with green roofs die before 65, and yet individual a, or individual b, survives the age of 65. What is logically excluded by the accidental universal is only the *conjunctive* supposition that a is an inhabitant of a house with a green roof and survives the age of 65. It is not denied that "$a \in B \cdot b \in B$," where a and b happen to be the only objects that have property A, is the ground, indeed the conclusive ground, on which the accidental universal "all A are B" is asserted; what is denied is that any *atomic* statements, or conjunctions of such, are analytically entailed by a universal statement, regardless of whether it is accidental or lawlike. The same confusion of the meaning of the universal statement with the ground on which it is asserted is involved in the following interpretation: $(a \in A) \cdot (a \in B) \cdot (b \in A) \cdot (b \in B) \ldots$ $(n \in A) \cdot (n \in B) \cdot (x)(x \in A \equiv x = a \lor x = b \lor \ldots \lor x = n)$. For clearly none of the atomic statements are entailed by the universal statement "all A are B."

But suppose that accidental universals were characterized pragmatically rather than semantically, in terms of the nature of the evidence which makes them warrantedly assertable. Thus P. F. Strawson [20] suggests that only the knowledge that all the members of A have been observed and found to be B constitutes a good reason for asserting an accidental universal "all A are B." Now, Strawson cannot mean *conclusive* evidence by "good reason," since as long as there remain unobserved members of the subject class the evidence for a lawlike [21] generalization is not conclusive either. He must therefore be making the more audacious claim that observations of a part of the subject class of an accidental universal cannot even make it *probable* that its unobserved members are likewise positive instances. He is then taking the same position as Nelson Goodman, who holds that if "all A are B" is accidental, it does not make sense to say that the evidence that observed members of A are B's *confirms* the prediction that unobserved members of A are likewise B's. But this criterion is highly counterintuitive. If 10 apples are picked out of a basket filled with apples and are found to be rotten without exception, it will be inductively rational to predict that the next apple that will be picked is likewise rotten. Yet, it may be just an accidental fact that all the apples in the basket are

206

rotten. It is not necessary to assume that somebody deliberately filled the basket with rotten apples, though the circumstances may make this hypothesis plausible. It is possible, for instance, that somebody who made random selections (with closed eyes) of apples from a larger basket in order to fill up a smaller basket had the misfortune to get nothing but rotten ones though there were quite a few good specimens in the larger basket.

An attempt to define the law-accident distinction in pragmatic rather than semantic terms, i.e., in terms of the kind of evidence leading one to assert the respective kinds of propositions, while retaining extensional logic for the formulation of the asserted propositions, has likewise been made by R. B. Braithwaite.[22] He says as much as that the assertion of a contrary-to-fact conditional causally presupposes acceptance of an instantially confirmed law from which the conditional component (the other component is the negation of the antecedent) is deducible, but that the *truth-condition* [23] of the contrary-to-fact conditional is expressible in extensional logic: $(p \supset q) \cdot \sim p$. There are two major objections to this approach: In the first place, contrary-to-fact conditionals with identical antecedents and contradictory consequents (e.g., "if he had come, he would have been shot," "if he had come, he would not have been shot") are *logically compatible* on this analysis; whereas one should think that their logical incompatibility is a guiding criterion of adequacy for the semantic (not pragmatic) analysis of contrary-to-fact conditionals.[24] Braithwaite in fact is saying that all contrary-to-fact conditionals whatever are true, though not all of them would be asserted by people confronted with the choice between asserting or denying them. But if a person honestly denies "p" and is familiar with the conventional meaning of "p", then he does not believe the proposition expressed by "p"; yet, if the proposition expressed by "if A had happened, B would have happened" is simply the proposition that A did not happen (notice that "$\sim p$" is logically equivalent to "$\sim p \cdot (p \supset q)$"), how could anyone who recognizes the conditional as contrary to fact fail to believe it? But secondly, Braithwaite merely postpones the difficulty facing the extensional analysis to the presupposed laws. For, as explained earlier, these may themselves be counterfactual, accepted not because of derivability from instantially confirmed laws but because of extrapolation to an ideal limit. When Galileo asserted that in a vacuum all bodies fall with the same acceleration, he was not led to this assertion by a belief in the derivability of the asserted generalization from "higher level hypotheses." Galileo's law is indeed deducible from "higher level hypotheses," but at least one of these (the law of universal gravitation) was accepted not because of instantial confirmation but just because Galileo's law, together with other "derived laws" (Kepler's laws), was derivable from it.

Braithwaite's extensional analysis of "law", or "lawlike hypothesis", in terms of the notion of a hypothetico-deductive system, is moreover untenable for the following reason. If "all A are B" is supported just by instantial evidence (induction by "simple enumeration"), he says, then it is not lawlike. In order to be lawlike, it must be deducible from well-confirmed higher level hypotheses (it must be supported, in other words, by what Kneale has aptly called "secondary induction"). But since the "highest" hypotheses usually do not admit of instantial confirmation, on account of their postulating entities or events that are not directly observable, what is the condition of their lawlikeness? Braithwaite's answer is that they are lawlike because testable consequences are deducible from them. What it all seems to amount to is that "all A are B"—restricting ourselves, like Braithwaite, to this form of law for the sake of simplification—is lawlike if and only if it is capable of being supported by indirect confirmation, not just by instantial confirmation, i.e., either by instantial confirmation of more general statements from which it follows or by instantial confirmation of less general statements that follow from it. Notice that we need as defining condition indirect confirmability, not actual indirect confirmation, otherwise "lawlike" would be a time-dependent predicate,[25] which does not seem to be Braithwaite's intention.

But on this analysis there are no accidental universals at all. Consider, for instance, (1) "all men now in this room are bald," as compared with (2) "all tall men now in this room are bald," where actually some of the men now in this room are tall and some are not. Clearly (2) is deducible from (1), and there is more instantial evidence for (1) than for (2). This is exactly analogous to Braithwaite's argument (op. cit., p. 302) that "all men are mortal" is regarded as a law of nature because it is deducible from "all animals are mortal", for which generalization there is more instantial evidence. And consider this statement: "If . . . there is evidence for [an hypothesis] which is independent of its instances, such as the indirect evidence provided by instances of a

208

same-level general proposition subsumed along with it under the same higher-level hypothesis, then the general proposition will *explain* its instances in the sense that it will provide grounds for believing in their truth independently of any direct knowledge of such truth" (p. 303). It is thus that Braithwaite wants to tie the notion of law to the notion of explanation. But he is just engaged in a merry-go-round, since we do not accept a subsumptive syllogism as an explanation unless its major premise is lawlike. Referring back to an example already used, let us assume that not only the inhabitants of green-roofed house H, but also the inhabitants of a house H' which is uniquely describable as, say, the only house in the United States built by a Chinese architect, died before 65 without exception. Then there is more instantial evidence for "all the inhabitants of H or of H' die before 65" than for "all the inhabitants of H die before 65," which follows from the former statement. Yet, we would not accept it as an explanation of the fact that Mr. X died before 65, that he inhabited H and that all inhabitants of H died before that age, if we consider it just *coincidental* that all the inhabitants of H died before 65.

Surprisingly, Braithwaite cites Julius Weinberg [26] as giving a similar analysis. But actually there seems to be a fundamental difference in that Weinberg seems to include the belief in a confirmed law from which the singular contrary-to-fact conditional is deducible in the *analysis* of the latter, whereas Braithwaite takes it, in my terminology, to be causally presupposed by its assertion. Weinberg maintains that "if this vase had been dropped, it would have broken" asserts implicitly "I believe that vases of a given sort break if dropped because I have such and such evidence and I later and independently know a vase of the required sort which has not been dropped." Although I suspect that Weinberg, like other writers on the contrary-to-fact conditional, simply confused the concepts of "causal presupposition" and of "truth-condition" of an assertion,[27] it seems to me likely that he used "asserts implicitly" in the sense in which to say "A implicitly asserted q in asserting p" is to say that q is *entailed* by p. Indeed, unless Weinberg meant that such belief statements are entailed by contrary-to-fact conditionals, it would be irrelevant for him to raise, as he does, the question whether belief statements are analyzable by means of extensional logic in connection with the question whether contrary-to-fact conditionals are so analyzable. Now, it is a simple reflection that the contrary-to-fact conditional about the vase could be true in a universe devoid of minds and hence of beliefs; surely "nobody believes that any vases break under any circumstances, but if this vase were dropped it would break" expresses a logical possibility. That the assertion of such a statement is *pragmatically* contradictory is an entirely different matter. Would Weinberg say that a man who asserts that it will rain *implicitly asserts* the proposition that he believes that it will rain because it is unlikely or perhaps even logically impossible—depending on the sense of "assert" (cf. note 11 above)—that he should assert the former proposition unless the latter proposition were true? But surely the propositions that it rains at t and that A does not believe (at a time before t) that it rains at t [28] are logically compatible.

All these considerations point to the conclusion that extensional logic is inadequate for the formulation of laws, and therefore for explicit definition of disposition concepts. If so, an extensionalist who frowns on "causal necessity" as an obscure notion, will have to introduce dispositional predicates into his ideally clear language by means of a device suggested by Carnap some twenty years ago: *reduction sentences.* In order to preclude vacuous applicability of dispositional predicates (cf. p. 198), Carnap, who at that time was firmly committed to the thesis of extensionality, proposed in *Testability and Meaning* to replace explicit definitions of the form $Q_3(x) = (t)(Q_1(x,t) \supset Q_2(x,t))$ by reduction sentences of the form $(x)(t)(Q_1(x,t) \supset (Q_3(x) \equiv Q_2(x,t)))$. Such reduction sentences do, indeed, overcome the paradox of vacuous applicability, since neither "Q_3" nor "$\sim Q_3$" is applicable to x if x has not been subjected to the test operation Q_1. Furthermore, the method of reduction sentences did not, as it might seem at first blush, entail the equally unacceptable consequence that there are no grounds for attributing a disposition to an object prior to performance of the relevant test operation upon it. For, as Carnap pointed out, if Q_1 has been performed upon several members of a class K and led to the result Q_2, the reduction sentence permits us to ascribe the disposition to them, and hence we may inductively infer that other members of K which have not yet been subjected to Q_1 likewise have that disposition.

Nevertheless, one of my main arguments against D_2, viz., that it involves a confusion of truth-conditions and conditions of verification, semantic meaning and pragmatic meaning, is equally applicable to Carnap's reduction sentences. My argument was that the intuitive meaning of dispositional predicates is such that it is logically possible for an object to have a disposition which is never manifested at all. Now, the above reduction sentence does not, indeed, entail that it is self-contradictory to suppose that an object has Q_3 while nothing at all satisfies the function "$(\exists t)Q_1x,t$"; but it entails instead that such a supposition is meaningless. Thus Carnap writes in Testability and Meaning: [29] "If a body b consists of such a substance that for no body of this substance has the test-condition . . . ever been fulfilled, then neither the predicate nor its negation can be attributed to b." Out of context, this statement is ambiguous. Does it simply mean that on the mentioned conditions we do not know whether or not b has the disposition, but that nevertheless the law of the excluded middle is applicable to the dispositional predicate, i.e., either "Q_3b" or "$\sim Q_3b$" is true? Or does it mean that both of these formally contradictory sentences are meaningless in that case? It seems to me obvious that the principle of empiricism, that synthetic sentences are meaningful only if they are in principle confirmable, together with the method of reduction sentences entails the latter alternative. It is the very essence of a reduction sentence that it determines the meaning of the reduced term only relative to the test condition. By adding further reduction sentences for the same term we can increase its range of significant applicability, but no amount of factual knowledge could ever provide us with grounds for deciding the question whether an object which satisfies none of the alternative test conditions has the property designated by the term if nothing has ever satisfied any of these conditions, in the same sense in which it is on semantic grounds undecidable whether or not the square root of two is a prime number: "prime" is defined only for natural numbers. Of course, if dispositional predicates were literally "introduced" into a language, without any antecedent meaning, there would be nothing paradoxical about this consequence; it would be just a matter of stipulation how the range of significant application is to be delimited. But I am concerned to criticize the method of reduction sentences as a method of explicating the intuitive meanings of dispositional predicates, on the ground that the intuitive meaning of "soluble", for example, is such that it makes sense to suppose that even in a universe in which this disposition is never manifested some things are soluble and some are not.[30]

It might be supposed that once we abandon the extensional language and replace material implication by causal implication [31] for the formulation of "operational" definitions, all these difficulties are easily solved. For the distinctive property of causal implication as compared with material implication is just that the falsity of the antecedent is no ground for inferring the truth of the causal implication. But the defect of D_1, that it makes the extensions of dispositional predicates undesirably large, would simply give way to the no less serious defect that their extensions are either too large or too small, if the non-extensional definition schema for dispositional predicates took the simple form $Ox,t \rightarrow Rx,t$. For if the arrow signifies that the antecedent predicate designates a property which is *causally sufficient* for the property designated by the consequent predicate, then either everything or nothing has the defined disposition. This follows from the fact that if the antecedent of a causal implication expresses a sufficient condition for the kind of event expressed by the consequent, then *individual constants occur vacuously in causal implications*. "$Oa,t_0 \rightarrow Ra,t_0$" entails "$Ob,t_0 \rightarrow Rb,t_0$" and "$Oa,t_1 \rightarrow Ra,t_1$", and so forth. Hence, if anything satisfies the definiens at some time, then everything satisfies it at any time, and so everything has the defined disposition at all times. By contraposition, if something does not satisfy the definiens at some time, then nothing satisfies it at any time, and so nothing has the defined disposition.[32] Indeed, the test operation by which a disposition is defined is never causally sufficient to bring about the manifestation of the disposition; the effect will occur only if the operation is performed on an object with specified characteristics. Thus, it is "x is immersed in aqua regia and x is gold" which causally implies "x dissolves," not "x is immersed in aqua regia" by itself. This consideration suggests the following improvement [33] on D_2:

$$Dx =_{df} (\exists f)[fx \cdot (t)(y)(fy \cdot Oy,t \rightarrow Ry,t)] \qquad (D_3)$$

It will be noticed that in contrast to D_2, no instantiation claim is implicit in a dispositional statement according to D_3—which is all to the good. It is true that Wedberg's objection applies here too: if "$Ox \supset Rx$" is taken as a value of "fx", then anything satisfies the definiens, since Burks defines "causal implication" in such a way that strict (analytic) implication is a special case of it (Reichenbach's term for this inclusive concept is "nomological implication"). But it is easy to protect D_3 against this popular line of attack by either restricting the predicate variable to properties which do not satisfy the definiens tautologically, or so defining causal implication that only synthetic implications count as causal.[34]

Before turning to the major question I wish to discuss in the remainder of this essay, viz., whether the transition to a non-extensional language of causal implication involves an abandonment of Hume's regularity theory of causation and therefore a breach with a basic tenet of empiricism, let us see whether our new definition schema meets the requirement of extensional equivalence of definiendum and definiens. According to it, in ascribing a disposition to an object one asserts that it has some property by virtue of which the reaction R may be predicted to follow realization of test condition O in accordance with a causal law.[35] However, the premise that x is subjected to test condition O is insufficient for the prediction of R for two reasons: not only must one ascertain, as already pointed out, that x has a certain intrinsic property, like being gold, or being sugar, or being hydrogen, or having molecular structure H_2SO_4, but further certain environmental conditions must be fulfilled at the time of the experiment which are usually referred to by the safety clause "other things being equal" if they are not known in detail. For example: suppose we define "x is inflammable" as "x has some intrinsic property (e.g., chemical nature) such that anything with this intrinsic property would burn whenever it is heated." On this definition nothing is inflammable, since the antecedent of the universal causal implication does not mention the presence of oxygen, which is a necessary condition for burning. We need a special variable in order to leave the possibility open that we do not have an exhaustive knowledge of such relevant environmental conditions. We cannot bring them within the range of the same variable as is used for the intrinsic properties, because intrinsic properties are relatively stable, time-independent,[36] unlike such transient properties as "being surrounded by oxygen" (consider, for example, the intrinsic property of a sample of gas "being composed of hydrogen molecules": does it even make sense to suppose that the same sample of gas has the property at one time and not at another time?). At any rate, if we express the disposition by a time-independent predicate, we have to use time-independent predicates for the intrinsic properties too, but we need time-dependent predicates for the changeable environmental conditions. Hence the following definition schema for time-independent dispositions might plausibly be proposed:

$$Dx =_{df} (\exists\theta)(\exists\psi)[\theta x \cdot (y)(t)(\theta y \cdot \psi y,t \cdot Oy,t \rightarrow Ry,t)]^{37} \quad (D_4)$$

It is true that if we knew all the environmental conditions that are necessary and jointly sufficient for the occurrence of state R in a thing of specified kind θ, the second predicate variable would not be needed. But since the only criterion of the completeness of such knowledge is just that there are no exceptions to the universal causal implication, which it is impossible to know with theoretical certainty, this variable is indispensable for the analysis of disposition concepts in terms of causal implication. On the other hand, if we wish to use "disposition" in such a way that to say that things have dispositions does not entail that their successive states are governed by causal laws but only that they are governed by statistical laws, then we may simply replace causal implication by probability implication in the definiens. The environmental predicate variable would then be unnecessary.

As far as I can see, D_4 is perfectly satisfactory—if we can rest satisfied with the use of the causal arrow as a *primitive* logical constant. But has Hume written in vain? Should we not at least attempt to reduce the concept of causal implication to the concept of "constant conjunction"? Or is the admission of the inadequacy of extensional logic for the definition of disposition concepts and formulation of contrary-to-fact conditionals tantamount to the admission that causal connection cannot be defined in terms of contingent "constant conjunction"? Several writers have assumed without argument that Hume's regularity theory stands and falls with the possibility of formulating causal laws in an extensional language. Thus Burks writes: "Consider the question: Can causal propositions be adequately translated into an extensional language (e.g. that of *Principia Mathematica*)? The first point to note is that this question is a technical reformulation of a very old metaphysical one: Can the concept of causal connection be defined in terms of ideas of matter-of-fact and constant conjunction, i.e. can causal potentialities be reduced to actualities?" [38] Similarly Braithwaite thinks that in order to defend Hume he must show that the use of subjunctive conditionals can be accounted for without surrendering the extensional analysis of "if a thing is A, then it is B" as simply "there are no A's which are not B's." [39] I wish to show that this view is mistaken.

214

According to the regularity theory, to say that the heating of a block of ice (H) causes it to melt (M) [40] is to say that every instance of H is followed by an instance of M, which implies that not only all past instances of H were followed by an instance of M but also that any future instance of H will be followed by an instance of M. Can this assertion be formulated extensionally? Using "seq(y,x)" for "y follows x", its extensional formulation would read: $(x)(Hx \supset (\exists y)(seq(y,x) \cdot My))$, where the variables range over events that may be characterized by predicates, such as "being the heating of a block of ice" (H) or "being the melting of a block of ice" (M).[41] Now, according to this formulation, the prediction that any future instance of H is followed by an instance of M would be vacuously true if there were no future instances of H. But the conditional predictions which according to the regularity theory are implicit in any causal judgment are not vacuously confirmable; they are subjunctive conditionals, like "if any instance of H should occur again, it would be followed by an instance of M." As Strawson has pointed out, we do not use "all A are B" in such a way that its truth follows from the nonexistence of A's; rather, if there are no A's, one normally does not attach any truth-value to "all A are B"; and if one does, then not because the subject class is empty, but because the statement was intended as a subjunctive conditional which is indirectly confirmable through inductive reasoning.

Further, that the Humean analysis of causation is not expressible in extensional logic is evident from the consideration that the modal concept of *conceivable circumstances* is needed to express it adequately. This may be shown by analyzing a passage from J. S. Mill, the empiricist who explicitly espoused Hume's doctrine of causation as against the "metaphysicians" who look for mysterious ties in the course of natural events:

When we define the cause of any thing (in the only sense in which the present inquiry has any concern with causes) to be "the antecedent which it invariably follows," we do not use this phrase as exactly synonymous with "the antecedent which it invariably *has* followed in our past experience." Such a mode of conceiving causation would be liable to the objection very plausibly urged by Dr. Reid, namely, that according to this doctrine night must be the cause of day, and day the cause of night; since these phenomena have invariably succeeded one another from the beginning of the world. But it is necessary to our using the word cause, that we should believe not only that the antecedent always has been followed by the consequent, but that as long as the present constitution of things endures, it always *will* be so. And this would not be true of day and night. We do not believe that night will be followed by day under all imaginable circumstances, but only that it will be so *provided* the sun rises above the horizon. . . . This is what writers mean when they say that the notion of cause involves the idea of necessity. If there be any meaning which confessedly belongs to the term necessity, it is *unconditionalness*. . . . That which will be followed by a given consequent when, and only when, some third circumstance also exists, is not the cause, even though no case should ever have occurred in which the phenomenon took place without it.[42]

Let us see whether this idea of "unconditionalness" can be expressed in extensional terms. Consider the following causal proposition: the lowering of the temperature of a sample of gas G to x degrees causes it to condense. If in fact every instance of the described temperature change is followed by the described effect, we would nevertheless not be justified in calling it the "cause" of the effect, according to Mill's conception of cause as *unconditionally* invariable antecedent. For we know that the drop of temperature (T) would not be followed by condensation (C) if the gas were not subject to a certain minimal pressure (P). The latter is the "third circumstance" mentioned in the concluding sentence of my citation. Now, if in fact this circumstance accompanies every instance of T, then the extensional implication "$(x)(Tx \supset (\exists y)(Cy \cdot seq(y,x)))$" is equivalent to the extensional implication "$(x)(Tx \cdot Px \supset (\exists y)(Cy \cdot seq(y,x)))$". Therefore, if the assertion of "constant conjunction," which according to Hume and Mill a causal proposition reduces to, could be expressed extensionally, there would be (on the assumption that every instance of T is in fact accompanied by an instance of P) no ground for identifying the cause of C with the complex condition (T · P) rather than with the simpler condition T. If in fact the earth continues to rotate forever and the sun continues to radiate light forever, then day is an invariable antecedent of night, but it is not an unconditionally invariable antecedent because day *would* become everlasting on some part of the globe the moment the earth ceased to rotate (provided that solar radiation were to continue). To put it in general terms, even though C may *in fact* be regularly followed by E it may not be a cause of E because the following subjunctive regularity assertion may not be true: if at any time C were to occur, it would be followed by E. And this assertion would be false if another subjunctive regularity assertion were true: if at any time C were to occur together with C', or in the absence of C", then E would not follow. Notice that the intended meaning of "C is followed by E under all conceivable circumstances" cannot be rendered by "the proposition that C is invariably followed by E holds in all logically possible worlds," for then the causal law would be logically necessary, which is precisely what Hume and his followers have denied. It rather means "there are no cases of C not being followed by E and there are no conditions C' (logically compatible with C and E) such that C would not be followed by E if C' were present." [43] It is obvious, therefore, that we need the subjunctive conditional in order to give a plausible formulation of the regularity theory, like the one offered by Mill.

It may be replied that once it is admitted that causal propositions do not just assert that such and such conditions are *in fact* always followed by such and such effects, defeat for the regularity theory has been conceded. That one is free to so use the term "regularity theory" that the regularity theory can be true only if causal propositions can be expressed by extensional implications, without the use of non-extensional connectives, cannot be reasonably disputed. Yet, if the core of the regularity theory is taken to be the claim that causal propositions are, explicitly or implicitly, universal propositions which are not logically necessary, i.e., cannot be known by analysis of concepts and application of logical principles alone but are warrantedly assertable only on the basis of empirical evidence, then it does not by any means entail extensionalism. To say that the concept "causally (not logically) sufficient condition" cannot be expressed in terms of material implication [44] is perfectly compatible with saying that a causal law can be known only through inductive generalization or deduction from universal propositions which themselves are knowable only through inductive generalization. That causal laws can be known only, directly or indirectly, on the basis of inductive generalization, may superficially seem to conflict with the "uniformity axiom" of the logic of causal propositions, viz., that any singular causal implication *entails* the corresponding universal implication. For this suggests the following analogy between *causal* and *logical* connection between attributes. If a propositional function "Qx" is logically entailed by a propositional function "Px", then of course the singular proposition "Qa" is entailed by the singular proposition "Pa". But conversely, the entailment proposition " 'Pa' entails 'Qa' "

217

entails the entailment proposition "$(x)(Px$ entails $Qx)$". Briefly: individual constants occur vacuously in entailment statements. And as has been explicitly stated by Burks,[45] the same holds *mutatis mutandis* for causal implication. It is tempting to conclude from this analogy that causal implication is a species of entailment which a superior intellect could discover without the aid of induction.[46] But he who succumbs to this temptation, simply overlooks that there is absolutely nothing in the logic of causal implication that indicates that there is any other evidential basis for the assertion of a causal implication "$Pa \rightarrow Qa$" than conjunctions like "$Pb \cdot Qb \cdot Pc \cdot Qc \ldots Pn \cdot Qn$";[47] and the inference from the conjunction to the implication is obviously inductive.

In his careful and instructive article "Dispositional Statements" (*loc. cit.*), Burks invites empiricists to meet the following challenge: ". . . if a philosopher holds that the concept of causal necessity is irreducible to extensional concepts, he should ultimately either show that it is a complex concept or abandon concept-empiricism" (p. 188). Without wishing to commit myself to "empiricism" in all the senses of this term (which I suspect would be a commitment that no lover of consistency could incur), I propose to meet Burks' challenge by defining "causal implication" in terms of the nonlogical constant "seq"—meaning either just temporal contiguity, so that "action at a distance" would be logically possible, or both temporal and spatial contiguity, as expressed for example by differential laws of motion—together with the logical concept of *natural* implication which is involved in conditional sentences expressing causal connections as well as in conditional sentences that do not express causal connections. Using "NI" for "naturally implies", we have simply: $Pa \rightarrow Qa =_{df} (x)(Px \text{ NI } (\exists y)(Qy \cdot seq(y,x)))$. The properties of natural implication may be stated by a set of axioms for natural implication which is like Burks' except that strict implication is not considered a case of natural implication, i.e., natural implications are contingent statements although they are non-extensional with respect to the constituent statements and predicates. The distinguishing property of natural implication is that the truth of the implication is not entailed by the falsity of its antecedent (resp., by the emptiness of the antecedent predicate), and accordingly "$pNIq$" is incompatible with "$pNI \sim q$" provided "p" expresses a logical possibility.[48] Examples of natural implications that are not causal implications are laws of coexistence, as contrasted with laws of succession (dynamic laws): all sugar is soluble in water, all ravens are black, and so forth. Notice that a statement of the form "all A are B" is translatable into a natural implication (in the subjunctive mood: for any x, x would be a B if it were an A) only if it is taken to be incompatible with "no A are B." But, so it may be asked, is not the only condition on which "all A are B" is incompatible with "no A are B" the condition that either statement has existential import? And if so, how can universal contrary-to-fact conditionals like the law of inertia and the other examples adduced earlier be regarded as natural implications in the specified sense?

This argument, however, is based on the assumption that "all A are B" must be analyzable either into "there are no A's that are not B's" or into "there are no A's that are not B's, and there are A's." On the former interpretation, "all A are B" is compatible with "no A are B"—which is counterintuitive; on the latter interpretation there is incompatibility, but on this interpretation "all A are B" cannot express a true contrary-to-fact conditional of universal character. The argument, of course, presupposes that "all A are B" has a clear meaning only if it can be translated into an extensional language, and therefore begs the question. Extensional logic assumes the incompatibility of "all things have P" and "this thing does not have P" ("(x)Px" and "$\sim$Pa") as intuitively evident, and derives the compatibility of "all A are B" and "no A are B" on the basis of an extensional analysis of these statement forms. Since it is thus indispensable anyway that some relations of incompatibility and entailment, like the incompatibility between "everything is P" and "this is not P," be axiomatically asserted, there can be no objection in principle to our asserting axiomatically that "all A are B" and "no A are B," taken as natural implications, are incompatible provided it is logically possible that there should be A's. This intuitive incompatibility derives from the fact that to assert a natural implication is to express a habit of expectation. In saying "if the sun comes out, then it will get warmer" one expresses the habit of associating the idea of rising temperature with the idea of the breaking of sunshine through the cloudy sky, which association of ideas derives, as Hume noted, from a repeated concomitance of the corresponding sense impressions. In saying "if the sun comes out, then it will get colder (and hence not warmer)" one would express the habit of associating the idea of dropping temperature with the idea of increased solar radiation.

But these two habits cannot exist in the same mind at the same time. As an explanation of the origin of the intuitive feeling of incompatibility in question this may seem to be circular: for isn't to say that A has the habit of associating idea I_1 with idea I_2, to say that if I_1 were evoked in A, then I_2 would also be evoked in A? In other words, isn't to ascribe a habit to a human being to ascribe a *disposition* to him, and have we not argued that to attribute a disposition to an object is to assert a *natural implication*? However, the point is that the *manifestation* of such a mental disposition consists not just in I_1 being immediately followed by I_2 but also in the occurrence of an introspectable urge or inclination, which Hume called a "gentle force of association." To assert the occurrence of such an inclination is not to assert an implication. And the proposition that a mind cannot, in one and the same phase of its history, be both in the occurrent state described by "inclining from I_1 to some determinate form of non-I_2" and in the occurrent state described by "inclining from I_1 to I_2," is therefore not a special case of the incompatibility of natural implications whose psychological origin is in question.

It seems to me, then, that the use of a primitive concept of natural implication for the formulation of causal connections is perfectly consistent with Hume's theory of causation. I do not know what could be meant by saying that there is a *necessary connection* between antecedent and consequent of a true natural implication, if it does not just mean that in asserting such an implication one manifests a strong habit of association. The statements "if a block of ice is sufficiently heated, then it *necessarily* melts" and "if any block of ice were at any time sufficiently heated, then it would melt" assert the same fact, however they may differ in emotive pictorial meaning. This insight of Hume and the logical empiricists remains valid, whether or not an extensional analysis of the contrary-to-fact conditional, and therewith of the concept of "disposition", is feasible.

NOTES

[1] In this context "knowledge" is used in the weak sense in which "p is known to be true" entails that there is evidence making it highly probable that p, not the stronger claim that there is evidence making it *certain* that p.

[2] I have slightly changed Carnap's way of putting the counterintuitive consequence, in accordance with my using "Dx,t" instead of "Dx".

[3] There seems to be fairly universal agreement now among philosophers of science that the simple kind of explicit definition of disposition concepts in terms of material

implication is inadequate, precisely because we want to be able to say of an object which is not subjected to the test operation by which a disposition D is defined that it does *not* have D. One exception to this trend might, however, be noted: Gustav Bergmann maintains ("Comments on Professor Hempel's 'The Concept of Cognitive Significance,'" *Proceedings of the American Academy of Arts and Sciences*, July 1951, pp. 78–86) that such explicit definitions nevertheless provide adequate analyses of the disposition concepts—in a sense of "adequate analysis" which is obscure to me. Referring to Carnap's example of the match which is burned up before ever being immersed in water and therefore would be soluble by the criticized definition of "soluble", he says "I propose to analyze the *particular* sentence 'the aforementioned match is (was) not soluble' by means of two sentences of the ideal schema, the first corresponding to 'This match is (was) wooden,' the second to the law 'No wooden object is soluble.'" In what sense do these two sentences provide an *analysis* of "soluble"? Bergmann is simply deducing "the match is not soluble" from two well-confirmed premises, and is therefore perhaps giving a correct *explanation* of the fact described by the sentence, but since "soluble" reappears in the major premise—as it must if the syllogism is to be valid!—its meaning has not been analyzed at all. It is one thing to give grounds for an assertion, another thing to analyze the asserted proposition.

⁴ See D. J. O'Connor, "The Analysis of Conditional Sentences," *Mind*, July 1951, p. 354. Also, the Finnish philosopher E. Kaila once attempted to escape from Carnap's conclusion that disposition concepts are not explicitly definable by proposing that "Dx" be taken as neither true nor false in case x is not subjected to O (which proposal, incidentally, is consonant with Carnap's proposal of introducing dispositional predicates by reduction sentences, as we shall see later): "Wenn-So," *Theoria*, 1945, Part II.

⁵ This has been called the "paradox of confirmation." See C. G. Hempel, "Studies in the Logic of Confirmation," *Mind*, January, April 1945; and R. Carnap, *Logical Foundations of Probability*, Section 87 (Chicago: Univ. of Chicago Press, 1950).

⁶ For a lucid warning against this confusion, see R. Carnap, "Truth and Confirmation," in H. Feigl and W. Sellars (eds.), *Readings in Philosophical Analysis* (New York: Appleton-Century-Crofts, 1949).

⁷ Indirect confirmation of a conditional is distinguished from (a) direct confirmation, consisting in the verification of the conjunction of antecedent and consequent, (b) vacuous confirmation, consisting in the verification of the negation of the antecedent.

⁸ D is here assumed to be an intrinsic disposition in the sense explained on p. 198. The above schema is, with a slight alteration, copied from Anders Wedberg's "The Logical Construction of the World" (*Theoria*, 1944, Part III, p. 237), who cites it for purposes of criticism from Kaila's *Den maenskliga kunskapen*. A variant of this definition schema has more recently been proposed by Thomas Storer: "On Defining 'Soluble'," *Analysis*, June 1951.

⁹ The latter restriction has been suggested to me by Michael Scriven.

¹⁰ For example, the painstaking attempt made by B. J. Diggs, in "Counterfactual Conditionals" (*Mind*, October 1952), to achieve an extensional analysis of the counterfactual conditional is guided by this idea.

¹¹ One might, though, take the more moderate view that warranted assertion of counterfactual conditionals merely involves statistical determinism, i.e., belief in the existence of a statistical law relative to which the consequent is inferable from the antecedent with a probability sufficiently high to warrant practical reliance on the conditional. But on either view singular counterfactual conditionals derive their warrant from a *law*, whether causal or statistical.

¹² Notice that while "A says 'p'" does not entail, but at best confers a high probability upon "A believes that p," the latter proposition is entailed by "A asserts that p,"

according to my usage of "assert" as an intentional verb. I am not denying, of course, that there may be a proper purely behavioristic sense of "assert"; nor do I deny that "A asserts that p" may properly be so used that it is compatible with "A does not believe that p." My usage may be explicated as follows: A believes that p and utters a sentence expressing the proposition that p.

[12] This seems to be overlooked by O'Connor who, following Broad, concludes his analysis of conditional sentences (*loc. cit.*) with the claim that "a particular contrary-to-fact conditional has exactly the same meaning as the corresponding universal indicative statement." The examples given by him indicate that by the universal statement corresponding to the "particular" contrary-to-fact conditional he means the universal conditional of which the latter is a substitution instance. Obviously, it might be true to say "if the trigger of the gun had been pulled, the gun would have fired" though there are exceptions to the generalization "any gun fires if its trigger is pulled." The singular conditional is elliptical; in asserting it one presupposes the presence in the particular situation of various causal conditions which the antecedent does not explicitly mention. (See, on this point, my article "Philosophical Analysis, Translation Schemas and the Regularity Theory of Causation," *Journal of Philosophy*, October 9, 1952, and my book *Analytische Erkenntnistheorie*, Chapter IV A (Vienna: Springer Verlag, 1955); also R. Chisholm, "Law Statements and Counterfactual Inference," *Analysis*, April 1955).

[14] It might be objected that the law of inertia can be formulated in such a way that it is not contrary to fact: if no *unbalanced* forces act on a body, then it is at rest or in uniform motion relative to the fixed stars. But when the law is used for the derivation of the orbit of a body moving under the influence of a central force, it is used in the contrary-to-fact formulation since the tangential velocities are computed by making a thought experiment: how would the body move at this moment if the central force ceased to act on it and it moved solely under the influence of its inertia?

[15] For further elaboration of this argument against the extensional interpretation of laws, see my article "Reduction Sentences and Disposition Concepts," in P. A. Schilpp (ed.), *The Philosophy of Rudolf Carnap* (forthcoming).

[16] Notice that a property may fail to be purely general in this sense even if it is not defined in terms of a particular object, e.g., "being the highest mountain."

[17] This criticism applies to C. G. Hempel and P. Oppenheim's explication of "law" relative to a simplified extensional language system, in "Studies in the Logic of Explanation," *Philosophy of Science*, April 1948; reprinted in H. Feigl and M. Brodbeck (eds.), *Readings in the Philosophy of Science* (New York: Appleton-Century-Crofts, 1953). R. Chisholm makes the same criticism, in "Law Statements and Counterfactual Inference," *Analysis*, April 1955.

[18] "A Note on Natural Laws and So-Called 'Contrary-to-Fact Conditionals,'" *Mind*, January 1949.

[19] He could hardly mean it just in the sense of "$(\exists y)(y \,\epsilon\, A \cdot x = y)$", for this says nothing else than "$x \,\epsilon\, A$", and so does not amount to one of alternative interpretations of "$x \,\epsilon\, A$".

[20] *Introduction to Logical Theory* (London: Methuen; New York: Wiley, 1952), p. 199.

[21] A lawlike statement is a statement which expresses a law if it is true.

[22] *Scientific Explanation* (Cambridge: Cambridge Univ. Press, 1953), Chapter 9.

[23] The truth-condition of a sentence is that state of affairs whose existence is the necessary and sufficient condition for the truth of the sentence. One might instead speak simply of the *proposition* expressed by a sentence, if it were not for the purpose of emphasizing the connection between the concepts of truth and of semantic meaning (reference).

[24] Strictly speaking, they are incompatible only if the antecedent describes a logical possibility. But contrary-to-fact conditionals with self-contradictory antecedents are

analytic, and we are here concerned only with conditional sentences that express empirical propositions. Cf. the following statement by H. Reichenbach, in *Nomological Statements and Admissible Operations* (Amsterdam: North-Holland Publishing Company, 1953). "Introduction": "Assume we say 'if a had happened, then b would have happened.' If this is to be a reasonable implication, it should be required that the contrary implication 'if a had happened, then not-b would have happened' be not true."

[25] A predicate "P" is time-dependent if only statements of the form "x is P at time t," not statements of the form "x is P," are complete.

[26] "Contrary-to-Fact Conditionals," *Journal of Philosophy*, January 1951.

[27] By the truth-condition of an assertion I mean of course the truth-condition of the asserted sentence.

[28] I deliberately use "unusual" tenseless sentences in order not to contaminate propositions with pragmatic properties of assertion events, such as their temporal relation to the asserted facts.

[29] *Philosophy of Science*, October 1936, p. 445.

[30] A more detailed discussion of reduction sentences, especially in connection with the analytic-synthetic dualism that has been branded a "dogma of empiricism," is contained in my articles "Reduction Sentences and Open Concepts," *Methodos*, Vol. 5, No. 17, and "Reduction Sentences and Disposition Concepts," in P. A. Schilpp (ed.), *The Philosophy of Rudolf Carnap*, forthcoming. See also similar comments by Hempel, in "The Concept of Cognitive Significance: A Reconsideration" (*American Academy of Arts and Sciences*, July 1951; and "A Logical Appraisal of Operationism" (*Scientific Monthly*, October 1954).

[31] See A. W. Burks, "The Logic of Causal Propositions," *Mind*, July 1951, for an axiomatic definition of causal implication.

[32] In "On the Presuppositions of Induction," *Review of Metaphysics*, June 1955, A. W. Burks formulates a "uniformity" axiom to the effect that a universal causal implication is logically equivalent to any substitution instance of itself; or, equivalently, that any two substitution instances of a universal causal implication are equivalent. This is another way of characterizing causal implication, since obviously "$Fa \supset Ga$" does not entail "$(x)(Fx \supset Gx)$".

[33] Cf. A. W. Burks, "Dispositional Statements," *Philosophy of Science*, July 1955. The same non-extensional analysis has been proposed by W. Sellars, in the course of discussions held at the Minnesota Center for Philosophy of Science.

[34] For this reason I am not impressed by the defeatist argument presented by Jan Berg in "On Defining Disposition Predicates," *Analysis*, March 1955.

[35] It should be noted that my discussion is here restricted to what may be called "causal" dispositions, in contradistinction to what may be called "probabilistic" dispositions.

[36] By a time-independent property I here mean a property which a thing has either all the time or never at all. This usage should be distinguished from the usage in which a time-independent property is a property P such that sentences of the form "x has P at time t" are meaningless (thus Carnap argues in "Truth and Confirmation," *op. cit.*, that "true" is time-independent in this sense). To say of a disposition that it is time-independent in the former sense is to assert an empirical law, as explained on p. 198.

[37] The schema for time-dependent dispositions, like "electrically charged", "elastic", "kindly disposed toward X", is analogous except that all predicate constants and predicate variables carry the time variable as second argument.

[38] "The Logic of Causal Propositions," *op. cit.*, p. 364.

[39] *Scientific Explanation*, *op. cit.*, p. 296.

[40] Following Burks, I shall here assume for the sake of simplicity that what is called the "cause" is a sufficient condition. It is well known that the events which are

actually identified as "causes," both in everyday life and in science, are not strictly sufficient conditions for their alleged effects. For a detailed discussion of problems created by this circumstance for an adequate formulation of an analysis of causal judgments in terms of "constant conjunction," see my article "Philosophical Analysis, Translation Schemas and the Regularity Theory of Causation," *op. cit.*, or my book *Analytische Erkenntnistheorie*, loc. cit.

[41] If we want to express the idea that cause and effect are successive states of the same thing, as in the above example, a more complicated symbolism is needed. But this would not affect the question at issue.

[42] *System of Logic*, Book III, Chapter V, section 6.

[43] C' may be a negative condition, in which case it would be more natural to speak of the necessary absence of a specified condition. For example, in order for the day-night-day sequence to continue it is necessary that no opaque body interpose itself between sun and earth in such a way that no sunlight could reach any part of the earth's surface at any time.

[44] The following consideration serves as a striking demonstration of the inadequacy of extensional logic for the definition of the concepts "sufficient condition" and "necessary condition" as used in everyday life and science. We often have occasion to say that a certain disjunction of conditions is a necessary condition for a given effect though neither condition by itself is necessary. Thus a college professor may announce to his class that in order to pass his course they must either write a passing term paper or pass a final examination, but that it is not necessary to write a passing term paper, nor is it necessary to pass a final examination. Now, the extensional definition of " 'q' expresses a necessary condition for 'p' " is $p \supset q$. Hence the professor's statement would take the form $(p \supset q \vee r) \cdot \sim(p \supset q) \cdot \sim(p \supset r)$. But since this conjunction entails $(p \cdot \sim q \cdot \sim r)$, which contradicts the first conjunct, it is self-contradictory!

[45] Cf. "On the Presuppositions of Induction," *Review of Metaphysics*, June 1955.

[46] This seems to be the view W. Kneale takes of laws of nature. As Kneale himself notes in *Probability and Induction* (Oxford: The Clarendon Press, 1949), p. 71, the view was held by Locke: though man cannot attain to certain knowledge of the laws of nature, as he can only generalize from instances, an angel who knew the "real essences" of natural kinds would see the same sort of necessary connection between causal antecedent and causal consequent as we see between "being a Euclidean triangle" and "being a triangle whose angle-sum equals 180°."

[47] Of course we may justifiably assert "Pa → Qa" even if no instance of P has ever been observed, on the evidence "Ra · Qa · Rb · Qb" etc., where P and R are similar properties (e.g., let Px = x is water subjected to a temperature exceeding 150°, and Rx = x is coffee subjected to a temperature exceeding 155° and Qx = x boils).

[48] In Burks' system the specified incompatibility, moreover, holds only if the antecedent is *physically* possible; accordingly there are paradoxes of causal implication analogous to the familiar paradoxes of material and strict implication. This additional proviso, however, has such queer consequences as that "if ice were denser than water, it would not float" and "if ice were denser than water, it would still float" are compatible.

Counterfactuals, Dispositions, and the Causal Modalities

Introduction

(i) Although the following essay attempts to deal in a connected way with a number of connected conceptual tangles, it is by no means monolithic in design. It divides roughly in two, with the first half (Parts I and II) devoted to certain puzzles which have their source in a misunderstanding of the more specific structure of the language in which we describe and explain natural phenomena; while the second half (Parts III and IV) attempts to resolve the more sweeping controversy over the nature of the connection between 'cause' and 'effect,' or, in modern dress, the logical status of 'lawlike statements.'

(ii) The essay begins with a case analysis of a puzzle, taken from recent philosophical literature, relating to the analysis of counterfactual conditionals, statements of the form "If that lump of salt had been put in water, it would have dissolved." The diagnosis of this puzzle, which occupies the whole of Part I, shows it to rest on a misunderstanding of the conceptual framework in terms of which we speak of what *things do* when *acted upon* in certain ways in certain kinds of *circumstance*. Although the puzzle is initially posed in terms of examples taken from everyday life, the logical features of these examples which, misunderstood, generate the puzzle, are to be found in even the more theoretical levels of the language of science, and the puzzle is as much at home in the one place as in the other. For the framework in which *things* of various *kinds* (e.g. matches, white rats) *behave* ('respond') in various ways (catch fire, leap at a door) when acted upon ('submitted to such and such stimuli') under given conditions (presence of oxygen, 24 hours of food deprivation) is far more basic than the distinctions between metrical and non-metrical concepts, molar and micro-things,

Wilfrid Sellars

observable and unobservable properties, empirical generalizations and theoretical assumptions, which seem, at first sight, to introduce such a gulf between pre-scientific and scientific discourse.

(iii) If Part I is primarily 'critical' in its orientation, calling attention in only the most general terms to the above mentioned logical features of the framework presupposed by counterfactuals such as "If that match had been scratched, it would have lighted," and subjunctive conditionals such as "If that piece of salt were put in water, it would dissolve," Part II attempts a constructive account which, though necessarily brief and schematic, highlights those features of this framework which seem to have caused the most trouble. Postponing for later treatment (Parts III and IV) the classical puzzle about the 'connection' between 'cause' and 'effect,' it explores the logic of expressions for *things*, for *kinds* of things, for the *causal properties* of things, as well as the distinction between *properties* and *states*. It offers an analysis of the relation between thing-kinds and the traits in terms of which we identify things as belonging to them which illuminates both the nature and, which is more important, the *limitations* of the explanations provided by generalizations of the form "Things of kind K behave thusly when such and such is done to them under such and such conditions." I have italicized the word "limitations" because it is, in my opinion, the considerations advanced at the end of Part II which provide the key to a correct interpretation of the role of theoretical explanations and the status of theoretical ('unobservable') entities.

(iv) The second half of the essay (Parts III and IV) is devoted to an attempt to disentangle and resolve the issues matted together in the centuries long debate between the 'constant conjunction' (or 'regularity') and the 'entailment' (or 'necessary connection') interpretations of 'causality.' Part III attempts a sympathetic reconstruction of the controversy in the form of a debate between a Mr. C (for Constant Conjunction) and a Mr. E (for Entailment) who develop and qualify their views in such a way as to bring them to the growing edge of the problem. Although it is primarily designed to pose the problem in a way which reflects the philosophical commitments and concerns of the participants in the great debate, Part III also develops some of the themes and distinctions which are put to use in the constructive analysis which follows in Part IV. In particular, it contains a brief discussion of the force of probability statements (section 60), an examination of

226

what it might mean to say that the world is 'in principle' describable without using either prescriptive or modal expressions (sections 79–80), and some remarks on the supposed 'metalinguistic' status of modal statements (sections 81–82).

(v) Of the fourth and final part of the essay I shall say only that it offers an account of lawlike statements and of the inductive reasoning by which we support them which shows, in my opinion, how the logical insights of Mr. E can be reconciled with the naturalistic, empiricist tradition defended (if in too narrow and oversimplified a form) by Mr. C.

I. Counterfactuals

1. In his important paper on counterfactual conditionals,* Nelson Goodman interprets his problem as that of "defining the circumstances under which a given counterfactual holds while the opposing counterfactual with the contradictory consequent fails to hold." † As examples of such opposing counterfactuals, he gives "If that piece of butter had been heated to 150 F, it would have melted," and "If that piece of butter had been heated to 150 F, it would not have melted."

2. After a quick survey of some varieties of counterfactual and related statements, he finds that "a counterfactual is true if a certain connection obtains between the antecedent and the consequent," ‡ and turns to the task of explaining this connection. He points out, to begin with, that "the consequent [of a counterfactual] seldom follows from the antecedent by logic alone," § and never in the case of the empirical counterfactuals with which he is primarily concerned. Nor, in the case of the latter, does the consequent follow from the antecedent alone by virtue of a law of nature. For "the assertion that a connection holds is made on the presumption that certain circumstances not stated in the antecedent obtain."

When we say

If that match had been scratched, it would have lighted, we mean that the conditions are such—i.e., the match is well made, is dry enough,

---

* Nelson Goodman, "The Problem of Counterfactual Conditionals," *Journal of Philosophy*, 44:113–28 (1947); reprinted in his book, *Fact, Fiction and Forecast* (Cambridge, Mass.: Harvard Univ. Press, 1955), pp. 13–34. Page references in the following are to *Fact, Fiction and Forecast*.
† *Op. cit.*, p. 14.
‡ *Ibid.*, p. 16.
§ *Ibid.*, p. 16.

oxygen enough is present, etc.—that "That match lights" can be inferred from "That match is scratched." Thus the connection we affirm may be regarded as joining the consequent with the conjunction of the antecedent and other statements that truly describe the relevant conditions. Notice especially that our assertion of the counterfactual is *not* conditioned upon these circumstances obtaining. We do not assert that the counterfactual is true if the circumstances obtain; rather, in asserting the counterfactual we commit ourselves to the actual truth of the statements describing the requisite relevant conditions. (p. 17)

"There are," he concludes, "two major problems, though they are not independent and may even be regarded as aspects of a single problem . . . The first . . . is to define relevant conditions: to specify what sentences are meant to be taken in conjunction with the antecedent as a basis for inferring the consequent." * The second is to define what is meant by a law of nature. For

even after the particular relevant conditions are specified, the connection obtaining will not ordinarily be a logical one. The principle that permits inference of

>That match lights

from

>That match is scratched. That match is dry enough.
>Enough oxygen is present. Etc.

is not a law of logic but what we call a natural or physical or causal law. (p. 17)

3. Goodman first takes up the problem of relevant conditions. He has implied, in the passages just quoted, that whenever we assert a counterfactual, we have in mind a *specific* set of relevant conditions, those conditions, indeed, which the relevant law of nature requires to obtain in order that we may infer "That match lights" from "That match is scratched." Instead, however, of focusing attention on these *specific* conditions, and exploring their bearing on the truth or falsity of the counterfactual, Goodman begins from scratch. Thus he writes,

It might seem natural to propose that the consequent follows by law from the antecedent and a description of the actual state-of-affairs of the world, that we need hardly define relevant conditions because it will do no harm to include irrelevant ones. (pp. 17–18)

points out that

if we say that the statement follows by law from the antecedent and

---

* *Ibid.*, pp. 16–17, *passim.*

all true statements, we encounter an immediate difficulty: among true sentences is the negate of the antecedent, so that from the antecedent and all true sentences everything follows. Certainly this gives us no way of distinguishing true from false counterfactuals. (p. 18)

and embarks on the task of so narrowing the class of true auxiliary sentences that we can account for this difference. A compact but lucid argument, in which he introduces a series of restrictions on the membership of this class, leads him to the following tentative rule:

. . . a counterfactual is true if and only if there is some set S of true sentences such that S is compatible with C [the consequent of the counterfactual in question] and with ∼C [the contradictory consequent], and such that A · S is self-compatible [A being the antecedent] and leads by law to C; while there is no set S′ compatible with C and with ∼C, and such that A · S′ is self-compatible and leads by law to ∼C. (p. 21)

4. It is at this point that Goodman explodes his bomb.

The requirement that A · S be self-compatible is not strong enough; for S might comprise true sentences that although *compatible with A,* were such that *they would not be true if A were true.* For this reason, many statements that we would regard as definitely false would be true according to the stated criterion. As an example, consider the familiar case where for a given match M, we would affirm

(i) If match M had been scratched, it would have lighted,
but deny

(ii) If match M had been scratched, it would not have been dry.
According to our tentative criterion, statement (ii) would be quite as true as statement (i). For in the case of (ii), we may take as an element in our S the true sentence

Match M did not light,
which is presumably compatible with A (otherwise nothing would be required along with A to reach the opposite as the consequent of the true counterfactual statement (i)). As our total A · S we may have

Match M is scratched. It does not light. It is well made.
Oxygen enough is present . . . etc.;
and from this, by means of a legitimate general law, we can infer

It was not dry.
And there would seem to be no suitable set of sentences S′ such that A · S′ leads by law to the negate of this consequent. Hence the unwanted counterfactual is established in accord with our rule.

"The trouble," Goodman continues, without pausing for breath,

is caused by including in our S a true statement which although compatible with A would not be true if A were. Accordingly we must exclude such statements from the set of relevant conditions; S, in addition to satisfying the other requirements already laid down, must be not merely compatible with A but 'jointly tenable' or *cotenable* with A. A is cotenable with S, and the conjunction A·S self-cotenable, if it is not the case that S would not be true if A were. (pp. 21–22)

5. This new requirement, however, instead of saving the rule leads it to immediate shipwreck.

. . . in order to determine whether or not a given S is cotenable with A, we have to determine whether or not the counterfactual "If A were true, then S would not be true" is itself true. But this means determining whether or not there is a suitable S_1, cotenable with A, that leads to ~S and so on. Thus we find ourselves involved in an infinite regressus or a circle; for cotenability is defined in terms of counterfactuals, yet the meaning of counterfactuals is defined in terms of cotenability. In other words, to establish any counterfactual, it seems that we first have to determine the truth of another. If so, we can never explain a counterfactual except in terms of others, so that the problem of counterfactuals must remain unsolved. (p. 23)

As of 1947, Goodman, "though unwilling to accept this conclusion, [did] not . . . see any way of meeting the difficulty." * That he still regards this difficulty as genuine, and the line of thought of which it is the culmination philosophically sound, is indicated by the fact that he has made "The Problem of Counterfactual Conditionals" the starting point of his recent re-examination † of the same nexus of problems. Indeed, Goodman explicitly tells us that the four chapters of which this new study consists, and of which the first is a reprinting of the 1947 paper, "represents a consecutive effort of thought on a closely integrated group of problems," ‡ and that this first chapter contains "an essentially unaltered description of the state of affairs from which the London lectures took their departure." §

6. It is my purpose in the opening sections of this essay, devoted as it is to fundamentally the same group of problems, to show that Goodman's puzzle about cotenability arises from a failure to appreciate the force of the verbal form of counterfactuals in actual discourse, and of

---

* *Ibid.*, p. 23.

† *Fact, Fiction and Forecast.* This book, of which the first part is a reprinting of the 1947 paper, contains the University of London Special Lectures in Philosophy for 1953.

‡ *Op. cit.*, p. 7.

§ *Ibid.*, p. 9.

the general statements by which we support them; and that this failure stems, as in so many other cases, from too hasty an assimilation of a problematic feature of ordinary discourse to a formalism by reference to which we have succeeded in illuminating certain other features.

7. Let me begin by asking whether it is indeed true that in "the familiar case where for a given match M, we would affirm

(i) If match M had been scratched, it would have lighted"

we would "deny

(ii) If match M had been scratched, it would not have been dry."

Goodman himself points out in a note that "Of course, some sentences similar to (ii), referring to other matches under special conditions may be true." * Perhaps he has something like the following case in mind:

Tom: If M had been scratched, it would have been wet.
Dick: Why:
Tom: Well, Harry is over there, and he has a phobia about matches. If he sees anyone scratch a match, he puts it in water.

But just how is Goodman's "familiar case" different from that of the above dialogue? Why are we so confident that (ii) is false whereas (i) is true? Part of the answer, at least, is that we are taking for granted in our reflections that the only features of the case which are relevant to the truth or falsity of (ii) are such things as that the match was dry, that it was not scratched, that it was well made, that sufficient oxygen was present, that it did not light, "etc." † and that the generalization to which appeal would properly be made in support of (ii) concerns only such things as being dry, being scratched, being well made, sufficient oxygen being present, lighting, etc. For as soon as we modify the case by supposing Tom to enter and tell us (a) that if M had been scratched, Harry would have found it out, and (b) that if Harry finds out that a match has been scratched, he puts it in water, the feeling that (ii) is obviously false disappears.

8. In asking us to consider this "familiar case," then, Goodman, whether he realizes it or not, is asking us to imagine ourselves in a

* *Ibid.*, p. 33 (note 7 to p. 21).

† Goodman's "etc." should not mislead us. Its scope, though vague, is limited by the context, and does not include, positively or negatively, every possible circumstance, e.g., the presence of a pyrophobe.

situation in which we are to choose between (i) and (ii) knowing (a) that only the above limited set of considerations are relevant; and (b) that scratching dry, well-made matches in the presence of oxygen, etc. causes them to light. It is, I take it, clear that if we did find ourselves in such a situation, we would indeed accept (i) and reject (ii).

To call attention to all this, however, is not yet to criticize Goodman's argument, though it does give us a better understanding of what is going on. Indeed, it might seem that since we have just admitted that once we are clear about the nature of the case on which we are being asked to reflect, we would, in the imagined circumstances, accept (i) but reject (ii), we are committed to agree with Goodman that the criterion under examination is at fault. For according to it would not (ii) be true?

9. It is not my purpose to defend Goodman's tentative criterion against his criticisms. There are a number of reasons why it won't do as it stands, as will become apparent as we explore the force of counterfactuals in their native habitat. I will, however, in a sense, be defending it against the specific objection raised by Goodman. For it is because he *misinterprets* the fact that we would accept (i) but reject (ii) that he is led to the idea that the criterion must be enriched with a disastrous requirement of cotenability. And once this fact is properly interpreted, it will become clear that while there is *something* to Goodman's idea that a sound criterion must include a requirement of cotenability, this requirement turns out to be quite harmless, to be quite free of regress or paradox.

10. But is it, on second thought, so obvious that even if we were in the circumstances described above, we would reject (ii)? After all, knowing that M didn't light, but was well made, that sufficient oxygen was present, etc. and knowing that M wasn't scratched but was dry, would we not be entitled to say,

> (iii) If it had been true that M was scratched, it would also have been true that M was not dry?

The fact that this looks as though it *might* be a long-winded version of (ii) gives us pause.

If, however, we are willing to consider the possibility that (ii) is after all true, the reasoning by which Goodman seeks to establish that if the tentative criterion were sound, (ii) as used in our "familiar case" would be true, becomes of greater interest. The core of this reasoning is the following sentence,

As our total A · S we may have

> Match M is scratched. It does not light. It is well made.
> Oxygen enough is present . . . etc.

and from this, by means of a legitimate general law, we can infer

> It was not dry. (pp. 21–22)

But although Goodman assures us that there is a "legitimate general law" which permits this inference, he does not take time to formulate it, and once we notice this, we also notice that he has nowhere taken time to formulate the "legitimate general law" which authorizes (i). The closest he comes to doing this is in the introductory section of the paper, where he writes,

When we say

> If that match had been scratched, it would have lighted

we mean that the conditions are such—i.e., the match is well made, is dry enough, oxygen enough is present, etc.—that "That match lights" can be inferred from "That match is scratched." (p. 17)

11. Now the idea behind the above sentence seems to be that the relevant law pertaining to matches has the form

> (x)(t) x is a match · x is dry at t · x is scratched at t · *implies* · x lights at t

(where, to simplify our formulations, the conditions under which matches light when scratched have been boiled down to being dry.) And it must indeed be admitted that if this were the "legitimate general law" which authorizes

> If M had been scratched, it would have lighted

given M *was dry* and M *was not scratched*, there would be reason to expect the *equivalent* "legitimate general law"

> (x)(t) x is a match · x does not light at t · x is scratched at t · *implies* · x is not dry at t

to authorize

> If M had been scratched, it would not have been dry

given M *did not light* and M *was not scratched*.

Or, to make the same point from a slightly different direction, if we were to persuade ourselves that the laws which stand behind true counterfactuals of the form,

If x had been . . . it would have - - -

are of the form,

$$(x)(t) \ A(x,t) \cdot B(x,t) \supset C(x,t)$$

we would, in all consistency, expect the equivalent laws

$$(x)(t) \ A(x,t) \cdot \sim C(x,t) \supset \sim B(x,t)$$
$$(x)(t) \ B(x,t) \cdot \sim C(x,t) \supset \sim A(x,t)$$

to authorize counterfactuals of the same form. And if we were to persuade ourselves that

[Given that M was dry, then, although M was not scratched,] if M had been scratched, it would have lighted

has the form

[Given that x was A at t, then, although x was not B at t,] if x had been B at t, x would have been C at t

we would expect the equivalent general laws to authorize such counterfactuals as

[Given that M did not light, then, although M was not scratched,] if M had been scratched, it would not have been dry

and

[Given that M did not light, then, although M was not dry,] if M had been dry, it would not have been scratched.

12. But as soon as we take a good look at these counterfactuals, we see that something is wrong. For in spite of the fact that "M was not dry" can be inferred from "M was scratched" together with "M did not light," we most certainly would not agree that—given *M did not light* and *M was not scratched*—

If M had been scratched, it would not have been dry.

What is wrong? One line of thought, the line which leads to cotenability takes Goodman's "familiar case" as its paradigm and, after pointing out that we are clearly entitled to say

(1) [Since M was dry,] if M had been scratched, it would have lighted

234

but not

(2) [Since M did not light,] if M had been scratched, it would not be dry,

continues somewhat as follows:

(1) is true
(2) is false
According to (1) M would have lighted if it had been scratched. But (2) presupposes that M did not light.
Thus (1) being true, a presupposition of (2) would not have been true if M had been scratched.
So, (1) being true, a presupposition of (2) would not have been true if its 'antecedent' had been true.
Consequently, (1) being true, the truth of (2) is incompatible with the truth of its 'antecedent'—surely a terrible thing to say about any conditional, even a counterfactual one . . .

and concludes, (A) that the falsity of (2) follows from the truth of (1); (B) in knowing that (1) itself is true we must be knowing that there is no true counterfactual according to which a presupposition of (1) would not have been true if *its* [the new counterfactual's] antecedent had been true; and, in general (C) that in order to know whether any counterfactual, Γ, is true we need to know that there is no true counterfactual, Γ', which specifies that the S required by Γ' would not have been the case if Γ's antecedent had been true. In Goodman's words, ". . . in order to determine whether or not a given S is cotenable with A, we have to determine whether or not the counterfactual 'If A were true, then S would not be true' is itself true. But this means determining whether or not there is a suitable S_1, cotenable with A, that leads to $\sim$S and so on. Thus we find ourselves involved in a regressus or a circle . . ."

13. Now there are, to say the least, some highly dubious steps in the reasoning delineated above. I do not, however, propose to examine it, but rather to undercut it by correctly locating the elements of truth it contains. That there is *something* to the above reasoning is clear. The truth of (1) *does* seem to be incompatible with the truth of (2); and the falsity of (2) *does* seem to rest on the fact that if M had been scratched, it would have lighted.

Perhaps the best way of separating out the sound core of the above reasoning is to note what happens if, instead of exploring the logical relationship between the two counterfactuals (1) and (2), we turn our attention instead to corresponding subjunctive conditionals not contrary to fact in a new "familiar case" which differs from Goodman's in that these subjunctive conditionals rather than counterfactuals are appropriate. Specifically, I want to consider the "mixed" subjunctive conditionals,

> (1') If M is dry, then if M were scratched, it would light,

and

> (2') If M does not light, then if M were scratched, it would not be dry.

Is it not clear as in Goodman's case that (1') is true but (2') false? Indeed, that the falsity of (2') is a consequence of the truth of (1')? Here, however, there is no temptation to say that (2') is false for the reason that in order for it to be true a state of affairs would have to obtain which would not obtain if M were scratched. For (2'), unlike (2) does not require as a necessary condition of its truth that M does not light.

14. How, then, is the incompatibility of (2') with (1') to be understood? The answer is really very simple, and to get it, it is only necessary to ask 'Why would we reject (2')?' For to this question the answer is simply that it is just not the case that by scratching dry matches we cause them, provided they do not light, to become wet. And how do we know this? Part of the answer, of course, is the absence of favorable evidence for this generalization; not to say the existence of substantial evidence against it. But more directly relevant to our *philosophical* puzzle is the fact that in our "familiar case" we are granted to know that scratching dry matches causes them to light. And if this generalization is true—and it must be remembered that we are using "x is dry" to stand for "x is dry and x is well made, and sufficient oxygen is present, etc."—then the other generalization *can't* be true. The two generalizations are, in a very simple sense, incompatible. For if scratching dry matches causes them to light, then the expression 'scratching dry matches *which do not light*' describes a kind of situation which cannot (physically) obtain. And we begin to suspect that Goodman's requirement of cotenability mislocates the sound idea that (to use a notation which, whatever its shortcomings in other respects, is adequate for the purpose of making *this* point) if it is a law that

$$(x) \, Ax \cdot Sx \cdot \supset \cdot Cx$$

then it can't—*logically* can't—be a law that

$$(x) \, Ax \supset \sim Sx$$

15. But we have not yet pinpointed Goodman's mistake. To do so we must take a closer look at our reasons for rejecting (2'). We said above that we would reject it simply because it is not the case that by scratching dry matches we cause them to become wet. Perhaps the best way of beginning our finer grained analysis is by making a point about our two subjunctive conditionals (1') and (2') which parallels a point which was made earlier about counterfactuals (1) and (2).

Suppose that the "legitimate general law" which authorizes (1') had the form

$$(x)(t) \, A(x,t) \cdot S(x,t) \cdot \supset \cdot C(x,t);$$

would not (2') be authorized by

$$(x)(t) \, A(x,t) \cdot \sim C(x,t) \cdot \supset \cdot \sim S(x,t)?$$

and hence—in view of the logical equivalence of these two general implications—be true if (1') is true? Clearly we must do some thinking about the form of the "legitimate general laws" which authorize subjunctive conditionals of the form

if x were . . . it would - - -

and which stand behind contrary-to-fact conditionals of the form

if x had been . . . it would have - - -.

This thinking will consist, essentially, in paying strict attention to the characteristics of subjunctive conditionals, counterfactuals and lawlike statements in their native habitat, rather than to their supposed counterparts in PMese.

16. We pointed out above that if we were asked why we would reject (2') in the context in which it arose, we would say that it is not the case that scratching dry matches causes them to become wet, if they don't light. We now note that if (1') were challenged we would support it by saying that scratching dry matches does cause them to light, or that matches light when scratched, provided they are dry, or, perhaps, that if a dry match is scratched it will light, or something of the sort. Is it proper to represent these statements by the form

$$(x)(t) \, F(x,t) \cdot G(x,t) \cdot \supset \cdot H(x,t)?$$

If we leave aside for the moment the fact that there is something odd about the expression "x is a match at t," and focus our attention on the other concepts involved, it does not take much logical imagination to see that while 'there is no law against' representing "x is scratched at t" by "$Sc(x,t)$", "x is dry at t" by "$D(x,t)$", and "x lights at t" by "$L(x,t)$", to do so is to obscure rather than make manifest the logical form of "If a dry match is scratched, it lights." For it is by no means irrelevant to the logic of this generalization that matches *begin to burn* when they are scratched. And it is a familiar fact that

As B when Ded—provided the circumstance, C, are propitious,

concerns something *new* that A's *begin to do* when *changed* in a certain respect in certain *standing conditions*—which need not, of course, be 'standing still.'

17. I do not, by any means, wish to suggest that all empirical generalizations are of the above form. Clearly,

Eggs stay fresh longer if they are not washed,

which authorizes the counterfactual

If this egg had not been washed, it would have stayed fresh longer,

is not of this form. But our problem, after all, is that of understanding just why it is clear that—in Goodman's "familiar case"—we would affirm

(i) If M had been scratched, it would have lighted

but reject

(ii) If M had been scratched, it would not have been dry,

and to do this we must get the hang of generalizations of the former kind.

18. Now, *being dry* is obviously not the same thing as *becoming dry*, nor *beginning to burn* as *burning*, and though we can imagine that someone might say "matches burn when scratched," this would, strictly speaking, be either incorrect or false—incorrect if it was intended to express the familiar truth about matches; false if it was intended to express the idea that matches burn when they are *being scratched* as iron rusts while exposed to moisture. (Having made this point, I can now rephrase it by saying that if it were correct to use "matches burn when scratched" in the former sense, this would simply mean that "burn" has an *idiomatic* use in which it is equivalent to "begin to burn".)

With this in mind, let us examine the apodosis of Goodman's (ii), namely, ". . . it (M) would not have been dry." If we suppose that this is intended to have the force of "would have *become wet*", we can, indeed, assimilate

If M had been scratched, it would not have been dry

to the form

If x had been *Ded*, it would have *Bed*

of which (i) is such a straightforward example. For *becoming wet* would seem to be a legitimate example of *B-ing*.

But while there are true generalizations to the effect that doing certain things to matches in certain favorable circumstances causes them to become wet, none of them seem to involve scratching. Again, a match which *becomes wet* must have *been dry*, and approaching Goodman's "familiar case"—as we do—in the knowledge that scratching dry (etc.) matches causes them to light, we cannot consistently say both

> [Since M was dry, etc.,] if M had been scratched, it would have lighted

and

> [Since M was dry, etc.,] if M had been scratched, it would have become wet

unless we suppose that the circumstances in which scratching dry matches causes them to become wet (the *etc.* of the second 'since-' clause) differs in at least one respect from the circumstances in which scratching dry matches causes them to light (the *etc.* of the first 'since-' clause). And it is clearly no help—in the absence of this supposition—to add to the second counterfactual the proviso, "provided M does not light"; for this proviso, given the truth of the first counterfactual, is physically inconsistent with the conjunction of the antecedent of the second counterfactual with the 'since-' clause on which it rests.

19. If, therefore, we interpret ". . . it (M) would not have been dry" as ". . . it (M) would have become wet," we run up against the fact that a generalization is implied which is not only patently false, but *inconsistent*—given the stipulations of the case—with one which we know to be true. And this is, as we have already noted, the sound core of Goodman's cotenability requirement. Two counterfactuals cannot both be true if they imply logically inconsistent generalizations. If one counterfactual is true, no counterfactual which involves an ante-

cedent-cum-circumstances which is specified to be physically self-incompatible by the generalization implied by the first counterfactual can *also* be true. On the other hand, cotenability *thus understood* leads to no "infinite regressus or . . . circle," for while one has not confirmed a generalization *unless* one has *disconfirmed* logically incompatible generalizations, this does not mean that *before* establishing one thing one must *first* establish something else, *and so on.* For the process of confirming a generalization *is* the process of disconfirming logically incompatible generalizations.

20. Suppose, however—as is indeed obvious—that we are not to interpret ". . . would not have been dry" as ". . . would have become wet"; does another interpretation of (ii) lie within groping distance? The answer is Yes—but, as before, on condition that we are prepared to make certain changes in its wording. Let us begin this groping with an examination of—not (ii) but—the closely related counterfactual,

If M had been scratched without lighting, then it . . .

then it *what?* Should we say ". . . *would* not have been dry"? or ". . . *could* not have been dry"? Clearly the latter. The difference, in this context, between 'w' and 'c' is all important. It is the difference between

(A) Matches *will not* be (stay) dry, if they are scratched without lighting

and

(B) Matches *cannot* be dry, if they do not light when scratched.

(A) introduces, as we have seen, a new generalization into our "familiar case"—one which is inconsistent with

(C) Matches *will* light when scratched, provided they are dry,

which is the generalization implied by (i). (B), on the other hand, far from being inconsistent with (C) would seem to be just another version of it.

And it is clear, on reflection, that (C) is the only 'will-' statement which expresses the fact that scratching dry matches causes them to light. Thus, we can say that

A dry match will light when scratched

but not

A match which does not light when scratched *will* not be dry.

To be sure, we can say—with a little license—

> A match which does not light when scratched will be found not to be dry

so that the above claim is not quite true. But the point being made is clear enough, and, in any case, we shall be examining the 'exception' in a moment.

21. We begin, therefore, to suspect that corresponding to generalizations of the form

> Bing As causes them to D—provided C

there is only one correctly formed counterfactual of the form "If x had been Yed it would have . . . " namely

> [Since C,] if this A had been Bed, it would have Ded

which is not to say that each such generalization might not authorize a number of counterfactuals having a different form. Beating about the bushes for other asymmetries pertaining to our familiar generalization about matches, we notice that while it tells us that scratching matches causes them to light, it doesn't tell us the cause of matches not being dry; and that while it enables us to explain the fact that a match lighted on a certain occasion by pointing out that it was scratched and was dry, it doesn't enable us to explain the fact that a match was not dry by pointing out that it was scratched without lighting.

On the other hand, the generalization does enable us to explain how we know that a given match was not dry. "I know that it wasn't dry, because it didn't light when scratched." "M can't have been dry, because it was scratched, but did not light." "Since M was scratched, but did not light, it can't have been dry." "M was scratched without lighting, so it wasn't dry." All these point to the hypothetical

> (M was scratched without lighting) implies (M was not dry),

and, indeed, to the general hypothetical

> The fact that a match is scratched without lighting implies that it was not dry.

22. I have already pointed out how misleading it is to characterize the "legitimate general law" which authorizes the counterfactual

> If M had been scratched, it would have lighted

241

as a "principle which permits the inference of

>That match lights

from

>That match is scratched. That match is well made. Enough oxygen is present. Etc." *

For the fact that if there is a principle which authorizes the inference of S_3 from $S_1 \cdot S_2$, there will also be a principle which authorizes the inference of $\sim S_2$ from $S_1 \cdot \sim S_3$ leads one to expect that the same general fact about matches which, in Goodman's "familiar case," supports the above counterfactual, will also support

>If M had been scratched, it would not have been dry,

an expectation which is the ultimate source of the puzzlement exploited by Goodman's paper.

23. This is not to say that it is *wrong* to interpret our generalization about matches as a "season inference ticket." It is rather that the connection between the generalization and the counterfactual, "If M had been scratched, it would have lighted," rests on features of the generalization which are not captured by the concept of a season inference ticket, and which, therefore, the logical form of a general hypothetical does not illuminate. Thus, while

>(m)(t) m is scratched at t · m is dry at t · *implies* · m lights at t †

does, *in a sense*, have the force of "dry matches light if scratched," or "scratching dry matches causes them to light," this mode of representation must be supplemented by a commentary along the lines of the above analysis, if its relation to "If M had been scratched, it would have lighted" is to be understood; while if our familiar fact about matches is assimilated without further ado to the form

$$(x)(t) A(x,t) \cdot B(x,t) \cdot C(x,t) \ldots \cdot \supset \cdot L(x,t)$$

all chance of clarity has been lost.

24. We have connected the fact that scratching a match is *doing* something to it, with the fact that we expect

>. . . if M had been scratched . . .

---

* *Fact, Fiction and Forecast*, p. 17.

† I have used the so-called 'tenseless present'—a typical philosophical invention—to simplify the formulation of this general hypothetical, without, in this context, doing it too much violence.

to be preceded, at least tacitly, by an expression referring to *standing conditions*, thus

[Since M was dry,] . . .

and to be followed by an expression referring to a *result*, thus

. . . it would have lighted.

It is important to bear in mind that the distinction between the *standing conditions*, the *doing* and the *result* is an *objective* one. It is not relative to a particular way of formulating the general fact that dry matches light when scratched. The equivalent formulas

$$(x)(t) \ D(x,t) \supset \cdot Sc(x,t) \supset L(x,t)$$
$$(x)(t) \sim L(x,t) \supset \cdot Sc(x,t) \supset \sim D(x,t)$$
$$(x)(t) \sim L(x,t) \supset \cdot D(x,t) \supset \sim Sc(x,t)$$

do *not* give us three different ways of cutting up the above fact about matches into a standing condition, a doing and a result or *consequence*; although, in a purely logical sense, "$\sim L(x,t)$" may be said to formulate a 'condition' under which "$(x)(t) \ Sc(x,t) \supset \sim D(x,t)$" holds, and "$Sc(x,t)$" and "$\sim D(x,t)$" respectively to be the 'antecedent' and the 'consequent' of this implication.

The fact that "$D(x,t)$" formulates a 'condition' in a sense in which "$\sim L(x,t)$" does not, is, though obvious, the key to our problem. For it is just because "If M were scratched . . ." and "If M had been scratched . . ." are expressions for somethings being done to something (in a certain kind of circumstance) that we expect them to be followed, not just by a 'consequent,' but by (expressions for) a consequence, and also expect the context to make it clear just what conditions or circumstances are being implied to obtain. There is, however, a manner of formulating this same content which does not evoke these expectations, and which *does* focus attention on specifically logical relationships. Consider, for example, the following conditionals,

> If it were the case that M was scratched without lighting, it would be the case that M was not dry.
> If it had been the case that M was scratched without lighting, it would have been the case that M was not dry.

Clearly, to wonder what else would have to be the case, if it were the case that M was scratched without lighting, is not the same thing as to wonder what the *consequence* of striking a match would be, given that it failed to light.

Does this mean that in our familiar case, we would accept

> If it had been the case that M was scratched, it would have been the case that M was not dry (or would not have been the case that M was dry)

although we reject

> If M had been scratched, it would not have been dry?

The answer is *almost* Yes. We are getting 'warmer,' though there is still work to be done. I shall introduce the next step by discussing examples of quite another sort.

25. Consider the following (where n is a number, perhaps the number of planets):

> (1) If n were divisible by 3 and by 4, it would be divisible by 12
> (2) If n were divisible by 3, then if n were divisible by 4, it would be divisible by 12
> (3) Since n is divisible by 3, if n were divisible by 4, it would be divisible by 12
> (4) Since n is divisible by 3, if n had been divisible by 4, it would have been divisible by 12

and then the following (where n is, say, the number of chess pieces on a side):

> (5) If n were not divisible by 12, but divisible by 3, it would not be divisible by 4
> (6) If n were not divisible by 12, then if n were divisible by 3, it would not be divisible by 4
> (7) Since n is not divisible by 12, if n were divisible by 3, it would not be divisible by 4
> (8) Since n is not divisible by 12, if n had been divisible by 2, it would not have been divisible by 4.

The crucial step, in each series, is from the first to the second, i.e. from (1) to (2), and from (5) to (6). (1) and (5) are clearly true. What of the others? What, to begin with, shall we say about (2)? The point is a delicate one. At first glance, it looks quite acceptable, a sound inference ticket. But would we not, perhaps, be a bit happier if it read

> (2') If n were divisible by 3, then if it were *also* divisible by 4, it would be divisible by 12?

What of (3)? It calls attention to the argument,

> n is divisible by 3
> So, if n were divisible by 4, it would be divisible by 12.

(Call the conclusion of this argument C_1.) The principle of the argument is the complex hypothetical (2). And the question arises, How does this argument differ from one that would be authorized by (1)? Consider the argument

> n is divisible by 3
> So, if it were *also* divisible by 4, it would be divisible by 12.

There is clearly a sense in which the conclusion of this argument (call it C_2) is more cautious than that of the preceding argument. For C_2 carries with it a reference to, and a commitment to the truth of, its premise, which is lacking in C_1. The difference can be put by noting that while C_1, as a conclusion, may imply that one has *come to know that* 'n is divisible by 12' can be inferred from 'n is divisible by 4' *by virtue of knowing that* n is divisible by 3; it does not imply that what one has come to know is {that 'n is divisible by 12' can be inferred from 'n is divisible by 4' *given that n is divisible by 3*}. And by not implying this, indeed by implying that what one has come to know is that 'n is divisible by 12' can *without qualification* be inferred from 'n is divisible by 4,' it is false. To infer from p the legitimacy of the inference *from q to r*, is not the same thing at all as to infer from p the legitimacy of the inference *from q to r, given p*.

26. In the symbolism of modal logic, there is all the difference in the world between '$p \cdot q \cdot < \cdot r$' and '$p < (q < r)$' even though the corresponding formulas in the system of material implication are equivalent. The former authorizes the argument

> I. p
> So, $q \supset r$

but not, as does the latter

> II. p
> So, $q < r$

And while argument II defends the subjunctive conditional

> If q were the case, r would be the case

argument I does not. The only resembling subjunctive conditional defended by the assertion *that p*, and an appeal to '$p \cdot q \cdot < \cdot r$' is

> If q were the case as *well as p*, r would be the case

245

and while this latter carries with it the assertion *that* p, it does not do so in the same way as does

> [Since p is the case,] if q were the case, r would be the case.

For this points to argument II with its stronger conclusion.

27. Turning back to our two lists of conditional statements about numbers, we can now see that the counterfactual corresponding to (1) is not (4), but rather

> (4') Since n is divisible by 3, if it had *also* been divisible by 4, it would have been divisible by 12

On the other hand, (4) does correspond to (2). Again, (6) has the same force as (5) only if it is interpreted as

> (6') If n were not divisible by 12, then if it were *also* the case that it *was* divisible by 3, it would not be divisible by 4.

and (5) authorizes (8) only if it is interpreted as

> (8') Since n is not divisible by 12, if it had *also* been the case that it *was* divisible by 3, it would not have been divisible by 4.

28. It is worth noting, in this connection, that it is not only in cases like our match example, where we are dealing with particular matters of fact, that a generalization may enable us to explain *how we know* a fact, without enabling us to explain the fact itself. Thus, while

> If n is divisible by 3 and 4, it is divisible by 12

enables us to explain the fact that a certain number is divisible by 12 ("It is divisible by 12 because it is divisible by 3 and by 4."), it does not enable us to explain the fact that a certain number is not divisible by 4, though it does enable us to explain how we happen to know that the number is not divisible by 4. ("I know that it is not divisible by 4, because though it is divisible by 3, it is not divisible by 12." "He knows that it is not divisible by 4, because he knows that though it is divisible by 3, it is not divisible by 12." "It can't be divisible by 4, because, though it is divisible by 3, it is not divisible by 12.") It would simply be a mistake to say, "It is not divisible by 4, because, though divisible by 3, it is not divisible by 12."

One is tempted to put this by saying that just as one explains a particular matter of empirical fact by 'showing how it comes about,' and not, simply, by subsuming it under the 'consequent' of a general hypothetical, the 'antecedent' of which it is known to satisfy, so one explains such a fact as that a certain number is divisible by 12, or not divisible by 4, not simply by subsuming it under the 'consequent' of any old mathematical truth under the 'consequent' of which it can be subsumed, but only by applying a mathematical truth which, so to speak, takes us in the direction of the 'genesis' of the property in question in the mathematical order, i.e. which starts us down (or up?) the path of what, in a neatly formalized system, would be its 'definition chain.' Certainly "n is divisible by 12, because it is divisible by 3 and by 4" has something of this flavor, while "n is not divisible by 4, because, though divisible by 3, it is not divisible by 12" does not. But to say anything worthwhile on this topic, one would have to say a great deal more than there is space for on this occasion.

29. Now the moral of these mathematical examples is that the counterfactual most resembling Goodman's (ii) which *is* authorized by our (simplified) generalization about matches, is, explicitly formulated,

> (ii′) *Since M did not light*, if it had *also* been the case that it was scratched, it would have been the case that it was not dry,

and it would be correct to boil this counterfactual down to

> If it had been the case that M was scratched, it would have been the case that M was not dry

only if the context makes it clear that there is a tacit *also* in the statement, and indicates in what direction the additional presupposition is to be found.

Why, then, it may be asked, should we not conclude that (i) itself is simply a shorter version, appropriately used in certain contexts, of

> (i′) *Since M was dry*, if it had *also* been the case that M was scratched, it would have been the case that M lighted?

(Clearly it is not a shorter version of

> Since M was dry, if it had *also* been scratched . . .

for *this* would imply that something else must be *done* to the match besides scratching it, to make it light.)

The answer should, by now, be obvious. It is part of the logic of generalizations of the form

> Xing Y's causes them to Z, provided . . .

247

that when we say

If *this* Y had been Xed, it would have Zed,

it is understood that it is because *this* Y was in certain (in principle) specifiable circumstances that it would have Zed if it had been Xed. In other words, the fact that it is proper to say, simply

If M had been scratched, it would have lighted

rests on the relation of the statement to the *objective* distinction between *standing conditions*, what is *done* and its *result*.

30. If, however, the framework of our discussion has been adequate for the purpose of dispelling the specific perplexities generated by Goodman's formulation of his first problem, we must, before we turn our attention to his second problem, namely, that of the 'connection' between the antecedent and the consequent of a law of nature construed as a general hypothetical, build this framework into some sort of overall constructive account of the logical form of what, for the time being, we shall lump together as 'causal generalizations in actual usage.'

II. Thing-Kinds and Causal Properties

31. I shall begin this constructive account of causal generalizations with some remarks which grow quite naturally out of the first part of this essay. Suppose we have reason to believe that

Φ-ing Ks (in circumstances C) causes them to ψ

(where K is a kind of thing—e.g., match). Then we have reason to believe of a particular thing of kind K, call it x_1, which is in C, that

x_1 would ψ, if it were Φ-ed.

And if it were Φ-ed and did ψ, and we were asked "Why did it ψ?" we would answer, "Because it was Φ-ed"; and if we were then asked, "Why did it ψ when Φ-ed?" we would answer "Because it is a K." If it were then pointed out that Ks don't always Φ when ψ-ed, we should counter with "They do if they are in C, as this one was."

31. Now, there is clearly a close connection between

x_1 is (water-) soluble

and

If x_1 were put in water, it would dissolve.

So much so, that it is tempting to claim, at least as a first approximation, that statements of these two forms have the same sense. I believe that this claim, or something like it, would stand up under examination—indeed, that the prima facie case in its favor is so strong that to defend it is simply to weed away misunderstandings. Unfortunately, "simply" to weed away misunderstandings is not a simple job. For most of them spring from misguided efforts to fit causal discourse into an overly austere, indeed procrustean, empiricism. And it will not be until the conclusion of the fourth and final section of this essay—in which I shall attempt to clarify certain fundamental issues pertaining to scientific inference—that we will, I believe, be in a position to accept the 'obvious' with good philosophical conscience.

32. Perhaps the simplest way to come to grips with puzzles about causal properties is to represent the analysis of concepts like '(water-) soluble' by the schema

$$D(x,t) =_{Df} \Phi(x,t) \text{ implies } \psi(x,t)$$

(where '$\Phi(x,t)$' and '$\psi(x,t)$' are informally construed as the counterparts, respectively, of 'x is scratched at t' and 'x lights at t') and then ask "What is the force of the term 'implies' in this context?" For this question calls attention to the fact that to attribute a property of the sort we are considering to an object is to be prepared *in that context* to infer 'it ψs' from 'it is Φ-ed.' And if the phrase "in that context" poses, in a sense, our original problem all over again, there may be some gain in the reformulation.

Now, any answer to this question must account for the fact that we think of *being Φ-ed* as the cause of ψ-*ing*. The pellet of salt dissolves *because* it is put in water, just as, in our earlier example, the match lights *because* it is scratched. This suggests that to attribute to an object a 'disposition' of which the 'antecedent' is *being Φ-ed* and the 'consequent' ψ-*ing*, is to commit oneself to the idea that there is a general causal fact, a law, shall we say, which relates *being Φ-ed* to ψ-*ing*.

On the other hand, it is perfectly clear that this law is not to the effect that Φ-*ing* anything causes it to ψ, i.e. that

$$(x)(t) \ \Phi(x,t) \text{ implies } \psi(x,t)$$

For when we say of a piece of salt that it is soluble, we are certainly not committing ourselves to the idea that everything, e.g. a stone, dissolves in water. And, indeed, the argument of the first part of this essay has made it clear that if, when we attribute a 'disposition' to an object, we are committing ourselves to the existence of a general fact involving ψ-ing and being Φ-ed, this general fact has the form Φ-ing Ks (in C) causes them to ψ.

And reflection on the fact that when we attribute a 'disposition' to an object we think of being Φ-ed as the cause of ψ-ing calls attention to the fact that words like "dissolves", "ignites", etc. are words for *results*. To say of something that it has *dissolved* is to say more than that, having been placed in water, it has disintegrated and disappeared, but is recoverable, say, by evaporation. It is to imply that it has disintegrated *because* it was placed in water. It is no accident that alongside such a word as "soluble" we find the word "dissolves". And this, in turn, suggests that it is no accident that alongside such a word as "soluble" there is the fact that we know such general truths as that *salt dissolves in water*.

33. Let us, therefore, work for the time being with the idea that when we ascribe a 'disposition' to a thing, we are committing ourselves to the idea that there is a general fact of the form

> Whenever and wherever a thing of kind K is Φ-ed (in favorable circumstances) it ψs.

And let us limit our discussion to those cases in which the things referred to are correctly classified by a thing-kind word in actual usage, and in which the causal properties in question are similarly enshrined in discourse. In other words, let us examine the logic of 'disposition terms' in a framework which abstracts from the fact, so annoying to logicians, that human discourse is discourse for *finding things out* as well as for expressing, in textbook style, what we already know.

34. Let us suppose, then, that to ascribe the causal property $D(x,t)$ to x_1 now, where (it is also supposed that)

$$D(x,t) =_{Df} \Phi(x,t) \text{ implies } \psi(x,t)$$

is to commit oneself to the idea that x_1 belongs to a kind of thing, K, and is in a kind of circumstance, C, such that if one knew which kind was K, and which kind was C, one would be in a position to reason

> x_1 is K, and is in C
> So, if it were also the case that $\Phi(x_1, \text{now})$, it would be the case that $\psi(x_1, \text{now})$

thus,

> x_1 is a pellet of salt . . .
> So, if x_1 were put in water, it would dissolve.

Now, the "also" in the above reasoning schema reminds us that the first part of this essay has made it clear that

> If x were Φ-ed, it would ψ

is correctly transcribed into the technical language of logic by neither an unqualified

$$\Phi(x_1, \text{now}) \supset \psi(x_1, \text{now})$$

which is obvious, nor by

$$\Phi(x_1, \text{now}) \longrightarrow \psi(x_1, \text{now})$$

where '$\longrightarrow$' is the basic symbol for 'causal implication.' The root idea behind modal connectives is *inferability*, and, as we saw, once we turn from ordinary discourse to logistical formulations, the above subjunctive conditional must, in the first instance (i.e. neglecting, for the moment, all the other respects in which such formulations are misleading), be represented by the schema

> . . . if it were *also* the case that $\Phi(x_1, \text{now})$, then it would be the case that $\psi(x_1, \text{now})$

where the *also* makes it clear that the above attempt to represent the conditional by an unqualified modal statement simply won't do.

35. On the other hand, our analysis has also made it clear that the force of a subjunctive conditional is, at bottom, a modal force. It rests on such inference-authorizing general truths as 'salt dissolves in water' (or, to mention an example of a kind which is excluded from the restricted framework of the present discussion, '(In the northern hemisphere) floating needles point to the northernmost regions of the earth)'. And though we shall not come to grips with the 'causal modalities' until the concluding section of this essay, it is not unreasonable to assume, provisionally, that these general truths are properly represented, in the technical language of modal logic, by the form

$$(x)(t) : K(x) \cdot C(x,t) \cdot \longrightarrow \cdot \Phi(x,t) \supset \psi(x,t)$$

If so, it would be natural to suggest that

> If x_1 were Φ-ed, it would ψ

as presupposing a general fact of this form, should be transcribed by an implication symbol which has a modal force without being the basic symbol for causal implication. It might, for example, be represented by the use of a shorter arrow, thus

$$\Phi(x_1, now) \longrightarrow \psi(x_1, now).$$

36. But before we follow up this suggestion, let me call attention to the fact, which has undoubtedly been noticed, that the above general hypothetical contains the expression 'K(x)', and not, as might have been expected, the expression 'K(x,t)'. This formulation embodies the fact that where 'K' is a thing-kind word, it is misleading to represent both 'x is a K' and, say, 'x is red' by the same form, 'F(x,t)'. The point is simply that *being a K* is logically related to the self-identity of a thing, x, at different times, in a way in which *being red* is not. It might be put by saying that where 'K' is a thing-kind word in a given context of discourse, if at *any* time it is true of x that it is a K, then if x were to cease to be a K, it would cease to be x, i.e. would cease to be (full stop). Or, to put it less paradoxically, *being a K* is not something that a thing *is at a time*, though it may be *true at a time* that it is a K. "Can't we say that x was a *child* at t, and subsequently a *man* at t'?" But 'child', as Aristotle saw, is not a thing-kind term in the sense in which 'man' (human being) is a thing-kind term. *Child* and *grown-up* are not sub-kinds of *man* (human being), as *man* and *dog* are sub-kinds of *animal*.

How we classify objects depends on our purposes, but within a given context of discourse, the identity of the things we are talking about, their coming into being and ceasing to be, is relative to the *kinds* of that context.

37. I shall have more to say about thing-kind words in a moment. But first let us put the suggestion of section 36 to work in the analysis of 'disposition terms.' With the introduction of the symbol '$\longrightarrow$' we would seem to be in a position to answer the question "What kind of implication belongs in the schema

$$D(x,t) =_{Df} \Phi(x,t) \ implies \ \psi(x,t)?"$$

by simply rewriting it as

$$D(x,t) =_{Df} \Phi(x,t) \longrightarrow \psi(x,t).$$

But if we do so, we must not forget that it is only because we have informally been construing '$\Phi(x,t)$' as 'x is Φ-ed at t' and '$\psi(x,t)$' as 'x ψs at t' that we can go from

$$\Phi(x_1, now) \longrightarrow \psi(x_1, now)$$

to

If x_1 were Φ-ed, it would ψ

as contrasted with

If it were *also* the case that $\Phi(x_1, now)$, it would be the case that $\psi(x_1, now)$.

In other words, the informal commentary with which we have been surrounding our use of logistical expressions is essential to their correct interpretation as a transcription of causal discourse. This commentary is associated with a division of the functions which appear in this transcription into four categories with a different category of sign designs for each category (thus, 'K$_1$' 'K$_2$' . . . 'K$_n$'; 'C$_1$' 'C$_2$' . . . 'C$_n$'; 'Φ_1' 'Φ_2' . . . 'Φ_n'; 'ψ_1' 'ψ_2' . . . 'ψ_n') such that expressions for kinds of things are transcribed by a 'K', expressions for kinds of circumstances by a 'C', expressions—roughly—for something done to a thing by a 'Φ' and expressions for what it does in return by a 'ψ'. Thus, the form 'F(x,t)' has a different *logic* depending on whether 'F' is representing a 'C', a 'Φ', or a 'ψ'. And, indeed, if we read 'F(x,t)' as 'x is F at t,' we should not be under the illusion that "at t" means the same whether 'F' is a 'C', a 'Φ', or a 'ψ'; or, for that matter—if we were to elect to represent 'x is a K' by 'K(x,t)'—a 'K'.

Thus it will not do simply to propose

$$D(x,t) =_{Df} f_2(x,t) \longrightarrow f_3(x,t)$$

as the technical transcription of

x is soluble at t *if and only if*, if x were placed in water at t, x would (begin to) dissolve at t

stipulating only that expressions of the form

$$f_1(x_1,t_1) \longrightarrow f_2(x_1,t_1)$$

imply the truth of a statement of the form

$$(x)(t) f_3(x,t) \cdot f_1(x,t) \longrightarrow f_2(x,t)$$

and the truth of

$$f_3(x_1,t_1).$$

For, in the absence of such additional stipulations as have been associated with our division of descriptive functions into four categories, the above transcription procedures would generate Goodman's paradox.

38. Now we could, of course, abandon the attempt to capture the force of such subjunctives as

If M were scratched, it would light

in our technical language, and limit ourselves instead to conditionals of the form

If p were the case, q would be the case,

abandoning the device of contextual implication, and putting all implications into the direct content of what is said. This would mean that the counterpart of

If this were put in water, it would dissolve

would no longer be

$$\Phi(x_1, now) \longrightarrow \psi(x_1, now)$$

but rather something like

$$(\exists K)(\exists C) :: K(x_1) \cdot C(x_1,t_1) :. (x)(t) : K(x,t) \cdot C(x,t) \cdot \longrightarrow . \\ \Phi(x,t) \supset \psi(x,t)$$

i.e., there is a kind of thing and a circumstance such that x_1 is of that kind and is now in that circumstance, and such that if anything of that kind is ever in that circumstance, then if it is Φ-ed, it ψs. For the only way in which the contextual implications of the above subjunctive conditional could become part of the direct content of what is asserted, is by the use of existential qualification over thing-kind and circumstance variables.*

On the other hand, if our technical language does distinguish between the four classes of function, there is no reason why we should not introduce a symbol, '$\longrightarrow$', together with the contextual stipulations described above. The issue is partly a matter of what we want our technical language to do. If our aim is the limited one of *rewriting* ordinary causal property and subjunctive conditional discourse in a symbolism sprinkled with 'Φ's, 'ψ's, etc., then this purpose is readily achieved by introducing as many categories of, and logics for, symbolic expressions as are necessary to reproduce the complexity of ordinary usage. If, on

---

* For a careful analysis of dispositional concepts along these lines, see Burks (6). The above account, however, was independently developed in Minnesota Center for Philosophy of Science memoranda during 1953–1954.

the other hand, our aim is in some sense to analyze or reconstruct ordinary usage, then, instead of simply creating, so to speak, a symbolic code for ordinary causal discourse, we will seek to introduce these special categories of expression with their special 'logics,' in terms of a smaller number of initial categories and a basic framework of logical principles. This effort, presumably, would be guided, not so much by abstract considerations of formal elegance, as by reflection on the scientific use the product is to have. Of course, once the appropriate derivative categories had been introduced, it would then be possible to introduce the symbol '$\longrightarrow$' as before. This time, however, our transcriptions of causal discourse would be far more than a simple rewriting in logistical symbols.

39. Now it might be thought that the task of constructing our four categories of function, K, C, Φ, and ψ out of more primitive descriptive functions, including, among others, a function '$f(x,t)$' * (e.g. '$Red(x,t)$'), is a straightforward one, if not downright easy. That this is not the case; that this task is not only not easy, but that it may spring from a misconception, will emerge, I believe, in the following paragraphs.

40. We pointed out above that when one makes explicit the presuppositions of a statement to the effect that a certain object, x, has a certain causal property D (of the kind we are considering) at time t. thus, '$D(x_1,t_1)$', one gets something like

$$(\exists K)(\exists C) :: K(x_1) \cdot C(x_1t_1) :. (x)(t) : K(x,t) \cdot C(x,t) \cdot \longrightarrow \cdot$$
$$\Phi(x,t) \supset \psi(x,t)$$

Bearing in mind our stipulations of an ideal universe of discourse containing a fixed and known and named variety of thing-kinds, and a fixed and known and named variety of causal properties, let us use this form as a means of calling attention both to certain distinctions among causal properties, and to certain additional questions of philosophical interest.

41. It is clear, to begin with, that the above formula imposes serious restrictions on the sort of thing that is to count as a 'dispositional property.' The first thing to note is that it captures only one of the uses of the terms we are considering, for we not only speak, as above, of an individual thing as having a certain causal property; we also ascribe causal properties to thing-kinds.

When we say of salt, for example, that it is (water-) soluble, we are

---

* Or, perhaps, '$f(x,s,t)$'—thus 'x is red at place s and time t.'

clearly not ascribing this property to the thing-kind *at a time*. This would, indeed, be logical nonsense. The statement that salt is soluble has the form '$D(K)$' and not '$D(K,t)$'. How, then, shall we represent the connection between the two type levels? Shall we say

$$D(K) \equiv (x) K(x) \text{ implies } D(x)$$

or

$$D(K) \equiv (x)(t) K(x) \text{ implies } D(x,t)?$$

Actually, of course, these two formulas are equivalent, provided we stipulate that

$$D(x) \equiv (t) D(x,t).$$

But the question calls attention to the fact that not only do we say "salt is soluble" rather than "salt is soluble at t," we also say "This is soluble" rather than "This is soluble at t," or, to put it somewhat differently, "This is soluble" does not have the force of "This is soluble *now*." This suggests that the schema

$$D(x,t) \equiv \Phi(x,t) \longrightarrow \psi(x,t)$$

does not do justice to the logic of words for causal properties in ordinary usage. Just as something is of a kind, period, and not of a kind at a time, so something has a causal property, *period*.* As a matter of fact, this seems to be the heart of the distinction between *properties* (causal or otherwise) and *states*. Expressions for states have the form '$F(x,t)$'; those for properties the form '$F(x)$'. And what would correspond in ordinary usage to the '$D(x,t)$' of the above schema is '(the state of) being such that if it were Φ-ed, it would ψ.' Thus, *being magnetized* is a state.† We implied above that not all properties are causal properties. The point will be developed shortly. It must now be added, though the point is less likely to be controversial, that not all states have the form '(the state of) being such that if it were Φ-ed, it would ψ.' The state of *being red* at a certain time would seem to be a good example of what might be called an "occurrent" as contrasted with a "causal" state.

* For a related distinction, see Bergmann (3).

† Yet it would be an oversimplification, of course, to say that the form '$F(x,t)$' represents exactly the force of ordinary expressions to the effect that a certain thing is in a certain state. For when we say, for example, of a certain object that it is red, or magnetized, we imply that it has been and will continue to be red or magnetized for an unspecified period; otherwise we would say, "It is red (or magnetized) *now*" or ". . . for the moment."

42. Now if the above remarks are sound, they highlight anew the central role in causal discourse of thing-kind concepts. For *this* is soluble, *period*, rather than soluble-at-t, just because we are thinking of *this* as belonging to a soluble thing-kind. But to make these remarks stick, we must draw certain distinctions. For, to begin with, it might be said that *malleable* is a causal property, and yet a thing can be malleable at one time but not malleable at another. The rough and ready answer to this objection is that the term 'malleable' is ambiguous, and that in one sense of 'malleable', malleability may be a causal property of *iron*, while in another sense it may be a state of *this* (piece of) iron, which was not (in this sense) malleable a moment ago. But to spell this out calls for some remarks on the notion of a *capacity*.

43. It is not my purpose to botanize causal characteristics, to draw, for example, the familiar distinctions between 'active' and 'passive' powers, between quantitative (metrical or non-metrical) and non-quantitative causal properties, or between causal characteristics of various levels (illustrated by the distinction between *being magnetized* and *being magnetizable*). For the philosophical perplexities with which we are concerned arise when the attempt is made to understand even the most 'elementary' members of this family. Thus, our immediate purposes will be achieved by reflection on the distinction between a *disposition* (as this term is currently used) and a *capacity*.

As a first approximation, this distinction can be put by saying that to say of a certain kind of thing that it has the capacity to $\psi, \Gamma\psi$, is to say that *there is* a combination of a *circumstance*, C, and a *something done*, Φ, which results in the ψ-ing of that kind of thing. Thus, roughly,

$$\Gamma\psi\,(K) = {}_{\text{Df}}(\exists C)(\exists\Phi) :. (x)(t) : K(x) \cdot C(x,t) \cdot \longrightarrow \cdot$$
$$\Phi(x,t) \supset \psi(x,t)$$

This reference to circumstances calls to mind the fact that on our account of dispositions to date, to ascribe a disposition to a thing is to imply that the thing *is actually in* a favorable circumstance, the C of '$(x)(t) K(x) \cdot C(x,t) \cdot \longrightarrow \cdot \Phi(x,t) \supset \psi(x,t)$.' It might not have been in C (or in any other favorable circumstance, C'), in which case a presupposition of the ascription would not obtain. This means, however, that we must reconsider the schema

$$D(K) \equiv (x)(t)\, K(x) \text{ implies } D(x,t)$$

which tells us that if K has D, then any thing of kind K is always in a circumstance such that if it were Φ-ed, it would ψ. This suggests that what we want, instead, is the function '$D_c(K)$', where

$$D_c(K) \equiv (x)(t) \, K(x) \cdot C(x,t) \cdot \text{implies } D(x,t)$$

which amounts to the concept of being disposed to ψ if Φ-ed when the circumstances are C. Only if things of kind K would ψ if Φ-ed in any circumstances whatever, would it be proper to ascribe to K a property of the form $D(K)$ as contrasted with $D_c(K)$.

44. The next point I wish to make can best be introduced by considering an example which takes us somewhat away from the 'ideal' universe of discourse in which we have been operating. It takes its point of departure from the fact that according to our original account of disposition terms, to ascribe a disposition to an object at a certain time, thus, "$D(x_1,t_1)$", is to imply the existence of a general fact such that *if* one *knew it*, and *if* one *knew* a certain fact about the circumstances of x_1 at t_1, and if one knew that x_1 had been Φ-ed at t_1, one would be in a position to reason

x_1 was a K
x_1 was in C at t_1
x_1 was Φ-ed at t_1
So, x_1 ψ-ed at t_1

And this raises the question, Are we not often in a position to ascribe with reason a disposition to an object, although we are not in a position to subsume the object under a generalization of the appropriate form—that is to say of the form, 'Ks ψ when Φ-ed in C'?

Suppose, for example, that the only chemical substances we have so far found to dissolve in water are salt, sugar and a few others, and that they all share the property of forming large white crystals. And suppose that by a chemical reaction which we can repeat at will, we produce large white crystals which consist neither of salt, sugar, nor any of the other substances in our list of soluble chemicals. Suppose, finally, that in the absence of any reason to the contrary we conclude that this new substance (do we also *conclude* that it is a substance?) is soluble.

Now, one way of interpreting the above reasoning is by saying that from the idea that all known soluble substances share the property of forming large white crystals, we drew the inductive conclusion that the product of this chemical reaction, as also having the property of forming large white crystals, (probably) belongs in its turn to a soluble thing-kind, though we did not yet know *what* soluble thing-kind (*what* substance). We were not, the interpretation would continue, in a position to reason,

> This is a K
> So, if it were put in water, it would dissolve

though we were in a position to reason,

> This has the property λ
> Things having the property λ (probably) belong to a soluble thing-kind
> So, if this were put in water, it would (probably) dissolve.

(where λ is the property of forming large white crystals).

'But,' it might be asked, 'instead of concluding that if something has the property λ, then it (probably) belongs to a soluble thing-kind, i.e. that

$$(x) \lambda (x) \text{ implies (in all probability) } (\exists K) \, Sol(K) \cdot K(x)$$

why not conclude that λ *itself* is a soluble thing-kind? The suggestion is, in other words, that the proper conclusion of the above inductive inference, instead of being that having the *property* λ implies that *there is* a thing-kind K, such that

$$(x)(t) K(x) \cdot \longrightarrow \cdot \Phi(x,t) \supset \psi(x,t)$$

should rather be, simply, that λ is *itself* the *thing-kind* in question, a thing-kind of which salt, sugar, etc., are sub-kinds. Our thing-kind generalization would be

$$(x)(t) \lambda(x) \cdot \longrightarrow \cdot \Phi(x,t) \supset \psi(x,t)$$

and 'Sol(λ)' would be the counterpart of 'Sol(salt)'.

45. The answer is, in principle, straightforward. Words for thing-kinds not only embody a great deal of empirical knowledge, which is obvious, but they have quite a different role in discourse from that of expressions for properties, e.g., 'forming large crystals', or 'being white'. We might be tempted to locate this difference between, say, 'salt' and 'λ' by saying that while they both stand for properties, the property of being *saline* fits into a scheme of classification which organizes our chemical knowledge into a perspicuous whole. And, of course, it is true that thing-kind words do go along with ways of *classifying* things. But this is only part of the story, and is quite misleading if taken for the whole.

To bring this out, let us suppose someone to ask, "Can we not

Wilfrid Sellars

imagine that λ might have been the identifying property of a thing-kind; and if so, would we not then be in a position to say 'x₁ is (a sample of) λ' as we now say 'x₁ is (a sample of) salt'?" But the change from 'x is λ' ('x is large crystal forming') to 'x is a λ' gives the show away. For if 'λ' were to acquire this use, it would no longer be the same term, as when John the miller became John Miller, the word "miller" acquired a new use.*

46. Words for thing-kinds have a special logic which is ill-represented by the schema

$$K(x) =_{Df} (t) P_1(x,t) \cdot P_2(x,t) \cdot \ldots P_n(x,t)$$

(where 'P' is a neutral term which ranges over both 'causal' and 'non-causal' characteristics.) There is, indeed, a sense in which a thing-kind word 'means' a certain set of characteristics; but, as elsewhere, the term 'means' is unilluminating. One must get down to cases and see just how words for thing-kinds are related to words for causal properties and to words for such items as color, shape, and number of legs.

Now, the basic flaw in the above schema is that it assimilates the logic of thing-kinds to that of complex properties. The point is not simply that thing-kind concepts are vague in a way which makes inapplicable the model of a set of separately necessary and jointly sufficient defining criteria. For while there are important differences between thing-kind and property expressions with respect to the applicability of this model, the difficulty of finding separately necessary and jointly sufficient criteria is not limited to expressions for thing-kinds. Indeed, the problem of vagueness had been discussed for some time in terms of such examples as 'bald', before the pervasiveness of the problem became apparent. The point is the more radical one that the relation of a thing-kind word to the criteria for belonging to that kind of thing is different in principle from the relation of words for characteristics of things to the criteria for the presence of these characteristics. "Lemon" and "bald" may both be vague, but they are so in radically different ways.†

* For a further discussion of thing-kind expressions which construes them as common names of the individuals belonging to the kinds, and compares the irreducibility of a thing-kind to its 'criterion characteristics' with the irreducibility of proper names to the definite descriptions which are the criteria for their application, see my "Form and Substance in Aristotle: an Exploration," *Journal of Philosophy*, forthcoming, fall 1957.

† For basic discussions of vagueness and 'open texture,' see Kaplan (10), Kaplan and Schott (11), Pap (13), Waismann (20), and Wittgenstein (22).

47. One way of attempting to put this point is by saying that words for kinds of thing continue, in an important sense, to have the same meaning in spite of significant changes in their so-called defining traits, whereas words for characteristics do not. Thus, one might begin by claiming that a shift in the criteria for baldness would amount to the substitution of a new concept for the old one. Suppose, for example, that evolution diminishes man's initial endowment of hair; might not the word "bald" come to be so used that one would have to have less hair than today in order to be called bald? And would not the word have changed its meaning? This, of course, is much too simple. Yet the very way in which it is too simple throws light on thing-kind words. For the term 'bald' is not a cold descriptive term; bald people are not merely people with a 'small' amount of hair, nor is it simply a matter, say, of having a small proportion of the original endowment (in which case there need have been no change of meaning to begin with). The logic of 'bald' involves the idea that being bald is not the sort of thing one would choose; and this theme is a continuing theme in its use.

48. This idea of a continuing theme illuminates the 'meaning' of thing-kind words. It is the role of these words in explanation which accounts for the fact that it can be reasonable to say "That wasn't really gold" in spite of the fact that the object in question was correctly called gold according to the criteria used at the time the claim that is being disputed was made. And the statement that the object really wasn't gold is not to be construed as a queer way of saying that the word "gold" no longer means exactly what it did. It is the *regulative* connection of thing-kind words with the schema

Ks ψ when Φ-ed, in appropriate circumstances

which guides them through the vicissitudes of empirical knowledge.

This feature of the tie between a thing-kind word and the criteria by which one identifies members of the kind throws new light on the logic of general truths concerning thing-kinds. If thing-kind words were adequately represented by the schema

$$K(x) =_{Df} (t) P_1(x,t) \cdot P_2(x,t) \ldots P_n(x,t)$$

then general truths of the form

$$(x) K(x) \cdot implies \cdot (t) \Phi(x,t) \supset \psi(x,t)$$

261

would, viewed more penetratingly, have the form

$$(x)(t) P_1(x,t) \cdot P_2(x,t) \ldots P_n(x,t) \cdot implies \cdot \Phi(x,t) \supset \psi(x,t)$$

Now, if P_1, $P_2 \ldots P_n$ were 'occurrent' rather than 'causal' characteristics, there would be relatively little in all this to puzzle us. But it is clear on reflection that the criteria for belonging to a thing-kind are by no means limited to non-causal characteristics; and once we realize this, we begin to be puzzled.

For, we wonder, how is it to be reconciled with the idea, on which we earlier laid such stress, that when a soluble object dissolves in water, the fact that it is put in water *causes* it to dissolve? We took this at the time to mean that while there is no general causal fact to the effect that *anything* put in water dissolves, the soluble object has *some* character such that it is a general fact that anything having this character which is *also* put in water, dissolves. If we now ask, Can this character be *another* causal property or set of causal properties, or include a causal property? we are strongly tempted to say No—partly because we are tempted to think of the fact that the object has this additional character as a *part cause* (and hence of the fact that it is put in water as *really* only itself a *part cause* of the dissolving), and then to wonder how a causal property can be a *cause*; and partly because we smell the beginnings of a circle. If, on the other hand we try to fall back on the idea that the general fact in question is of the form

$$(x)(t) O(x,t) \cdot implies \cdot \Phi(x,t) \supset \psi(x,t)$$

(where O neither is nor includes a causal characteristic), we are confronted by the brute fact that we *don't know any such general facts*.

49. Now part of the solution to this puzzle consists in recognizing that even if the fact that the object was put in water is not the complete explanation of the fact that it dissolved, the putting in water was not, for this reason, only a *part cause* of the dissolving. Thus, when we explain the fact that a piece of salt dissolved in water by calling attention to the fact that it *was* a piece of salt, we are not implying that being a piece of salt is a *part cause* (along with being put in water) of the dissolving. More, indeed, must be known of an object than the mere fact that it was put in water, in order to infer that it dissolved. But such thing-kind generalizations as "Salt dissolves in water" include this more not by specifying additional part causes, but by restricting their scope to identifiable kinds of thing, in identifiable kinds of circumstance.

50. But the philosophically more exciting part of the solution consists in distinguishing between the causal properties of a certain kind of thing, and the theoretical explanation of the fact that it has these causal properties. For while causal generalizations about thing-kinds provide perfectly sound explanations, in spite of the fact that thing-kinds are not part-causes, it is no accident that philosophers have been tempted to think that such a phenomenon as salt dissolving in water must "at bottom" or "in principle" be a "lawfully evolving process" describable in purely episodic terms. Such an "ideal" description would no longer, in the ordinary sense, be in causal terms, nor the laws be causal laws; though philosophers have often muddied the waters by extending the application of the terms 'cause' and 'causal' in such wise that any law of nature (at least any nonstatistical law of nature) is a 'causal' law.*

It would be a serious mistake to think that a mode of explanation, in particular, ordinary causal explanation, which enables us to give satisfactory answers to one family of questions, cannot be such as by its very nature to lead us on to new horizons, to new questions calling for new answers of a different kind. The plausibility of the 'positivistic' interpretation of theoretical entities rests on a failure to appreciate the way in which thing-kind generalizations by bunching rather than explaining causal properties point beyond themselves to a more penetrating level of description and explanation; it rests, that is, on a failure to appreciate the promissory note dimension of thing-kind expressions. The customary picture of the relation of 'observational' to 'theoretical' discourse is upside down. The 'primacy' of molar objects and their observable properties is methodological rather than ontological. It is the ultimate task of theory to re-create the observational frame in theoretical terms; to make available in principle a part of itself (at a highly derived level, of course) for the observational role—both perceptual, and, by containing a micro-theory of psychological phenomena, introspective.†

51. We said above that the picture of the world in terms of molar things and their causal properties (a) points beyond itself to a picture of the world as pure episode, and (b) leads, by its own logic, to the

* Cf. Collingwood (8), Feigl (9), and Russell (23).

† For an elaboration of this theme, and a more complete discussion of the nature and status of theories, see my essay "Empiricism and the Philosophy of Mind," in Volume I of Minnesota Studies in the Philosophy of Science, particularly sections 39–44 and 51–55.

introduction of unobserved entities. It is important to see that these two 'demands,' though related, do not coincide. For micro-theories themselves characteristically postulate micro-*thing-kinds* which have fundamentally the same logic as the molar *thing kinds* we have been considering. And if they *do* take us *on the way* to a process picture of the world, they do not take us all the way. For even if a 'ground floor' theory in terms of micro-micro-things were equivalent to a pure process theory by virtue of raising no questions concerning the causal properties of these micro-micro-things to which it could not provide the answer, it would not for that reason be a pure process theory. For the logical form of a *thing* theory is, after all, characteristically different from that of a theory whose basic entities are spatio-temporally related *events*, or overlapping *episodes*.

52. The conception of the world as pure process, which is as old as Plato, and as new as Minkowski, remains a regulative ideal; not simply because we cannot hope to know the manifold content of the world in all its particularity, but because science has not yet achieved the very concepts in terms of which such a picture might be formulated. Only those philosophies (New Realism, Neo-Thomism, Positivism, certain contemporary philosophies of common sense and ordinary usage, etc.) which suppose that the final story of "what there is" must be built (after submitting them to a process of epistemological smelting and refinement) from concepts pertaining to the perceptible features of the everyday world, and which mistake the methodological dependence of theoretical on observational discourse for an intrinsically second-class status with respect to the problems of ontology, can suppose the contrary.

53. Important though these broader implications of our analysis may be, to follow them up would take us far beyond the scope of this essay. Our task is to quarry some of the stones for this more ambitious enterprise. Let us, therefore, conclude the present section of this essay with some remarks on the distinction between the *identifying* traits and the *properties* of thing-kinds.

Suppose, to begin with, that a certain kind of thing, K_1, has a certain causal characteristic, P_1, which is not one of its identifying traits. One might be tempted to think that the assertion that K_1 has P_1 is equivalent to the assertion that anything having the traits by which K_1 is identified, has P_1. If our argument to date is sound, however, this idea would be incorrect—as assimilating thing-kind expressions to expressions for complex characteristics. On the other hand, it is quite true that the momentary cash value of the idea that K_1 has P_1 is the idea that the traits by virtue of which K_1 is identified are conjoined with P_1. It is important to note, however, that not all the identifying traits of a thing-kind need be directly relevant to its possession of a given causal characteristic. Indeed, we are often in a position to formulate generalizations which, prima facie, have the form

$$(x) P_n (x) \cdot \ldots P_{n + m}(x) \cdot \longrightarrow \cdot (t) \Phi(x,t) \supset \psi(x,t)$$

where $P_n \ldots P_{n + m}$ constitute a proper subset of the identifying traits of a thing-kind, and where this group of traits may be found in several thing-kinds. The existence of generalizations having (prima facie) this form encourages the mistaken idea that thing-kind generalizations are special cases of such generalizations, cases in which the set of traits in question has acquired the status of a thing-kind concept by virtue of being given a place in a classificatory scheme.

The truth of the matter is rather that the generalizations represented above exist within a framework of identifiable thing-kinds, and that far from it being the case that generalizations pertaining to thing-kinds are a special case of generalizations pertaining to sets of characteristics, the latter are abstractions from generalizations pertaining to thing-kinds, and are, implicitly, of the form

$$(x)(K) :. K(x) \text{ implies } P_n \ldots P_{n + m}(x) : \text{implies} :$$
$$(t) \Phi(x,t) \supset \psi(x,t)$$

54. Finally, what of the case where a causal property is one of the identifying traits of a thing-kind? What are we to make of the formula

$$(x)(t) K(x) \cdot C(x,t) : \text{implies} \cdot \Phi(x,t) \supset \psi(x,t)$$

(where ψ-ing when Φ-ed (in C) is an identifying trait of K)? We seem to be confronted with a dilemma. Either the remaining identifying traits of K imply the presence of this trait—in which case there is no point to including it among the identifying traits—or they do not, in which case how can a generalization of the above form be anything other than a tautology? But surely when we suggested that

If x_1 were Φ-ed, it would ψ

points beyond itself to

$F(x_1, \text{now})$, and (x_1, now)

265

So if it were also the case that $\Phi(x_1, \text{now})$ it would be the case that $\psi(x_1, \text{now})$

we were thinking of the relation between F and ψ-*ing when* Φ-*ed* as synthetic and empirical!

It might be thought that the solution to this puzzle is to be found in the idea that the *remaining* identifying traits imply (perhaps only with high probability) that objects having them ψ when Φ-ed (in C), so that our reasoning, instead of the above, is (roughly)

x_1 is $(K - P_1)$ [where P_1 is the property of ψ-ing when Φ-ed (in C)]
and x_1 is now in C
So, if it were also the case that $\Phi(x_1, \text{now})$, it would be the case that $\psi(x_1, \text{now})$.

But it does not seem to be true that the identifying traits of a thing-kind need be highly correlated with each other. What is true, and the key to the answer, is that as a complete group they belong together by virtue of their correlation with non-identifying traits. They belong together, that is to say, by virtue of the fact that the thing-kind they identify has causal properties which belong to it *as a matter of empirical fact.*

The 'empirical' element, then, in the connection between *being a K* and ψ-*ing when* Φ-*ed (in C),* where ψ-*ing when* Φ-*ed (in C)* is an identifying trait of K enters in with what might be called the 'methodological distance' between thing-kind words and identifying traits to which we have called attention, a distance which enables them to play their characteristic role, both in the organization of empirical knowledge at a time, and in the search for new knowledge. It is this methodological dimension which enables a reference to being a K in circumstances C to authorize a subjunctive conditional, even though, as far as *cash value* is concerned, '$(x)(t) K(x) \cdot C(x,t) \cdot implies \cdot \Phi(x,t) \supset \psi(x,t)$' is a tautology.

III. Causal Connection: The Dialectic of the Controversy

55. I propose next to discuss a number of questions which, though they must inevitably arise in any discussion of subjunctive conditionals or causal properties, have been either postponed outright or answered most provisionally in the preceding sections of this essay. The general

theme of these questions, as well as the appropriate apperceptive mass of philosophical perplexity, can readily be called to mind by referring to the perennial debate as to whether or not 'causality' is to be construed as a 'necessary connection' of logically distinguishable states of affairs.

56. It will be useful to begin by reflecting on the general pattern of this controversy. It has tended to organize itself around two 'polar' positions. Each is a 'straightforward' answer to the question, What is the relation between the two kinds of state of affairs, A and B, which we have in mind when we speak of them as causally connected? These answers are, respectively, (1) "The relation consists in a constant conjunction of A with B"; (b) "The relation is a logical relation of entailment—in an inclusive but proper sense of this phrase—between A and B." Needless to say, once these 'straightforward' answers have been given, each is immediately surrounded with a host of qualifications and 'clarifications' designed to counter the standard objections from the opposite camp.*

Now, the only way to resolve the perplexities embodied in this controversy is to 'join' it, while maintaining—to adopt and adapt a metaphor from aesthetics—an appropriate 'philosophical distance.' And perhaps the easiest way to put ourselves into the picture is to ask, Why would anyone be moved to say that causal connection is a quasi-logical relation of entailment?

First, why entailment? Mr. Entailment's answer is simple enough. "Because when we say that A and B are causally related, we mean that if a case of A were to exist, a case of B would exist; we mean that there are cases of B because there are cases of A; in short, we reason from the existence of a case of A to the existence of a case of B. And if this is what we have in mind, does it not amount to the idea that the existence of an A-situation entails the existence of a B-situation?" To which Mr. E adds, "The sheer idea that there have been and will be no A-situation unaccompanied by B-situations, while, it does, indeed, imply that anything identical with one of the past, present or future A-situations—granted there be such—would have a B-situation as its

* The most recent, and, in many respects, the best, presentation of the entailment side of the controversy is to be found in Kneale (12); but see also Broad (7). For equally effective presentations of the regularity analysis, see Ayer (1), Braithwaite (4), Reichenbach (16, 17), and Weinberg (24).

companion, simply does not imply that if an A-situation *were* to occur, it *would* have a B-situation as its companion."

Why quasi-logical (or, as we put it above, logical in a broad, if proper sense)? Again Mr. E has a ready answer. "Actually it might better be called 'natural' or 'physical' entailment, for while any entailment is a logical relation, we can distinguish within the broad class of entailments between those which are, and those which are not, a function of the specific empirical contents between which they obtain. The latter are investigated by general or formal logic (and pure mathematics). Empirical science, on the other hand, to the extent that it is a search for *laws*, is the search for entailments of the former kind. (Putative) success in this search finds its expression in statements of the form 'It is (inductively) probable that A physically entails B.' "

57. Mr. C(onstant Conjunction), as is typical in debates of this kind, opens his case with an attack. "Whatever *else*, if anything, it may mean to say that A 'physically entails' B, it is surely a *necessary* condition of the truth of 'A physically entails B' that A be constantly conjoined with B. In short,

$$E_p(A,B) \text{ logically implies } (x) \, Ax \supset Bx \, *$$

It would, however, I am prepared to admit, be a mistake simply to *equate* lawlike statements with statements affirming constant conjunctions. Something more must, indeed, be said. It is this *more* which finds unhelpful expression in your phrase 'physical entailment'.

"To begin with," continues Mr. C, "the statement 'A-situations cause B-situations' differs from the technical formula '(x) Ax ⊃ Bx' in that it carries with it the contextual implication that the conjunction of A with B is not simply a matter of there being no As. There may be secondary senses of 'law' in which a statement may formulate a law and yet, strictly speaking, be vacuously satisfied, but they have a derivative status which is to be explicated in terms of their relation to non-vacuous conjunctions. More important is the fact that a basic lawlike statement carries with it the further implication that *it is accepted on inductive grounds*, and, in particular, that it is not accepted on the ground that all the As which (in all probability) ever will have existed *have been examined and found to be B*. The statement, in short, *sticks its neck*

---

* The form '(x) Ax ⊃ Bx' will be used for simplicity of formulation, leaving the reference to time as something to be 'understood'; to say nothing of the complexities discussed in the first two parts of this essay.

out.* It is this neck-sticking-out-ness (to use a Tolmanism) which finds its expression in the subjunctive mood. Thus, when I say 'If this were an A-situation, it would be accompanied by a B-situation,' this statement not only gives expression to the idea that A is constantly conjoined with B, but does so in a way which has these contextual implications."

58. Mr. C concludes his initial say with the following two comments on Mr. E's contention: (a) "I am ill at ease in this vocabulary of 'entailments,' 'necessary connections,' and, to tell the truth, modal expressions generally. It does seem to me, however, that if one is going to use this vocabulary, one should use it, and not pick and choose. Isn't an entailment the sort of thing one 'sees?' Doesn't one describe an inference in these terms by saying that the person who (correctly) drew the inference not only believed the premises, but 'saw' that the premises entailed the conclusion? But ever since the collapse of extreme rationalism, philosophers of your stripe have hastened to admit that one doesn't 'see' these 'physical entailments,' but merely concludes that (probably) there is a relation of physical entailment between, say, A and B. Surely, however, an entailment which can't be 'seen' is an entailment which can't do entailment work, which can't serve the purpose you want it to serve, namely that of authorizing inference." (b) "If, on the other hand, you are prepared to say, in the context of discovering empirical laws, that we do come to 'see' physical entailments, you must face up to the fact that we 'see' formal entailments by understanding the meanings of the terms of our discourse. Yet it is obviously not by reflecting on the meanings of empirical terms that we discover empirical laws."

Both of these points are telling ones, and together they appear to confront Mr. E with an insuperable dilemma: either physical entailments can't be 'seen'—in which case they are not entailments; or they can be 'seen'—in which case they are not empirical.

59. As far as the first horn of this dilemma is concerned, I think that we, from our 'philosophical distance,' must agree that it won't do at all to claim that we make inferences of the form

x_1 is A
So, x_1 is B

* Cf. Goodman's opening characterization of lawlike statements in the second part of his paper on counterfactuals in Fact, Fiction and Forecast, pp. 24ff., particularly p. 26.

which are not enthymematic forms of

(x) x is A ⊃ x is B
x_1 is A
So, x_1 is B;

add that the validity of such inferences is to be explicated in terms of a 'physical entailment' between A and B; and then deny that we can 'see' that A entails B. If one is going to explain our thinking in causal matters by using the idea of physical entailment, one must do more than defend the idea that "there are" such entailments; one must make plausible the idea that these entailments play a role in causal reasoning analogous to the role of 'formal' entailments in less problematic forms of inference. This, of course, does not mean that one is precluded from speaking of unknown (not unknowable) physical entailments, any more than the fact that we can 'see' formal entailments precludes us from speaking of unknown formal entailments.

60. Now, Mr. E *might* reply to all this—and I say 'might' because we are on the point of taking over the argument—as follows: "To conclude, 'It is (inductively) *probable* that A physically entails B' is simply to conclude (inductively) that A physically entails B. If Jones concludes (inductively) that A physically entails B, and we think him right in so doing, we shall say that he has come to see that A physically entails B, thus borrowing for metaphorical use from perceptual discourse the endorsing form 'x sees that p'."

This hypothetical reply, while it won't do as it stands, is a step in the right direction. It has, to begin with, the fundamental merit of recognizing that to say "(So) *probably* p" is not to attribute a relational property to a state of affairs, i.e. that of 'standing in the probability relation' to certain implied facts. It is to assert that p, but contextually imply that one has good reasons of an empirical kind for asserting it. In other words, "Probably p" says that p, but indicates something about the grounds on which one says that p.

And if this is the case, the fact that our knowledge of the laws of nature is expressed by the form

(In all probability) p

has not the slightest tendency to show that what we are really knowing is facts of the form

Prob(p,e)

i.e., p is probable on evidence e, and that it is facts of this form which are our reasons for asserting that p. Our reason for asserting that p is that e, not that prob(p,e). And the knowledge expressed by

> (In all probability) p,

where it is properly endorsed as knowledge, is not the knowledge that prob(p,e), but the knowledge that p. And this fundamental point about the phrase 'in all probability' is untouched by the fact that 'p' may be, in a suitably broad sense, a statistical proposition. Nor does it require us to deny that there are such facts as that prob(p,e), as is readily seen once one recognizes the ubiquitous role in discourse of the context ". . . it is a fact that . . ." and its cousin ". . . it is true that. . . ." Consider the sentence

> It is true that debts ought to be paid, but Jones is in such a tight spot that . . . .

Do we really think that this should be edited with raised-eyebrow quotation marks to read

> It is 'true' that . . . ?

61. Thus, if laws of nature are, as Mr. E insists, of the form

> Being A physically entails being B,

the fact that the knowledge of such a law would be properly expressed by

> (In all probability) being A physically entails being B

does not mean that what is known is 'the probability of the existence of a relation of physical entailment between being A and being B.' To say that Jones knows that A causes B, and add that this knowledge is, of course, inductive, is not to say that Jones knows a probability fact about A causing B, but simply to say that his knowledge that A causes B is probable knowledge, i.e. the kind of knowledge we get in empirical science, as contrasted with the kind of knowledge we get in, say, pure mathematics.

On the other hand, Mr. E was going a bit fast when he went from the sound idea that the inductive character of scientific knowledge is compatible with the claim that it is the physical entailments themselves which are known, to the idea that it is compatible with the claim that these entailments are 'seen.' It simply does not seem proper to speak of an entailment as 'seen' when the knowledge of the entailment is probable knowledge in the sense characterized above. Thus, if it were true that entailments had to be 'seen' and not merely *known* in order to authorize inferences, subjunctive conditionals, etc., Mr. E would not yet be out of the woods.

Yet that some progress has been made is indicated by the fact that if we were asked, Would not the *knowledge* that A entails B authorize the inference from 'this is A' to 'this is B' even if the entailment were physical entailment, and the knowledge that it obtains the probable knowledge of inductive science? the only thing that would keep us from answering "Yes" is doubt about the very idea, presupposed by the question, that there is such a thing as the 'probable knowledge of physical entailments'; indeed, that there is such a thing as physical entailment.

62. Thus, even if Mr. E's thesis has been reformulated in such a way as to meet some of the objections leveled against it by Mr. C, we have not yet come to grips with the most searching challenge of all, namely, Why introduce the concept of physical entailment at all? Mr. C, it will be remembered, argued

1. that whatever *else* it may be, the idea that A physically entails B is, *at least in part,* the idea that A is constantly conjoined with B;
2. that while it would indeed be incorrect to say that 'A causes B' simply amounts to 'A is constantly conjoined with B,' the latter *with certain qualifications* will do the job;
3. that these qualifications amount, at bottom, to the idea that 'A causes B' says that

$$(x) Ax \supset Bx$$

and *implies* that the latter is asserted on inductive grounds.

Of these three contentions, the first would seem to be common ground, for Mr. E and his colleagues are typically prepared to grant without further ado that to say that *being* A physically entails *being* B is equivalent to saying that

It is physically necessary that A be constantly conjoined with B

or, in current logistical symbolism,

$$\boxed{\text{c}}\,\{(x) Ax \supset Bx\}$$

where '$\boxed{\text{c}}$' has the sense of 'it is causally necessary that', and where '$\boxed{\text{c}}\{(x) Ax \supset Bx\}$' logically implies '$(x) Ax \supset Bx$'.* From this point of view, the difference between Messrs. E and C with respect to the second

---

* For a lucid presentation of the fundamentals of a logic of the causal modalities, see Burks (5); also Reichenbach (15, 17) and von Wright (19).

of the above three contentions is simply which 'qualifications' are the right ones. And from this point of view, the outcome of the controversy hinges, therefore, on the third contention.

63. How are we to come to grips with it? As far as I can see, the best way is to begin by noting that Mr. C is, by implication, granting what is surely the case, namely that *in the absence of the contextual implications which he has introduced*, '(x) Ax ⊃ Bx' *pure and simple* cannot with any plausibility be claimed to authorize either 'If anything were A, it would be B,' or 'If x_1 were A, it would be B,' though it clearly would authorize subjunctive conditionals which might easily be confused with the above, namely

> If anything were identical with one of the things which are (have been or will be) A, it would be B

and

> If x were identical with one of the things which are (have been or will be) A, it would be B.

The principle which relates the latter conditionals to '(x) Ax ⊃ B(x)' is the Leibnitz-Russell principle

$$x = y \cdot \supset \cdot (\Phi) \Phi x \supset \Phi y$$

a principle which authorizes such reasonings as

> Tom is tall
> So, if I were Tom, I would be tall

64. It can readily be seen that where K is a class given by a listing of its members, thus

$$(x) \, x \, \epsilon \, K =_{Df} x = x_1 \, v \, x = x_2 \, v \, . \, . \, . \, x = x_n$$

and where the function 'Φx' has the definition

$$\Phi x =_{Df} \Phi' x \cdot x \, \epsilon \, K$$

where, in other words, the class of the things which are Φ contains a reference to a denotatively specified set of individuals, the proposition

$$(x) \, \Phi x \supset \psi x$$

while it does, indeed, authorize the subjunctive conditional

> If anything were Φ, it would be ψ

it does so only because the latter has the sense of

If anything were identical with one of the things which are Φ, it would be ψ.

It is tempting to conclude with Popper (14) that where the class of Φ is an open class, i.e. a class which is not defined in terms of a denotatively specified set of individuals, then

(x) Φx ⊃ ψx

authorizes not simply

If anything were identical with one of the things which are (have been or will be) Φ, it would be ψ.

but

If anything were Φ, it *would be* ψ

as well.

65. But how are we to test the claim that 'A causes B' can be construed as '(x) Ax ⊃ Bx' with or without the stipulation that the former contextually implies that the speaker has inductive grounds for his statement? The proper move would seem to be a thought experiment. Thus, Mr. C's claim amounts to the idea that it would be a 'howler' to affirm that (x) Ax ⊃ Bx, implying, in so doing, that one has good inductive grounds for making the statement, while denying in the same breath that *if anything were A it would be B*. If, therefore, we can construct in imagination a situation in which it would be quite proper to do this, the claim will have been refuted.

Suppose that we had good grounds for believing that all planets revolving around a central sun rotate in the same direction as they revolve, provided that the planets and the sun around which they revolve have had a common origin. *Suppose* also that we had good grounds to believe that it was extremely improbable that a body could join a solar system from outside without gravitating directly to the sun; in short that it was extremely unlikely that a planet could have originated from outside. *Suppose*, however, that we had good grounds for believing that a material object of whatever size which revolves around another object, rotating as it does so, *need not* rotate in the same direction as it revolves. *Suppose*, finally, that no planet has ever been observed to rotate in a direction other than that in which it revolves.

Given all the above suppositions, and postponing for the moment any question as to their legitimacy and mutual consistency, would we not be in a position to say

(In all probability) all planets *in point of* (contingent) fact rotate in the same direction as they revolve but deny that

> (In all probability) if anything were a planet, it would rotate
> in the same direction as it revolves?

that is, in the language of the controversy, with 'Px' for 'x is a planet'
and 'Rx' for 'x rotates in the same direction as it revolves', to affirm

> (In all probability) (x) Px $\supset$ Rx

but reject

> (In all probability) (x) if it were the case that Px, it would be
> the case that Rx?

though not, of course, reject

> (In all probability) if anything were identical with one of the
> planets which have existed or ever will exist, it would rotate in
> the same direction as it revolves.

On the other hand, since one of our suppositions is that we have
good grounds for believing it to be extremely improbable that a body
could come into a solar system without gravitating directly to the sun,
we could say (could we not?) that

> (In all probability) under the circumstances which (in all proba-
> bility) obtain, i.e. that all planets have originated and will origi-
> nate within their solar systems, if anything were a planet, it
> would rotate in the same direction as it revolves

for this mobilizes the two ideas (1) that

> (In all probability) all planets in point of fact originate within
> their solar systems

and (2) that

> (In all probability) all planets which originate within their solar
> system rotate of physical necessity in the same direction as
> they revolve

in a way which is analogous to that in which

> [Since (p $\supset$ q) is the case] if p were also the case, r would be
> the case

mobilizes 'p $\supset$ q' and '(p $\cdot$ q) < r'.

66. We shall shortly see that things are not quite so simple; indeed
that our thought experiment simply will not do as it stands, for reasons
which the reader may already have spotted. But let us work with it
for a moment before submitting it to criticism, as it will enable us
to bring into our argument themes from many current discussions of
the distinction between 'necessary' and 'accidental' constant conjunctions.

67. There are, however, two difficulties, one minor, one of major
import, which should at least be looked at before we continue. To
take the minor point first, it is clear that if the only way in which

we could come to know that

$$\Diamond\text{-}\{(\exists x)\, Px \cdot \sim Rx\}$$

i.e., 'It is physically possible that $(\exists x)\, Px \cdot \sim Rx$', were by inferring this from

$$(\exists x)\, Px \cdot \sim Rx$$

we could never be in a position to say both

$$(x)\, Px \supset Rx$$

and

$$\Diamond\text{-}\{(\exists x)\, Px \cdot \sim Rx\}$$

Evidence which would warrant the affirmation of a constant conjunction would *ipso facto* warrant the denial that exceptions were physically possible; and the idea that '$\boxed{c}\text{-}\{(x)\, Ax \supset Bx\}$' had the force of '(In all probability) $(x)\, Ax \supset Bx$' would have survived our thought experiment for the simple reason that the latter would be internally inconsistent.

In general, if

(In all probability) $(x)\, Ax \supset Bx$

had the form

Observed As have, without exception, been B
So, (in all probability) $(x)\, Ax \supset Bx$

and

(In all probability) $\Diamond\text{-}\{(\exists x)\, Ax \cdot \sim Bx\}$

had the form

$(\exists x)\, Ax \cdot \sim Bx$
So, $\Diamond\text{-}\{(\exists x)\, Ax \cdot \sim Bx\}$

one could not simultaneously have inductive reasons for affirming both a constant conjunction and the (physical) possibility of an exception.

68. On the other hand, to mention a point of major significance it must be admitted that where 'A' and 'B' are *unlocalized* predicates, predicates, that is, which do not contain covert references to particular times, places or things, there are, to put it mildly, serious difficulties about the idea that one could have reason to assert both

$$\Diamond\text{-}\{(\exists x)\, Ax \cdot \sim Bx\}$$

and

$$\sim(\exists x)\, Ax \cdot \sim Bx$$

276

Nor do these difficulties depend on the idea that, in general,

(In all probability) $\diamondsuit\{(\exists x)\,Ax \cdot \sim\!Bx\}$

has the form

$(\exists x)\,Ax \cdot \sim\!Bx$
So, $\diamondsuit\{(\exists x)\,Ax \cdot \sim\!Bx\}$

For the time being I shall simply look these difficulties in the face and walk on, as I shall also do in the case of the related problem of how the supposition (whatever its analysis) that 'It is extremely likely that a body entering a solar system from without would gravitate directly to the sun' where this does *not* mean 'It is inductively probable that *all* bodies entering a solar system from without would gravitate directly to the sun' could authorize

(In all probability) *all* planets have as a contingent matter of fact originated within their solar system, and will continue to do so

as contrasted with

(In all probability) *most* planets have originated (or will originate) within their solar system.

69. Let us suppose, therefore, that Mr. C does not, for the moment, seize on these weaknesses in our thought experiment. Let us suppose, indeed, that, for the moment, he finds our thought experiment convincing, and abandons the simple idea that

$(x)\,Ax \supset Bx$

has the force of

(In all probability) $(x)\,Ax \supset Bx$.

It would be a mistake, however, to conclude that having left this bastion, he has no option but to join forces with an already chastened Mr. E. Indeed, he has one more qualification up his sleeve which might do the trick without amounting to full surrender.

What this qualification might be is suggested by the argument of the preceding section. After all, even if the use of modal language in connection with empirical phenomena arouses one's philosophical anxieties, the fact remains that in our unperplexed moments we *do* speak of this or that as a 'necessary consequence' of something else, as 'physically possible,' etc. It is only sensible, therefore, to look to the inter-relationships of modal expressions for a clue to the presuppositions of lawlike statements. Of these inter-relationships, the following are the most promising:

(1) $\diamondsuit$⊣{(∃x) Ax · ∼Bx}⊢ : < : ∼[c]⊣{(x) Ax ⊃ Bx}⊢

(2) [c]⊣{(x) Ax · Cx : ⊃ ∼Bx}⊢ : < : $\diamondsuit$⊣{(∃x) Ax · Cx · ∼Bx}⊢
   : < $\diamondsuit$⊣{(∃x) Ax · ∼Bx}⊢
   : < : ∼[c]⊣{(x) Ax ⊃ Bx}⊢

(1) immediately suggests the idea that to assert that (in all probability) A causes B is to imply that one has good inductive reason for claiming that

(In all probability) (x) Ax ⊃ Bx

and does *not* have good inductive reason for claiming that

(In all probability) $\diamondsuit$⊣{(∃x) Ax · ∼Bx}⊢.

It correspondingly suggests that to assert that (in all probability) A is constantly conjoined with B, but deny that A causes B, is to imply that although one has good inductive ground for claiming that

(In all probability) (x) Ax ⊃ Bx

one *also* has good reason for claiming that

(In all probability) $\diamondsuit$⊣{(∃x) Ax · ∼Bx}⊢

But this suggestion is clearly of little use to Mr. C as it stands, for by explaining the claim that the constant conjunction between A and B is or is not *necessary* in terms of the idea that exceptions are or are not *possible*, it does nothing to ease his anxieties about the causal modalities generally. On the other hand, if we replace, in each case, '(in all probability) $\diamondsuit$⊣{(∃x) Ax · ∼Bx}⊢' by '(in all probability) (∃x) Ax · ∼Bx', on the ground that if it is true that

$\diamondsuit$⊣{(∃x) Ax · ∼Bx}⊢ : < : ∼[c]⊣{(x) Ax ⊃ Bx}⊢

((1) above) it is equally true that

(∃x) Ax · ∼Bx : < : ∼[c] (x) Ax ⊃ Bx

the suggestion, thus modified, fails to accomplish its mission; for to assert that (in all probability) A has B for its constant companion, but deny that A causes B obviously cannot be to imply that there is sufficient inductive reason to warrant the assertion of *both* the constant conjunction *and the existence of exceptions*. While to assert that A causes B is to deny not just the *existence* of exceptions, but the (physical) *possibility* of exceptions.

70. The second relationship, (2), is more promising. This time the suggestion is the twofold one that (a) to assert that (in all probability) A is constantly conjoined with, but does not cause, B, is to imply that while one has good inductive reasons for claiming that

(In all probability) (x) Ax ⊃ Bx

one knows about a character C such that one is entitled to say

(In all probability) (x) Ax · Cx : ⊃ ~Bx

though not, of course, on the grounds that one has observation knowledge to the effect that

(∃x) Ax · Cx · ~Bx

It correspondingly suggests (b) that to assert that (in all probability) A causes B is to imply that one has good inductive grounds for claiming that (in all probability) (x) Ax ⊃ Bx, and knows of no characteristic C, such that one is entitled to say

(In all probability) (x) Ax · Cx : ⊃ ~Bx.

71. Now the first part, (a), of this suggestion involves the obvious difficulty that since, *ex hypothesi*, A and B are *constantly* (if contingently) conjoined, the generalization which, according to it, is contextually implied, namely, '(in all probability) (x) Ax · Cx : ⊃ ~Bx', is implied to be vacuously true. But if this implied generalization concerning the characteristic C amounts, simply, to

(In all probability) ~(∃x) Ax · Cx · Bx

it is difficult to see how the idea that 'A is constantly, but contingently, conjoined with B' implies that we know of a characteristic C of which *this* is true, and illuminates the force of the assertion; while if we replace '(in all probability) (x) Ax · Cx : ⊃ ~Bx' by '(in all probability) [c]⊣(x) Ax · Cx : ⊃ ~Bx}' we are once again explicating the force of one modal expression ('(physically) possible') by another ('(physically) necessary').

72. As for part (b) of the suggestion, I shall limit myself to pointing out that when we claim that A is not merely *constantly conjoined* with, but *causes*, B, we seem to be implying not simply that we *know* of no characteristic C such that we are entitled to say that

(In all probability) (x) Ax · Cx : ⊃ ~Bx

(though we are, of course, implying *at least* this) but that *there is no*

279

such *characteristic*. I limit myself to this remark because the discussion initiated by our 'thought experiment' has served its purpose—which was not, it will be remembered, to *prove* anything, but to introduce certain themes, and it is time to approach our problem from new directions.

73. Let us leave Mr. C for a moment and return to our chastened Mr. E, a Mr. E who is willing, indeed, eager, to go as far as he can to meet his critics; if only he can preserve the 'core'—however small it may be—of his original position. Instead of continuing to press him back step by step, however, I shall present him without further ado in his 'last ditch.' As a matter of fact, I shall begin by having him retreat *too* far, as, indeed, he might be expected to do under the momentum of the argument.

74. Like Mr. C, he now seeks to illuminate the idea that A causes B in terms of the contextual implications of causal statements. Unlike Mr. C, however, he interprets the significance of the causal modalities *not* in terms of the reasoning

> I. . . .
> So (in all probability) (x) Ax $\supset$ Bx
> II. (x) Ax $\supset$ Bx
> Ax$_1$
> So, (of logical necessity) Bx$_1$

but in terms of the reasoning

> I' . . .
> So (in all probability) if anything were A it would be B
> II' Ax$_1$
> So (of physical necessity) Bx$_1$

In short, he takes the causal modalities at their face value.

On the other hand, while he takes 'being A *physically* necessitates (entails) being B' as having the same sort of job as 'being C logically necessitates (entails) being D', he is no longer moved to say *in either case* that 'necessity is a relation between properties.' Not that he is moved to deny this; for he is well rehearsed in the rubric "You can say that . . . is a --- if you like, but * * *"; and he has learned that insight may be divided from itself in such clashes as those between 'There are abstract entities,' 'There is a unique meaning-relation of aboutness or reference,' and 'Obligation is a unique togetherness of a person, a situation, a possible action' on the one hand, and 'There really are no such things' on the other. He has also learned that to pull this insight together, it is necessary to explore the way in which many dimensions of discourse come together in the use of the expressions 'under analysis.' (This depth-psychological expression is, as frequently noted, a useful metaphor; a philosophical analysis is barely under way when 'surface' techniques of definition—a family which includes 'definition in use'—have been brought to bear on the problem.)

75. In keeping with the above, Mr. E begins his last ditch stand by saying that the statement 'Being A physically entails being B' (which we shall abbreviate, from now on, to 'A P-entails B') contextually implies that the speaker feels himself entitled to infer that something is B, given that it is A.

76. But why, it may be asked, does he say 'feels,' and not that . . . the speaker *believes* himself entitled to infer that something is B, given that it is A? And could we not extort from him the 'admission' that the speaker believes this because he believes that A P-entails B? If so, the enterprise is doomed from the start.

77. Now, if Mr. E were to replace 'feels' by 'believes', he would, of course, have to point out that 'believes' in this context does not imply 'does not know'. For if it did, he would be back on the road to making physical entailments the sort of thing one 'believes is there' but cannot know. On the other hand, it would be misleading to say that the statement 'A P-entails B' contextually implies that the speaker knows that he is entitled to infer that something is B, given that it is A, not only because 'knows' implies, among other things, that we would agree with the statement—which could be gotten around by putting it in inverted commas as representing something the speaker would claim—but because, as Cook Wilson emphasized, an unqualified statement may express a mere 'thinking without question' that something is the case. And even if the statement '(*In all probability*) A P-entails B' could correctly be said to imply that the speaker knows (or 'knows') that he is entitled to infer that something is B, given that it is A, the same could scarcely be said of '(*Probably*) A P-entails B' and '(*It is more probable than not*) that A P-entails B.'

78. Suppose, then, Mr. E were to replace 'feels' by 'thinks'. Could he be forced into the stultifying 'admission' that if the speaker thinks himself entitled to infer that something is B, given that it is A, it is because he thinks that A P-entails B? Mr. E is quite unmoved by this line of

questioning, for he has up his sleeve the idea that thinking oneself entitled to draw this inference is somehow *the same thing* as thinking that A P-entails B—though this does not mean, he hastens to add, that one can simply *equate* 'A P-entails B' with 'One is entitled to infer that something is B, given that it is A.'

In any event, what Mr. E actually said was that 'A P-entails B' contextually implies that the speaker *feels* himself entitled to infer that something is B, given that it is A. And what he has in mind is the idea, to be found in many recent discussions of prescriptive discourse, that instead of the *feeling* that one ought to do A consisting of a *thinking* that one ought to do A *plus* a tendency to be moved to do A from this thought, the thinking that one ought to do A is a way of being moved to do A. Not, as early emotivism had it, because *thinking that one ought to do A* isn't really *thinking*, but merely a matter of having a 'pro-attitude' towards the doing of A (or an 'anti-attitude' towards the not-doing of A), but because 'to have the concept of obligation' is *both* to *reason* from and to the idea that people ought to do certain things, and to *intend* that they do them. And it is both of these *not* because it is each of them separately, but because *thinking* that people ought to do certain things *is intending that they do them*, where the intentions embody a certain pattern of *reasoning*.*

79. Now, once it is granted—and the point cannot be argued here—that empiricism in moral philosophy is compatible with the recognition that 'ought' has as distinguished a role in discourse as descriptive and logical terms, in particular that we *reason* rather than 'reason' concerning *ought*, and once the tautology 'The world is described by descriptive concepts' is freed from the idea that the business of all non-logical concepts is to describe, the way is clear to an *ungrudging* recognition that many expressions which empiricists have relegated to second-class citizenship in discourse, are not *inferior*, just *different*.

Clearly, to use the term 'ought' is to-prescribe rather than describe. The naturalistic 'thesis' that the world, including the verbal behavior of those who use the term 'ought'—and the mental states involving the concept to which this word gives expression—can, 'in principle,' be de-

---

* The above remarks are necessarily brief. For an expanded account, along the above lines, of statements of the form 'Jones thinks that x ought to do A,' see my essay "Imperatives, Intentions and the Logic of 'Ought'," *Methodos*, 8, 1956; also R. M. Hare, *The Language of Morals*, (Oxford: The Clarendon Press, 1952).

scribed without using the term 'ought' or any other prescriptive expression, is a logical point about what is to count as a description *in principle* of the world. For, whereas in ordinary discourse to state what something *is*, to describe something as Φ (e.g., a person as a criminal) does not preclude the possibility that an 'unpacking' of the description would involve the use of the term 'ought' or some other prescriptive expression, naturalism presents us with the ideal of a *pure* description of the world (in particular of human behavior), a description which simply says what things *are*, and never, in any respect, what they *ought* or *ought not* to be; and it is clear (as a matter of simple logic) that neither 'ought' nor any other prescriptive expression *could* be used (as opposed to *mentioned*) in such a description.

80. An essentially similar point can be made about modal expressions. To make first hand use of these expressions is to be about the business of *explaining* a state of affairs, or *justifying* an assertion. Thus, even if to state that p entails q is, in a legitimate sense, to state that something is the case, the primary use of 'p entails q' is not to state that something is the case, but to explain *why* q, or justify the assertion *that* q. The idea that the world can, in principle, be so described that the description contains no modal expression is of a piece with the idea that the world can, in principle, be so described that the description contains no prescriptive expression. For what is being called to mind is the ideal of a statement of 'everything that is the case' which, however, serves, *through and through, only* the purpose of stating what is the case. And it is a logical truth that such a description, however many modal expressions might properly be used in *arriving at* it, or in *justifying* it, or in showing the *relevance* of one of its components to another, could *contain* no modal expression.

81. It is sometimes thought that modal statements do not describe states of affairs in the world, because they are *really* metalinguistic. This won't do at all if it is meant that instead of describing states of affairs in the world, they describe linguistic habits. It is more plausible if it is meant that statements involving modal terms have the force of *prescriptive* statements about the use of certain expressions in the object language. Yet there is more than one way to 'have *the force of*' a statement, and a failure to distinguish between them may snowball into serious confusion as wider implications are drawn. Is 'p entails q' *really* the same as a statement to the effect, say, that one *ought* not to commit

oneself to 'not-q' unless one abandons 'p'? But one can know that Turks, for example, ought to withdraw '. . .' when they commit themselves to '- - -' without knowing the language, whereas the statement 'p entails q' contextually implies that the speaker not only knows the language to which 'p' and 'q' belong, but, in particular, knows how to use 'p' and 'q' themselves. A related point may illuminate the situation. The semantical statement

'Rot' (in German) means red

is not *really* the statement

'Rot' (in German) translates into 'red' (in English)

for the simple reason that whereas both štatements are in English, and hence cannot be made without knowing English, the former cannot properly be made unless the speaker understands not only English, but, in particular, the English word 'red'—and presupposes that the person spoken to does also—whereas the latter can quite properly be made by— and to—an English-speaking person who does not know how to use the word 'red'. One is tempted to put this by saying that in the semantical statement 'red' is functioning both as 'red' and as ' 'red' '. But when one reflects on the fact that it translates into French as

'Rot' (en Allemand) veut dire *rouge*

one wonders if it is helpful to say that it *mentions* the English word 'red' at all.

Shall we say that modal expressions are metalinguistic? Neither a simple 'yes' nor a simple 'no' will do. As a matter of fact, once the above considerations are given their proper weight, it is possible to acknowledge that the idea that they are metalinguistic in character over-simplifies a fundamental insight. For our present purposes, it is sufficient to say that the claim that modal expressions are 'in the metalanguage' is not too misleading if the peculiar force of the expressions which occur alongside them (represented by the 'p' and the 'q' of our example) is recognized, in particular that they have a 'straightforward' translation into other languages, and if it is also recognized that they belong not only 'in the metalanguage,' but in discourse about *thoughts* and *concepts* as well.*

* For further discussion of the rubric " '. . .' means - - -" and for an interpretation of the framework of thoughts and concepts as a quasi-theoretical framework of which the role in discourse pertaining to the explanation of overt human behavior

82. The above remarks may serve to reconcile us somewhat to Mr. E's suggestion that 'thinking (or feeling) oneself entitled to infer that something is B, given that it is A' is somehow the same thing as 'thinking that A P-entails B.' "Well, then," it may be said, "if all Mr. E wishes to claim is that on occasion we 'know' ourselves 'entitled to infer' that something is B, given that it is A, what is all the fuss about?" *The fuss is about the inverted commas around 'know' and 'entitled to infer'.*

We have learned the hard way that the core truth of 'emotivism' is not only compatible with, but absurd without, *ungrudging* recognition of the fact, so properly stressed (if mis-assimilated to the model of describing) by 'ethical rationalists,' that ethical discourse *as ethical discourse* is a mode of rational discourse. It is my purpose to argue that the core truth of Hume's philosophy of causation is not only compatible with, but absurd without, *ungrudging* recognition of those features of causal discourse as a mode of rational discourse on which the 'metaphysical rationalists' laid such stress but also mis-assimilated to describing.

IV. Toward a Theory of the 'Causal' Modalities

83. It is in the spirit of the concluding paragraphs of Part III that Mr. E now suggests that the distinction between 'A is constantly conjoined with, but does not cause, B' and 'A causes B' is to be interpreted in terms of the idea that statements of the second form imply that *simply from the fact that something is* A one is entitled to infer that it is B, whereas statements of the first form, whatever else they may do, imply that one is *not* entitled to infer *simply from the fact that something is* A that it is also B. He insists, of course, that the idea that one is entitled to infer that something is B *simply* from the fact that it is A *is exactly that,* and not 'at bottom,' as Mr. C would have it, the idea of the enthymeme obtained from

$(x) Ax \supset Bx$
Ax_1
So, Bx_1

by 'suppressing' the major premise even with the proviso that the major premise has been accepted on inductive grounds, and, perhaps, that it

is logically prior to its role in 'self-awareness' or 'introspection,' see my essay "Empiricism and the Philosophy of Mind," in Volume I of *Minnesota Studies in the Philosophy of Science,* especially sections 30–31; also the Appendix on Intentionality and the Mental at the end of the present volume.

is related in certain ways to other inductively supported propositions of this or related forms. In short, Mr. E insists that the 'season inference ticket'

If anything were A, it would be B

is actually an *inference ticket*, and not, so to speak, a *letter of credit* certifying that one has a major premise and a *formal* inference ticket at home. And this means that he conceives of induction not in terms of the model

. . .

So, (in all probability) (x) Ax ⊃ Bx

but, rather, the model

. . .

So, (in all probability) if anything were A, it would be B.

He conceives of induction as establishing principles *in accordance with which* we reason, rather than major premises *from which* we reason.

84. It is a simple consequence of this analysis that Mr. E finds a looser connection between the statement 'A causes B' and the idea that there is good inductive reason to suppose that A and B are constantly conjoined than did Mr. C in the later stages of his argument. For, although 'If anything were A, it would be B' is the sort of thing which is properly justified by inductive argument, it is, on the entailment view, even in its least metaphysical form, an oversimplification to say that the claim to have been reached by inductive reasoning is part of the force of the statement 'A causes B.'

As a parallel Mr. E might offer the fact that although moral principles are indeed the sort of thing that is properly justified by relating their espousal to the general welfare, it would be most misleading to say that we simply mean by 'If one has promised to do something, then, *ceteris paribus*, one ought to do it' something that has this sort of justification. Not that it would be 'sheer error' to say this, for it points to an important truth; the trouble is that it gives too simple a picture of the reasonableness of the appeal to general welfare in morals.

85. It is now high time that I dropped the persona of Mr. E, and set about replying to the challenge with which Mr. C ended his first critique of the entailment theory. This challenge, which Mr. E has simply ignored, presents the view I propose to defend with its crucial test. "How," it runs, "unless we view causal arguments as enthymemes,

can the terms 'implies', 'necessitates', 'impossible', etc., with which they are sprinkled, have other than a *metaphorical* use in these contexts, in view of the fact that the paradigm cases in which these expressions occur are cases in which to know entailments is simply to understand the language by which they are expressed?"

86. But, to begin with, even in the case of 'analytic inference' the situation is not quite as simple as this challenge supposes. For it would seem quite possible to understand an entailment statement in mathematical discourse without knowing its truth value. To this the reply would presumably be that to understand the meaning of mathematical expressions is, in part, to know certain procedures; and that while one can indeed understand a given segment of mathematical discourse without knowing all the entailments which one might come to know by following the appropriate procedures, one comes to know such entailments as one does come to know simply by virtue of the fact that one has understood the expressions involved, i.e., has known (and followed) these procedures. If this *is* the reply, then the challenge would appear to consist, at bottom, of the idea that the paradigm cases of entailment are cases to which *armchair* procedures are appropriate.

Thus understood, the challenge is met by *drawing a distinction* and by *reflecting*, in the spirit of the later Wittgenstein, *on the idea of 'meaning.'* The distinction is between the *antecedent* 'meanings' of 'A' and 'B' in terms of which one formulates the evidence which points to a certain inductive 'conclusion' (actually the decision to espouse the inference ticket 'If anything were A, it would be B') and what one *subsequently* 'understands' by these terms when one uses them in accordance with this decision. The point of this distinction is that while one does not inductively establish that A P-entails B by armchair reflection on the *antecedent* 'meanings' of 'A' and 'B', to establish by induction that A P-entails B is to *enrich* (and, perhaps, otherwise modify) the use of these terms in such wise that to 'understand' what one now 'means' by 'A' and 'B' *is* to know that A P-entails B.

If to establish by induction that A causes B were to establish that (in all probability) $(x) Ax \supset Bx$, perhaps as a member of a set of inductive conclusions, there would be little reason to say that to establish by induction that A causes B is to decide on empirical grounds to give a new use to 'A' and 'B'. If, however, it is, as I am arguing, a matter of deciding to adopt a new principle of inference, then there is every reason to say that to establish by induction that A causes B is to modify the use of 'A' and 'B' and, indeed, to modify it in such a way that these terms can properly be said to have acquired a new 'meaning.'

Here two warnings are in order: First, the new 'meanings' do not involve a change in explicit definition. B has not, in *this* sense become 'part of the meaning of' 'A'. Yet the new role played by 'B' and 'A' does warrant the statement that the 'meaning' of 'A' involves the 'meaning' of 'B'; for they are now 'internally related' in a way in which they were not before.

Second, the relation between the new and the old 'meanings' of 'A' and 'B' is a *logical* rather than a purely historical one; as long, that is, as the espousal of this new inference ticket retains its character as a scientific decision. For in spite of the fact that in science as in life "You can't go home again," and one never quite returns to old 'meanings' (though the historian of science can unearth them), scientific terms have, as part of their logic a 'line of retreat' as well as a 'plan of advance'—a fact which makes meaningful the claim that in an important sense A and B are the 'same' properties they were 'before.' And it is this strategic dimension of the use of scientific terms which makes possible the *reasoned* recognition of what Aldrich (2) has perceptively called "renegade instances," and gives inductive conclusions, in spite of the fact that, as principles of inference, they relate to the very 'meaning' of scientific terms, a corrigibility which is a matter of 'retreat to prepared positions' rather than an irrational 'rout.' The motto of the age of science might well be: *Natural philosophers have hitherto sought to understand 'meanings'; the task is to change them.*

87. If the above argument is successful, it explains how one can grant that 'knowing that A P-entails B' has the connection with 'understanding the meaning of "A" and "B" ' which Mr. C requires of 'knowing that one state of affairs entails another,' without being committed to the absurdities of classical rationalism. In doing so it explains why one feels uncomfortable about saying that one *sees* that one state of affairs P-entails another. For the metaphor of *seeing* and *coming to see*, taken from a paradigm case of *non-inferential* knowledge, is clearly inappropriate where, instead of exploring implications within a *status quo* of 'meanings,' one is reasoning one's way into a decision to change the *status quo*. (As a matter of fact, we have recently come to appreciate that the extent to which even the discovery of new logico-mathematical

entailments is a matter of working within the framework of antecedent usage was greatly exaggerated by classical philosophies of mathematics.)

But if it is inappropriate to speak, in scientific contexts, of *seeing* physical entailments, it by no means follows that it is inappropriate to speak of *knowing* that one state of affairs physically entails or necessitates another. And it is the fact, to which we have already called attention, that empirically minded philosophers who have developed interpretations of causality along entailment lines (among others, C. D. Broad and W. C. Kneale) have taken for granted that entailments which can't be 'seen' can't be *known* which has given their views such an air of paradox and put them unnecessarily on the defensive. There *is*, indeed, an implicit contradiction in the idea of explaining scientific reasoning in terms of unknowable relations of entailment which one *opines* to be *there*. Mr. C was certainly entitled to expostulate, 'If our science doesn't require us to know them, why put them there to be known by the angels? It is, as I see it, a primary virtue of the account we have been developing, that it lacks this unwelcome feature of classical entailment interpretations of causality.

88. It is high time that we reminded ourselves that our controversy between Messrs. E and C has been carried on in a very rarified atmosphere. Among other things, it has been formulated in terms of a supposed distinction between physically contingent and physically necessary constant conjunctions, where both are *truly universal* in scope; i.e. contain no reference, overt or covert, to particular places, times or objects. In a certain sense, this was unavoidable. The initial stages, at least, of an attempt to resolve a classical controversy must take 'theses' and 'antitheses' as it finds them, and not change the subject. Yet the story is not complete until some effort has been made to tie these abstractly formulated issues to the features of actual discourse, scientific and prescientific, which gave rise to them. But before discussing the 'universality,' in the above sense, of scientific generalizations, I shall touch all too briefly on a topic which, though at first sight it serves only to *supplement* our account of inductive inference, will actually lead us to the more penetrating account of lawlike statements as material rules of inference.

I have in mind the problem of interpreting those inductions of which the conclusion, instead of having the form '(In all probability) All As are B,' have instead the form '(In all probability) the proportion of

As which are B is n/m.' For, it may well be asked, unless you are going to interpret all 'statistical' inductive conclusions (in a suitably broad sense of 'statistical') as belonging to the category of 'accidental,' as opposed to 'nomological' generalizations, you face the problem of explaining how statistical nomologicals can be interpreted as physical entailments or analogous to physical entailments.

89. Can we find anything in the field of statistical induction which resembles

> . . .
> So, (in all probability) A P-entails B [i.e. that something is B may reasonably be inferred, given that it is A]?

The obvious suggestion is

> n/m of observed As have been (found to be) B
> So, (in all probability) K is a restricted class of As P-entails that n/m of its members are B * [i.e. that n/m of the members of K are B may reasonably be inferred, given that K is a restricted class of As].

(By speaking of K as a 'restricted' class of As, I mean that K is a finite class of As the membership of which is specified in terms of a place and/or a time and/or an individual thing.)

There are many respects in which this formulation would have to be tidied up and qualified to meet the demands of a theory of primary statistical induction. In so far as they are of a kind which must be taken into account by any such theory, I can safely leave them to the reader. There is, however, one objection which is, at first sight, fatal to the above suggestion. Suppose that of m hitherto observed cases of A, n have been found to be B. According to the theory under consideration, we argue

> . . .
> So, (in all probability) that K is a restricted class of As P-entails that n/m of the members of K are B.

Suppose, however, that we subsequently examine a new restricted class of As, K_1, and find that n'/m' of the members, m' in number, of K_1

---

* A more realistic account would have, instead of 'n/m', 'a proportion approximating to n/m', and would give some indication of how the closeness of the approximation relates to the 'size' of the evidence and to other features of the inductive situation. But I am leaving out of account all 'secondary' inductions, for I am attempting to put my finger on a logical point which relates to the very concept of inductive inference.

are B. We then reason, according to the theory, and taking into account this new evidence,

> $n + n'/m + m'$ of the observed cases of A have been B
> So, (in all probability) K is a restricted class of As P-entails that $n + n'/m + m'$ of the members of K are B.

But have we not just examined a restricted class of As, namely K_1, and found the proportion of Bs to be, not $n + n'/m + m'$, but, rather, n'/m'? How can it be reasonable to say that

> (In all probability) that K is a restricted class of As P-entails that $n + n'/m + m'$ of the members of K are B

when we know that not $n + n'/m + m'$, but n'/m', of the members of K_1, which we have just examined, are B? After all, can we reasonably say that p entails q, when we know that p is true and q false?

90. Before we attempt to answer this objection, let us note that if it could be answered, and if the above account is essentially correct, then statistical induction, like the induction of logically universal laws, would yield principles in accordance with which we would move from empirical proposition to empirical proposition. In other words, we would not be faced with the problem of how to get from 'limits of frequencies' in an infinite reference class, or even from frequencies in classes which are stipulated to be finite but of unspecified numerosity, to empirical propositions concerning the ratio with which a quaesitum property occurs in a restricted class of objects having the reference property. For the view we are proposing so formulates the conclusions of primary statistical inductions that they concern the inference of finite, restricted empirical matter of fact from finite, restricted empirical matter of fact.

91. But what of the objection? We must begin by granting that if the conclusions of primary statistical induction were of the form

> . . .
> So, (in all probability) that K is any restricted class of As P-entails that n/m of its members are B

the objection would be unanswerable. When, however, we reflect that the point of induction is to give us a rational grip on unobserved or, better, in a suitably broad sense, unexamined cases, a ray of hope appears. Suppose, then, we try

> . . .
> So, (in all probability) that K is any unexamined restricted class of As P-entails that n/m of its members are B.

At first sight this formulation is open to the objection that it makes a physical entailment of the fact of being a restricted class, K, of As *hinge on K's being unexamined*. This strikes us, at first sight, as of a piece with saying that causal laws are of the form 'unexamined As cause B.' Actually, however, the situation is not as bad as it looks, for the first two parts of this essay have made it abundantly clear that the word 'cause' as actually used has a meaning which is not captured in *toto* by the notion of physical entailment. Thus, if we have permitted ourselves in these last two sections to use such locutions as 'A causes B' and to treat them as equivalent (from Mr. E's standpoint) to 'A physically entails B,' this has been dialectical license. Once, however, we bear in mind that not even in the conclusion of non-statistical inductions, as we have formulated them, is 'physically entails' intended to have the force of 'causes', but to have the force, roughly, of 'entails in a way which essentially involves the specific empirical subject matter to which reference is made', the above paradox vanishes, as is readily seen if, instead of the above, we write

. . .

> So, that n/m of the members of K are B may reasonably be inferred, given that K is an unexamined restricted class of As.

And, indeed, concerning what sort of classes does one wish to draw inferences, if not unexamined ones, unexamined, that is, in the respect under consideration?

Statements of the form 'The chance that x_1 is B is n/m' imply that the individual in question, whether a thing (e.g. a planet, a marble) or an event (e.g. an election, the drawing of a marble), is being considered as a member of a restricted class K of, say, As, where there is reason to think (perhaps because one has examined them, perhaps by the 'use' of a statistical inference ticket) that the proportion of Ks which are B is n/m. The statistical inference ticket itself, namely 'That the proportion of Bs in K is n/m can reasonably be inferred, given that K is an unexamined, restricted class of As' corresponds, therefore, to the statement '(In all probability) the chance that an A is B is n/m.'

That the proportion of Bs in a specific restricted class of As is n/m is, of course, either true or false as a matter of empirical fact. On the other hand, the question as to the applicability of the terms 'true' or 'false' to the conclusions of inductive inferences is considerably more complex. What can be said is that it is undoubtedly the fact that it would at the very least be *misleading* to say of the conclusion of yesterday's carefully and correctly drawn inference that it was false, on the ground that negative evidence turned up this morning, which gives aid and comfort to the idea that the conclusions of carefully and correctly drawn inductive inferences are logically true, and hence to the conception that probability is a relation of the form $prob(p,e)$.*

92. Whether or not this account of primary statistical induction would substantially survive all criticism, I think it has some merit. And if it is sound (in its general lines) it provides welcome reinforcement for the idea that the 'conclusions' of primary non-statistical inductions are decisions to espouse inference tickets. But more than this it provides us, as we shall see in a moment, with an important clue to the evaluation of the idea (so dear to Mr. C's heart) that the conclusions of primary non-statistical induction either *are* or *include* statements about all things, everywhere and every-when.

This can best be brought out by imagining the following objection to be brought against our treatment of Mr. C: "It is simply absurd to suppose that where 'A' and 'B' contain no overt or covert reference to particular times, places or individuals, one could have reason to suppose that

$$\Diamond\{(\exists x)\, Ax \cdot \sim Bx\}$$

without having reason to suppose that

$$(\exists x)\, Ax \cdot \sim Bx.$$

After all, *all things everywhere and every-when* is a pretty large order, and there is an air of unreality about challenging Mr. C to explain the 'fact' that one could have reason, on occasion, to believe in physical possibilities that are *never* actualized. Take the example around which you built your 'thought experiment' (section 65). The idea was, if I understand it, that we might be entitled to believe that $(x)\, Px \supset Rx$ is a constant but (physically) contingent conjunction, because we might be entitled to explain this constant conjunction in terms of the two ideas, (1) that *as a (physically) contingent matter of fact* all planets have arisen and will arise from inside their solar system; and (2) that as a matter of *physical necessity* all inside-originating planets have the

* This paragraph and the one which immediately precedes it were stimulated by a helpful discussion with Michael Scriven of the compatibility of the above treatment of statistical induction with the view, which he wished to defend, that statements about the likelihoods of individual events are empirically true or false.

property P. In other words, the idea was that we might be entitled to assert that planets which originate from outside, although there happen to be none, need not rotate as they revolve.

"But," the objection continues, "unless I am very much mistaken, the idea that we could be entitled to believe, on inductive grounds, both that

> It is physically possible for planets to originate from outside their solar system

and that

> Nowhere and no-when does any planet so originate

simply won't do. And if so, you have not really challenged Mr. C's interpretation of 'A causes (or physically necessitates) B' as an unrestricted generalization of the form

> Everywhere and every-when A is conjoined with B

as contextually implying that the speaker has inductive grounds for his assertion."

93. We are now in a position to concede that this objection rests on a sound insight; one, however, which gives neither aid nor comfort to the constant conjunction interpretation of causality. The truth it sees, and which must be conceded, is that one, indeed, could not have inductive reason to assert both

$$\text{(In all probability) } (x)\, Ax \supset Bx$$

and

$$\diamondsuit\text{-}\{(\exists x)\, Ax \cdot \sim Bx\}\text{-}$$

where the scope of the former statement is *unrestricted* in the sense indicated.* What point could there be to a distinction between state-

---

* This statement must be qualified, once the theoretical dimension of scientific reasoning is taken into account, by mentioning such possible exceptions are represented by the following: Suppose that we knew on *theoretical* grounds that the universe was one 'heart beat' of expansion and contraction, and that a certain kind of event B could take place, given an event of kind A, only when and if the universe went through a certain pattern P in its expansion. Suppose, further, that whether or not the universe goes through this pattern depends on the initial state of the universe, the theory defining a class of alternative initial states some of which do, some of which do not, eventuate in P. Suppose, finally, that observation provides reason to believe that the universe did go through P. We conclude that it is a *physically contingent* fact that A was constantly conjoined with B, and will continue (if vacuously) to be so, but that it is a matter of physical necessity that A was and will be constantly conjoined with B in the presence of P.

ments of unrestricted constant conjunction and lawlike statements, if one is never in a position to assert the physical possibility of exceptions, while denying that they actually occur?

94. Or, to put it somewhat differently, what point can there be to an extension to the universe as a whole (everywhere and every-when) of the distinction we can readily draw, in more restricted contexts, between uniformities which depend on the presence of an additional factor, and those which do not? After all, in evaluating the uniformities found in restricted contexts, we can point beyond them in certain cases, the 'physically contingent cases,' to the fact that the uniformity is absent when the circumstances are different. This procedure, however, makes no sense when extended to the universe as a whole, everywhere and every-when.

95. What shall we say? Actually, the clue to the answer is to be found in what might be thought to be the very strength of the objection. "This procedure makes no sense when extended to the universe as a whole, everywhere and every-when." For Mr. C has been construing the primary induction of non-statistical laws to the effect that A causes B, as a limiting case of coming to know that the members of a restricted class of As are, without exception, B; the limiting case, that is, in which the relevant class is the class of all As in the universe as a whole, every-when and everywhere. This, however, if our argument to date is sound, is simply not so. He has been reinforced in this mistake by the idea that the primary induction of non-statistical laws is a limiting case of the primary induction of statistical laws. But while in a certain sense this latter idea is quite correct, it is so only if primary statistical induction is construed as we have been construing it. These two points hang neatly together, for on our account the idea that the induction of non-statistical laws is a special case of statistical induction amounts to the idea that the former is to be represented by the schema

> Observed As have been found, without exception, to be B
> So, (in all probability) that K is an unexamined, restricted class of As P-entails that the proportion of Bs in K is 1.

or

> . . .
> So, that the proportion of Bs in K is unity can reasonably be inferred, given that K is an unexamined, restricted class of As.

And, of course, the difference between this case, and the case of primary statistical induction is that if a hitherto unexamined restricted class, K_1, of As turns out, on examination, to include As which are not B, no future induction which includes the members of K_1 among its data can hope to establish once again that the proportion of Bs within an unexamined restricted class K can reasonably be inferred to be unity (as opposed to 'can reasonably be inferred to approximate unity' or 'can reasonably be inferred to be the closer to unity, the larger the membership of K'). It is in this sense, and in this sense only that new evidence is more threatening to non-statistical than to statistical primary induction.

96. To the objection that to take this line is to formulate causal laws in terms of what is entailed by the fact that K is an *unexamined* class of A's, whereas we surely think that (in general) the fact of being un-observed is irrelevant to the *effects* things have, it is sufficient to point out once again that we are analyzing not the specific force of 'causes', but the logical character of modal expressions in scientific explanation, and that to put 'P-entails' in the above context does not require us to say that 'A causes B on *condition that it is unobserved*,' but only that 'the idea that A P-implies B commits one to the reasonableness of the inference with respect to any *unexamined*, restricted class K of As, that its members are, without exception, B.'

97. Viewed in this light, our problem no longer appears as that of distinguishing within the class of statements of the form

$$(x) \ Fx \supset Gx$$

between those which formulate laws and those which formulate 'acci-dental but unrestricted conjunctions.' For if our interpretation of in-ductive reasoning is correct, it is just a mistake to suppose that lawlike statements are statements of the form '$(x) \ Fx \supset Gx$' at all, *with or with-out contextual implications*. It is even misleading to say that they imply statements of this form, though we did not demur when Mr. C made this claim at an early stage of his argument. The relation between

A P-entails B

and the function

$$\sim[x \ is \ A \cdot \sim(x \ is \ B)]$$

which we are tempted to put by saying that

A P-entails B $: < : (x) \ Ax \supset Bx$

or by representing 'A P-entails B' by '$\boxed{c}\{(x) \ Ax \supset Bx\}$', where, in each case '(x) Ax ⊃ Bx' formulates a statement about everything, everywhere and every-when, consists rather in the fact that our decision to espouse the inference ticket which is the lawlike statement, would be logically undermined were we to find *anywhere* or *anywhen* a restricted class of As, the members of which were not uniformly B.

My point, of course, is not that we *couldn't* use '(x) Ax ⊃ Bx' to represent lawlike statements. It is, rather, that given that we use this form to represent general statements which do not have a lawlike force, to use it *also* to represent lawlike statements is to imply that lawlike statements are a *special case* of non-lawlike statements. It is therefore particularly important to note that I am not claiming that all restricted generalizations, i.e. generalizations of which the subject term is a *localized* term, are unlawlike. It may, indeed, be true that all unrestricted generalizations *which we can have reason to assert* are lawlike. But not all lawlike statements which we can have reason to assert are unrestricted generalizations. And the logical form of even a restricted lawlike generalization is obscured rather than clarified by representing it by '(x) fx ⊃ gx'.

98. It would be incorrect to say that *any* statement of the form "All . . . are ---' is a mere abbreviation for a conjunction of singular statements. Yet some statements of this form, those which, as we informally say, commit themselves only to what is the case, are *in principle* completely confirmable by confirming each of a finite set of singular statements. This does not mean, of course, that to do the latter *is the same thing* as to do the former; for, as was pointed out above, these 'all-' statements are not shorthand for the conjunction of these singular statements. To illustrate, we can in principle completely confirm such statements as 'All the people in this room are tall' (made on a particular occasion) by confirming each of a set of singular statements to the formulation of which the original statement is (in the circumstances in which it was made) a guide. But, once again, the conjunction of these singular statements does not have the force of the original statement.

Now it is such 'all-'statements as these (let us call them *descriptive* 'all-'statements) which authorize only 'subjunctive identicals' as contrasted with subjunctive conditionals proper. Thus, 'All the people in this room are tall' authorizes 'If anyone were (identical with) one of the people who are in this room, he would be tall'; but not 'If anyone were in this room he would be tall.' To be sure, if we knew that *being tall* was, for one reason or another, a necessary condition of getting into the room, then we would know that if anyone were in the room, he would be tall; but the correct way to imply that if anyone were in the room he would be tall is *not* by saying 'All the people in this room are tall,' but rather by saying 'All the people in this room are, of necessity, tall.' And to say this is not to claim that it is a law that being in the room entails by itself being tall, but simply that the state of affairs asserted by the descriptive 'all-'statement can be shown to be a necessary consequence of certain other facts about the situation.

The fact that descriptive 'all-'statements can be *reasonably* believed to be true without complete confirmation—that they can, in a broad sense, be established by *inductive* reasoning—has given aid and comfort to the idea that lawlike statements are a special class of descriptive 'all-' statements. To have this idea, however, is, among other things, to be puzzled as to why, where our knowledge that all the men in this room are tall is, in a broad sense, 'inductive,' we can't say 'If anyone were in this room, he would be tall' or '. . . it would be the case that he was tall.' The explanation can't consist in the fact that the 'all-'statement is restricted in its scope to less than the whole universe, for statements can be so restricted and yet authorize subjunctive conditionals proper (as opposed to counter-identicals, e.g. 'If anyone were identical with one of the persons who are in this room, he would be tall.') Nor is the explanation that the reasoning which supports the statement is of the same sort as that by which we support lawlike statements, but that the grounds are *weaker*, not strong enough to support a lawlike statement. The explanation is rather that the 'inductive' reasoning—the 'crime detection' reasoning—by which we support restricted 'all-'statements which are not lawlike is *not* the same sort of thing as the reasoning by which we support lawlike statements, as can be readily seen by comparing the reasoning by which, from a Holmesian variety of clues, we might establish that all the people who walked down a certain muddy road yesterday were farmers, with the following, dated 1500,

> All observed free-floating needles in these latitudes which have been stroked by stone S have, without exception, pointed to the North
> So, that the members of K will point to the North can reasonably be inferred given that K is an unexamined, restricted

class of free-floating needles which have been stroked by stone S.

To make the same point the other way around, if the reasoning by which a restricted 'all-'statement (e.g. 'All the people in that room are tall') has been established were of the form

All of the people in that room whose height has been ascertained have proved, without exception, to be tall
So, (in all probability) all the people in that room are tall

or were a straightforward derivation of this 'all-'statement by specification from a more general 'all-'statement which had been established by an argument of the above form, then 'All the people in that room are tall', would be the (misleading) formulation of a lawlike statement. For while lawlike statements may be accepted without reason, or for reasons which do not have the form of an inductive argument in the narrow or 'primary' sense, all 'all-'statements which are accepted on inductive grounds in the narrow or 'primary' sense are, however restricted in their scope they may be, without exception lawlike. It is because we already know so much about people, rooms, size, etc. antecedent to raising the question 'Are all the people in the next room tall?' that we would reject the above argument as a bad one. And while the argument by which, in a given case, the statement 'All the people in that room are tall' is supported might, as we have seen, be such as to authorize 'If anyone were in that room, he would be tall (i.e. it would be the case that he was tall),' it need not be.*

To sum up, lawlike statements are not a special case of descriptive 'all-'statements. In particular, they are not descriptive 'all-'statements which are unrestricted in scope, i.e. not localized by reference to particular places, times, or objects. Indeed, do we ever make descriptive 'all-'statements about the whole universe everywhere and every-when? As philosophers we can imagine ourselves doing so; but the idea that we are doing so everytime we make an unrestricted lawlike statement is a product of bad philosophy.

99. A related point can be made about statistical laws. Thus, suppose

---

* This paragraph was added after Mr. Gavin Alexander correctly pointed out that the distinction between the 'crime detection' reasoning—inductive 'in a broad sense'—by which we support restricted 'all-'statements which are not lawlike, and the reasoning by which we support even restricted lawlike statements, is so central to my argument that it should not be referred to cavalierly as something that "can readily be seen."

that on grounds of analogy or extrapolation, as contrasted with direct induction from planetary observations, we reasoned

> . . .
> So, that, say, 99/100 of the members of K originate inside their solar system may reasonably be inferred, given that K is an unexamined restricted class of planets.

Granted that our statistical knowledge about planets, thus interpreted, does not entail that there are any planets, does it not, perhaps, entail that if there are any, then some 1/100 of the number of all planets everywhere and every-when have succeeded in joining their solar systems from without? Is it not *incompatible* with the idea that there never has been nor never will be a planet which succeeds in joining its solar system from without?

The answer, in terms of our analysis, is that there is, indeed, such an incompatibility; not, however, because the statistical law is a statement of the form

> The proportion of Bs among As in the past, present and future of the universe is n/m

or its more sophisticated variants (Reichenbach, Von Mises) designed to make sense of the relative frequency of a quaesitum property in an infinite reference class, but because to accept the law is to be prepared to infer, with respect to any unexamined restricted class of planets, that the proportion of its members which originate from outside the solar system to which they belong is 1/100.

100. In the case of both statistical and non-statistical primary inductions, then, our account has freed us from the idea, disturbing even to those who have believed themselves committed to it, that if induction is to be reasonable, it must be reasonable to move from 'observed As have been found to be B in the proportion n/m (where n may equal m),' to '(In all probability) everywhere and every-when the proportion of As which are B is n/m.'

101. Does any place remain, after all this has been said, for the idea of a *physically contingent* but *unrestricted* constant conjunction? The answer is that even if one is never, can—logically—never be in a position to say

> . . .
> So, (in all probability) A is as a *matter of physically contingent fact* constantly accompanied by B

one may well be in a position to say

> . . . So, there need not have been nor need there ever be exceptions to the conjunction of B with A, in spite of the fact that (in all probability) there are exceptions, and that (in all probability) A does not P-entail B.

We must here, as elsewhere, draw a distinction between what we are committed to concerning the world by virtue of the fact that we have reason to make a certain assertion, and the force, in a narrower sense, of the assertion itself. Idealism is notorious for the fallacy of concluding that because there must be minds in the world in order for us to have reason to make statements about the world, therefore there is no sense to the idea of a world which does not include minds; the idea, that is, that things might have been such that there were no minds. Surely there is a parallel fallacy in the argument that since we can have no reason to suppose that the relationship between A and B is contingent, which is not a reason for supposing there to be As which are not B, there is no sense to the idea that things *might* have so worked out that A was constantly but contingently conjoined with B!

And just as it throws light on the status of mind in the universe to point out that it makes sense to speak of a universe which contains no minds; so it throws light on the concept of a law of nature to point out that it makes sense to speak of a universe in which there are uniformities which, although physically contingent, are without exception. Surely, to be in a position to say

> . . .
> So, (in all probability) A · C P-entails B; whereas A · C′ P-entails ~B

or, more simply,

> . . .
> So, (in all probability) A is P-compatible with both B and ~B

is to be in a position to say that, *although in the nature of the case we have reason to think that they have not done so*, things might have so worked out that A was constantly conjoined with B (or, for that matter, with ~B). And where our reason for thinking that A is compatible with both B and ~B is *not* that we have observed As which are B and As which are ~B, but consists, rather, in considerations of extrapolation and analogy, we are in a position to say that, although in the nature of the case we have reason to think they have not done so, things may actually be such that A is constantly conjoined with B (or ~B).

102. To take the causal modalities at their face value, that is to say, to interpret statements concerning what is physically necessary or possible or impossible as belonging to the object language of scientific (and everyday) discourse, which statements, however intimately they may be related to such metalinguistic statements as they may, *in some sense*, imply, are nevertheless not themselves 'really' metalinguistic, is certainly to court serious philosophical perplexity. Even a dyed in the wool empiricist might be willing to go along with the idea that specific statements of the form 'A P-entails B' are non-descriptive statements which contextually imply that the speaker feels entitled to infer that something is B, given that it is A; it is when he is confronted with statements of the form

> *There is* a property which P-entails B

or, above all, by such statements as

> *There exist* causal connections which have not yet been discovered

and

> For every kind of event E *there is* a kind of event E' such that the occurrence of E' P-entails the contiguous occurrence of E

that his anxiety is likely to reach serious proportions.

It is as though someone who had taken the early emotivist line in ethics had been carefully talked into the idea that 'ought' is a perfectly good concept, though not a descriptive one, and that 'Everybody ought to keep promises' contextually implies a wish, on the speaker's part, that promise keeping were a universal practice, and was then confronted with such statements as

> *There are* obligations which have not yet been recognized

and

> Some of the things we think of as obligations are not obligations.

103. It is therefore important to realize that the presence in the object language of the causal modalities (and of the logical modalities and of the deontic modalities) serves not only to express *existing* commitments, but also to provide the *framework* for the thinking by which

we reason our way (in a manner appropriate to the specific subject matter) into the making of new commitments and the abandoning of old. And since this framework essentially involves quantification over predicate variables, puzzles over the 'existence of abstract entities' are almost as responsible for the prevalence in the empiricist tradition of 'nothing-but-ism' in its various forms (emotivism, philosophical behaviorism, phenomenalism) as its tendency to assimilate all discourse to describing.

This is not the occasion for an exploration of the problem of 'abstract entities.' * It is, however, essential to my purposes to urge that an ungrudging recognition of the role in discourse of such contexts as

$$(\exists \Phi) \ldots \Phi \ldots$$

is the very foundation of sound philosophy. Empiricists have tended to be reasonably comfortable with such statements as

The German word 'rot' means the quality red

by virtue of construing them, correctly, as having something like the force of

The German word 'rot' has—in an appropriate sense—the same role or use as our one-place predicate 'red'.

and, in general, by thinking of the rubric 'there is a quality, relation, property, etc., such that . . .' as a framework device which uses what Wittgenstein (in the Tractatus) called 'formal concepts' to represent in a language certain features of its use, features the formulation of which would belong in a metalanguage. It is when the empiricist is confronted with such statements as

There are qualities which no one has yet experienced
There are numbers for which no designation exists in our language

not to mention the examples of the preceding paragraph, that he is tempted either to regress to a more primitive empiricism, or to cross the lines and join forces with the more empirically minded metaphysicians.

104. It has been, on the whole, a presupposition of contemporary empiricism that the range of variables is to be interpreted in terms of

---

* I have discussed this problem in an essay, "Empiricism and Abstract Entities," to appear at a future date in The Philosophy of Rudolf Carnap, (New York: Tudor, forthcoming).

existing conceptual resources. This presupposition found its most explicit expression in the formulas (Wittgenstein, 20)

$$(x) \, fx = fa \cdot fb \cdot fc \, \ldots$$
$$(\exists x) \, fx = fa \, v \, fb \, v \, fc \, \ldots$$

Built on a distinction between expressions which *name* (the 'a', 'b', 'c', etc. of the above formulas) and expressions which, *though they may present the appearance of names*, are to be analyzed as 'shorthand' for definite descriptions, this presupposition amounted to the idea that our language refers to the members of a certain category of entity, in this case particulars—which, to free the logical point I am making from phenomenalistic associations, I shall suppose to be physical objects—by virtue of (a) the names it contains, and (b) by virtue of the descriptive phrases of the form 'the x which is R to a' which can be formulated in it. And while reference to a *particular* physical object is, indeed, by name or by description, the idea that reference to physical objects *in general* exists by virtue of names supplemented by definite descriptions, where the variable x in the description is interpreted in the spirit of the above formulas can readily be seen to involve the paradoxical consequence that the range of describable objects, and hence the range of reference of the language (with respect to physical objects) coincides with the range of *named* objects.

It is obvious, indeed, that only in an 'ideally complete' language which did contain names for all physical objects could there be a *cash value* equivalence between '(x) fx' and 'fa $\cdot$ fb $\cdot$ fc . . .' We are tempted to put this by saying that *as matters stand* the use of variables and the device of quantification gives language a direct reference to physical objects which supplements the reference provided by names. To do so, however, is to become puzzled—particularly if, following Quine, we are tempted to construe all designations of individuals as descriptions.

105. The solution of this puzzle lies in the fact that the logic of variables and quantification involves not only the *momentary* crystalized content of the language at a *cross section* of its history, but also its character as admitting—indeed demanding—modification, revision, in short, development, in accordance with rational procedures. In the case of variables the values of which are descriptive constants, these rational procedures can be summed up in the single word 'Induction.' But the point is of more general import, as can be seen by reflecting

on the logic of number variables in the context of the history of mathematics since, say, 1600.

106. The above remarks on variables are designed to introduce the concluding theme of this essay. For they make it clear that the force of such expressions as 'There is a characteristic such that . . .', i.e.

$$(\exists \Phi) \ldots \Phi \ldots$$

is likewise misunderstood if they are interpreted as mobilizing the *existing* stock of 'primitive descriptive predicates' of our language at this cross section of its history. Rather they embody the idea of the predicates it will be reasonable to *introduce* (or to *discard*) as well as of those which express our imperfect achievements to date.

But it is this fact which enables us to make sense of the idea that

> There are causal connections which have not yet been discovered.

For we have not yet fully faced the question: What can be meant by speaking of the 'existence' of an *unknown entailments?* It is the willingness to accept this way of talking which—in the absence of the distinctions we have been drawing—leads directly to rationalistic metaphysics. It is the unwillingness to accept rationalistic metaphysics which—in the absence of the distinctions we have been drawing—leads directly to Humean metaphysics.

107. Is the idea that every change has a cause a super-hypothesis? An induction from inductions? Or is it, perhaps, an a priori truth? It is certainly not the latter if we mean by an a priori truth the sort of thing that *could* be established by induction but is *fortunately* exempt from having to run the inductive gauntlet because of our progress at rational intuition. For the 'Causal Principle' isn't the sort of thing that *could* be established by induction. It isn't a hypothesis about the world—not because it is about nothing, but because it no more has the business of describing than do specific causal propositions. Not that it is like specific causal propositions, only more abstract; its force, as we shall see, is of quite another kind.

The first thing to see, is that it is a logical truth that there can be no *descriptive* statement which stands to 'Every event has a cause' as 'This A is B,' 'That A is B,' etc. stand to 'All A is B.' That is to say, there can be none if our analysis of lawlike statements is correct. And if so, then the idea of an inductive argument of which the conclusion is

Wilfrid Sellars

'. . . So, (in all probability) every event has a cause' is logical nonsense.

And once one abandons the idea that the causal principle is a super-description of the world, one is no longer confronted by the need to choose between the alternatives, (a) that it is an induction from inductions (thus implicitly committing ourselves to the regularity analysis of lawlike statements), and (b) that it is a rational intuition. And we find ourselves in a position to acknowledge the truth in the claim that we know a priori—i.e. other than by induction—that every change has a cause. For not all *knowing* is knowing how to describe something. We *know* what we *ought to do* as well as what the circumstances *are*.

The indicative sentence "Every change has a cause" and its more sophisticated counterparts, bring every descriptive term which has or will be introduced into the language of science within the scope of the question 'What is its cause?' And while it is, indeed, true that circumstances can be imagined in which it would be unreasonable to continue the search for causes in a certain domain of problems, it would be simply incorrect to express the decision to abandon this search by means of the sentence '(In all probability) such and such a kind of event has no cause.' It would, of course, be equally incorrect to express the decision to press on in all areas of science, based on success after success in past investigations, by the sentence, '(In all probability) every kind of event has a cause.' The *economic* (in the broadest sense) issue 'to continue or not to continue?' must not be confused with an issue concerning the causal principle. To say that a certain kind of event has no cause is not to express a pessimistic view of the outcome of an investigation; if it didn't express philosophical confusion, it would be to abdicate.

108. For the causal principle gives expression to features of our language (indeed, of our mind) which are independent of success or failure, of optimism or pessimism, of the economics of intellectual effort. Among other things, it gives expression to the fact that although describing and explaining (predicting, retrodicting, understanding) are *distinguishable*, they are also, in an important sense, *inseparable*. It is only because the expressions in terms of which we describe objects, even such basic expressions as words for the perceptible characteristics of molar objects * locate these objects in a space of implications, that they *describe* at all,

* For an elaboration of this point, see my essay "Empiricism and the Philosophy of Mind," in the first volume of *Minnesota Studies in the Philosophy of Science*, particularly sections 35–38.

rather than merely label. The descriptive and the explanatory resources of language advance hand in hand; and to abandon the search for explanation is to abandon the attempt to improve language, *period*.

Once the development of human language left the stage when linguistic changes had *causes*, but not *reasons*, and man acquired the ability to reason about his reasons, then, and this is a logical point about having the ability to reason about reasons, his language came to permit the formulation of certain propositions which, incapable of proof or disproof by empirical methods, draw, in the heart of *language militant*, a picture of *language triumphant*. Kant's conception that reason is characterized by certain regulative ideals contains a profound truth which empiricism has tended to distort into the empirical psychology of the scientific enterprise.

February 24, 1957

REFERENCES

1. Ayer, A. J. "What is a Law of Nature?" *Revue Internationale de Philosophie*, 56:144–165 (1956).
2. Aldrich, Virgil. "Renegade Instances," *Philosophy of Science*, 3:506–514 (1936).
3. Bergmann, Gustav. "Dispositional Properties," *Philosophical Studies*, 6:77–80 (1955).
4. Braithwaite, R. B. *Scientific Explanation*. Cambridge: Cambridge Univ. Press, 1953.
5. Burks, Arthur. "The Logic of Causal Propositions," *Mind*, 60:363–382 (1951).
6. Burks, Arthur. "Dispositional Statements," *Philosophy of Science*, 22:175–193 (1955).
7. Broad, C. D. *Examination of McTaggart's Philosophy*, Vol. I. Cambridge: Cambridge Univ. Press, 1934.
8. Collingwood, R. G. "On the So-Called Idea of Causation," *Aristotelian Society Proceedings*, 38:85–112 (1937–38).
9. Feigl, Herbert. "Notes on Causality," in H. Feigl and M. Brodbeck (eds.), *Readings in the Philosophy of Science*. New York: Appleton-Century-Crofts, 1953.
10. Kaplan, Abraham. "Definition and Specification of Meaning," *Journal of Philosophy*, 43:281–288 (1946).
11. Kaplan, Abraham, and H. F. Schott. "A Calculus for Empirical Classes," *Methodos*, 3:165–188 (1951).
12. Kneale, William. *Probability and Induction*. New York: Oxford Univ. Press, 1949.
13. Pap, Arthur. "Reduction Sentences and Open Concepts," *Methodos*, 5:3–30 (1953).
14. Popper, Karl. "A Note on Natural Laws and So-Called 'Contrary to Fact Conditionals,' " *Mind*, 58:62–66 (1949).
15. Reichenbach, Hans. *Elements of Symbolic Logic*. New York: Macmillan, 1947.
16. Reichenbach, Hans. *Theory of Probability*. Berkeley: Univ. of California Press, 1949.

17. Reichenbach, Hans. *Nomological Statements and Admissible Operations.* Amsterdam: North-Holland Publishing Co., 1954.
18. Von Wright, G. H. *An Essay in Modal Logic.* Amsterdam: North-Holland Publishing Co., 1951.
19. Waismann, F. "Verifiability," *Aristotelian Society Proceedings, Supplementary Volume XIX,* 119–150 (1945). Reprinted in Anthony Flew (ed.), *Logic and Language.* New York: Philosophical Library, 1951.
20. Wittgenstein, Ludwig. *Tractatus Logico-Philosophicus.* London: Routledge and Kegan Paul, 1922.
21. Wittgenstein, Ludwig. *Philosophical Investigations.* Oxford: Blackwell, 1953.
22. Russell, Bertrand. "On the Notion of Cause," in *Mysticism and Logic.* London: George Allen & Unwin, 1929. Reprinted in H. Feigl and M. Brodbeck (eds.), *Readings in the Philosophy of Science.* New York: Appleton-Century-Crofts, 1953.
23. Weinberg, Julius. "Contrary to Fact Conditionals," *Journal of Philosophy,* 48: 517–528 (1951).

————— H. GAVIN ALEXANDER —————

General Statements as Rules of Inference?

Several philosophers recently have suggested that it is often profitable to regard universal general statements as rules of inference, as material rules rather than formal rules, as P-rules of our language rather than L-rules (to use Carnap's terms). The view is held in different forms. At one extreme there is the comparatively innocuous claim that in some contexts general statements perform a rule analogous to that of deductive rules of inference; at the other, there is the contention that implicit in both everyday language and scientific discourse are P-rules of inference which are in some sense more fundamental than the general statements which can be derived from them.

The considerations which have led philosophers to take up these various connected positions can be listed under four heads. First, there is the fact—noted already by Descartes and Locke—that in everyday discourse we seldom argue in explicit syllogisms. In the same field of ordinary discourse there are the familiar difficulties in interpreting universal statements extensionally. Second, there is the general problem of induction. The old view according to which we need a supreme major premise for all inductive inferences is unattractive, and this is said to be avoided if one treats general laws as principles rather than premises. The third line of argument is the one which has been strongly advocated by Toulmin—that in scientific practice, deductions are not made from laws but in accordance with them. Fourth—although obviously closely related to the first—is the puzzle of counterfactual conditionals: if general statements did not have the force of rules of inference, it would be impossible to derive counterfactual conditionals from them.

It may be interesting to examine the validity of these four lines of thought. As we shall see, there are considerable difficulties that have not been so clearly stated.

H. Gavin Alexander

"This egg has been boiling for six minutes now, and so it will be hard."

"President Eisenhower is a man; therefore he is mortal."

Traditional logic books treat these as enthymemes of the first order, that is as syllogisms with their major premises suppressed. Critics of traditional logic claim that it is pointless and even misleading to try to squeeze all inference into the strait jacket of the syllogistic forms. Among such critics Mill held that in arriving at the conclusion that Eisenhower is mortal we do not need to presuppose that all men are mortal; all we need to do is argue by analogy with cases such as Socrates and the Duke of Wellington, both of whom have died. Contemporary philosophers such as Ryle and Black, on the other hand, say that we infer directly from the single premise to the conclusion, using a non-logical rule of inference.*

Mill's view clearly will not do by itself. Similarity is an incomplete predicate and therefore in order to know that Eisenhower is mortal, we have to know in what important respects he is like Socrates and the Duke of Wellington. It is not in being more than five feet long or in weighing more than 140 pounds; it is in being a man, or perhaps an animal. So in a way we do presuppose a major premise. The contemporary view is much more plausible. Certainly one of the main functions of general laws is to enable us to infer from one singular statement to another; and this function is so important that it is tempting to follow Ryle and call general laws *inference tickets*.

But if we thus abolish the traditional category of enthymemes of the first order, why should we not do the same with enthymemes of the second order? "All cows are ruminants; so Flossie is a ruminant." "All cows are mammals; therefore, Flossie is a mammal." Following Ryle and Black we now say that it is wrong to regard these as syllogisms with a suppressed minor premise, "Flossie is a cow." No, these are direct inferences which have a rule of inference corresponding to "Flossie is a cow." It might be thought that this is too particular to be a rule of inference. But this is not the case, for we have already seen that there are two different inferences in which it can be used as a governing rule

* J. S. Mill, *System of Logic*, Book II, Chapter III. G. Ryle, " 'If', 'So', and 'Because' " in *Philosophical Analysis*, ed. M. Black, pp. 323–340. M. Black, *Problems of Analysis*, pp. 191ff.

of inference, and there are obviously infinitely many more. The rule can in fact be put in logical form as $(\Phi)[\{(x) \cdot (x \text{ is a cow}) \supset \Phi x\} \supset \Phi$ Flossie]. A possible objection is that though it is quite common to suppress minor premises and thus to use a special rule of inference, this is not so frequent as the use of a general statement as a principle of inference. This may be true, but the difference is not very considerable. In fact, both general statements and singular statements are sometimes used as conclusions of arguments (inductive or deductive) to 'state facts,' sometimes as explicit or implicit steps in an argument. If we wish to say that in the latter use the general statements are principles of inference whenever they are not explicitly stated, then there is no reason why we should not say the same about the singular statements. If, as I would suggest, this seems an excessive multiplication of rules of inference, then the fault lies at the beginning. The traditional account in terms of enthymemes seems preferable to an account that considers only the explicit form of the argument.

This is not the only difficulty of the Ryle-Black approach. No one has shown more clearly than Ryle himself that the vocabulary suitable for talking about rules is different from that suitable for statements. Statements can be true or false, probable or improbable; rules can be correct or incorrect, useful or useless.* Normally we say that some general statements are true, others false, or that some are probably true. If then we wish to say that general statements are rules of inference, it has to be shown that by saying that they are correct rules we are doing much the same as when we said that the corresponding general statements were true. What then does it mean to say that some rules are correct, others incorrect? It cannot mean, as it does with rules of grammar, that correct rules are the ones which are accepted and conformed to by the majority (or by the French Academy). The correctness or incorrectness of these P-rules must somehow depend on empirical facts. The only possible meaning is that a rule is correct if the world is such that by following the rule we arrive at true conclusions.

Thus instead of saying that a general statement is universally true, we say that the corresponding rule of inference always enables us to reach true conclusions from true premises; instead of saying that most Φ's are ψ's, we say that the rule of inference $(x)(\Phi x \supset \psi x)$ usually enables

---

* But see the paper by M. Scriven in this volume where he argues that rules can be true or false.

H. Gavin Alexander

us to reach a true conclusion when we are given a true premise of the form Φx. But if this is accepted, it becomes obvious that one of the advantages we had hoped for has been lost. Certainly some philosophers, like Ramsey, have been puzzled by the logic of general statements which are so obviously not truth-functional and have hoped that the puzzle might be bypassed by regarding general statements as rules of inference. But we have only been able to do this at the cost of bringing in other general statements; for we now have the general statement that in all cases the use of the rule of inference enables us to arrive at true conclusions. So we are no better off.*

Of course, this difficulty might be avoided by holding that, when we say a rule is correct, all that we mean is that it is a rule observed by all users of a certain language (in the philosophical sense of language), and that when we say a rule is probably correct, what we mean is that it might be useful to adopt this as a rule of our language. This would be to make such rules meaning rules or what are normally called analytic truths. This line of thought is the one put forward by Wilfrid Sellars. It is closely connected with the problem of counterfactual conditionals and will therefore be discussed in the last part of this paper. At the moment it is sufficient to notice that it goes considerably beyond the arguments of writers like Ryle and Black and therefore cannot be used by them as a way out of this difficulty unless they are willing to change much of their account. Unless they are prepared to deny that there are any purely empirical general statements or rules—that is statements (or rules) which are not true (or correct) *ex vi terminorum*—then it must follow that there are some general statements, either in the object language or the metalanguage, which cannot be interpreted as rules.

II

I have thus been claiming that it is unhelpful and, in fact, misleading to speak of material rules of inference rather than of implied major premises. But a strong argument against this position can be drawn from a discussion of induction. Many classical logicians regarded inductive inferences as concealed deductive arguments with a suppressed major premise about the uniformity of nature. In this case, however, such an analysis appears artificial. The only apparent alternative is to

---

* I owe the substance of this paragraph to a remark made in discussion by Dr. W. Rozeboom.

regard inductive inferences as arguments governed by a non-deductive rule of inference—and if we allow a non-deductive rule of inference here, why not accept them elsewhere? Another advantage claimed by Braithwaite and Black * for this approach is that it may enable us to show that induction can be justified inductively without arguing in a circle. Unfortunately, when one examines this last claim, one realizes that it raises considerable difficulties which make the principle-of-inference interpretation of induction as unpalatable as the suppressed-major-premise view.

In his exposition, which is rather more easily summarized than Braithwaite's, Black does not actually subscribe to the view that there is a single supreme inductive rule or principle. He does however consider two forms of a rule which is a very strong candidate for such a position. Rule 1 (R_1) is to argue from *All examined A's have been B* to *All A's are B*. R_2 is to argue from *Most A's examined in a wide variety of conditions have been found to be B* to (probably) *The next A will be B*. Now it is possible to construct the following self-supporting argument:

(a_1) All examined instances of the use of R_1 in arguments with true premises have been instances in which R_1 has been successful.

Hence, all instances of the use of R_1 in arguments with true premises are instances in which R_1 is successful.

This argument uses R_1 to reach the conclusion that R_1 is always successful; a similar argument can clearly be constructed for R_2. The obvious criticism is that these arguments are circular. But, Black points out, this is not quite so obvious as it seems at first. A circular argument, in the usual sense, is either one in which one of the premises is identical with the conclusion or else one in which it is impossible to get to know the truth of one of the premises without first getting to know the truth of the conclusion. But here there is only one premise, which is clearly independent of the conclusion, so that the argument is not circular in the usual way. At this point Braithwaite cites the difference in a deductive system between a rule of inference and a formula, and remarks that the rule of detachment may be used in order to derive the formula $p \cdot (p \supset q) \supset q$.

But in spite of this analogy, one is reluctant to accept this self-sup-

* R. B. Braithwaite, *Scientific Explanation*, Chapter IX. Cambridge: Cambridge Univ. Press, 1953. Max Black, *Problems in Analysis*, pp. 191–208. Ithaca, N.Y.: Cornell Univ. Press, 1954.

porting 'justification' of induction. One reason is that if one accepts this, then it seems one would also have to accept arguments like the following:

> Rule 4: to argue from *The Pope speaking ex cathedra says p* to *p*.
> (a_4) The Pope speaking *ex cathedra* has stated that whenever the Pope speaks *ex cathedra* what he says is true.
> *Hence whatever the Pope says ex cathedra is true.*
> Or Rule 5: to argue from *The Bible states that p* to *p*.
> (a_5) In 2 Tim. 3:16 it is stated that all scripture is given by inspiration of God and is profitable for doctrine, hence etc.*

These are clearly circular and yet they seem of exactly the same form as Black's argument.

Wesley Salmon has given an even more convincing reason for rejecting Black's argument as a possible justification of induction.† This is that by citing the same evidence as Black would give in support of R_2 one could produce a self-supporting argument for R_3: to argue from *Most examined A's have been B* to *(probably) The next A will* NOT *be B*. Salmon thus holds that Black's arguments are in fact circular although not in the usual way. He writes:

For an argument to establish its conclusion, either inductively or deductively, two conditions must be fulfilled. First, the premises must be true, and second, the rules of inference used by the argument must be correct. . . . Unless we are justified in accepting the premises as true and in accepting the rules of inference as correct, the argument is inconclusive. . . . To regard the facts in the premises as evidence for the conclusion is to assume that the rule of inference used in the argument is a correct one. And [in the case of the self-supporting arguments] this is precisely what is to be proved.

But this view has difficulties of its own. One is that it involves us in something very similar to the principle of the uniformity of nature. Before, writers like Mill wanted such a principle as a major premise; now, writers like Salmon want it as a metastatement telling us that the principle of inductive inference is always (or usually) successful. The difference here is minimal.

A second difficulty in Salmon's account lies in its application to deduction. For according to him, in order to reach conclusions deductively, we must have a justification of the rules of inference. Now it is not

* Cf. *Westminster Confession of Faith*, Chapter 1.
† "Should We Attempt to Justify Induction?" *Philosophical Studies*, April 1957.

easy to see that deductive rules can be justified. It is true that Reichenbach purports to give a justification of the rule of detachment in his *Elements of Symbolic Logic;* * but all that he succeeds in showing is that it is inconsistent to admit that a statement 'If . . . then . . .' can be represented by p ⊃ q (where '⊃' is defined truth-functionally) and at the same time to assert both the hypothetical statement and its antecedent but deny its consequent. Actually we only can tell that a given statement in words can be represented by p ⊃ q, if we first see that it would be falsified if the antecedent were true and the consequent false. But even if we were to grant the validity of Reichenbach's 'justification,' we should still be left with the paradoxical conclusion that no deductive arguments were conclusive before Reichenbach's time. God has not been so sparing to men as to make them barely two-legged creatures and left it to Reichenbach to enable them to reach conclusions.

We thus seem to have reached an impasse. For the three theories of inductive inference that we have considered are all untenable. Mill's view that all inductive arguments are enthymemes, with the suppressed major premise that nature is uniform, seems completely artificial as an analysis of the inference from 'Usually when the wind goes round to the S.W. with a falling glass, rain follows' to 'Probably when the wind next goes round to the S.W., etc.' Black avoids this artificiality by regarding this and similar arguments as valid because of material rules of inference. But this leads to the conclusion that there are a large number of non-circular self-supporting arguments such as our two theological examples—which is absurd. Salmon escapes this absurdity by demanding that the rules of inference be justified. But if this demand is extended to ALL rules of inference, it makes nonsense of deduction. If it is applied only to non-deductive rules, it completely spoils the analogy that is being drawn between these so-called material rules of inference and the genuine (deductive) rules of inference. The one positive conclusion that one can draw from the statement of this impasse is that here also the introduction of the idea of material rules of inference raises more difficulties than it solves.

However it may be possible to be slightly more constructive and to indicate a way of escape from this puzzling situation. Here it is perhaps illuminating to consider a special use of the concept of necessity. 'All men are mortal, President Eisenhower is a man, so President Eisenhower

* P. 66. New York: Macmillan, 1947.

H. Gavin Alexander

is necessarily mortal' or 'he must be mortal.' Here the word 'must' does nothing more than signal the fact that this is the conclusion of a deductive argument. Often we use the same phrasing without ever stating the premises—'He must be ill' or 'It must be going to rain.' Here the function of 'must' is again to indicate that these statements could be exhibited as the conclusions of deductive arguments. If asked why, we would outline the argument by quoting either the major or the minor premise or both: 'He's pale and shivering and can't concentrate,' 'Always when the wind goes to the S.W. and the glass is falling, rain follows.' Thus to say in this sense of 'must' 'A must be B' is not to say that A and B are connected by some special sort of close tie; it is only to say that A is B, and that a deductive argument which has as a conclusion 'A is B' can be constructed with acceptable premises.

I would suggest that 'probably' plays a somewhat similar role. When we say 'It will probably rain' what we mean is that it is possible to construct an argument of the form 'Usually when conditions x, y, z hold, rain follows within 24 hours; conditions x, y, z hold now; therefore it will probably rain.' When we say 'All observed A's are B; therefore it is probable that all A's are B' we mean that it is possible to construct an argument of the form 'Usually generalizations made on the basis of evidence of such and such a kind have proved true; our observations of A's which are B constitute evidence of this kind; therefore it is probable that all A's are B.' This is the basic use of 'probable.' The frequency concept of probability is a derived use which makes the concept more precise, but at the price of making it inapplicable in those situations where it is impossible to gather statistics.

On this view there is a rule of inference which enables one to move from 'Most A's have been B' to 'Probably this A is B.' But it is a rule of inference which is deductive rather than inductive. There is now no problem of justifying the move, any more than there is a problem of justifying the move from 'Most A's have been B' to 'It is reasonable to expect this A to be B.' The moves are valid because of the meanings of the phrases 'probable' and 'reasonable expectation.'

One can also see that on this analysis Black's self-supporting arguments become less perplexing. Now it is necessary to distinguish the two different cases separately—first, the inference to '(Probably) all uses of R_1 will be successful' where R_1 is the rule of arguing from all observed cases to all cases; and second, the inference to 'Probably the next use of R$_2$ will be successful' where R$_2$ is the rule of arguing from most observed cases to the next case. The second of these arguments is now non-circular but unexciting—just as unexciting as any other case of immediate inference. The first argument is, however, invalid if the conclusion contains the word 'probably' and illegitimate if it does not contain it. For if it contains the word 'probably' then, as we have seen above, the implication is that we could construct an argument with a higher order generalization which stated that most other general hypotheses posited on the basis of an amount of evidence similar to that which we possess here have not been disproved later. But clearly this particular case is unique so that it is quite impossible to formulate a generalization about similar cases. So the claim implied by the word 'probably' cannot be fulfilled and the argument is therefore invalid.

If, on the other hand, the word 'probably' is omitted, then the argument conforms to no pattern of inference at all—except the pattern of inference of arguments contained in the induction chapters of logic textbooks. Except when we are discussing induction, we never argue from 'All observed A's are B' to 'All A's are B' but rather to 'Probably all A's are B' or 'It is reasonable to assume that . . .' or 'We can expect . . .' It is true that if the generalizations continue to be confirmed we will drop the qualifying phrase, but this is either because we cease to question the truth of the generalization and instead use it as a premise for other arguments or else because we see that the generalization can be seen as a particular case of a higher order generalization. The words 'probably' and 'necessarily' (in the sense I have discussed above) are used to indicate the line of argument we have followed; when we go on toward some different conclusion starting from this first conclusion as a premise, then we no longer need these indicator words.

III

It is impossible within the space of a few pages to discuss at all adequately the way in which laws function in natural science. The most that can be done is to indicate some of the lines of thought that have led writers such as Toulmin to conclude that natural laws are more like rules than like statements.

One possible argument, though not one that is now often explicitly held, is that science is interested in the prediction and control of nature. Now all prediction and all control must involve singular statements.

Thus general laws only function as steppingstones or rules of inference, which enable us to move from the set of singular observation statements to prediction statements. This argument is clearly inconclusive. For it is not clear that the intermediate general truths are rules rather than statements. And further, the account only applies to some scientists, especially applied scientists. Many pure scientists are just interested in discovering laws of nature or general truths—and truths or statements, not just patterns of inference.

Another argument that I think has influenced Toulmin starts from the fact that many scientific laws are such that no one conceivable state of affairs would count as a conclusive refutation. I have suggested elsewhere * that this is one of the main considerations that has led Kneale to call natural laws 'principles of natural necessitation' and Quine to posit a continuum from particular empirical statements at one end to the laws of logic at the other. But although it may be impossible to refute laws of nature—they are abandoned rather than refuted—it is possible to give evidence in their support. But it is clearly impossible (logically) to give evidence for rules—one can give evidence for the statement that certain rules are observed; one can give empirical grounds in support of the claim that certain rules should be accepted; but one cannot give evidence for the rules themselves. And it does not make sense to say rules are true—whether true empirically or true *ex vi terminorum*. The fact that scientific laws are not refutable in the same way as empirical generalizations must be explained by discussing the way in which the statements of science hang together (cf. Duhem and Quine) and cannot be verified or falsified individually, rather than by evading the issue by calling them rules.

It is also possible that some writers who take this view of scientific laws have been influenced by the same sort of consideration that we considered above—that in drawing an inference the law is usually not stated explicitly. Thus in Britain one might look at an electric light bulb, see that it was marked 60 watts, and then say, 'It must have a resistance of about 880 ohms.' This is clearly drawn by means of the formula, derived from Ohm's Law, 'Power $= E^2/R$,' but this formula is not stated. Thus it could be said that this formula served as a principle of inference rather than as a suppressed premise. But equally the argument depends on the fact that the standard British power supply

* "Necessary Truths," forthcoming in *Mind*.

is 230 volts. If this is a suppressed premise rather than a rule of inference, the same can equally well be said of the law that the power dissipated (in watts) is equal to the square of the voltage divided by the resistance in ohms.

The principal argument used by Toulmin * is more interesting than any of these. It is that "laws of nature tell us nothing about phenomena, if taken by themselves, but rather express the form of a regularity whose scope is stated elsewhere" (*Introduction to the Philosophy of Science*, p. 86). As it stands this is unexceptionable; for, at most, it represents a slight narrowing of normal scientific usage in confining the name *law* to the mathematical formula which is, as it were, the core of the statement. But Toulmin goes on to draw a parallel between these laws—in his narrow sense—and rules or principles. "In this respect, laws of nature resemble other kinds of laws, rules, and regulations. These are not themselves true or false, though statements about their range of application can be" (p. 79). On p. 93 he cites with approval Ryle's metaphorical phrase 'inference-ticket', and on p. 102 he also claims that there is a similarity between laws of nature and principles of deductive inference.

Now as a matter of scientific usage, it is just false to say that the statement of a law never mentions its scope.† If one thumbs through a textbook of optics, one finds the following statements:

"Kirchoff's law of radiation states that the ratio of the radiant emittance to the absorptance is the same for all bodies at a given temperature."

"Bouguer's law of absorption states that in a semi-transparent medium layers of equal thickness absorb equal fractions of the intensity of the light incident upon them, whatever this intensity may be."

"According to Stokes' law, the wavelength of the fluorescent light is always longer than that of the absorbed light."

"Fermat's principle should read: the path taken by a light ray in going from one point to another through any set of media is such as to render its optical path equal, in the first approximation, to other paths closely adjacent to the actual one."

In all these the scope is included in the statement of the law. But

* S. E. Toulmin, *Introduction to the Philosophy of Science*. London: Hutchinson's Univ. Libr.; New York: Longmans, Green and Co., 1953.

† This has been pointed out by reviewers of Toulmin's book, e.g., M. Scriven in *Philosophical Review*, 64:124–128 (1955) and E. Nagel in *Mind*, 63:403–412 (1954).

it is true that Toulmin's account does apply in some cases. Thus, as he points out, a textbook will say, "In calcite, Snell's law of refraction holds for one ray but not for the other"; it does not say that when calcite was discovered, Snell's law was found to be not strictly true. Does it follow from this that Snell's law is a rule or an inference license?

The first thing to be noticed here is that any scientific law—unlike simple generalizations of natural history—is multiply general; that is if we were to represent it by a logical formula, we would need several quantifiers. At the first stage Snell's law gives us a formula which sums up the relations between the angles of refraction and the angles of incidence for all angles of incidence. Second, Snell's law—if we use the name now to include not only the formula but the statements of its scope—tells us that for all different specimens of the same two media, the formula holds and the constant of proportionality between the sines of the angles is the same. Third, Snell's law tells us that the formula holds for all—or almost all—transparent media but that the constant of proportionality is different for different pairs of media. And perhaps fourth one might say this was true at all times. Thus *theoretically* the law could be falsified in four different ways: (1) by finding, say, that the refractive index of substances varied systematically with time; (2) by finding a transparent medium for which the law did not hold; (3) by finding that there were certain pieces of flint glass which, though identical in all other respects, had different refractive indexes; (3a) by finding that there were certain pieces of flint glass identical in all other respects with normal specimens for which the relation was $\sin^2 i/\sin^2 r = \text{constant}$; (4) by finding that all previous observations had been wildly mistaken, and that the law which held for all transparent media was $\sin^2 i/\sin^2 r = \text{constant}$. Now because of this multiple generality of law statements, it is understandable that a shortcoming in one respect should not lead us to abandon it altogether.

In practice, the fourth kind of 'falsification' will always be such that the first formula will be a valid first approximation to the more accurate formula. There will therefore be cases in which the law in its first inaccurate form will still be used. The third kind of falsification never, I believe, occurs in the physical sciences. Two specimens will never differ in only one respect, and therefore if two pieces of glass have different refractive indexes we know they will exhibit other differences so that they cannot be called instances of the same kind of glass. 'Falsification' in the second way is not infrequent; as in the case of abnormal refraction, we do not abandon the law completely but note that its scope is restricted. The first kind of disproof has never yet been observed, but if Whitehead is right it may sometime be found.

But this feature of multiple generality is not confined to the physical sciences. As a British visitor to the United States, I am expected to report some general facts about American university life. These reports could be doubly general, that is, true about all (or most) students or faculty on all (or most) campuses. Basing my reports on my observations on the Minnesota campus, I might reach conclusions such as "Almost all men undergraduate students dress informally, with no ties and no jackets (coats)" or "Most full professors and university administrators wear dark suits." An American friend will then tell me that the latter generalization is true of all American campuses, but that the former only holds in the Midwest. So what I might do is make generalizations like those in the accompanying list.

Generalization	Scope
All professors dress formally	Everywhere
Undergraduates dress very informally	Midwest
Undergraduates take outside work in term time	Not in liberal arts colleges

Now if I constructed such a list, Toulmin would presumably say that the sentences on the left were rules or inference licenses. But this is ridiculous. If anything they are analogous to propositional functions. That is, they are incomplete statements which can be completed by either supplying a particular context, e.g., 'on the Harvard campus' or else by quantifying, 'on all campuses', 'on some campuses', or 'on most campuses'.

This, I think, is sufficient to show that Toulmin's argument is invalid. But there is still a problem as to the way we apply laws to particular situations. Nagel, for instance, points out that we can infer the motion of a projectile from the laws of mechanics. This, presumably, might be done by treating the projectile as a homogeneous body of mass m, assuming that the air resistance is a simple function of the velocity and can be represented by a simple force acting in the line of motion, and neglecting any effects due to the spin of the projectile. We then write down the equations, substitute in the initial conditions, and deduce that the projectile will land one thousand yards away in the direction in which it was fired.

This deduction therefore takes two steps. The first is to the intermediate conclusion that certain laws, and only these laws, are applicable to this instance; the second is the deduction made by substituting initial conditions into these laws. Often the first step proves to be unjustified as in the case when one applies the simple laws of mechanics to the flight of a cricket ball or baseball and reaches the conclusion that such balls never 'swerve in the air.' Sometimes the deduction may be wrong because the formula used in the deduction is only true to a first approximation and in this particular case the second order differences are important.

But an exactly similar account would apply to my deduction that Franklin Smith usually wears a T shirt. First, I would notice that he was an undergraduate at a Midwestern state university; then I would see which laws held for Midwestern state university campuses and draw my deduction. Of course, in this example, both steps of the inference are of the same kind and both are very obvious. In the case of the projectile, the first step is by means of a verbal argument, the second by mathematical reasoning. It is therefore understandable that the attention of scientists should have been focused on the second stage and that as a consequence philosophers of science should have been misled into thinking that the mathematical formula by itself was the law. In fact, the formula by itself is only a formula; when the scope is supplied it becomes part of a statement. But in no sense is it like a rule.

IV

A. The fourth argument in support of material rules of inference is one put forward by Wilfrid Sellars and expressed most clearly in his paper "Inference and Meaning." * Briefly, it is that subjunctive conditionals are expressions in the material mode of material rules of inference in the formal mode. He writes thus:

" 'If anything were red and square, it would be red' cannot plausibly

---

* *Mind*, 62:313–338 (1953). Professor Sellars' paper in this volume completes, and also to some extent modifies, the theory outlined in his earlier article. Since I wrote the present paper before his paper for this volume was completed, I have only discussed in the text his earlier article. Thus some of my criticisms are not applicable to his present views, and some of them have been implicitly countered by some of his arguments.

be claimed to assert the same as '(In point of fact) all red and square things are red'; this subjunctive conditional conveys the same information as the logical rule permitting the inference of *x is red* from *x is red and x is square*" (p. 323).

" 'If there were to be a flash of lightning, there would be thunder' gives expression to some such rule as '*There is thunder at time t + n* may be inferred from *there is lightning at time t*' " (p. 323).

"Whenever we assert a subjunctive conditional of the latter form ('if x were A, x would be B'), we would deny that it was merely in point of fact that all A's are B" (p. 324).

"Unless some way can be found of interpreting such subjunctive conditionals in terms of logical principles of inference, we have established not only that they are the expression of material rules of inference, but that the authority of these rules is not derivative from formal rules" (p. 325).

"Material transformation rules determine the descriptive meaning of the expressions of a language within the framework established by its logical transformation rules. In other words where 'ψa' is P-derivable from 'Φa', it is as correct to say that '$\Phi a \supset \psi a$' is true by virtue of the meanings of 'Φ' and 'ψ', as it is to say this where 'ψa' is L-derivable from 'Φa' " (p. 336).

Thus Sellars' view, as expressed in his 1953 paper, is that a necessary and sufficient condition for a generalization to provide grounds for asserting a subjunctive conditional is that the generalization shall be the expression in the object language of a material rule of inference. That is, the generalization has either to be one that contains the word *necessarily* explicitly or else has to be in such a context that *necessarily* is implied. Generalizations of this kind can then be said to be true *ex vi terminorum*, if we take the widest possible concept of meaning; for such generalizations can all be ranged in a continuum which ends at one extreme in 'truths' such as 'All bachelors are unmarried.'

It appears then that we can place all possible generalizations into four classes. At what might be termed the lower extremity, we have those generalizations which can only be established by complete enumeration—of these the standard example is 'All the coins in my pocket were minted after 1940.' From this first class one can only derive what Goodman calls *counter-identical conditionals* such as 'If this coin had been identical with one of the coins in my pocket, it would have been minted after 1940.'

The second class contains those empirical generalizations which are arrived at by genuine induction but which are not 'necessarily true,' not expressions of material rules of inference. These are the truths which Sellars regards as "merely true in point of fact." They also are below the salt, for from them, Sellars holds, one can again derive nothing stronger than counter-identical conditionals. A special subclass of such generalizations would appear to be general statements which mention a particular individual.

The third class—which, as we have seen, merges into the tautologies of which the fourth class is made up—comprises the laws of nature, necessary truths which hold by virtue of the meanings of the words. From such statements (and from the tautologies) one can derive genuine counterfactuals.

(It is however important to realize that one cannot always derive the most usual type of counterfactual. Thus, if one assumes that solar disturbances are a necessary and sufficient condition for the occurrence some 24 hours later of auroral displays, we can assert that 'If solar disturbances had occurred on Tuesday, auroral displays would have taken place on Wednesday.' On the other hand, it would sound odd to say 'If auroral displays had taken place on Wednesday, solar disturbances would have occurred on Tuesday.' Rather we would say 'If auroras had occurred, *this would have meant that* solar disturbances had occurred.' Similarly we might on the basis of our knowledge of segregation in the United States in general and Jonesville in particular, say "If Smith had been colored, he would have lived in northeast Jonesville." But we should not say, "If Smith had lived in northeast Jonesville, he would have been colored"; we could only say, "If . . . it would have meant that . . .")

It is however easy to show that this theory, as I have interpreted it, is untenable. For consider the case of a husband who, after twenty years of a happy marriage, remarks to his wife 'You would have been furious if you had been there. The youths were torturing that cat out of pure sadistic pleasure.' Here we have an example of a counterfactual being asserted by the husband—let us call him Mr. Smith—because he knows by experience that his wife becomes angry whenever she sees wanton cruelty to animals. I would suggest that this is clearly a generalization of the second class. It mentions an individual; it does not explicitly or implicitly include the adverb 'necessarily'; and it can by no stretch of the imagination be said to be true *ex vi terminorum* because of the meaning of "Mrs. Smith". Yet the counterfactual is clearly a genuine one.*

It might be suggested in reply that although this generalization is empirical, the counterfactual really rests on a more fundamental generalization, some psychological law about the reaction of certain types of people in certain circumstances. But this is unplausible. Are we going to say that Mr. Smith is able to make such counterfactual statements about his wife because he has majored in psychology at college, but that poor Mr. Brown, married equally long and equally happily, is unable to do so because he never has opened a psychology textbook or even attended a university? Or are we going to say Mr. Brown *implicitly* knows and relies on the psychological law even though he explicitly refuses to assent to the law when it is quoted to him?

It is true that one might say that both Mr. Smith and Mr. Brown are making the assumption that their respective wives have acted in consistent ways and will continue to do so. But this would only be to refer to the assumption of the uniformity of nature, the assumption which may be said to be implicit in every generalization reached by genuine ampliative induction and thus implicit in every generalization of the second group. In fact, this line of defense would make the second class empty, for it would ascribe a necessary nomological connection to each and every generalization in virtue of the fact that it was reached by ampliative induction.

There is an even simpler argument which enables us to reach this same conclusion. If one considers any particular counterfactual such as 'If this stone had been released, it would have fallen' or 'If Grey had clearly and publicly explained Britain's foreign policy, the first war would never have occurred,' one sees that the way in which one would justify such assertions is exactly similar to the way in which one would justify a prediction. Mr. Dulles, knowing that President Eisenhower is about to announce the Eisenhower doctrine, tries to predict what world reaction will be; Mr. Smith, seeing his small son about to drop a stone out of the window, predicts what will happen; and the way in which they

---

* Professor Sellars now admits that his 1953 paper did not take into account these singular counterfactuals, and that it would be misleading to say that generalizations corresponding to these singular counterfactuals were true *ex vi terminorum*. His paper in this volume makes it clear that he is willing to say such generalizations are in a way necessary and that he therefore does not need to have recourse to either of the arguments I discuss in the two succeeding paragraphs.

do so is the same as the way in which counterfactuals are established. The only difference is that predictions can usually be conclusively verified (or falsified) later; counterfactual conditionals never can be. Now it is obvious that in predicting the future we use empirical generalizations (of the second class); it is clear to me that we also use them in order to arrive at counterfactuals.

We have now seen that having the characteristics of the third class is not a necessary condition for a generalization to give rise to subjunctive conditionals. I want to go on to make the stronger claim that the third class, as defined by Sellars, is empty, that there are no laws of necessary connection. My claim is that when a generalization includes the word *necessarily* or when we say a general statement is necessary, one of a variety of different things is meant. One use is that mentioned above. We often say 'All A's are necessarily B' when we are claiming not only that 'All A's are B' but also that this fact can be justified by a deductive argument from a more general premise which is accepted by the speaker and usually by the listeners also. This is exactly the same as particular statements such as 'It must be going to rain.' Closely allied to this is the case when the generalization is justified by reference to considerations of a different kind as when we say, 'All voters are necessarily over 21' because of the law that no one under 21 may vote. Also similar is the case when the generalization is justified by reference to the meaning of the constituent words—the case of tautologies. What is common to all these is that in inserting the word *necessarily* we are indicating that our assertion is not based on examination of individual A's which are B, and that it is therefore useless to search for A's which are not B.

This, I believe, covers all the cases in which the word *necessarily* is actually included in the sentence itself. The same claim could conceivably be made by saying that the general statement 'All A's are B' was necessary—but this would sound rather unnatural. There are, however, other situations in which philosophers might call a general statement necessary, although they would hesitate to insert the modal adverb *necessarily* in the object-language sentence. These are the cases, mentioned above, when a scientific generalization becomes so well established that no one conceivable state of affairs would be taken as constituting a refutation of it. This is what is sometimes called the functional or the pragmatic a priori. But this sort of necessity consists in the way in which scientists regard certain laws, the way in which they use them; it is not in any way an 'intrinsic property' of the statements. And since, if questioned, scientists would cite empirical evidence in support of these laws, it would, as we have seen, be misleading to say that they were true *ex vi terminorum*.

B. There is, however, another way in which some philosophers have attempted to distinguish a special class of 'necessary' or 'basic' laws. This distinction is most easily explained by considering a universe which consists of a perfect billiard table and two perfect billiard balls in motion on it. It might be the case that because of the initial conditions, these two balls would never collide. If so, then the statement that these balls would never collide would be lawlike inasmuch as it would always be true, but yet it would be different from, say, the laws of reflection which hold for the collisions of the balls with the cushions. These latter laws could be called *basic* or *necessary*, the former *structure dependent* or *contingent*.

Here we have a view which is nearer to Kneale's than to Sellars'. For it might seem that such basic laws would be 'principles of natural necessitation' to use Kneale's phrase. That is, we would almost seem to have here a concept of metaphysical necessity instead of the concept of pragmatic necessity discussed by Sellars.

The difficulty about this distinction is that of applying it to our actual universe. For until, like God, we know all the secrets of the universe, it will be impossible to know which laws are structure dependent and which are not. If, for example, the Mach-Einstein program were carried through, then some of the basic laws of mechanics would be shown to be structure dependent. A second possible criticism of this distinction is that its persuasiveness is only superficial. Examples like the billiard table make the distinction appear important because experience in our actual universe has taught us that the laws of collision hold for all billiard tables and for other collisions as well, not just for the one table; the fact that the balls never meet we know would never hold for every table. That is, in considering the simple billiard table universe we tacitly bring in our knowledge of our actual multi-billiard-table universe. If—to formulate a rather outrageous counterfactual—I were one of the two billiard balls (and still possessed means of making observations), I might distinguish the two types of law but neither would seem more *basic* or more *necessary* than the other. "The laws

327

of collision might have been different, the initial conditions might have been different—but both are what they are."

Finally it should be noticed that even if one did accept this distinction, it would not coincide with the distinction Sellars wants to draw between his second and third class of general statements. For it is, I think, clear that psychological laws, sociological laws, biological laws, and possibly, as we have seen, even the laws of mechanics are structure dependent. There cannot be many basic laws remaining. If it were only these basic (and probably as yet unknown) laws that give rise to counterfactuals, then counterfactuals would be confined to the pages of the most recondite physics books, instead of being a pervasive feature of our ordinary language.

C. Thus the word *necessary* (and its cognates), when included in a general statement in the object language or used in the metalanguage to describe an object-language generalization, is ambiguous. When included in the statement it signals a claim about the way in which the generalization is justified; in the other cases when used about the generalization, it says something about the role the generalization plays in scientific theory. And, if this explanation is correct, we need no longer look for ties of necessary connection or even for statements (other than tautologies) true *ex vi terminorum*, or for object-language expressions of logically prior material rules of inference.

Actually some of the plausibility of Sellars' argument is due to the misleading use of the phrase *in point of fact*. We are left with the impression that the only alternative to his view of generalizations as expressions of material rules of inference is to take them as generalizations which are 'in point of fact true.' But though in one sense an empiricist would accept this, it is unintentionally misleading because we often use the phrase *in point of fact* to distinguish between general statements which can only be validated by perfect induction—'all the coins in my pocket were minted after 1940'—and those which are reached by ampliative induction. Of course, any empiricist would admit that, if and when we find them, the basic laws of the universe will, in a sense, be true in point of fact. But this is only to deny that they are tautologies, 'principles of natural necessitation' (whatever that may mean), or rules. It is not to deny that these laws fit into a very complex theoretical system and that they are such that they are not easily refutable by direct empirical evidence. And, more important, it is not to assert that they only *happen* to be true or are true *by chance*—for this notion of chance only applies *within* a universe in which either the basic laws are indeterministic or else are so complex that men do not know them; the notion cannot meaningfully be applied to the universe as a whole. When one realizes this, one sees that there is no need to accept Sellars' third category of generalizations. Empirical generalizations of differing scope and generality are sufficient for prediction, retrodiction, explanation, and the formation of counterfactual conditionals; what more could one ask for?

We have thus seen how unsatisfactory are most of the arguments that have been put forward in support of the thesis that material rules of inference are an indispensable feature of our language. The strongest argument is that which starts from the fact that we often argue directly from particular premise to particular conclusion without stating any major premise. If one wished to construct a logic that represented the way we explicitly argued, then one would have to recognize material rules of inference. But does the idea of such a logic make sense? We have seen that it would also have to be applied to what previously have been regarded as enthymemes of the second order. It is however clear that such a logic would have to be so complicated as to be completely unwieldy—do we not before using logic often 'put statements into logical form,' that is, say that statements of different grammatical form have the same logical form? A logic which considered all the different ways arguments might be put would be very different from any present logic, and it would almost certainly be a logic which would be of little philosophical use.

If then one rejects the idea of such a logic, very little remains to be said in favor of material rules of inference, inference licenses, or inference tickets. In fact, I fail to see that these terms are of any use in a philosophical investigation of the way in which we talk, either in science or everyday discourse.

Persons

I

In the *Tractatus* (5.631–5.641), Wittgenstein writes of the I which occurs in philosophy, of the philosophical idea of the subject of experiences. He says first: "The thinking, presenting subject—there is no such thing." Then, a little later: "*In an important sense there is no subject.*" This is followed by: "The subject does not belong to the world, but is a limit of the world." And a little later comes the following paragraph: "There is [therefore] really a sense in which in philosophy we can talk non-psychologically of the I. The I occurs in philosophy through the fact that the 'world is my world.' The philosophical I is not the man, not the human body, or the human soul of which psychology treats, but the metaphysical subject, the limit—not a part of the world." These remarks are impressive, but also puzzling and obscure. Reading them, one might think: Well, let's settle for the human body and the human soul of which psychology treats, and which is a part of the world, and let the metaphysical subject go. But again we might think: No, when I talk of myself, I do after all talk of that which has all of my experiences, I do talk of the subject of my experiences—and yet also of something that is part of the world in that it, but not the world, comes to an end when I die. The limit of *my* world is not—and is not so thought of by me—the limit of *the* world. It may be difficult to explain the idea of something which is both a subject of experiences and a part of the world. But it is an idea we have: it should be an idea we can explain.

Let us think of some of the ways in which we ordinarily talk of ourselves, of some of the things which we ordinarily ascribe to ourselves. They are of many kinds. We ascribe to ourselves *actions and intentions* (I am doing, did, shall do this); *sensations* (I am warm, in pain); *thoughts and feelings* (I think, wonder, want this, am angry, disappointed, contented); *perceptions and memories* (I see this, hear the other, remember that). We ascribe to ourselves, in two senses, position: *location* (I am on the sofa) and *attitude* (I am lying down). And of course we ascribe to ourselves not only temporary conditions, states, and situations, like most of these, but also enduring characteristics, including such physical characteristics as height, coloring, shape, and weight. That is to say, among the things we ascribe to ourselves are things of a kind that we also ascribe to material bodies to which we would not dream of ascribing others of the things that we ascribe to ourselves. Now there seems nothing needing explanation in the fact that the particular height, coloring, and physical position which we ascribe to ourselves, should be ascribed to *something* or *other*; for that which one calls one's body is, at least, a body, a material thing. It can be picked out from others, identified by ordinary physical criteria and described in ordinary physical terms. But it can seem, and has seemed, to need explanation that one's states of consciousness, one's thoughts and sensations, are ascribed *to the very same thing* as that to which these physical characteristics, this physical situation, is ascribed. Why are one's states of consciousness ascribed to the very same thing as certain corporeal characteristics, a certain physical situation, etc.? And once this question is raised, another question follows it, viz.: Why are one's states of consciousness ascribed to (said to be of, or to belong to) anything at all? It is not to be supposed that the answers to these questions will be independent of one another.

It might indeed be thought that an answer to both of them could be found in the unique role which each person's body plays in his experience, particularly his perceptual experience. All philosophers who have concerned themselves with these questions have referred to the uniqueness of this role. (Descartes was well enough aware of its uniqueness: "I am *not* lodged in my body like a pilot in a vessel.") In what does this uniqueness consist? Well, of course, in a great many facts. We may summarize some of these facts by saying that for each person there is one body which occupies a certain *causal* position in relation to that person's perceptual experience, a causal position which is in various ways unique in relation to each of the various kinds of perceptual experience he has; and—as a further consequence—that this body is also unique for him as an *object* of the various kinds of perceptual experience which he has. This complex uniqueness of the single body appears, moreover, to be a contingent matter, or rather a cluster of contingent matters; we can, or it seems that we can, imagine many peculiar combinations of dependence and independence of aspects of our perceptual experience on the physical states or situation of more than one body.

Now I must say, straightaway, that this cluster of apparently contingent facts about the unique role which each person's body plays in his experience does not seem to me to provide, by itself, an answer to our questions. Of course these facts explain something. They provide a very good reason why a subject of experience should have a very special regard for just one body, why he should think of it as unique and perhaps more important than any other. They explain—if I may be permitted to put it so—why I feel peculiarly attached to what in fact I call my own body; they even might be said to explain why, granted that I am going to speak of one body as mine, I should speak of this body (the body that I do speak of as mine) as mine. But they do not explain why I should have the concept of myself at all, why I should ascribe my thoughts and experiences to anything. Moreover, even if we were satisfied with some other explanation of why one's states of consciousness (thoughts and feelings and perceptions) were ascribed to something, and satisfied that the facts in question sufficed to explain why the "possession" of a particular body should be ascribed to the same thing (i.e., to explain why a particular body should be spoken of as standing in some special relation, called "being possessed by" to that thing), yet the facts in question still do not explain why we should, as we do, ascribe certain corporeal characteristics not simply to the body standing in this special relation to the thing to which we ascribe thoughts, feelings, etc., but to the thing itself to which we ascribe those thoughts and feelings. (For we say "I am bald" as well as "I am cold," "I am lying on the hearthrug" as well as "I see a spider on the ceiling.") Briefly, the facts in question explain why a subject of experience should pick out one body from others, give it, perhaps, an honored name and ascribe to it whatever characteristics it has; but they do not explain why the experiences should be ascribed to any subject at all; and they do not explain why, if the experiences are to be ascribed to something, they and the corporeal characteristics which might be truly ascribed to the favored body, should be ascribed to the same thing. So the facts in question do not explain the use that we make of the word "I", or how any word has the use that word has. They do not explain the concept we have of a person.

II

A possible reaction at this point is to say that the concept we have is wrong or confused, or, if we make it a rule not to say that the concepts we have are confused, that the usage we have, whereby we ascribe, or seem to ascribe, such different kinds of predicate to one and the same thing, is confusing, that it conceals the true nature of the concepts involved, or something of this sort. This reaction can be found in two very important types of view about these matters. The first type of view is Cartesian, the view of Descartes and of others who think like him. Over the attribution of the second type of view I am more hesitant; but there is some evidence that it was held, at one period, by Wittgenstein and possibly also by Schlick. On both of these views, one of the questions we are considering, namely "Why do we ascribe our states of consciousness to the very same thing as certain corporeal characteristics, etc.?" is a question which does not arise; for on both views it is only a linguistic illusion that both kinds of predicate are properly ascribed to one and the same thing, that there is a common owner, or subject, of both types of predicate. And on the second of these views, the other question we are considering, namely "Why do we ascribe our states of consciousness to anything at all?" is also a question which does not arise; for on this view, it is only a linguistic illusion that one ascribes one's states of consciousness at all, that there is any proper subject of these apparent ascriptions, that states of consciousness belong to, or are states of, anything.

That Descartes held the first of these views is well enough known. When we speak of a person, we are really referring to one or both of two distinct substances (two substances of different types), each of which has its own appropriate type of states and properties; and none of the properties or states of either can be a property or state of the other. States of consciousness belong to one of these substances, and not to the other. I shall say no more about the Cartesian view at the moment—what I have to say about it will emerge later on—except to note again that while it escapes one of our questions, it does not escape, but indeed invites, the other: "Why are one's states of consciousness ascribed at all, to any subject?"

The second of these views I shall call the "no-ownership" or "no-subject" doctrine of the self. Whether or not anyone has explicitly held this view, it is worth reconstructing, or constructing, in outline.* For the errors into which it falls are instructive. The "no-ownership" theorist may be presumed to start his explanations with facts of the sort which illustrate the unique causal position of a certain material body in a person's experience. The theorist maintains that the uniqueness of this body is sufficient to give rise to the idea that one's experiences can be ascribed to some particular individual thing, can be said to be possessed by, or owned by, that thing. This idea, he thinks, though infelicitously and misleadingly expressed in terms of ownership, would have some validity, would make some sort of sense, so long as we thought of this individual thing, the possessor of the experiences, as the body itself. So long as we thought in this way, then to ascribe a particular state of consciousness to this body, this individual thing, would at least be to say something contingent, something that might

---

* The evidence that Wittgenstein at one time held such a view is to be found in the third of Moore's articles in Mind on "Wittgenstein's Lectures in 1930–33" (Mind, 1955, especially pp. 13–14). He is reported to have held that the use of "I" was utterly different in the case of "I have a tooth-ache" or "I see a red patch" from its use in the case of "I've got a bad tooth" or "I've got a matchbox." He thought that there were two uses of "I" and that in one of them "I" was replaceable by "this body." So far the view might be Cartesian. But he also said that in the other use (the use exemplified by "I have a tooth-ache" as opposed to "I have a bad tooth"), the "I" does not denote a possessor, and that no ego is involved in thinking or in having tooth-ache; and referred with apparent approval to Lichtenberg's dictum that, instead of saying "I think," we (or Descartes!) ought to say "There is a thought" (i.e., "Es denkt").

The attribution of such a view to Schlick would have to rest on his article "Meaning and Verification," Pt. V (Readings in Philosophical Analysis, H. Feigl and W. Sellars, eds.). Like Wittgenstein, Schlick quotes Lichtenberg, and then goes on to say: "Thus we see that unless we choose to call our body the owner or bearer of the data [the data of immediate experience]—which seems to be a rather misleading expression—we have to say that the data have no owner or bearer." The full import of Schlick's article is, however, obscure to me, and it is quite likely that a false impression is given by the quotation of a single sentence. I shall say merely that I have drawn on Schlick's article in constructing the case of my hypothetical "no-subject" theorist; but shall not claim to be representing his views.

Lichtenberg's anti-Cartesian dictum is, as the subsequent argument will show, one that I endorse, if properly used. But it seems to have been repeated, without being understood, by many of Descartes' critics.

The evidence that Wittgenstein and Schlick ever held a "no-subject" view seems indecisive, since it is possible that the relevant remarks are intended as criticisms of a Cartesian view rather than as expositions of the true view.

be, or might have been, false. It might have been a misascription; for the experience in question might be, or might have been, causally dependent on the state of some other body; in the present admissible, though infelicitous, sense of "belong", it might have belonged to some other individual thing. But now, the theorist suggests, one becomes confused: one slides from this admissible, though infelicitous, sense in which one's experiences may be said to belong to, or be possessed by, some particular thing, to a wholly inadmissible and empty sense of these expressions; and in this new and inadmissible sense, the particular thing which is supposed to possess the experiences is not thought of as a body, but as something else, say an ego.

Suppose we call the first type of possession, which is really a certain kind of causal dependence, "having$_1$", and the second type of possession, "having$_2$"; and call the individual of the first type "B" and the supposed individual of the second type "E". Then the difference is that while it is genuinely a contingent matter that *all my experiences are had$_1$ by B*, it appears as a necessary truth that *all my experiences are had$_2$ by E*. But the belief in E and in having$_2$ is an illusion. Only those things whose ownership is logically transferable can be owned at all. So experiences are not owned by anything except in the dubious sense of being causally dependent on the state of a particular body. This is at least a genuine relationship to a thing, in that they might have stood in it to another thing. Since the whole function of E was to own experiences in a logically non-transferable sense of "own", and since experiences are not owned by anything in this sense, for there is no such sense of "own", E must be eliminated from the picture altogether. It only came in because of a confusion.

I think it must be clear that this account of the matter, though it contains some of the facts, is not coherent. It is not coherent, in that one who holds it is forced to make use of that sense of possession of which he denies the existence, in presenting his case for the denial. When he tries to state the contingent fact, which he thinks gives rise to the illusion of the "ego," he has to state it in some such form as "All my experiences are had$_1$ by (uniquely dependent on the state of) body B." For any attempt to eliminate the "my", or some other expression with a similar possessive force, would yield something that was not a contingent fact at all. The proposition that *all* experiences are causally dependent on the state of a single body B, for example, is just false. The theorist means to speak of all the experiences had by a certain person being contingently so dependent. And the theorist cannot consistently argue that "all the experiences of person P" means the same thing as "all experiences contingently dependent on a certain body B"; for then his proposition would not be contingent, as his theory requires, but analytic. He must mean to be speaking of some class of experiences of the members of which it is in fact contingently true that they are all dependent on body B. And the defining characteristic of this class is in fact that they are "my experiences" or "the experiences of some person," where the sense of "possession" is the one he calls into question.

This internal incoherence is a serious matter when it is a question of denying what prima facie is the case: that is, that one does genuinely ascribe one's states of consciousness to something, viz., oneself, and that this kind of ascription is precisely such as the theorist finds unsatisfactory, i.e., is such that it does not seem to make sense to suggest, for example, that the identical pain which was in fact one's own might have been another's. We do not have to seek far in order to understand the place of this logically non-transferable kind of ownership in our general scheme of thought. For if we think of the requirements of identifying reference, in speech, to particular states of consciousness, or private experiences, we see that such particulars cannot be thus identifyingly referred to except as the states or experiences of some identified person. States, or experiences, one might say, owe their identity as particulars to the identity of the person whose states or experiences they are. And from this it follows immediately that if they can be identified as particular states or experiences at all, they must be possessed or ascribable in just that way which the no-ownership theorist ridicules, i.e., in such a way that it is logically impossible that a particular state or experience in fact possessed by someone should have been possessed by anyone else. The requirements of identity rule out logical transferability of ownership. So the theorist could maintain his position only by denying that we could ever refer to particular states or experiences at all. And this position is ridiculous.

We may notice, even now, a possible connection between the no-ownership doctrine and the Cartesian position. The latter is, straightforwardly enough, a dualism of two subjects (two types of subject). The former could, a little paradoxically, be called a dualism too: a dualism of one subject (the body) and one non-subject. We might surmise that the second dualism, paradoxically so called, arises out of the first dualism, nonparadoxically so called; in other words, that if we try to think of that to which one's states of consciousness are ascribed as something utterly different from that to which certain corporeal characteristics are ascribed, then indeed it becomes difficult to see why states of consciousness should be ascribed, thought of as belonging to, anything at all. And when we think of this possibility, we may also think of another: viz., that both the Cartesian and the no-ownership theorist are profoundly wrong in holding, as each must, that there are two uses of "I" in one of which it denotes something which it does not denote in the other.

III

The no-ownership theorist fails to take account of all the facts. He takes account of some of them. He implies, correctly, that the unique position or role of a single body in one's experience is not a sufficient explanation of the fact that one's experiences, or states of consciousness, are ascribed to something which *has* them, with that peculiar non-transferable kind of possession which is here in question. It may be a necessary part of the explanation, but it is not, by itself, a sufficient explanation. The theorist, as we have seen, goes on to suggest that it is perhaps a sufficient explanation of something else: viz., of our confusedly and mistakenly *thinking* that states of consciousness are to be ascribed to something in this special way. And this suggestion, as we have seen, is incoherent: for it involves the denial that someone's states of consciousness are anyone's. We avoid the incoherence of this denial, while agreeing that the special role of a single body in someone's experience does not suffice to explain why that experience should be ascribed to anybody. The fact that there is this special role does not, by itself, give a sufficient reason why what we think of as a subject of experience should have any use for the conception of himself as such a subject.

When I say that the no-ownership theorist's account fails through not reckoning with all the facts, I have in mind a very simple but, in this question, a very central, thought: viz., that it is a necessary condition of one's ascribing states of consciousness, experiences, to oneself, in the way one does, that one should also ascribe them (or be pre-

337

pared to ascribe them) to others who are not oneself.* This means not less than it says. It means, for example, that the ascribing phrases should be used in just the same sense when the subject is another, as when the subject is oneself. Of course the thought that this is so gives no trouble to the non-philosopher: the thought, for example, that "in pain" means the same whether one says "I am in pain" or "He is in pain." The dictionaries do not give two sets of meanings for every expression which describes a state of consciousness: a first-person meaning, and a second- and third-person meaning. But to the philosopher this thought has given trouble; indeed it has. How could the sense be the same when the method of verification was so different in the two cases—or, rather, when there *was* a method of verification in the one case (the case of others) and not, properly speaking, in the other case (the case of oneself)? Or, again, how can it be right to talk of ascribing in the case of oneself? For surely there can be a question of ascribing only if there is or could be a question of identifying that to which the ascription is made? And though there may be a question of identifying the one who is in pain when that one is another, how can there be such a question when that one is oneself? But this last query answers itself as soon as we remember that we speak primarily to others, for the information of others. In one sense, indeed, there is no question of my having to *tell who it is* who is in pain, when I am. In another sense I may have to *tell who it is*, i.e., to let others know who it is.

* I can imagine an objection to the unqualified form of this statement, an objection which might be put as follows. Surely the idea of a uniquely applicable predicate (a predicate which *in fact* belongs to only one individual) is not absurd. And, if it is not, then surely the most that can be claimed is that a necessary condition of one's ascribing predicates of a certain class to one individual (oneself) is that one should be prepared, or ready, on appropriate occasions, to ascribe them to other individuals, and hence that one should have a conception of what those appropriate occasions for ascribing them would be; but not, necessarily, that one should actually do so on any occasion.

The shortest way with the objection is to admit it, or at least to refrain from disputing it; for the lesser claim is all that the argument strictly requires, though it is slightly simpler to conduct it on the basis of the larger claim. But it is well to point out further that we are not speaking of a single predicate, or merely of some group or other of predicates, but of the whole of an enormous class of predicates such that the applicability of those predicates or their negations determines a major logical type or category of individuals. To insist, at this level, on the distinction between the lesser and the larger claims is to carry the distinction over from a level at which it is clearly correct to a level at which it may well appear idle or, possibly, senseless.

The main point here is a purely logical one: the idea of a predicate is correlative with that of a range of distinguishable individuals of which the predicate can be significantly, though not necessarily truly, affirmed.

What I have just said explains, perhaps, how one may properly be said to ascribe states of consciousness to oneself, given that one ascribes them to others. But how is it that one can ascribe them to others? Well, one thing is certain: that if the things one ascribes states of consciousness to, in ascribing them to others, are thought of as a set of Cartesian egos to which only private experiences can, in correct logical grammar, be ascribed, then this question is unanswerable and this problem insoluble. If, in identifying the things to which states of consciousness are to be ascribed, private experiences are to be all one has to go on, then, just for the very same reason as that for which there is, from one's own point of view, no question of telling that a private experience is one's own, there is also no question of telling that a private experience is another's. All private experiences, all states of consciousness, will be mine, i.e., no one's. To put it briefly: one can ascribe states of consciousness to oneself only if one can ascribe them to others; one can ascribe them to others only if one can identify other subjects of experience; and one cannot identify others if one can identify them only as subjects of experience, possessors of states of consciousness.

It might be objected that this way with Cartesianism is too short. After all, there is no difficulty about distinguishing bodies from one another, no difficulty about identifying bodies. And does not this give us an indirect way of identifying subjects of experience, while preserving the Cartesian mode? Can we not identify such a subject as, for example, "the subject that stands to that body in the same special relation as I stand to this one"; or, in other words, "the subject of those experiences which stand in the same unique causal relation to body N as my experiences stand to body M"? But this suggestion is useless. It requires me to have noted that my experiences stand in a special relation to body M, when it is just the right to speak of my experiences at all that is in question. (It requires me to have noted that my experiences stand in a special relation to body M; but it requires me to have noted this as a condition of being able to identify other subjects of experience, i.e., as a condition of having the idea of myself as a subject of experience, i.e., as a condition of thinking of any experience as mine.) So long as we persist in talking, in the mode of this explanation, of experiences on the one hand, and bodies on the other, the most I may be allowed to have noted is that experiences, all experiences, stand in a special relation to body M, that body M is unique in just this way, that this is what makes body M unique among bodies. (This "most" is, perhaps, too much—because of the presence of the word "experiences".) The proffered explanation runs: "Another subject of experience is distinguished and identified as the subject of those experiences which stand in the same unique causal relationship to body N as my experiences stand to body M." And the objection is: "But what is the word 'my' doing in this explanation? (It could not get on without it.)"

What we have to acknowledge, in order to begin to free ourselves from these difficulties, is the *primitiveness* of the concept of a person. What I mean by the concept of a person is the concept of a type of entity such that *both* predicates ascribing states of consciousness *and* predicates ascribing corporeal characteristics, a physical situation, etc. are equally applicable to a single individual of that single type. And what I mean by saying that this concept is primitive can be put in a number of ways. One way is to return to those two questions I asked earlier: viz., (1) why are states of consciousness ascribed to anything at all? and (2) why are they ascribed to the very same thing as certain corporeal characteristics, a certain physical situation, etc.? I remarked at the beginning that it was not to be supposed that the answers to these questions were independent of each other. And now I shall say that they are connected in this way: that a necessary condition of states of consciousness being ascribed at all is that they should be ascribed to the *very same things* as certain corporeal characteristics, a certain physical situation, etc. That is to say, states of consciousness could not be ascribed at all, *unless* they were ascribed to persons, in the sense I have claimed for this word. We are tempted to think of a person as a sort of compound of two kinds of subject—a subject of experiences (a pure consciousness, an ego), on the one hand, and a subject of corporeal attributes on the other.

Many questions arise when we think in this way. But, in particular, when we ask ourselves how we come to frame, to get a use for, the concept of this compound of two subjects, the picture—if we are honest and careful—is apt to change from the picture of two subjects to the picture of one subject and one non-subject. For it becomes impossible to see how we could come by the idea of different, distinguishable, identifiable subjects of experiences—different consciousnesses—*if this idea is thought of as logically primitive, as a logical ingredient in the compound idea of a person, the latter being composed of two subjects.*

For there could never be any question of assigning an experience, as such, to any subject other than oneself; and therefore never any question of assigning it to oneself either, never any question of ascribing it to a subject at all. So the concept of the pure individual consciousness—the pure ego—is a concept that cannot exist; or, at least, cannot exist as a primary concept in terms of which the concept of a person can be explained or analyzed. It can only exist, if at all, as a secondary, non-primitive concept, which itself is to be explained, analyzed, in terms of the concept of a person. It was the entity corresponding to this illusory primary concept of the pure consciousness, the ego-substance, for which Hume was seeking, or ironically pretending to seek, when he looked into himself, and complained that he could never discover himself without a perception and could never discover anything but the perception. More seriously—and this time there was no irony, but a confusion, a Nemesis of confusion for Hume—it was this entity of which Hume vainly sought for the principle of unity, confessing himself perplexed and defeated; sought vainly because there is no principle of unity where there is no principle of differentiation. It was this, too, to which Kant, more perspicacious here than Hume, accorded a purely formal ("analytic") unity: the unity of the "I think" that accompanies all my perceptions and therefore might just as well accompany none. And finally it is this, perhaps, of which Wittgenstein spoke when he said of the subject, first, that there is no such thing, and, second, that it is not a part of the world, but its limit.

So, then, the word "I" never refers to this, the pure subject. But this does not mean, as the no-ownership theorist must think and as Wittgenstein, at least at one period, seemed to think, that "I" in some cases does not refer at all. It refers, because I am a person among others. And the predicates which would, per impossible, belong to the pure subject if it could be referred to, belong properly to the person to which "I" does refer.

The concept of a person is logically prior to that of an individual consciousness. The concept of a person is not to be analyzed as that of an animated body or of an embodied anima. This is not to say that the concept of a pure individual consciousness might not have a logically secondary existence, if one thinks, or finds, it desirable. We speak of a dead person—a body—and in the same secondary way we might at least think of a disembodied person, retaining the logical benefit of individuality from having been a person.*

IV

It is important to realize the full extent of the acknowledgment one is making in acknowledging the logical primitiveness of the concept of a person. Let me rehearse briefly the stages of the argument. There would be no question of ascribing one's own states of consciousness, or experiences, to anything, unless one also ascribed states of consciousness, or experiences, to other individual entities of the same logical type as that thing to which one ascribes one's own states of consciousness. The condition of reckoning oneself as a subject of such predicates is that one should also reckon others as subjects of such predicates. The condition, in turn, of this being possible, is that one should be able to distinguish from one another (pick out, identify) different subjects of such predicates, i.e., different individuals of the type concerned. And the condition, in turn, of this being possible is that the individuals concerned, including oneself, should be of a certain unique type: of a type, namely, such that to each individual of that type there must be ascribed, or ascribable, both states of consciousness and corporeal characteristics. But this characterization of the type is still very opaque and does not at all clearly bring out what is involved. To bring this out, I must make a rough division, into two, of the kinds of predicates properly applied to individuals of this type. The first kind of predicate consists of those which are also properly applied to material bodies to which we would not dream of applying predicates ascribing states of consciousness. I will call this first kind M-predicates: and they include things like "weighs 10 stone", "is in the drawing room", and so on. The second kind consists of all the other predicates we apply to persons. These I shall call P-predicates. And P-predicates, of course, will be very various. They will include things like "is smiling", "is going for a walk", as well as things like "is in pain", "is thinking hard", "believes in God", and so on.

So far I have said that the concept of a person is to be understood as the concept of a type of entity such that both predicates ascribing states of consciousness and predicates ascribing corporeal characteristics, a physical situation, etc. are equally applicable to an individual entity

* A little further thought will show how limited this concession is. But I shall not discuss the question now.

of that type. And all I have said about the meaning of saying that this concept is primitive is that it is not to be analyzed in a certain way or ways. We are not, for example, to think of it as a secondary kind of entity in relation to two primary kinds, viz., a particular consciousness and a particular human body. I implied also that the Cartesian error is just a special case of a more general error, present in a different form in theories of the no-ownership type, of thinking of the designations, or apparent designations, of persons as *not* denoting precisely the same thing, or entity, for all kinds of predicate ascribed to the entity designated. That is, if we are to avoid the general form of this error we must *not* think of "I" or "Smith" as suffering from type-ambiguity. (If we want to locate type-ambiguity somewhere, we would do better to locate it in certain predicates like "is in the drawing room", "was hit by a stone", etc., and say they mean one thing when applied to material objects and another when applied to persons.)

This is all I have so far said or implied about the meaning of saying that the concept of a person is primitive. What has to be brought out further is what the implications of saying this are as regards the logical character of those predicates in which we ascribe states of consciousness. And for this purpose we may well consider P-predicates in general. For though not all P-predicates are what we should call "predicates ascribing states of consciousness" (for example, "going for a walk" is not), they may be said to have this in common, that they imply the possession of consciousness on the part of that to which they are ascribed.

What then are the consequences of this view as regards the character of P-predicates? I think they are these. Clearly there is no sense in talking of identifiable individuals of a special type, a type, namely, such that they possess both M-predicates and P-predicates, unless there is in principle some way of telling, with regard to any individual of that type, and any P-predicate, whether that individual possesses that P-predicate. And, in the case of at least some P-predicates, the ways of telling must constitute in some sense logically adequate kinds of criteria for the ascription of the P-predicate. For suppose in no case did these ways of telling constitute logically adequate kinds of criteria. Then we should have to think of the relation between the ways of telling and what the P-predicate ascribes (or a part of what it ascribes) always in the following way: we should have to think of the ways of telling as signs of the presence, in the individual concerned, of this different thing (the state of consciousness). But then we could only know that the way of telling was a sign of the presence of the different thing ascribed by the P-predicate, by the observation of correlations between the two. But this observation we could each make only in one case, namely, our own. And now we are back in the position of the defender of Cartesianism, who thought our way with it was too short. For what, now, does "our own case" mean? There is no sense in the idea of ascribing states of consciousness to oneself, or at all, unless the ascriber already knows how to ascribe at least some states of consciousness to others. So he cannot (or cannot generally) argue "from his own case" to conclusions about how to do this; for unless he already knows how to do this, he has no conception of *his own case*, or *any case* (i.e., any subject of experiences). Instead, he just has evidence that pain, etc. may be expected when a certain body is affected in certain ways and not when others are.

The conclusion here is, of course, not new. What I have said is that one ascribes P-predicates to others on the strength of observation of their behavior; and that the behavior criteria one goes on are not just signs of the presence of what is meant by the P-predicate, but are criteria of a logically adequate kind for the ascription of the P-predicate. On behalf of this conclusion, however, I am claiming that it follows from a consideration of the conditions necessary for any ascription of states of consciousness to anything. The point is not that we must accept this conclusion in order to avoid skepticism, but that we must accept it in order to explain the existence of the conceptual scheme in terms of which the skeptical problem is stated. But once the conclusion is accepted, the skeptical problem does not arise. (And so with the generality of skeptical problems: their statement involves the pretended acceptance of a conceptual scheme and at the same time the silent repudiation of one of the conditions of its existence. This is why they are, in the terms in which they are stated, insoluble.) But this is only half the picture about P-predicates.

Now let us turn to the other half. For of course it is true, at least of some important classes of P-predicates, that when one ascribes them to oneself, one does not do so on the strength of observation of those behavior criteria on the strength of which one ascribes them to others. This is not true of all P-predicates. It is not, in general, true of those which carry assessments of character and capability: these, when self-ascribed, are in general ascribed on the same kind of basis as that on which they are ascribed to others. And of those P-predicates of which it is true that one does not generally ascribe them to oneself on the basis of the criteria on the strength of which one ascribes them to others, there are many of which it is also true that their ascription is liable to correction by the self-ascriber on this basis. But there remain many cases in which one has an entirely adequate basis for ascribing a P-predicate to oneself, and yet in which this basis is quite distinct from those on which one ascribes the predicate to another. (Thus one says, reporting a present state of mind or feeling: "I feel tired, am depressed, am in pain.") How can this fact be reconciled with the doctrine that the criteria on the strength of which one ascribes P-predicates to others are criteria of a logically adequate kind for this ascription?

The apparent difficulty of bringing about this reconciliation may tempt us in many directions. It may tempt us, for example, to deny that these self-ascriptions are really ascriptions at all; to assimilate first-person ascriptions of states of consciousness to those other forms of behavior which constitute criteria on the basis of which one person ascribes P-predicates to another. This device seems to avoid the difficulty; it is not, in all cases, entirely inappropriate. But it obscures the facts, and is needless. It is merely a sophisticated form of failure to recognize the special character of P-predicates (or at least of a crucial class of P-predicates). For just as there is not (in general) one primary process of learning, or teaching oneself, an inner private meaning for predicates of this class, then another process of learning to apply such predicates to others on the strength of a correlation, noted in one's own case, with certain forms of behavior, so—and equally—there is not (in general) one primary process of learning to apply such predicates to others on the strength of behavior criteria, and then another process of acquiring the secondary technique of exhibiting a new form of behavior, viz., first-person P-utterances. Both these pictures are refusals to acknowledge the unique logical character of the predicates concerned.

Suppose we write 'Px' as the general form of propositional function of such a predicate. Then according to the first picture, the expression which primarily replaces "x" in this form is "I", the first-person singular pronoun; its uses with other replacements are secondary, derivative, and shaky. According to the second picture, on the other hand, the primary

345

replacements of "x" in this form are "he", "that person", etc., and its use with "I" is secondary, peculiar, not a true ascriptive use. But it is essential to the character of these predicates that they have both first- and third-person ascriptive uses, that they are both self-ascribable otherwise than on the basis of observation of the behavior of the subject of them, and other-ascribable on the basis of behavior criteria. To learn their use is to learn both aspects of their use. In order to *have* this type of concept, one must be both a self-ascriber and an other-ascriber of such predicates, and must see every other as a self-ascriber. And in order to *understand* this type of concept, one must acknowledge that there is a kind of predicate which is unambiguously and adequately ascribable *both* on the basis of observation of the subject of the predicate *and* not on this basis (independently of observation of the subject): the second case is the case where the ascriber is also the subject. If there were no concepts answering to the characterization I have just given, we should indeed have no philosophical problem about the soul; but equally we should not have our concept of a person.

To put the point—with a certain unavoidable crudity—in terms of one particular concept of this class, say, that of depression, we speak of behaving in a depressed way (of depressed behavior) and also of feeling depressed (of a feeling of depression). One is inclined to argue that feelings can be felt, but not observed, and behavior can be observed, but not felt, and that therefore there must be room here to drive in a logical wedge. But the concept of depression spans the place where one wants to drive it in. We might say, in order for there to be such a concept as that of X's depression, the depression which X has, the concept must cover both what is felt, but not observed, by X and what may be observed, but not felt, by others than X (for all values of X). But it is perhaps better to say: X's depression *is* something, one and the same thing, which is felt but not observed by X and observed but not felt by others than X. (And, of course, what can be observed can also be faked or disguised.) To refuse to accept this is to refuse to accept the structure of the language in which we talk about depression. That is, in a sense, all right. One might give up talking; or devise, perhaps, a different structure in terms of which to soliloquize. What is not all right is simultaneously to pretend to accept that structure and to refuse to accept it; i.e., to couch one's rejection in the language of that structure.

It is in this light that we must see some of the familiar philosophical difficulties in the topic of the mind. For some of them spring from just such a failure to admit, or fully appreciate, the character which I have been claiming for at least some P-predicates. It is not seen that these predicates could not have either aspect of their use (the self-ascriptive and the non-self-ascriptive) without having the other aspect. Instead, one aspect of their use is taken as self-sufficient, which it could not be, and then the other aspect appears as problematical. And so we oscillate between philosophical skepticism and philosophical behaviorism. When we take the self-ascriptive aspect of the use of some P-predicate (say, "depressed") as primary, then a logical gap seems to open between the criteria on the strength of which we say that another is depressed, and the actual state of depression. What we do not realize is that if this logical gap is allowed to open, then it swallows not only his depression, but our depression as well. For if the logical gap exists, then depressed behavior, however much there is of it, is no more than a sign of depression. And it can become a sign of depression only because of an observed correlation between it and depression. But whose depression? Only mine, one is tempted to say. But if only mine, then not mine at all. The skeptical position customarily represents the crossing of the logical gap as at best a shaky inference. But the point is that not even the syntax of the premises of the inference exists if the gap exists.

If, on the other hand, we take the other-ascriptive uses of these predicates as self-sufficient, we may come to think that all there is in the meaning of these predicates, as predicates, is the criteria on the strength of which we ascribe them to others. Does this not follow from the denial of the logical gap? It does not follow. To think that it does is to forget the self-ascriptive use of these predicates, to forget that we have to do with a class of predicates to the meaning of which it is essential that they should be both self-ascribable and other-ascribable to the same individual, when self-ascriptions are not made on the observational basis on which other-ascriptions are made, but on another basis. It is not that these predicates have two kinds of meaning. Rather, it is essential to the single kind of meaning that they do have that both ways of ascribing them should be perfectly in order.

If one is playing a game of cards, the distinctive markings of a certain card constitute a logically adequate criterion for calling it, say, the

Queen of Hearts; but, in calling it this, in the context of the game, one is also ascribing to it properties over and above the possession of those markings. The predicate gets its meaning from the whole structure of the game. So it is with the language which ascribes P-predicates. To say that the criteria on the strength of which we ascribe P-predicates to others are of a logically adequate kind for this ascription is not to say that all there is to the ascriptive meaning of these predicates is these criteria. To say this is to forget that they are P-predicates, to forget the rest of the language-structure to which they belong.

V

Now our perplexities may take a different form, the form of the question "But how can one ascribe to oneself, not on the basis of observation, *the very same thing* that others may have, on the basis of observation, a logically adequate reason for ascribing to one?" And this question may be absorbed in a wider one, which might be phrased: "How are P-predicates possible?" or "How is the concept of a person possible?" This is the question by which we replace those two earlier questions, viz.: "Why are states of consciousness ascribed at all, ascribed to anything?" and "Why are they ascribed to the very same thing as certain corporeal characteristics, etc.?" For the answer to these two initial questions is to be found nowhere else but in the admission of the primitiveness of the concept of a person, and hence of the unique character of P-predicates. So residual perplexities have to frame themselves in this new way. For when we have acknowledged the primitiveness of the concept of a person and, with it, the unique character of P-predicates, we may still want to ask what it is in the natural facts that makes it intelligible that we should have this concept, and to ask this in the hope of a non-trivial answer.* I do not pretend to be able to satisfy this demand at all fully. But I may mention two very different things which might count as beginnings or fragments of an answer.

And, first, I think a beginning can be made by moving a certain class of P-predicates to a central position in the picture. They are predicates, roughly, which involve doing something, which clearly imply intention or a state of mind or at least consciousness in general, and which indi-

---

* I mean, in the hope of an answer which does not merely say: Well, there are people in the world.

cate a characteristic pattern, or range of patterns, of bodily movement, while not indicating at all precisely any very definite sensation or experience. I mean such things as "going for a walk", "furling a rope", "playing ball", "writing a letter". Such predicates have the interesting characteristic of many P-predicates that one does not, in general, ascribe them to oneself on the strength of observation, whereas one does ascribe them to others on the strength of observation. But, in the case of these predicates, one feels minimal reluctance to concede that what is ascribed in these two different ways is the same. And this is because of the marked dominance of a fairly definite pattern of bodily movement in what they ascribe, and the marked absence of any distinctive experience. They release us from the idea that the only things we can know about without observation, or inference, or both, are private experiences; we can know also, without telling by either of these means, about the present and future movements of a body. Yet bodily movements are certainly also things we can know about by observation and inference.

Among the things that we observe, as opposed to the things we know without observation, are the movements of bodies similar to that about which we have knowledge not based on observation. It is important that we understand such observed movements; they bear on and condition our own. And in fact we understand them, we interpret them, only by seeing them as elements in just such plans or schemes of action as those of which we know the present course and future development without observation of the relevant present movements. But this is to say that we see such movements (the observed movements of others) as *actions*, that we interpret them in terms of intention, that we see them as movements of individuals of a type to which also belongs that individual whose present and future movements we know about without observation; that we see others, as self-ascribers, not on the basis of observations, of what we ascribe to them on this basis.

Of course these remarks are not intended to suggest how the "problem of other minds" could be solved, or our beliefs about others given a general philosophical "justification." I have already argued that such a "solution" or "justification" is impossible, that the demand for it cannot be coherently stated. Nor are these remarks intended as a priori genetic psychology. They are simply intended to help to make it seem intelligible to us, at this stage in the history of the philosophy of this subject, that we have the conceptual scheme we have. What I am suggesting is that it is easier to understand how we can see each other (and ourselves) as persons, if we think first of the fact that we act, and act on each other, and act in accordance with a common human nature. "To see each other as persons" is a lot of things; but not a lot of separate and unconnected things. The class of P-predicates that I have moved into the center of the picture are not unconnectedly there, detached from others irrelevant to them. On the contrary, they are inextricably bound up with the others, interwoven with them. The topic of the mind does not divide into unconnected subjects.

I spoke just now of a common human nature. But there is also a sense in which a condition of the existence of the conceptual scheme we have is that human nature should not be common, should not be, that is, a community nature. Philosophers used to discuss the question of whether there was, or could be, such a thing as a "group mind." And for some the idea had a peculiar fascination, while to others it seemed utterly absurd and nonsensical and at the same time, curiously enough, pernicious. It is easy to see why these last found it pernicious: they found something horrible in the thought that people should cease to have toward individual persons the kind of attitudes that they did have, and instead have attitudes in some way analogous to those toward groups; and that they might cease to decide individual courses of action for themselves and instead merely participate in corporate activities. But their finding it pernicious showed that they understood the idea they claimed to be absurd only too well. The fact that we find it natural to individuate as persons the members of a certain class of what might also be individuated as organic bodies does not mean that such a conceptual scheme is inevitable for any class of beings not utterly unlike ourselves.

Might we not construct the idea of a special kind of social world in which the concept of an individual person has no employment, whereas an analogous concept for groups does have employment? Think, to begin with, of certain aspects of actual human existence. Think, for example, of two groups of human beings engaged in some competitive but corporate activity, such as battle, for which they have been exceedingly well trained. We may even suppose that orders are superfluous, though information is passed. It is easy to imagine that, while absorbed in such activity, the members of the groups make no references to individual persons at all, have no use for personal names or pronouns. They do, however, refer to the groups and apply to them predicates analogous to those predicates ascribing purposive activity which we normally apply to individual persons. They may, in fact, use in such circumstances the plural forms "we" and "they"; but these are not genuine plurals, they are plurals without a singular, such as we use in sentences like these: "We have taken the citadel," "We have lost the game." They may also refer to elements in the group, to members of the group, but exclusively in terms which get their sense from the parts played by these elements in the corporate activity. (Thus we sometimes refer to what are in fact persons as "stroke" or "tackle".)

When we think of such cases, we see that we ourselves, over a part of our social lives—not, I am thankful to say, a very large part—do operate conceptual schemes in which the idea of the individual person has no place, in which its place is taken, so to speak, by that of a group. But might we not think of communities or groups such that this part of the lives of their members was the dominant part—or was the whole? It sometimes happens, with groups of human beings, that, as we say, their members think, feel, and act "as one." The point I wish to make is that a condition for the existence, the use, of the concept of an individual person is that this should happen only sometimes.

It is absolutely useless to say, at this point: But all the same, even if this happened all the time, every member of the group would have an individual consciousness, would be an individual subject of experience. The point is, once more, that there is no sense in speaking of the individual consciousness just as such, of the individual subject of experience just as such: for there is no way of identifying such pure entities.* It is true, of course, that in suggesting this fantasy, I have taken our concept of an individual person as a starting point. It is this fact which makes the useless reaction a natural one. But suppose, instead, I had made the following suggestion: that each part of the human body, each organ and each member, had an individual consciousness, was a separate center of experiences. This, in the same way, but more obviously, would be a useless suggestion. Then imagine all the intermediate cases, for instance these. There is a class of moving natural objects, divided into groups, each group exhibiting the same charac-

---

* More accurately: their identification is necessarily secondary to the identification of persons.

teristic pattern of activity. Within each group there are certain differentiations of appearance accompanying differentiations of function, and in particular there is one member of each group with a distinctive appearance. Cannot one imagine different sets of observations which might lead us, in the one case, to think of the particular member as the spokesman of the group, as its mouthpiece; and in the other case to think of him as its mouth, to think of the group as a single *scattered* body? The point is that as soon as we adopt the latter way of thinking then we want to drop the former; we are no longer influenced by the human analogy in its first form, but only in its second; and we no longer want to say: "Perhaps the members have consciousness." To understand the movement of our thought here, we need only remember the startling ambiguity of the phrase "a body and its members".

VI

I shall not pursue this attempt at explanation any further. What I have been mainly arguing for is that we should acknowledge the logical primitiveness of the concept of a person and, with this, the unique logical character of certain predicates. Once this is acknowledged, certain traditional philosophical problems are seen not to be problems at all. In particular, the problem that seems to have perplexed Hume * does not exist—the problem of the principle of unity, of identity, of the particular consciousness, of the particular subject of "perceptions" (experiences) considered as a primary particular. There is no such problem and no such principle. If there were such a principle, then each of us would have to apply it in order to decide whether any contemporary experience of his was his or someone else's; and there is no sense in this suggestion. (This is not to deny, of course, that one person may be unsure of his own identity in some way, may be unsure, for example, whether some particular action, or series of actions, had been performed by him. Then he uses the same methods (the same in principle) to resolve the doubt about himself as anyone else uses to resolve the same doubt about him. And these methods simply involve the application of the ordinary criteria for *personal* identity. There remains the question of what exactly these criteria are, what their relative weights are, etc.; but, once disentangled from spurious questions, this is one of the easier problems in philosophy.)

---

* Cf. the Appendix to the *Treatise of Human Nature.*

352

Where Hume erred, or seems to have erred, both Kant and Wittgenstein had the better insight. Perhaps neither always expressed it in the happiest way. For Kant's doctrine that the "analytic unity of consciousness" neither requires nor entails any principle of unity is not as clear as one could wish. And Wittgenstein's remarks (at one time) to the effect that the data of consciousness are not owned, that "I" as used by Jones, in speaking of his own feelings, etc., does not refer to what "Jones" as used by another refers to, seem needlessly to flout the conceptual scheme we actually employ. It is needlessly paradoxical to deny, or seem to deny, that when Smith says "Jones has a pain" and Jones says "I have a pain," they are talking about the same entity and saying the same thing about it, needlessly paradoxical to deny that Jones can confirm that he has a pain. Instead of denying that self-ascribed states of consciousness are really ascribed at all, it is more in harmony with our actual ways of talking to say: For each user of the language, there is just one person in ascribing to whom states of consciousness he does not need to use the criteria of the observed behavior of that person (though he does not necessarily not do so); and that person is himself. This remark at least respects the structure of the conceptual scheme we employ, without precluding further examination of it.

The Significance of Experience of the Individual for the Science of Psychology

The present essay consists substantially of a paper presented as part of a symposium on current behavioristic theory and methodology.* It was expected that my contribution might approach the subject from the contrasting point of view of Gestalt theory. Initially, the two theories differed in a number of basic ways. Central among these differences were these: at the methodological level, their systematic treatments of conscious experience; at the empirical level, their differential stress upon the factor of organization; at the theoretical level, their differing stresses upon "peripheral" factors vs. "brain" processes, and the general properties of those central brain processes—i.e., their atomistic vs. field character. On the one hand, Gestalt psychologists have, within the last twenty-five years, failed to increase markedly the specificity of their statements concerning the detailed properties of Gestalt processes and their determining conditions. Certain neo-behavioristic theories, on the other hand, have incorporated into their systems functional equivalents of such processes (cf. Hull's afferent neural interaction, 10). Others have so modified their original stresses as to obscure any general differences between theirs and the Gestalt position. Only the first-mentioned difference still remains fundamental—namely, the difference accorded, at least in practice, to the scientific status of experience. It is this difference that I propose to examine, in its relation to the potential content of the science of psychology. The word "experience" will here be used to refer in a general way to what has variously been termed awareness, conscious or direct experience, the phenomenal world, or, though I dislike the term, simply consciousness.

* A symposium held at the Minnesota Center for Philosophy of Science. University of Minnesota, May 17, 1954.

I shall contend that the difference in point of view involved still remains of the greatest importance, and that, if maintained, the long-range consequences of the dominant behavioristic emphasis will prove crippling for the development of psychology. Let us assume that psychology aims toward an understanding of all, including the most valued and most specifically human levels, of behavior and experience. Let us also assume that psychology as a science attempts, in an increasingly adequate fashion, to characterize the most significant features, at all levels, of the events we regard as psychological; to identify their determining conditions; and, most essentially, to state with increasing specificity the interrelations between such events and their conditions—that is, to formulate psychological laws.

We shall not be concerned with problems of the logical characteristics of the linguistic structure of science but rather with the basis in observation which is presupposed by any such analysis. The question which I propose to consider is the following: How is the actual and potential achievement of the aims of science just mentioned influenced by the practicing scientist's formal view of the role of experience in science? To restate the problem: What is the relation that may obtain at a stage of development of a science comparable to the present state of psychology between the breadth of its observation base and the character of its content in terms of functional relationships? In particular, we shall consider the limitations which a marked restriction of the range of experience regarded as scientifically usable or legitimate may have both upon the further development of psychology as a science and also upon the interrelationships between scientific psychology and other branches of knowledge concerning human behavior, such as the humanities.

What I have to say has little direct bearing upon the hygienic analyses of previous improprieties in the use of language in science which have been vigorously furthered by the philosophers of science in recent decades. I wish to point out, however, some of the unfortunate consequences which have resulted from acceptance by psychologists of these methodological emphases without viewing them in proper perspective to the psychologist's total task as a scientist. As a scientist, his total task involves the discovery, as well as the ordering and the verification of relevant knowledge. The psychologists' methodology of verification indeed needed re-analysis. Here I am concerned chiefly to inquire into the consequences for psychology of the quasi-emotionally based rejection of direct experience for other aspects of his scientific task.

Although the historical development of the behavioristic view of the status of conscious or direct experience in the science of psychology is well known, reference here to certain aspects of it is instructive. Titchener envisaged the primary tasks of psychology as the analytical description of conscious experience and the specification of its determining conditions. Watson reacted against this exclusive interest in the analysis of experience rather than of behavior. In itself this was a healthy reaction to Titchener's radical restriction of the subject matter of psychology. Unfortunately Watson's own initial denial of the existence of conscious experience constituted just as drastic an amputation upon the body of psychology—one which in its practical consequences was not reversed by his later formal admission of its existence. For the "ontological" status of conscious experience as a vital aspect of many of the events constituting the referents of psychological constructs was still implicitly denied, as was its "functional" status as a direct observation base of psychology. However complex his own reasons for this rejection of experience, his most valid scientific one was the failure of the refined Titchenerian "introspective" method to yield consistent results especially when applied to the analysis of complex experiences.

Clearly, consistency or inter-individual agreement in observation is, in some sense, a central and irreducible requirement of scientific method, and the full force of Watson's criticism has never been adequately dealt with by his theoretical opponents. There has been too much of a tendency to insist upon the desirability, and even in general terms the necessity, of recognizing phenomenal reality or direct experience; not enough of a detailed spelling out of a convincing methodological rationale. Such a rationale must adequately recognize and analyze the potential sources of error and discriminate the conditions of observation under which the experiential aspects of reality as reported can and cannot be assimilated into the interrelated system of functional relationships constituting psychological science. Only thus can the hard core of the Watsonian critique be satisfactorily met. The extent to which it can be met is after all not an a priori matter or one to be decided autistically, however great the felt urgency to make science "meaningful," but one which must be decided empirically, and with full recognition of its difficulties. The extent to which experiential variables may be assimilated into the body of psychological science *might* in practice have proven to be limited to the necessary but qualitatively trivial role of perceived pointer readings in physics. The argument in favor of this possibility is on its face persuasive. How can any event, such as a particular experience of an individual, directly accessible only to one person and thus absolutely private, and, as a unique event, uncheckable, serve as a basis for the establishment of scientific laws? Such a possibility appears in principle incompatible with the accepted supra-individual or public character of science. It has thus been frequently assumed that only those events which in principle can be simultaneously observed by multiple observers whose independent reports in turn may be observed and compared, also by multiple observers termed experimenters—only such events may be accepted as constituting a legitimate observational basis for science.

In general methodological discussions, the original observational basis is often almost taken for granted without any detailed specification of assumed conditions. Thus, it is assumed that, under so-called standard, but frequently unspecified conditions, any normal person will see a green field as green, and the oaks on its edges as spreading out in three-dimensional space. Or, it may be proposed—if reports on green fields or oaks on their edges are not in complete agreement "let us get back to the pointer readings of the physical scientist—where agreement is assured." Psychologists, however, perhaps shocked by such an epistemologically uncritical position, and impressed by the possible lacks in correspondence between one's experience and one's report of it, have frequently taken a radically opposed position. They have insisted that only verbal reports by the observing subject of his own experience, including that of another's behavior, or perhaps better, written statements concerning experience or behavior, or, even better, graphic records of the consequences of such behavior are public and, therefore, safe starting points for the science of psychology. Thus, observable written words or sentences have become acceptable scientific data, but the individual's experiences to which they may refer, that is, the experiential referents of those words, are disenfranchised as private and, therefore, illegitimate.

Let us examine in more detail whether such an intransigent insistence upon the criterion of interobserver agreement with respect to the particular observations upon which science rests is either necessary or desirable. Let us also examine the conditions under which the criterion may be applied without hampering scientific advance. Unfortunately for us, philosophers of science have discussed this problem chiefly in terms of physical science. It is therefore worthwhile to consider briefly the differential consequences for physics and for psychology of the two just suggested restricted observational bases (i.e., pointer readings and verbal reports).

In physics, it has gradually become possible to make many data-yielding experimental observations by reading the dials of scientific instruments, the so-called pointer readings. This is a type of perceptual situation specifically designed to maximize accuracy of observation and thus also interobserver agreement in the report of observation. Physics has achieved primary reliance upon such a type of observational situation only after a long period of development. At present, this type has definite advantages and sets only minor restrictions on the investigation of a wide range of physical events. This present state of affairs depends, however, upon several basic facts. The specificity of inferences permitted by the detailed character of current physical knowledge makes it possible to connect physically and deductively that part of the situation observed (the instrument dial) with the actual events in the physical systems being studied in such a way that almost any process may be determinately related to standard physical instruments (the character of whose internal structure and processes is of course known in complete detail). Secondly, the perceptual experience involved is reduced to that of displacement of a pointer on the dial or scale of a measuring instrument. Apparently, for such perceptions to yield inter-individual consistency of report, the only important preconditions within the observer are adequate visual acuity, attention, and a minimal level of verbal articulateness. Finally, the physicist uses perceptual experiences in any case solely as *indifferent indicators* of the events in which he is directly interested. Accuracy and consistency of report are his only concerns and he can and does ignore the particular phenomenal properties on which the report is based. They are mere epistemological handles necessary for the check of his theory against reality, but the *locus of his scientific concern* is elsewhere. As Pratt (15) points out, the present physicist leaves the level of observation almost immediately, further descriptive analysis of the experienced world would profit him little if at all, and the experiences against which he does check his scientific inferences have no intimate or intrinsic relationship or correspondence with his scientific (explanatory) constructs.

With regard to each of these considerations, current psychology differs radically from current physics. The first and most vital difference consists in the content of the two sciences. In contrast to physics, psychology is interested in the experience and behavior of, and events within, the human organism, not in external events per se. The processes intervening between external stimulus conditions and reactive behavior are certainly complex. No human behavior can be adequately explained without reference to them. And in the vastly important class of primarily endogenously regulated actions, they provide the major key to understanding and prediction of behavior. (Furthermore, one of the currently most misleading practices in psychology is that of assuming that an explanation is provided by functional relationships between external independent and dependent variables affecting a system, itself consisting of a complex set of variables which are merely kept constant in the experimental situation.) Experience or awareness is presumably more directly dependent upon these intervening processes than is overt behavior, including verbal report. This remains true even though we have difficulty in specifying any basic postulate, such as that of isomorphism, expressing in detail the form of this dependence. And it is extremely likely that clues as to the properties of these intermediate processes may be yielded by sensitive phenomenal description. However, wholly aside from this heuristic consideration, the phenomenal characteristics of our perceptual and other behavior in themselves constitute an aspect of the universe with which it is the peculiar task of psychology to deal scientifically.

Secondly, the lack of specificity in the functional relations constituting present psychology does not permit us to construct observational situations in which important features of complex human activities are unambiguously linked via recording apparatus to simple pointer readings characterizable only in terms of a physical-thing language. To take aspects of peripheral behavior as indicators of central events with the same specificity as pointer readings are taken by physics would require that our knowledge of the effector processes intervening between them and these central processes (i.e., those underlying the experience or constituting the implicit behavior) be as detailed and determinate as that of the processes of the interior of the physical measuring instruments connecting its moving pointer to the relevant properties of the physical event in which the physicist is interested. In such cases these effector processes (or these plus the recording instrument) are for the psychologist or the physiologist the equivalent of the measuring instrument alone for the physicist. They mediate between the events observed and the events constituting, in the particular experiment, the locus of concern of the scientist. In the case of psychology as in physics, the experimenter's locus of concern is operationally determinable by the terms of the hypothesis he proposes to test and by the type of generalization he makes of his experimental findings (i.e., of the laws they are taken to define). If we are interested in relating to their determining conditions the significant features of human and animal behavior, including the perceptual activity of experiencing, we cannot limit ourselves to observations determined primarily by external conditions. All psychologically relevant experience is in some degree, and most of it is in a marked degree, conditioned by internal states and processes of the individual. Therefore, restriction of observational situations to those in which the role of internal determinants is minimized, as in the observations of physics, disastrously limits the range of psychological events that can be directly reported.

It is true that psychology has gained by utilizing observational situations similar to those of physics. Concentration of experimental attention on kinds or aspects of behavior especially of animals capable of being connected to physical measuring instruments has permitted the determination of quantitative and quasi-quantitative relationships of great interest. We are concerned here, however, with the consequences of too exclusive a utilization of such situations. Carried to the extreme to which much methodological discussion would indicate as desirable, it would result in the exclusion, in principle, of all experience in the production of which differences in past experience, in special capacities, in present motivation, or in personality, would play a significant role, as well as those differences in receptor equipment and attention affecting observation in standard physical situations. Thus would be excluded all the more complex experiences of everyday life, all those constituting the working data of the clinical psychologist, and the whole range of artistically creative experiences as well as those which constitute the subject matter of the humanistic disciplines. In other words, in the interest of achieving scientific objectivity, description of all most characteristically human experience is avoided as failing to achieve the criterion of general inter-observer agreement so frequently insisted upon as scientifically necessary. (See Spence, 16, for a forceful recent restatement of this point.)

I should like to suggest that this criterion, as generally stated, *is not a necessary one for scientific observation.* Rather, developments in our knowledge of perception provide the *possibility, in principle, of transcending the difficulties raised by inter-individual variability in reports on experience.* Since science seeks to formulate systems of functional interrelationships (laws) between certain characteristics of events and their relevant conditions, the "objectivity" required by science means only that *under given specifiable and manipulable conditions, repeatable events* (in the present context, repeatable experiences) *can be shown to recur.* Whether or not we can directly check the individual occurrence of a particular experience becomes therefore of only minor importance if the experience uniformly recurs under adequately specified conditions. Furthermore, specification of the conditions need not, as in physics, be primarily in terms of the external situation. It may require, in addition, a detailed and even elaborate specification of personal, or organismic, conditions. Adequate specification of the relevant personal variables will at present often not be possible without further research. However, present technical difficulties should not obscure the matter of the methodological principle here involved. Techniques of experimental manipulation and control of internal variables will increase in adequacy with increasing knowledge both of perceptual and effector processes (just as with physics the development of precision of laws and measuring instruments has been a circular process). Manipulation of the conditions under which, for instance, occurrence of musical experiences of specified characteristics may be predicted, may involve years of training of a person of defined musical abilities. The number of such persons available for experimental subjection to controlled auditory stimulus events might not be large. However, this would not, in principle, invalidate the scientific objectivity or repeatability of the functional relationships that might be obtained with this limited number of observers possessing specified characteristics. Again an observation need not be repeatable by any given person picked randomly from the street, or from the classroom, in order for it to serve as an adequate basis for establishment of psychological laws. It is required only that it be repeatable under specifiable external and internal conditions, even though, practically, this may limit its repetition to a very restricted set of persons. I am, therefore, suggesting that the *more general* and, to me, acceptable, objective intended by the current criterion of "public character of individual observations" or of interobserver agreement would be better and more flexibly served by the substitution of the *criterion of repeatability of obtained functional relationships between specified experiences and specified conditions* (external and internal).

The importance of specification of hitherto unstressed internal conditions may be illustrated by reference to the recent work of one of my colleagues, Dr. M. Gaffron. Her observations on the effect of right-left mirror-image reversals in painting and etchings provide striking phenomenal indications of processes which may enter in a very basic way into the perception of three-dimensional space (3, 4). Individual subjects are variously sensitive toward the various components of the complex phenomenal effects of right-left reversal. Such effects include shifts in the felt location of the observer within the picture space, the direction from which individuals within the picture space are felt to be perceived, the internal groupings of such individuals as determined by spatial arrangement or by their personal inter-relationships. Such felt differences indicate the necessity of investigating laterality and the complexities of brain dominances in human observers. The effects of hitherto neglected factors of laterality may not only explain variations in the results of such perceptual experiments but, upon more adequate specification, may lead to the discovery of new dimensions of human experience.

Paradoxically, considering Titchener's position, the possibility of incorporating phenomenal observations of complex experiences into lawful relationships (i.e., into science) will depend upon the developments of techniques of diagnosis (projective and other techniques of so-called clinical or individual difference psychology) of internal, personal variables, and upon techniques of controlling them, as much as upon the controls of external stimulus variables. It will also depend upon the development of a more adequate knowledge of the processes of perceptual learning.

We thus urge the advantage of a broadened range of phenomenal experiences upon which psychology may be based, and obversely, deny that they need be limited only to those upon which general intersubjective agreement can be obtained. A more extreme form of the position here rejected lies in the contention that the difficulties of phenomenal observation and report can best be avoided by recourse to so-called objective experimentation with animals.

It has been asserted that in objective experiments with rats Lashley has demonstrated the major facts concerning perceptual grouping, figure-ground differentiation and the like, originally reported by Wertheimer, Rubin, and Köhler in human "introspective" experiments. The implication that human reports on experience were therefore dispensable is incorrect. Science consists of far more than confirming already observed relationships. Strategically the important advance was the initial identification or discovery of these experiences at the human level. This constituted the pre-condition for their subsequent check at the animal level. As the original human observations in the history of the psychology of simple perceptual forms have historically preceded confirmation of similar functional relationships at the animal level, so we may expect that identification of the characteristics of more complex experiences of greater human significance will be made by observers sensitized to such features of their own experience. The work of Michotte and his co-workers on the phenomenal characteristics of the perception of "mechanical causality," "reality," and "permanence" provide illustrations (14). Furthermore, such observations will not be invalidated if they are never confirmed at the animal level.

An examination of some of the ways in which useful descriptive categories have originated would be relevant to the present argument. The standard sensory attributes such as pitch or loudness distinguished within the Wundtian-Titchenerian tradition arose out of a tendency to identify the simplest dimensions of uncomplicated experience. Doubtless, knowledge of the dimensions of physical stimuli played a certain role in their initial identification. But such a phenomenal dimension as tonal volume scarcely arose in this way. Contrariwise, the initial specification of the phenomenal characteristics of such experiences as figure-ground by Rubin or the varieties of apparent movement by Wertheimer arose from a free unrestricted description of their experiences. Later, general acceptance of these phenomenal categories came after sufficient determination of their stimulus conditions and formulation of adequate instructions enabled other observers consistently to identify and report these features in their own experiences. I suggest that twentieth-century sensory psycho-physics has exploited the capital of phenomenological distinctions made in the nineteenth century—and am apprehensive that no new comparable wealth of phenomenal distinctions relevant to more complex perceptions is being presently accumulated.

At times mixtures of physiological theory, of physical conceptions of the stimulus, and of properly naive phenomenal description have yielded valuable new distinctions. One illustration is that of perceptual segregation, introduced by Wertheimer and Köhler. It was probably derived in part from speculations as to brain functioning. The more recent suggestions by Gibson that surfaces, edges, and texture gradients constitute the basic phenomenal dimensions of three-dimensional space doubtless derive in part from a geometrical and physical analysis of the characteristics of the optical stimulus (5, 6).

There is no reason why the constructive role of phenomenological description should be confined to the area of perception as traditionally conceived. Quite to the contrary, I would urge that its more systematic extension to other areas would provide a powerful tool to initial identification of significant variables, and, in the idiom of my colleague S. Koch, further the pre-conditions for incipient theory. McLeod (12, 13) and Asch (1) have strongly argued this point with regard to social psychology. Fritz Heider (8, 9) has shown the possibilities of identification of different action attributes. Koch has recently illustrated the forcefulness with which a set of personal phenomenal observations may be brought to bear upon the general mode of thinking about motivational processes (11). That certain central systematic motivational concepts (e.g., Lewin's *Aufforderungscharacter*, Murray's press) have had phenomenal overtones may have been neither wholly unintentional nor without virtue.

A further potential empirical gain stemming from the present argument is the factual contribution which would result from more systematic phenomenal characterizations of the less usual kinds of experience; that is, those kinds traditionally regarded as scientifically unusable because of lack of sufficient intersubjective agreement in reporting them. Such experiences would typically occur in situations in which some type of internal factor plays an unusually predominant role, or in which the total situation is one which for practical and humanitarian reasons would not be experimentally instituted. Acute situations of great danger, of great stress, of unusual deprivation, of drug addiction or administration, are examples of one type. Psychiatrically or neuropathologically abnormal individuals, both in chronic and in acute situations such as that of brain operation, provide further examples. Observations under such conditions are by no means lacking but their systematic utilization has been. The point to be made here is that the potential advantage to be gained by more systematic use of those unusual situations is, in principle, the same as that widely recognized in the area of complex motivation. There, discovery of important features of the interplay of motives in normal situations has been gained by attention to their exaggerated manifestations under abnormal conditions. In the present context, it is suggested that phenomenal dimensions, as for instance that of reality-unreality, which in usual experience may not vary enough to be noticed, may exhibit themselves more clearly under unusual conditions. Further examples of the same point are provided by instances of experience dependent upon rare characteristics of the observer such as exceptional training or special talent, particularly as combined in the creative artist or thinker of high capacity.

Psychology need not fall prey to the common attitude that genuine values in a democratic framework are limited only to those achievable by all men. It has much to gain by consciously seeking to identify and determine the conditions of the more rarely occurring experiences even if they only occur with more differentiated human beings. We may expect that their identification will be followed, if more slowly, by a specification of their conditions, which would constitute the occasion of their assimilation by psychological science. This is not to suggest that there are no limitations to such scientific assimilation. There well may be inherent limitations derived from the special attitudes under which some types of experience occur and those necessary for adequate observation and verbal report. Here, I have been more concerned to point out that such limitations may be far more closely approximated than to attempt to determine their exact character. For fuller exploitation of phenomenal experiences under unusual conditions, it is clear that fuller knowledge of the interrelationships between experience and the report on it is required.

A few remarks may be made as to general conditions which would be favorable to the discovery of new phenomenal characteristics. It is quite probable that individuals vary considerably in their awareness of the phenomenal dimensions or characteristics of experience. Such awareness may well be decreased by the inevitable emphasis developed in scientific activity upon conceptual categorization and enhanced by a certain reluctance immediately to categorize experience in terms of the characteristics traditionally recognized in the language of technical psychology or of everyday language. Let us refer to individuals capable of freeing themselves from traditional categorization, as experientially sensitive observers. Certainly an increased number of such among psychologists would be desirable.

Another precondition for progress in phenomenal observation is a more general trust in one's own experience. Recent generations of psychology students are extraordinarily reluctant to trust any of their own descriptions of their own experience not immediately confirmed by the reports of any happenstance bystander quite without reference to whether certain conditions of training, attitude, motivation, and the like are required for occurrence of the phenomenal characteristic in question. This is apt to be accompanied by a corresponding uncritical acceptance of the significance of verbal reports of others provided considerable agreement is exhibited among them, often without even raising the question of the character of the relationship between the words of the report and their referents in the experience of the individual. This is reflected also in the frequent uncritical acceptance of graphic records without adequate consideration of their relation to the underlying events. All of these features stem from the neglect of experience of the individual as having direct scientific status in current psychology.

One of the most urgent technical questions involves the relationship between experience and its various indicators. A major source of confusion stems from the identification of a property of experience with its most frequent indicator—the verbal report—that is, of identifying a red experience with the report "it is red," or of the felt experience of the plastic character of a piece of sculpture with the report "it is plastic." Explicit justification of this practice on operational grounds (see Stevens, 17) seems not to be currently maintained (2, 15, 16) and yet, in practice, as Boring has recently indicated (2), actual concern is apt to be deflected from the experiential referent to its operational index, the report. And, since the "report" is publicly observable and is a "response," it tends to be regarded as the significant end term of the functional relationship being established. It is also frequently treated as a sheer response, with neglect of its referent, phenomenal experience. However one may protest that this constitutes an unnecessary distortion of the essentials of the behavioristic analysis, there remains the incontrovertible historical fact of pragmatic significance that, within the last thirty years, no new phenomenological distinctions have arisen out of investigations by any behavioristically oriented psychologists.

Furthermore, since the behavioristic formulation shifts the burden of scientific responsibility from the report of the subject to the report of the experimenter, no incentive exists for a more adequate analysis of the processes intervening between occurrence of and report on experience. Fortunately for the behaviorist, there exists no need within his formulations to search for *le mot juste*—to adequately characterize any of his experiences. The current attitude is that it is the behavior that counts—and that means the report, not its forgotten referent, the experience.

Yet, obviously, a more intensive analysis of the interrelation of language and experience is required. Even a more central and general problem, however, lies in the analysis of meaning in behavior, not only linguistic behavior. Thus, it is often strictly irrelevant whether an observer reports in verbal terms the presence of a phenomenal characteristic, or presses a key after an appropriate verbal instruction from the experimenter. There is thus a functional equivalence of the role of verbal instruction and of verbal report. The meaning of the key-pressing behavior may be identical with that of a verbal characterization. And, under certain conditions often achieved only with laborious effort, this meaning may be established by non-verbal training methods. A specification of these conditions would be equivalent to a statement of the conditions under which language develops. But these problems cannot be further pursued here.

One final comment concerning the current devaluation of free unrestricted description in experimental phenomenal analysis. Graham has characterized free description as being on the level of casual conversation and recognizes only reports highly restricted by instructions as of scientific value (7). This ignores the role played by free description of experience in the essential developmental stage of identification of new phenomenal categories. Initially, the individual psychological observer need not be able by himself to specify a particular phenomenal dimension which nevertheless he may be perfectly capable of reporting if requested by the experimenter to do so through appropriate instructions. But before the determining conditions of an experience can be established, at any level of parametric detail, the significant phenomenal characteristics of the experience must first be identified. And this is in a sense a creative task. I am by no means identifying this task with the whole task of science. But in the early stages, it may constitute a very critical phase of scientific advance, and psychology in most of its fields is in such an early stage of development.

To recapitulate, I have stressed the significance of our conscious experiences for the science of psychology in respect both to the development of new knowledge and to the character of the content of psychology. Discussions of scientific method, particularly in the context of behavioristic psychology, have tended to stress problems of testability, of concepts and of functional relations, relatively neglecting the extent to which either the concepts or functional relations investigated correspond to those aspects of the universe which in some sense are most central and significant for the area of reality with which the science deals. I have contended that an acceptance of the necessity, in principle, of general intersubjective agreement on individual observations, and a too exclusive concern with verbal reports as such rather than with the experiences to which they refer, have together enormously narrowed the range of experiences regarded as legitimately accessible to psychological science. Among other consequences, this has resulted in an unfortunate and unnecessarily wide gap between psychological science and the humanities as branches of knowledge; it has limited advances in areas of scientific psychology itself even outside that of perception, notably in those of motivation and social psychology.

Great technical difficulties in specifying the relations between experience and report still remain. It is my conviction that these technical difficulties are soluble with sufficient insight and experimental effort, but that a general precondition of their solution resides in a change in the climate of opinion in which psychologists work. Such a change would involve a more general trust in observation of one's own experience, and an increased recognition of the scientific legitimacy of the observation of more rarely occurring experiences provided that the conditions of such experiences are specifiable. Finally, and this I cannot overstress, such a change would involve clearer recognition that full development of psychology as a science requires that a sufficient number of its scientific observers and experimenters must themselves be highly developed in those characteristics which are most essentially and significantly human.

REFERENCES

1. Asch, S. E. *Social Psychology*. New York: Prentice-Hall, 1952.
2. Boring, E. G. "A History of Introspection," *Psychological Bulletin*, 50:169–189 (1953).
3. Gaffron, M. "Right and Left in Pictures," *Art Quarterly*, 13:312–331 (1950).
4. Gaffron, M. "Some New Dimensions in the Phenomenal Analysis of Visual Experience," *Journal of Personality*, 24:285–307 (1956).
5. Gibson, J. J. *The Perception of the Visual World*. Cambridge, Mass.: Riverside Press, 1950.
6. Gibson, J. J. "The Perception of Visual Surfaces," *American Journal of Psychology*, 63:367–384 (1950).
7. Graham, C. H. "Visual Perception" in S. S. Stevens (ed.), *Handbook of Experimental Psychology*, pp. 868–920. New York: Wiley, 1951.
8. Heider, F. "Social Perception and Phenomenal Causality," *Psychological Review*, 51:358–374 (1944).
9. Heider, F., and M. Simmel. "An Experimental Study of Apparent Behavior," *American Journal of Psychology*, 57:243–259 (1944).
10. Hull, C. L. *Principles of Behavior*. New York: D. Appleton-Century Co., 1943.
11. Koch, S. "Behavior as 'Intrinsically' Regulated: Work Notes towards a Pretheory of Phenomena called 'Motivational,'" in M. R. Jones (ed.), *Nebraska Symposium on Motivation*. Lincoln: Univ. of Nebraska Press, 1956.
12. MacLeod, R. B. "The Phenomenological Approach to Social Psychology," *Psychological Review*, 54:193–210 (1947).
13. MacLeod, R. B. "The Place of Phenomenological Analysis in Social Psychological Theory," in J. H. Rohrer and M. Sherif (eds.), *Social Psychology at the Crossroads*, pp. 215–241. New York: Harper, 1951.
14. Michotte, A. *La Perception de la Causalité*. Louvain: l'Institute superieur de Philonoptue, 1946.
15. Pratt, C. C. *The Logic of Modern Psychology*. New York: Macmillan, 1948.
16. Spence, K. W. "The Empirical Basis and Theoretical Structure of Psychology," *Philosophy of Science*, 24:97–108 (1957).
17. Stevens, S. S. "Psychology: The Propaedeutic Science," *Philosophy of Science*, 3:90–103 (1936).

The "Mental" and the "Physical"

I. A Preliminary Survey of Some Perplexities and Their Repression

Tough-minded scientists tend to relegate the mind-body problem to the limbo of speculative metaphysics. Perhaps after trying a bit, but with questionable success to square themselves with the puzzle, they usually take one or the other of two attitudes. Either the puzzle is left to the philosophers to worry about, or else it is bluntly declared a pseudoproblem not worth pondering by anybody. Yet, the perplexities crop up again and again, often quite unexpectedly, if not in central issues of substantive scientific research, then certainly, and at least in connection with the attempts to formulate adequately and consistently the problems, the results, and the programs of scientific inquiry. The disputes regarding the very subject matter and definition of psychology furnish a poignant illustration. Is it *mental experience* or is it *behavior*?

The behaviorist revolution in psychology, as well as its opposite philosophical counterpart, the phenomenalistic point of view in epistemology, each in its way, tried to obviate the problem. But all sorts of perplexities keep bedeviling both parties. The problem may be repressed, but repression produces symptoms, logical symptoms such as paradoxes or inconsistencies in this case. The behaviorist psychologist assimilates his method to that of the "objective" natural sciences. Scientific psychology, as the well known saying goes, having first lost its soul, later its consciousness, seems finally to lose its mind altogether. Behaviorism, now after more than forty years of development, shows of course many signs of mitigation of its originally rather harsh and radical position. It has availed itself of various clothings from the storehouse of philosophical garments. But despite the considerably greater scientific and logical sophistication in recent treatments of the issue, it is somewhat

370

depressing to note that the main philosophical positions still are these: materialism, mentalism, mind-body interactionism, evolutionary emergence theories, psychoneurophysiological parallelism (epiphenomenalism, isomorphism, double aspect theories), and neutral monism. Characteristically, the phenomenalist and the behaviorist positions, refined descendants or variants respectively of the mentalistic and the materialistic philosophies, have been most forcefully advocated by the positivists of the last and of the present century. Positivism, more distinctly than any other point of view, with its notorious phobia of metaphysical problems and its marked tendency toward reductionism, was always ready to diagnose the mind-body puzzle as a *Scheinproblem*. Small wonder then that phenomenalism (or neutral monism) on the one hand, and physicalism on the other, have been the favored positions in various phases of the history of the positivistic outlook.

In the philosophy of the enlightenment of the eighteenth century we find the outspoken and clear-headed phenomenalism of Hume, but also the equally explicit, though more "simpliste" French materialism, especially of Baron d'Holbach. The German positivists of the nineteenth century, led by Mach and Avenarius, were essentially Humeans. And so was Bertrand Russell in one of the earlier phases of his epistemological odyssey. It was the combined influence of Russell's phenomenalism (or neutral monism) and of the logic of *Principia Mathematica* which led Carnap in his early work *Der Logische Aufbau der Welt* (1928) to elaborate in considerable detail and with remarkable precision a logical reconstruction of the relation between psychological and physical concepts. He chose as a basis for this reconstruction a set of neutral experiential data and showed how the concepts of various scientific disciplines can be constituted as logical constructions erected on a basis of concepts which refer to elements and relations of that (subjectless) raw material of immediate experience. Carnap's attempt was thus a culminating point in the series of positivistic-phenomenalistic epistemologies. But certain grave objections and difficulties soon made Carnap abandon this scheme and replace it by another, different in basis and structure. His new reconstruction is physicalistic in that the basic elements and relations are the designata of an intersubjective observation language (viz., the physicalistic thing-language). The difference in logical structure is due mainly to the recognition that the Russellian hierarchy of types does not adequately explicate the category mistakes which

371

undoubtedly give rise to some (though by no means all) mind-body puzzles.

The physicalist views of Lashley (192), Carnap (62, 64, 66, 67), Hempel (146), Black (37, 38), Quine (268), Ryle (294), Skinner (321), and Wilfrid Sellars (315), though differing in many more or less important respects among each other, are primarily motivated by a basic doubt about the possibility of a purely phenomenal language. The observation language of everyday life, we are told, is rooted in the intersubjective terms whose usage we acquired in the learning situations of a common, public context of labeling things, properties, relations, states, events, processes, and dispositions. Subjective or "mentalistic" terms, this group of thinkers claims, are introduced and their usage learned on an intersubjective basis. Remove this intersubjective basis and you have deprived psychological concepts not only of their scientific significance, but you are left with nothing more than ineffable raw feels or with exclamations devoid of cognitive significance.

But the problems will not completely yield to this reductive approach. Introspection, though admittedly often unreliable, does enable us to describe elements, aspects, and configurations in the phenomenal fields of direct experience. When the doctor asks me whether I have a pain in my chest, whether my mood is gloomy, or whether I can read the fine print, he can afford to be a behaviorist and test for these various experiences in a perfectly objective manner. But *I* have (or do not have) the pain, the depressed mood, or the visual sensations; and I can report them on the basis of direct experience and introspection. Thus the question arises inevitably: how are the raw feels related to behavioral (or neurophysiological) states? Or, if we prefer the formal mode of speech to the material mode, what are the *logical* relations of raw-feel-talk (phenomenal terms, if not phenomenal language) to the terms and statements in the language of behavior (or of neurophysiology)?

No matter how sophisticated we may be in logical analysis or epistemology, the old perplexities center precisely around this point and they will not down. Many philosophical positions at least since the eighteenth century were primarily motivated, I strongly suspect, by the wish to avoid the mind-body problem. Moreover, the central significance of the problem for any *Weltanschauung* burdens its clarification with powerful emotions, be they engendered by materialistic, idealistic or theological prepossessions. Schopenhauer rightly viewed the mind-body problem as the "*Weltknoten*" (world knot). It is truly a cluster of intricate puzzles—some scientific, some epistemological, some syntactical, some semantical, and some pragmatic. Closely related to these are the equally sensitive and controversial issues regarding teleology, purpose, intentionality, and free will.

I am convinced, along with many contemporary philosophical analysts and logicians of science, that *all* of these problems have been unnecessarily complicated by conceptual confusions, and to that extent are gratuitous puzzles and pseudoproblems. But I feel that we have not yet done *full* justice to any of them. Repression by reductionist philosophies (positivism, phenomenalism, logical behaviorism, operationism) is fortunately going out of fashion and is being replaced by much more detailed and painstaking analyses, of both the (Wittgensteinian) "ordinary language" and the (Carnapian) "reconstructionist" types.

Collingwood once said "people are apt to be ticklish in their absolute presuppositions; [they] blow up right in your face, because you have put your finger on one of their absolute presuppositions." One might add that philosophers are hypersensitive also in their repressed perplexities. A puzzle which does not resolve itself within a given favored philosophical frame is repressed very much in the manner in which unresolved intrapersonal conflicts are repressed. I surmise that psychologically the first kind may be subsumed under the second. Scholars cathect certain ideas so strongly and their outlook becomes so ego involved that they erect elaborate barricades of defenses, merely to protect their pet ideas from the blows (or the slower corrosive effects) of criticism. No one can be sure that he is not doing this sort of thing in a particular case, and I claim no exception for myself. The best one can do is to proceed with candor and to subject oneself to ruthless criticism as often as feasible and fruitful. Techniques of self-scrutiny are nothing new in philosophy, but implemented by modern depth-psychological tools they could surely be made much more effective. In this candid spirit, I shall begin by putting my cards quite openly on the table; in the next two sections I shall indicate what I consider the sort of requirements for an adequate solution of the mind-body problems. I have no doubt whatever that some philosophers or psychologists will differ from me even in these first stages. All I can do then is to try, first to make these requirements as plausible as I can, and second, to analyze and evaluate the assets and the liabilities of some of the various proposed solutions as fully as space permits.

II. The Scientific and the Philosophical Strands in the Mind-Body Tangle

A first indispensable step toward a clarification of the issues is to separate the scientific from the epistemological questions pertaining to the relations of the mental to the physical. Epistemology is here understood in the modern sense of a logical analysis of concepts and statements and of the closely related logical reconstruction of the validation of knowledge claims. Some of the pertinent statements themselves are, however, essentially of a scientific nature in that they fall under the jurisdiction of empirical evidence. It is right here where we find a fundamental parting of the ways. Biologists, psychologists (and with them, many philosophers) hold deep convictions, one way or another, on the autonomy or non-autonomy of the mental. The strongest contrast is to be found between those who hold interactionistic views regarding the mental and the physical, and those who reject interactionism and hence espouse either parallelism (e.g., in its currently favored form, isomorphism) or some emphatically monistic view. Interactionism as well as parallelism are of course forms of dualism. The main difference and dispute between these two points of view is at present not fully decided by the evidence. But I think this is an issue to which empirical evidence is ultimately and in principle relevant.

Vitalists or interactionists like Driesch, McDougall, J. B. Pratt, Ducasse, Kapp, *et al.* hold that biological concepts and laws are not reducible to the laws of physics, and hence—a fortiori—that psychological concepts and laws are likewise irreducible. Usually this doctrine is combined with a theory of the emergent novelty of life and mind. But there are others who restrict emergence to the mental, i.e. they hold a reducibility view in regard to the biological facts. "Reducibility" is here understood to mean the same as "explainability"; and has no necessary connection with the introducibility (empirical anchorage) of biological or psychological concepts on the basis of physicalistic *observation* terms. As Carnap (67) has pointed out clearly, the thesis (*his* thesis) of the unity of the *language* of science does not in any way prejudice the issue of the unitary explainability of biological and psychological facts (or laws) on the basis of physical *theory*. Philosophers should certainly not assume that such a basic scientific issue can be settled merely by logical analysis. It is *logically* conceivable that biological, psychological, and social phenomena (as well as their regularities) may not be explainable in terms of those physical or physicochemical laws (and theoretical assumptions) which are sufficient for the explanation and prediction of inorganic phenomena (and their regularities).

Logical parallels to such irreducibilities are clearly evident even *within* physics. The "mechanistic" (Newtonian) premises of explanation are now viewed as entirely insufficient for the explanation of electromagnetic radiation, of the dynamics of intra-molecular and intra-atomic processes, and of the interaction of electromagnetic radiation and the particles of matter. Nineteenth century physics added the fundamentally new concepts and laws of electromagnetics; and these in turn were drastically modified and supplemented by the relativity and quantum theories of our century. It is conceivable that homologous emendations may be required for the explanation of the phenomena of life and mind. Contemporary dualists, be they vitalists, emergentists, interactionists, or parallelists, maintain that such an enrichment of the conceptual system of science will be indispensable. Their arguments are based primarily on the traditionally captivating evidence of teleological processes, purposive behavior, psychosomatics, and the mnemonic and intentional features of perception, cognition, thought, desire, and volition. And some apparently very persuasive arguments point simply to the existence (occurrence) of immediate experience, i.e., the raw feels or hard data of the directly given. They maintain that these data, though *related* to behavior and neurophysiological processes, are not *reducible* to, or *definable* in terms of, purely physical concepts; and that their occurrence is not predictable or explainable on the basis of physical laws and physical descriptions only.

At this point the distinction between the scientific and the philosophical aspects of the mind-body problems becomes imperative. "Irreducibility" may mean non-derivability from a specified set of premises; but in other contexts it may mean non-translatability (non-synonymy, non-equivalence in the *logical* sense). To illustrate: many physical phenomena of sound or heat are derivable from the kinetic theory of molecular motion. In this sense certain parts of acoustics and of thermodynamics are reducible to mechanics, with a high degree of approximation at least within a certain limited range of the relevant variables.

But the phenomena of heat radiation (and similarly those of optics, electricity, magnetism, and chemistry) are not reducible to mechanics. Whitehead speculatively maintained that the laws pertaining to the motion of electrons in living organisms differ fundamentally from the laws of electrons in the context of inorganic lifeless bodies. In a similar vein the physicist Elsasser (95, 96, 97), following some suggestions contained in Bergson's views on organic life and memory, regards the physical laws as special or limiting cases of biological laws. This is a drastic reversal of the "Victorian" outlook according to which macro-regularities are (usually) explainable in terms of basic micro-laws.*

As a student of the history and the methodology of modern science, and impressed as I am with the recent advances of biophysics, biochemistry, and neurophysiology, I am inclined to believe strongly in the fruitfulness of the physicalistic research program (involving micro-explanations) for biology and psychology. But qua analytic philosopher my intellectual conscience demands that I do not prejudge the issues of reducibility (explainability) in an a priori manner. Beyond the sketchy empirically oriented arguments which I am going to submit presently, I shall address myself later on primarily to the logical and epistemological aspects of the mind-body problem.

Along empirical lines I believe there are differences, in principle capable of test, between parallelism and interactionism (and/or emergentism). Psycho-neurophysiological parallelism is here understood as postulating a one-one, or at least a one-many, simultaneity-correspondence between the mental and the physical. Parallelism as customarily conceived clearly rules out a many-one or a many-many correspondence. This latter type of correspondence, if I may speak for a moment about the *motivation* rather than the evidential substantiation (confirmation), is generally unpalatable to the scientific (especially the "Victorian") point of view, because it would obviously limit the predictability of mental events from neurophysiological states of the organism. But given a "dictionary," i.e., more properly speaking, a set of laws correlating in one-one or many-one fashion physical and mental states, physical determinism is not abrogated.

* I have dealt elsewhere (106, 108, 112, 113, 115, 116) with the logic and methodology of such explanations. See also the important articles by E. Nagel (230, 232); Hempel and Oppenheim (152); Kemeny and Oppenheim (177); Oppenheim and Putnam (in the present volume).

Two important qualifying remarks are in order here: (1) By "physical determinism" I mean, of course, that degree of precise and specific in-principle-predictability that even modern quantum physics would allow as regards the macro- and some of the micro-processes in organisms. (2) By "physical" I mean * the type of concepts and laws which suffice in principle for the explanation and prediction of inorganic processes. If emergentism is *not* required for the phenomena of organic life, "physical" would mean those concepts and laws sufficient for the explanation of inorganic as well as of biological phenomena. In accordance with the terminology of Meehl and Sellars (221), I shall henceforth designate *this* concept by "physical$_2$" in contradistinction to "physical$_1$", which is practically synonymous with "scientific", i.e., with being an essential part of the coherent and adequate descriptive and explanatory account of the spatio-temporal-causal world.

In view of what was said above about the *empirical* character of the interaction and the emergence problems, the concepts of mental states might well be physical$_1$ concepts, in that they could be introduced on the basis of the intersubjective observation language of common life (and this includes the observation language of science). Just as the concept of the magnetic field, while not denoting anything directly observable, can be introduced with the help of postulates and correspondence rules (cf. Carnap, 73), so it is conceivable that concepts of vital forces, entelechies, "diathetes" (cf. Kapp, 172, 173, 174), and mental events might be given their respective meanings by postulates and correspondence rules. Of course, the question remains whether such ("emergent") concepts are really needed and whether they will do the expected job in the explanation and prediction of the behavior of organisms, subhuman or human. My personal view, admittedly tentative and based on the progress and partial success of physicalistic micro-explanation (implemented by Gestalt and cybernetic considerations), is to the effect that physical$_2$ laws will prove sufficient. But, having abandoned the all too narrow old meaning criteria of the earlier logical positivists, I would not for a moment wish to suggest that the doctrines of emergence or of interactionism are scientifically meaningless.

Let us then return to the empirically testable difference between interactionism and emergentism on the one hand, and parallelism on

---

* In *this* context only; other meanings of "physical" will be listed and discussed in sections IV and V.

the other. An obvious and picturesque analogy or model for the inter-actionist view may be suggested here to provide a more vivid background. Billiard balls are in motion on a billiard table, and their motions are, we assume, predictable on the basis of mechanical laws (Newton's, supplemented by the laws of friction and of partially elastic collision). But imagine now a mischievous boy standing by, once and again pushing this or that ball or lifting some ball from the table. The mechanical laws, combined with a statement of initial conditions for the balls and the table, at a given moment, will then no longer suffice for the prediction of the course of the balls. The system in this case is of course an open one. If we could proceed to a larger closed system including the boy, with information about his shifting desires and so forth, deterministic predictability might be restored. (Since prediction of the boy's actions is precisely the issue at stake, I shall not beg any questions here and shall leave the boy's behavior unexamined for the moment.) This model is merely to illustrate a good clear meaning of "interaction". The boy watches the balls and his actions are in part influenced by their momentary distribution and motions on the board. The events on the board are in turn influenced by the boy's actions. From the point of view of ordinary usage, it is proper to employ the word "interaction" perhaps only when we deal with causal relations directed both ways between two continuants (things, organisms, persons, etc.).

But even a theory of emergence, such as the one suggested, though not definitely endorsed, by Meehl and Sellars (221), is confirmable in principle by showing that $physical_2$ determinism does not hold. Mental states or raw feels, be they regarded as states of an interacting substantial mind (or soul) or as values of emergent scientific variables, would in any case entail a breach in $physical_2$ determinism. The system of neurophysiological events inasmuch as it is describable in $physical_2$ terms would have to be regarded as open not only in the usual way, i.e., in regard to the extraneural, let alone extradermal, events, but it would also be open in regard to the set of mental events with which they are assumed to be causally (functionally) related in a way that would make them radically different from a set of mere epiphenomena. Now, while it is admittedly difficult at present to test for the implied breach in $physical_2$ determinism, the idea is not metaphysical in the objectionable sense that empirical evidence could not conceivably confirm or disconfirm it.

Much depends in this issue upon just how the "interactors" or the "emergents" are conceived. Traditional vitalism, culturally and historically perhaps a descendant of more primitive forms of animism, stresses the capricious nature of vis vitalis and of anima. (In our model the boy by the billiard table is assumed to exercise "free" choice.) But interaction need not be indeterministic in the wider system. The wind and the waves of the sea genuinely interact; even if the wind's influence is quantitatively greater, the waves do have some effect upon the air currents nearby. But though precise prediction of detail is practically extremely difficult because of the enormous complexities of the situation, this type of interaction is in principle deterministically * analyzable in terms of the functional relations of the two types of variables. Even the individual "free" or "capricious" momentary choices of our boy might be predictable in principle; but here the practical feasibility is far beyond the horizon of current psychology. At best only some statistical regularities might be formulated.

Determinism, inasmuch as it is allowed for by current physical theory, is also the presupposition of the sophisticated conception of emergence as presented in the essay by Meehl and Sellars. Here we have no interacting things or substances, but scientific variables intertwined in such a way that certain values in the range of one set of variables are functionally so related to the values of the variables in the other set, that the relations in the second set are nomologically different from what they would be if the values of the first set are zero. More concretely, once mental states have emerged, their very occurrence is supposed to alter the functional relations between the neurophysiological (physical$_2$) variables in a manner in principle susceptible to confirmation. While my (scientific) predilections are completely incompatible with this ingenious and fanciful assumption, I do consider it scientifically meaningful. I just place my bets regarding the future of psychophysiology in the "Victorian" direction. And I admit I may be woefully wrong.†

* Again it is only to the extent that hydrodynamics and aerodynamics for macro-processes are (approximately) deterministic.

† In his earlier formulations of the general theory of relativity Einstein endorsed the so-called Mach principle, according to which centrifugal and inertial forces are the effects of accelerations relative to the total masses of the fixed-stars-universe. But, impelled by what he considered cogent physical and mathematical arguments, he later ascribed those effects to a relatively independently existing "Führungsfeld" (guiding field). I mention this merely as a somewhat remote logically parallel case from an entirely different domain of science. Naturally, my expectation here is that something

Herbert Feigl

With the foregoing remarks I hope to have indicated clearly enough that I consider these basic issues as essentially scientific rather than philosophical. But a full clarification and analysis of the precise meanings and implications of, respectively, parallelism, isomorphism, interactionism, and the various forms, naive or sophisticated, of emergentism is a *philosophical* task. I shall now develop the philosophical explication of the factual-empirical meaning of these assorted doctrines a little further and bring out their salient epistemological points. Parallelism and isomorphism, now that we have recovered from the excesses of positivism and behaviorism, are generally considered as inductively confirmable hypotheses. Reserving more penetrating epistemological analyses, especially of the "immediate experience" and "other minds" problems, until later, I assume for the present purpose and in the vein of the recent positions of Ayer (15, 18) and Pap (243, 248) that the ψ-Φ (i.e., psycho-neurophysiological) relations or correspondences can be empirically investigated; and that mental states (raw feels) may by analogy be ascribed to other human beings (and higher animals), even if in the case of those "others" they are inaccessible to *direct* confirmation.

Parallelism, then, in its strongest form assumes a one-to-one correspondence of the ψ's to the Φ's. It is empirically extremely likely that these correspondences are *not* "atomistic" in the sense that there is a separate law of correspondence between each discernible ψ_i and its correlate Φ_i. It is quite plausible that, for example, different intensities of a phenomenally given tone (e.g., middle C), at least within a given range, are correlated with corresponding values in a limited range of some variable(s) of the neural processes in the temporal lobe of the brain.

Isomorphism as understood by the Gestalt psychologists (Wertheimer, Köhler, and Koffka) and the cyberneticists (Wiener, McCulloch, Pitts, etc.) assumes an even more complete one-one correspondence between the elements, relations, and configurations of the phenomenal fields with their counterparts in the neurophysiological fields which characterize portions of cerebral, and especially cortical, processes. As mentioned before, this sort of approach would also countenance a one-many correspondence of ψ's and Φ's. In that case, mental states would

of Mach's principle, even if in strongly modified form, will be salvaged. Powerful inertial forces as effects of a self-existent metrical field seem extremely implausible to me.

(with the help of the ψ-Φ "dictionary") still be uniquely inferable from neurophysiological descriptions. But many-one or many-many correspondences, even if expressed in terms of statistical laws, would seriously restrict such inferences from specific Φ's to specific ψ's. I know of no good empirical reasons for assuming anything but one-one correspondence; or one-many if very exact and detailed Φ-descriptions are used, and if account is to be taken of the limited introspective discernibility of the ψ's from one another.

Interactionism, as I understand (but reject) it, would entail a many-one or many-many correspondence. Arthur Pap (242, p. 277), however, argued that there is no empirically confirmable difference between parallelism and interactionism. This, he thought, is because lawful relations or functional dependencies are the modern scientific equivalent of the cause-effect relation. Temporal succession, he maintains, is not a criterion of causal connection. While I admit that the most general conception of the causal relation is simply that of a (synthetic) sufficient condition,* and is thus free of any connotation regarding the temporal succession of cause and effect; and though I also agree that in the case of ψ-Φ relation it would seem rather fantastic to assume anything like a time difference, I think that the interaction hypothesis differs in its empirical meaning from parallelism or isomorphism in that it entails a breach of physical$_2$ determinism for the Φ's. This, if true, could in principle be confirmed by autocerebroscopic evidence. For example, the experience of volitions as directly introspected would not be correlated in one-to-one (or one-many) fashion with simultaneous cortical states as observed (really inferred) by looking upon the screen of a cerebroscope,† and regularly succeeded by certain processes in the efferent nerves of the brain, ultimately affecting my muscles or glands, and thus ensuing in some act of behavior. This is the sort of most direct evidence one could ever hope for, as regards the confirmation of ψ-Φ action. If the idea of *interaction*, i.e., action both ways between the ψ's and the Φ's, is entertained, then there should be sensations (produced by the

---

* And in the laws of classical mechanics and electrodynamics of sufficient and necessary condition.

† This, for the time being, of course, must remain a piece of science fiction (conceived in analogy to the doctors' fluoroscope) with the help of which I would be able to ascertain the detailed configurations of my cortical nerve currents while introspectively noting other direct experiences, such as the auditory experiences of music, or my thoughts, emotions, or desires.

Herbert Feigl

chain of processes usually assumed in the causal theory of perception, but) not strictly correlated with the terminal cortical events.

Characteristically, philosophers have been emphasizing much more the action of "mind on matter"—as in voluntary behavior, or in the roles of pleasure, pain, and attention—than that of "matter on mind." This asymmetrical attitude usually comes from preoccupation with the freewill puzzle, or related to this, from some remnants of theological ideas in the doctrines of an ideal ("noumenal") self. But the freewill puzzle—even if some details of its moral aspects still await more clarification—has in its scientific aspects been satisfactorily resolved by making the indispensable distinctions between causality and compulsion (and indeterminism and free choice). The perennial confusions underlying the freewill perplexity, truly a scandal in philosophy, have been brilliantly exposed by empiricist philosophers.*

The main reasons why most psychophysiologists (and along with them many philosophers) reject the hypothesis of ψ-Φ-many-one or many-many correspondence are these:

1. Normal inductive extrapolation from the successes of psychophysiology to date makes it plausible that an adequate theory of animal and human behavior can be provided on a neurophysiological basis. Most physiologists therefore favor ψ-Φ parallelism or epiphenomenalism. Parallelism, I repeat, is here understood as the assertion of the one-one (or, at least, one-many) ψ-Φ correspondence, and not, as by Wundt and some philosophers, as the doctrine of double causation, i.e., involving parallel series of events with temporal-causal relations corresponding (contemporaneously) to one another on both sides. Causality in the mental series is by far too spotty to constitute a "chain" of events sufficiently regular to be deterministic by itself. Epiphenomenalism in a value-neutral scientific sense may be understood as the hypothesis of a one-one correlation of ψ's to (some, not all) Φ's, with determinism (or as much of it as allowed for by modern physics) holding for the Φ-series, and of course the "dangling" nomological relations connecting the Φ's with the ψ's. According to this conception voluntary action as well as psychosomatic processes, such as hysteria, neurotic symptoms,

---

* Hobbes, Locke, and especially Hume, Mill, Sidgwick, Russell, Schlick (301); and Dickinson S. Miller, cf. the superb article he published under the pseudonym "R. E. Hobart" (157). See also C. L. Stevenson (329); University of California Associates (339); A. K. Stout (330); and Francis Raab (271).

and psychogenic organic diseases (e.g., gastric ulcers) may ultimately quite plausibly be explained by the causal effects of cerebral states and processes upon various other parts of the organism; only the cerebral states themselves being correlated with conscious (or unconscious *) mental states.

2. While the cultural and historical roots of the epiphenomenalist doctrine may be the same as those of traditional materialism, we can disentangle what is methodologically sound and fruitful in the materialistic point of view from what is cognitively false, confused, or meaningless. The fundamental methodological reason for the rejection of interactionism, or the (equivalent) adoption of ψ-Φ-one-one (or one-many) correspondence as a working hypothesis or research program, however, is this: If the ψ's are not inferable on the basis of intersubjectively accessible (observed, or usually, inferred) Φ's, then their role is suspiciously like that of a *deus ex machina*. The German biologist-philosopher Driesch admitted this candidly, and thereby gave his case for vitalism away. He said that the intentions of the entelechy could be inferred only *post factum*, but could not be predicted from antecedent physical conditions. This is just like the case, in our crude analogy, of the capricious boy at the billiard table. After he has removed a ball we may say that he intended (perhaps!) to avoid a collision of the red ball with the white one. According to the vitalist interactionist doctrine, the volitions of the boy are in principle unpredictable on the basis of any and all antecedent conditions in his organism and the environment. Interactionism so conceived assumes causal relations between the elements in the series of mental states, the series of physical states, but also some crossing from the set of mental states to the physical ones and vice versa. In the model of the wind and the waves, we have precisely this sort of schema exemplified. But notice the crucial difference. A closed system (or a system with known initial and boundary conditions) is here conceivable in which all relevant variables are ascertainable *intersubjectively* and *antecedently* to the prediction of later states of the system; whereas in the case of ψ-Φ interaction, intersubjective and antecedent confirmation of the ψ-states is *ex hypothesi* excluded.

The flavor of the theological arguments from design and of primitive animistic explanations of nature and human behavior permeates inter-

* The terminological question whether to speak of the unconscious as "mental" will be discussed in sections IV and V.

actionistic explanations. They are at best ·ex *post facto* explanations. This sort of explanation, while not as satisfactory as explanations that also have *predictive* power, is nevertheless quite legitimate and is frequently the best we can provide in complex situations. Earthquakes are notoriously unpredictable (i.e., *practically* unpredictable), but once we observe a certain case of large scale destruction, its explanation in terms of an earthquake is perfectly legitimate even if the precise location of each piece of rubble in the shambles is far from predictable. Biologists are satisfied with evolutionary (retrospective) explanations of the emergence of a new species, even though they could never have predicted this emergence in any specific detail. Given the species in the Cambrian epoch, and given the principles of genetics and of Neo-Darwinian evolution, nobody could inductively infer the emergence of the chimpanzee or of the orchid; nevertheless, the very partial explanations of the theory of evolution are scientifically significant, acceptable, and helpful. Explanations of historical phenomena like wars, revolutions, and new forms of art furnish another illustration for the same type of *ex post facto* explanations. Finally, for an example in the psychological domain, if we find that a man has written dozens of letters of application for a certain type of job, we infer that he was impelled by a desire for such a job, even if we could not have predicted the occurrence of this desire on the basis of antecedent and intersubjectively confirmable conditions.

It is important, however, to notice again the decisive difference between explanations for which it is at least in principle conceivable that they could be predictive (as well as retrodictive), and those which *ex hypothesi* are *only* retrodictive. Scientists are predominantly interested in enlarging the scope of predictive explanations. The opposition against vitalism then stems from a reluctance to admit defeat as regards predictability. And the opposition against ψ-Φ interactionism stems furthermore from the reluctance to admit antecedents which are only subjectively accessible into the premises (regarding initial conditions) for predictive inferences. Expressing the same idea positively, we may say that it is part of the methodology or of the over-all working hypothesis of modern science that prediction, to the extent that it is possible at all (taking account of the basic quantum indeterminacies), is always in principle possible starting from *intersubjectively* confirmable statements about initial conditions. Scientists have, on the whole, adjusted themselves to the limitations involved in *statistical* prediction and *probabilistic* explanation. Very likely nothing better will ever be forthcoming in any area except in the few where classical determinism holds with a high degree of approximation. Of course, a logical distinction should be made between those cases in which the restriction to probabilistic predictability is a consequence of the complexity of the situation, and those in which the *theoretical* postulates of a given domain are themselves formulations of statistical laws. Although one can never be sure that this distinction is correctly drawn or that the dividing line will remain in the same place during the progress of science, the distinction *can* be drawn tentatively in the light of theories well confirmed at a given time.

But scientists are radically opposed to the admission of *purely subjective* factors or data (conceived as in principle inaccessible to intersubjective confirmation) as a basis for prediction or explanation. This would indeed be scientifically meaningless, if not even statistical relations of subjective states to antecedent or consequent intersubjective observables could be assumed. If they *are* assumed, then the subjective states are not *purely* subjective or "private" in the radical sense intended by some interactionists. The "emergent" raw feels in the interpretation by Meehl and Sellars are of course subjective only in the sense that they can be the objects of direct introspective verification, but they are also intersubjective (physical$_1$) in the sense that they can be assumed (posited, inferred, hypothetically constructed) by scientists who do not have the same sort of raw feels in the repertory of their own direct experience. This is so, for example, in the case of a congenitally blind scientist, equipped with modern electronic instruments who could establish the (behavioristic) psychology of vision for subjects endowed with eyesight. The blind scientist could thus confirm all sorts of statements about visual sensations and qualities—which in his knowledge would be represented by "hypothetical constructs." But if *ex hypothesi* all connections of the subjective raw feels with the intersubjectively accessible facts are radically severed, then such raw feels are, I should say by definition, excluded from the scope of science. The question whether discourse about such absolutely private raw feels makes sense in any sense of "sense" will be discussed later.

The upshot of this longish discussion on the difference between the scientific and the philosophical components of the mind-body problems is this: If interactionism or any genuine emergence hypotheses

Herbert Feigl

are sensibly formulated, they have empirical content and entail incisive limitations of the scope of physical$_2$ determinism. Interactionism is more difficult to formulate sensibly than is the (Meehl-Sellars) emergence hypothesis. In one form it requires substances (things, continuants or systems of such) for a normal use of the term "interaction," and in this form there seems little scientific evidence that would support it. I have read a great many arguments by metaphysicians attempting to support the idea of a totally (or partially) immaterial "self." But I have never been able to discern any good *cognitive* reasons beneath their emotionally and pictorially highly charged phrases. Whatever role the self (in Freudian terms perhaps the total superego, ego, and id-structure) may play in the determination of human conduct, it may yet very well be explained by a more or less stable structure of dispositions due to some constitutionally inherited, maturationally and environmentally modified, and continually modulated structure of the organism (especially the nervous and endocrine systems).

In another form interactionism (without a self) would require "spontaneously" arising mental states, i.e., an indeterminism not even limited by statistical regularities, and this again is neither supported by empirical evidence, nor advisable as a regulative idea for research. Nor is it required for the solution of the freewill problem, or for an account of the causal efficacy of mental events in the course of behavior. As regards the emergence hypothesis (à la Meehl and Sellars), this clearly makes sense, but whether it is really needed for the explanation of behavior is an open question. In the spirit of the normal procedures of scientific induction and theory construction I remain conservative in thinking that the rule of parsimony (Ockham's razor, or Newton's first *regula philosophandi*) warns us not to multiply entities (factors, variables) beyond necessity. If the necessity should become evident in the progress of research, I shall cheerfully accept this enrichment of the conceptual apparatus of science; or, ontologically speaking, this discovery of new entities in our world. In the meantime, I remain skeptical about emergence, i.e., optimistic about the prospects of physical$_2$ determinism. And, as I shall argue from the point of view of epistemology in sections IV and V, the sheer existence of raw feels is not a good reason for holding an emergence doctrine.

Another philosophical issue which needs careful separation from the scientific problems among the mind-body tangles is that of the "intentionality" of the mental. (For expository reasons the discussion of this issue will be reserved for section IV *F*.)

III. Requirements and Desiderata for an Adequate Solution of the Mind-Body Problem. A Concise Statement of the Major Issues

If the title of this section were not already a bit too long, I should have added, "as *I* view these requirements and desiderata, and as *I* conceive the adequacy of a solution." All I can say by way of extenuation of my personal biases in this matter is that I have concerned myself seriously and repeatedly with the problem for about thirty-six years; that I have studied most of the contributions from thinkers of many lands in modern and recent philosophy and science; and that this is my fourth published attempt to arrive at an all around satisfactory clarification. There have often been moments of despair when I tried ineffectively to do justice to the many (apparently) conflicting but impressive claims coming from ever so many quarters. It is, then, with a heavy sense of intellectual responsibility and not without some misgivings that I proceed to enumerate the following requirements, desiderata, and considerations which seem to me the conditions (or at least *some* of the conditions) that may serve as criteria of adequacy for a solution of the problem; a solution that is to be satisfactory from the point of view of contemporary science as well as in the light of modern philosophical analysis. I concede unblushingly that in some respects I share here the attitude of some of the (shall I say, epistemologically not too naive) metaphysicians who have wrestled with the problem and have tried to provide a solution that is *synoptic* in that it would render a just, consistent, and coherent account of all relevant aspects and facets of the issue.

Here, then, is my list of requirements and desiderata (or "conservanda" and "explicanda"):

1. The terms "mental" and "physical" are precariously ambiguous and vague. Hence a first prerequisite for the clarification and the adequate settlement of the main issues is an analytical study of the meanings of each of these two key terms, and a comparative critical appraisal of the merits and demerits of their various definitions and connotations. Due attention will also be given to the (partly) terminological question as to whether to include under "mental" beside the directly experienced

and introspectible also the unconscious states and processes of depth-psychological theories (Freudian or Neo-Freudian). All this will be undertaken in the next section of this essay.

2. In the light of what was said in the preceding section about the scientific (empirical) components of the mind-body problem, an analysis of the mind-body relation is to be sought which does justice to the arguments for the sort of mind-body unity which impresses itself increasingly upon the majority of psychologists, psychophysiologists, and psychiatrists of our time. Although the question of evolutionary as well as of logical "emergence" cannot be decided by a priori philosophical considerations, vitalistic and interactionist doctrines appear on empirical and methodological grounds as suspect and undesirable. Just what the alleged facts of parapsychology (telepathy, clairvoyance, precognition, psychokinesis, etc.) may imply for the mind-body problem is still quite unclear. Here too, it seems to me, any speculations along the lines of interactionism are—to put it mildly—premature, and any theological interpretations amount to jumping to completely unwarranted conclusions. My own attitude in regard to the experiments (statistical designs) on extrasensory perception, etc. is that of the "open mind." The book by Soal and Bateman (325) and its discussion by M. Scriven (305) present evidence and arguments which can not lazily or cavalierly be shrugged off. The chances of explaining the "facts" away as due to experimental or statistical error, let alone as outright hoax or fraud, seem now rather remote. But even granting these facts, I think that efforts should be made to explain them first by revisions and emendations in the *physical* theory of behavior before we indulge in speculations about immaterial souls or selves. These remarks clearly reveal my bias in favor of a naturalistic, if not monistic, position. That and how this position differs from "crass materialism," the bugbear of idealistic and spiritualistic metaphysicians, will be explained later on.

3. Any solution of the mind-body problem worth consideration should render an adequate account of the efficacy of mental states, events, and processes in the behavior of human (and also some subhuman) organisms. It is not tendermindedness or metaphysical confusions, I trust, which impel this repudiation of a materialistically oriented epiphenomenalism. Admittedly, the testimony of direct experience and of introspection is fallible. But to maintain that planning, deliberation, preference, choice, volition, pleasure, pain, displeasure, love, hatred, at-

tention, vigilance, enthusiasm, grief, indignation, expectations, remembrances, hopes, wishes, etc. are not among the causal factors which determine human behavior, is to fly in the face of the commonest of evidence, or else to deviate in a strange and unjustifiable way from the ordinary use of language. The task is neither to repudiate these obvious facts, nor to rule out this manner of describing them. The task is rather to analyze the logical status of this sort of description in its relation to behavioral and/or neurophysiological descriptions. In the pursuit of this objective it will of course be necessary to avoid both interactionism and epiphenomenalism; and it will moreover be desirable to formulate the solution in such a way that it does not presuppose emergentism (in the sense of physical$_2$ indeterminism), although the door to a scientifically formulated emergentism need not be closed.

In this same connection justice should be rendered to what is meaningful and scientifically defensible in the notion of free will or free choice. If our personality-as-it-is at the moment of choice expresses itself in the choice made; if our choices accord with our most deeply felt desires, i.e., if they are not imposed upon us by some sort of compulsion, coercion, or constraints such as by brute physical force, by other persons (or even only by components of our personality which we do not acknowledge as the "core" deemed centrally our "self"), then we are "free" in the sense that we are the doers of our deeds, the choosers of our choices, the makers of our decisions. In other words, it is in this case that our central personality structure is a link in the causal chain of our behavior, predominantly, even if not exclusively, effective in the determination of our conduct. This sort of freedom (in the superb formulation of R. E. Hobart-Dickinson Miller) "*involves determinism and [is] inconceivable without it.*" *

4. A most important *logical* requirement for the analysis of the mind-body problem is the recognition of the *synthetic* or *empirical* character of the statements regarding the correlation of psychological to neurophysiological states. It has been pointed out time and again † that the early reductionistic logical behaviorism failed to produce an adequate and plausible construal of mentalistic concepts by explicit definition on the basis of purely *behavioral* concepts. (In the less adequate material

* Cf. R. E. Hobart (157).
† Cf. F. Kaufmann (175), N. Jacobs (163), C. I. Lewis (196), E. Nagel (230), A. Pap (243), *et al.*

mode this might be put by bluntly saying that mind is not identifiable with behavior.) For a long time, however, I was tempted to identify, in the sense of *logical* identity, the mental with the neurophysiological, or rather with certain configurational aspects of the neural processes. It was in this sense that I (103) suggested a *double-language* theory of the mental and the physical. But if this theory is understood as holding a *logical translatability* (analytic transformability) of statements in the one language into statements in the other, this will certainly not do. Interlinguistic translations like *"Il ne fait pas beau temps"* into "The weather is not fine" are analytic if the respective meanings are fixed with the help of syntactical and semantical metalanguages common to both French and English. Similarly the geocentric description of the pure kinematics of the planetary system is analytically translatable into the corresponding heliocentric description, precisely because we avail ourselves here of transformation rules in a four-dimensional geometry (i.e., kinematics).

But the question which mental states correspond to which cerebral states is in *some* sense (to be analyzed epistemologically later on) an empirical question. If this were not so, the intriguing and very unfinished science of psychophysiology could be pursued and completed by purely a priori reasoning. Ancient and primitive people had a fair amount of informal and practical psychological knowledge, but the fact that mental states are closely associated with cerebral states was unknown to them. Aristotle held that the seat of our feelings and emotions is the heart (and this has survived in the traditions of poetic discourse). But to say that Aristotle was wrong means that we have now empirical evidence which proves that the emotions are linked to brain processes. It is therefore imperative to preserve the *synthetic* character of the assertion of this knowledge claim, whatever specifically may prove to be its most clarifying formulation.

If any of my readers should be hard-boiled behaviorists or "crass" materialists, it will be difficult to convince them that there is a problem at all. I can do no more than to ask them such persuasive or *ad hominem* questions as, Don't you want anesthesia if the surgeon is to operate on you? And if so, what you want prevented is the occurrence of the (very!) raw feels of pain, is it not? If you have genuine concern and compassion for your fellow human beings (as well as perhaps for your dogs, horses, etc.), what is it that you object to among the consequences of cruel treatments? Is it not the pains experienced by these "others"? It could not be merely their physical mutilation and consequent malfunctioning. Moral condemnation of wanton cruelty presupposes the meaningfulness of the ascription of direct experience to others. Subjective experience in *this* sense cannot be *logically* identical with states of the organism; i.e., phenomenal terms could not explicitly be defined on the basis of physical$_1$ or physical$_2$ terms.

It should be noted that we repudiate the *logical* translatability thesis not because of the possibility, definitely contemplated, of a one-many-ψ-Φ correspondence. One could always formulate such a correspondence with the help of a general equivalence between statements containing single ψ-predicates on the one side and disjunctions of statements containing several and various Φ-predicates on the other. It is rather the *logical necessity* of the equivalence which is here rejected. The equivalence must be construed as logically contingent.

5. Consonant with the spirit of the preceding discussions, but now to be stated explicitly, are three very closely related *epistemological* requirements. To list them first very briefly, they are:

(a) the need for a *criterion of scientific meaningfulness* based on *intersubjective* confirmability;

(b) the recognition that epistemology, in order to provide an adequate reconstruction of the confirmation of knowledge claims must employ the notion of immediate experience as a confirmation basis; (the "given" cannot be entirely a myth!) "Acquaintance" and "Knowledge by Acquaintance," however, require careful scrutiny;

(c) the indispensability of a *realistic*, as contrasted with operationalistic or phenomenalistic, interpretation of empirical knowledge in general, and of scientific theories in particular.

(ad a) It is generally agreed that scientific knowledge claims must not only be intersubjectively communicable (intelligible), but also intersubjectively testable. The following considerations will illustrate the point. If the stream of my conscious experience continued beyond the death and decay of my body, then this may be verifiable by me (in some, none too clear, sense of "me"; but I shall let this pass for the moment). If such survival were, however, not even extremely indirectly or incompletely confirmable by others; if it were in no way lawfully connected with, and thus not inferable from, any feature of life (mine or that of others) before death, then, while the statement in question may be said to have subjective meaning, it could not become part of science in the sense in which "science" is commonly understood.*

(ad b) Recent behavioristic and physicalistic arguments to the contrary notwithstanding, I am still convinced that purely phenomenal statements make sense and are the ultimate epistemic basis of the confirmation (or disconfirmation) of knowledge claims. By this I do not at all wish to suggest that phenomenal statements are infallible ("incorrigible"), nor that they necessarily have a higher degree of certainty than intersubjectively confirmable statements about the ordinary objects of our common life environment. I grant that, especially for the purposes of the philosophy of *science*, it is more useful to choose the physicalistic thing language for the confirmation basis of knowledge claims. But when I judge, e.g., that a certain pain is increasing, or that I hear a certain ringing sound (no matter whether this sound-as-experienced is causally due to a doorbell, a police car siren, to "buzzing in my ear," or to a hallucination), then that certain *it* which may later find its place in the causal structure of the world is first of all, and taken by itself, a *datum of direct experience*. Whether I get to it "post-analytically," or whether I simply *have* it, pre-analytically; that is to say, whether I arrive at it by a kind of analysis starting from "seeming," "appearing," "looks like" ("sounds like," etc.) sentences; or whether I can by simultaneous introspection (self-observation) or immediate retrospection, ascertain the occurrence of a certain datum, I have no doubt that talk about phenomenal data and phenomenal fields makes sense; and that in a rational reconstruction of the confirmation of ordinary observation statements, we can (if we wish) penetrate to this deepest level of evidence.†

I have not been convinced by the arguments of Popper (258) that the search for "hard data" is doomed to failure, that the "given" is like a bottomless swamp. Nor am I convinced that a purely private language ‡ is inconceivable. Of course, if by "language" one means an in-

---

* For a fuller discussion of the scientific meaning criterion cf. my articles (103, 105, 109, 110, 114, 116) and Carnap (64, 67, 73). For stimulating discussions of the meaning of "disembodied minds" see Aldrich (6) and Lewy (199).

† For persuasive arguments along these lines, cf. B. Russell (284, 287); H. H. Price (264); C. I. Lewis (195, 197, 198); Ayer (12, 13, 18); N. Goodman (135, 136, 137). For an incisive critique of the "incorrigibility" arguments, cf. K. R. Popper (258); R. Carnap (62, 64); H. Reichenbach (273, 276); M. Black (38); J. Epstein (98).

‡ Cf. the symposium by Ayer and Rhees (16, 278).

strument of interpersonal communication, then the idea of an absolutely private language is self-contradictory. But, granting that in the normal case the capacity for using a language is acquired by education, it is not *logically* inconceivable that a child growing up in complete solitude might devise his own symbolism not only for the objects and events in its environment *but also* for the *raw feels* of its direct experience. Such a child might well come to use terms for various aches, pains, itches, tickles, moods, emotions, etc. I do not for a moment deny that the use of such subjective terms, in the usual and normal case, is acquired through trial and error learning, and in this process largely inculcated in the child by other persons who *tell* him, e.g., "now you are tired," "now you are glad," "you must have an awful pain." Such *tellings* by others are guided by the facial expressions, vocal emissions, posture, etc., i.e., generally by the observable behavior of the child (and by test condition → test result sequences in its behavior, involving both environmental stimulus situations and a variety of responses).*

In sum, I believe that there is an indispensable place for "acquaintance" and "knowledge by acquaintance" in a complete and adequate epistemology. A more detailed account and analysis of the meanings of these terms will be given in the two subsequent sections of the present essay.

(ad c) The last epistemological requirement, to be briefly discussed here, is that of a realistic, rather than phenomenalistic or operationalistic, reconstruction of knowledge. With the current liberalization of the criterion of empirical meaningfulness † the narrower positivism of the Vienna Circle has been definitively repudiated, and is being replaced by a ("hypercritical") realism. No longer do we identify the meaning of a statement with its method of verification. Nor do we consider the meaning of a concept as equivalent with the set of operations which in test situations enable us to determine its (more or less likely) applicability. Instead we distinguish the evidential (or confirmatory) basis from the factual content or reference of a knowledge claim. Early and crude forms of behaviorism identified mental states with their (sic!) observable symptoms. Embarrassment might then mean *nothing but* blushing. But refinements and corrections were introduced in due

* Cf. Carnap (62, 63); Skinner (320, 321); Wittgenstein (357).
† Cf. Carnap (64, 73); Hempel (149, 151); Feigl (105, 106, 109, 110, 112, 114, 116); Ayer (18); A. Pap (243, 246, 248). Also Grünbaum (139); Feyerabend (119).

course. Mental states were considered "logical" constructions based on observable behavior; and statements about mental states were considered logically translatable into statements about actual or possible behavior, or into statements (or sets of statements) about test conditions and ensuing test results concerning behavior. Mental traits were considered as correlation clusters of their (*sic!*) symptoms and manifestations, and so forth.

But even such a refined or "logical" behaviorism is now rejected as an inadequate reconstruction. It was realized that those behavioral test condition → test result conditionals are to be *derived* from the laws and postulates regarding central states. Such derivations or explanations have been eminently successful in the physical and in some of the biological sciences. In the atomic theory, or in the theory of genes, for example, it is becoming increasingly possible to derive the macro-regularities, regarding, e.g., chemical compounding, or Mendelian heredity from lawlike postulates and existential hypotheses. The central states of molar behavior theory (or the "factors" in the factor analysis of personality traits) are, however, unspecified as regards their neurophysiological basis. This is comparable to the early stages of the atomic theory when nothing was known about the mass and the structure of individual atoms, or to the early stages of the theory of heredity when Mendel's "units" were not as yet identified with the genes, located and spatially ordered in specific ways, within the chromosomes of the germ cells.

There is little doubt in my mind that psychoanalytic theory (or at least some of its components) has genuine explanatory power, even if any precise identification of repression, ego, superego, ego, id, etc. with neural processes and structures is still a very long way off. I am not in the least disputing the value of theories whose basic concepts are not in any way micro-specified. What I am arguing is that even *before* such specifications become possible, the meaning of scientific terms can be explicated by postulates and correspondence rules (cf. Carnap, 73), and that this meaning may later be greatly enriched, i.e. much more fully specified, by the addition of *further* postulates and correspondence rules.*

* For a defense of psychological theory without explicit reference to micro-levels, cf. Lindzey (200). The logic of theoretical concepts in psychology has been discussed in some detail by McCorquodale and Meehl (213); Feigl (113); Cronbach and Meehl (79); Ginsberg (133, 134); Maze (212); Seward (317); Rozeboom (283); Scriven (306).

After the recovery from radical behaviorism and operationism, we need no longer hesitate to distinguish between *evidence* and *reference*, i.e., between manifestations or symptoms on the one hand, and central states on the other; no matter whether or not central states are micro-specified (neurophysiologically identified).

The meaning of scientific statements consists indeed in their truth conditions. But "truth conditions" does not mean the same as "confirming evidence". (The only possible exceptions to this are the directly and completely confirmable singular statements regarding immediately observable situations.) A *theory* is required to tell us which observations form confirming evidence for scientific statements about matters inaccessible to direct observation. It is in the light of such theories that we can then specify how much support a given bit of evidence lends to a specified hypothesis.

In section V, I shall return to the crucial questions of reduction and identification. There I shall discuss the logical nature of the relation between mentalistically, behaviorally, and neurophysiologically characterized central states.

No elaborate arguments should here be required for a realistic interpretation of the statements about the "physical" objects of everyday life or of theoretical physics.* In the explanatory context (or the "nomological net") concepts pertaining to the unobservables are related to, but not identifiable with, the observables which constitute the evidential data for the confirmation of statements about the unobservables. For example, spectral lines, cloud chamber tracks, scintillations on screens, Geiger counter indications, etc. are the evidential data which, in a complete logical reconstruction, must be conceived as *nomologically* connected with the aspects of atomic and subatomic particles which they confirm. Less exciting, but logically analogous, is the analysis of statements of common life about ordinary (partly or wholly observable) objects. Here the perceived perspectives of mountains, trees, clouds, etc., or the instrument indications of air pressure, wind currents, air moisture, etc., are to be interpreted as evidence related to what is evidenced, by the geometrical-optical laws underlying the projections in visual perception, or the physical laws which explain the operation of barometers, anemometers, hygrometers, etc.

* Cf. B. Russell (288); R. B. Braithwaite (48); Kneale (179); L. W. Beck (24); Feigl (110, 111, 114).

6. The "meat" of an adequate solution of the mind-body problem will consist in a specific analysis of the characteristics and the relations between the attributes of the mental (especially the phenomenal) and the *physical* (specifically the neurophysiological). It should be clear from the outset that, if a complete solution of these problems is ever going to be achieved, it will arise out of a combination of the results both of scientific research and of philosophical analysis. In all these questions the two components are so intimately bound up with one another, that neglecting either of them seriously jeopardizes the whole endeavor. The philosophical aspects will be given a further analysis in the next section where I shall try to sort out the various meanings and the attached connotations of the terms "mental" and "physical". The most controversial, tangled and perplexing questions concern, of course, the distinctions made rightly or wrongly in the Cartesian and in the subsequent dualistic tradition between the *mental* and the *physical* in terms of the various alleged criteria listed in the accompanying table.

Mental	Physical
subjective (private)	objective (public)
nonspatial	spatial
qualitative	quantitative
purposive	mechanical
mnemic	non-mnemic
holistic	atomistic
emergent	compositional
intentional	"blind"; nonintentional

Practically all the perennial perplexities of the mind-body problem center around the listed contrasts. The dualists make *prima facie* an excellent showing. The more enlightened monists have always realized that any argument in favor of an identification (in *some* sense!) of the mental and the physical is faced with serious difficulties. Small wonder then that many of the more sophisticated analytic philosophers of the present age either embrace some form of dualism (usually parallelism), or else declare the issue between monism and dualism a pseudoproblem engendered by logical or terminological confusions. I do not share this outlook. In the following section I shall prepare the ground for an "identity" theory, and I shall present my formulation as well as my arguments in section V.

IV. Sorting Out the Various Meanings of "Mental" and "Physical". A Comparative and Critical Analysis

Much of the trouble with the mind-body problem arises out of the ambiguities and vaguenesses of the terms "mental" and "physical". Some of their connotations have been briefly indicated in the juxtapositions listed toward the end of the preceding section. I shall now attempt to analyze these and other meanings more closely, and to point out the merits and demerits of the various actual and possible usages of "mental" and "physical". Philosophers of the modern age clearly differ as to what constitutes the central core or (if there be such clarity!?) the *criteria* of the mental and the physical. Some philosophers fasten primarily upon one pair of distinctions, others on a different pair as of primary significance.

A. *"Subjective" versus "Objective"*. The juxtaposition of "subjective" and "objective" has been the source of endless and badly confused controversies throughout the ages. There is nevertheless something significant and worth preserving in this distinction. To say that a twinge of pain experienced by person A is "subjective" or "private" to him may simply mean that another person B, observing A's behavior, may *infer* A's pain, but does not *have* it, i.e. he does not directly experience it. Dentists do not have the toothaches of their patients. In one sense this is clearly analytic (tautological).* It is analytic for reasons analogous to those which make it self-contradictory to say that I am growing my wife's hair. (Schizophrenics are known to make assertions of this sort.) "I am eating with my wife's teeth" is merely funny, but not self-contradictory. "Dentists always suffer toothaches when their drill comes near the pulpa of their patient's tooth" is synthetic, but empirically false. "I am listening through my wife's ears" if meant literally (not metaphorically) is a border line case, depending on specific detailed interpretation. "I am enjoying Mozart's music exactly as my wife does" is synthetic and may even be rendered as "I have the *same* musical experience as does my wife." (Remarks about the two meanings of "same" will follow presently.)

The case is a trifle more complex for perception. Two persons sitting next to each other in the concert hall are said to hear the same music,

* This is now even admitted by Ayer (18) who had earlier (15) held it was synthetic. His earlier position was, however, incisively criticized by Pap (243, 248) and Wating (341).

or at a given moment the same tones or chords, produced by the pianist on the stage. But the facts of the case are really not fundamentally different from the first example. A does not *have* B's musical experience (or vice versa), even if their auditory discrimination, musical appreciation, etc., does not differ in any discernible way. They may be said to hear the same sounds, to be both equally impressed or thrilled by them; but common sense as well as scientific reasoning clearly indicates that their *experiences* are numerically different. Fundamentally this case does not differ from, e.g., the case of two thermometers immersed next to each other in the same glass of water. It is perfectly proper to say that these instruments indicate the *same* physical condition. It is also perfectly proper to say that the two thermometers not only indicate *but also* "have" the "same" temperature. (This is logically quite like saying that two marbles have the same color.) But it would be most improper and paradoxical to say that the *events* taking place in the one thermometer are *identical* with those in the other. This is not the place for a discussion of Plato's problem of the "one and the many." Suffice it to point out that the phrases "the same as" and "identical with" are ambiguously used. "Sameness" or "identity" may mean complete similarity, as in the case of the two musical experiences, or in the case of the two thermometric indications. But "sameness" or "identity" in other contexts means the numerical oneness of the individual referent of , e.g., two different names, or of two different unique characterizations (Russellian descriptions). I conclude then that it makes perfectly good sense to speak of the subjectivity or privacy of immediate experience. *Numerically* different but *qualitatively* identical (indistinguishable) experiences may be had by two or more persons, the experiential events being "private" to each of the distinct persons.

Terminological trouble, however, arises immediately when we take a scientific attitude toward direct experience and try to confirm, describe, or explain it "objectively." Is it not an "objective" fact of the world that Eisenhower experienced severe pain when he had his heart attack? Is it not a public item of the world's history that Churchill during a certain speech experienced intense sentiments of indignation and contempt for Hitler? Of course! What is meant here is simply that statements about facts of this sort are in principle *intersubjectively confirmable* and could thus be incorporated in a complete historical account of the events of our universe. To be sure, there are cases in which confirmation is *practically* outright impossible. The last thoughts and feelings of a man immediately before his death, especially in a case of complete paralysis, or of death occurring through electrocution, may be inferable only with scant reliability. But this is not different from the case (cf. Carnap, 67, p. 419f) of the confirmation of the electric charge of a specific raindrop that fell into the Pacific Ocean in a place far removed from any observers. Our current liberal formulation of the empiricist meaning criterion countenances all statements of this sort as perfectly meaningful. They do not fundamentally differ from other less difficult-to-confirm statements about, e.g., the "true thoughts" of a liar or play actor. Modern devices, such as the lie detector, and various clinical-psychological techniques enable us to test for such "private" events with increasing (though generally only relatively low) reliability.

The foregoing considerations suggest that the terms "subjective" or "private" at least in one of their commonly proper and serviceable usages are not to be considered as logically incompatible with "objective" or "public" in the sense of "in-principle-intersubjectively confirmable". Private states in this philosophically quite innocuous sense are then simply *central* states. (Whether these are ultimately to be conceived mentalistically or neurophysiologically may be disregarded for the moment; but this will of course be discussed quite fully later.) "Subjective" or "private" in this sense may then designate the referents of direct introspective reports, and it will be understood that these same referents may well be more indirectly characterized by descriptions involving inference from behavioral symptoms or test results of experiments on behavior. In those cases of subhuman animal behavior in which we don't hesitate to speak of experienced pains, gratifications, rage, expectations, etc., there are of course no introspective reports. But other aspects of such behavior are in many respects so similar to the human case that the ascription of raw feels is usually justified on the basis of analogy. Here again, the "private" means the central state which causally effects (or at least affects) the overt and publicly observable behavior.

The terms "subjective" and "objective" are indeed mutually exclusive if they are used in a quite familiar but different way. In designating some impressions, opinions, beliefs, value judgments, etc. as "subjective," we sometimes contrast them with the "objective truth," or "objective reality." If, e.g., my friend maintains that the room is cold,

I am inclined to argue with him by pointing to the thermometer (which reads, say, 74°); and perhaps by explaining his "impression" by the fact that he is too scantily dressed, or that he is sick, or suffers from anxieties, etc. Similarly in the more drastic cases of dreams, illusion, delusion, etc. we criticize some (interpretive) *judgments* as based on *"merely subjective"* evidence. And it should go without saying that disagreements in aesthetic value judgments may often be explained on the basis of individual or cultural differences. "De gustibus non est disputandum" is our final resort if no objectively justifiable standard can be agreed upon.* But wherever beliefs *can* be criticized as, e.g., "biased," "too optimistic," "too pessimistic," etc., there are standards, such as those of normal inductive inference, which may indeed justify the rejection or correction of such "all too subjective" convictions. Here "subjective" and "objective" are indeed incompatible, although of course there may well again be an "objective" explanation of the genesis of "subjective beliefs."

There is, however, also a philosophical and speculatively extended sense of "subjective" or "private". In this very special and highly problematic sense it is assumed that there may be subjective states which are in principle inaccessible to intersubjective confirmation. Here we had better speak explicitly of *"absolute* subjectivity" or *"absolute* privacy." It is *this* sense which is entertained in some of the more radically interactionistic forms of dualism. And it is this sense which by definition is incompatible with "objectivity" understood as intersubjective confirmability. As I have indicated before, I no longer insist that a doctrine involving the notion of *absolute* privacy is entirely devoid of *cognitive* meaning. But I am inclined to regard it as *scientifically* meaningless. To recapitulate: if the scientific enterprise is defined as necessarily requiring *intersubjective* confirmability of knowledge claims, then this follows immediately and quite trivially.

Now, I think it is an essential aspect of the basic working program and of the working hypotheses of science that there is nothing in existence which would in principle escape intersubjective confirmation. Allowances have already been made for the (sometimes) insuperable *practical* difficulties of even the most incomplete and indirect confirmations. But the optimistic outlook that inspires the advance of

---

* On the meaning and the limits of the justification of norms, cf. my essay (109).

science and informs its heuristic principles,* does not tolerate the (objectively) unknowable or "un-get-at-able." No matter how distant, complicated, or indirect the connection of scientific concepts with some (intersubjective) evidential bases may be, they would not be concepts of empirical science (as contrasted with the concepts of pure logic or mathematics) unless they could in some such fashion be "fixed" by "triangulation in logical space." The "fix" we are able to obtain may be as indefinite as it is when theoretical concepts (like those of the positron, the neutrino, or the meson in physics; that of the unit of heredity; or of memory traces; of the superego, of general paresis, or of schizophrenia in biology, psychology, or psychiatry) were first tentatively introduced by only very sketchily formulated postulates. The concepts of absolutely subjective or completely private data, however, are so conceived that they can be applied only on the basis of the direct experiences contained in a given stream of consciousness. A completely "captive mind" † might experience senselike qualities, thoughts, emotions, volitions, etc., but they would (ex hypothesi) not in any way, i.e., not even through weak statistical correlations, be connected with the publicly observable behavior or the neurophysiological processes of an organism.

While it is difficult to spin out this yarn in a consistent (let alone plausible) fashion, I do not think it impossible, in the sense that it would necessarily involve some self-contradictions. There are philosophers who have been concerned with an analysis of the meaning of the "continuance of a pure (immaterial) stream of experience after bodily death"; or with the problem of the "inverted spectrum" (Could pure sensory-like qualia like red and green, blue and yellow, be systematically interchanged for different persons, despite a complete similarity in their discriminatory and linguistic behavior, as well as in their neurophysiological processes?). Speculations of this sort were declared taboo and absolutely meaningless by the early logical positivists. They were compared with assertions about absolute space and time, the (Lorentzian) ether, the "bond" between cause and effect, or the existence of a metaphysical substance, over and above anything that could be verifiably known by science about spatio-temporal relations, coordinate

* Some philosophers rather speak of them as "metaphysical presuppositions"; for my criticisms of this interpretation of science cf. (110, 114).

† The idea and the phrase are Hilary Putnam's.

transformation, functional relations between observable properties or measurable magnitudes, or relations of compresence of various observable properties. There is no doubt that this positivistic cleansing of the Augean stables of metaphysics had a most salutary effect. But positivists (temperamentally often negativists), in their zeal and eagerness to purge the scientific enterprise of meaningless as well as superfluous elements, have often overshot their goal. A redressing of the balance has become necessary, and we pursue nowadays responsible analyses of, e.g., causal necessity * which are perfectly compatible with the basic antimetaphysical insights of Hume. Similarly as regards the notion of absolute privacy, it is illuminating to conceive it at least as a logical possibility, and then to state as clearly as feasible the reasons which can be adduced for rejecting the idea for our world as we have come to conceive of it in our science to date.

The notion of absolutely private data of experience, if such data are to be *described*, would require a purely phenomenal or absolutely private language. Such a language, by definition and *ex hypothesi*, could not serve as an instrument of communication. Even a completely solitary humanlike individual could not engage in audible (or visible, etc.) symbolic activities. Not even soliloquies in this physically expressible form would then be possible. For *ordinary* soliloquies, amounting to more than the unexpressed thoughts of a private thinker, are expressible, and the very expressions would provide (no matter how unreliable) clues to the "inner" thought processes.†

Now, of course, if by a "language" one means what is *customarily* meant by it (viz., an instrument or vehicle of intersubjective communication), then an absolutely private language is ruled out by definition. Language as we know it and use it is indeed not absolutely private in the sense explained. But *that* it is intersubjective reflects a basic empirical feature of our world, or at least a basic feature of our-world-as-we-conceive-it in common life and in science. But I must postpone discussion of the fuller implications of this feature until I present my dénouement of the "world knot" in the final section. For the present I submit that by a "language" one is not compelled to mean an instrument of interpersonal communication. The idea of the soliloquy (*intra-*

* Cf. Burks (59); W. Sellars (312, 313, 314).
† For an extremely lucid and succinct discussion of this point cf. P. E. Meehl (219).

personal communication) may be restricted and modified in such a manner that it refers to unexpressed and inexpressible thoughts. This preserves a sufficient "family resemblance" with the ordinary notion of language. Such an absolutely private language would still enable the solitary thinker silently to label the qualities of his direct experience and to think silent thoughts which have the logical form of declarative (singular, universal, etc.) statements. I could, for example, with the help of remembrance, think that extreme anger always gradually subsides, that a given tone-as-heard is increasing in intensity, etc. Knowledge thus formulated in a private language may well be called "knowledge by acquaintance." It is true that ordinary discourse entertains a much wider conception of knowledge by acquaintance. There it covers knowledge based on, and not essentially transcending, the observations (amplified by very moderate and limited inferences). Thus we can quite properly say that we know the properties of sticks and stones, of apples and oranges, the manners and mannerisms of our close friends "by acquaintance."

But this ordinary concept of acquaintance is not very sharply defined. Having actually seen Winston Churchill for a few seconds (when on July 10, 1954, he emerged from 10 Downing Street in London and entered his black limousine, holding his cigar and waving to the assembled small crowd), am I entitled to say that I know him "by acquaintance"? Would I know Churchill "by acquaintance" if I had seen him (or rather his image) only in the cinema newsreels? I leave it to the linguistically more sensitive and subtle Oxford analytic philosophers to decide these questions, or else to tell me that "knowledge by acquaintance" is a hazy notion, involving "slippery slopes" in various directions. (Anyway, the latter alternative is what I consider the best analysis of the ordinary usage of the term.)

For a philosophical usage of the term, however, I suggest that "knowledge by acquaintance" be understood as knowledge involving no inferential components—or, if this be chimerical, then knowledge involving only that minimum of inference which is present when only memory is utilized for the recognition of similarities and differences. It is in this sense that I could assert on the basis of acquaintance, "Ah, there is that peculiar smell again; I don't know what causes it, I don't even know how to label it; it is so different from any fragrances of flowers, perfumes, cigar smoke, burnt toast, tangerines, etc. that I can't even place it in a multidimensional scheme of the rank orders of smells; but I know I have experienced this smell before and I am (subjectively) sure I would recognize it in the future if I were to experience it again."

As I have said earlier, I make no claim for the infallibility of knowledge by acquaintance. Our world, being what it is, is such that corrections of subjective-experience judgments (knowledge claims made on the basis of direct acquaintance) are definitely possible from the vantage point of intersubjective observation. Moreover, it should require no reminder that I quite emphatically want to distinguish *acquaintance* from *knowledge by acquaintance*. "Acquaintance as such" (in the philosophically restricted sense) is to mean simply the direct experience itself, as lived through, enjoyed, or suffered; *knowledge* by acquaintance, however, is propositional. Knowledge claims of any sort may be valid or invalid; the statements which formulate such knowledge claims are either true or false. In the case of practically all knowledge claims which have scientific status, the confirmation of their truth is incomplete and indirect. Knowledge by acquaintance, however, is direct and complete in the following sense: it seems utterly inappropriate to ask someone what his evidence is for asserting that he, e.g., feels at the moment elated, depressed, anxious, dizzy, hot, cold, and so on through the various modalities and qualities.

The philosophically much misused and over-exploited term "self-evident" might well be redefined and restricted to just such reports of immediate introspection or self-observation. With this, possibly unwise, terminological suggestion I do not wish to imply any doctrine of "incorrigibility" in regard to such protocols of immediate experience. I grant that even such protocol statements may be in error; and not only for the generally admitted reasons such as possible slips of the tongue or the pen; but also because the predicates or relational words used in such statements, if they are what they are intended to be, viz. universals, presuppose for their correct application even in the "absolutely private" language (as fancied above) at least the reliability of memory. This alone would ensure that the same term is applied to an experienced quality of the same kind as before. Otherwise a protocol statement would simply amount to what would in effect be a first introduction of the predicate in question by stipulative-ostensive definition; * i.e., it

* The notion of "ostensive definition" is of course highly problematic. In contradistinction to what "definition" (explicit, contextual, recursive, abstractive, condi-

would amount to the resolution to use the same term on future occasions sufficiently similar to the present one. But on the occasion of the first use of a new term, the sentence containing it would be true only in the extremely restricted (very much like *analytic*) sense that "Λ," the label which I arbitrarily apply to the completely and incomparably new fragrance that I am just experiencing, designates the quality experienced during each of the moments of its temporary occurrence of finite duration.

There are other uncertainties besides the ones mentioned in the use of (available) predicates for the qualia of immediate experience. Am I to describe the way I feel at a given moment as "happy", "joyous", "merry", "gay", "frolicsome", "blithe", "debonair", "light hearted", "buoyant", "bright", "animated", "gleeful", "hilarious", "jolly", or what?

It is time to draw some conclusions from this discussion. There is one meaning of "mental" in which it coincides with one meaning of "subjective". Let us call this meaning "phenomenal". In so calling it we may leave for later the question as to whether what is phenomenally given and phenomenally labeled is always also indirectly characterizable in an intersubjectively meaningful terminology. In any case we have isolated one contrasting (though not necessarily incompatible) pair of meanings for "mental" and "physical": the phenomenal (i.e., the subjectively confirmable) and the intersubjectively confirmable (i.e., the physical₁ in the terminology suggested above). The meaning of "mental" (synonymous with "phenomenal") looms large in introspective and phenomenological psychology. It is also prevalent in Gestalt-psychological descriptions of the configurations in phenomenal fields.

But in the "depth-psychological" statements of the psychoanalytic schools of thought, "mental" includes also subconscious, and some unconscious, states and processes. Since these are described largely with the help of metaphors and similes taken from the phenomenal (disregarding here those from the physical, e.g., mechanical, hydraulic, etc.) sphere, and inasmuch as detailed neurophysiological descriptions are

tional, coordinative, or even implicit) generally means, ostensive definitions cannot be rendered in speech, writing, or printing. "Definition" in its normal use always means specification of the meaning of some symbol by recourse to the meanings of other symbols. "Ostensive definitions" (if this phrase is to be retained at all) had therefore better be regarded as the establishment or acquisition of a linguistic habit, the inculcation of a bit of rule-governed linguistic behavior. In an absolutely private language it may amount to the stipulation of a rule which associates certain thoughts or images with specific other items or aspects of direct experience.

still lacking, it will be well to remember that the word "mental" as commonly employed by present-day psychologists covers both phenomenal and non-phenomenal states and events. The justification for the inclusion of the subconscious ("preconscious") and the unconscious in the realm of mind comes of course from some other attributes traditionally considered as criteria of mentality. We shall turn to those other attributes. The one which (for philosophical-historical reasons) will be taken up first is, however, not as essential in this connection as are some of the others further down the list.

B. *Non-Spatial versus Spatial.* The Cartesian distinction of res *cognitans* and res *extensa* still provides some philosophers of our age with what they consider one of their most powerful arguments in favor of a radical dualism. Mental states and events in contradistinction to physical bodies, so they claim, have neither a location, nor are they characterizable as having shapes or sizes. The apparent plausibility of this doctrine seems to me to derive mainly from (1) a confusion, and (2) inattention to phenomenal spatiality and its relations to physical spatiality. The confusion becomes evident in rhetorical questions asked by dualists, such as "where is the feeling of motherly love located?" "how many inches is it long?" "is it square or pentagonal?" I must confess I have little patience with these silly games. The feeling of motherly love is a universal, an abstract concept, and it makes as little sense to ask about its spatial location as it does in regard to the (physical) concept of temperature. We have here a category mistake of the crudest sort, a confusion between universals and individuals. It makes sense to ask about the location of individual things or events, but it is simply nonsense to ask about the location of a concept (properties or relations in abstracto).

The same sort of nonsense arises if, after hearing the sentence "the mental depression finally left him," someone asks, "Where did it go?" This sort of question can come only from taking the initial (metaphorical) statement as literally as we take "his wife finally left him." Concepts, whether they designate occurrent or dispositional properties, do not as such have spatial location; or rather it makes no sense to ascribe any such to them. But concepts which are constituents of singular (specific descriptive) statements * are applied to individuals. We

* I.e., sentences containing proper names or coordinates.

say "Anthony Eden felt depressed after the failure of the Egyptian campaign." In this case there is quite clearly a location for the feeling of depression. It is in the person concerned! The question of location becomes then more sensible, but logically also more delicate, if we ask it of individual mental states.

Using "mental" for the time being in the sense of "phenomenal", we had better—and without too much ado—introduce the indispensable distinction between phenomenal space(s) and physical space. I am perhaps not too acute in matters of phenomenological description but it does seem to me that my feelings and emotions pervade large parts of my body-as-I-experience it. William James has given us some striking illustrations of this. In the phenomenal field of the subject, specific feelings may be located at least vaguely or diffusely in some not very sharply delimited part of the organism. My feelings or sentiments of elation, depression, delight, disgust, enthusiasm, indignation, admiration, contempt, etc. seem to me to be spread roughly through the upper half or two-thirds of my body.

Sounds and smells, at least in the usual situations of "veridical" perceptions seem to be partly outside, partly inside the phenomenal head. Colors are usually perceived as surface qualities of extradermal objects, or in the case of looking at the skin of one's own arms or legs, as surface qualities of those limbs. Colors seen when pressing one's eyelids (closed eyes) are vaguely located either immediately in front of one's eyes, or even inside them. Similarly musical sound images (especially in the eidetic's case) appear either inside one's head or seem to come from the outside as in a concert hall. The taste of an apple is clearly experienced within the mouth. The stars as seen on a cloudless night are tiny bright spots on a fairly distant dark background. These bright spots clearly have spatial relations to one another. A given small portion of the sky-as-perceived is an approximately plane surface with the twinkling stars distributed in certain constellations. If for the moment we may use the names of the stars as proper names for the bright spots in the visual field, we may well say that, e.g., Sirius is to the left and far below the three stars of Orion's belt. There is no question then that we are "acquainted" with the elements and relations in visual space.

A detailed discussion of the relations of visual, tactual, kinesthetic, and auditory "spaces" among each other is a task of phenomenal psychology. For our purposes it is sufficient to notice that "spatiality" means qualitatively quite different things for the various sense modalities. But *physical* space, in the sense in which the science of physics (including, of course, astronomy) understands it, is something radically different. The astronomers' measurements and inferential interpretations have provided us with an account of the three-dimensional array of the stars in "objective" space. This three-dimensional order is most properly considered as a conceptual system which can be only inadequately visualized or imaged phenomenally. I don't for a moment deny that in our rooms or in a landscape we *perceive* directly at least some of this three-dimensional order. (In the case of the stars, we don't.) But what is present in perception at any given moment is always a particular perspective and not the geometrical order which we must *assume* (together with certain laws of geometrical optics) in order to *explain* the peculiarities of any (or all) particular perspectives.

I shall not labor the obviously analogous case of time. Phenomenal time and physical time differ from, and are related to, each other very much like phenomenal space and physical space. Experienced durations may seem very long in the case of tiresome waiting, while time packed full with exciting events seems to "pass quickly." But the physically measured durations may be exactly the same. The *psychological* relativity of (phenomenal) time must of course not be confused with the (Einsteinian) *physical* relativity of simultaneity and duration which, in the nature of the case, is not directly observable at all.*

We conclude then that *mental* data have their own (phenomenal) kinds of spatiality; and that *physical* space is a theoretical construction introduced to explain the features and regularities of phenomenally spatial relations. The exact and detailed derivation, even only of the perspectival aspects of visual spatiality is a quite complex matter, involving geometrical, physical, psychophysical, and psychophysiological laws. Our arguments have so far disproved only the Cartesian contention that the mental is non-spatial. To put it very strongly, mental events as directly experienced and phenomenally described *are* spatial. Physical bodies geometrically characterized in their measurable positions, orientations, shapes, and sizes are not spatial (in the *visual*, or generally,

---

* Except, of course, for such cases as the traveling and returning twin brother, which, though strictly implied by the well-confirmed principles of Einstein's theory, has not been susceptible to direct check thus far (because of obvious practical difficulties).

phenomenal) sense at all. "Space" in the physical sense is an abstract theoretical ordering system. The reader who accepts my arguments may nevertheless maintain that the emphasized distinction between phenomenal and physical spatiality (and temporality) reaffirms all the more convincingly the dualism of the mental and the physical. My rebuttal of this contention will be given in the concluding sections. Suffice it here to suggest that if by "physical" we do not understand a kind, type, part, or aspect of reality, but rather a method, language, or conceptual system, then there is no room for a dualistic opposition of mental and physical events or processes, let alone substances.

C. *Quality versus Quantity.* Another time-honored distinction between the mental and the physical is made in terms of the qualitative and the quantitative. This distinction also is fraught with the danger of various confusions. A prima facie plausible argument maintains that, e.g., the qualities of colors-as-experienced, sounds-as-heard, odors-as-sensed, heat-intensities-as-felt, etc. are undeniably and fundamentally different from the quantitatively measurable wave lengths of light radiation, the frequencies and energies of sound waves, the chemical compositions of odorous substances, the mean kinetic energies of the molecules, etc. Of course, they are. But the argument misses the essential point. What the physicist measures are quantitative aspects of stimuli or stimulus patterns. These stimuli produce, under certain ("normal") circumstances, certain qualitatively characterizable sensations within the phenomenal fields. The familiar freshman's question, "Is there a sound when on a lonely island, with neither men nor beasts present, a tree falls to the ground?" is quickly clarified by the distinction between the sound waves (vibrations in the air) and sounds-as-heard. The dualistic argument would, however, be strictly to the point if it concerned the distinction between the sense-qualities-as-experienced and the "correlated" cortical processes in the brain of the experiencing subject. These cortical processes could be quantitatively described in a completed neurophysiology. Various more or less localized patterns of nerve currents ("firings" of neurons, etc.) would be the object of a "physical" description. Just which phenomenal qualities correspond to which cortical-process patterns has to be determined by empirical investigation. In our previous discussion of "conservanda" and "explicanda" we have not only admitted, but insisted upon, the *synthetic* character of the statements which formulate these correlations. Reserving fuller arguments for monism again for the final sections, a few preliminary critical observations are in order at this point:

(a) Purely phenomenal descriptions are generally not restricted to a merely qualitative form. Semiquantitative or rank-ordering ("topological") descriptions are possible at least among the qualities within each modality of experience. "My pain is increasing"; "this (sensed) blue is darker than that"; "my embarrassment was worse than any I had ever felt before"—these examples illustrate semiquantitative singular statements. Universal statements of this form can also be made, e.g., "Purple is more bluish than scarlet." "D is higher in pitch than C." Universal statements of this sort can be organized in topological arrays of one, two, three (or more) dimensions, as in the tone scale, the color pyramid, the prism of odors, etc. Moreover, there are cases of remarkable intersubjective agreement even in purely introspective judgments of the *metrical* relations of given qualities or intensities among each other. S. S. Stevens,* for example, found by careful experimentation that subjects agreed on what was the mid-point in a series of sounds of varying intensities. Shapes, sizes, distances, durations—all-as-directly-experienced are often susceptible to metrical estimates far surpassing in accuracy anything the uninformed might ever expect.

As regards the differences among such experiential modalities as colors, sounds, and smells, or between larger classes such as the sense qualities and the emotions, it must of course be recognized that they differ qualitatively from one another; and no merely quantitative distinction will serve as a criterion to characterize their different generic features. Dualists have tried to utilize this as an argument by asking, Why should there be more than one basic quality (or modality, for the matter of that), if all of the manifold phenomenal data are to be nothing but the subjective aspects of basically homogeneous brain processes? But the answer may well be that there are sufficient topographical, configurational, and quantitative differences even among those "homogeneous" neural processes.

(b) The magnitudes determined by physical measurement, and syntactically represented in scientific language by *functors*,† differ among each other in a way that can hardly be called anything but "qualita-

---

* Cf. his article in the *Handbook of Experimental Psychology* (S. S. Stevens, ed.). New York: Wiley, 1951.

† Cf. Carnap (65, 68); Reichenbach (274).

tive". What else can we say about the differences between, e.g., mass, temperature, pressure, electric current intensity, electromotoric force, gravitational field intensity, etc.? What is it that is, respectively, indicated by thermometers, manometers, ammeters, voltmeters, etc.? I think it is entirely justifiable to speak of these scientific variables as *qualitatively* different. To be sure, they are not directly experienced qualities. But is there any good reason for restricting the term "quality" to the phenomenally given?

I conclude that the attempt to define "mental" and "physical" in terms of the distinction qualitative-quantitative begs the question. It makes perfectly good sense to speak of mental quantities and of physical qualities.

D. "Purposive" versus "Mechanical". Along with *direct experience*, it is perhaps *intelligence* which makes up the most important characteristic of the commonsense concept of mentality. And intelligence is usually and most basically characterized as the capacity of utilizing means toward the attainment of ends. One trouble with this characteristic is that common language is apt to describe as "intelligent" even the instinctive behavior of many animals. In the case of, e.g., social insects (termites, ants, bees, etc.) the behavior is stunningly purposive, highly organized, and intricate; and yet we hesitate to ascribe sentience or subjective experience (raw feels) even only remotely resembling our own to these entirely different organisms. Moreover, the current *scientific* use of the word "intelligence" tends to be restricted to those evolutionary levels and species in which learning combined with ingenious (inventive) and symbolic behavior plays a dominant role. Pigeons, rats, cats, dogs—those favorite laboratory animals of the behavioristic psychologists—show (in each species) marked individual differences in the speed and the scope of their learning. Anthropoid apes, like the chimpanzees, are famous (ever since W. Köhler's original experiments) for their inventiveness—in addition to their commonly known capacities for imitation. Genuinely *linguistic* behavior, involving syntactical, semantical, and pragmatic features, seems to be restricted to *homo sapiens*; the so-called language of the bees (which is apparently instinctive and lacking in syntactical and semantical flexibility) does not seem to be an exception.

If intelligence or just purposiveness were chosen as the sole criterion of mentality, then it would be hard to draw a sharp line anywhere within the realm of organic life. Even in the kingdom of plants we find processes whose teleological characteristics are not fundamentally different from the features of purposive behavior in the lower animals. Of course, if one deliberately makes the (often suggested and no doubt helpful) distinction between two types of teleology, one of them involving *conscious* aims, and the other excluding them, and designates only the former as "purposive," then the empirical evidence suggests (but does not force upon us) the decision to call "intelligent" only the behavior of the higher animals, or perhaps to restrict the label "intelligence" to human beings (i.e., if and when they behave in a genuinely *sapient* manner).

It becomes clear then that the scope of the two criteria (*sentient* and *sapient*) is not necessarily the same. The two concepts are not coextensive. The situation has been further complicated in our age by the construction of "intelligent" machines. Logical reasoning, mathematical proofs and computations, forecasting, game playing, etc. are all being performed by various and usually highly complex electronic devices. Here the temptation to ascribe "raw feels" becomes even weaker than in the case of the lower animals.* Inductively it is plausible that sentience requires complex organic processes.

Descartes was perhaps not completely wrong in restricting mentality to human beings. If "mind" is understood as the capacity for reflective thought, then indeed we may have reason to deny minds (in *this* sense!) to animals (and perhaps even to electronic computers!). The issue is difficult to decide, because the connotations of "reflective thought" are numerous and indefinite. But if it connotes a *conjunction* of sentience, learning capacity, spontaneity (free choice), purposiveness (in the sense of goal directedness), original inventiveness, intentionality (in the sense of symbolic reference), and the ability to *formulate rules* of behavior (practical, moral, linguistic, etc.), then *mind* (in this sense) is clearly the prerogative of man.

All the foregoing considerations need not disturb us. They merely lead to the scarcely surprising conclusion that the term "mental" in ordinary and even scientific usage represents a whole family of concepts; and that special distinctions like "mental$_1$", "mental$_2$", "mental$_3$",

---

* Cf. however, the remarkable and stimulating discussion of the robot problem by Scriven (304). We shall return to this issue in connection with the scrutiny of the analogy argument for "other minds" in section V.

etc. are needed in order to prevent confusions. (We shall return to a brief discussion of "intentionality" in subsection *F*.)

As far as the original distinction of *purposive* versus *mechanical* is concerned, it scarcely helps in the definition of the mental versus physical distinction. If "purposive", despite our warnings, is taken as synonymous with "teleological", then we have a distinction, which, though it becomes rather irrelevant to the mental-physical issue, is not useless in the natural sciences and in technology. But then it can no longer be considered as either sharply exclusive, nor as particularly enlightening. The flow of a river toward the sea is a mechanical and non-teleological phenomenon, but the functioning of servomechanisms is mechanical as well as teleological, and the functioning of the heart is teleological and presumably "mechanical" in the same (wider) sense in which complex servomechanisms operating by negative feedback are regulative *physical* devices. In short, the phrase "teleological mechanisms", in our age of cybernetics is no longer a contradiction in terms.

E. "Mnemic", "Holistic", "Emergent" versus "Non-Mnemic", "Atomistic", "Compositional". This bundle of contrasts has often been associated with the distinction of the mental and the physical. Fortunately, except for one facet of the emergence issue, discussion can be quite brief. The *mnemic* as a criterion of mind was stressed especially by Bertrand Russell. But long before him, the physiologist Ewald Hering (and his disciple Semon) considered the mnemic as a general property of all organic matter. Even in inorganic matter there are more or less permanent modifications of dispositional properties which can be effected by various influences. Certain features of elasticity and of magnetic hysteresis are "mnemic" in this sense. And of course the storage of information in present-day computing machines clearly shows that mnemic features, just as the "purposive-intelligent" features, need not coincide with mentality in the sense of sentience or awareness.

The holistic aspects of the phenomenal fields were brought to the fore by the Gestalt psychologists. But almost from the beginning, this school of thought (especially ever since W. Köhler's book on *Physical Gestalten*, 1920) emphasized the idea of the isomorphism of phenomenal with neurophysiological configurations. Thus again, without the addition of the criterion of immediate experience we do not obtain a distinction between the mental and the physical configurations or "organic wholes" or "dynamic Gestalten."

Herbert Feigl

Inseparably connected with holism and the Gestalt philosophy is the doctrine of emergence. The old slogan "the whole is greater than the sum of its parts" has of course no very clear meaning. Much of its obscurity is due to the lack of a definition of the phrase "the sum of the parts". Recent analyses * of the still controversial significance of "organic wholeness" and of "emergent novelty" have contributed a great deal to the clarification of the issues. There is no imperative need for us to enter into details here. It will be sufficient for our concerns to realize that in modern natural science no sharp distinction can be made between *resultants* (as in the composition, i.e. vectorial addition of forces or velocities) and *emergents*. In the explanation of the properties and the behavior of complexes and wholes we always need laws of composition—be they as simple as the straightforward arithmetical addition of volumes, masses, electric charges, etc., or slightly more complicated as is vector addition, (or just a trifle more involved as is the relativistic "addition" formula for velocities), or extremely complex as are the so far not fully formulated composition laws which would be required for the prediction of the behavior of organisms on the basis of a complete knowledge of their microstructure and the dynamic laws interrelating their component micro-constituents.

Modern quantum physics, on a very basic level, employs laws which have "organismic" character, as for instance the exclusion principle of W. Pauli † which holds even for single atoms. It is conceivable that much of what is called "emergent novelty" on the chemical and biological levels of complexity may ultimately be explained in terms of the organismic or holistic features of the laws of atomic and molecular dynamics; and that, given those basic micro-laws, the only composition laws (which scientists often take for granted like "silent partners") are simply the postulates and theorems of geometry and kinematics. This is indeed my own, admittedly risky and speculative, guess; that is to say, I believe that once quantum dynamics is able to explain the facts and regularities of organic chemistry (i.e. of non-living, but complex compounds) it will in principle also be capable of explaining the facts and regularities of organic life. But no matter whether these conjectures

* Schlick (299); Nagel (232, 235); Henle (153); Bergmann (28, 34); Hempel and Oppenheim (152); Rescher and Oppenheim (277); Pap (244).
† Cf. the clarifying discussion by Margenau (208); and the stimulating, but perhaps somewhat speculative, ideas of Kaila (169).

prove correct or incorrect, emergent novelty from a logical or methodological point of view simply means the impossibility of the derivation of the laws of complexes ("wholes") from the laws that are sufficient to predict and explain the behavior of their constituents in relative isolation. Thus, the laws that are sufficient to account for the motion of free electrons (as in cathode rays, and traversing electric or magnetic fields) are clearly insufficient to account for the behavior of electrons when they are constituents of atoms.

It stands to reason, that in order to "glean" (i.e., to ascertain) the laws of nature, scientists can't afford to stop their investigations on a very low level of complexity. In some cases we are lucky in that from such a very low level of complexity upwards to higher complexities of any degree, no new *physical* laws (but only geometrical composition laws) are required. This holds, for example, for the law of the lever which remains applicable even for the most complex system of pulleys. It also holds for the law of gravitation and the laws of motion (both in their Newtonian form). The "many bodies problem" is unsolved only in the mathematical sense that no single set of simultaneous equations has as yet been found for the prediction of the motions in complex star systems. But successive approximations can be computed to any desired degree of accuracy. In other cases (as with the behavior of electrons) we could never glean all the relevant laws below a certain level of complexity. And I have admitted (in section II) that it is always *logically* conceivable that our scientific theories may have to be amended and enriched by the introduction of new basic concepts (variables), and this is of course tantamount to the introduction of new (lawlike) postulates and/or existential hypotheses.

We have seen that the mnemic, teleological, holistic, and emergent features are not adequate as criteria of mentality, because these features characterize even inorganic structures and processes. Emergence as conceived by most dualists, however, refers to the evolutionary novelty and the (physical$_2$) underivability of *sentience* or *raw feels*. The whole issue therefore turns again upon the criterion of *subjective experience*. The issue can be brought out by questions such as the following: Suppose we could predict the detailed chemical structure of an entirely new perfume which will be manufactured in Paris in the year 1995. Suppose, furthermore, that we could equally exactly predict the neurophysiological effects of this perfume on the mucous membranes of a human nose, as well as the resulting cortical processes in the person thus smelling the perfume. Could we then also predict the quality of the experienced fragrance? The usual answer to this question is in the negative, because it is assumed that the fragrance in question will be an "emergent novelty." But behaviorists, and physicalists generally, need not take such a pessimistic view. For given the presuppositions of our questions it should also be possible to predict the answers to questionnaire items like "Is the fragrance more similar to Chanel 5 or to Nuit d'Amour?" That is to say, we should be able to predict the location of the quality in the topological space of odors, provided we have a sufficiency of psychophysiological correlation laws to make this particular case one of interpolation or (limited) extrapolation.

The issue can however be made more poignant if we are concerned with the prediction of qualities within an entirely new modality. In the case of the congenitally blind who by a cataract operation suddenly attain eyesight, the experience of colors and (visual) shapes is a complete novelty. Suppose that all of mankind had been completely blind up to a certain point in history, and then acquired vision. Presupposing physical$_2$ determinism we should (according to my basic conjecture) in principle be able to predict the relevant neural and behavioral processes, and thus to foretell all the discriminatory and linguistic behavior which depends upon the new cortical processes (which correspond to the emergent, novel qualities of experience). What is it then that we would not or could not know at the time of the original prediction? I think the answer is obvious. We would not and could not know (then) the color experiences *by acquaintance;* i.e., (1) we would not *have* them; (2) we could not *imagine* them; (3) we could not *recognize* (or *label*) them as "red", "green", etc., even if by some miracle we suddenly had them, except by completely new stipulations of designation rules.*

I conclude that the central puzzle of the mind-body problem is the logical nature of the correlation laws connecting raw feel qualities with neurophysiological processes. But before we tackle this difficult question, a glance at one more issue is required.

F. *"Intentional"* versus *"Non-intentional"*. The mental life of (at least) the adult *homo sapiens* is characterized by the capacity for *awareness*—in addition to the occurrence of mere raw feels. (We credit some

---

* Cf. Pap's discussion of absolute emergence (244).

animals and certainly young children with the latter in any case.) To have an experience, and to be aware of having it, is a distinction which I think cannot be avoided, even if in a given case it may be very difficult to decide whether awareness actually supervened. This is one of the notoriously difficult questions of phenomenological description. But assuming the distinction, it is fairly plausible that awareness is impossible without some sort of symbolism, even if it be the "silent" symbolism of imagery or (if there be such) of imageless thought. It is here where the idea of "*intention*" (not in the sense of purpose, end-in-view, or resolution, but) in the sense of *reference* becomes essential.

I shall try to show that the scientifically relevant issues regarding interactionism versus parallelism (or epiphenomenalism) should be carefully separated from the philosophical issues which stem from the "intentional" features of mind, stressed by Brentano and the phenomenological schools of thought. According to this point of view the most fundamental difference between the mental and the physical consists in the fact that the mental life consists of *acts directed upon objects*, no matter whether these objects exist in the world, or are pure concepts, or figments of the imaginations. It is true that dualism in the Cartesian tradition has emphasized the intentional as well as the raw feel features of mind. The mind-body problems in the larger sense therefore have customarily included such questions as, Can we give a physical (1 or 2, in this case) account of how thoughts, beliefs, desires, sentiments, etc. can be *about* something? Can we give a naturalistic translation of the language of reasoning as it occurs in arguments, i.e., discourse in which we give *reasons* intended to support knowledge claims, or value judgments? I think it has become increasingly clear * that the answer must be in the negative; but not because human behavior involving "higher thought processes" is not in principle capable of physical (at least physical$_1$) explanation and prediction; but rather because the problem is one of the logical reducibility or irreducibility of discourse involving *aboutness* (i.e., intentional terms), to the language of behavioral or neurophysiological description. Now it seems fairly obvious that such discourse, just like discourse involving *ought-ness* (i.e., normative discourse) is *not* logically translatable into purely factual statements. The relation of designation (formalized in pure

* Cf. especially Wilfrid Sellars (310, 311).

semantics) is not an empirical relation, but a construct of semantical discourse.

Personally, I therefore consider the problem of intentionality not as part of the psycho-physical but rather as a part of the psycho-logical problem, i.e., as part of the relation of psychological to the logical forms of discourse. This becomes even more evident because, assuming the ultimate possibility of a full neurophysiological account of behavior (including linguistic behavior), we should then have the problem of relating the *physiological* to the logical forms of discourse. If many writers permit themselves nowadays to speak of "thinking machines" (electronic computers, chess playing machines, etc.), then it is equally justified to pursue the problem of the relation between the *mechanical* (or the electrical) and the logical. In the case of the machines, it is ourselves who have built them in such a way that in their functioning they conform to certain rules of logical, mathematical, or semantical operations. In the case of human beings we have nervous systems which through education and training acquire the dispositions toward certain types of symbolic behavior which in actual operation then is more or less in conformity with certain rules.

But the abstract statement of a rule is not to be confused with the formulation of the (statistical) empirical regularity of the symbolic behavior. An illicit inference or a computation mistake is a *violation* of a *rule*, it is not an instance which would disconfirm a law of behavior. The recent phase of the clarification of these issues was in essence initiated by Husserl and Frege in their critique of *psychologism*, i.e., of the confusion of logical with psychological discourse. The pan-empiricist position of, e.g., John Stuart Mill who regarded logical truths as on a par with the truths of the natural sciences, was thus effectively and definitively refuted. Later, very much needed refinements of the anti-psychologistic position were added by Carnap (65, 68, 69, 71, 72), and a full study of the logical status of rules and rule-governed behavior has been contributed by W. Sellars (*loc. cit.*).

No matter what the most clarifying analysis of rule-governed symbolic behavior in its relation to the rules as such may turn out to be, there can be no doubt that if physical (at least physical$_1$) determinism is to be maintained, the following will have to hold: A person's brain state when thinking, e.g., about Napoleon's defeat at Waterloo must qualitatively or structurally differ from the brain state of the same person (or, for that matter, of other persons) when thinking about Caesar's crossing of the Rubicon. This aspect of the psychology and physiology of thought is definitely relevant for our problem.

V. Mind-Body Identity. Explications and Supporting Arguments

With due trepidation I shall now proceed to draw the conclusions from the preceding discussions, and to present the dénouement of the philosophical tangles. There are many points on which I have sincere and serious doubts. There is yet a great deal of analytic work to be done on several puzzling aspects for which I can at present only sketch the sort of solution which seems to me especially plausible.

A. *Review of the More Basic Meanings and Connotations of "Mental" and "Physical". Conclusions regarding their Respective Merits and Demerits.* The surveys and discussions of the preceding sections have paved the way for a summary and systematic appraisal of various characteristics which have been proposed as defining criteria of the mental and the physical. Outstanding candidates among the criteria of mind are (1) direct experience and (2) intelligence. "Direct experience" is synonymous with one sense of "subjectivity", viz. sentience, raw feels, or phenomenal givenness. "Intelligence" connotes learning capacity, purposive (goal directed) behavior and—on the human level—intentionality (symbolic behavior). Although the two criteria have in fact a certain area of coincidence, this coincidence (or overlap) is not a matter of logical necessity. By and large then, the two criteria of mentality define two entirely different concepts.

"Mind" as we have come to suspect all along, is an ambiguous term, or at best a group of concepts with family resemblances (in Wittgenstein's sense). The major components of the connotation of "intelligence" may be attributed not only to the higher animals but also to the "thinking machines" which we generally consider not only as lifeless but also as devoid of sentience. Direct experience, on the other hand, may well be attributed to some of the lower animals, babies, idiots, and to the severely insane; but in each of these classes at least some, if not all, of the marks of intelligence are lacking. Furthermore, it is customary in contemporary psychology to classify the unconscious (deeply repressed) traumata, anxieties, wishes, conflicts, etc. as mental. This again indicates that direct experience is not the criterion here, even if—according to the psychoanalytic doctrine—deeply repressed matters are *potentially* conscious, in that they can be brought to the fore of awareness by special techniques. Hypnotic and posthypnotic phenomena also often involve deeply unconscious processes, which because of their other similarities with the conscious processes are unhesitatingly classified as mental.

One might suppose that the term "physical" (to which we have paid thus far only sporadic attention) is much more definite in meaning than the term "mental". Unfortunately, the contrary is the case. There are some superficial and entirely inadequate definitions of "physical" which need only be mentioned in order to be promptly dismissed. For example, to define "physical" as the "outer" aspect (in contradistinction to the "inner" mental life) is to use misleading metaphors. "Inside" and "outside", "internal" and "external" have a good clear meaning in ordinary usage. What is literally inside, e.g., the skin of a person is most of his body (i.e., the body minus the skin) and that's "physical" in at least one very good sense of the term. After all, anatomy and physiology are concerned with the physical structure and the functions of organisms. *Inside* the skull is the brain of man, and that is "physical" in the same well understood sense.

Similarly unhelpful is the definition of the "physical" as the *mechanical*-compositional, as contrasted with the *purposive*-holistic. We have already repudiated this sort of definition-by-contrast, by pointing out that "mechanical" in the strict sense of "characterizable by the concepts and laws of Newtonian mechanics" designates only a narrow subclass of the class of *physical* events or processes, using "physical" (comprising also electrodynamic, relativistic, and quantum-theoretical characteristics) in the sense of modern physics. And if by "purposive" we mean no more than by "teleological" and "holistic", then there are innumerable teleological mechanisms, many of them with typical features of organic wholeness, both in nature and among the artifacts of technology. If "purposive" is understood in the narrower and more fruitful sense, then it involves intelligence (and this, on the human level, includes intentionality).

But the fact *that* there are (human) organisms functioning intelligently and displaying (symbolic) behavior which indicates intentional acts is describable in an intersubjective ("physical$_1$") manner and therefore again does not support a definition-by-contrast between the physical (in this case physical$_1$) and the mental. It remains true, however, that among the objects and processes describable in physical$_1$ terms, there are differences at least of degree (often of very considerable degree) if not of a fundamental, evolutionary-emergent type, as between the structure and the dynamics of electrons, atoms, molecules, genes, viruses, and unicellular and multicellular organisms. The tremendous differences between, e.g., a simple inorganic structure and a human being are therefore not in the least denied. As Castell (74) puts it, the solar system and an astronomer thinking about it, are in many essential respects very dissimilar indeed. (But the dualistic conclusions drawn by Castell seem to me nevertheless *non sequiturs*.)

The foregoing considerations suggest some of the more fruitful definitions of "physical". "Physical$_1$" may be defined as the sort of objects or processes which can be described (and possibly explained or predicted) in the concepts of a language with an intersubjective observation basis. This language or conceptual system is—in our sort of world—characterized by its spatio-temporal-causal structure. This is so fundamental a feature of our world that it is extremely difficult to imagine an alternative kind of world in which intersubjectivity is *not* connected with this feature. One can understand, but need not concede, Kant's contentions regarding the synthetic a priori character of this "presupposition." * The concept of "physical$_1$" is closely related to but by no means equivalent with one of the primary meanings of "physical" in ordinary language, viz. observable by sense perception. In its most natural usage "observable by sense perception", clearly comprises the solid and liquid objects of our environment; it includes of course our own bodies; it includes a trifle less clearly the air (which can be felt if it moves with sufficient speed; or other gases if they can be smelled); it includes less obviously some of the dispositional properties of various sorts of matter (such as their hardness, elasticity, solubility, fusibility, etc.); and it scarcely includes electric or magnetic fields, atoms and electrons, or the secret thoughts of other persons.

But in one usage "observable by sense perception" does comprise the feelings, emotions, and even some of the (dispositional) personality traits of other persons. For example, we say, "I could see how disappointed he was." "I can see that he is a depressive person," etc. But these are usages, which from the point of view of logical analysis are perhaps

* For a critique of this rationalistic position, cf. Pap (242); Nagel (233); Reichenbach (275); Feigl (114).

not fundamentally different from the case of a physicist, who (looking at a cloud chamber photograph of condensation tracks) says, "Here I see the collision of an electron with a photon." Such (extended) "observation statements" urgently demand a logical analysis into their *directly* verifiable, as contrasted with interpretive and inferential components. Logical analysis, pursuing as it should, an epistemological reconstruction, must therefore be distinguished from phenomenological description.

From the point of view of a phenomenological description, the "preanalytic data" of the clinical psychologist contain his direct impression of (some of) the personality traits of his clients; just as the experienced physician's judgments may be based on his direct impression of the disease (diabetes, multiple sclerosis, Parkinson's disease, etc.) of his patient. Phenomenological description is a subtle and interesting matter, but philosophically much less relevant than it is often supposed to be. By a little exercise of our analytic abilities we can, and for epistemological purposes we must, separate the directly verifiable situation (the patient is very slow in all his movements, hangs his head, speaks with a very low voice; or: he has dry skin; his breath has a fruity smell; his hands tremble; etc.) from the inferential interpretations, i.e., the conclusions regarding his mental or physical illness.

Inasmuch as the use of terms like "psychoneurosis" is established, and diagnoses of psychoneuroses can hence be confirmed, on an intersubjective basis, the *concept* of psychoneurosis is evidently a physical$_1$ concept. At least partial *explanations* of the behavior and the subjective experience of psychoneurotics have also been given on a physical$_1$ (roughly: behavioristic) basis. We can plausibly explain neurotic dispositions by tracing them causally to the childhood situations of the patient (not necessarily neglecting some of his biologically inherited constitutional traits). And we can predict his anxieties, depressed moods, etc. on the basis of such intersubjectively confirmable information as, e.g., about a preceding period of highly "id-indulgent," overbearing, or hostile behavior. These "physical$_1$" explanations do not differ fundamentally from explanations of, e.g., the growth of plants or the behavior of lower animals. That a plant grows poorly may be explained by the sandy soil in which it is rooted, the lack of rainfall, etc. The behavior (or some aspects of it) of an amoeba may be explained by the thermal and chemical conditions of its immediate environment.

The distinction between psychoneuroses and "physical" nervous disorders originates from the same commonsense considerations that have traditionally led to the contrast of "states of mind" and states of the body. No matter whether normal or abnormal processes are concerned, whenever scientifically or philosophically innocent people speak of something as being "in the mind" or "merely in the mind," this means apparently that it is not directly accessible to sensory observation. But, it is also positively characterized by the fact that these "states of mind" can (usually) be reported by those who have them, and that they can (sometimes) be influenced by talking. Sticks and stones cannot be made to move by merely talking to them.* Persons (having minds!) can be made to do things by suggestions, propaganda, requests, commands, etc., often by just giving them certain bits of information.

But important and interesting as is this sort of difference, in its scientific aspects it no longer establishes a fundamental difference between inanimate things and minded persons. Modern robots have been constructed which emit information about their "inner" (physical!) states, and they can be made to do things by speaking to them. But if intellectually acute and learned men † discuss seriously the problem as to whether robots really have a mental life (involving thoughts and/or feelings), there must be a question here that clearly transcends the obviously scientific and technological issue as to whether robots can be constructed which in their behavior duplicate all essential features (of course, one must ask: which ones and how completely?) of human behavior. If by "thinking" one means a kind of performance which, starting with "input" premises yield "output" conclusions of deductive or inductive inference, and consists (at least) in certain observable relations between input and output, then there is no doubt that certain types of robots or computers do think. If one means by "feeling" what the logical (or illogical?) behaviorists mean, then it is at least conceivable (cf. Scriven, 304) that there might be machinelike structures (artificially made, or even naturally existing on some other stars) which behave (respond, etc.) in every way as if they had feelings and emotions.‡

* This still seems safe to assert even in view of the alleged but highly questionable "facts" of psychokinesis.

† Cf. Turing (338); MacKay (216); Spilsbury (326); Scriven (304).

‡ The question in this form is by no means new. William James discussed it in his *Principles of Psychology* (Vol. I) by means of the example of the "automatic sweetheart." He was severely criticized by E. A. Singer (319) who, ironically enough,

Herbert Feigl

Here the question is clearly of the same logical nature as the queries: "Do butterflies feel?" "Do fishworms, when put on the hook, feel pain?" "Do plants have feelings?" "Do human embryos, four months old, have any direct experience?" I shall try to clarify the nature of these questions in the following subsection. For the moment it must suffice to point out that here we have to do with the distinction between "mental" (in the sense of *sentience*) and *physical₁*. *Intelligence*, in contrast to sentience, is clearly definable in physical₁ terms. But as to whether sentience is so definable is perhaps the central perplexity among the mind-body puzzles.

But now to complete our analysis of the meanings of "physical": We have distinguished "physical₁" and "physical₂". By "physical₁ terms" I mean *all* (empirical) terms whose specification of meaning essentially involves logical (necessary or, more usually, probabilistic) connections with the intersubjective observation language, as well as the terms of this observation language itself. Theoretical concepts in physics, biology, psychology, and the social sciences hence are all—at least—physical₁ concepts. By "physical₂" I mean the kind of theoretical concepts (and statements) which are sufficient for the *explanation*, i.e., the deductive or probabilistic derivation, of the observation statements regarding the inorganic (lifeless) domain of nature. If my conjecture (discussed above) is correct, then the scopes of *theoretical* "physical₁" and "physical₂" terms are the same. *If*, however, there is genuine emergence, i.e., logical underivability, in the domains of organic, mental, and/or social phenomena, then the scope of "physical₂" terms is clearly narrower than that of "physical₁" theoretical terms.

Within the category of "physical₁" terms, it is clearly important to distinguish observation terms from theoretical terms; and among the latter several levels may methodologically, if not logically, be distinguished. For example, the concepts of classical thermodynamics form one level, and the concepts of statistical or molecular mechanics (in terms of which those of thermodynamics, with certain modifications,

appealed to James' own principle of pragmatism (derived from Peirce's meaning criterion which anticipated the essentially equivalent later operationist and logical-positivist formulations of the criterion). But E. A. Singer in turn was incisively criticized by D. S. Miller (224), who many years later (226) attacked on the same grounds the much more subtle linguistic behaviorism expounded in Gilbert Ryle's *The Concept of Mind*.

424

can be defined) form a "higher" level. The concepts of molar behavior theory are related analogously to those of the higher level of neurophysiology; and so on *mutatis mutandis*, throughout the various fields of scientific theories.

We conclude that to say "x is physical" is highly ambiguous. There is first the obvious distinction between the physical *languages* (physical language designators) and physical *objects* (physical language designata). This distinction carries through the two further distinctions and does not, for our purposes, require elaborate discussion. To illustrate, an electromagnetic field, just as the planet Jupiter, are *designata* of physical language *terms*. However, the *observation* terms of the physical$_1$ language serve also as the evidential basis of the physical$_1$ or physical$_2$ theoretical languages. *Theoretical* terms are here conceived as not *explicitly* definable on the basis of observation terms (cf. Carnap, 73; Feigl, 110; Sellars, 315), but as specified by postulates and by correspondence rules relating them to the terms of the observation language. And, to restate this in different words, *if* there is no genuine emergence in the logical sense above the level of lifeless phenomena, then there is no basic distinction between the theoretical terms of the physical$_1$ and physical$_2$ languages. That is to say that the theoretical terms of biology and psychology are explicitly definable on the basis of the theoretical concepts of physics in the same sense as the theoretical terms of chemistry (e.g., the chemical bond) are nowadays explicitly definable on the basis of the theoretical terms of the physical$_2$ language (i.e., of the atomic and quantum theories).

The central questions of the mind-body problem then come down to this: are the concepts of introspective psychology—relating to phenomenal data or phenomenal fields—definable on the basis of physical$_1$ theoretical terms, and if so, are they also definable on the basis of physical$_2$ (theoretical) terms? The first question is a matter for *philosophical* analysis. The second question is, at the present level of scientific research, undecided, though my personal (admittedly bold and risky) guess is that future scientific progress will decide it affirmatively. We turn now to a discussion of the first question primarily, but occasional remarks about the second question will also be ventured.

B. *The Inference to Other Minds.* Behaviorism and phenomenalism display interesting similarities as well as fundamental differences. According to logical behaviorism, the concepts of *mental* states, disposi-

Herbert Feigl

tions, and events are logical constructions based on (physical₁) characterizations of behavior. According to the more recent formulations of physicalism (Feigl, 113, 116; Carnap, 73; Sellars, 315) the "logical construction" thesis is inadequate and has to be replaced by an analysis in terms of postulates and correspondence rules. Very simply and very roughly, this means—in the material mode of speech—that for physicalism mental states are inferential ("illata," cf. Reichenbach, 273). Contrariwise, modern phenomenalism (Carnap, 60; Ayer, 12; Goodman, 135) had maintained that the concepts of *physical* things, states, dispositions, and events are logical constructions based on concepts designating the phenomena of immediate experience. And in the "revised" version of phenomenalism, i.e., a genuinely *realistic* epistemology based on phenomenal data, a doctrine which should not be called "phenomenalism" at all, the concepts of physical objects are inferential ("hypothetical constructs," "illata"). But this doctrine is in many of its tenets consonant with classical critical realism (von Hartmann, Külpe, Schlick, R. W. Sellars, D. Drake, C. A. Strong, J. B. Pratt, A. O. Lovejoy, G. Santayana). In contradistinction to critical realism, there is the earlier doctrine of *neutral monism* developed by the neorealists, especially E. B. Holt and Bertrand Russell (before his later critical realism), and historically rooted in the positivism and empiriocriticism of Hume, Mill, Mach, and Avenarius. Russell (284, 287) was the primary influence in Carnap's early epistemology (60, 61); and this sort of neutral monism was also adopted in prefatory philosophical remarks of some psychologists like E. C. Tolman (336), C. C. Pratt (260), and others.

The distinctive mark of neutral monism is a conception of the "given" which is (1) subjectless, i.e., it does not allow for the use of the personal pronoun "I"; and (2) is "neutral" in the sense that the given is characterizable as *neither* "mental" *nor* "physical." It maintains that both mentalistic concepts (the concepts of psychology) and physical concepts (those of physics) are logically constituted out of the more basic concepts designating neutral data. Psychology and physics are here understood as more or less systematic knowledge both on the level of common life, and on the more advanced level of science. Disregarding some technical logical questions, the *data* upon which the construction is based turn out to be items of immediate experience (sentience) and are thus "mental" after all, in one of the two senses of "mental" which we have been at pains to explicate.

This is not the place to review the many arguments * which have been advanced in the refutation of phenomenalism. If an epistemology with a phenomenal basis can at all be worked out satisfactorily, then these data have to be conceived as *lawfully* related to the physical objects of everyday life. This means that the doctrine of logical constructionism or reductionism, i.e., of the *explicit* definability of physical concepts in terms of phenomenal concepts, has to be abandoned. The logical relations involved here are *synthetic*, and the translatability thesis is not just utopian (owing to the always admitted complexities), but completely inadequate, if not quixotic. I remain unimpressed with the significance of Craig's theorem (cf. Hempel's essay in the present volume) in this connection. An infinite set of postulates is *not* what phenomenalists ever had in mind. And I believe there are other grave objections to that sort of a translatability doctrine. The kind of translatability which Craig's theorem allows for concerns only the empirical content of theories in the sense of all conceivable evidential (confirming) statements, but not in the sense of the *factual reference* of the postulates (and, hence, of the theorems).

Mutatis mutandis, it is now realized in many philosophical and psychological quarters † that the thesis of the translatability of statements about mental states (in phenomenal language) into statements about peripheral behavior (in *descriptive*, not theoretical physical₁ language) must also be repudiated.

With this firmly established orientation, the inference of sentience (raw feels) in other organisms seems prima facie restored to its original form as an argument from analogy. I have no doubt that *analogy* is the essential criterion for the ascription of sentience. But a closer look at the logic of the inference will prove worthwhile. The inference from peripheral behavior to central processes, very much like the inference from skulls to brains contained in them, is intersubjectively confirmable, and this in the sense that independent intersubjective evidence for the truth of these conclusions is in principle available. Just this is, of course,

* Cf. Freytag (128); Külpe (191); Broad (50, 51); Schlick (298); Reichenbach (273); Pap (248); Lovejoy (204); R. W. Sellars (307); W. S. Sellars (308); B. Russell (288); Kneale (179); Beck (24); Feigl (110, 111); Berlin (35); Watling (342); Braithwaite (48); E. J. Nelson (237, 238); and now, after a drastic change in outlook, even Ayer (18) is close to a critical realist position.

† Cf. Hempel (146); Carnap (64, 67, 73); Kaufmann (175); Jacobs (163); Pap (242, 243, 245, 248); Ayer (18); Feigl (113, 116); Cronbach and Meehl (79); Scriven (306).

Herbert Feigl

not the case for the conclusions regarding mental states, if by mental states (sentience, raw feels) one means something that is not identifiable (i.e., not explicitly definable in physical$_1$ terms) with either overt-behavioral or central-neural states or processes.* If, contrary to the suggested orientation, such identifications could be made, i.e., if explicit definition could plausibly be given as an analysis of the meaning of phenomenal terms, then indeed no analogical inferences would be required. Nevertheless, considerations of analogy would be *suggestive*, though never decisive, for the *terminological* conventions according to which we apply or refrain from applying phenomenal terms to the behavior of animals and plants (let alone lifeless things).

If, however, phenomenal terms are logically irreducible to physicalistic terms, then parallelistic (epiphenomenalist) dualism is the most plausible alternative view. But *interactionistic* dualism is empirically much less defensible, and its methodological orientation too defeatist, to be acceptable to the current scientific outlook (cf. section II, above). And epiphenomenalism also has generally been considered objectionable because it denies the causal efficacy of raw feels; and because it introduces peculiar lawlike relations between cerebral events and mental events. These correlation laws are utterly different from any other laws of (physical$_2$) science in that, first, they are nomological "danglers," i.e., relations which connect intersubjectively confirmable events with events which ex hypothesi are in principle not intersubjectively and independently confirmable. Hence, the presence or absence of phenomenal data is not a difference that could conceivably make a difference in the confirmatory physical$_1$-*observational* evidence, i.e., in the publicly observable behavior, or for that matter in the neural processes observed or inferred by the neurophysiologists. And second, these correlation laws would, unlike other correlation laws in the natural sciences, be (again ex hypothesi) absolutely underivable from the premises of even the most inclusive and enriched set of postulates of any future theoretical physics or biology.

No wonder then that after a period of acquiescence with epiphenomenalism during the last century (T. H. Huxley, et al.), the behaviorist

* This is my way of stating succinctly the puzzle of "Other Minds" as it is understood in the long (unfinished) sequence of agonizing articles by John Wisdom (354), and in many other authors' publications, notably: Carnap (61, 62); Schlick (299); Ayer (15, 18); Austin (10); Pap (243, 248); Hampshire (141); Watling (341); Mellor (223).

movement in psychology took hold, and exercised an unprecedented influence in so many quarters. Behaviorists, in their way, repressed the problem in that they either *denied* the existence of raw feels (materialism); or in that they *defined* them in physical$_1$-observation terms (logical behaviorism); or they maintained that the subject matter of scientific and experimental psychology can be nothing but behavior (methodological behaviorism), which leaves the existence of raw feels an open question, but as of no relevance to science. Our previous discussions have, I trust, clearly indicated that behaviorism in the first sense is absurdly false; in the second sense it is inadequate as a logical analysis of the meaning of phenomenal terms; and in the third sense, it is an admittedly fruitful but limited program of research, but it entails no conclusion directly relevant to the central philosophical issue.

The repudiation of radical behaviorism and of logical behaviorism entails the acceptance of some sort of parallelistic doctrine. Recent arguments for this position * are prima facie highly persuasive. The basic point is simply that each of us knows his own states of immediate experience by acquaintance, and that by analogical reasoning we can infer similar, though never directly inspectable, states of experience in others. Direct inspection of the mental states of others is now generally considered a *logical* impossibility. For example, the subjunctive conditional, "If I were you, I would experience your pain," is not merely counterfactual, but counterlogical in that the antecedent of the conditional involves an outright inconsistency. The air of plausibility of the mentioned subjunctive conditional derives from entirely other, quite legitimate types of subjunctive conditionals, such as "If I had a broken leg (as you do), I should feel pain"; or "If I had (some traits of) your personality, flattery would please me." The logical grammar of personal proper names (or pronouns) however is such that it is downright self-contradictory to say (in a reasonably constructed and interpreted language) that Smith is Jones, or that I am you. The Mont Blanc cannot conceivably be identical with Mt. Everest!

Indirect verification or confirmation of statements regarding the mental states of other persons is however clearly possible once we have established laws regarding the correlation of the Φ's with the ψ's for our own case. And as we have pointed out, these laws could in prin-

* By Pap (243); Hampshire (141); Watling (341); Ayer (18).

ciple be most directly established with the help of an autocerebroscope. On the level of common life, of course, the correlations between neural and mental states are totally unknown. But a great many behavioral *indicators* are constantly being used in the (probabilistic) ascription of mental states. Logical analysis (Carnap, 73; Scriven, 306; Feyerabend, 119; Watling, 342; Feigl, 110, 111, 112, 114) has, I think, quite convincingly demonstrated the need for distinguishing the evidential bases from the factual reference of concepts and statements. The behavioral indicators serve as evidential bases for the ascription of mental states. Only the person who experiences the mental state can *directly* verify its occurrence. But there is no reason whatever to assume that when A reports his mental state, and B talks about it on the basis of behavioral evidence (or, if this is feasible, on the basis of neurophysiological evidence), that what they are talking about is not the very same mental state. This is indeed the way in which ordinary communication is understood. For example, if the doctor tells me a moment before lancing my abscess, "This will hurt," it is I who can directly verify this prediction. Moreover, most of us have learned from childhood on how to conceal our thoughts, feelings, sentiments, how to dissimulate, play-act, etc. And so we can justifiably say that behavioral symptoms do *not reliably* indicate mental states. In the light of the basic principles of normal induction and analogy, involving symmetry considerations, solipsism (with its arbitrary asymmetries) must be regarded as an absurdly false, rather than as a meaningless doctrine.

If we had completely adequate and detailed knowledge of the neural processes in human brains, and the knowledge of the one-one, or at least one-many ψ-Φ correlation laws, then a description of a neural state would be completely reliable evidence (or a genuine criterion) for the occurrence of the corresponding mental state. If these central neural events are essential intermediate links in the causal chain which connects stimuli with responses, then these central states are (probabilistically) inferable from stimulus-response situations. In this respect they have a logical status similar to the mental states as they are inferred from behavior in everyday life, or as the basis of psychological test situations. One may therefore wonder whether two steps of inference are really needed for a full logical reconstruction of the scientific ascription of mental states to other persons; the first step being the one from overt behavior to central neural events, and the second step being the one from neural events to mental states. I shall return to this question in subsection E, where I shall discuss the arguments for and against the identification of raw feels with the denotata of certain theoretical physical$_1$ (or physical$_2$) concepts.

C. *The Cognitive Roles of Acquaintance.* Various meanings of "acquaintance" and of "knowledge by acquaintance" were sorted out in section IV A. Our present concern is with the roles of acquaintance and of knowledge by acquaintance in the enterprise of science, especially in psychology. The first question I wish to discuss concerns the cognitive "plus," i.e., the alleged advantages of knowledge by acquaintance over knowledge by description. We may ask, for example, what does the seeing man know that the congenitally blind man could not know. Or, to take two examples from Eddington (93, 94), What could a man know about the effects of jokes if he had no sense of humor? Could a Martian, entirely without sentiments of compassion or piety, know about what is going on during a commemoration of the armistice? For the sake of the argument, we assume complete physical (1 or 2) predictability and explainability of the behavior of humans equipped with vision, a sense of humor, and sentiments of piety. The Martian could then predict all responses, including the linguistic utterances of the earthlings in the situations which involve their visual perceptions, their laughter about jokes, or their (solemn) behavior at the commemoration. But *ex hypothesi*, the Martian would be lacking completely in the sort of *imagery* and *empathy* which depends on familiarity (direct acquaintance) with the kinds of *qualia* to be imaged or empathized.

As we have pointed out before, "knowledge *of*," i.e., "acquaintance with," qualia is not a necessary condition for "knowledge *about*" (or knowledge by inference of) those qualia. A psychiatrist may know a great deal *about* extreme states of manic euphoria or of abject melancholic depression, without ever having experienced anything anywhere near them himself. In this case, of course, it must be admitted that the psychiatrist can get an "idea" of these extreme conditions by imaginative extrapolation from the milder spells of elation or depression which he, along with all human beings, does know by acquaintance. But the case is different for observers who are congenitally deprived of acquaintance with an entire modality of direct experience. This is the case of the congenitally blind or deaf, or that of our fancied Martian who has no emotions or sentiments of any kind. But I think it is also the case of human beings endowed with the entire repertory of normal sensory and emotional experience, when they introduce theoretical concepts in their science, such as the electromagnetic or gravitational fields, electric currents, and nuclear forces. We are "acquainted" with the perceptible things, properties, and relations on the relevant evidential bases which suggest the introduction of these concepts into the system of science generally, or which justify their special application in particular instances of observation.

In the context of the present discussion it does not matter very much whether we use the narrower, philosophical notion of direct acquaintance (restricted to the qualia of raw feels) or the wider commonsense or physicalistic notion of acquaintance (which includes the directly observable properties and relations of the objects in our everyday life environment). I think it does make sense to say that we do not know by acquaintance the "nature" of electric currents or of the forces within the nuclei of atoms. And although the congenitally blind have no acquaintance with color qualities or visual shapes, they may nevertheless come to have knowledge by inference at least of the neural correlates among the processes in the occipital lobes of the brains of persons with eyesight. The "intrinsic nature" of those neural processes remains unknown by acquaintance to the blind scientist, just as the "intrinsic nature" of electric currents remains unknown to scientists who have eyesight, and who have seen electrical machines and wires, have been tickled or shocked by electric currents, have seen electric sparks, have felt the heat produced by electric currents, have read voltmeters and ammeters, have observed the chemical and magnetic effects of electric currents, etc.

I trust my readers will not charge me with obscurantist tendencies. I do not at all share the view (e.g., Bergson's) that *genuine* knowledge is to be found only in direct acquaintance or intuition. Bergson, in his *Introduction to Metaphysics*, paradoxically claimed that metaphysics—the intuitive knowledge of intrinsic reality—is "the science that dispenses with symbols altogether." I wish to assert, quite to the contrary, that genuine knowledge is *always symbolic*, be it knowledge by acquaintance as formulated in direct introspective report sentences, or be it knowledge by description as, e.g., in the hypotheses of modern nuclear physics. If we knew all about electricity, magnetism, nuclear forces, etc., i.e., if we had a complete set of laws concerning those matters—this would be all we could possibly wish to know within the scientific enterprise. Anything added to this by way of "acquaintance" would be cognitively irrelevant imagery. Such imagery might be welcome from a poetic or artistic point of view. It might occasionally be helpful heuristically or didactically, but even in this regard it amounts only to pictorial bywork, and is often dangerously misleading. "Thou shalt not make unto thee any graven image . . ."

Our world, being what it is, can of course be known by description, in any of its parts or aspects, only on the basis of a foothold somewhere in direct acquaintance. This, it seems to me, is one of the cornerstones of any empiricist epistemology, old or new. But the new empiricism of recent times has come to recognize that it matters little just which areas of acquaintance are available or actually utilized for the "triangulation" of facts or entities outside the scope of direct acquaintance. The congenitally blind-deaf person, I stress again, could in principle construct and confirm a complete system of the natural sciences (including astronomy!) and the social sciences (including the psychology of vision and hearing, as well as the psychology of art and music appreciation!). It should go without saying that such a person, like Helen Keller, would normally depend upon information received from persons endowed with visual and auditory perception.

But, supposing such a human being could survive a long time as a solitary observer and was equipped with supreme intelligence and ingenuity, then one can well conceive of various modern instruments and devices (involving photoelectric cells, amplifiers, electromagnetic indicators, etc.) he could invent which would serve him in the detection of the stars, the chemical constitution of various substances, the behavior of animals, and so on—all accessible to him ultimately through, e.g., tactual pointer readings of one sort or another. All this is merely a picturesque way of saying that the "nomological net," i.e., the system of scientific concepts and laws, may be "tacked down" in a variety of alternative ways, either in several sense modalities (as in the normal case), or even in only one of them. To be sure, "triangulation of entities in logical space" is much easier and much more secure in the normal case. But, as we have pointed out, normal, unaided perception by itself is also quite insufficient for the confirmation of our knowledge regarding radio waves, infrared, ultraviolet, gamma radiations, cosmic rays, the molecular and atomic structure of matter, the motions and other physical and chemical characteristics of stars and galaxies, etc. Intricate instruments and ingenious theoretical constructions are indispensable in the case of normal (multimodal) perception as well. The difference between persons equipped with all normal sense organs and the deaf-blind is only one of degree, or of the speed with which they would, respectively, attain knowledge about the world in which they are embedded and of which they are parts.

Similar considerations apply to the advantages held by fully equipped persons in regard to psychological and linguistic or descriptive-semantical knowledge. If I have been trained by normal education to apply phenomenal terms (like "red", "green", "lilac fragrance", "rose fragrance", "sweet", "sour", etc.) to qualia of my own direct experience, then I can predict much more readily the application of these terms by other persons in the presence of certain specifiable visual, olfactory or gustatory stimuli. But predictions of this sort are based upon analogical inference; and they are in principle dispensable, because the discriminatory and verbal behavior of other persons is open to intersubjective test. Moreover, if we had a complete neurophysiological explanation of discriminatory and verbal responses we could derive these responses from the cerebral states which initiate them, and which, in turn were engendered by sensory stimulation. Analogously, whatever reliability empathetic understanding in common life, or "clinical intuition" in the psychologist's practice, may have is ultimately to be appraised by intersubjective tests. But the speed with which empathy or intuition do their work depends upon the breadth and the richness of the "experience" of the judge. It also depends upon his use of critical controls.

If the psychologist's personality type is radically different from that of his subject, he will have to correct (often to the point of complete reversal) his first intuitions. For example, an extremely extrovert person will find it difficult to "understand" an extreme introvert, and vice versa. If, however, the personalities are very similar, intuition may "click" readily, and it may even be frequently quite correct. The role of direct acquaintance in all these cases simply amounts to having in one's own experience features and regularities with which one is quite familiar, and which are hence speedily projected and utilized in the interpretation of the behavior of other persons. I conclude that the advantages of direct acquaintance pertain to the *context of discovery* (cf. Reichenbach, 273) and not to the context of justification. All the examples discussed do not differ in principle from the obvious examples of persons with "wide experience" as contrasted with persons with "narrow experience," in the most ordinary meaning of these terms. Someone thoroughly familiar with the weather patterns of Minnesota, or with the conduct of business in the Congress of the United States (to take two very different illustrations of the same point) will have the advantages of much speedier inferences and (usually) more reliable predictions than someone who has had no opportunity of long range observations in either case.

The philosophically intriguing questions regarding acquaintance are, I think, of a different sort. They are best expressed by asking, e.g., What is it that the blind man cannot know concerning color qualities? What is it that the (emotionless) Martian could not know about human feelings and sentiments? If we assume complete physical (i.e., at least physical$_1$) predictability of human behavior, i.e., as much predictability as the best developed physical science of the future could conceivably provide, then it is clear that the blind man or the Martian would lack only *acquaintance* and *knowledge by acquaintance* in certain areas of the realm of qualia. Lacking acquaintance means *not having* those experiential qualia; and the consequent lack of knowledge by acquaintance simply amounts to being unable to label the qualia with terms used previously by the subject (or by some other subject) when confronted with their occurrence in direct experience. Now, mere *having* or *living through* ("erleben") is not *knowledge* in any sense. "Knowledge by acquaintance," however, as we understand it here, is propositional, it does make truth claims; and although it is not infallible, it is under favorable circumstances so reliable that we rarely hesitate to call it "certain." It remains in any case the ultimate confirmation basis of *all* knowledge claims.

In many of the foregoing discussions we have suggested that what one person *has* and *knows by acquaintance* may be identical with what someone else *knows by description*. The color experiences of the man who can see are known to him by acquaintance, but the blind man can have inferential knowledge, or knowledge by description *about* those same experiences. After all, this is true as regards an individual color experience even if the other person is endowed with eyesight. The other person does not and could not conceivably have the numerically identical experience (see p. 397f above). Why should we then not conclude that the behavioristic psychologist can "triangulate" the direct experiences of others? I think that indeed he does just that if he relinquishes the narrow peripheralist position, i.e., if he allows himself the introduction of theoretical concepts which are only logically connected with, but never explicitly definable in terms of, concepts pertaining to overt molar behavior. These acquaintancewise possibly unknown states which the behaviorist must introduce for the sake of a theoretical explanation of overt behavior, and to which he (no longer a "radical" behaviorist) refers as the central causes of the peripheral behavior symptoms and manifestations, may well be *identical* with the referents of the phenomenal (acquaintance) terms used by his subject in introspective descriptions of his (the subject's) direct experience. As remarked before, in ordinary communication about our respective mental states, we make this assumption of identity quite unquestioningly. It took a great deal of training in philosophical doubt for learned men to call this assumption into question.

But philosophical doubt, here as elsewhere,* while stimulating in the search for clarity, is ultimately due to conceptual confusions. We have learned how to avoid these confusions, and thus to return with a good philosophical conscience to (at least *some* of) the convictions of commonsense. We have learned that philosophical doubts, unlike ordinary empirical doubts, cannot be removed by logical or experimental demonstration. What *can* be demonstrated logically is only the exploitation of certain misleading extensions of, or deviations from, the sensible and fruitful use of terms in ordinary or scientific language. Thus to doubt whether we can at all have knowledge about the "private" experience of other persons is merely the philosophical extension of the ordinary and quite legitimate doubts that we may have in specific instances, for example, when we ask "Is he really as disappointed as his behavior would seem to indicate?" This is to confuse practical difficulties of knowing with (allegedly) basic impossibilities. Once one becomes fully aware of the disease of philosophical skepticism, it becomes possible to cure oneself of it by a sort of self-analysis (*logical* analysis is what I have in mind here; but in certain cases psychoanalysis may help too, or may even be indispensable).

Granting then that the *referents* of acquaintance terms and physical$_1$ theoretical terms may in some cases be identical, this does not by itself

* As, e.g., in the problems of induction, the trustworthiness of memory, the veridicality of perception, etc.

decide the issue between monism and dualism. As we have seen in the previous subsection, the inference to other persons' raw feels can be *logically* differentiated from the inference to their central nervous processes. Dualistic parallelism or epiphenomenalism is entirely compatible with the assertion of the identity of the subjectively labeled mental state with the intersubjectively inferred state which is needed for the explanation of molar behavior. The mental state is logically distinguishable from the "correlated" neurophysiological state. Indeed (as pointed out in section III 4), it makes no sense to talk of *correlation*, or in any case not the usual sense, if the relation of "correlation" were that of *identity*. We shall tackle this crucial point in the next two subsections.

Before we proceed to the discussion of identity and identification, let us however summarize some important conclusions from our discussion of *acquaintance*. The data of direct experience function in three roles: First, in the use of typical patterns and regularities of one person's data for the intuitive or empathetic ascription of similar patterns and regularities of direct experience (or even of unconscious processes) to other persons, these data *suggest*, but by themselves are never a sufficiently strong *basis of validation* for knowledge claims about the mental life of other persons. Further clinical, experimental, or statistical studies of the behavior of those persons are needed in order to obtain a scientifically respectable degree of confirmation for such inferences. Second, nevertheless, and this is philosophically even more important, the first-person data of direct experience are, in the ultimate epistemological analysis, the *confirmation basis of all* types of factual knowledge claims. This is simply the core of the empiricist thesis over again. But third, the data are also *objects* (targets, referents) of *some* knowledge claims, viz. of those statements which concern nothing but the occurrence of raw feels or whatever regularities (if any!) can be formulated about raw feels in purely phenomenal terms. For examples of the latter, I mention the three-dimensional ordering of color qualia according to hue, brightness, and saturation; the regularities regarding the gradual (temporal) fading of intense emotions like joy, rage, exultation, embarrassment, regret, grief, etc.; the lawful correlations between, e.g., the experienced contents of daydreams and the attendant emotions of hope or fear. In all these cases, no matter whether the raw feels are our own or someone else's, they are the *objects* of our knowledge claims or the *referents* of certain terms in the sentences which describe them. I emphasize this

Herbert Feigl

point because recent empiricist epistemologies in their concern with the confirmation bases of our knowledge claims, and with observation statements which formulate the confirming (or disconfirming) evidence, have tended to neglect consideration of those cases in which the target of the knowledge claim is a state or a regularity of direct experience. Evidence and reference coincide only in the case of statements about the immediate data of first-person experience. But they are clearly distinct in all other cases, such as those in which the object of reference is a state of affairs in the world outside the observer (or else anatomically physiologically inside his own skin), no matter whether it be the state of inorganic things, or processes in organisms. Even the direct experience of oneself at a time distinct from the present moment, and of course the direct experience of other organisms or persons are numerically distinct from the data of the confirming evidence. In short, the data of immediate experience function either as verifiers or as referents of knowledge claims.

D. Reduction and Identification in Scientific Theories. In order to decide whether the mental and the physical can in some sense be identified, it is indispensable to cast at least a brief glance at the logic of reduction and identification in the sciences, especially in physics, biology, and psychology. Although these reflections will not provide us with the complete solution of the problem, they will be helpful and suggestive.

It was pointed out and briefly discussed in section II that the advance of scientific theories consists essentially in the reduction of a variety of originally heterogeneous observable facts and regularities to a unitary set of explanatory concepts and postulates. Customarily it is said, for example, that visible light is electromagnetic radiation (within a certain interval of wave lengths); that table salt is NaCl; that magnetized iron is an aggregate of iron atoms with a characteristic spin of certain of their electrons; that the transmitters of hereditary traits are the genes in the chromosomes of the germ cells; that (at least) short range memory traces are reverberating circuits in cerebral cell assemblies, etc. The "is" and the "are" in these sentences represent identities. But these identities differ in their mode of certification from the analytic identities of pure logic and mathematics. For extremely simple illustrations consider the general theorem of set theory "$[S \lor T] = -[-S \cdot -T]$" or the specific arithmetical identity "$\sqrt{64} = 2^3$" which hold by virtue of presupposed definitions and the principles of logic or arithmetic.

But the identities established in the factual sciences are confirmed on the basis of empirical evidence. This is very like the empirically ascertainable identity of Shakespeare (or could it be Marlowe?) with the author of *Hamlet*, or the identity of the author of *Hamlet* with the author of *King Lear*. Of course there are also such empirically ascertainable identities as those of Tully and Cicero, of William Thompson and Lord Kelvin, or of the evening star and the morning star. In the examples just given we have (extensional) identities of individuals labeled or uniquely described in two or more ways. When it comes to properties (universals), the identity may be either intensional or extensional. An illustration of the first is, e.g., the identity of d♯ and e♭ in the well tempered scale of music. An illustration of the second is the identity of the chemical element with atomic number or nuclear charge 20 with calcium characterized as a constituent of limestone, of atomic weight 40, having a melting point of 810° C., a specific heat of 0.169 at 20° C., etc.

In the case of analytic identities of individuals or of properties we may speak of the synonymy of names or predicates, respectively. (This applies, of course, also to two-place, three-place, etc. predicates, i.e., to dyadic, triadic, etc. relations. Thus, e.g., "earlier than" is logically synonymous with "temporally precedent to" or with the converse of the relation "later than"). The identity of the class of rational animals with the class of featherless bipeds (disregarding plucked birds), or with the class of laughing animals (disregarding hyenas), is *extensional* and *empirical*. Of course, extensional identity, be it logically necessary or empirical, is implied by intensional identity, but not vice versa. There is no longer any reason to be puzzled about identity being a *relation*. The proper explication of identity consists simply in the recognition that one and the same individual (or universal) may be designated by different labels or described by different characterizations. This could (but need not) be formulated by saying that the relation of identity fully explicated, amounts to a triadic relation between labels (L), or descriptions (D) and a referent (R). The following diagrams represent the simplest paradigmatic situations.

$$L_1 \longrightarrow R \longleftarrow L_2 \text{ or } L \longrightarrow R \longleftarrow D \text{ or } D_1 \longrightarrow R \longleftarrow D_2$$

Since I am not a nominalist, having remained unconvinced by the arguments of Quine, Goodman, and White (269, 242), I see no objection to introducing *universals* as referents of predicates or relations. And since I am not a Platonic realist either, I am quite willing to consider talk about universals as a convenient *façon de parler*, rather than as a matter of profound "*ontological*" significance. In my previous example I regarded "d♯" and "e♭" as different labels for the same *kind* of musical tone-as-heard. Similarly I see no reason whatever to deny that "calcium" and "element of atomic number 20" designate the same *kind* of substance. This amounts to saying that the identity of universals, if it is not based on the *logical* synonymy of intensions, can amount only to an *extensional* (in this case, empirical) *equivalence* of two classes.

Prima facie the identifications achieved by scientific laws and theories appear to be cases of co-extensiveness, i.e., of extensional equivalence. This is certainly the case with identifications based on empirical laws. A metal characterized in terms of its thermal conductivity may be identical with the metal characterized by its electric conductivity. The ascertainment of the identity, in this case, depends upon the validity of the Wiedemann-Franz law according to which there is a linear relationship between the two kinds of conductivity. Now, while I grant that the word "*identity*" has only one meaning, and this is the meaning defined by the (properly understood) Leibniz principle of *identitas indiscernibilium*, the *modes* of *ascertainment* of identity are for our purposes the essential consideration. I shall therefore take the terminological liberty of speaking of different kinds of identity, viz., (1) logical, (2) empirical; and under (2) I shall distinguish (a) accidental, (b) nomological, (c) theoretical identities. In more precise but also more cumbersome language this would amount to distinguishing the various modes of ascertainment of identity, or the types of validity that assertions of identity may have.

The identity of the class of rational animals with the class of featherless bipeds may be considered not only as logically contingent, but as empirically accidental; in the same sense as we consider it empirically accidental that the city which is the seat of the United States Government is identical with the city in which on January 17, 1956, at 11:00 a.m. the temperature was (say) 43° F., the barometric pressure 30 inches, and the relative humidity 89 per cent. The referent of these descriptions is the one city of Washington, D.C. This is identity of individuals. Nomological identities rest on empirical laws; theoretical identities depend upon the postulates and definitions of a scientific theory. Since all types of identity, except the logical, are established on the basis of empirical evidence, they must therefore be formulated in *synthetic* statements.

There is, however, the temptation to regard certain well established *theoretical* identities as analytic. For example, if "gas pressure" is *defined* in terms of the sum of the momenta delivered by the molecules of a gas to the walls of its container, then of course within the context of the kinetic theory of gases, the identification of pressure with the sum of the molecular momenta is *analytic*. But, as Ernest Nagel (230) has made clear, if we mean by "the pressure of a gas" that property of it which is measurable by manometers, and which has a variety of well-known lawful connections with the volume, the temperature, etc. of the gas, and thus "manifests" itself in a variety of ways, then clearly it was a *discovery*, yielding *new* information, that revealed to us the relation of gas pressure (the "macro"-concept) to certain aspects of molecular motion. This is clearly synthetic. The interesting point which makes it so tempting to view the relation as analytic is, however, worth a little discussion. It is not simply the much vaunted arbitrariness of defini-tions.* It is rather that the macro-properties and macro-regularities of gases can be *derived* † from the assumptions of the molecular-kinetic theory. A full fledged micro-theory of thermal conduction, convection, diffusion, etc. thus enables us, among other things, to derive the regu-larities of such indicating instruments as the manometers, thermometers, etc. The expansion of the volume of the gas in the gas thermometer is an immediate logical consequence of the (assumed) increase in the average velocities of the molecules making up the gas, and the initial and boundary conditions which characterize the micro-state of the in-strument. Quite analogous considerations apply to the electron theory of electric currents and the measurements of electromotive force and current intensity with the help of such indicating instruments as the voltmeter and the ammeter.

* What is arbitrary in definitions is usually very uninteresting and inconsequential, in contrast to what is *not* arbitrary.

† It was customary to assume that these derivations are *deductive*. But some of the premises in this case are *statistical* laws; hence some of the derivations of descrip-tive-observational or empirical-regularity conclusions are probabilistic. Strict deduc-tions, however, can be found in *classical* thermodynamics, *classical* electrodynamics, in the theory of relativity and other examples of "classical" scientific theories. Even in statistical mechanics some derivations are strictly deductive, others so *highly* probable that for practical purposes they can be considered as ("nearly") deductive.

Herbert Feigl

The explanation of the macro-behavior of organisms is sought along methodologically similar lines. Neurophysiological laws and neural-endocrine-muscular, etc. states will presumably suffice for the explanation of even as complex and intricate behavior as that of human beings. Disregarding the ultimately (possibly inevitable) *statistical* aspects of some of the laws or of the assumptions about initial and boundary conditions, the neurophysiology of the future (3000 A.D.?) should provide complete deductive derivations of the behavior symptoms of various central states whose ψ-correlates are the familiar sensations, perceptions, thoughts, beliefs, desires, volitions, emotions, and sentiments (known by acquaintance and described in phenomenal language). Perhaps I should make clear that I am here trying not so much to convince my readers of the feasibility of what he may consider an entirely utopian and quixotic program for science. I am rather concerned to argue *conditionally*, i.e., *if* this physicalistic program can be carried out, then there would be something like an *empirical* identification of the referents of molar behavior theory concepts with the referents of some neurophysiological concepts. In its logical and methodological aspects this would be quite analogous to the identification of, e.g., the property of magnetism (as conceived in the *macro*-theories of physics) with certain micro-structures and processes involving electron spins, etc., ascribed to the atom and quantum dynamics of ferromagnetic substances. These identifications, like all others of a similar kind * appear as analytic only because of the mentioned relations of deducibility which we know (or believe) to hold between the micro-theoretical and macro-nomological or macro-descriptive propositions.

But a more accurate analysis reveals invariably a synthetic-empirical feature *somewhere* in the context of such scientific explanations. Just where this feature is located depends largely on the nature of the logical reconstruction by means of which we analyze those explanations. In the case of the length of the mercury column in a thermometer, or the volume of the gas in a gas thermometer, the derivation of their (respective) expansions under the condition of increasing heat intensity is so direct that the "identity" appears deceptively as a *logical* one. But even here, empirical regularities enter in. In addition to considerations of the

* E.g., table salt = NaCl; Units of heredity = Genes; Light = electromagnetic waves; the chemical bond = electromagnetic forces playing between the atoms within a molecule; memory traces = reverberating neural circuits; etc., etc.

442

respective thermal expansion coefficients of gases or mercury as compared with those of the glass of the instruments, there are the laws of geometrical optics regarding the paths of the light rays, and the laws of psychophysics and of psychophysiology concerning the visual perception of the mercury column or of the indicator (e.g., a drop of ink) of the gas thermometer.

Just where we decide to put the boundary (or "partition") between the data of observation and the inferred state of affairs is thus a matter of convenience in epistemological reconstruction. But somewhere we must put it, if we are not to lose sight of the *empirical* character of the relation between the *data* and the *illata*. In one reconstruction the data statements concern the observables of common life. This is the epistemology favored by thinkers like Popper, Carnap, Reichenbach, Hempel, Ryle, Black, Skinner, and W. Sellars. They all agree in *this* respect even if they differ sharply in others. They all accept in one way or another an intersubjectvie (physicalistic) thing-language as the basis of epistemological reconstruction. Bertrand Russell, in his later works, is about the only thinker who has made a valiant attempt to combine acceptance of a *phenomenal* basis with a *realistic* (non-phenomenalistic) reconstruction. This means that, as a realist, he has long ago abandoned the earlier phenomenalistic translatability doctrine, and has ever since regarded the relation between physical object statements and phenomenal data statements as one of probabilistic inference. I believe this position still needs considerable logical clarification, but I also believe that it is basically sound, in that it pursues the epistemological analysis down to data which involve only that minimum of inference which knowledge by acquaintance requires. (This was more fully discussed in the preceding subsection.)

No matter where the line is drawn between observables and inferred entities, the most adequate reconstruction, it seems to me, has to be rendered in any case in terms of nomological nets. To return to the temperature example, we may say that the intensity of heat in an oven is *indicated* by various observable effects, but is not identical with any single one of them, nor is it identifiable with a disjunction (or other logical function) of the observable indications. The intensity of heat is nomologically, and hence *synthetically*, related to the indications of indicators. This is not to be confused with the quite obviously synthetic character of the functional or statistical relations between the indications themselves. Empiricists, positivists, and operationists have of course always stressed the empirical character of these correlations.

But even when theories (spelling out nomological networks) are adumbrated only in the form of extremely vague "promissory notes," the practice of scientific thinking clearly demonstrates that theoretical concepts (hypothetical entities) are never reducible to, or identifiable with, observable data (or logical constructions thereof). When, e.g., the spirochaete *treponema pallida,* was still undiscovered, the "disease entity" *general paresis* was conceived as the *causative* factor which "produces" the various symptoms of that disease. Examples of this sort could be multiplied indefinitely from all the sciences. Theoretical concepts are "anchored" in the observables, but are not logically (explicitly) definable in terms of the observables. To be sure, it is the "congruence," "consilience," "convergence," or whatever one wishes to call the testable correlations between the observables that allows for the introduction of fruitful theoretical concepts. It is indeed this consilience which provides the empirical basis for the specification of the meaning of theoretical concepts. Abstract postulates alone determine only their logical or mathematical structure, but never their *empirical* significance.

New evidential bases, such as the microscopic bacteriological findings, provide additional, and usually crucially important, "fixes" upon the theoretical concepts. Nevertheless they amount essentially to enrichments of the nomological net, and thus to a revision of the "weights" of the various other indicators. Thus, in present day pathology, the presence of the spirochaete is a *criterion* of general paresis, and even if many of the usual symptoms were absent, the disease would be ascribed to a patient if a sufficient concentration of the spirochaetes in the nerve tissues were verified. The fact that the bacteriological evidence is correlated with the (more "superficial") symptoms is of course something that only observations could have confirmed. But this need not prevent us from saying that the disease entity *general paresis* as construed *before,* or *independently* of, the evidence for the presence of the spirochaete, can be rightfully *identified* with the disease characterized with the help of the bacteriological evidence.

I conclude that it is proper to speak of "*identification*," not only in the purely formal sciences where identity consists in the *logical* synonymy of two or more expressions, but also in those cases in which the mode of ascertainment is empirical. The important consequence for our problem is then this: Concepts of molar behavior theory like habit strength, expectancy, drive, instinct, memory trace, repression, superego, etc., may yet be identified in a future psychophysiology with specific types of neural-structure-and-process-patterns. The identification, involving as it will, factual discoveries, is empirical in its mode of certification, but it is an identification nonetheless.

E. *Arguments Concerning the Identification of Sentience with Neural Events.* I shall now present, as explicitly as I can, the reasons for an empirical identification of raw feels with neural processes. I shall also discuss several apparently trenchant arguments that have been advanced against this identity theory of the mental and the physical. It will be advisable first to state my thesis quite succinctly, and to elaborate the arguments for and against it afterwards.

Taking into consideration everything we have said so far about the scientific and the philosophical aspects of the mind-body problem, the following view suggests itself: The raw feels of direct experience as we "have" them, are empirically identifiable with the referents of certain specifiable concepts of molar behavior theory, and these in turn (this was argued in the preceding subsection *D*) are empirically identifiable with the referents of some neurophysiological concepts. As we have pointed out, the word "mental" in present day psychology covers, however, not only the events and processes of direct experience (i.e., the raw feels), but also the unconscious events and processes, as well as the "intentional acts" of perception, introspective awareness, expectation, thought, belief, doubt, desire, volition, resolution, etc. I have argued above that since *intentionality* as such is to be analyzed on the one hand in terms of pure semantics (and thus falls under the category of the *logical*, rather than the psychological), it would be a category mistake of the most glaring sort to attempt a neurophysiological identification of this aspect of "mind." But since, on the other hand, intentional acts as occurrents in direct experience are introspectively or phenomenologically describable in something quite like raw-feel terms, a neural identification of *this* aspect of mind is prima facie not excluded on purely logical grounds. Unconscious processes, such as those described in psychoanalytic theory, are methodologically on a par with the concepts of molar behavior theories (as, e.g., instinct, habit strength, expectancy, drive, etc.) and hence offer in principle no greater difficulties for neurophysiological identification than the concepts of molar behavior

445

theory which refer to *conscious* events or processes (e.g., directly experienced sensations, thoughts, feelings, emotions, etc.). As we have repeatedly pointed out, the crux of the mind-body problem consists in the interpretation of the relation between raw feels and the neural processes. The questions to be discussed are therefore these:

1. What does the identity thesis assert about the relation of raw feels to neural events?

2. What is the difference, if there is a difference, between psychophysiological parallelism (or epiphenomenalism) and the identity thesis?

3. Can the identity thesis be defended against empirical arguments which support an interactionistic dualism?

4. Can the identity thesis be defended against philosophical arguments which support dualism on the grounds of the alleged fundamental differences between the properties of direct experience and the features of physical (neurophysiological) processes?

Since I have already paved the way for at least partial replies to question 3, and to some extent also to 4, I shall now primarily concentrate on questions 1 and 2, and discuss the other issues more briefly whenever they will be relevant.

The identity thesis which I wish to clarify and to defend asserts that the states of direct experience which conscious human beings "live through," and those which we confidently ascribe to some of the higher animals, are identical with certain (presumably configurational) aspects of the neural processes in those organisms. To put the same idea in the terminology explained previously, we may say, what is *had-in-experience*, and (in the case of human beings) *knowable by acquaintance*, is identical with the object of *knowledge by description* provided first by molar behavior theory and this is in turn identical with what the science of neurophysiology *describes* (or, rather, will describe when sufficient progress has been achieved) as processes in the central nervous system, perhaps especially in the cerebral cortex. In its basic core this is the "double knowledge" theory held by many modern monistic critical realists.*

---

* Especially Alois Riehl, Moritz Schlick, Richard Gätschenberger, H. Reichenbach, Günther Jacoby, Bertrand Russell, Roy W. Sellars, Durant Drake, and C. A. Strong. To be sure, there are very significant differences among these thinkers. Russell has never quite freed himself from the neutral monism (phenomenalism) of his earlier neorealistic phase. R. W. Sellars and, following him on a higher level of logical sophistication, his son, Wilfrid, have combined their realistic, double-knowledge view with a doctrine of evolutionary emergence. Opposing the emergence view, Strong and Drake, originally influenced by F. Paulsen, adopted a panpsychistic metaphysics. My own view is a development in more modern terms of the epistemological outlook common

This view does not have the disadvantages of the Spinozistic doctrine of the unknown or unknowable *third* of which the mental and the physical are aspects. The "mental" states or events (in the sense of raw feels) are the referents (denotata) of both the phenomenal terms of the language of introspection, as well as of certain terms of the neurophysiological language. For this reason I have in previous publications called my view a "double-language theory." But, as I have explained above, this way of phrasing it is possibly misleading in that it suggests a purely analytic (logical) translatability between the statements in the two languages. It may therefore be wiser to speak instead of *twofold access* or *double knowledge*. The identification, I have emphasized, is to be *empirically* justified, and hence there can be no *logical* equivalence between the concepts (or statements) in the two languages.

On superficial reflection one may be tempted to regard the identification of phenomenal data with neurophysiological events as a case of the *theoretically* ascertainable identities of the natural sciences. "Theoretical identity" (explicated in section V D) means the sameness of the referent (universal or particular) of two or more *intersubjective* descriptions. For example, it is the atomic micro-structure of a crystal which is indicated ("described") by the optical refraction index, the dielectric constant, the magnetic permeability coefficient, and in greater detail evidenced by X-ray diffraction patterns. Similarly, the various behavioral indications for habit strength refer to a certain, as yet not fully specified, neurophysiological structure in a brain, which may ultimately be certified by more direct histological evidence. Logical Behaviorism admits only intersubjectively confirmable statements and hence *defines* mentalistic (phenomenal) terms explicitly on the basis of molar behavioral theoretical concepts. Thus, to ascribe to a person the experience of, e.g., an after-image amounts, within the intersubjective frame of reference, to the ascription of a hypothetical construct (theoretical concept), anchored in observable stimulus and response variables. This

to Riehl, Schlick, Russell, and to some extent of that of the erratic but brilliant Gätschenberger. The French philosopher Raymond Ruyer (289, 290) especially before he turned to a speculative and questionable neovitalism (293) held a similar view. Among psychologists W. Köhler (182, 183), E. G. Boring (40), and D. K. Adams (1), again differing in many important respects, hold similar monistic positions. Personally, I consider sections 22–35 in Schlick (298) as the first genuinely perspicacious, lucid and convincing formulation of the realistic-monistic point of view here defended. It is to be hoped that an English translation of this classic in modern epistemology will eventually become available.

theoretical concept may then later be identified, i.e., come to be regarded as *empirically* co-referential with the more detailed and deductively more powerful neurophysiological concept.

The empirical character of the identification rests upon the extensional equivalences, or extensional implications, which hold between statements about the behavioral and the neurophysiological evidence. In our example this means that all persons to whom we ascribe an after-image, as evidenced by certain stimulus and response conditions, also have cerebral processes of a certain kind, and vice versa. In view of the uncertainties and inaccuracies of our experimental techniques we can at present, of course, assert only a statistical correlation between the two domains of evidence. That is to say, the equivalences or implications are, practically speaking, only probabilistic. But in any case, the correlations as well as the theoretical identification of the referents indicated by various items of evidence are formulated in *intersubjectively* confirmable statements.

The identification of raw feels with neural states, however, crosses what in metaphysical phraseology is sometimes called an "ontological barrier." It connects the "subjective" with the "intersubjective." It *identifies* the referents of subjective terms with the referents of certain objective terms. But in my view of the matter there is here no longer an unbridgeable gulf, and hence no occasion for metaphysical shudders. Taking into account the conclusions of the preceding analyses of "privacy", "acquaintance", "physical", and of "identification", private states known by direct acquaintance and referred to by phenomenal (subjective) terms can be described in a public (at least physical$_1$) language and may thus be empirically identifiable with the referents of certain neurophysiological terms. Privacy is capable of public (intersubjective) description, and the objects of intersubjective science can be evidenced by data of private experience.

The application of phenomenal terms in statements of knowledge by acquaintance is *direct*, and therefore the verification of such statements (about the present moment of subjective experience) is likewise immediate. Phenomenal terms applied to other persons or organisms are used *indirectly*, and the confirmation of statements containing phenomenal terms (thus used) is *mediated* by rules of inference, utilizing various strands in the nomological net as rules of inference. Judging by the structure of one's own experience, there seems to be no reason to assume the existence of *absolutely* private mental states; i.e., there are presumably no "captive minds" in our world. This is of course a basic ontological feature of nature as we have come to conceive it. It is an *empirical* feature of a very fundamental kind, similar in its "basic frame" character to the $3 + 1$ dimensionality of space-time, or to the causal order of the universe. Such frame principles do not differ in kind, although they differ in degree of generality, from the postulates of scientific theories. Their adoption is essentially regulated by the rules of the hypothetico-deductive method.

Logical empiricism as it has come to be formulated in recent years (Carnap, 70, 73; Feigl, 116) recognizes the difference between direct observation (knowledge-by-acquaintance) statements and inferential statements as a *contextual* difference between direct and indirect confirmation. It does not matter precisely where, in our epistemological reconstruction, we draw the line between the observable and the inferred entities. But wherever we do draw it, the scope of the directly experienceable or of the directly observable depends on the identity of the experiencing and/or observing subject.* What is directly verifiable for one subject is only indirectly confirmable for another. And these very statements (expressed in the preceding two sentences) may be formalized in a pragmatic, intersubjective metalanguage.

Having formulated and in outline explicated the identity thesis, we now have to attend to several important points of philosophical interpretation. I reject the (Spinozistic) double aspect theory because it involves the assumption of an unknown, if not unknowable, neutral ("third") substance or reality-in-itself of which the mental (sentience) and the physical (appearance, properties, structure, etc.) are complementary aspects. If the neutral third is conceived as unknown, then it can be excluded by the principle of parsimony which is an essential ingredient of the normal hypothetico-deductive method of theory construction. If it is defined as *in principle* unknowable, then it must be repudiated as factually meaningless on even the most liberally inter-

* As I understand Dewey and other pragmatists, as well as contextualists like S. C. Pepper (254, 255), this point has been explicitly recognized by them. Cf. also the discussions by analytic philosophers, such as Hampshire (141), Watling (341), and Ayer (18). An exact logical account of the linguistic reflection of direct versus indirect verifiability has been given in the analysis of egocentric particulars (token-reflexive, indexical terms) by B. Russell (286), Reichenbach (274), Burks (58), W. Sellars (308, 312), and Bar-Hillel (20).

preted empiricist criterion of significance. But our view does not in the least suggest the need for a neutral third of any sort. This will now be shown more explicitly.

If a brain physiologist were equipped with the knowledge and devices that may be available a thousand years hence, and could investigate my brain processes and describe them in full detail, then he could formulate his findings in neurophysiological language, and might even be able to produce a complete microphysical account in terms of atomic and sub-atomic concepts. In our logical analysis of the meanings of the word "physical" we have argued that the physical sciences consist of knowl-edge-claims-by-description. That is to say that the objects (targets, ref-erents) of such knowledge claims are "triangulated" on the basis of various areas of observational (sensory) evidence. What these objects are acquaintancewise is left completely open as long as we remain within the frame of *physical* concept formation and theory construction. But, since in point of empirical fact, I am directly acquainted with the qualia of my own immediate experience, I happen to know (by acquaintance) what the neurophysiologist refers to when he talks about certain con-figurational aspects of my cerebral processes.

There is a danger at this point to lapse into the fallacies of the well-known doctrine of structuralism, according to which physical knowledge concerns only the *form* or *structure* of the events of the universe, where-as acquaintance concerns the *contents* or *qualia* of existence.* This doctrine is to be repudiated on two counts. First, by failing to distin-guish acquaintance (the mere *having* of data, or the capacity for imaging *some* of them) from *knowledge* by acquaintance (propositions, e.g., about similarities or dissimilarities, rank-orders, etc., of the qualia of the given), the doctrine fails to recognize that even introspective or phe-nomenological knowledge claims are *structural* in the very same sense in which *all* knowledge is structural, i.e., that it consists in the formu-lation of *relations* of one sort or another. Second, the realistic interpre-tation of physical knowledge which we have defended implies that what-ever we "triangulate" from various bases of sensory observation is to be considered as "qualitative" in a generalized sense of this term. In the vast majority of cases the qualitative content of the referents of physi-cal descriptions is *not* "given," i.e., it is not part of a phenomenal field.

* This doctrine has been espoused in various forms by Poincaré (257), Eddington (93), C. I. Lewis (195), Schlick (299), *et al.*

But it is a given content in the case of certain specifiable neurophysiological processes.

If one wishes to trace the historical origins of this view, one might find it, if not in Aristotle, then certainly in Kant who came very close to saying that the experienced content is the Ding-an-sich which corresponds to the brain process as known in the spatio-temporal-causal concepts of natural science.* To put it more picturesquely, in the physical account of the universe as provided in the four-dimensional Minkowski diagram, there are sporadically some very small regions (representing the brains of living and awake organisms) which are "illuminated by the inner light" of direct experience or sentience. This view differs from panpsychism which assumes that the "internal illumination" pervades all of physical reality. But the panpsychists' hypothesis is inconsistent with the very principles of analogy which they claim to use as guides for their reasoning. If one really follows the analogies, then it stands to reason that the enormous differences in behavior (and neural processes) that exist between, e.g., human beings and insects, indicate equally great differences in their corresponding direct experience or sentience. Fancying the qualities of sentience of the lower animals is best left to poetic writers like Fechner, Bergson, or Maeterlinck. As regards the mental life of robots, or of Scriven's (304) "androids," I cannot believe that they could display all (or even most) of the characteristics of human behavior unless they were made of the proteins that constitute the nervous systems—and in that case they would present no puzzle.

The identity view here proposed has met with a great deal of resistance, especially on the part of modern analytic philosophers. To be sure, there are identifications which are "above suspicion." For example, it has been suggested that a legitimate form of empirical identification is to be found in such paradigms as the identity of the "visual" with the "tactual" penny (or the visual, tactual, and olfactory rose; or the visual, tactual, and auditory bell). In each of these examples one may distinguish the various domains of sensory evidence from the particular thing (or thing-kind) that the evidence indicates or refers to. Phenomenalists will, of course, be quick to point out that there is no sense in talking of a thing existing over and above the actual and possible "evidential" data and their important correlations. But from my realistic

* Cf. I. Kant, Critique of Pure Reason, section on "The Paralogisms of Pure Reason."

point of view it makes perfectly good sense to explain in terms of physical, psychophysical, and psychophysiological theories how, e.g. a bell by reflecting light, producing sound waves and being a solid, hard body affects our retina, cochlea, and our tactile nerve endings (under specifiable perceptual conditions) and thus produces the visual, tactual, and auditory data in our direct experience. This is indeed the "causal theory of perception" so much maligned by phenomenalists.

We grant that as empiricists we must ultimately justify the causal theory of perception (which is indeed a *scientific* theory, and not an epistemological analysis) by reference to the evidential data which confirm it. And this we can do, no matter whether our own perceptions are concerned (in the egocentric perspective) or those of others (in the "side view" or lateral perspective that we obtain by observing the stimuli, central processes and responses pertaining to other persons). The various sensory "aspects" of the bell are thus to be conceived as the effects which the bell, considered either on the common sense level, or on the micro-level of scientific analysis, has upon our sense organs and finally on our awareness (this last effect empirically identifiable with processes in various cortical areas). Since the phenomenalist thesis of the translatability of physical object statements into data statements is untenable, epistemological analysis must "dovetail" with the causal (scientific) theory of perception and render justice to the latter by an explicit reconstruction of the *nomological* (not purely logical!) relations between the data and the illata. This is still *conceptual* analysis, in that it retraces the relations between the concepts of stimulus objects and the concepts pertaining to the central (cortical-mental) processes in the perceiving organisms.

Our ψ-Φ identification, however, *cannot* be conceived according to the paradigm of the identity of stimulus objects (like the bell, or the rose). The analogy is misleading in that we have, in the case of stimulus objects physical descriptions of them which together with the empirical laws of psychophysics and psychophysiology enable us (in principle) to derive their various sensory "appearances." Far from requiring an unknown or unknowable "third" or "neutral propertyless substance," ordinary knowledge and especially scientific theory contains a great deal of information about the nature and structure of stimulus objects. The situation in the ψ-Φ case is fundamentally different: We don't have two kinds of *evidence* for one and the same entity (event, process, etc.). In direct acquaintance we have, we experience the datum (it is not evidenced, it is evident!), and we identify it with a physical process which we posit as an illatum whose existence is asserted on the basis of multifarious data in other evidential domains.

It should now be clear how the view here proposed differs from the Spinozistic double aspect doctrine. The data of experience are the reality which a very narrow class of neurophysiological concepts denotes. I admit this sounds very "metaphysical." And I shall no doubt be accused of illegitimately extending the ordinary meaning of "denotation". I am fully aware that I am extending the meaning. But I plead that this does not involve my view in paradoxes or needless perplexities. It is true that in common parlance, as well as in the widely accepted philosophical usage, we would say that a term like "neural process in the occipital lobe" denotes a pattern of nerve currents, and not a visual experience. But this remark obviously comes down to the true but trivial semantical assertion that a term designates its designatum; (e.g., "neuron" designates neuron!).

A specification of meaning can be attained through semantic designation rules only if the meaning of the translation equivalent of the definiendum is already understood in the metalanguage. Obviously, according to the commonly accepted usage of the word, a "denotatum" is the referent of proper names, and (except for the null cases) also of predicates, relations, etc. A genuine specification of meaning for empirical terms can be achieved only by a combination of semantical, syntactical and pragmatic rules. The last two types of rules are particularly important. The syntactical rules specify the relations of concepts to one another, and the pragmatic ones make clear which concepts pertain to a basis of direct evidence. The realistic interpretation of empirical concepts depends on an appropriate analysis especially of the roles of proper names (and in scientific languages of coordinates) and of individual-variables (coordinate-variables).*

Taking these analyses into account, we can recognize the valid elements in the older critical realistic epistemology of perceptual and conceptual reference. A physical object or process as perceived in common life, or as conceived in science, is the referent of certain symbolic representations. I submit that it is the preoccupation with the confirmatory

---

* Cf. especially W. Sellars (308); H. Feigl (110, 111); Bar-Hillel (20).

evidence which has misled positivists and some pragmatists (all of them phenomenalists, radical empiricists, or operationists) to identify the meaning of physical object statements with the actual and/or possible data which, according to our view, merely constitute their evidential bases. Worse still, even sophisticated analytic philosophers tend to confuse the meaning of physical concepts with the perceived or imaged appearance of physical things. No wonder then that we are told that the identity of certain neurophysiological states (or features thereof) with raw feels is a logical blunder. If the denotatum of "brain process (of a specified sort)" is thus confused with the appearance of the gray mass of the brain as one perceives it when looking into an opened skull, then it is indeed logically impossible to identify this appearance with the raw feels, e.g., of greenness or of anxiety.

It would be a similarly bad logical blunder to identify such raw feels with the scientific (heuristic or didactic) tinkertoy models of complex molecular structures (as of amino acids, or proteins) displayed by chemistry instructors in their courses. I don't know whether I should call these blunders "category mistakes." The first one simply consists in the confusion of evidence with the evidenced, or of the indicator with the indicated. What mistake does one make if one confuses smoke with fire, footprints with a man walking, certain darkish spots on an X-ray photograph with tuberculosis? It is strange that of all people it should be the analytic philosophers (who would expose *these* fallacies with ruthless irony) who do not see that they are making the same sort of mistake in thinking that physical-object concepts denote the perceptual appearance of physical things.

As I have been at pains to point out (in section IV), the only consistent and philosophically fruitful meaning of "physical" (more precisely, of "physical$_1$") is that of a conceptual system anchored in sensory observation and designed for increasingly comprehensive and coherent explanations of the intersubjectively confirmable facts of observation. This conceptual system or any part of it is in principle non-intuitive (*unanschaulich* as the Germans call it, i.e., unvisualizable). Hence, an identification of a small subset of its referents with something directly given and knowable by acquaintance is in principle left completely open. In point of fact, the imagery commonly, and sometimes helpfully, employed in the thinking of theoretical physicists, biologists, or neurophysiologists consists primarily of *pictorial appeals*. These are at best intellectual crutches, fruitful only heuristically or didactically, and not to be confused with conceptual meanings. The fallacy of "introjection" * which was so vigorously criticized by Avenarius (the empiriocriticist of the last century) consists in the *pictorial* ascription of raw feels to other organisms. As we have seen, such ascriptions indeed clash with the (equally pictorial) ascriptions of physical-appearance properties to other persons or animals.

In the perceptual awareness of other organisms we are confronted with their *behavior*, i.e., their responses, facial expressions, tone of voice, gait, posture, linguistic utterances, etc., but never with their raw feels. Raw feels do not and cannot be fitted into the appearance picture. They must therefore be conceived as the subjective counterpart of these appearances. As such they are inferentially attainable but not perceptually accessible. At an earlier point we have already discussed the phenomenology of the alleged intuitive or empathetic apprehension of the mental states of other organisms. Since we must recognize intuitive or empathetic ascriptions as fallible and corrigible, they have to be regarded as *inferential* from the point of view of *logical* reconstruction (i.e., in the context of justification), no matter how immediate, "self-evident," compelling, or convincing they may be *psychologically*.

That "introjection" in this sense leads to absurdities becomes especially clear when we consider the ascription of phenomenal fields, e.g., of visual spatiality to other persons. Unless we are solipsists, there is every good reason in the world to ascribe to others the same sort of "life space" (phenomenal environment) which we find so distinctly within our own experience. But if we think of other persons in terms of their appearance in our own phenomenal environment, then it is impossible to ascribe (pictorially) to them also the particular perspectives that they perceive of their environment (or of parts of their own bodies). The fallacy is just as gross as in the case of expecting to find in the brain of another person looking at a green tree a little picture of that tree. But pictorial thinking is one thing, and conceptual thinking is quite another. For *conceptual* ascription, however, there is no difficulty. The *concepts* of neurophysiology are non-intuitive and must not be confused with their logically irrelevant pictorial connotations. These connotations lend, psychologically speaking, a certain "root flavor" to

* The term "introjection" as used by R. Avenarius has nothing to do with the well-known homonymous psychoanalytic concept.

these concepts. But once the pictorial appeals connected with the evidential roots of our physical or neurophysiological concepts are dismissed as irrelevant, they no longer pre-empt those places in the conceptual system of which we may then say that they denote some raw feels.

For these reasons I think that once the proper safeguards are applied, no category mistakes are made if we combine phenomenal and physical terms, as indeed we do quite ingenuously not only in ordinary discourse but also in the language of psychology. There is no reason why we should not say, e.g., "The anticipation of success quickened his pace"; "Morbid and tormenting thoughts caused his loss of appetite"; "Touching the hot stove caused intense pain"; "His repressed hostilities finally produced a gastric ulcer"; etc. Category mistakes do arise from confusions of universals with particulars; or of dispositions with occurrents. The first sort of category mistake certainly consists in a violation of the Russellian rule of types. I am not sure whether the second sort can always be reduced to the first. But the original diagnosis made especially by Carnap in his early (phenomenalistic) work (60) of the mind-body perplexities as Russellian-type confusions is no longer acceptable. Physical concepts are *not* logical constructions out of phenomenal concepts.

A more serious objection to identification comes from reflections upon Leibniz's principle of the identity of indiscernibles. Since we have not only admitted, but repeatedly emphasized the *empirical* nature of the ψ-Φ identification, one may well ask how we can speak of *identity* if its confirmation requires the observation of empirical regularities. The most direct confirmation conceivable would have to be executed with the help of an autocerebroscope. We may fancy a "compleat autocerebroscopist" who while introspectively attending to, e.g., his increasing feelings of anger (or love, hatred, embarrassment, exultation, or to the experience of a tune-as-heard, etc.) would simultaneously be observing a vastly magnified visual "picture" of his own cerebral nerve currents on a projection screen. (This piece of science fiction is conceived in analogy to the fluoroscope with the help of which a person may watch, e.g., his own heart action.) Along the lines of the proposed realistic interpretation he would take the shifting patterns visible on the screen as evidence for his own brain processes. Assuming the empirical core of parallelism or isomorphism, he would find that a "crescendo" in his anger, or in the melody heard, would be corresponded by a "crescendo" in the "correlated" cortical processes. (Similarly for "accelerandos," "ritardandos," etc. Adrian's and McCulloch's experiments seem to have demonstrated a surprisingly simple isomorphism of the shapes of geometrical figures in the visual field with the patterns of raised electric potentials in the occipital lobe of the cortex.) According to the identity thesis the directly experienced qualia and configurations are the realities-in-themselves that are denoted by the neurophysiological descriptions. This identification of the denotata is therefore *empirical*, and the most direct evidence conceivably attainable would be that of the autocerebro-scopically observable regularities.

Any detailed account of the ψ-Φ identities is a matter for the future progress of psychophysiological research. But in the light of the scanty knowledge available even today, it is plausible that only certain types of cerebral processes in some of their (probably configurational) aspects are identical with the experienced and acquaintancewise knowable raw feels. A "psychological physiology" * which frames hypotheses about neural structures and processes on the basis of a knowledge of the characteristics and the regularities in the changes of phenomenal fields must therefore always remain extremely sketchy. Knowledge by acquaintance of phenomenal fields alone cannot possibly yield more than a few strands of the total nomological net of neurophysiological concepts required for the explanation of molar behavior. The identification is therefore restricted to those elements, properties, or relations in the neural processes which (in dualistic parlance) are the "correlates" of the raw feels. In our monistic account this is tantamount to the identity of the denotata directly labeled by phenomenal terms, with the *denotata* of neural descriptions. These latter denotata are acquaintancewise unknown to the neurophysiologist, except if he uses the autocerebroscope himself.

Now it is clear that neural correlates (to speak for the sake of easier exposition once more dualistically) are denoted by concepts which are much richer in meaning than the corresponding phenomenal concepts. The neurophysiological concepts refer to complicated, highly ramified patterns of neuron discharges, whereas their raw-feel correlates may be simple qualities or relations in a phenomenal field. How can, e.g., a uniform patch of greenness, a single musical tone, a stinging pain be identical with a complex set of neural events? Here again it is essential to distinguish between the *scientific* and the *philosophical* components of

---

* Advocated by W. Köhler (184, 185) and critically discussed by C. C. Pratt (260).

this question. Our psychophysiological ignorance is still too great to permit anything more than bold guesses on the scientific side.

There has been talk of "thresholds" and "fusion"; i.e., it is assumed that raw feels emerge only if the intensities of the neural patterns have reached a certain degree; and that complex neural patterns may be "fused" so that the emerging quality "appears" simple and uniform. This sort of talk, though dangerously apt to mislead, is not entirely illegitimate. Talk of thresholds, limens, and fusion is of course quite customary and proper in *psychophysics*, but its extension to *psychophysiology* is precarious. It makes perfectly good sense, and is true, to say that the white and black sectors on a swiftly rotating disk phenomenally fuse and yield a uniformly gray appearance. It makes perfectly good sense also, and is equally true, that the intensity of physical stimuli (like light, sound, pressure on one's skin, concentration of chemical substances in the air, etc.) must surpass a certain lower limiting value, if they are to effect a sensation in any of the various modalities (sight, hearing, touch, smell, etc.).

If these facts have any analogies in the intra-cerebral sphere, it would have to be assumed that one area of the cortex "taps" or "scans" other areas and could thus not come to react unless the input reaches a certain intensity. Likewise, one would have to assume that the effect in the second area reflects only certain gross features of the intricate and multifarious process patterns in the first. These would be the analogues of psychophysical thresholds and fusions. Finally, one may assume that the second area (which corresponds to the sensing of the raw feels) is connected with another area corresponding respectively to awareness or judgment (as in introspection) and finally to a motoric area of the cortex which innervates expressive responses or speech.* May I say again that I don't for a moment insist on the scientific adequacy of this particular model. I am not trying to do armchair neurophysiology. All I am concerned to point out is that models are conceivable which would enable us to remove the obstacles arising from the apparent disparities of phenomenal unity versus physical multiplicity; phenomenal spatialities and physical space; phenomenal time and physical time; phenomenal purposiveness and physical causality; etc. I am now going to outline these considerations very briefly.

---

* I am indebted to R. Carnap for suggesting (in conversations) this sort of brain model.

W. Köhler (182, 183, 185) and R. Ruyer (290, 292, 293) have convincingly shown that the notorious Cartesian perplexities regarding spatiality can be removed by closer attention to the facts of psychophysiology combined with a logical clarification of the distinction between phenomenal space(s) and physical space. (We have laid the groundwork for this in section III B). The surface of objects "physically" outside my skin naturally appears in my visual space as external to the visual appearance of those parts of my body which I can see. There is histological and physiological evidence for a relatively simple projection of the excitation patterns in the retina of the eye, in the area of the occipital lobe of the cerebral cortex. The projection, in its physical and geometrical aspects, is similar to the sort of projection one gets on the screen of a periscope inside a submarine. Not only parts of the surrounding surface of the sea and of other ships, but also parts of the (surfacing) submarine itself are projected upon the screen. Similarly, when I lie on a couch I find not only the appearances of tables, chairs, walls, and windows within my visual field, but I find these object appearances phenomenally outside that part of my phenomenal body (chest, arms, hands, legs, feet) which is also included in my visual field. These simple reflections show that some of the older philosophical puzzles about the outward projection of visual percepts from my mind or brain into the external world are gratuitous, based on confusions, and resolvable by proper attention to the scientific facts on the one hand and to the meanings of spatial terms and phraseologies on the other.

The resolution of the perplexities regarding phenomenal versus physical time, as well as experienced purposiveness versus physical or physiological causality proceeds quite analogously. In the phenomenally temporal "projection" we locate ends-in-view at some distance in the future, and then go about attaining these ends by action, i.e. by the utilization of means. If, e.g., I decide to attend a lecture, I may have to go through a long chain of acts, such as walking to my garage, starting my car, driving to the auditorium, and getting seated there. My actions are clearly goal directed, but there is no need for the myth about the later events (the goal) influencing my antecedent behavior. My behavior is guided, controlled, or modulated by the goal *idea* which is contemporaneous with my instrumental acts, or possibly precedes them. What in the phenomenal description appears like a future event in my life career determining my current behavior, becomes in the causal account the effect of one part of my cerebral processes upon another. Of course in this case, just as in the case of memory (recollection), our thinking is essentially mediated by symbols; and therefore "intentionality" (cf. section IV F) plays an important role here. But the symbolic *representation* of past events or of future events is effected by processes occurring now; i.e., these representations are causal factors in the determination of current behavior. Just as there is no need for a curious notion of "final" causes (or, in Lecomte de Noüy's phrase, of "telefinality"), there is no need for the assumption of a literal presence of the past in present recollections. Whatever the adequate and detailed neurophysiological account of memory traces may ultimately turn out to be, it is these memory traces and not some direct and mysterious apprehension of past events which will causally account for the facts of recollection and of the modification of behavior through learning processes.

Similar considerations would seem to apply to the perennial puzzles concerned with the problems of the nature of the "*self*," i.e., the unity of the *ego*, or the unity of consciousness. Here, as in the other puzzles just discussed, the phenomenological descriptions may be correlated with the neurophysiological explanations. Phenomenally there may or may not be a "central core," the "I," in all my experiences. We may admit, following Hume and the later empiricists in the Humean tradition, that there is no distinct element, datum, or impression that could properly be regarded as the self. But it is hard to deny that in the directly given data and in their succession throughout experienced time, there is a certain feature of centralization, coordination, organization, or integration—the reader may choose whichever term seems most suitable. This unitary organization seems to rest on the ever-present potentialities of recollecting a great many events or sequences of events of one's (sic!) past; the ever present possibility of the occurrence of somatic data (referring to one's own body); the existence of a set of dispositions or behavior tendencies, including those ascribed (psychoanalytically) to the superego (i.e., in plain language our set of values and ideals as incorporated in one's conscience); and finally that conception of one's self which is largely a result of the realization of one's own character and personality, adequately or often very inadequately derived from interpretations of one's own behavior and one's social role as perceived by oneself or by others in the social context.

Whichever of these aspects are in some sense phenomenally "given"—

460

and I suggest a good many may well be so given—these aspects very likely "correspond" to (or according to my view, are identical with) certain relatively stable patterns of cerebral structures and functions. In the pathological cases of split or of alternating personalities (of the Sally Beauchamp, or of the Dr. Jekyll and Mr. Hyde varieties), it has often been suggested that we deal with cerebral subsystems, each having "organic unity" in itself, but only one of them dominating in the determination of behavior during certain intervals of time. If according to psychoanalytic theory large parts of the *id* as well as of the *super-ego* are unconscious, this may well be interpreted by assuming that certain portions of the cerebral processes are blocked off (this corresponds to "repressed") from the areas of awareness and of verbal report.

Having rendered plausible the *scientific* feasibility of at least a *parallelistic* account of some of the striking and remarkable features of mental life, I return now to the *philosophical* or *logical* crux of the *identity* thesis. We have stressed that the (empirical!) identification of the mental with the physical consists in regarding what is labeled in knowledge by acquaintance as a quale of direct experience as identical with the denotatum of some neurophysiological concept. The scientific evidence for parallelism or isomorphism is then *interpreted* as the *empirical* basis for the identification. The step from parallelism to the identity view is essentially a matter of philosophical interpretation. The principle of parsimony as it is employed in the sciences contributes only one reason in favor of monism. If isomorphism is admitted, the dualistic (parallelistic) position may be retained, but no good grounds can be adduced for such a duplication of realities, or even of "aspects" of reality. The principle of parsimony or of inductive (or hypothetico-deductive) simplicity does oppose the operationistic predilection for speaking of two (or more) concepts if the evidential facts, though completely correlated, are qualitatively heterogeneous.

Our view of "triangulation" under such conditions of convergence has, I trust, shown the operationist view to be by far too restrictive. But there is still the *logical* question how concepts with such fundamentally different evidential bases can be interpreted as (empirically) identifiable. In the case of the concept of the electric current (cf. above section V C) as measured by its magnetic, chemical or thermal, etc. effects, the identification of the several operationally introduced concepts is plausible enough. But, it will again be asked, how can we speak

461

of identity in the entirely different psychophysiological case where one of the concepts is characterized by the direct applicability of subjective acquaintance terms and the other (the physiological) is introduced on an intersubjective basis and thus has its evidential roots in the sensory data of any qualified observer? I think the answer is not so difficult any more. If we first consider "acquaintance" in its ordinary usage, we can certainly say that Anthony Eden is *acquainted* with Queen Elizabeth II, and I am not (never having had the opportunity of meeting her). Nevertheless, I can lay claim to some knowledge about the Queen, based on newspaper reports, pictures, and the like. It is surely the *same* person that Eden and I know, each in his way. Closer to the point, I know by acquaintance what it is to have an eidetic musical-image experience (I occasionally "hear with my inner ear" entire passages from symphonies, string quartets, etc. in their full tone colors). Someone else lacking this sort of experience does not know it by acquaintance, but he can know *about* it, especially if he is a skillful experimental psychologist. It would be unparsimonious to assume that the psychologist and I are *referring* to two different (but correlated) processes.

Now, direct acquaintance with "private" raw feels is describable also in the intersubjective language of science. Its ultimate explanation may again have to refer to various cerebral areas, one of which (speaking for ease of exposition again dualistically) "corresponds" to *sensing*, another to *judging*, and possibly another yet corresponds to (introspective) *reporting*. I conclude that acquaintance statements differ only in the type and domain of *evidence*, but not in regard to their *reference*, from certain neurophysiological statements. Since the neural apparatus of introspection differs most markedly from that of (external) perception, it should not be surprising that knowledge by acquaintance (now taken in its *narrow* epistemological sense) is so much more crude, undetailed, and imprecise, than knowledge based on sense perception, especially when this is aided by the instruments of science.

Direct awareness, as we have pointed out before, usually furnishes only qualitative or topological orderings of the contents of phenomenal fields. It could not by itself inform us about the cerebral localization of subjective experience. A very crude (but, if taken literally, I fear highly misleading) analogy might help illuminate this point. A man lost in a jungle perceives the trees and undergrowth in his immediate environment. But the location of this very same part of the jungle can be determined in a much more accurate and encompassing manner by a cartographer making his measurements from the vantage point of an airplane or balloon high above the jungle. This simile is misleading, of course, in that *both* the lost wanderer *and* the cartographer use sensory perception as evidential bases for their knowledge claims. This clearly differs from the case in which I report (or "avow" as Ryle puts it), e.g., a feeling of anxiety and a behavioral psychologist infers my anxiety from the "symptoms," or a neurophysiologist recognizes it in the "corresponding" cerebral processes. Nevertheless, I fail to see that the difference, important though it is in many ways, affects the argument for the identification of the *referents* of the introspective avowal, with those of the two scientific descriptions.

I conclude that ψ-Φ identity as I conceive it is then still an identity of indiscernibles as defined by Leibniz and Russell. But as the clarification of the "paradox of analysis" (cf. Feyerabend, 120) and of related puzzles about belief sentences should by now have made amply clear, mutual substitutivity even of *logically* synonymous expressions holds only in non-pragmatic contexts. The *empirical* synonymy of ψ and Φ terms (or, more cautiously perhaps, their empirical *co-reference*) a fortiori does not allow for substitutivity in pragmatic contexts. By this I mean that the "*salva veritate*" condition is fulfilled only in contexts of substitution which do *not* depend on what we *know*, or what *evidence* we have for our knowledge claims. As we pointed out before, there are or were many people (primitive, ancient, etc.) who have no idea of the association of mental life with cerebral processes. But it is nevertheless as justifiable to speak of identity here as it is in the case of "Walter Scott = the author of the Waverley novels," regardless of whether this fact is known or unknown to a given person. In this particular and well-worn example the identity concerns an individual. But, not being a nominalist, I see no difficulties in the identity of a universal, named or described in various ways. Psychophysiological identity may be identity of particulars (*this* twinge of pain with a specific cerebral event at a certain time), or of universals (pain of a certain *kind*, and a *type* of cerebral process).

I am finally going to tackle more specifically and pointedly the question: What is the difference that makes a difference between the parallelism and the identity doctrines? The pragmatist-positivist flavor of this question suggests that it concerns empirically testable differences. But I have already admitted that there are no such differences and that there could not be any, as far as conceivable empirical evidence is concerned. Is the identity thesis then a piece of otiose metaphysics? Whether it is metaphysics depends of course on what one means by "metaphysics". As I see it, the question is not only similar, but indeed intimately related, to such "metaphysical" issues as realism versus phenomenalism, or the modality versus the regularity view of causality. As most philosophers nowadays realize, these issues, unlike disputes regarding *scientific* theories cannot be decided by empirical tests. These questions concern the explication of the meaning of concepts and assumptions. They are a subject matter for logical analysis.

As to whether there is a tenable meaning of "causal necessity" related to regularity, but not reducible to it, is a highly controversial issue today. My own reflections favor a view of causal modalities (possibility, necessity, impossibility) which explicates the use of these terms metalinguistically, and nevertheless does not conflict with Hume's basic, and in my opinion irrefutable, contention; viz., that (if I may put it in my own way) the only *evidence* we can ever have for the assertion of causal connections must be observed regularities. There is, as I see it, no *test* for causal necessity over and above the tests for regularity. But this does not preclude *meaning* from the distinction between *accidental* and *necessary* universal synthetic statements. A world is conceivable in which a certain metal with a high melting point (say, e.g., platinum) everywhere and always in the infinite history of that world occurs in the solid state, simply because the temperature in that world "happens" never anywhere to surpass a certain upper limit. In such a world the universal statement "$(x,y,z;t)(Pt_{xyzt} \supset S_{xyzt})$," i.e., "platinum is everywhere and always solid" would be a true universal statement. But the counterfactual conditional "if the temperature *were* ever to reach or surpass a certain value, platinum *would* melt" might even be deducible from the basic laws of physics of that world. The universal statement in question is accidentally true. It is not a consequence of a basic *law* of nature; its truth depends on certain contingent features of the initial and boundary conditions of the fancied world. This shows that there are meaningful distinctions for which no conceivable empirical test could be designed.

Even closer to our problem is the issue between realism and phenomenalism. As I have shown elsewhere (110), there is again no *testable* difference between these two interpretations of factual knowledge, but there are excellent reasons for the repudiation of phenomenalism and hence for the acceptance of a realistic epistemology. To relegate the issue to the limbo of metaphysics is a lazy man's way of saving himself the troubles of careful analysis. But close attention to the logic of evidence and reference shows that phenomenalism, even in its most liberal forms does not and cannot substantiate its translatability doctrine; and that only a view which relates phenomenal evidence *synthetically* to statements about physical objects is ultimately tenable.

It is precisely because realists locate both the *evidence* and the *evidenced* within the nomological net, that they can give a more adequate account of the relation between "the knower and the known" than positivists, pragmatists, or operationists have ever been able to provide. And it is for this very same reason, that our view of the nature of physical concepts enables us to identify *some* (of course very few only!) of their referents with the referents of raw feel terms. Dazzled by the admittedly tremendous importance of the evidential basis for our knowledge claims, positivists have regrettably neglected the very *objects* of those knowledge claims. They have myopically flattened them into the surface of evidence, and thus prevented themselves from giving a viable account of the concepts of physics; and they have merely evaded or repressed the mind-body problem which they thought would vanish if their "reductions"—phenomenalistic or behavioristic—were accepted. Ingenious and tempting though their more sophisticated endeavors of reduction have been, they did not succeed. This is why I felt that an explicit reinstatement and defense of a realistic solution of the mind-body problem would be timely and worthwhile.

VI. A Budget of Unsolved Problems. Suggestions for Further Analyses and Research

Although I have proposed what I believe to be at least a fairly circumspect sketch of an adequate solution of the mind-body problems, there are a number of specific component issues which require a great deal of further clarification and investigation. Since I am more interested in the continuing endeavors in this field than in having said the "last word" about it (that's almost inconceivable, in philosophy at any rate!), I shall now attempt to state and discuss succinctly a number of questions to which I have no entirely satisfactory answer at present. I should be immensely pleased if others were to take up these questions in their own work.

Herbert Feigl

The foregoing analyses and discussions were intended to bring to a level of full awareness many of the repressed difficulties of our problem. I have been especially concerned to separate, as well as I could, the scientific from the philosophical issues. And I have tried to show that there are no *insuperable* logical difficulties for an identity theory of the mental and the physical. I shall again divide the discussion into two parts. The first (*A, B, C*) will be concerned with open *philosophical* questions and difficulties. The second (*D*) will appraise much more briefly the acceptability of identity theory in the light of possibly forthcoming heterodoxical *scientific* discoveries.

A. *Is There a Phenomenal Language? The Relations of Meaning, Evidence, and Reference.* The central core of the proposed solution rests upon the distinction between evidence and reference. No matter what indirect (behavioral) evidence we use for the ascription of mental states, the mental state ascribed is not to be confused with the evidence which only lends support to the ascription. A fortiori, we must eliminate the still worse confusion of the pictorial appeals (attached to evidential terms) with the conceptual meaning or the reference of neurophysiological concepts. The only case in which pictorial appeals or imagery may be thought to play an essential role in knowledge claims is at the ultimate phenomenal basis of the confirmation of all knowledge claims. And, as we have pointed out, if and only if these knowledge claims are so extremely restricted as to refer exclusively to a currently experienced datum, then—in this very special case—evidence and reference coincide. "Now green", "now anger", "now green spot on a gray background", "stinging pain suddenly increasing", etc. might be examples. The last example shows that the indexical term "now" need not appear in the phenomenal sentence; but of course the sentence is in the present tense, and this is presumably equivalent with the occurrence of the indexical "now".

It is difficult to decide whether indexical terms (i.e., egocentric particulars like "now", "I", "here", "this") are indispensable constituents of singular phenomenal sentences. There are, of course, many examples of *universal* statements which contain only *phenomenal* terms as descriptive signs (in addition to purely logical signs): "Orange is more similar to red than it is to green"; "Whatever is colored is extended (in the visual field)"; "Anger always subsides after some time"; etc. There is also the difficult question whether phenomenal sentences

466

can contain proper names (or something like topological coordinates) for elements in the phenomenal fields. One of my examples suggested that one might use proper names for the small bright spots on the dark background of a visual field and thus describe their relative positions in terms of such relations as "to the left of", "above", and "far below" It seems clear that there is a danger of logical paradoxes, engendered by category mistakes, if we try to mix phenomenal sentences of this sort with the usual behaviorally based ascriptions of mental states to organisms. In these behavioral ascriptions the organism (or the person?) is the individual which is represented by the subject term of the sentence; the predicate is then something like "sees green", "sees an array of bright spots on a dark background". There can then be no direct translation of sentences in which the subject terms denote elements in a phenomenal field, into sentences in which the subject terms denote individual organisms. But perhaps there can be an *empirical* coreference between statements about some (configurational) aspects of neural fields and those about phenomenal fields.

The precise logical explication of empirical identity or coreference is fraught with many difficulties. Some of these stem from the tendency to think of *meaning* as *intension*, and then to conceive of intension in terms of its simplest picturable examples. *Blueness* is an intension indeed, but what are the intensions of "energy", "entropy", "electric field strength", "electric charge", "neuron discharge", "reverberating neural circuit"? In all these other cases the intensions are non-intuitive and can be specified only by postulates and correspondence rules. Similarly non-intuitive are the elements of the corresponding extensions, or the denotata. It does seem to me that we can rightly say that both the intension and the extension of the theoretical concepts of the physical sciences are largely unknown by acquaintance, and that only a very small selection of them can therefore be identified with the intensions and extensions of concepts-by-acquaintance. But of course the latter presuppose the existence of a phenomenal language. It has indeed been seriously questioned as to whether there is a phenomenal language at all. In the usual, and full-fledged sense, "language" means a symbolic system with specifiable syntactical (formation and transformation) rules, semantical (designation) rules, and pragmatic (verification) rules. Scraps and bits of phenomenal phraseology seem to fulfill these requirements, but an overall system like that of the physical language does not seem attainable.

Herbert Feigl

The difficulties are further complicated by the question on which level of analysis we are to specify elements and relations described by phenomenal sentences. There is a long history of objections against the Hume-Mach-Russell-Price analysis of experience into "hard" and "soft" data. Phenomenologists, Gestalt psychologists, and more recently many analytic philosophers have raised serious objections not only against the atomism or elementarism of the sense-data doctrine, but also against *any* doctrine of immediacy or of the given.*

I have throughout this essay maintained and argued that genuinely phenomenal or acquaintance terms are indispensable, not only for the reconstruction of the indirect confirmation of practically all our knowledge claims, but also as labels for the referents of some knowledge claims—whether they are about my own raw feels or that of other humans or animals. I have allowed for the possibility that the "hard data" (i.e., those data which we can talk about with a minimum of inference) are not preanalytically but only postanalytically "given." But on just what level of psychological, introspective, phenomenological, or logical analysis we find those data which stand in the required one-one correspondence to neural events, is an open question. With W. Köhler I am inclined to think that an analysis which stops at a relatively simple configurational level (but does not proceed further to "atomize" the given) may well yield the desired items on the ψ-side of the ψ-Φ isomorphism. But phenomenal description, even of the Gestalt type, is no easy matter.

B. *Unitary or Dual Language Reconstruction?* In most of the crucial parts of the present essay I have taken a unitary language to be the ideal medium of epistemological reconstruction. By this I mean the following: Both the phenomenal terms (designating raw feel data) and the illata terms (designating unobservables) occur in the language of commonsense or of science, and they are connected by strands in the nomological net. I believe that if this sort of unitary language is constructed with care, category mistakes can be avoided. This reconstruction differs essentially from the dual language reconstruction pursued by Carnap

---

* For some impressive arguments against atomism see W. Köhler (183, 184, 185), Brunswik (56), Wallraff (340); and against immediacy, Lean (193), Chisholm (75), Wittgenstein (357), Rhees (278), Quinton (270), W. Sellars (315). Others like Ryle (294), Black (38) and Quine (268) have denied the possibility of a phenomenal language altogether. W. Sellars admits phenomenal concepts only as theoretical terms in a language of behavior theory.

and W. Sellars (cf. their essays 73, 315). Purely phenomenal terms are there excluded, presumably owing to their conviction that category mistakes as well as solipsism would be unavoidable if we chose a phenomenal basis of reconstruction. But with the reinstatement of realism, i.e., with the insistence on the *synthetic* character of the strands in the nomological net, solipsism is no longer a consequence, and category mistakes can be avoided if we dismiss pictorial appeals as cognitively irrelevant, and if we take care to distinguish sharply between universals and particulars, among phenomenal as well as among non-phenomenal terms.

I admit, of course, that there are certain distinct advantages in the dual language reconstruction. All evidential statements are there couched in terms of the observation language; and the observation language is conceived as *intersubjectively* meaningful right from the beginning. The connections between the observation language and the theoretical language are formulated with the help of correspondence rules. This type of reconstruction is very illuminating in the analysis of the meaning and the confirmation of scientific theories. But, as I have pointed out, it does not do full justice to statements *about* the data of direct experience, whether they are one's own or someone else's. In our unitary language the "partition" between the data and the illata is located very differently. The correspondence rules in the unitary language would ultimately be statements of ψ-Φ correlations, i.e., of the raw-feel denotations of neurophysiological terms. Since precise knowledge of these correlations is only a matter of hope for a future psychophysiology, the unitary language is largely in the "promissory note" stage. It is therefore not very illuminating if our epistemological reconstruction is to reflect the progress of knowledge in our very unfinished and ongoing scientific enterprise. For this purpose, the dual language reconstruction is much more adequate.

But if we are satisfied with relatively low probabilities for the strands in the nomological net, the unitary reconstruction might do the job too. As a sketch for a reconstruction of an ideally finished science, however, the unitary language approach is preferable. What this would amount to can at present be indicated only by some sort of "science-fiction" illustration: Suppose that we had a complete knowledge of neurophysiology and that we could order all possible human brain states (if not metrically, then at least topologically) in a phase space of n dimensions. Every point in this phase space would then represent a fully specific type of brain state. And, taking isomorphism for granted, a subset of these points would also represent the total set of possible mental states.

Suppose further that we could teach children the vocabulary of the language of brain states. If this requires n-tuples of numbers, then simple expressions like "17-9-6-53-12" (or even abbreviatory symbols for these) might be inculcated in the child's language. If we took care that these expressions take the place of all introspective labels for mental states, the child would immediately learn to speak about his own mental states in the language of neurophysiology. Of course, the child would not know this at first, because it would use the expression, e.g., "17-9-6-53-12" as we would "tense-impatient-apprehensive-yet hopefully-expectant." But having acquired this vocabulary, the child, when growing up and becoming a scientist, would later have no trouble in making this terminology coherent with, and part of, the conceptual system of neurophysiology, and ultimately perhaps with that of theoretical physics. Of course, I not only admit, but I would stress, that in this transformation there is a considerable change in the meaning of the original terms. But this change may be regarded essentially as an enormous enrichment, rather than as a radical shift or a "crossing of ontological barriers." In other words, introspection may be regarded as an approach to neurophysiological knowledge, although by itself it yields only extremely crude and sketchy information about cerebral processes. This sort of information may concern certain Gestalt patterns, certain qualitative and semiquantitative distinctions and gradations; but it would not, by itself, contain any indication of the cerebral connections, let alone localizations.

C. *One-one Correspondence and the "Riddle of the Universe."* The isomorphism of the mental and the physical consists, according to our interpretation, in a one-one correspondence of elements and relations among the phenomenal data with the elements and relations among the referents of certain neurophysiological terms. And we proposed to explain this isomorphism in the simplest way possible by the assumption of the identity of phenomenal data with the referents of (some) neurophysiological terms. The question arises whether the identity view could be held if we were, for empirical reasons, forced to abandon ψ-Φ-one-one correspondence and to replace it by a doctrine of one-many correspondence. As was pointed out previously, the physicalistic predictability of the occurrence of mental states would in principle still be unique, if one-many correspondence holds true. Comparison with an example of the identification of purely physical concepts may shed some light on this issue. Macro-temperature, as thermometrically ascertained, corresponds in one-many fashion to a multitude of micro-conditions, viz., a very large set of molecular states. Strictly speaking, this correspondence holds between one state description on the macro-level with a specifiable infinite disjunction of state descriptions pertaining to the micro-level. Since, as we have also pointed out, this correspondence is empirically ascertained, there is here as little reason to speak of logical identity as in the ψ-Φ case. Nevertheless, we have seen that it makes sense, and what sense it makes, to regard the relation of temperature to mean molecular kinetic energy as an example of a theoretical identity.

In the mind-body case, just as in the temperature case, prediction of the ensuing micro- (and ultimately even macro-) constellations on the basis of information about, respectively, the mental state, or the macro-temperature state, could not be unique under the supposition of one-many correspondence. This is obvious for the temperature example in the light of the principles of statistical mechanics. Analogously, the precise behavior subsequent to the occurrence of a specified mental state would not be predictable either. This is not too disturbing by itself. After all, even if one-one correspondence held true, the neural correlates of a mental state would form only a very insignificant part of the relevant total initial conditions. Talk of identity in the case of one-many correspondence, however, would seem unjustified, because here we are (ex hypothesi) acquainted with the phenomenal datum, and the corresponding disjunction of cerebral states could not plausibly be identified with that individual datum.

Even if one-one correspondence is assumed, there is an intriguing objection * against the identity view. According to the view presented in section V, there is no empirically testable difference between the identity and the parallelism doctrines. We said that the step toward the identity view is a matter of philosophical interpretation. But, so the objection maintains, if identity is assumed, it would be logically impossible to have a stream of direct experience (a "disembodied mind")

---

* Raised in Minnesota Center for Philosophy of Science discussions by Mr. H. Gavin Alexander.

survive bodily death and decay. It is further asserted that this would not be a logically entailed consequence of parallelism. For it could well be maintained that the one-one correspondence holds only during the life of the person, but that as drastic an event as bodily death marks the limits of this correspondence. Mental states could then occur independently of physical correlates.

Thus it would seem as if our *philosophical* identity theory implied consequences which are testably different from those of parallelism. This is quite paradoxical. My tentative reply to this argument is twofold. First, ψ-Φ identification being empirical, it could of course be mistaken. But if the identity does hold, then survival is indeed logically impossible. This is logically quite analogous to the conditional: *If* the law of the conservation of energy holds, then a *perpetuum mobile* (of the "first kind") is thereby logically excluded. But, of course, the energy law has only empirical validity and might some day be refuted by cogent empirical evidence. Second, and perhaps more important, the parallelism doctrine, as I understand it, holds that there is a ψ-Φ-one-one correspondence and that this correspondence is a matter of *universal* and irreducible law. This seems to me to exclude disembodied minds just as much as does the identity thesis. I therefore think that the identity thesis is a matter of epistemological and semantic interpretation, and does not differ in empirical consequences from a carefully formulated parallelism.

Another perplexity was formulated in Leibniz's monadology, and in different form presented by E. Dubois-Reymond as one of his famous unsolvable "riddles of the universe." If I may put the core of the puzzle in modern form, it concerns the *irreducible* (synthetic) character of the ψ-Φ correlations. Wherever we find co-existential or correlational regularities in nature, we hope to find a unitary explanation for them, and in many cases scientific theories have provided fruitful and well-confirmed explanations of this sort. But in the case of the ψ-Φ correlation we seem to be confronted with a fundamentally different situation. There is no plausible *scientific* theory anywhere in sight which would explain just why phenomenal states are associated with brain states. Many philosophers have resigned themselves to regard the ψ-Φ correlations as "ultimate," "irreducible," "brute facts." Since any explanation presupposes explanatory premises which at least in the context of the given explanation must be accepted, and since even the introduction of higher explanatory levels usually reaches its limit after three or four "steps up," one might as well reconcile oneself to the situation, and say that "the world is what it is, and that's the end of the matter." Now, I think that it is precisely one of the advantages of the identity theory that it removes the duality of two sets of correlated events, and replaces it by the much less puzzling duality of two ways of knowing the same event—one direct, the other indirect.

Nevertheless, there are some "brute facts" also according to the identity theory. But they are located differently. Besides the basic physical laws and initial conditions, there are according to our view the only empirically certifiable identities of denotation of phenomenal and of physical terms. But this identity cannot be formulated in laws or law-like sentences or formulas. The identity amounts merely to the common reference of acquaintance terms on the one hand and unique physical descriptions on the other. Any other way of phrasing the relation creates gratuitous puzzles and avoidable perplexities. For example, it is misleading to ask, "Why does a mental state 'appear' as a brain state to the physiologist?" The brain-state-as-it-appears-to-the-physiologist * is of course analyzable into phenomenal data forming part of the direct experience of the physiologist. The "brute fact" simply consists in this, that the phenomenal qualities known by acquaintance to one person are known (indirectly) by description to another person on the basis of phenomenal (evidential) data which, in the vast majority of cases, are qualitatively quite different from the data had by, or ascribed to, the first person. I see nothing paradoxical or especially puzzling in this account of the matter.

A little reflection upon the autocerebroscopic situation shows clearly that the correspondence between, e.g., musical-tones-as-directly-experienced and certain excitation patterns in the temporal lobes of one's brain as represented by visual patterns (perceived on the screen) is simply a correlation between patterns in two phenomenal fields. The conceptual neurophysiological account of the visual data in this case consists in explanatory hypotheses about cerebral processes which are causally responsible for the production of the image on the screen, and these are in turn causally responsible for the emergence of certain patterns in the visual field. Strictly speaking, and in the light of physical

* No matter whether the physiologist observes someone else's brain, or—autocerebroscopically—his own.

473

laws, there must even be a minute time lag between the moment of the occurrence of a neural event in the temporal lobe and its "representation" via the autocerebroscope in one's own visual field. The experienced patterns in the visual field are in this situation the *causal* consequences of (among other things) the auditory data. Disregarding the small time lag we could here speak of a parallelism indeed. But this is a parallelism between the data (or patterns) in different sense modalities; or, in the case of visual experience autocerebroscopically "represented" by other visual data, within one and the same modality. (May I leave it to the reader to think this through and to find out for himself that this special case of autocerebroscopy does not involve any paradoxical consequences.)

Another puzzle that may be raised is the question as to whether the proposed identity theory does not involve the undesirable consequences of *epiphenomenalism*. It should be obvious by now that our solution of the mind-body problem differs quite fundamentally from materialistic epiphenomenalism in that: (1) it is *monistic*, whereas epiphenomenalism is a form of dualistic parallelism; (2) the "physical" is interpreted as a conceptual system (or as the realities described by it), but not as the primary kind of existence, to which the mental is appended as a causally inefficacious luxury, or "shadowy" secondary kind of existence; (3) quite to the contrary, mental states experienced and/or knowable by acquaintance are interpreted as the very realities which are also denoted by a (very small) subset of physical concepts. The efficacy of pleasure, pain, emotion, deliberation, volitions, etc. is therefore quite definitely affirmed. In this respect monism shares the tenable and defensible tenets, without admitting the objectionable ones, of interactionism.

Speaking "ontologically" for the moment, the identity theory regards sentience (qualities experienced, and in human beings knowable by acquaintance) and other qualities (unexperienced and knowable only by description) the basic reality. In avoiding the unwarranted panpsychistic generalization, it steers clear of a highly dubious sort of inductive metaphysics. It shares with certain forms of idealistic metaphysics, in a very limited and (I hope) purified way, a conception of reality and combines with it the tenable component of materialism, viz., the conviction that the basic laws of the universe are "physical." This means especially, that the teleology of organic processes, the goal directedness or purposiveness of behavior are macro-features, and that their explanation can be given in terms of non-teleological concepts and laws which hold for the underlying micro-levels. In other words, the monistic theory here proposed does not require irreducibly teleological concepts in its explanatory premises.

In this connection there is, however, a perplexity which may give us pause. Inasmuch as we consider it a matter of empirical fact and hence of logical contingency just which physical (neurophysiological) concepts denote data of direct experience (raw feels), one may wonder whether the causal efficacy of raw feels is satisfactorily accounted for. There are countless teleological processes in organic life which, unless we be panpsychists or psychovitalists, must be regarded as occurring without the benefit of sentience. For examples, consider the extremely "ingenious" processes of reproduction, growth, adaptation, restitution, and regeneration, which occur in lower organisms as well as in many parts of human organisms. On the other hand, the causal efficacy of attention, awareness, vigilance, pleasure, pain, etc. on the human level is so striking that one is tempted, with the panpsychists, to assume some unknown-by-acquaintance qualities quite cognate with those actually experienced.

The new puzzle of epiphenomenalism would seem to come down to this: An evolutionary, physiological, and possibly physical explanation of adaptation, learning, abient or adient, goal-directed behavior can be given without any reference whatever to raw feels. The distribution of raw feels over the various possible neural states could be entirely different from what in fact it is. For example, raw feels might be associated with the peristaltic movements of the stomach or with coronary self-repair, and not with cortical processes. But, I repeat, such different distribution of raw feels or even their complete absence would still not prevent an adequate explanation of teleological behavior. Of course if we accept the *actual* distribution, i.e., the total set of ψ-Φ-correlation rules as ultimate parallel laws, and interpret these according to the identity theory, then we can quite legitimately speak of the efficacy of raw feels. This is so, because the raw-feel terms are then precisely in those loci of the nomological net where science puts (what dualistic parallelism regards as) their neural correlates. But if the biopsychological explanations offered by the theories of evolution and of learning can thus incorporate the efficacy of raw feels, those theories presuppose, but do not by themselves explain, the ψ-Φ correlations.

Herbert Feigl

That pleasure or satisfaction reinforces certain forms of adient behavior can be formulated in the manner of the law of effect (cf. Meehl,
220). But in the ultimate neurophysiological derivation of this empirical law of behavior, the correlation of pleasure or gratification with
certain cerebral states is not required. Behaviorists, especially "logical
behaviorists," have taken too easy a way out here in simply *defining*
the pleasurable as the behaviorally attractive and the painful as the
behaviorally repellent. The "illumination" of certain physically described
processes by raw feels is plainly something a radical behaviorist cannot
even begin to discuss. But if the *synthetic* element in the ψ-Φ relations
that we have stressed throughout is admitted, then there is something
which purely physical theory does not and cannot account for. Is there
then a kind of "brute fact" which our monistic theory has to accept
but for which there is possibly no explanation, in the same sense as
there can be (within a naturalistic empiricism) no explanation for the
fact that our world is what it is in its basic laws and conditions? Possibly, however, I see a riddle here only because I have fallen victim to
one of the very confusions which I am eager to eliminate from the mind-
body problem. Frankly, I suspect some sort of "regression" rather than
"repression" has engendered my bafflement. If so, I should be most
grateful for "therapeutic" suggestions which would help in clearing up
the issue. Possibly, the solution may be found in a direction which
appears plausible at least for the somewhat related puzzle of the "inverted spectrum."

This ancient conundrum, we have seen, is not satisfactorily "dissolved" by Logical Behaviorism. A "captive mind" is logically conceivable, and might know by acquaintance that his sense qualia do not
stand in one-one correspondence to his autocerebroscopically ascertained
neural states. If physical determinism is assumed, then it is true that
such knowledge would have to remain forever private and uncommuni-
cable. But under these conditions a systematic interchange of the qualia
for one person at different times and as between different persons is
logically conceivable. It would of course ex *hypothesi* not be intersubjectively confirmable, and thus never be a possible knowledge claim of
science. But the logical conceivability of the inverted spectrum situation
demonstrates again the empirical character of the ψ-Φ correspondence.
This empirical character is, however, (as we have also emphasized) extremely fundamental in that it is closely bound up with the basic prin-

476

ciple of causality or of "sufficient reason." Systematic interchange of qualia for the same sort of neural states would be something for which, ex hypothesi, we could not state any good reasons whatever.

Furthermore, there is a grave difficulty involved in the assumption that a captive mind could even "privately" know about the interchange. Normal recollection by memory presumably involves (at least) quasideterministic neural processes. The captive mind could be aware of the inverted spectrum type of interchange of qualia only if we assume some peculiar breach in normal causality. If the captive mind is to *know* that today the correlation of raw feels with neural states differs from what it was yesterday, he would have to *remember* yesterday's correlations. But how could this be possible if memory depends upon modifications in the neural structures of the cortex? These considerations show clearly that under the supposition of normal physical causality the systematic interchange would remain unknowable even to the private captive mind. (Converse, but otherwise analogous, puzzles arise for the assumption of the survival of a private stream of experience beyond bodily death. How could such a private mind have knowledge about the continuance of his "physical" environment?)

All these reflections seem to me to indicate that in our world at least, there is nothing that is in principle inaccessible by "triangulation" on an intersubjective (sensory) basis. The *having* of raw feels is not knowledge at all, and knowledge by acquaintance does not furnish any truths which could not in principle also be confirmed indirectly by persons other than the one who verifies them directly. The ψ-Φ-identity theory as I understand it, makes explicit this "ontological" feature of our world. The criterion of scientific meaningfulness formulated in terms of intersubjective confirmability, far from being an arbitrary decree or conventional stipulation, may thus be viewed as having ontological significance—but "ontological" in the harmless sense of reflecting an inductively plausible, basic characteristic of our world.

Empirical identity, as I conceive it, is "weaker" than logical identity but "stronger" than accidental empirical identity, and like theoretical identity stronger than nomological identity in the physical sciences (just as causal necessity is weaker than logical necessity, but stronger than mere empirical regularity). If the coreference of a phenomenal term with a neurophysiological term is conceived as something more than mere extensional equivalence, if it is conceived as characteristic of the basic nature of our world (just as the basic natural laws characterize our kind of world and differentiate it from other kinds), then perhaps the inference from a neural state to its ("correlated") raw feel is at least as "necessary" (though of course not purely deductive) as is the inference from, e.g., the atomic structure of a chemical compound to its macro-physical and chemical properties.

I hope that readers sympathetic to my admittedly speculative gropings will try to formulate in logically more precise and lucid form what I have been able to adumbrate only so vaguely. Such readers should in any case keep in mind one of the ideas which seem to me indispensable for an adequate solution of the phenomenalism-realism as well as the mind-body problems: The paradigm of symbolic designation and denotation is to be seen in the relation of a token of a phenomenal term to its raw-feel referent. All non-phenomenal descriptive terms of our language, i.e., all physical terms (no matter on which level of the explanatory hierarchy) designate (or denote) entities which—within the frame of physical knowledge—are unknown by acquaintance. But if our "hypercritical" realism is accepted, we must ascribe denotata to all those physical terms which designate individuals, properties, relations, structures, fields, etc., i.e., entities which can justifiably be said to be *described* (i.e., uniquely characterized) on the basis of evidential data by Russellian descriptions on one or the other level in the hierarchy of logical types. "To exist" means simply to be the object of a true, uniquely descriptive statement. But since such descriptive knowledge (on a sensory evidential basis) by itself never enables us *deductively* to infer the acquaintance qualities of its objects, there is always a possibility for some sort of *modal* identification of a *datum* with a specifiable *descriptum*. This is the central contention of the present essay.

D. *Some Remarks on the Philosophical Relevance of Open Scientific Questions in Psychophysiology.* There are many problems of predominantly *scientific* character among the various mind-body puzzles. These await for their solution the further developments of biology, neurophysiology, and especially of psychophysiology.* We have touched on

* The following works and articles strike me as especially important, or at least suggestive, in these fields: Boring (40); Köhler (183, 184); Wiener (349); Hebb (145); Herrick (154); Adrian (3, 4, 5); Brain (46); Eccles (92); Ashby (9); McCulloch (214, 215); von Foerster (122, 123); Blum (39); Brillouin (49); Culbertson (80); Colby (76); Gellhorn (132); Krech (188, 189). Northrop's (240) exuberant and enthusiastic appraisal of the significance of cybernetics for the mind-body prob-

many of these issues in various parts and passages of the present essay. Speaking (again for ease of exposition only) the language of parallelism, there are, e.g., the following issues to be decided by further research concerning the specific ψ-Φ correspondences:

1. The problem of the cerebral *localization* of mental states and functions: Classical and recent experiments indicate quite specific localization for many processes. On the other hand, the findings of Lashley, Köhler, and others demonstrate a principle of mass action or of the equipotentiality of various cerebral domains.

2. The problem of the relation of phenomenal (visual, tactual, kinaesthetic, auditory, etc.) spatialities to physical space: The time-honored puzzle regarding (Lotze's) "local signs" is, as far as I know, not completely resolved. The question is by what neural mechanisms are we able to localize narrowly circumscribed events (like sensations of touch or of pain) more or less correctly on our skin or within our organism? Can we assume projection areas in the cortex which through learning processes come to interconnect afferent neural impulses in the different sensory modalities, and thus enable us to localize, e.g., visually what is first given as a tactual or pain sensation?

3. The problem of the nature of memory traces: Current fashion makes much of the reverberating circuits in neural structures. But it seems that while this explanation may do for short-range memory, it is probably not sufficient for long-range memory. Whether the lowering of neural or synaptic resistance is to be explained by "neurobiotaxis," by thickenings of the bud ends of dendrites, or by some chemical (quantum-dynamical) change in the neurons, is at present quite dubious.

4. The problem of the "specious present": The fact that the direct experience of one conscious moment embraces the events in a short stretch of finite duration, and not just an "infinitesimal" of physical time, presents a puzzle that is intriguing especially from a philosophical point of view. It is difficult, but I think not impossible to conceive of scanning mechanisms which "take note" of freshly accumulated traces, and even involve an extrapolative aspect as regards the immediate future.

5. The problem of the recollection of ordered sequences of past experiences: How can a brain process at a given time provide a correct

lem indicates at least one philosopher's response to the challenge of this new borderland discipline.

simultaneous representation of such a sequence? Philosophers are used to distinguishing a sequence of remembrances from the remembrance of a sequence of events. It seems that the latter can in certain instances occur in one moment of the specious present. Thus I seem to be aware of the sequence of themes and developments in the first movement of Beethoven's Seventh Symphony, and this awareness does not seem to require a quick internal rehearsal. It seems to be "all there at once." I also can, usually with fair reliability, recall the temporal sequence of many events in my life (various voyages, lecture engagements, first, second, third, etc. visits to Paris, and so on). Is it again some sort of "scanning" mechanism which might account for this? Driesch (87) considered it outright impossible to conceive any neurophysiological mechanism which would explain these phenomena, and believed that only a dualistic interactionism (involving a strictly immaterial mind or self, consonant with the rest of his vitalistic doctrines) could render justice to them. While I know of no obviously workable neural model that would do the trick, I think that Driesch, here as elsewhere, declared the defeat of naturalistic explanations prematurely. Present-day scientific findings and scientific theorizing have in so many cases shown the feasibility of physicochemical explanations of biological phenomena, so that we have good reasons to expect a successful solution of the problem of remembrance of past event-sequences.

6. The problems of "quality," "fusion," and "thresholds": I have dealt with these as best I could above (section V E), but there is no doubt that future research is needed in order to provide an adequate explanation for these striking phenomena.

7. The problems of "wholeness" (Gestalt), teleological functioning and purposive behavior: These also were discussed above (section IV E). The contributions of Gestalt theory and its doctrine of isomorphism have been largely absorbed in current psychophysiology (cf. especially Hebb, 145). Similarly significant and hopeful are the analyses of negative feedback processes as provided by cybernetics. The doctrines of "General Systems Theory," though related in spirit to cybernetics, Gestalt theory, and mathematical biophysics, are however very dubious from a logical point of view (cf. Buck, 57). We have also discussed the related issue of emergent novelty. If "absolute emergence" (Pap, 244) is a fact, then perhaps some such account as that given by Meehl and Sellars (221) may be considered seriously. I still expect that future

scientific research will demonstrate the sufficiency of physical$_2$ explanations. But if I should be wrong in that, a theory involving genuine emergence would seem to be a much more plausible alternative than dualistic interactionism. Such a theory would, however, have important philosophical implications. Inference to mental states would rest on presupposed nomological relations between physical$_2$ brain events and mental states which could be defined only in terms of the *theoretical* concepts of a physical$_1$ language. There would still be empirical identity between the referents of some (theoretical) physical$_1$ terms and the referents of phenomenal terms, but the scientific explanation of behavior would be markedly different from purely physical$_2$ explanations. Some of the philosophical puzzles of the mind-body problem might be resolved even more plausibly under this hypothesis. For example, the question regarding the "inverted spectrum" could be answered, quite straightforwardly, on the basis of normal inductive or analogical inference. Directly given qualia, represented by (theoretical) physical$_1$ terms in our scientific account would then be functionally related to those brain processes which are described in physical$_2$ (theoretical) terms. The principle of sufficient reason would then tell us that to assume any deviation from the highly confirmed functional relationships between mental states and physical$_2$ brain states would be just as arbitrary as, e.g., the assumption that some electric currents are associated with magnetic fields of an entirely different structure than are others (despite the complete similarity of the electric currents in every other respect). As I have indicated before, the validity of the emergentist theory falls in any case under the jurisdiction of future empirical research.

8. The problem of a neurophysiological account of *selfhood*: This important though controversial notion describes a form of organization or integration of experiences and dispositions which on the neural side corresponds first to the relatively stable structure of the brain and the other parts of the nervous system, as well as to certain unified forms of functioning. To what extent the psychoanalytic concepts of the ego, superego, and id may be "identified" with such structures and functions is still very unclear. Very likely, the psychological notions will appear only as first crude approximations, once the detailed neurophysiological facts are better known.

9. The problems of neurophysiological theories which will account for the unconscious processes assumed by various "depth psychologies,"

especially psychoanalysis: One of the philosophically intriguing questions here is whether we can explicate such psychoanalytic concepts as "repressed wishes", "unconscious anxiety", "Oedipus complex", etc. as *dispositions*, or whether unconscious *events* also need to be assumed. Even outside the sphere of Freudian preoccupations, there are for instance the often reported cases of "waking up with the solution of a mathematical problem." One wonders whether the brain did some "work" during sleep, and if so, whether "unconscious thoughts" might not be part of a first-level explanation of this sort of phenomenon. I am inclined to think that *both* dispositions *and* events are required, and that the future development of science may well produce more reliable neurophysiological explanations than the currently suggested (and suggestive) brain models (cf. Colby, 76).

10. Much more problematic than all the questions so far discussed in this section are the implications of the alleged findings of *psychical research*. Having been educated in the exercise of the scientific method, I would in the first place insist on further experimental scrutiny of those findings. But if we take seriously the impressive statistical evidence in favor of telepathy, clairvoyance, and precognition, then there arises the extremely difficult problem of how to account for these facts by means of a scientific theory. I know of no attempt that gives even a plausible suggestion for such a theory. All hypotheses that have been proposed so far are so utterly fantastic as to be scientifically fruitless for the present. But logical analyses (e.g., C. D. Broad, 52; M. Scriven, 304) which make explicit in which respects the facts (*if* they are facts!) of psychical research are incompatible with some of the guiding principles of ("Victorian"!) science are helpful and suggestive. It is difficult to know whether we stand before a scientific revolution more incisive than any other previous revampings of the frame of science, or whether the changes which may have to be made will only amount to minor emendations.

Concluding Remark. An essential part of the justification of the philosophical monism proposed in this essay depends upon empirical, scientific assumptions. Only the future development of psychophysiology will decide whether these assumptions are tenable. Since I am not a laboratory scientist (though I did some laboratory work in physics and chemistry in my early years), I cannot responsibly construct psychophysiological hypotheses. Nor did I intend to close the doors to alternative philosophical views of the relations of the mental to the physical. What I did try to show, however, is that monism is

(1) still very plausible on scientific grounds,
(2) philosophically defensible in that it involves no insurmountable logical or epistemological difficulties and paradoxes.

I realize fully that I could deal only with some of the perplexities which have vexed philosophers or psychologists throughout the ages, and especially in recent decades. Just where the philosophical shoe pinches one, just which problems strike one as important—that depends, of course, on a great many more or less accidental personal, educational, or cultural factors. Despite my valiant efforts to deal with what strike *me* as important and baffling questions, I may of course not even have touched on other facets which some of my readers might consider as *the* essential problems of mind and body. May others come and deal with them!

NOTE AND REFERENCES

Since this essay has almost the dimensions of a monograph, I feel I should acknowledge my sincere indebtedness to the countless philosophers and scientists who have helped me by their publications as well as (in many instances) by personal discussion or correspondence to reach whatever clarity I may claim to have achieved. It is impossible to mention them all, but some stand out so distinctly and prominently that I should list them. Naturally, I have learned from many of these thinkers by way of disagreement and controversy. In any case none of them is to be held responsible for whatever may be wrong or confused in my views. My first acquaintance with philosophical monism goes back to reading the work of Alois Riehl (279); I found essentially the same position again in Moritz Schlick (298), some of whose work I had studied before I became his student in Vienna in 1922. I have profited enormously (although he may well think, not sufficiently) from discussions with my kind and patient friend R. Carnap intermittently throughout more than thirty years. During my Vienna years (1922–30) I was greatly stimulated by discussions also with Schlick, Wittgenstein, Victor Kraft, Otto Neurath, E. Kaila, Karl Popper, Edgar Zilsel, et al. I was greatly reinforced in my views by my early contact with the outstanding American critical realist C. A. Strong (in Fiesole, Italy, 1927 and 1928). Along similar lines I found corroboration in the work of Roy W. Sellars, Durant Drake, Richard Gätschenberger, and in some of the writings of Bertrand Russell. Discussions (and many controversies) during my American years, beginning in 1930, with E. G. Boring, S. S. Stevens, P. W. Bridgman, C. I. Lewis, A. N. Whitehead, H. M. Sheffer, V. C. Aldrich, S. C. Pepper, E. C. Tolman, C. L. Hull, B. F. Skinner, K. Lewin, E. Brunswik, W. Köhler, Albert Einstein, H. Reichenbach, F. C. S. Northrop, and Philipp Frank, proved most stimulating.

During the last three and a half years of the activities of the Minnesota Center for Philosophy of Science I had the tremendous advantage of intensive discussions not only with my colleagues Paul E. Meehl, Wilfrid Sellars, and Michael Scriven, each of whom disagrees with me on several different fundamental points, and each for different reasons, but I also profited from discussions with such visitors or collaborators as Gilbert Ryle, C. D. Broad, Anthony Flew, Peter Strawson, Ernest Nagel, C. G. Hempel, A. Kaplan, Arthur Pap, Herbert Bohnert, Henry Mehlberg, Hilary Putnam,

Herbert Feigl

Gavin Alexander, William Rozeboom, and Adolf Grünbaum. Last, but not least, I owe a great debt of gratitude to my students at Minnesota who during many a year of seminar work in the philosophical problems of psychology have helped me through their criticisms to arrive at clearer formulations of my ideas and to eliminate various difficulties, mistakes, and confusions. It has been a veritable Odyssey of ideas for me, and I am by no means sure I have "arrived"!

In the following rather ample bibliography I have tried to assemble references not only to those materials actually discussed or quoted in my essay, but also a great deal of what seemed to me of systematic significance for future philosophical work in the area. With the appalling volume of philosophical writings in recent decades, many a valuable book or article becomes all too soon forgotten, and many go entirely unnoticed. Scholars or students who wish to tackle the "world knot" may find most of these books or articles stimulating, and many of them illuminating.

As regards my earlier publications on the mind-body problem, I now regard my presentation (103) of 1934 as partly confused. The later rather compact presentation (112) of 1950 presents on the whole an adequate preview and summary of my present outlook (though I am no longer satisfied with some of the illustrative analogies used there). A fuller discussion of my identity theory in relation to Carnap's present (largely unpublished) version of physicalism and to the issues of the empiricist criterion of factual meaningfulness is contained in my essay˜ (116) in the forthcoming Carnap volume of P. A. Schilpp's Library of Living Philosophers.

1. Adams, D. K. "Learning and explanation," *Learning Theory, Personality Theory, and Clinical Research: The Kentucky Symposium*, pp. 66–80. New York: Wiley; London: Chapman & Hall, Ltd., 1954.
2. Adams, G. P., J. Loewenberg, and S. C. Pepper (eds.). *The Nature of Mind*, University of California Publications in Philosophy, Vol. 19, 1936 (especially articles by P. Marhenke and S. C. Pepper).
3. Adrian, E. D. *The Mechanism of Nervous Action*. Philadelphia: Univ. of Pennsylvania Press, 1932.
4. Adrian, E. D. *The Physical Background of Perception*. Oxford: The Clarendon Press, 1947.
5. Adrian, E. D., F. Bremer, H. H. Jasper (consulting eds.), and J. F. Delafresnaye (ed. for the Council). *Brain Mechanisms and Consciousness: a Symposium—Council for International Organizations of Medical Sciences*. Springfield (Ill.): Charles C. Thomas, 1954.
6. Aldrich, V. C. "Messrs. Schlick and Ayer on Immortality," *Philosophical Review*, 47:209–213 (1938). Reprinted in H. Feigl and W. Sellars, *Readings in Philosophical Analysis*. New York: Appleton-Century-Crofts, 1949.
7. Aldrich, V. C. "What Appears?" *Philosophical Review*, 63:232–240 (1954).
8. Alexander, P. "Complementary Descriptions," *Mind*, 65:145–65 (1956).
9. Ashby, W. R. *Design for a Brain*. New York: Wiley, 1952.
10. Austin, J. L. "Other Minds," *Aristotelian Society Supplementary Volume*, 20: 148–187 (1946). Reprinted in A. G. N. Flew, *Logic and Language* (2nd series) 123–58. Oxford: Blackwell; New York: Philosophical Library, 1953.
11. Avenarius, R. *Der Menschliche Weltbegrift*. Leipzig: Reisland, 1912.
12. Ayer, A. J. *Language, Truth and Logic*. New York: Oxford Univ. Press, 1936; 2nd ed., London: Gollanz, 1946.
13. Ayer, A. J. *The Foundations of Empirical Knowledge*. New York: Macmillan, 1940.
14. Ayer, A. J. "The Physical Basis of Mind: A Philosophers' Symposium II," in Peter Laslett (ed.), *The Physical Basis of Mind*, pp. 70–74. New York: Macmillan, 1950.
15. Ayer, A. J. "One's Knowledge of Other Minds," *Theoria*, 19:1–20, Part 1–2 (1953).

16. Ayer, A. J. "Can There be a Private Language?" A Symposium, *Aristotelian Society Supplementary Volume*, 28:63–76 (1954).
17. Ayer, A. J. "Phenomenalism," in A. J. Ayer, *Philosophical Essays*. New York: St. Martin's Press, 1954.
18. Ayer, A. J. *The Problem of Knowledge*. New York: St. Martin's Press, 1956.
19. Bakan, D. "A Reconsideration of the Problem of Introspection," *Psychological Bulletin*, 51:106–118, March 1954.
20. Bar-Hillel, Y. "Indexical Expressions," *Mind*, 63:359–379 (1954).
21. Beck, L. W. "The Psychophysical as a Pseudo-Problem," *Journal of Philosophy*, 37:561–571 (1940).
22. Beck, L. W. "The Principle of Parsimony in Empirical Science," *Journal of Philosophy*, 40:617–633 (1943).
23. Beck, L. W. "Secondary Quality," *Journal of Philosophy*, 43:599–610 (1946).
24. Beck, L. W. "Constructions and Inferred Entities," *Philosophy of Science*, 17: 74–86 (1950). Reprinted in H. Feigl and M. Brodbeck (eds.), *Readings in the Philosophy of Science*, pp. 368–381. New York: Appleton-Century-Crofts, 1953.
25. Berenda, C. W. "On Emergence and Prediction," *Journal of Philosophy*, 50: 269–274 (1953).
26. Bergmann, G. "On Physicalistic Models of Non-physical Terms," *Philosophy of Science*, 7:151–158 (1940).
27. Bergmann, G. "On Some Methodological Problems of Psychology," *Philosophy of Science*, 7:205–219 (1940). Reprinted in H. Feigl and M. Brodbeck (eds.), *Readings in the Philosophy of Science*, pp. 627–636. New York: Appleton-Century-Crofts, 1953.
28. Bergmann, G. "Holism, Historicism and Emergence," *Philosophy of Science*, 11:209–221 (1944).
29. Bergmann, G. "The Logic of Psychological Concepts," *Philosophy of Science*, 18:93–110 (1951).
30. Bergmann, G. "The Problem of Relations in Classical Psychology," *Philosophical Quarterly*, 2:140–152 (1952).
31. Bergmann, G. "Theoretical Psychology," *Annual Review of Psychology*, 4:435–458 (1953).
32. Bergmann, G. "Sense and Nonsense in Operationism," *Science Monthly*, 79: 210–214 (1954).
33. Bergmann, G. "Intentionality," *Archivio di Filosofia*, 6:177–216 (1955).
34. Bergmann, G. *Philosophy of Science*. Madison: Univ. of Wisconsin Press, 1957.
35. Berlin, I. "Empirical Propositions and Hypothetical Statements," *Mind*, 59:289–312 (1950).
36. Bichowsky, F. R. "Factors Common to the Mind and to the External World," *Journal of Philosophy*, 37:18 (1940).
37. Black, M. "Linguistic Method in Philosophy," *Philosophical and Phenomenological Research*, 8:4 (1948). Reprinted in M. Black, *Language and Philosophy*. Ithaca: Cornell Univ. Press, 1949.
38. Black, M. "Symposium: Phenomenalism." *Science, Language, and Human Rights*. American Philosophical Association, Vol. 1, Philadelphia: Univ. of Pennsylvania Press, 1952.
39. Blum, H. F. *Time's Arrow and Evolution*. Princeton: Princeton Univ. Press, 1955.
40. Boring, E. G. *The Physical Dimensions of Consciousness*. New York, London: The Century Co., 1933.
41. Boring, E. G. "Psychophysiological Systems and Isomorphic Relations," *Psychological Review*, 43:565–587 (1936).
42. Boring, E. G. "A Psychological Function is the Relation of Successive Differentiations of Events in the Organism," *Psychological Review*, 44:445–461 (1937).

43. Boring, E. G., *et al.* Symposium on Operationism. *Psychological Review,* 52: 241–294 (1945).

44. Boring, E. G. "Mind and Mechanism," *American Journal of Psychology,* 59: 173–192 (1946).

45. Boring, E. G. "A History of Introspection," *Psychological Bulletin,* 50:169–189 (1953).

46. Brain, W. R. *The Contribution of Medicine to Our Idea of Mind.* Cambridge: Cambridge Univ. Press, 1952.

47. Braithwaite, M. "Causal Laws in Psychology," A Symposium, *Aristotelian Society Supplementary Volume,* 23:45–60 (1949).

48. Braithwaite, R. B. *Scientific Explanation.* Cambridge: Cambridge Univ. Press, 1953.

49. Brillouin, L. *Science and Information Theory.* New York: Academic Press, 1956.

50. Broad, C. D. *Perception, Physics, and Reality.* Cambridge: Cambridge Univ. Press, 1914.

51. Broad, C. D. *The Mind and Its Place in Nature.* London: Routledge & Kegan Paul, 1925.

52. Broad, C. D. "The Relevance of Psychical Research to Philosophy," *Philosophy,* 24:291–309 (1949). Reprinted in C. D. Broad, *Religion, Philosophy, and Psychical Research.* New York: Harcourt, Brace, 1953.

53. Brodbeck, M. "On the Philosophy of the Social Sciences," *Philosophy of Science,* 21:140–156 (1954).

54. Brunswik, E. "The Conceptual Focus of Some Psychological Symptoms," in P. L. Harriman (ed.), *Twentieth Century Psychology.* New York: Philosophical Library, 1946.

55. Brunswik, E. "Points of View," in *Encyclopedia of Psychology* (P. L. Harriman, ed.). New York: Philosophical Library, 1946.

56. Brunswik, E. "The Conceptual Framework of Psychology," *International Encyclopedia of Unified Science,* Vol. 10. Chicago: Univ. of Chicago Press, 1952.

57. Buck, R. C. "On the Logic of General Behavior Systems Theory," in H. Feigl and M. Scriven (eds.). *Minnesota Studies in the Philosophy of Science,* Vol. I, *The Foundations of Science and the Concepts of Psychology and Psychoanalysis,* pp. 223–238. Minneapolis: Univ. of Minnesota Press, 1956.

58. Burks, A. W. "Icon, Index and Symbol," *Philosophical and Phenomenological Research,* 9:673–689 (1949).

59. Burks, A. W. "The Logic of Causal Propositions," *Mind,* 60:363–382 (1951).

60. Carnap, R. *Der Logische Aufbau der Welt.* Berlin: Weltkreis, 1928.

61. Carnap, R. *Scheinproblem in der Philosophie.* Berlin: Weltkreis, 1928.

62. Carnap, R. "Psychologie in Physikalischer Sprache," *Erkenntnis,* 3:107–142 (1933).

63. Carnap, R. "Les Concepts Psychologiques et les Concepts Physiques, sont-ils Foncièrement Différents?" *Revue de Synthèse,* 10:43–53 (1935).

64. Carnap, R. "Testability and Meaning," *Philosophy of Science,* 3:420–468 (1936); 4:1–40 (1937). Also reprinted by Graduate Philosophy Club, Yale University, New Haven, Conn., 1950. Also reprinted in H. Feigl and M. Brodbeck (eds.), *Readings in the Philosophy of Science,* pp. 47–92. New York: Appleton-Century-Crofts, 1953.

65. Carnap, R. *The Logical Syntax of Language.* New York: Harcourt, Brace, 1937.

66. Carnap, R. *The Unity of Science.* London: Kegan Paul, 1938.

67. Carnap, R. "Logical Foundations of the Unity of Science," *International Encyclopedia of Unified Science,* Vol. I, No. 1 (R. Carnap and C. W. Morris, eds.). Chicago: Univ. of Chicago Press, 1938, 42–62. Reprinted in H. Feigl and W. Sellars (eds.), *Readings in Philosophical Analysis,* pp. 408–423. New York: Appleton-Century-Crofts, Inc., 1949.

68. Carnap, R. "Foundations of Logic and Mathematics," *International Encyclopedia of Unified Science*, Vol. I, No. 3. Chicago: Univ. of Chicago Press, 1939. A part ("The Interpretation of Physics") is reprinted in H. Feigl and M. Brodbeck (eds.), *Readings in the Philosophy of Science*, pp. 309–318. New York: Appleton-Century-Crofts, 1953.

69. Carnap, R. *Introduction to Semantics*. Cambridge (Mass.): Harvard Univ. Press, 1942.

70. Carnap, R. "Empiricism, Semantics, and Ontology," *Revue Internationale de Philosophie*, 4:20–40 (1950). Reprinted in P. P. Wiener (ed.), *Readings in the Philosophy of Science*, pp. 509–521. New York: Scribner, 1953. Also reprinted in L. Linsky (ed.), *Semantics and the Philosophy of Language*, pp. 208–230. Urbana (Ill.): Univ. of Illinois Press, 1952.

71. Carnap, R. "Meaning and Synonymy in Natural Languages," *Philosophical Studies*, 6:33–47 (1955).

72. Carnap, R. *Meaning and Necessity*, 2nd edition. Chicago: Univ. of Chicago Press, 1956.

73. Carnap, R. "The Methodological Character of Theoretical Concepts," in *Minnesota Studies in the Philosophy of Science*, Vol. I, pp. 38–76. Minneapolis: Univ. of Minnesota Press, 1956.

74. Castell, A. "The Critical and the Mechanical," *The Philosophical Review*, 60:1 (1951).

75. Chisholm, R. M. "Verification and Perception," *Revue Internationale de Philosophie*, 17:1–17 (1951).

76. Colby, K. M. *Energy and Structure in Psychoanalysis*. New York: Ronald Press Co., 1955.

77. Copi, I. M. "A Note on Representation in Art," *Journal of Philosophy*, 52:346–349 (1955).

78. Cory, D. "Are Sense-Data 'in' the Brain?" *Journal of Philosophy*, 65:533–548 (1948).

79. Cronbach, L. J., and P. M. Meehl. "Construct Validity in Psychological Tests," *Psychological Bulletin*, 52:281–302 (1955). Reprinted in H. Feigl and M. Scriven (eds.), *Minnesota Studies in the Philosophy of Science*, Vol. I, pp. 174–204. Minneapolis: Univ. of Minnesota Press, 1956.

80. Culbertson, J. T. *Consciousness and Behavior*. Dubuque (Iowa): W. C. Brown Co., 1950.

81. Dennes, W. R. "Mind and Meaning," in G. P. Adams, J. Loewenberg, and S. C. Pepper (eds.), *The Nature of Mind*, pp. 1–30. Berkeley: Univ. of California Press, 1936.

82. Deutsch, K. W. "Mechanism, Teleology, and Mind: The Theory of Communications and Some Problems in Philosophy and Social Science," *Philosophical and Phenomenological Research*, 12:185–223 (1951).

83. Dewey, J. *Experience and Nature*. LaSalle (Ill.): Open Court Pub. Co., 1926.

84. Dewey, J. "Conduct and Experience," in C. Murchison (ed.), *Psychologies of 1930*. Worcester (Mass.): Clark Univ. Press, 1930.

85. Drake, D. *Mind and its Place in Nature*. New York: Macmillan, 1925.

86. Drake, D. *Invitation to Philosophy*. Chicago: Houghton Mifflin Co., 1933.

87. Driesch, H. *Mind and Body*. London: Methuen, 1927.

88. Driesch, H. *Philosophische Gegenwartsfragen*. Leipzig: Verlag Emmanuel Reinicke, 1933.

89. Ducasse, C. J. "On the Attributes of Material Things," *Journal of Philosophy*, 31:57–72 (1934).

90. Ducasse, C. J. *Nature, Mind, and Death*. LaSalle (Ill): Open Court Pub. Co., 1951.

Herbert Feigl

91. Ducasse, C. J. "Demos on 'Nature, Mind and Death,'" *The Review of Metaphysics*, 7:290–298 (1953).
92. Eccles, J. C. *The Neurophysiological Basis of Mind*. Oxford: The Clarendon Press, 1953.
93. Eddington, A. S. *The Nature of the Physical World*. New York: Macmillan, 1928.
94. Eddington, A. S. *Science and the Unseen World*. New York: Macmillan, 1929.
95. Elsasser, W. M. "Quantum Mechanics, Amplifying Processes, and Living Matter," *Philosophy of Science*, 18:300–326 (1951).
96. Elsasser, W. M. "A Reformulation of Bergson's Theory of Memory," *Philosophy of Science*, 20:7–21 (1953).
97. Elsasser, W. M. *The Physical Foundation of Biology*. (Unpublished book manuscript completed in 1956.)
98. Epstein, J. "Professor Ayer on Sense-Data," *Journal of Philosophy*, 53:401–415 (1956).
99. Farrell, B. A. "Causal Laws in Psychology," A Symposium, *Aristotelian Society Supplementary Volume*, 23:30–44 (1949).
100. Farrell, B. A. "Critical Notice on 'The Concept of Mind' by Gilbert Ryle," *British Journal of Psychology*, 40:159–164 (1950).
101. Farrell, B. A. "Experience," *Mind*, 59:170–198 (1950).
102. Farrell, B. A. "Intentionality and the Theory of Signs," *Philosophical and Phenomenological Research*, 15:500–511 (1955).
103. Feigl, H. "Logical Analysis of the Psychophysical Problem," *Philosophy of Science*, 1:420–445 (1934).
104. Feigl, H. "Moritz Schlick," *Erkenntnis*, 7:393–419 (1938).
105. Feigl, H. "Logical Empiricism," in D. D. Runes (ed.), *Twentieth Century Philosophy*, New York: Philosophical Library, 1943, pp. 371–416. Reprinted in H. Feigl and W. Sellars, *Readings in Philosophical Analysis*. New York: Appleton-Century-Crofts, 1949. Reprinted (in part) in M. Mandelbaum, et al., *Philosophic Problems*, pp. 3–26. New York: Macmillan, 1957.
106. Feigl, H. "Operationism and Scientific Method," *Psychological Review*, 52:250–259 (1945). Reprinted in H. Feigl and W. Sellars (eds.), *Readings in Philosophical Analysis*, pp. 498–509. New York: Appleton-Century-Crofts, 1949.
107. Feigl, H. "Naturalism and Humanism," *American Quarterly*, 1:135–149 (1949). Reprinted in H. Feigl and M. Brodbeck (eds.), *Readings in the Philosophy of Science*, pp. 8–18. New York: Appleton-Century-Crofts, 1953.
108. Feigl, H. "Some Remarks on the Meaning of Scientific Explanation," in H. Feigl and W. Sellars (eds.), *Readings in Philosophical Analysis*, pp. 510–514. New York: Appleton-Century-Crofts, 1949.
109. Feigl, H. "De Principiis Non Disputandum . . .? On the Meaning and the Limits of Justification," in M. Black (ed.), *Philosophical Analysis*, pp. 119–156. Ithaca (N.Y.): Cornell University Press, 1950.
110. Feigl, H. "Existential Hypotheses: Realistic Versus Phenomenalistic Interpretations," *Philosophy of Science*, 17:35–62 (1950).
111. Feigl, H. "Logical Reconstruction, Realism and Pure Semiotic," *Philosophy of Science*, 17:186–195 (1950).
112. Feigl, H. "The Mind-Body Problem in the Development of Logical Empiricism," *Revue Internationale de Philosophie*, 4:64–83 (1950). Reprinted in H. Feigl and M. Brodbeck (eds.), *Readings in the Philosophy of Science*, pp. 612–626. New York: Appleton-Century-Crofts, 1953.
113. Feigl, H. "Principles and Problems of Theory Construction in Psychology," in W. Dennis (ed.), *Current Trends of Psychological Theory*, pp. 174–213. Pittsburgh: Univ. of Pittsburgh Press, 1951.
114. Feigl, H. "Scientific Method Without Metaphysical Presuppositions," *Philo-*

sophical Studies, 5:17–19 (1954). Reprinted with minor alterations in H. Feigl and M. Scriven (eds.), Minnesota Studies in the Philosophy of Science, Vol. I, pp. 22–37. Minneapolis: Univ. of Minnesota Press, 1956.

115. Feigl, H. "Functionalism, Psychological Theory, and the Uniting Sciences: Some Discussion Remarks," Psychological Review, 62:232–235 (1955).

116. Feigl, H. "Physicalism, Unity of Science and the Foundations of Psychology," in P. A. Schilpp (ed.), The Philosophy of Rudolf Carnap. New York: Tudor (forthcoming).

117. Feigl, H., and M. Brodbeck (eds.). Readings in the Philosophy of Science. New York: Appleton-Century-Crofts, 1953.

118. Feigl, H., and W. Sellars (eds.). Readings in Philosophical Analysis. New York: Appleton-Century-Crofts, 1949.

119. Feyerabend, P. K. "Carnap's Theorie der Interpretation theoretischer Systeme," Theoria, 21:55–62 (1955).

120. Feyerabend, P. K. "A Note on the Paradox of Analysis," Philosophical Studies, 7:92–96 (1956).

121. Findlay, J. N. "Is There Knowledge by Acquaintance?" A Symposium, Aristotelian Society Supplementary Volume, 23:111–128 (1949).

122. Förster, H. Das Gedächtnis. Vienna: Franz Deuticke, 1948.

123. Förster, H. (ed.). Conferences on Cybernetics, Vols. 6–9. New York: Josiah Macy, Jr. Foundation, 1949–1952.

124. Frank, L. K., et al. Teleological Mechanisms. New York: The New York Academy of Sciences, 1948.

125. Frank, P. Modern Science and its Philosophy. Cambridge (Mass.): Harvard Univ. Press, 1949.

126. Frank, P. G. Philosophy of Science. New York: Prentice-Hall, 1957.

127. Frenkel-Brunswik, E. "Psychoanalysis and the Unity of Science," Proceedings of the American Academy of Arts and Sciences, 80:271–350 (1954).

128. Freytag, W. Der Realismus und das Transzendenzproblem. Halle: Niemeyer, 1902.

129. Fritz, C. A., Jr. "Sense Perception and Material Objects," Philosophical and Phenomenological Research, 16:303–316 (1956).

130. Gätschenberger, R. Symbola. Karlsruhe: G. Braun, 1920.

131. Gätschenberger, R. Zeichen, die Fundamente des Wissens. Stuttgart: Frommann, 1932.

132. Gellhorn, E. Physiological Foundations of Neurology and Psychiatry. Minneapolis: Univ. of Minnesota Press, 1953.

133. Ginsberg, A. "Hypothetical Constructs and Intervening Variables," Psychological Review, 61:119–131 (1954).

134. Ginsberg, A. "Operational Definitions and Theories," Journal of General Psychology, 52:223–245 (1955).

135. Goodman, N. The Structure of Appearance. Cambridge: Harvard Univ. Press, 1951.

136. Goodman, N. "Sense and Certainty," Philosophical Review, 61:160–167 (1952).

137. Goodman, N. "The Revision of Philosophy," in S. Hook (ed.), American Philosophers at Work, pp. 75–92. New York: Criterion Books, 1956.

138. Grossmann, R. S. "Zur Logischen Analyse des Neobehaviorismus," Psychologische Rundschau, Band VI/4:246–260 (1955).

139. Grünbaum, A. "Operationism and Relativity," Scientific Monthly, 79:228–231 (1954).

140. Guthrie, E. R. "Purpose and Mechanism in Psychology," Journal of Philosophy, 21:25 (1924).

141. Hampshire, S. "The Analogy of Feeling," Mind, 61:1–12 (1952).

Herbert Feigl

142. Hart, H. L. A. "Is There Knowledge by Acquaintance?" A Symposium, Aristotelian Society Supplementary Volume, 23:69–90 (1949).
143. Hathaway, S. R. "Clinical Intuition and Inferential Accuracy," Journal of Personality, 24:223–250 (1956).
144. Hayek, F. A. "The Facts of the Social Sciences," Ethics, 54:1 (1943).
145. Hebb, D. O. The Organization of Behavior, A Neuropsychological Theory. New York: Wiley, 1949.
146. Hempel, C. G. "The Logical Analysis of Psychology," Revue de Synthèse, 10: 27–42 (1935). Reprinted in H. Feigl and W. Sellars (eds.), Readings in Philosophical Analysis, pp. 373–384. New York: Appleton-Century-Crofts, 1949.
147. Hempel, C. G. "The Concept of Cognitive Significance: A Reconsideration," Proceedings of the American Academy of Arts and Sciences, 80:61–77 (1951).
148. Hempel, C. G. "Fundamentals of Concept Formation in the Empirical Sciences," International Encyclopedia of Unified Science, Vol. II, No. 7. Chicago: Univ. of Chicago Press, 1952.
149. Hempel, C. G. "Problems and Changes in the Empiricist Criterion of Meaning," Revue Internationale de Philosophie, 4:41–63 (1950). Reprinted in L. Linsky (ed.), Semantics and the Philosophy of Language. Urbana: Univ. of Illinois Press, 1952.
150. Hempel, C. G. "Reflections on Nelson Goodman's The Structure of Appearance," Philosophical Review, 62:108–116 (1953).
151. Hempel, C. G. "A Logical Appraisal of Operationism," Scientific Monthly, 79:215–220 (1954).
152. Hempel, C. G., and P. Oppenheim. "The Logic of Explanation," Philosophy of Science, 15:135–175 (1948). Reprinted in H. Feigl and M. Brodbeck (eds.), Readings in the Philosophy of Science, pp. 319–352. New York: Appleton-Century-Crofts, 1953.
153. Henle, P. "The Status of Emergence," Journal of Philosophy, 39:486–493 (1942).
154. Herrick, C. J. The Evolution of Human Nature. Austin: Univ. of Texas Press, 1956.
155. Hervey, H. "The Private Language Problem," Philosophical Quarterly, 7:63–79 (1957).
156. Heymans, G. Einführung in die Metaphysik. Leipzig: Barth, 1921.
157. Hobart, R. E. "Free Will as Involving Determinism and Inconceivable Without It," Mind, 43:1–26 (1934).
158. Hofstadter, A. "Professor Ryle's Category-Mistake," Journal of Philosophy, 48: 257–270 (1951).
159. Holt, E. B. The Concept of Consciousness. London: G. Allen and Co., Ltd., 1914.
160. Hospers, J. An Introduction to Philosophical Analysis. New York: Prentice-Hall, 1953.
161. Hughes, G. E. "Is There Knowledge by Acquaintance?" A Symposium, Aristotelian Society Supplementary Volume, 23:91–110 (1949).
162. Hull, C. L. "Mind, Mechanism, and Adaptive Behavior," Psychological Review, 44:1–32 (1937).
163. Jacobs, N. "Physicalism and Sensation Sentences," Journal of Philosophy, 34:22 (1937).
164. Jacoby, G. Allgemeine Ontologie der Wirklichkeit, Vol. 2. Halle: Niemeyer, 1955.
165. James, W. Principles of Psychology. New York: H. Holt and Co., 1890.
166. Juhos, B. Die Erkenntnis und ihre Leistung. Vienna: Springer-Verlag, 1950.
167. Kaila, E. "Beiträge zu einer Synthetischen Philosophie," Annales Universitatis Aboensis, 4:9–208 (1928).

168. Kaila, E. "Physikalismus und Phänomenalismus," *Theoria*, 8:85–125 (1942).
169. Kaila, E. "Terminalkansalität als die Grundlage eines Unitarischen Naturbegriffs," *Acts Philosophica Fennica*, 10:7–122 (1956).
170. Kaplan, A. "Definition and Specification of Meaning," *Journal of Philosophy*, 63:281–288 (1946).
171. Kaplan, A. and H. F. Schott. "A Calculus for Empirical Classes," *Methodos*, 3:165–190 (1951).
172. Kapp, R. O. *Science vs. Materialism*. London: Methuen, 1940.
173. Kapp, R. O. *Mind, Life, and Body*. London: Constable, 1951.
174. Kapp, R. O. *Facts and Faith: The Dual Nature of Reality*. New York: Oxford Univ. Press, 1955.
175. Kaufmann, F. *Methodology of the Social Sciences*. New York: Oxford Univ. Press, 1944.
176. Keller, F. S. *The Definition of Psychology*. New York: Appleton-Century-Crofts, 1937.
177. Kemeny, J. G., and P. Oppenheim. "On Reduction," *Philosophical Studies*, 7:6–19 (1956).
178. King, H. R. "Professor Ryle and the Concept of Mind," *Journal of Philosophy*, 48:9 (1951).
179. Kneale, W. "Induction, Explanation, and Transcendent Hypotheses," in W. Kneale, *Probability and Induction*, pp. 92–110. Oxford: The Clarendon Press, 1949. Reprinted in H. Feigl and M. Brodbeck (eds.), *Readings in the Philosophy of Science*, pp. 353–367. New York: Appleton-Century-Crofts, 1953.
180. Kneale, W. *Probability and Induction*. Oxford: The Clarendon Press, 1949.
181. Köhler, W. "Bemerkungen zum Leib-Seele-Problem," *Deutsche Medizinische Wochenschrift*, 50:1269–1270 (1924).
182. Köhler, W. "Ein altes Scheinproblem," *Die Naturwissenschaften*, 17:395–401 (1929).
183. Köhler, W. *The Place of Values in a World of Facts*. New York: Liveright, 1938.
184. Köhler, W. *Dynamics in Psychology*. New York: Liveright, 1940.
185. Köhler, W. *Gestalt Psychology*. New York: Liveright, 1947.
186. Köhler, W. "Direction of Processes in Living Systems," in P. G. Frank (ed.), *The Validation of Scientific Theories*, pp. 143–150. Boston: Beacon Press, 1954.
187. Kraft, V. *The Vienna Circle* (translated by A. Pap). New York: Philosophical Library, 1953.
188. Krech, D. "Dynamic Systems, Psychological Fields, and Hypothetical Constructs," *Psychological Review*, 57:283–290 (1950).
189. Krech, D. "Dynamic Systems as Open Neurological Systems," *Psychological Review*, 57:345–361 (1950).
190. Krikorian, Y. H. (ed.). *Naturalism and the Human Mind*. New York: Columbia Univ. Press, 1944.
191. Külpe, O. *Die Realisierung*. Leipzig: S. Hirzel, 1912.
192. Lashley, K. S. "Behaviorism and Consciousness," *Psychological Review*, 30:346 (1923).
193. Lean, Martin. *Sense Perception and Matter*. London: Routledge and Kegan Paul, 1953.
194. Lecomte Du Noüy, P. *Human Destiny*. New York: Longmans, Green and Co., 1947.
195. Lewis, C. I. *Mind and the World Order*. New York: Scribner, 1929.
196. Lewis, C. I. "Some Logical Considerations Concerning the Mental," *Journal of Philosophy*, 38 (1941). Reprinted in H. Feigl and W. Sellars (eds.), *Readings in Philosophical Analysis*, pp. 385–392. New York: Appleton-Century-Crofts, 1949.

Herbert Feigl

197. Lewis, C. I. An Analysis of Knowledge and Valuation. LaSalle (Ill.): Open Court Pub. Co., 1946.
198. Lewis, C. I. "The Given Element in Empirical Knowledge," Philosophical Review, 61:168–175 (1952).
199. Lewy, C. "Is the Notion of Disembodied Existence Self-Contradictory?" Proceedings of the Aristotelian Society, 43:59–78 (1942–1943).
200. Lindzey, G. "Hypothetical Constructs, Conventional Constructs, and Use of Physiological Data in Psychological Theory," Psychiatry, 16:27–33 (1953).
201. Littman, R. A. "Mr. Ryle on 'Thinking,'" Acta Psychologica, 10:381–384 (1954).
202. London, I. D. "Free Will as a Function of Divergence," Psychological Review, 55:41–47 (1948).
203. London, I. D. "Quantum Biology and Psychology," Journal of General Psychology, 46:123–149 (1952).
204. Lovejoy, A. O. The Revolt Against Dualism. New York: Norton & Co., 1930.
205. Mace, C. A. "Causal Laws in Psychology," A Symposium, Aristotelian Society Supplementary Volume, 23:61–68 (1949).
206. Mach, E. The Analysis of Sensations. LaSalle (Ill.): Open Court Pub. Co., 1914.
207. Madden, E. N. "Discussion—Science, Philosophy and Gestalt Theory," Philosophy of Science, 20:329–331 (1953).
208. Margenau, H. The Nature of Physical Reality. New York: McGraw-Hill Book Co., 1950.
209. Margenau, H. "The Exclusion Principle and Its Philosophical Importance," Philosophy of Science, 11:187–208 (1944).
210. Marhenke, P. "The Constituents of Mind," in G. P. Adams, J. Loewenberg, and S. C. Pepper (eds.), The Nature of Mind, pp. 171–208. Berkeley: Univ. of California Press, 1936.
211. Marx, M. H. (ed.). Psychological Theory. New York: Macmillan, 1951.
212. Maze, J. R. "Do Intervening Variables Intervene?" Psychological Review, 61: 226–234 (1954).
213. MacCorquodale, K., and P. E. Meehl. "On a Distinction between Hypothetical Constructs and Intervening Variables," Psychological Review, 55:95–107 (1948).
214. McCulloch, W. S. "Brain and Behavior," in Current Trends in Psychological Theory, pp. 165–178. Pittsburgh: Univ. of Pittsburgh Press, 1951.
215. McCulloch, W. S. "Mysterium Iniquitatis—of Sinful Man Aspiring into the Place of God," in P. G. Frank (ed.), The Validation of Scientific Theories, pp. 159–170. Boston: Beacon Press, 1954.
216. MacKay, D. M. "Mentality in Machines," A Symposium, Aristotelian Society Supplementary Volume, 26:61–86 (1952).
217. MacLeod, R. B. "The Phenomenological Approach to Social Psychology," Psychological Review, 54:193–210 (1947).
218. MacLeod, R. B. "New Psychologies of Yesterday and Today," Canadian Journal of Psychology, 3:199–212 (1949).
219. Meehl, P. E. "A Most Peculiar Paradox," Philosophical Studies, 1:47–48 (1950).
220. Meehl, P. E. "On the Circularity of the Law of Effect," Psychological Bulletin, 47:53–75 (1950). Reprinted as "Law and Convention in Psychology," in H. Feigl and M. Brodbeck (eds.), Readings in the Philosophy of Science, pp. 637–659. New York: Appleton-Century-Crofts, 1953.
221. Meehl, P. E., and W. Sellars. "The Concept of Emergence," in H. Feigl and M. Scriven (eds.), Minnesota Studies in the Philosophy of Science, Vol. I, pp. 239–252. Minneapolis: Univ. of Minnesota Press, 1956.
222. Mehlberg, H. "Positivisme et Science," Studia Philosophica, 3:211–294 (1948).

223. Mellor, W. W. "Three Problems about Other Minds," *Mind*, 65:200–218 (1956).
224. Miller, D. S. "Is Consciousness 'A Type of Behavior'?" *Journal of Philosophy*, 8:322–327 (1911).
225. Miller, D. S. "The Pleasure-Quality and the Pain-Quality Analysable, not Ultimate," *Mind*, 38:150, 215–218 (1929).
226. Miller, D. S. " 'Descartes' Myth' and 'Professor Ryle's Fallacy,' " *Journal of Philosophy*, 48:9 (1951).
227. Miller, J. G. *Unconsciousness*. New York: Wiley, 1942.
228. Morris, C. W. *Six Theories of Mind*. Chicago: Univ. of Chicago Press, 1932.
229. Morris, C. W. *Signs, Language, and Behavior*. New York: Prentice-Hall, 1946.
230. Nagel, E. "The Meaning of Reduction in the Natural Sciences," in R. C. Stauffer (ed.), *Science and Civilization*, pp. 99–138. Madison (Wis.): Univ. of Wisconsin Press, 1949. Reprinted in P. P. Wiener (ed.), *Readings in the Philosophy of Science*, pp. 531–548. New York: Scribner, 1953.
231. Nagel, E. "Are Naturalists Materialists?" *Journal of Philosophy*, 42:515–553 (1945). Reprinted in E. Nagel, *Logic Without Metaphysics*, pp. 19–38. Glencoe (Ill.): The Free Press, 1956.
232. Nagel, E. "Mechanistic Explanation of Organismic Biology," *Philosophical and Phenomenological Research*, 11:3 (1951). Reprinted in S. Hook (ed.), *American Philosophers at Work*, pp. 106–120. New York: Criterion Books, 1956.
233. Nagel, E. *Sovereign Reason*. Glencoe (Ill.): The Free Press, 1954.
234. Nagel, E. "Naturalism Reconsidered," *Proceedings and Addresses of the American Philosophical Association*, 28:5–17 (1954–1955). Reprinted in E. Nagel, *Logic Without Metaphysics*, pp. 3–18. Glencoe (Ill.): The Free Press, 1956.
235. Nagel, E. "A Formalization of Functionalism," in E. Nagel, *Logic Without Metaphysics*, pp. 247–283. Glencoe (Ill.): The Free Press, 1956.
236. Nagel, E., and C. G. Hempel. "Symposium: Problems of Concept and Theory Formation in the Social Sciences." *Science, Language, and the Human Rights*. American Philosophical Association, Vol. I. Philadelphia: Univ. of Pennsylvania Press, 1952.
237. Nelson, E. J. "A Defense of Substance," *Philosophical Review*, 56:491–509 (1947).
238. Nelson, E. J. "The Verification Theory of Meaning," *Philosophical Review*, 63:182–192 (1954).
239. Northrop, F. S. C. *The Logic of the Sciences and the Humanities*. New York: Macmillan, 1947.
240. Northrop, F. S. C. "The Neurological and Behavioristic Psychological Basis of the Ordering of Society by Means of Ideas," *Science*, 107:411–417 (1948).
241. O'Connor, D. J. "Awareness and Communication," *Journal of Philosophy*, 52:505–514 (1955).
242. Pap, A. *Elements of Analytic Philosophy*. New York: Macmillan, 1949.
243. Pap, A. "Other Minds and the Principle of Verifiability," *Revue Internationale de Philosophie*, No. 17–18, Fasc. 3–4 (1951).
244. Pap, A. "The Concept of Absolute Emergence," *British Journal for the Philosophy of Science*, 2:8 (1952).
245. Pap, A. "Semantic Analysis and Psycho-Physical Dualism," *Mind*, 61:242 (1952).
246. Pap, A. "Reduction-Sentences and Open Concepts," *Methodos*, 5:17 (1953).
247. Pap, A. "Das Leib-Seele-Problem in der Analytischen Philosophie," *Archiv für Philosophie*, Band 5, Heft 2, 113–129 (1954).
248. Pap, A. *Analytische Erkenntnistheorie*. Vienna: Springer, 1955.
249. Pap, A. "Synonymy, Identity of Concepts and the Paradox of Analysis," *Methodos*, 7:115–128 (1955).

250. Paulsen, F. *Introduction to Philosophy*. New York: H. Holt and Co., 1895.
251. Penelhum, T. "Hume on Personal Identity," *Philosophical Review*, 64:571–589 (1955).
252. Pepper, S. C. "Emergence," *Journal of Philosophy*, 23:241–245 (1926).
253. Pepper, S. C. "A Criticism of a Positivistic Theory of Mind," in G. P. Adams, J. Loewenberg, and S. C. Pepper (eds.), *The Nature of Mind*, pp. 211–232. Berkeley: Univ. of California Press, 1936.
254. Pepper, S. C. "The Issue Over the Facts," in *Meaning and Interpretation*. Berkeley: Univ. of California Press, 1950.
255. Pepper, S. C. *A Neural Identity Theory*. (Unpublished manuscript)
256. Place, U. T. "Is Consciousness a Brain Process?" *British Journal of Psychology*, 47:44–50 (1956).
257. Poincaré, H. *The Foundations of Science*. New York: The Science Press, 1929.
258. Popper, K. R. *Logik der Forschung*. Vienna: Springer, 1935.
259. Popper, K. R. "Language and the Body-Mind Problem," *Proceedings of the 11th International Congress of Philosophy*, 7:101–107 (1953).
260. Pratt, C. C. *The Logic of Modern Psychology*. New York: Macmillan, 1939.
261. Pratt, J. B. *Matter and Spirit*. New York: Macmillan, 1922.
262. Pratt, J. B. "The Present Status of the Mind-Body Problem," *The Philosophical Review*, 65:144–156 (1936). Reprinted in *Proceedings and Addresses of the American Philosophical Association*, 9:144–166 (1935).
263. Pratt, J. B. *Personal Realism*. New York: Macmillan, 1937.
264. Price, H. H. *Perception*. London: Methuen, 1932.
265. Prince, M. "The Identification of Mind and Matter," *Philosophical Review*, 13:445–451 (1904).
266. Pumpian-Mindlin, E. (ed.). *Psychoanalysis as a Science* (with essays by E. R. Hilgard, L. S. Kubie, and the editor). Stanford: Stanford Univ. Press, 1952.
267. Putnam, H. "Mathematics and the Existence of Abstract Entities," *Philosophical Studies*, 7:81–88 (1956).
268. Quine, W. V. "On Mental Entities," in the *Proceedings of the American Academy of Arts and Sciences*, 80:3 (1950), Contributions to the Analysis and Synthesis of Knowledge.
269. Quine, W. V. "On What There Is," in W. V. Quine, *From a Logical Point of View*, pp. 1–19. Cambridge (Mass.): Harvard Univ. Press, 1953.
270. Quinton, A. M. "The Problem of Perception," *Mind*, 64:28–51 (1955).
271. Raab, F. V. "Free Will and the Ambiguity of 'Could,'" *Philosophical Review*, 64:60–77 (1955).
272. Rashevsky, N. "Is the Concept of an Organism as a Machine a Useful One?" in P. G. Frank (ed.), *The Validation of Scientific Theories*. Boston: Beacon Press, 1954.
273. Reichenbach, H. *Experience and Prediction*. Chicago: Univ. of Chicago Press, 1938.
274. Reichenbach, H. *Elements of Symbolic Logic*. New York: Macmillan, 1947.
275. Reichenbach, H. *The Rise of Scientific Philosophy*. Berkeley: Univ. of California Press, 1951.
276. Reichenbach, H. "Are Phenomenal Reports Absolutely Certain?" *Philosophical Review*, 61:147–159 (1952).
277. Rescher, N., and P. Oppenheim. "Logical Analysis of Gestalt Concepts," *British Journal for the Philosophy of Science*, 6:89–106 (1955).
278. Rhees, R. "Can There be a Private Language?" A Symposium, *Aristotelian Society Supplementary Volume*, 28:77–94 (1954).
279. Riehl, A. *Introduction to the Theory of Science and Metaphysics*. London: Kegan Paul, Trench and Co., 1894.

280. Roelofs, H. D. "A Case for Dualism and Interaction," *Philosophical and Phenomenological Research*, 15:451–476 (1955).
281. Rosenblueth, A., and N. Wiener. "Behavior, Purpose and Teleology," *Philosophy of Science*, 10:18–24 (1943).
282. Rosenblueth, A., and N. Wiener. "Purposeful and Non-Purposeful Behavior," *Philosophy of Science*, 17:318–326 (1950).
283. Rozeboom, W. R. "Mediation Variables in Scientific Theory," *Psychological Review*, 63:249–264 (1956).
284. Russell, B. *Our Knowledge of the External World*. New York: Norton & Co., 1929.
285. Russell, B. *The Analysis of Matter*. New York: Harcourt, Brace, 1927.
286. Russell, B. *An Inquiry Into Meaning and Truth*. New York: Norton & Co., 1940.
287. Russell, B. *The Analysis of Mind*. New York: Macmillan, 1921.
288. Russell, B. *Human Knowledge*. New York: Simon and Schuster, 1948.
289. Ruyer, R. *Esquisse d'une Philosophie de la Structure*. Paris: F. Alcan, 1930.
290. Ruyer, R. "Les Sensations Sont-elles dans Notre Tête?" *Journal de Psychologie*, 31:555–580 (1934).
291. Ruyer, R. *Elements de Psycho-Biologie*. Paris: Presses Univ. de France, 1946.
292. Ruyer, R. *La Conscience et le Corps*. Paris: Presses Univ. de France, 1950.
293. Ruyer, R. *Néo-Finalisme*. Paris: Presses Univ. de France, 1952.
294. Ryle, G. *The Concept of Mind*. London: Hutchinson's Univ. Libr., 1949.
295. Ryle, G. "The Physical Basis of Mind: A Philosophers' Symposium III," in P. Laslett (ed.), *The Physical Basis of Mind*, pp. 75–79. New York: Macmillan, 1950.
296. Samuel, V. "The Physical Basis of Mind: A Philosophers' Symposium I," in P. Laslett (ed.), *The Physical Basis of Mind*, pp. 65–69. New York: Macmillan, 1950.
297. Scheffler, I. "The New Dualism: Psychological and Physical Terms," *Journal of Philosophy*, 47:25 (1950).
298. Schlick, M. *Allgemeine Erkenntnislehre*. Berlin: Springer, 1925.
299. Schlick, M. *Gesammelte Aufsaetze*. Vienna: Gerold & Co., 1938.
300. Schlick, M. "De la Relation des Notions Psychologiques et les Notions Physiques," *Revue de Synthèse*, 10:5–26 (1935). Reprinted in English in H. Feigl and W. Sellars (eds.), *Readings in Philosophical Analysis*, pp. 393–407. New York: Appleton-Century-Crofts, 1949.
301. Schlick, M. *Problems of Ethics*. New York: Prentice-Hall, 1939.
302. Schlick, M. "Positivism and Realism," *Synthese*, Vol. 7, 6-B (1948–1949) in Communications of the Institute for the Unity of Science, Boston.
303. Schrödinger, E. *What is Life?* Cambridge: Cambridge Univ. Press, 1944.
304. Scriven, M. "The Mechancial Concept of Mind," *Mind*, 62:230–240 (1953).
305. Scriven, M. "Modern Experiments in Telepathy," *Philosophical Review*, 65:231–251 (1956).
306. Scriven, M. "A Study of Radical Behaviorism," in H. Feigl and M. Scriven (eds.), *Minnesota Studies in the Philosophy of Science*, Vol. I, pp. 88–130. Minneapolis: Univ. of Minnesota Press, 1956.
307. Sellars, R. W. *The Philosophy of Physical Realism*. New York: Macmillan, 1932.
308. Sellars, W. "Realism and the New Way of Words," *Philosophical and Phenomenological Research*, 8:601–634 (1948). Reprinted in H. Feigl and W. Sellars (eds.), *Readings in Philosophical Analysis*, pp. 424–456. New York: Appleton-Century-Crofts, 1949.
309. Sellars, W. "Aristotelian Philosophies of Mind," in V. J. McGill, M. Farber, and R. W. Sellars (eds.), *Philosophy for the Future*, pp. 544–570. New York: Macmillan, 1949.

Herbert Feigl

310. Sellars, W. "Mind, Meaning, and Behavior," *Philosophical Studies*, 3:83–94 (1952).

311. Sellars, W. "A Semantical Solution of the Mind-Body Problem," *Methodos*, 5:45–84 (1953).

312. Sellars, W. "Some Reflections on Language Games," *Philosophy of Science*, 21:204–228 (1954).

313. Sellars, W. "Is There a Synthetic A Priori?" *Philosophy of Science*, 20:121–138 (1953).

314. Sellars, W. "Inference and Meaning," *Mind*, 62:313–338 (1953).

315. Sellars, W. "Empiricism and the Philosophy of Mind," in H. Feigl and M. Scriven (eds.), *Minnesota Studies in the Philosophy of Science*, Vol. I, pp. 253–329. Minneapolis: Univ. of Minnesota Press, 1956.

316. Sellars, W. "Empiricism and Abstract Entities," in Schilpp (ed.), *The Philosophy of Rudolf Carnap*. Evanston (Ill.): Library of Living Philosophers (forthcoming). (Available in mimeographed form from the author.)

317. Seward, J. P. "The Constancy of the I-V: A Critique of Intervening Variables," *Psychological Review*, 62:155–168 (1955).

318. Sheldon, W. H. "Are Naturalists Materialists?" *Journal of Philosophy*, 43:197–209 (1946).

319. Singer, E. A. *Mind as Behavior*. Columbus (Ohio): R. G. Adams and Co., 1924.

320. Skinner, B. F. "The Operational Analysis of Psychological Terms," *Psychological Review*, 52:270–277 (1945). Reprinted in H. Feigl and M. Brodbeck (eds.), *Readings in the Philosophy of Science*, pp. 585–594. New York: Appleton-Century-Crofts, 1953.

321. Skinner, B. F. *Science and Human Behavior*. New York: Macmillan, 1953.

322. Smith, M. B. "The Phenomenological Approach in Personality Theory: Some Critical Remarks," *Journal of Abnormal and Social Psychology*, 45:516–522 (1950).

323. Smythies, J. R. *Analysis of Perception*. London: Routledge & Kegan Paul, 1956.

324. Snygg, D., and Combs, A. W. "The Phenomenological Approach and the Problem of 'Unconscious' Behavior: A Reply to Dr. Smith." *Journal of Abnormal and Social Psychology*, 45:523–528 (1950).

325. Soal, S. C., and F. Bateman. *Modern Experiments in Telepathy*. New Haven: Yale Univ. Press, 1954.

326. Spilsbury, R. J. "Mentality in Machines." A Symposium, *Aristotelian Society Supplementary Volume*, 26:27–60 (1952).

327. Stace, W. T. *Theory of Knowledge and Existence*. Oxford: Oxford Univ. Press, 1932.

328. Stevens, S. S. "Psychology and the Science of Science," *Psychological Bulletin*, 36:221–263 (1939). Reprinted in P. P. Wiener (ed.), *Readings in Philosophy of Science*, pp. 158–184. New York: Scribner, 1953.

329. Stevenson, C. L. *Ethics and Language*. New Haven (Conn.): Yale Univ. Press, 1944.

330. Stout, A. K. "Free Will and Responsibility," *Proceedings of the Aristotelian Society*, 37:213–230 (1937). Reprinted in W. Sellars and J. Hospers (eds.), *Readings in Ethical Theory*, pp. 537–548. New York: Appleton-Century-Crofts, 1952.

331. Stout, G. F. *Mind and Matter*. Cambridge (Eng.): Cambridge University Press, 1931.

332. Strong, C. A. *Essays on the Natural Origin of Mind*. London: Macmillan, 1930.

333. Taylor, R. "Comments on a Mechanistic Conception of Purposefulness," *Philosophy of Science*, 17:310–317 (1950).

334. Taylor, R. "Purposeful and Non-Purposeful Behavior: Rejoinder," *Philosophy of Science*, 17:327–332 (1950).
335. Tolman, E. C. "Psychology versus Immediate Experience," *Philosophy of Science*, 2:356–380 (1935).
336. Tolman, E. C. *Collected Papers in Psychology*. Berkeley: Univ. of California Press, 1951.
337. Tomas, J. "Can We Know the Contents of C. I. Lewis' Mind?" *Philosophical and Phenomenological Research*, 11:541–548 (1951).
338. Turing, A. M. "Computing Machinery and Intelligence," *Mind*, 59:433–460 (1950).
339. University of California Associates. "The Freedom of the Will," in *Knowledge and Society*. New York: D. Appleton-Century Co., 1938. Reprinted in H. Feigl and W. Sellars (eds.), *Readings in Philosophical Analysis*, pp. 594–615. New York: Appleton-Century-Crofts, 1949.
340. Wallraff, C. F. "On Immediacy and the Contemporary Dogma of Sense-Certainty," *Journal of Philosophy*, 50:2 (1953).
341. Watling, J. "Ayer on Other Minds," *Theoria*, 20:175–180 (1954).
342. Watling, J. "Inference from the Known to the Unknown," *Proceedings of the Aristotelian Society*, New Series 55:83–108 (1955).
343. Weber, A. O. "Gestalttheorie and the Theory of Relations," *Journal of Philosophy*, 35:589–606 (1938).
344. Weber, C. O. "Theoretical and Experimental Difficulties of Modern Psychology with the Body-Mind Problem," in P. L. Harriman (ed.), *Twentieth Century Psychology*, pp. 64–93. New York: Philosophical Library, 1946.
345. Weitz, M. "Professor Ryle's 'Logical Behaviorism,' " *Journal of Philosophy*, 48:9 (1951).
346. Wenzl, A. *Das Leib-Seele-Problem*. Leipzig: Verlag von Felix Meiner, 1933.
347. White, M. *Toward Reunion in Philosophy*. Cambridge (Mass.): Harvard Univ. Press, 1956.
348. Wiener, N. *Cybernetics*. New York: Wiley, 1948.
349. Williams, D. C. "Scientific Method and the Existence of Consciousness," *Psychological Review*, 41:461–479 (1934).
350. Wilson, N. L. "Designation and Description," *Journal of Philosophy*, 50:369–383 (1953).
351. Wilson, N. L. "In Defense of Proper Names Against Descriptions," *Philosophical Studies*, 4:73–78 (1953).
352. Wilson, N. L. "Property Designation and Description," *Philosophical Review*, 64:389–404 (1955).
353. Wisdom, J. "Other Minds," *Aristotelian Society Supplementary Volume*, 20:122–147 (1946).
354. Wisdom, J. *Other Minds*, Oxford: Blackwell, 1952.
355. Wisdom, J. O. "Mentality in Machines," A Symposium, *Aristotelian Society Supplementary Volume*, 26:1–26 (1952).
356. Wisdom, J. O. "Is Epiphenomenalism Refutable?" *Proceedings of the 2nd International Congress of the International Union for the Philosophy of Science*, 5:73–78 (1954).
357. Wittgenstein, L. *Philosophical Investigations*. London and New York: Macmillan, 1953.
358. Woodger, J. H. *Biological Principles*. London: Kegan Paul, Trench & Co., 1929.
359. Woodger, J. H. *Physics, Psychology and Medicine*. Cambridge: Cambridge Univ. Press, 1956.

When Shall We Use Our Heads Instead of the Formula?

My title question, "When should we use our heads instead of the formula?" is not rhetorical. I am sincerely asking what I see as an important question. I find the two extreme answers to this question, namely, "Always" and "Never," equally unacceptable. But to formulate a satisfactory answer upon the present evidence seems extraordinarily difficult.

I put the question in the practical clinical context. This is where Sarbin put it in his pioneering study (9) fourteen years ago, and this is where it belongs. Some critics of my book (5) have repudiated the whole question by saying that, always and necessarily, we use *both* our heads and the formula. No, we do not. In research, we use both; the best clinical research involves a shuttling back and forth between clever, creative speculation and subsequent statistical testing of empirical derivations therefrom. So far as I am aware, nobody has ever denied this. Even the arch-actuary George Lundberg approved of the clinician as hypothesis-maker. In research one cannot design experiments or concoct theories without using his head, and he cannot test them rigorously without using a formula. This is so obvious that I am surprised to find that people will waste time in discussing it. The clinical-statistical issue can hardly be stated so as to make sense in the research context, and I should have thought it clear that a meaningful issue can be raised only in the context of daily clinical activity.

In the clinical context, on the other hand, the question is sensible and of great practical importance. Here we have the working clinician or administrator, faced with the necessity to make a decision at *this* moment in time, regarding *this* particular patient. He knows that his evidence is inadequate. He can think of several research projects which, *had they* been done already, would be helpful to him in deciding the present case. If he is research-oriented he may even make a note of these research ideas and later carry them out or persuade someone else to do so. But none of that helps him now. He is in a sort of Kierkegaardian existential predicament, because he has to act. As Joe Zubin kept repeating when I last tangled with him on this subject, "Every clinical decision is a *Willensakt*." And so it is; but the question remains, how do we make our *Willensakts* as rational as possible, using limited information? What clinician X knows today and what he could find out by research in ten years are two very different things. The question "When shall we use our heads instead of the formula?" presupposes that we are about to make a clinical decision at a given point in time, and must base it upon what is known to us at that moment. In that context, the question makes perfectly good sense. It is silly to answer it by saying amicably, "We use both methods; they go hand in hand." If the formula and your head invariably yield the same predictions about individuals, you should quit using the more costly one because it is not adding anything. If they don't always yield the same prediction—and they clearly don't, as a matter of empirical fact—then you obviously can't "use both," because you cannot predict in opposite ways for the same case. If one says then, "Well, by 'using both,' I mean that we follow the formula except on special occasions," the problem becomes how to identify the proper subset of occasions. And this of course amounts to the very question I am putting. For example, does the formula tell us "Here, use your heads," or do we rely on our heads to tell us this, thus countermanding the formula?

Most decisions in current practice do not pose this problem because no formula exists. Sometimes there is no formula because the prediction problem is too open-ended, as in dream analysis; sometimes the very categorizing of the raw observations involves Gestalted stimulus equivalences for which the laws are unknown, and hence cannot be mathematically formulated (although the clinician himself exemplifies these laws and can therefore "utilize" them); in still other cases there is no formula because nobody has bothered to make one. In any of these three circumstances, we use our heads because there isn't anything else to use. This will presumably be true of many special prediction situations for years to come. The logical analysis of the first two situations— open-endedness and unknown psychological laws—is a fascinating subject in its own right, especially in relation to psychotherapy. But since our original question implies that a formula does exist, we will say no more about that subject here.

Suppose then that we have a prediction equation (or an actuarial table) which has been satisfactorily cross-validated. Let us say that it predicts with some accuracy which patients will respond well to intensive outpatient therapy in our VA clinic. We are forced to make such predictions because our staff-patient ratio physically precludes offering intensive treatment to all cases; also we know that a minority, such as certain latent schizophrenias, react adversely and even dangerously. The equation uses both psychometric and non-psychometric data. It may include what the Cornell workers called "Stop" items—items given such a huge weight that when present they override any combination of the remaining factors. It may be highly patterned, taking account of verified interaction effects.

So here is veteran Jones, whose case is under consideration by the therapy staff. The equation takes such facts as his Rorschach F+, his Multiphasic code, his divorce, his age, his 40 per cent service-connected disability, and grinds out a probability of .75 of "good response to therapy." (The logicians and theoretical statisticians are still arguing over the precise meaning of this number as applied to Jones. But we are safe in saying, "If you accept patients from this population who have this score, you will be right 3 times in 4.") Here is Jones. We want to do what is best for him. We don't *know for sure*, and we can't, by any method, actuarial or otherwise. We act on the probabilities, as everyone does who chooses a career, takes a wife, bets on a horse, or brings a lawsuit. (If you object, as some of the more cloud-headed clinikers do, to acting on "mere probabilities," you will have to shut up shop, because probabilities are all you'll ever get.)

But now the social worker tells us that Jones, age 40, said at the admission conference that his mother sent him in. The psychology trainee describes blocking and a bad F— on Rorschach VII; the psychiatrist adds his comments, and pretty soon we are concluding that Jones has a very severe problem with mother-figures. Since our only available therapist is Frau Dr. Schleswig-Holstein, who would traumatize anybody even without a mother-problem, we begin to vacillate. The formula gives us odds of 3 to 1 on Jones; these further facts, not in the equation, raise doubts in our minds. What shall we do?

In my little book on this subject, I gave an example which makes it too easy (5, p. 24). If a sociologist were predicting whether Professor X would go to the movies on a certain night, he might have an equation involving age, academic specialty, and introversion score. The equation might yield a probability of .90 that Professor X will go to the movies tonight. But if the family doctor announced that Professor X had just broken his leg, no sensible sociologist would stick with the equation. Why didn't the factor of "broken leg" appear in the formula? Because broken legs are very rare, and in the sociologist's entire sample of 500 criterion cases plus 250 cross-validating cases, he did not come upon a single instance of it. He uses the broken leg datum confidently, because "broken leg" is a subclass of a larger class we may crudely denote as "relatively immobilizing illness or injury," and movie-attending is a subclass of a larger class of "actions requiring moderate mobility." There is a universally recognized "subjective experience table" which cuts across sociological and theatrical categories, and the probabilities are so close to zero that not even a sociologist feels an urge to tabulate them! (That this is the correct analysis of matters can be easily seen if we ask what our sociologist would do if he were in a strange culture and had seen even a few legs in casts at the movies.)

I suppose only the most anal of actuaries would be reluctant to abandon the equation in the broken leg case, on the ground that we were unable to cite actual statistical support for the generalization "People with broken legs don't attend movies." But clinicians should beware of overdoing the broken leg analogy. There are at least four aspects of the broken leg case which are very different from the usual "psychodynamic" reversal of an actuarial prediction. First, a broken leg is a pretty objective fact, determinable with high accuracy, if you care to take the trouble; second, its correlation with relative immobilization is near perfect, based on a huge N, and attested by all sane men regardless of race, creed, color, or what school granted them the doctorate; third, interaction effects are conspicuously lacking—the immobilization phenomenon cuts neatly across the other categories under study; fourth, the prediction is mediated without use of any doubtful theory, being either purely taxonomic or based upon such low-level theory as can be provided by skeletal mechanics and common sense. The same cannot be said of such an inference as "Patient Jones has an unconscious problem with mother-figures, and male patients with such problems will not react well in intensive therapy with Frau Dr. Schleswig-Holstein."

When the physicists exploded the first atomic bomb, they had predicted a novel occurrence by theoretical methods. No actuarial table, based upon thousands of combinations of chemicals, would have led to this prediction. But these kinds of theoretical derivations in the developed sciences involve combining rigorously formulated theories with exact knowledge of the state of the particular system, neither of which we have in clinical psychology. Yet we must do justice to the basic *logical* claim of our clinician. I want to stress that he is not in the untenable position of denying the actuarial data. He freely admits that 75 per cent of patients having Jones' formula score are good bets for therapy. But he says that Jones belongs to the other 25 per cent, and therefore thinks we can avoid one of our formula's mispredictions by countermanding the formula in this case. There is nothing intrinsically wrong with this suggestion. Perhaps the clinician can identify a subclass of patients within the class having Jones' actuarial attributes, for which the success rate is less than .5. This would be perfectly compatible with the over-all actuarial data, provided the clinician doesn't claim it too often.

At this point the actuary, a straightforward fellow, proposes that we tabulate the new signs mentioned in staff conference as indicating this subclass before proceeding further. Here we again reduce our clinician to a hypothesis-suggestor, and seem to put the current prediction problem back on an actuarial basis. But wait. Are we really prepared to detail someone to do such "case-oriented" research every time a clinical prediction is made? Actually it is impossible. It would require a super-file of punch-cards of colossal N to be available in each clinic, and several major staff members doing nothing but running case-oriented minor studies while clinical conferences went into recess pending the outcomes.

However, this is a "practical" objection. Suppose we circumvent it somehow, so that when a sign or pattern is used clinically to support a counter-actuarial prediction, we can proceed immediately to subject the sign to actuarial test on our clinical files. There are serious difficulties even so. Unless the several staff members who produced these records had in mind all of the signs that anybody subsequently brings up, we have no assurance that they were looked for or noted. Anyone who has done file research knows the frustration of having no basis for deciding when the lack of mention of a symptom indicates its absence.

But even ignoring this factor, what if we find only three cases in the files who show the pattern? Any *split* among these three cases as to therapy outcome is statistically compatible with a wide range of parameter values. We can neither confirm nor refute, at any respectable confidence level, our clinician's claim that this pattern brings the success-probability from .75 to some value under .5 (he doesn't say how far under).

Here the statistician throws up his hands in despair. What, he asks, can you do with a clinician who wants to countermand a known probability of .75 by claiming a subclass probability which we cannot estimate reliably? And, of course, one wonders how many thousands of patients the clinician has seen to have accumulated a larger sample of the rare configuration. He also is subject to sampling errors, isn't he?

This brings us to the crux of the matter. Does the clinician need to have seen any cases of "mother-sent-me-in' and Card VII blockage who were treated by female therapists? Here we run into a philosophical issue about the nature of probability. Many logicians (including notably Carnap, Kneale, Sellars, and most of the British school) reject the view (widely held among applied statisticians) that *probability* is always *frequency*. Carnap speaks of "inductive probability," by which he means the logical support given to a hypothesis by evidence. We use this kind of probability constantly both in science and in daily life. No one knows how to compute it exactly, except for very simple worlds described by artificial languages. Even so, we cannot get along without it. So our clinician believes that he has inductive evidence from many different sources, on different populations, partly actuarial, partly experimental, partly anecdotal, that there is such a psychological structure as a "mother-surrogate problem." He adduces indirect evidence for the construct validity (1) of Rorschach Card VII reactions. I am not here considering the actual scientific merits of such claims in the clinical field, of which I take a rather dim view. But I think it important for us to understand the methodological character of the clinician's rebuttal. If Carnap and some of his fellow-logicians are right, the idea that *relative frequency* and *probability* are synonymous is a philosophical mistake.

Of course there is an implicit future reference to frequency even in this kind of inductive argument. Carnap identifies inductive probability with the betting odds which a reasonable man should accept. I take this to mean that if the clinician decided repeatedly on the basis of what he thought were high inductive probabilities, and we found him to be wrong most of the time, then he was presumably making erroneous estimates of his inductive probabilities. The claim of a high inductive probability implies an expectation of being right; in the long run, he who (correctly) bets odds of 7 to 3 will be able to point to a hit-rate of 70 per cent. But this future reference to success-frequency is not the same as the *present evidence* for a hypothesis. This seems a difficult point for people to see. As a member of a jury, you might be willing to bet 9 to 1 odds on the prisoner's guilt, and this might be rational of you; yet no calculation of frequencies constituted your inductive support in the present instance. The class of hypotheses where you have assigned an inductive probability of .9 should "pan out" 90 per cent of the time. But the assignment of that inductive probability to each hypothesis need not itself have been done by frequency methods. If we run a long series on Sherlock Holmes, and find that 95 per cent of his "reconstructions" of crimes turn out to be valid, our confidence in his guesses is good *in part just because they are his.* Yet do we wish to maintain that a rational man, ignorant of these statistics, could form no "probable opinion" about a *particular* Holmesian hypothesis based on the evidence available? I cannot think anyone wants to maintain this.

The philosophical recognition of a non-frequency inductive probability does not help much to solve our practical problem. No one has quantified this kind of probability (which is one reason why Fisher rejected it as useless for scientific purposes). Many logicians doubt that it can be quantified, even in principle. What then are we to say? The clinician thinks he has "high" (how high? who knows?) inductive support for his particular theory about Jones. He thinks it is so high that we are rationally justified in assigning Jones to the 25 per cent class permitted by the formula. The actuary doubts this, and the data do not allow a sufficiently sensitive statistical test. Whom do we follow?

Well, the actuary is not quite done yet. He has been surreptitiously spying upon the clinician for, lo, these many years. The mean old scoundrel has kept a record of the clinician's predictions. What does he find, when he treats the clinician as an empty decision-maker, ignoring the inductive logic going on inside him? Let me bring you up to date on the empirical evidence. As of today, there are 27 empirical studies in the literature which make some meaningful comparison between the predictive success of the clinician and the statistician. The predictive domains include success in academic or military training, recidivism and parole violation, recovery from psychosis, (concurrent) personality description, and outcome of psychotherapy. Of these 27 studies, 17 show a definite superiority for the statistical method; 10 show the methods to be of about equal efficiency; none of them show the clinician predicting better. I have reservations about some of these studies; I do not believe they are optimally designed to exhibit the clinician at his best; but I submit that it is high time that those who are so sure that the "right kind of study" will exhibit the clinician's prowess should do this right kind of study and back up their claim with evidence. Furthermore, a good deal of routine clinical prediction is going on all over the country in which the data available, and the intensity of clinical contact, are not materially different from that in the published comparisons. It is highly probable that current predictive methods are costly to taxpayers and harmful to the welfare of patients.

Lacking quantification of inductive probability, we have no choice but to examine the clinician's success rate. One would hope that the rule-of-thumb assessment of inductive probability is not utterly unreliable. The indicated research step is therefore obvious: We persuade the clinician to state the odds, or somehow rate his "confidence," in his day-by-day decisions. Even if he tends over all to be wrong when countermanding the actuary, he may still tend to be systematically right for a high-confidence subset of his predictions. Once having proved this, we could thereafter countermand the formula in cases where the clinician expresses high confidence in his head. It is likely that studies in a great diversity of domains will be required before useful generalizations can be made.

In the meantime, we are all continuing to make predictions. I think it is safe to say, on the present evidence, that we are not as good as we thought we were. The development of powerful actuarial methods could today proceed more rapidly than ever before. Both theoretical and empirical considerations suggest that we would be well advised to concentrate effort on improving our actuarial techniques rather than on the calibration of each clinician for each of a large number of different prediction problems. How should we meanwhile be making our decisions? Shall we use our heads, or shall we follow the formula? Mostly we will use our heads, because there just isn't any formula. But suppose

Paul E. Meehl

we have a formula, and a case comes along in which it disagrees with our heads? Shall we then use our heads? I would say, yes—provided the psychological situation is as clear as a broken leg; otherwise, very, very seldom.

EDITORS' NOTE. This article first appeared in the *Journal of Counseling Psychology,* Volume IV, Number 4 (Winter 1957). For the assignment of copyright, we are grateful to the editor, C. Gilbert Wrenn.

REFERENCES

1. Cronbach, L. J., and P. E. Meehl. "Construct Validity in Psychological Tests," *Psychological Bulletin,* 52:281–302 (1955). Reprinted in H. Feigl and M. Scriven (eds.), *Minnesota Studies in the Philosophy of Science,* Vol. I, pp. 174–204. Minneapolis: Univ. of Minnesota Press, 1956.
2. Humphreys, L. G., C. C. McArthur, P. E. Meehl, N. Sanford, and J. Zubin. "Clinical versus Actuarial Prediction," *Proceedings of the 1955 Invitational Conference on Testing Problems,* pp. 91–141.
3. McArthur, C. C. "Analyzing the Clinical Process," *Journal of Counseling Psychology,* 1:203–207 (1954).
4. McArthur, C. C., P. E. Meehl, and D. V. Tiedeman. "Symposium on Clinical and Statistical Prediction," *Journal of Counseling Psychology,* 3:163–173 (1956).
5. Meehl, P. E. *Clinical versus Statistical Prediction: A Theoretical Analysis and a Review of the Evidence.* Minneapolis: Univ. of Minnesota Press, 1954.
6. Meehl, P. E. "Comment on 'Analyzing the Clinical Process,'" *Journal of Counseling Psychology,* 1:207–208 (1954).
7. Meehl, P. E. "Wanted—A Good Cookbook," *American Psychologist,* 11:263–272 (1956). Reprinted as "Problems in the Actuarial Characterization of a Person," in H. Feigl and M. Scriven (eds.), *Minnesota Studies in the Philosophy of Science,* Vol. I, pp. 205–222. Minneapolis: Univ. of Minnesota Press, 1956.
8. Meehl, P. E., and A. Rosen. "Antecedent Probability and the Efficiency of Psychometric Signs, Patterns, or Cutting Scores," *Psychological Bulletin,* 52:194–216 (1955).
9. Sarbin, T. R. "A Contribution to the Study of Actuarial and Individual Methods of Prediction," *American Journal of Sociology,* 48:593–602 (1942).

Intentionality and the Mental

Introduction by Wilfrid Sellars

The traditional mind-body problem is, as Herbert Feigl has amply demonstrated in his contribution to this volume, a veritable tangle of tangles. At first sight but one of the 'problems of philosophy,' it soon turns out, as one picks at it, to be nothing more nor less than the philosophical enterprise as a whole. Yet if, to the close-up view of the philosopher at work, it soon becomes a bewildering crisscross of threads leading in all directions, it is possible to discern, on standing off, a number of distinguishable regions which, though but vaguely defined, provide relatively independent access to the whole. It is in this spirit that Feigl distinguishes, early in his essay,[1] some of the major component perplexities which go to make up this 'world knot.' It is only after drawing these distinctions, and indicating the general strategy with which he would approach the others, that he settles down to a painstaking analysis of the relation of what might be called 'sensory consciousness' (sensations, images, tickles, itches, etc.) to the body and, in particular, to the central nervous system.

Now it is not to be doubted that the task of clarifying conceptual puzzles concerning the status of sensory consciousness in the various frameworks (ordinary discourse, molar 'psychophysics,' the unified micro-theory of human behavior which, in outline, we can already dimly discern) in which it appears, is one of the most difficult and intriguing in philosophy. That it is often thought to be simple is but one more expression of the *simpliste* empiricisms which flourished in the thirties and, having made their contribution, are fading from the scene. On the other hand, as Feigl has emphasized, this task is, after all, but one strand in the world knot; and no collection of essays on philosophical topics pertaining to psychology can hope to be balanced, let alone complete, without some exploration of the other strands.

Of these other strands there are many, and most of them are well represented in the first two volumes of this series. There is, however, one major strand which, of central concern to the philosopher who wishes to locate the aims and methods of scientific psychology in the totality of discourse about 'docile organisms,' has received relatively short shrift—not because its importance was overlooked, but because it played a less controversial role in Center discussions than the more immediate issues of concept formation and theory construction in scientific psychology itself. This strand is known traditionally as the problem of 'intentionality,' that is to say, the problem of interpreting the status of the *reference* to objects and states of affairs, actual or possible, past, present or future, which is involved in the very meaning of the 'mentalistic' vocabulary of everyday life. Believing, desiring, intending, loving, hating, reasoning, approving—indeed, all characteristically human states and dispositions above the level of mere sensory consciousness—cannot be explicated without encountering such *reference* or *aboutness*. It lurks in such notions as that of 'behavioral' (as contrasted with 'geographical') environment, and in the non-technical use of such terms as 'goal', 'anticipatory', and 'expectancy' which have become technical terms in behavioristically oriented psychology. And while in their technical use

507

they may be explicitly introduced in terms of observables pertaining to overt behavior which no more contain the notion of reference or aboutness than do the observables of, say, physical theory, the problem remains of the relation between concepts so constructed and the mentalistic vocabulary with which the enterprise began.

This problem is, perhaps, best put in terms of a concrete example. Someone correctly and truly says, using the language of everyday life, "Jones believes that there is a round table in the room" ('There is a round table in his immediate behavioral environment'); and a (somewhat idealized) psychologist, using concepts which have been aseptically introduced on a basis of concepts pertaining to overt behavior, describes Jones by formulating the sentence "S is in behavioral state Φ." In some sense the psychologist is describing the same situation as is his common-sense counterpart. Now the situation as described by the latter includes *aboutness* or *reference*. Does the situation *as described by the psychologist* also include *aboutness* or *reference*? If so, it can only be because aboutness or reference is constructable out of the aseptic primitives to which he has restricted himself (together, of course, with the resources of logic and mathematics). If not, would it not (perhaps) follow that behavioristically oriented psychology *leaves something out* of its picture of what human beings are; that at most it describes the 'bodily' *correlates* of 'mental' states and dispositions, which later would constitute a unique set of facts accessible only to 'introspection' and beyond the scope of intersubjective science?

Now, I think that all psychologists who have reflected on the relation of mentalistic discourse to the deliberately contrived language of scientific psychology have had their hunches on this matter. These hunches have been built around two themes: (1) behavioristically oriented psychology is *not* doomed to give an incomplete picture of the human animal (at least as far as the 'higher processes' are concerned—the other fellow's tickles have caused more trouble); (2) the key to the behavioristic account of the 'higher processes' is verbal behavior. But these hunches, sound though they may be, and effective though they may be as dykes behind which to go about the journeyman task of building scientific psychology, do not answer the questions which must be faced now that the building has risen high enough to permit a view of the landscape outside.

It is clear that before one can hope to answer the question, 'Is behavioristics doomed to leave something out of its picture of the human animal, something which is included in the picture painted by ordinary mentalistic discourse?' he must have arrived at an understanding of the descriptive force of this mentalistic vocabulary. The simplest account, unfortunately incorrect, would be that mentalistic terms in ordinary usage are themselves built, albeit with an open texture and an informal reliance on the context of utterance more suitable to practical than to theoretical purposes, out of behavioral primitives. If so, the language of behavioristics would simply be "more of the same" and there could be no question of its leaving reference or aboutness out of its picture of human behavior.

But if the 'simplest account'—that of 'Philosophical Behaviorism'—won't do, then the problem exists in all its urgency. And there are not wanting those who insist that the only alternative to Philosophical Behaviorism is the view, as we put it, that a behavioristically oriented psychology can at most describe the 'bodily' correlates of 'mental' states and dispositions. (That this 'at most' would represent a magnificent achievement, nobody, of course, would deny.)

In my essay "Empiricism and the Philosophy of Mind," printed in the first volume of this series, I sought to answer these questions, though in little space, and as but one part of a far more complex argument. I offered an account of the logic of ordinary mentalistic discourse designed to show *in exactly what sense* it includes something (namely reference or aboutness) in its picture of human beings which is not to be found in the language of behavioristics. On the assumption that success in interpreting the force of such a basic mentalistic statement as "It suddenly occurred to

Jones that he was alone," or, in general, statements of the form "S had the thought that p," would provide the key to the understanding of such more complicated mental states and dispositions as believing, desiring, approving, and being self-centered, I attempted to explicate the status, in the mentalistic framework, of certain basic episodes which I called 'thoughts' (§§46–47).

Roughly my argument consisted of four stages. In the first I began by arguing (§§53–54) for the legitimacy of theoretical concepts in behavioristic psychology, and then (§56) suggested that our pre-scientific or common sense concepts of "inner" (mental) episodes began as something analogous to theoretical concepts introduced to explain certain forms of observable behavior. In the second (§§30–31) I explored the force of statements of the form illustrated by " 'Rot' (in German) means red" and argued that these statements, instead of describing words as standing in 'the meaning relation' to things, do not describe at all, but simply translate. In the third I characterized (§§51–52) the role of models in theory construction, and then (§§56–58) argued that it is the mode of discourse built around this translating rubric, in short semantical discourse, discourse about 'the meaning of a word', 'the truth of a statement', etc., which functioned as the model in the pre-scientific genesis of our everyday mentalistic framework. In the fourth and final stage I argued (§59) that though the framework of thoughts began as a 'theory' and was used as theories are used, it subsequently acquired, in a manner the general principle of which is readily understood, a reporting role.

I concluded by claiming that "this story helps us understand that concepts pertaining to such inner episodes as thoughts are primarily and essentially intersubjective, as intersubjective as the concept of a positron, and that the reporting role of these concepts—the fact that each of us has a privileged access to his thoughts—constitutes a dimension of the use of these concepts which is built on and presupposes this intersubjective status . . . It also makes clear that [the 'privacy' of 'inner episodes'] is not an 'absolute privacy.' For if it recognizes that these concepts have a reporting use in which one is not drawing inferences from behavioral evidence, it nevertheless insists that the fact that overt behavior is evidence for these episodes is built into the very logic of these concepts, just as the fact that the observable behavior of gases is evidence for molecular episodes is built into the very logic of molecule talk" (pp. 320–321).

As soon as the page proof was available, I sent a copy of this essay to Professor Roderick Chisholm, who has long shared my interest in the problem of intentionality, and has written penetratingly on the subject, though from a more conservative point of view. I was anxious to learn if this new twist to my argument would convince him of the essential soundness of my approach, as my previous papers on the topic had not. His friendly remarks encouraged me to make a further try for agreement, and the end result was the correspondence which is printed at the end of this Appendix, and is its raison d'etre. There was at the time no thought of publication, and it was only some months after the last of the letters had been written, when the present volume was already being prepared for the press, that the possibility was broached. Once the project was underway, Professor Chisholm kindly consented to edit his recent Aristotelian Society paper on 'Sentences about Believing' [2] for republication as a background for his side of the controversy.

NOTES

[1] Pp. 370ff of the present volume.

[2] Proceedings of the Aristotelian Society, 56:125–148 (1955–1956). A more complete account of his views is to be found in his book Perceiving: A Philosophical Study (Ithaca: Cornell Univ. Press, 1957).

Appendix

Sentences about Believing by Roderick M. Chisholm

1. "I can look for him when he is not there, but not hang him when he is not there."[1] The first of these activities, Brentano would have said, is *intentional*; it may take as its object something which does not exist. But the second activity is "merely physical"; it cannot be performed unless its object is there to work with. "Intentionality," he thought, provides us with a mark of what is psychological.

I shall try to reformulate Brentano's suggestion by describing one of the ways in which we need to use language when we talk about certain psychological states and events. I shall refer to this use as the "intentional use" of language. It is a kind of use we can avoid when we talk about non-psychological states and events.

In the interests of a philosophy contrary to that of Brentano, many philosophers and psychologists have tried to show, in effect, how we can avoid intentional language when we wish to talk about psychology. I shall discuss some of these attempts in so far as they relate to the sorts of things we wish to be able to say about *believing*. I believe that these attempts have been so far unsuccessful. And I think that this fact may provide some reason for saying, with Brentano, that "intentionality" is a mark of what is psychological.

2. In order to formulate criteria by means of which we can identify the "intentional" use of language, let us classify sentences as simple and compound. For our purposes I think it will be enough to say that a compound sentence is one compounded from two or more sentences by means of propositional connectives, such as "and", "or", "if-then", "although", and "because". A simple sentence is one which is not compound. Examples of simple sentences are "He is thinking of the Dnieper Dam," "She is looking for a suitable husband for her daughter," "Their car lacks a spare wheel," and "He believes that it will rain." I shall formulate three criteria for saying that simple declarative sentences are intentional, or are used intentionally.

(a) A simple declarative sentence is intentional if it uses a substantival expression—a name or a description—in such a way that neither the sentence nor its contradictory implies either that there is or that there isn't anything to which the substantival expression truly applies. The first two examples above are intentional by this criterion. When we say that a man is thinking of the Dnieper Dam, we do not imply either that there is or that there isn't such a dam; similarly when we deny that he is thinking of it. When we say that a lady is looking for a suitable husband for her daughter, we do not commit ourselves to saying that her daughter will, or that she will not, have a suitable husband; and similarly when we deny that the lady is looking for one. But the next sentence in our list of examples—"Their car lacks a spare wheel"—is not intentional. It is true that, if we affirm this sentence, we do not commit ourselves to saying either that there are or that there are not any spare wheels. But if we deny the sentence, affirming "Their car does not lack a spare wheel," then we imply that there is a spare wheel somewhere.

(b) We may describe a second type of intentional use by reference to simple sentences the principal verb of which takes as its object a phrase containing a subordinate verb. The subordinate verb may follow immediately upon the principal verb, as in "He is contemplating killing himself"; it may occur in a complete clause, as in "He believes it will rain"; it may occur in an infinitive, as in "He wishes to speak"; or it may occur in participial form, as in "He accused John of stealing the money" and "He asked John's brother to testify against him." I shall say that such a simple declarative sentence is intentional if neither the sentence nor its contradictory implies either that the phrase following the principal verb is true or that it is false.[2] "He is contemplating killing himself" is intentional, according to this second criterion, because neither it

NOTE: This article is reprinted, with revisions by the author, from *Proceedings of the Aristotelian Society*, 56:125–148 (1955–1956) with the kind permission of the author and the editors.

nor its denial implies either that he does or that he doesn't kill himself; similarly with our other examples. But "He prevented John from stealing the money" is not intentional, because it implies that John did not steal the money. And "He knows how to swim" is not intentional, because its denial implies that he isn't swimming.

Sometimes people use substantival expressions in place of the kind of phrases I have just been talking about. Instead of saying, "I want the strike to be called off," they may say, "The strike's being called off is what I want." The latter sentence could be said to be intentional according to our first criterion, for neither the sentence nor its contradictory implies either that "there is such a thing as" the strike's being called off, or that there isn't—that is to say, neither implies that the strike will be, or that it will not be, called off.

Many intentional sentences of our first type may be rewritten in such a way that they become instances of our second type. Instead of saying "I would like a glass of water," one may say "I would like to have a glass of water." And instead of saying "He is looking for the Fountain of Youth," one may say "He is trying to find the Fountain of Youth." But some sentences of the first type seem to resist such transformation into the second type; for example, "I was thinking about you yesterday."

(c) If we make use of Frege's concept of "indirect reference," which is, of course, closely related to that of "intentionality," we can add another important class of sentence to our list of those which are intentional.[3] "Indirect reference" may be defined, without using the characteristic terms of Frege's theory of meaning, in the following way: a name (or description) of a certain thing has an indirect reference in a sentence if its replacement by a different name (or description) of that thing results in a sentence whose truth-value may differ from that of the original sentence.[4] It is useful to interpret this criterion in such a way that we can say of those names (or descriptions), such as "the Fountain of Youth" and "a building half again as tall as the Empire State", which don't apply to anything, that they are all names of the same thing. Let us add, then, that a simple declarative sentence is intentional if it contains a name (or description) which has an indirect reference in that sentence. We can now say of certain *cognitive* sentences—sentences which use words such as "know", "remember", "see", "perceive", in one familiar way—that they, too, are intentional. I may see that Albert is here and Albert may be the man who will win the prize; but I do not now see *that* the man who will win the prize is here. And we all remember that although George IV knew that Scott was the author of Marmion he did not know that Scott was the author of Waverley.

(d) With respect to the intentionality of compound sentences—sentences constructed by means of propositional connectives from two or more sentences—it is enough to say this: a compound declarative sentence is intentional if and only if one or more of its component sentences is intentional. "I will be gratified if I learn that Albert wins the prize" is intentional, because the if-clause is intentional. But "The career of Ponce de Leon would have been most remarkable if he had found the Fountain of Youth" is not intentional, because neither of its components is intentional. (In order that this final criterion be applicable to sentences in the subjunctive, we should, of course, interpret it to mean a compound declarative sentence is intentional if and only if one or more of the component sentences of its indicative version is intentional.)

3. We may now formulate a thesis resembling that of Brentano by referring to intentional language. Let us say (1) that we do not need to use intentional language when we describe non-psychological, or "physical," phenomena; we can express all that we know, or believe, about such phenomena in language which is not intentional.[5] And let us say (2) that, when we wish to describe certain psychological phenomena—in particular, when we wish to describe thinking, believing, perceiving, seeing, knowing, wanting, hoping and the like—either (a) we must use language which

is intentional or (b) we must use a vocabulary which we do not need to use when we describe non-psychological, or "physical," phenomena.

I shall discuss this linguistic version of Brentano's thesis with reference to sentences about believing. I do not pretend to be able to show that it is true in its application to believing. But I think that there are serious difficulties, underestimated by many philosophers, which stand in the way of showing that it is false.

I wish to emphasize that my question does not concern "subsistence" or "the being of objects which don't exist." Philosophers may ask whether it is possible to think about unicorns if there are no unicorns for us to think about. They may also ask whether you and I can believe "the same thing" if there is no proposition or objective toward which each of our beliefs is directed. But I am not raising these questions. Possibly the feeling that the intentional use of language commits us to the assumption that there are such entities is one motive for seeking to avoid such use. But I wish to ask only whether we can avoid such use and at the same time say all that we want to be able to say about believing.

4. The first part of our thesis states that we do not need to use intentional language when we describe non-psychological, or "physical," phenomena. I do not believe that this statement presents any serious difficulty. It is true that we do sometimes use intentional sentences in non-psychological contexts. The following sentences, for example, are all intentional, according to our criteria, but none of them describe anything we would want to call "psychological": "The patient will be immune from the effects of any new epidemics" and "It is difficult to assemble a prefabricated house." But these sentences are not examples counter to our thesis. Anyone who understands the language can readily transform them into conditionals which are not intentional. (A compound sentence, it should be recalled, is intentional only if it has a component which is intentional.) Instead of using intentional sentences, we could have said, "If there should be any new epidemics, the patient would not be affected by them" and "If anyone were to assemble a prefabricated house, he would have difficulties." (Perhaps the last sentence should be rendered as "If anyone were to try to assemble a prefabricated house, he would have difficulties." In this version the sentence is intentional, once again, but since it contains the verb "to try" it can no longer be said to be non-psychological.)

I believe that any other ostensibly non-psychological sentence which is intentional can be transformed, in an equally obvious way, into a sentence conforming to our version of Brentano's thesis. That is to say, it will become a sentence of one of two possible types: either (a) it will be no longer intentional or (b) it will be explicitly psychological. Sentences about probability may be intentional, but, depending upon one's conception of probability, they may be transformed either into the first or into the second type. If I say "It is probable that there is life on Venus," neither my sentence nor its denial implies either that there is life on Venus or that there is not. According to one familiar interpretation of probability, my sentence can be transformed into a non-intentional sentence about frequencies—sentences telling about places where there is life and places where there isn't and comparing Venus with such places, etc. According to another interpretation, my sentence can be transformed into a psychological statement about believing—e.g., "It is reasonable for us to believe that there is life on Venus." Intentional sentences about tendencies and purposes in nature may be treated similarly. If we say, non-intentionally, "The purpose of the liver is to secrete bile," we may mean, psychologically, that the Creator made the liver so that it would secrete bile, or we may mean, non-intentionally, that in most live animals having livers the liver does do this work and that when it does not the animal is unhealthy.

There are people who like to ascribe beliefs, perceptions, plans, desires, and the like to robots and computing machinery. A computing machine might be said to believe, truly, that 7 and 5 are 12; when it is out of order, it may be said to make mistakes and possibly to believe, falsely, that 7 and 5 are 11. But such sentences, once again, are readily transformed into other sentences, usually conditionals, which are no longer intentional. If a man says that the machine believes 7 and 5 to be 11, he may mean merely that, if the keys marked "7" and "5" are pressed, the machine will produce a slip on which "11" is marked. Other intentional sentences about the attitudes of machines may be more complex, but I'm sure that, if they have been given any meaning by those who use them, they can be readily transformed into sentences which are not intentional. Indeed the ease with which robot sentences may be made either intentional or non-intentional may be one ground, or cause, for believing that sentences about the attitudes of human beings may readily be transformed in ways counter to our version of Brentano's thesis.

It should be noted, with respect to those universal sentences of physics which have no "existential import," that they are not intentional. It is true that the sentence, "All moving bodies not acted upon by external forces continue in a state of uniform motion in a straight line," does not imply either that there are, or that there are not, such bodies. But its contradictory implies that there are such bodies.

5. The second part of our version of Brentano's thesis states that, when we wish to describe anyone's believing, seeing, knowing, wanting, and the like, either (a) we must use language which is intentional or (b) we must use a vocabulary we don't need when we talk about non-psychological facts.

Perhaps the most instructive way of looking at our thesis is to contrast it with one which is slightly different. It has often been said, in recent years, that "the language of physical things" is adequate for the description of psychological phenomena—this language being any language whose vocabulary and rules are adequate for the description of non-psychological phenomena. If we do not need intentional language for describing physical things, then this counter-thesis—the thesis that the language of physical things is adequate for the description of psychological phenomena—would imply that we do not need intentional language for the description of psychological phenomena.

The easiest way to construct a non-intentional language for psychology is to telescope nouns and verbs. Finding a psychological verb, say "expects", and its grammatical object, say "food", we may manufacture a technical term by combining the two. We may say that the rat is "food-expectant" or that he "has a food-expectancy." Russell once proposed that, instead of saying "I perceive a cat," we say "I am cat-perceptive," and Professor Ryle has described a man seeing a thimble by saying that the man "is having a visual sensation in a thimble-seeing frame of mind." [6] Sentences about thinking, believing, desiring, and the like could readily be transformed in similar ways. But this way of avoiding intentional language has one serious limitation. If we wish to tell anyone what our technical terms mean, we must use intentional language again. Russell did not propose a definition of his technical term "cat-perceptive" in familiar non-intentional terms; he told us, in effect, that we should call a person "cat-perceptive" whenever the person takes something to be a cat. Our version of Brentano's thesis implies that, if we dispense with intentional language in talking about perceiving, believing, and expecting, we must use a vocabulary we don't need to use when we talk about non-psychological facts. The terms "food-expectancy", "thimble-seeing frame of mind", and "cat-perceptive" illustrate such a vocabulary.

I shall comment upon three general methods philosophers and psychologists have used in their attempts to provide "physical" translations of belief sentences. The first of these methods makes use of the concepts of "specific response" and "appropriate behavior"; references to these concepts appeared in the writings of the American "New Realists" and can still be found in the works of some psychologists. The second method refers to "verbal behavior"; its clearest statement is to be found in Professor Ayer's *Thinking and Meaning*. The third refers to a peculiar type of "fulfilment" or "satisfaction"; its classic statement is William James' so-called pragmatic theory of

Appendix

truth. I shall try to show that, if we interpret these various methods as attempts to show that our version of Brentano's thesis is false, then we can say that they are inadequate. I believe that the last of these methods—the one which refers to "fulfilment" or "satisfaction"—is the one which has the best chance of success.

6. When psychologists talk about the behavior of animals, they sometimes find it convenient to describe certain types of response in terms of the stimuli with which such responses are usually associated. A bird's "nesting responses" might be defined by reference to what the bird does in the presence of its nest and on no other occasions. A man's "rain responses," similarly, might be defined in terms of what he does when and only when he is in the rain. I believe we may say that some of the American "New Realists" assumed that, for every object of which a man can be said ever to be conscious, there is some response he makes when and only when he is in the presence of that object—some response which is *specific* to that object.[7] And they felt that the specific response vocabulary—"rain response", "fire response", "cat response"—provided a way of describing belief and the other types of phenomena Brentano would have called "intentional." This "specific response theory" is presupposed in some recent accounts of "sign behavior."

I think Brentano would have said that, if smoke is a *sign* to me of fire, then my perception of smoke causes me to *believe* that there is a fire. But if we have a specific response vocabulary available, we might say this: smoke is a sign to me of fire provided smoke calls up my *fire responses*. We might then say, more generally, that S is a sign of E for O provided only S calls up O's E-responses. But what would O's E-responses be?

What would a man's fire responses be? If smoke alone can call up his fire responses—as it may when it serves as a sign of fire—we can no longer say that his fire responses are the ways he behaves when and only when he is stimulated by fire. For we want to be able to say that he can make these responses in the presence of smoke and not of fire. Should we modify our conception of "fire response", then, and say that a man's fire responses are responses which are *like* those—which are *similar* to those—he makes when stimulated by fire? This would be saying too much, for in some respects every response he makes is like those he makes in the presence of fire. All of his responses, for example, are alike in being the result of neural and physiological events. But we don't want to say that all of the man's responses are fire responses. It is not enough, therefore, to say that a man's fire responses are similar to those he makes, or would make, in the presence of fire; we must also specify the respect in which they are similar. But no one, I believe, has been able to do this.

The problem isn't altered if we say that a man's fire responses constitute some part of those responses he makes in the presence of fire. More generally, the problem isn't altered if we introduce this definition: S is a sign of E provided only that S calls up part of the behavior that E calls up. It is not enough to say that the sign and the object call up some of the same behavior. The books in this room are not a sign to me of the books in that room, but the books in the two rooms call up some of the same behavior. And it is too much to say that S calls up all of the behavior that E calls up—that the sign evokes all of the responses that the subject makes to the object. The bell is a sign of food to the dog, but the dog, as we know, needn't eat the bell.

We might try to avoid our difficulties by introducing qualifications of another sort in our definition of *sign*. Charles E. Osgood proposes the following definition in the chapter entitled "Language Behavior," in *Method and Theory in Experimental Psychology* (New York: Oxford Univ. Press, 1953): "A pattern of stimulation which is not the object is a sign of the object if it evokes in an organism a mediating reaction, this (a) being some fractional part of the total behavior elicited by the object and (b) producing distinctive self-stimulation that mediates responses which would not occur without the previous association of nonobject and object patterns of stimulation" (p. 696). The second qualification in this definition—the requirement that there must have been a "previous association of nonobject and object" and hence that the thing signified must at least once have been experienced by the subject provides a restriction we haven't yet considered. But this restriction introduces a new set of difficulties. I have never seen a tornado, an igloo, or the Queen of England. According to the present definition, therefore, nothing can signify to me that a tornado is approaching, that there are igloos somewhere, or that the Queen of England is about to arrive. Hence the definition leaves one of the principal functions of signs and language unprovided for.

We may summarize the difficulties such definitions involve by reference to our attempt to define what a man's "fire responses" might be—those responses which, according to the present type of definition, are evoked by anything that serves as a sign of fire, and by reference to which we had hoped to define beliefs about fires. No matter how we formulate our definition of "fire responses", we find that our definition has one or another of these three defects: (1) a man's fire responses become responses that only fire can call up—in which case the presence of smoke alone will not call them up; (2) his fire responses become responses he sometimes makes when he doesn't take anything to be a sign of fire, when he doesn't believe that anything is on fire; or (3) our definitions will make use of intentional language.[8]

The "appropriate action" terminology is a variant of the "specific response" terminology. Psychologists sometimes say that, if the bell is a sign of food, then the bell calls up responses appropriate to food. And one might say, more generally, that a man believes a proposition p provided only he behaves, or is disposed to behave, in a way that is "appropriate to p," or "appropriate to p's being true." But unless we can find a way of defining "appropriate", this way of talking is intentional by our criteria. When we affirm, or when we deny, "The knight is acting in a way that is appropriate to the presence of dragons," we do not imply either that there are, or that there are not, any dragons.[9]

7. In the second type of definition we refer to the "verbal behavior" which we would ordinarily take to be symptomatic of belief. This time we try to describe a man's belief—his believing—in terms of his actual uses of words or of his dispositions to use words in various ways.

Let us consider a man who believes that the Missouri River has its source in the northern part of Montana. In saying that he believes this, we do not mean to imply that he is actually doing anything; we mean to say that, if the occasion arose, he would do certain things which he would not do if he did not believe that the Missouri had its source in northern Montana. This fact may be put briefly by saying that when we ascribe a belief to a man we are ascribing a certain set of dispositions to him. What, then, are these dispositions? According to the present suggestion, the man is disposed to use language in ways in which he wouldn't use it if he didn't have the belief. In its simplest form, the suggestion is this: if someone were to ask the man "Where is the source of the Missouri River?" the man would reply by uttering the words, "In the Northern part of Montana"; if someone were to ask him to name the rivers having their sources in the northern part of Montana, he would utter, among other things, the word "Missouri"; if someone were to ask "Does the Missouri arise in northern Montana?" he would say "Yes"; and so on.

We should note that this type of definition, unlike the others, is not obviously applicable to the beliefs of animals. Sometimes we like to say such things as "The dog believes he's going to be punished" and "Now the rat thinks he's going to be fed." But if we accept the present type of definition, we cannot say these things (unless we are prepared to countenance such conditions as "If the rat could speak English, he'd now say 'I am about to be fed' "). I do not know whether this limitation—the fact that the definition does not seem to allow us to ascribe beliefs to animals—should be counted as an advantage, or as a disadvantage, of the "verbal

515

behavior" definition. In any case, the definition involves a number of difficulties of detail and a general difficulty of principle.

The if-then sentences I have used as illustrations describe the ways in which our believer would answer certain questions. But surely we must qualify these sentences by adding that the believer has no desire to deceive the man who is questioning him. To the question "Where is the source of the Missouri?" he will reply by saying "In northern Montana"—provided he wants to tell the truth. But this proviso brings us back to statements which are intentional. If we say "The man wants to tell the truth" we do not imply, of course, either that he does or that he does not tell the truth; similarly, if we assert the contradictory. And when we say "He wants to *tell the truth*"—or, what comes to the same thing, "He doesn't want to *lie*"—we mean, I suppose, he doesn't want to say anything he *believes* to be false. Perhaps we should also add that he has no objection to his questioner *knowing* what it is that he believes about the Missouri.

We should also add that the man speaks English and that he does not misunderstand the questions that are put to him. This means, among other things, that he should not *take* the other man to be saying something other than what he is saying. If he took the other man to be saying "Where is the source of the *Mississippi?*" instead of "Where is the source of the Missouri?" he might reply by saying "In Minnesota" and not by saying "In Montana." It would seem essential to add, then, that he must not *believe* the other man to be asking anything other than "Where is the source of the Missouri?"

Again, if the man does not speak English, it may be that he will not reply by uttering any of the words discussed above. To accommodate this possibility, we might qualify our if-then statements in some such way as this: "If someone were to ask the man a question which, for him, had the same meaning as 'Where is the source of the Missouri?' has for us, then he would reply by uttering an expression which, for him, has the same meaning as 'In the northern part of Montana' has for us." [10] Or we might qualify our original if-then statements by adding this provision to the antecedents: "and if the man speaks English". When this qualification is spelled out, then, like the previous one, it will contain some reference to the meanings of words— some reference to the ways in which the man uses, applies, or interprets words and sentences. These references to the meanings of words and sentences—to their use, application, or interpretation—take us to the difficulty of principle involved in this linguistic interpretation of believing.

The sentences we use to describe the meanings and uses of words are ordinarily intentional. If I say, "The German word *Riese* means giant," I don't mean to imply, of course, either that there are giants or that there aren't any giants; similarly, if I deny the sentence. If we think of a word as a class of sounds or of designs, we may be tempted to say, at first consideration, that intentional sentences about the meanings and uses of words are examples which run counter to our general thesis about intentional sentences. For here we have sentences which seem to be concerned, not with anyone's thoughts, beliefs, or desires, but rather with the properties of certain patterns of marks and noises. But we must remind ourselves that such sentences are elliptical.

If I say, of the noises and marks constituting the German word *Riese*, that they mean giant, I mean something like this: "When people in Germany talk about giants, they use the word *Riese* to stand for giants, or to refer to giants." To avoid talking about things which don't exist, we might use the expression "gigantic" (interpreting it in its literal sense) and say: "People in Germany would call a thing *ein Riese* if and only if the thing were gigantic." And to make sure that the expression "to call a thing *ein Riese*" does not suggest anything mentalistic, we might replace it by a more complex expression about noises and marks. "To say 'A man calls a thing *ein Riese*' is to say that, in the presence of the thing, he would make the noise, or the mark, *ein Riese*."

Let us ignore all of the difficulties of detail listed above and let us assume, for simplicity, that our speakers have a childlike desire to call things as frequently as possible by their conventional names. Let us even assume that everything having a name is at hand waiting to be called. Is it true that people in Germany would call a thing *ein Riese*—in the present sense of "to call"—if and only if the thing were gigantic?

If a German were in the presence of a giant and took it to be something else—say, a tower or a monument—he would not call it *ein Riese*. Hence we cannot say that, if a thing were a giant, he would call it *ein Riese*. If he were in the presence of a tower or a monument and took the thing to be a giant, then he would call the tower or the monument *ein Riese*. And therefore we cannot say he would call a thing *ein Riese* only if the thing were a giant.

Our sentence "The German word *Riese* means giant" does not mean merely that people in Germany—however we may qualify them with respect to their desires—would call a thing *ein Riese* if and only if the thing were gigantic. It means at least this much more—that they would call a thing by this name if and only if they took the thing to be gigantic or *believed* it to be gigantic or *knew* it to be gigantic. And, in general, when we use the intentional locution, "People use such and such a word to mean so-and-so," part of what we mean to say is that people use that word when they wish to express or convey something they *know* or *believe*—or *perceive* or *take*—with respect to so-and-so.

I think we can say, then, that, even if we can describe a man's believing in terms of language, his actual use of language or his dispositions to use language in certain ways, we cannot describe his use of language, or his dispositions to use language in those ways, unless we refer to what he believes, or knows, or perceives.

The "verbal behavior" approach, then, involves difficulties essentially like those we encountered with the "specific response" theory. In trying to define "fire response", it will be recalled, we had to choose among definitions having at least one of three possible defects. We now seem to find that, no matter how we try to define that behavior which is to constitute "using the word *Riese* to mean giant," our definition will have one of these three undesirable consequences: (1) we will be unable to say that German speaking people ever mistake anything for a giant and call something which is *not* a giant *ein Riese*; (2) we will be unable to say that German speaking people ever mistake a giant for something else and refuse to call a giant *ein Riese*; or (3) our definition will make use of intentional language.

The final approach I shall examine involves similar difficulties.

8. One of the basic points in the grammar of our talk about states of consciousness, as Professor Findlay has observed, is that such states always stand opposed to other states which will "carry them out" or "fulfil" them.[11] The final approach to belief sentences I would like to discuss is one based upon this conception of *fulfilment*. I believe that, if we are to succeed in showing that Brentano was wrong, our hope lies here.

Let us consider a lady who reaches for the teakettle, *expecting* to find it full. We can say of her that she has a "motor set" which would be *disrupted* or *frustrated* if the teakettle turns out to be empty and which would be *fulfilled* or *satisfied* if the teakettle turns out to be full. In saying that the empty teakettle would disrupt or frustrate a "motor set," I am thinking of the disequilibration which might result from her lifting it; at the very least, she would be startled or surprised. But in saying that her set would be fulfilled or satisfied if the teakettle turns out to be full, I am not thinking of a positive state which serves as the contrary of disruption or frustration. Russell has introduced the terms "yes-feeling" and "quite-so feeling" in this context and would say, I think, that if the teakettle were full the lady would have a quite-so feeling.[12] Perhaps she would have such a feeling if her expectation had just been challenged—if someone had said, just before she lifted the teakettle, "I think you're mistaken in thinking there's water in that thing." And perhaps expectation always involves a kind of tension, which is relieved, or consummated, by the presence of its object. But we will be on surer ground if we describe the requisite fulfilment or satisfaction, in negative terms. To say that a full teakettle would cause fulfilment, or satisfaction, is merely to say that, unlike an empty teakettle, it would not cause disruption or frustration. The kind of "satisfaction" we can attribute to successful expectation, then, is quite different from the kind we can attribute to successful strivings or "springs of action."

Our example suggests the possibility of this kind of definition: "S expects that E will occur within a certain period" means that S is in a bodily state which would be frustrated, or disrupted, if and only if E were not to occur within that period. Or, if we prefer the term "fulfil", we may say that S is in a bodily state which would be fulfilled if and only if E were to occur within that period. And then we could define "believes" in a similar way, or perhaps define "believes" in terms of "being-disposed-to-expect".

I would like to remark, in passing, that in this type of definition we have what I am sure are the essentials of William James' so-called pragmatic theory of truth—a conception which has been seriously misunderstood, both in Great Britain and in America. Although James used the terms "fulfil" and "fulfilment", he preferred "satisfy" and "satisfaction". In his terms, our suggested definition of "believing" would read: "S believes that E will occur within a certain period" means that S is in a bodily state which would be *satisfied* if and only if E were to occur within that period. If we say that S's belief is *true*, that he is correct in thinking that E will occur within that period, then we imply, as James well knew, that E is going to occur in that period—and hence that S's belief will be satisfied. If we say that S's belief is false, we imply that E is not going to occur—and hence that S's belief will not be satisfied. And all of this implies that the man's belief is true if and only if he is in a state which is going to be satisfied. But unfortunately James' readers interpreted "satisfy" in its more usual sense, in which it is applicable to strivings and desirings rather than to believings.

Our definitions, as they stand, are much too simple; they cannot be applied, in any plausible way, to those situations for which we ordinarily use the words "believe", "take", and "expect". Let us consider, briefly, the difficulties involved in applying our definition of "believe" to one of James' own examples.

How should we re-express the statement "James believes there are tigers in India"? Obviously it would not be enough to say merely, "James is in a state which would be satisfied if and only if there are tigers in India, or which would be disrupted if and only if there are no tigers in India." We should say at least this much more: "James is in a state such that, if he were to go to India, the state would be satisfied if and only if there are tigers there." What if James went to India with no thought of tigers and with no desire to look for any? If his visit were brief and he happened not to run across any tigers, then the satisfaction, or disruption, would not occur in the manner required by the definition. More important, what if he came upon tigers and took them to be lions? Or if he were to go to Africa, *believing* himself to be in India—or to India, *believing* himself to be in Africa?

I think it is apparent that the definition cannot be applied to the example unless we introduce a number of intentional qualifications into the definiens. Comparable difficulties seem to stand in the way of applying the terms of this type of definition in any of those cases we would ordinarily call instances of believing. Yet this type of definition may have an advantage the others do not have. It may be that there are simple situations, ordinarily described as "beliefs" or "expectations," which can be adequately described, non-intentionally, by reference to fulfilment, or satisfaction, and disruption, or surprise. Perhaps the entire meaning of such a statement as "The dog expects to be beaten" or "The baby expects to be fed" can be conveyed in this manner. And perhaps "satisfaction" or "surprise" can be so interpreted that our ordinary beliefs can be defined in terms of "being disposed to have" a kind of expectation which is definable by reference to "satisfaction" or "surprise". And if all of these suppositions are true then we may yet be able to interpret belief sentences in a way which is contrary to the present version of Brentano's thesis. But, I believe, we aren't able to do so now.

9. The philosophers and psychologists I have been talking about seem to have felt that they were trying to do something important—that it would be philosophically significant if they could show that belief sentences can be rewritten in an adequate language which is not intentional, or at least that it would be significant to show that Brentano was wrong. Let us suppose for a moment that we cannot rewrite belief sentences in a way which is contrary to our linguistic version of Brentano's thesis. What would be the significance of this fact? I feel that this question is itself philosophically significant, but I am not prepared to answer it. I do want to suggest, however, that the two answers which are most likely to suggest themselves are not satisfactory.

I think that, if our linguistic thesis about intentionality is true, then the followers of Brentano would have a right to take some comfort in this fact. But if someone were to say that this linguistic fact indicates that there is a ghost in the machine I would feel sure that his answer to our question is mistaken. (And it would be important to remind him that belief sentences, as well as other intentional sentences, seem to be applicable to animals.)

What if someone were to tell us, on the other hand, that intentional sentences about believing and the like don't really say anything and that, in consequence, the hypothetical fact we are considering may have no philosophical significance? He might say something like this to us: "The intentional sentences of ordinary language have many important tasks; we may use the ones about believing and the like to give vent to our feelings, to influence the behavior of other people, and to perform many other functions which psychiatrists can tell us about. But such sentences are not factual; they are not descriptive; they don't say things about the world in the way in which certain non-psychological sentences say things about the world." I do not feel that this answer, as it stands, would be very helpful. For we would not be able to evaluate it unless the man also (1) gave some meaning to his technical philosophical expressions, "factual", "descriptive", and "they don't say things about the world", and (2) had some way of showing that, although these expressions can be applied to the use of certain non-psychological sentences, they cannot be applied to the use of those psychological sentences which are intentional.

Or suppose something like this were suggested: "Intentional sentences do not say of the world what at first thought we tend to think they say of the world. They are, rather, to be grouped with such sentences as 'The average carpenter has 2.7 children,' 'Charity is an essential part of our obligations,' and 'Heaven forbid,' in that their uses, or performances, differ in very fundamental ways from other sentences having the same grammatical form. We need not assume, with respect to the words which make sentences intentional, such words as 'believe', 'desire', 'choose', 'mean', 'refer', and 'signify', that they stand for a peculiar kind of property, characteristic, or relation. For we need not assume that they stand for properties, characteristics, or relations at all." We could ask the philosopher taking such a stand to give us a positive account of the uses of these words which would be an adequate account and which would show us that Brentano was mistaken. But I do not believe that anyone has yet been able to provide such an account.

NOTES

[1] L. Wittgenstein. *Philosophical Investigations*, p. 133e (London and New York: Macmillan, 1953).

Appendix

[2] This criterion must be so interpreted that it will apply to sentences wherein the verb phrases following the principal verb are infinitive, prepositional, or participial phrases; hence it must make sense to speak of such phrases as being true or false. When I say of the phrase, following the main verb of "He accused John of stealing the money," that it is true, I mean, of course, that John stole the money. More generally, when I say of such a sentence that the phrase following the principal verb is true, or that it is false, my statement may be interpreted as applying to that new sentence which is like the phrase in question, except that the verb appearing in infinitive or participial form in the phrase is the principal verb of the new sentence. I should add a qualification about tenses, but I do not believe that my failure to do so is serious. It should be noted that, in English, when the subject of an infinitive or of a participle is the same as that of the principal verb, we do not repeat the subject; although we say "I want John to go," we do not say "I want me to go" or "John wants himself to go." When I say, then, that the last two words of "I want to go" are true, my statement should be interpreted as applying to "I shall go."

[3] By adopting Frege's theory of meaning—or his terminology—we could make this criterion do the work of our first two. But I have made use of the first two in order that no one will be tempted to confuse what I want to say with what Frege had to say about meaning. The three criteria overlap to a considerable extent.

[4] If E is a sentence obtained merely by putting the identity sign between two names or descriptions of the same thing, if A is a sentence using one of these names or descriptions, if B is like A except that where A uses the one name or description B uses the other, then the one name or description may be said to have an *indirect reference* in A provided that the conjunction of A and E does not imply B.

[5] Certain sentences describing relations of comparison (e.g. "Some lizards look like dragons") constitute exceptions to (1). Strictly speaking, then, (1) should read: "we do not need any intentional sentences, other than those describing relations of comparison, when we describe non-psychological phenomena."

[6] See Russell's *Inquiry into Meaning and Truth* (American edition), p. 142 (New York: Norton & Co., 1940) and Ryle's *Concept of Mind*, p. 230 (London: Hutchinson's Univ. Libr., 1949).

[7] See Chapter 9 of E. B. Holt, *The Concept of Consciousness* (London: G. Allen and Co., Ltd., 1914).

[8] If we say that smoke signifies fire to O provided only that, as a result of the smoke, "there is a fire in O's *behavioral environment*," or "there is a fire *for O*," and if we interpret the words in the quotations in the way in which psychologists have tended to interpret them, our language is intentional.

[9] R. B. Braithwaite, in "Belief and Action," (*Proceedings of the Aristotelian Society*, Supplementary vol. XX, p. 10), suggests that a man may be said to believe a proposition p provided this condition obtains: "If at a time when an occasion arises relevant to p, his springs of action are s, he will perform an action which is such that, if p is true, it will tend to fulfill s, and which is such that, if p is false, it will not tend to satisfy s." But the definition needs qualifications in order to exclude those people who, believing the true proposition p that there are people who can reach the summit of Mt. Everest, and having the desire s to reach the summit themselves, have yet acted in a way which has not tended to satisfy s. Moreover, if we are to use such a definition to show that Brentano was wrong, we must provide a non-intentional definition of the present use of "wish", "desire", or "spring of action".

[10] See Alonzo Church's "On Carnap's Analysis of Statements of Assertion and Belief," *Analysis*, Vol. 10 (1950).

[11] "The Logic of Bewusstseinslagen," *Philosophical Quarterly*, Vol. 5 (1955).

[12] See *Human Knowledge* (American edition), pp. 148, 125 (New York: Simon and Schuster, 1948); compare *The Analysis of Matter*, p. 184 (New York: Harcourt, Brace, 1927).

Chisholm-Sellars Correspondence on Intentionality

July 30, 1956

PROFESSOR WILFRID SELLARS
Department of Philosophy
University of Minnesota
Minneapolis 14, Minnesota
DEAR SELLARS:

Thanks very much indeed for sending me the page proofs of your "Empiricism and the Philosophy of Mind." I have not yet had time to read all of it with care or to follow the entire thread of the argument, but I have read a good part of it and have looked through it all. I have seen enough to know that it is a challenging manuscript with which I should spend some time and that you and I are interested in pretty much the same problems. I agree with much of what you have to say about the "myth of the given" and with what you say about the "rightness" of statements or assertions. I would talk, though, about the rightness of believing rather than of saying, and this difference, I think, reflects the general difference between us in our attitude toward intentionality.

With respect to intentionality, I think you locate the issue between us pretty well on page 311. Among the central questions, as you intimate at the bottom of 319, are these: (1) Can we explicate the intentional character of believing and of other psychological attitudes by reference to certain features of language; or (2) must we explicate the intentional characteristics of language by reference to believing and to other psychological attitudes? In my Aristotelian Society paper [1] I answer the first of these questions in the negative and the second in the affirmative; see also my paper on Carnap in the recent *Philosophical Studies*.[2] I would gather that the fundamental difference between us concerned our attitude toward these two questions, and I don't feel clear about what your belief is in respect to the analysis of "semantical statements." . . .

With best wishes,
RODERICK M. CHISHOLM

August 3, 1956

PROFESSOR RODERICK CHISHOLM
Philosophy Department
Brown University
Providence, Rhode Island
DEAR CHISHOLM:

Your friendly remarks encourage me to call attention to some features of my treatment of intentionality which may not have stood out on a first reading. Their importance, as I see it, is that they define a point of view which is, in a certain sense, intermediate between the alternatives envisaged in your letter. I shall not attempt to summarize in a few words the complex argument by which, in the concluding third of my essay, I sought to recommend this analysis. It may be worthwhile, however, to state its essentials in a way which emphasizes the extent to which I would go along with many of the things you want to say.[3]

A-1. Unlike Ryle, I believe that meaningful *statements* are the expression of inner episodes, namely *thoughts*, which are not to be construed as mongrel categorical-hypothetical facts pertaining to overt behavior.

A-2. I speak of *thoughts* instead of *beliefs* because I construe *believing that p* as the disposition to have *thoughts that p*; though actually, of course, the story is more complicated. The *thought that p* is an episode which might also be referred to as the "*mental assertion*" *that p*. In other words, "having the thought that p" is not equivalent to "thinking that p" (as in "Jones thinks

521

that p") for the latter is a cousin of "believing that p" and like the latter has a dispositional force.

A-3. Thought episodes are essentially characterized by the categories of intentionality.

A-4. Thought episodes, to repeat, are not speech episodes. They are *expressed by* speech episodes.

A-5. *In one sense of* "because", statements are meaningful utterances because they express thoughts. In one sense of "because", Jones' statement, s, means *that p, because* s expresses Jones' thought *that p*.

So far I have been highlighting those aspects of my view which, I take it, are most congenial to your own ways of thinking. It is in the following points, if anywhere, that our differences are to be found.

A-6. Although statements mean states of affairs because they express thoughts which are about states of affairs, this *because* is not the *because* of analysis. Notice as something to keep in mind that physical objects move because the sub-atomic particles which make them up move; yet obviously the idea that physical objects move is not to be *analysed* in terms of the idea that sub-atomic particles move.

A-7. Thoughts, of course, are not theoretical entities. We have direct (non-inferential) knowledge, on occasion, of what we are thinking, just as we have direct (non-inferential) knowledge of such non-theoretical states of affairs as the bouncings of tennis balls.

A-8. Yet if thoughts are not theoretical entities, it is because they are more than *merely* theoretical entities.

A-9. In my essay I picture the framework of thoughts as one which was developed "once upon a time" as a *theory*[4] to make intelligible the fact that silent behavior could be as effective as behavior which was (as we should say) *thought through out loud* step by step.

A-10. But though we initially used the framework merely as a theory, we came to be able[5] to describe ourselves as having such and such thoughts without having to *infer* that we had them from the evidence of our overt, publicly accessible behavior.

A-11. The *model* for the theory is overt speech. Thoughts are construed as "inner speech"—i.e., as episodes which are (roughly) as like overt speech as something which is *not* overt speech can be.[6]

A-12. The argument presumes that the meta*linguistic* vocabulary in which we talk about linguistic episodes can be analysed in terms which do not presuppose the framework of mental acts; in particular, that

$$\text{". . ." means p}$$

is not to be analysed as

$$\text{". . ." expresses t and t is about p}$$

where t is a thought.

A-13. For my claim is that the categories of intentionality are nothing more nor less than the metalinguistic categories in terms of which we talk epistemically about overt speech as they appear in the framework of thoughts construed on the model of overt speech.

A-14. Thus I have tried to show in a number of papers—most successfully, I believe, in these lectures—that the role of

$$\text{". . ." means - - -}$$

can be accounted for without analysing this form in terms of mental acts.[7] . . .

Sincerely,
WILFRID SELLARS

August 12, 1956

DEAR SELLARS:

Thanks very much indeed for your letter of August 3, and for the clear statement of the essentials of your position. I think I can locate fairly well now the point at which we diverge.

I certainly have no quarrel with your first five points, and I can accept A-7 and A-8. As for A-6 and points that follow A-8, acceptability of these seems to depend upon A-12. If you could persuade me of A-12, perhaps you could persuade me of the rest.

I know that you have written at length about the thesis of paragraph A-12, but I do not think you have satisfied what my demands would be. In order to show that

". . ." means p

is not to be analysed as

". . ." expresses t and t is about p

your metalinguistic vocabulary must contain only locutions (1) which, according to the criteria of my Aristotelian Society paper,[8] are not intentional and (2) which can be defined in physicalistic terms. This is the point we would have to argue at length, for I believe you must introduce some term which, if it means anything at all, will refer to what you call thoughts. This term could be disguised by calling it "a primitive term of semantics" or "a primitive term of pragmatics", or something of that sort, but this would be only to concede that, when we analyze the kind of meaning that is involved in natural language, we need some concept we do not need in physics or in "behavioristics." Until you can succeed in doing what Carnap tried to do in the *Philosophical Studies* paper[9] I criticized last year[10] (namely, to analyse the semantics or pragmatics of natural language in the physicalistic vocabulary of a behavioristic psychology, with no undefined semantical terms and no reference to thoughts), I think I will remain unconverted to your views about intentionality.

Perhaps you will agree that if one rejects your paragraph A-12, then it is not unreasonable for him also to reject what you say on the bottom of page 319 of the lectures: "It must not be forgotten that the semantical characterization of overt verbal episodes is the primary use of semantical terms, and that overt linguistic events as semantically characterized are the model for the inner episodes introduced by the theory." . . .

Cordially yours,
RODERICK M. CHISHOLM

August 15, 1956

DEAR CHISHOLM:

. . . we have communicated so well so far, that I cannot forbear to make one more try for complete understanding (if not agreement).

You write, ". . . I believe you must introduce some term which, if it means anything at all, will refer to what you call thoughts. This term could be disguised by calling it 'a primitive term of semantics', or 'a primitive term of pragmatics', or something of the sort, but this would only be to concede that, when we analyse the kind of meaning that is involved in natural language, we need some concept we do not need in physics or in 'behavioristics.'" Now I certainly agree that semantical statements about statements in natural languages, i.e., statements in actual use, cannot be constructed out of the resources of behavioristics. I have insisted on this in a number of papers (e.g., "A Semantical Solution . . ."),[11] and, most recently in my essay[12] for the Carnap volume and my London lectures. I quite agree that one additional expression must be taken as primitive, specifically "means" or "designates" with its context

". . ." means - - -

What I have emphasized, however, is that although "means" is in a grammatical sense a "relation word," it is no more to be assimilated to words for descriptive *relations*

Appendix

than is "ought", and that though it is a "descriptive" predicate if one means by "descriptive" that it is not a logical term nor constructible out of such, it is not in any more interesting (or usual) sense a descriptive term.

I think that I have made these points most effectively in the Lectures, pp. 291–293, and 310. I mention them only because, since they are in a section which occurs much earlier than the section on *thoughts* which has been the subject of our correspondence to date, you may not have noticed them.

I am also sending under separate cover a mimeograph of my Carnap paper,[13] which discusses at length, pp. 30ff, the point about the irreducibility of "designates" to the concepts of formal logic.

Cordially yours,
WILFRID SELLARS

August 24, 1956

DEAR SELLARS:

The philosophic question which separates us is, in your terms, the question whether

(1) ". . ." means p

is to be analysed as

(2) ". . ." expresses t and t is about p.

I would urge that the first is to be analysed in terms of the second, but you would urge the converse. But we are in agreement, I take it, that we need a semantical (or intentional) term which is not needed in physics.

How are we to decide whether (1) is to be analysed in terms of (2), or conversely? If the question were merely of constructing a language, the answer would depend merely upon which would give us the neatest language. But if we take the first course, analysing the meaning of noises and marks by reference to the thoughts that living things have, the "intentionalist" will say: "Living things have a funny kind of characteristic that ordinary physical things don't have." If we take the second course, there could be a "linguisticist" who could say with equal justification, "Marks and noises have a funny kind of characteristic that living things and other physical things don't have."

Where does the funny characteristic belong? (Surely, it doesn't make one whit of difference to urge that it doesn't stand for a "descriptive relation." Brentano said substantially the same thing, incidentally, about the ostensible relation of "thinking about," etc.) Should we say there is a funny characteristic (i.e., a characteristic which would not be labelled by any physicalistic adjective) which belongs to living things—or that there is one which belongs to certain noises and marks?

When the question is put this way, I should think, the plausible answer is that it's the living things that are peculiar, not the noises and marks. I believe it was your colleague Hospers who proposed this useful figure: that whereas both thoughts and words have meaning, just as both the sun and the moon send light to us, the meaning of the words is related to the meaning of the thoughts just as the light of the moon is related to that of the sun. Extinguish the living things and the noises and marks wouldn't shine any more. But if you extinguish the noises and marks, people can still think about things (but not so well, of course). Surely it would be unfounded psychological dogma to say that infants, mutes, and animals cannot have beliefs and desires until they are able to use language.

In saying "There is a characteristic . . ." in paragraph 2 above, I don't mean to say, of course, that there are abstract entities.

I don't expect you to agree with all the above. But do you agree that the issue described in paragraph one is an important one and that there is no easy way to settle it? . . .

Cordially yours,
RODERICK M. CHISHOLM

INTENTIONALITY AND THE MENTAL

August 31, 1956

DEAR CHISHOLM:

Your latest letter, like the preceding ones, raises exactly the right questions to carry the discussion forward. (The points made in a fruitful philosophical discussion must, so to speak, be "bite size.") Let me take them up in order.

1. The contrast you draw between the "intentionalist" and the "linguisticist" is, in an essential respect, misleading. You write: ". . . if we take the first course, analyzing the meaning of noises and marks by reference to the thoughts that living things have, the 'intentionalist' will say: 'Living things have a funny kind of characteristic that ordinary physical things don't have.' If we take the second course, there could be a 'linguisticist' who could say with equal justification, 'Marks and noises have a funny kind of characteristic that living things and other physical things don't have.'

"Where does the funny characteristic belong? . . ." This is misleading because (although I am sure you did not mean to do so) it evokes a picture of the "linguisticist" as tracing the aboutness of thoughts to characteristics which marks and noises can have *as marks and noises* (e.g., serial order, composition out of more elementary marks and noises belonging to certain mutually exclusive classes, etc.). But while these "sign design" characteristics of marks and noises make it possible for them to function as expressions in a language, they do not, of course, constitute this functioning. Marks and noises are, in a primary sense, linguistic expressions only as "nonparrotingly" produced by a language-using animal.

2. Thus the "linguisticist" no less than the "intentionalist" will say that (certain) living things are able to produce marks and noises of which it can correctly be said that they *refer to* such and such and say such and such, whereas "ordinary physical things" are not. The problem, therefore, is not (as you put it), "Should we say that there is a funny characteristic (i.e., a characteristic which would not be labelled by any physicalistic adjective) which belongs to living things—or that there is one which belongs to certain noises and marks?" but rather, *granted* that the primary mode of existence of a language is in meaningful verbal performances by animals that can *think, desire, intend, wish, infer*, etc., etc., and granted (a) that these verbal performances *mean* such and such, and (b) that the *mental acts* which they *express* are *about* such and such; how are these concepts—*all of which pertain to certain living things rather than "ordinary physical things"*—to be explicated.

3. What persuades you that the "means" of

$$\text{". . ." means} \text{ - - -}$$

must stand for a *characteristic*, even if a "funny" one? If, like Brentano, you conclude (rightly) that it is only ostensibly a relation, must it therefore be a characteristic of some other kind, perhaps a kind all its own? (Perhaps you would prefer to say that it is *means-p* rather than *means* simpliciter which, in the case of propositions, is the characteristic.) I am not, of course, denying that the term "characteristic" can, with a certain initial plausibility, be extended to cover it. I do, however, claim that to use "characteristic" in such an extended way is to blur essential distinctions; but more of this in a moment.

I would be the last person to say that "the meaning of a term is its use," for there is no sense of "use" which *analyses* the relevant sense of "means". Yet this W—nian maxim embodies an important insight, and, used with caution, is a valuable tool. Suppose there were an expression which, though it clearly didn't designate an item belonging to one of your other ontological categories, you were reluctant to speak of as standing for a characteristic, though you granted that it played a systematic or ruleful role in discourse. What about "yes" as in "yes, it is raining." Suppose "yes" always occurred in the context "yes, p." Could we not even here make a meaningful use of the rubric " '. . .' means - - -," thus

$$\text{"Ja, p" means yes, p}$$

Appendix

and

"Ja" means yes.

(I take it that you would not be tempted to say that yes is a characteristic of propositions.) But if "yes" doesn't stand for a characteristic, the fact that

"x bedeutet y" means x means y

is not a conclusive reason for supposing that means is a characteristic. To be sure, from

"Bedeutet" means means

we can infer that

There is something (i.e., means) which "bedeutet" means. But that means is, in this broadest of senses, a 'something' tells us precious little indeed, for in this sense yes is a something too!

Where E is any expression in L, whatever its role, and E' is the translation of E in English, then we can properly say both

E (in L) means - - -

and

There is something, namely - - -, which E means,

where what goes in the place held by '- - -' is the English expression named by 'E', thus,

There is something, namely I shall, which "Ich werde" (in German) means

and

There is something, namely this which "dieser (diese, dieses)" (in German) means.

(In this last example, of course, the context brackets 'this' so that it is not playing its "pointing" role, though the semantical rubric mobilizes its pointing role in its own way.)

4. You write: ". . . the meaning of the words is related to the meaning of the thoughts just as the light of the moon is related to that of the sun. Extinguish the living things and the noises and marks wouldn't shine any more. But if you extinguish the noises and marks, people can still think about things (but not so well, of course)." Now I agree, of course, that marks in books and noises made by phonographs 'have meaning' only by virtue of their relation to 'living' verbal episodes in which language is the direct expression of thought (e.g., conversation, writing on a blackboard.) And, as I have emphasized in an earlier letter (3 August), I agree that 'living' verbal episodes are meaningful because they express thoughts. Our difference concerns the analysis of this 'because'.

Let me have another try at making the essential points. I have argued that it is in principle possible to conceive of the characteristic forms of semantical discourse being used by a people who have not yet arrived at the idea that there are such things as thoughts. They think, but they don't know that they think. Their use of language is meaningful because it is the expression of thoughts, but they don't know that it is the expression of thoughts; that is to say, they don't know that overt speech is the culmination of inner episodes of a kind which we conceive of as thoughts.

(Compare them, for a moment, with a people who have, as yet, no theoretical concepts in terms of which to give theoretical explanations of the observable behavior of physical objects. They are, nevertheless, able to explain particular events by means of that general knowledge which is embodied in dispositional concepts pertaining to thing kinds.)

Now, in order to communicate, such a people would, of course, have to appreciate both the norms which, by specifying what may not be said without withdrawing what, delimit the syntactical or 'intra-linguistic' structure of the language, as well as such facts as that, ceteris paribus, a person who says "This is green" is in the presence of

526

a green object, and a person who says "I shall do A" proceeds to do it. This understanding springs from the routines by which the language is learned and passed on from generation to generation by "social inheritance." It constitutes their mastery of the language.

If you grant that they could get this far without having arrived at the concept of a thought (though, of course, not without thinking), the crucial question arises, Could they come to make use of semantic discourse while remaining untouched by the idea that overt verbal behavior is the culmination of inner episodes, let alone that it is the expression of thoughts? To this question my answer is 'Yes.'

In your first letter you expressed agreement "with much of what [I] have to say about the 'myth of the given.'" Well, of a piece with my rejection of this myth is my contention that before these people could come to know noninferentially (by 'introspection') that they have thoughts, they must first construct the concept of what it is to be a thought.[14] Thus, while I agree with you that the rubric

". . ." means - - -

is not constructible in Rylean terms ('Behaviorese,' I have called it), I also insist that it is not to be analysed in terms of

". . ." expresses t, and t is about - - -.

My solution is that "'. . .' means - - -" is the core of a unique mode of discourse which is as distinct from the description and explanation of empirical fact, as is the language of prescription and justification.

I have probably lost you somewhere along the line. But, if not, from this point on the argument is clear. To put it in a way which artificially separates into stages a single line of conceptual development, thoughts began by being conceived of as theoretical episodes on the analogy of overt verbal behavior ("inner speech"). Men came, however, in a manner which I pictured in my Jonesean myth, to be able to say what they are thinking without having to draw theoretical inferences from their own publicly observable behavior.[15] They now not only think, but know that they think; and can not only infer the thoughts of others, but have direct (non-inferential) knowledge of what is going on in their own minds.

5. You write: "Surely it would be unfounded psychological dogma to say that infants, mutes, and animals cannot have beliefs, and desires until they are able to use language." Here I shall limit myself to a few brief points:

(a) Since I do not define thoughts in terms of overt verbal behavior, and grant that thought episodes occur without overt linguistic expression, there is, on my view, no contradiction in the idea of a being which thinks, yet has no language to serve as the overt expression of his thoughts.

(b) Not only do the subtle adjustments which animals make to their environment tempt us to say that they do what they do because they believe this, desire that, expect such and such, etc.; we are able to explain their behavior by ascribing to them these beliefs, desires, expectations, etc. But, and this is a key point, we invariably find ourselves qualifying these explanations in terms which would amount, in the case of a human subject, to the admission that he wasn't really thinking, believing, desiring, etc. For in the explanation of animal behavior the mentalistic framework is used as a model or analogy which is modified and restricted to fit the phenomena to be explained. It is as though we started out to explain the behavior of macroscopic objects, in particular, gases, by saying that they are made up of minute bouncing billiard balls, and found ourselves forced to add, "but, of course . . ."

(c) The use of the mentalistic framework as the point of departure for the explanation of animal behavior can be characterized as the approach "from the top down." Recent experimental psychology has been attempting an approach "from the bottom up," and while it is still barely under way, it has been made amply clear that discrimination is a far more elementary phenomenon than classification, and that

527

Appendix

chains of stimulus-response connections can be extremely complex and, in principle, account for such 'sophisticated' forms of adjustment as, for example, the learning of a maze, where these same adjustments, approached "from the top down" would be explained in terms of a qualified use of the framework of beliefs, desires, expectations, etc. To make this point in an extreme form, what would once have been said about an earthworm which comes to take the right hand turn in a T-shaped tube, as a result of getting a mild shock on turning to the left?

(d) I think you will agree with me that the ability to have thoughts entails the ability to do *some* classifying, see *some* implications, draw *some* inferences. I think you will also agree that it is a bit strong to conclude that a white rat must be *classifying* objects because it reacts in similar ways to objects which are similar in certain respects, and in dissimilar ways to objects which are dissimilar in certain respects; or that an infant must be *inferring* that his dinner is coming because he waves his spoon when his mother puts on his bib. While I do not wish to cut off, as with a knife, inner episodes which are below the level of thoughts, from inner episodes which are thoughts, I remain convinced that we approach the ability to have thoughts in the course of approaching the ability to use a language in inter-personal discourse, and that the ability to have thoughts without expressing them is a subsequent achievement.

(e) This brings me to my concluding point which, though last, is by no means least. It has been taken for granted in the above paragraphs that the languages the learning of which is the acquiring the ability to have thoughts, are languages in the sense of the highly conventionalized, socially sanctioned and inherited, systems of symbols, such as French, German, English, etc. (and the closely related 'sign languages' for handicapped persons). But it would be naive to suppose that the only forms of overt behavior which can play the role of symbols in the classifying, inferring, intending behavior of a human organism, are languages in this narrow sense. It is, therefore, even on my view, by no means impossible that there be a mature deaf-mute who has "beliefs and desires" and can "think about things (but not so well, of course)" though he has learned no *language*. I would merely urge (with W—n and others) that the overt behavior which has come to play the role of more conventional symbol-behavior must have been selectively *sanctioned* ("reinforced") by his fellows; and that a certain mode of behavior, B, can correctly be said to express the thought *that p,* only if B is the *translation* in his 'language' of the sentence in our *language,* call it S, represented by 'p'. This implies that B plays a role in his behavioral economy which parallels that of S in ours.

(f) I must add two footnotes to this "concluding point" which will relate it to what has gone before. The first concerns a topic of fundamental importance in current controversies about *meaning.* The mutual translatability of two expressions in actual usage is, with certain exceptions, an "ideal." By this I mean that whenever we make use of the rubric

E (in L) means - - -

we would, in most cases, have to admit that "strictly speaking" E and E' (see above, end of paragraph 3) "do not have quite the same meaning." Yet our use of this rubric is sensible for two reasons, of which the second is the more important. (a) The difference between the roles of E and E' may be irrelevant to the context in which this rubric is used. (b) This rubric, which treats E and E' as mutually translatable is the *base* or *point of departure* from which, by the addition of *qualifications,* we explain the use of expressions in L to someone who does not know how to use them.

(g) This second footnote is to point out that there is no substitute for the subtly articulated languages which have been developed over the millenia of human existence. To pick up a point made in (b) above, if we said of our deaf-mute that he had the thought *that p,* we would, do you not agree, find it necessary to add, *if pressed,* "but of course . . ."?

6. You write: "I don't expect you to agree with all the above." If I write "ditto," I am putting it mildly. On the other hand, though I don't agree with some of the things you say, I have attempted to make it clear that I do agree with a great deal of what you say, more than you might think possible, while remaining on my side of the fence.

Cordially,
WILFRID SELLARS

P.S. This really started out to be a letter!

September 12, 1956

DEAR SELLARS:

Thanks for your latest letter which I have enjoyed reading. I think the differences between us now seem to boil down to two points, both rather difficult to argue about.

First, we are apparently in some disagreement about what is meant by such terms as "analysis" and "explication". Consider the following sentences:

(B-1) The meaning of thoughts is to be analysed in terms of the meaning of language, and not conversely.

(B-2) Language is meaningful because it is the expression of thoughts—of thoughts which are about something.

(B-3) The people in your fable "come to make use of semantical discourse while remaining untouched by the idea that overt verbal behavior is the culmination of inner episodes, let alone that it is the expression of thoughts."

When I first wrote you I took (B-1) to be inconsistent with (B-2), but you affirm both (B-1) and (B-2). And apparently you take (B-3) to imply (B-1), but I accept (B-3) and deny (B-1).

Perhaps we could do better if we resolved not to use such technical terms as "analysis" and "explication". What would (B-1) come to then?

The second point of disagreement between us lies in the fact that I am more skeptical than you are about the content of such "solutions" as the one you propose on page 4. "My solution is that '". . ." means - - -' is the core of the unique mode of discourse which is as distinct from the description and explanation of empirical fact as is the language of prescription and justification." I am inclined to feel that the technical philosophical term "descriptive" is one which is very much over used, and I am not sure I can attach much meaning to it. Indeed I would be inclined to say that if the locution "Such and such a sentence is not descriptive" means anything at all, it means that the sentence in question (like "Do not cross the street" and "Would that the roses were blooming") is neither true nor false. But the sentence " 'Hund' means dog in German" is a sentence which is true. And anyone who denied it would be making a mistake—in the same sense, it seems to me, that he would be making a mistake if he said "Berlin is part of Warsaw." Hence it does not illuminate any of my problems to say that the sentence is not descriptive or that it embodies a unique mode of discourse.

But I hope we haven't reached an impasse quite yet.

Cordially yours,
R. M. CHISHOLM

September 19, 1956

DEAR CHISHOLM:

Many thanks for your letter of September 12 which, as usual, brings things back to a sharp focus. I shall take up the two points to which, as you see it, our differences "boil down" in the order in which you state them.

You ask what your sentence (B-1) would come to "if we resolved not to use such technical terms as 'analysis' and 'explication'." Good. I quite agree that these terms are dangerous unless carefully watched. "Analysis" now covers everything from definition to explanations of the various dimensions of the use of a term which are anything but definitions. Let me therefore begin by pointing out that I have been careful *not* to say that "the meaning of thoughts is to be analysed in terms of the meaning of language, and not conversely." This formulation stems from your letter of August 24,[16] and I should have taken exception to it in my last letter. I have, of course, denied that the meaning of language is to be analysed in terms of the meaning of thoughts—see, for example, paragraph A-12 in my letter of August 3—but the closest I have come to affirming the converse is when I wrote—paragraph A-13 in that letter—". . . the categories of intentionality are nothing more nor less than the metalinguistic categories in terms of which we talk epistemically about overt speech *as they appear in the framework of thoughts construed on the model of overt speech."* (No italics in the original.) Indeed, I have explicitly denied (point 5(b) in my letter of August 31)[17] that thoughts (and consequently their aboutness) are to be *defined* in terms of language. I have, however, argued that the aboutness of thoughts is to be *explained* or *understood* by reference to the categories of semantical discourse about language. It is only if "analysis" is stretched to (and, I think, beyond) the limits of its usefulness, that I would be prepared to accept your (B-1).

Let me interrupt the above train of thought to pull together some of the implications of the fable according to which the framework of thoughts was cooked up by Jones with semantical discourse about overt speech as his model. The fable has it, for example, that

x is a token of S and S (in L) means p

(where x ranges over overt linguistic episodes) was his model for

x is a case of T and T is the thought that p

(where x ranges over the inner episodes introduced by the 'theory.'). Now if I am correct in my interpretation of semantical statements, sentences of the form

S (in L) means p

as used by one of Jones' contemporaries *imply* but do not *assert* certain Rylean facts about the place of S in the behavioral economy of the users of L.

(They imply these facts in that "S (in L) means p" said by x would not be true unless the sentence named by 'S' plays the same Rylean role in the behavior of those who use L, as the sentence abbreviated by 'p' plays in the behavior of the speaker. They do not *assert* Rylean facts, for "S means p" is not (re-)constructible out of Rylean resources.)

The Rylean facts which, in this sense, 'underlie' semantical statements about the expressions of a language—and which must be appreciated not only by anyone who is going to be in a position to make semantical statements about the language, but also by anyone who is going to use the language to communicate with another user of the language—are (roughly) correlations between (a) environmental situation and verbal behavior, (b) verbal behavior and other verbal behavior and (c) verbal behavior and non-verbal behavior. And when semantical discourse about overt speech is taken as the model for the inner episodes which Jones postulates to account for the fact that the behavior of his fellows can be just as intelligent when they are silent as when (as we would put it) they think it through out loud, it is these correlations—*more accurately, these correlations as they would be if all such behavior were "thought through out loud"*—which are the effective model for the roles played by these inner episodes. It is these roles—though not, of course, the framework of intentionality which conveys them—which today we (reasonably) expect to interpret in terms of neurophysiological connections, as we have succeeded in interpreting the 'atoms,' 'molecules,' etc. of early chemical theory in terms of contemporary physical theory.[18]

I am beginning, however, to touch on topics which presuppose agreement on more fundamental issues (though the above may be useful as giving a more definite picture of the direction of my thought.) So back to your questions! Before this interruption I was making the point that I could not accept sentence (B-1) without qualifying it so radically that the term "analysis" would have to be stretched to the breaking point. In effect, then, we *both* deny (B-1). I, however, am prepared to accept a "first cousin" of (B-1). You, I take it, are not. Or are you? (See below.)

Again, though we both accept (B-2) *as a sentence*, I accept it only if the "because" it contains is (roughly) the "because" of theoretical explanation, whereas you have interpreted it as the "because" of analysis. How, then, will you interpret your acceptance of (B-2) now that we have "resolved not to use such technical terms as 'analysis' and 'explication' "? The sense in which I accept (B-2), on the other hand, is part and parcel of the sense in which I accept (B-1).

This brings me to the heart of the first part of this letter. In your letter of August 12 [19] you wrote, "I certainly have no quarrel with your first five points, and I can accept A-7 and A-8. As for A-6 and points that follow A-8, acceptability of these seems to depend upon A-12. If you could persuade me of A-12, perhaps you could persuade me of the rest." The question I wish to raise is this. You now write that you accept (B-3). You wrote on August 12 [20] that if I could persuade you of A-12 perhaps I could persuade you of the rest. *But doesn't (B-3) entail A-12?*

I turn now to "the second point of disagreement between us." Let me say right at the beginning that I share your mistrust of "solutions" of philosophical puzzles which simply find a new category for the expressions which raise them. It is because I believe that what I propose amounts to something more than this that I have ventured to call it a solution.

Perhaps the most important thing that needs to be said is that I not only *admit*, I have never *questioned* that

'Hund' means dog in German

is *true* in what, for our purposes, is exactly the same sense as

Berlin is part of Warsaw

would be if the facts of geography were somewhat different.

" 'Hund' means dog in German" is true ≡ 'Hund' means dog in German

just as

"Berlin is part of Warsaw" is true ≡ Berlin is part of Warsaw.

There is just no issue between us on this point. When I have said that semantical statements convey descriptive information but do not *assert* it, I have not meant to imply that semantical statements *only* convey and do not assert. They make semantical assertions. Nor is "convey", as I have used it, a synonym for "evince" or "express" as emotivists have used this term. I have certainly not wished to assimilate semantical statements to ejaculations or symptoms.

It might be worth noting at this point that, as I see it, it is just as proper to say of statements of the form "Jones ought to do A" that they are *true*, as it is to say this of mathematical, geographical or semantical statements. This, of course, does not preclude me from calling attention to important differences in the 'logics' of these statements.

I quite agree, then, that it is no more a solution of our problem simply to say that semantical statements are "unique," than it would be a solution of the corresponding problem in ethics simply to say that prescriptive statements are "unique." What is needed is a painstaking exploration of statements belonging to various (prima facie) families, with a view to discovering *specific* similarities and differences in the ways in which they behave. Only *after* this has been done can the claim that a certain family of statements is, in a certain respect, unique, be anything more than a promissory note. But while I would be the last to say that the account I have given of semantical and mentalistic statements is more than a beginning, I do think that it *is* a beginning, and that I have paid at least the first installment on the note.

I also agree that the term "descriptive" is of little help. Once the "journeyman" task (to use Ayer's expression) is well under way, it may be possible to give a precise meaning to this technical term. (Presumably this technical use would show some measure of continuity with our ordinary use of "describe".) I made an attempt along this line in my Carnap paper, though I am not very proud of it. On the other hand, as philosophers use the term today, it means little that is definite apart from the logician's contrast of "descriptive expression" with "logical expression" (on this use "ought" would be a descriptive term!) and the moral philosopher's contrast of "descriptive" with "prescriptive". According to both these uses, "S means p" would be a descriptive statement.

It is, then, the *ordinary* force of "describe", or something very like it, on which I have wished to draw when I have said that " 'Hund' means *dog* in German" is not a *descriptive* assertion. I have wished to say that there is an important sense in which this statement does not describe the role of "Hund" in the German language, though it *implies* such a description.

> (Remote parallel: When I *express the intention* of doing A, I am not *predicting* that I will do A, yet there is a sense in which the expression of the intention *implies* the corresponding prediction.)

Well, then, what *is* the business of such statements as " 'Hund' means *dog* in German"? I wish I could add to my previous attempts with which you are already familiar, but I can't, unless it be the following negative point. It is tempting (though it clearly won't do) to suppose that

> S₁: "Hund" means *dog* in German

really makes the same statement as

> S₂: "Hund" plays in German the same role as "dog" plays in English.

If so, it would describe the role of "Hund" as

> Tom resembles (in relevant respects) Dick

describes Tom. But a simple use of Church's translation test makes it clear that S₁ and S₂ are not equivalent. We who use "dog" (as an English word) use S₁ to explain to another user of "dog" the role of "Hund" in German, by holding out to him, so to speak, as an exhibit the word which plays the corresponding role in English, our language. And while a person could not correctly be said to have understood S₁ unless, *given that he uses the word* "dog," he knows that S₁ is true *if and only if* S₂ is true, nevertheless he can clearly know that S₂ is true without having that piece of knowledge the proper expression of which is " 'Hund' means *dog* in German." For he may know that S₂ is true without "having learned the word 'dog'."

> (Parallel: A person may know that Tom resembles (in relevant respects) Dick, without knowing what either Tom or Dick is like.)

Well, once again what turned out to be a short, clear-cut letter has gotten out of hand. Writing it has been helpful to me in clearing up some of my own ideas. I hope you find it of some use.

Cordially yours,
WILFRID SELLARS

October 3, 1956

DEAR SELLARS:

Excuse the delay in replying to your letter of September 19th.

I have the feeling that perhaps we should start again, for in formulating a reply to your letter I find that we are in danger of an impasse. You conclude the first part of your letter by asking "But doesn't B-3 entail A-12?" Since one of these sentences contains the technical term "analysis" which we decided to avoid, this question needs reformulation. I would not have said that B-3 entails A-12; hence we are using "analysis" in different ways. And, with respect to the second part of your letter, my natural temptation would be to say that the business of the sentence " 'Hund' means dog in German" where "German" is used to designate the language spoken by German people, is to tell us that German speaking people use the word "Hund" to express their thoughts about dogs. But saying this, of course, would not get us very far!

I think that everything I want to say is expressible in the following seven sentences:

(C-1) Thoughts (i.e., beliefs, desires, etc.) are intentional—they are about something.

(C-2) Linguistic entities (sentences, etc.) are also intentional.

(C-3) Nothing else is intentional.

(C-4) Thoughts would be intentional even if there were no linguistic entities. (This is a sentence about psychology. I concede that if we had no language, our thoughts would be considerably more crude than they are.)

(C-5) But if there were no thoughts, linguistic entities would not be intentional. (If there were no people, then the mark or noise "Hund"—if somehow occasionally it got produced—would not mean dog.)

(C-6) Hence thoughts are a "source of intentionality"—i.e., nothing would be intentional were it not for the fact that thoughts are intentional (When I used "because" in an earlier letter I meant it this way; I did not intend it, as you assumed, to be the "because" of analysis.)

(C-7) Hence—and this would be Brentano's thesis—thoughts are peculiar in that they have an important characteristic which nothing else in the world has—namely, the characteristic described in C-6.

Hospers' sun-moon analogy holds in all of this. For if we forget about stars and meteors, the above sentences will hold if "thoughts" is replaced by "sun", "linguistic entities" is replaced by "moon", and "are intentional" is replaced by "is a source of light".

Conceivably a man who was very well informed about the moon and knew very little about the sun could be helped in understanding the sun by learning of its resemblance to the moon. Such a man would be like the man of your fable. But the fact that there could be such a man, it seems to me, has no bearing upon the important astronomical truth expressed by C-7. And hence your fable, as I interpret it, does not lead me to question the truth of C-7.

Is there any hope now of our ever seeing eye to eye?

With best wishes,
R. M. CHISHOLM

October 19, 1956

DEAR CHISHOLM:

I admit that in the very letter in which I was agreeing that we should try to say what we want to say without relying on the technical term "analysis", I relied on this term to settle a point when I asked "But doesn't B-3 entail A-12?" I think you will agree, however, that if the point could have been settled in the framework of our earlier letters, we would be that much further along. We would now be trying to determine how matters stood when the point was restated without the use of this technical term. Although things haven't worked out that way, a word about the background of my argument may be useful.

I think that in my first letter I was so using the term "analysis" that to say that

Appendix

X is to be analysed in terms of Y entails that it would be incorrect to say of any-one that he had the concept of X but lacked the concept of Y. (The converse en-tailment does not seem to hold.) Thus, when, in A-12, I denied that

"..." means p

is to be analysed as

"..." expresses t, and t is about p

I intended, in effect, to deny that the fact that a person lacked the concept of a statement's expressing the thought that p would be a conclusive reason against sup-posing him to have the concept of a statement's meaning that p. And if that part of A-12, the negative part, which begins "in particular ..." and which says all that I wanted to say in advancing A-12, is interpreted in this manner, surely it *is* entailed by B-3. For what, in effect, does B-3 say? Let me try the following paraphrase:

> It is conceivable that people might have made semantical statements about one another's overt verbal behavior before they had arrived at the idea that there are such things as *thoughts* of which overt verbal behavior is the expression.

Thus, as I saw it, the fact that you formulated and accepted B-3, taken together with your earlier statement that if I could persuade you of A-12 perhaps I could persuade you of the rest, gave good grounds for hoping that we might be approaching a sub-stantial measure of agreement.

But even if we leave A-12 aside and stick with B-3, I think I can make my point. For once B-3 is granted, what alternatives are left for an account of the relation of the framework of thoughts and their aboutness to the framework of semantical state-ments about linguistic episodes? (Clearly it rules out the classical account according to which to say of a statement that it means that p is simply a concise way of saying that the statement expresses the thought that p.) One alternative, the alternative to which you seem to be committed, can be put—rather bluntly, to be sure—as fol-lows:

> To say of a verbal performance that it means that p is to attribute to the performance a certain property, namely the property of meaning that p, and hence the generic property of meaning *something*. It is conceivable that a people might have come to recognize this property of verbal performances, their own and those of others, without realizing that there are such things as thoughts (not that they haven't been thinking all along), just as they might have come to recognize the moon's property of being luminous with-out having discovered the sun. Subsequently they (introspectively) notice thoughts and, on examining them, discover that they have in common the property of being about something. Comparing this property with that of meaning something, they discover that they are, if not the same property, at least properties of the same sort, in that being about something (in the case of thoughts) and meaning something (in the case of linguistic ex-pressions) are alike ways of being intentional. They then establish that verbal expressions have the property of meaning something, and hence of being intentional, only if they stand in a certain relation to thoughts, whereas thoughts can have the property of being about something, and hence of being intentional, regardless of any relation they have to verbal expressions (though they also establish that thoughts above a certain level of crudity do not occur unless the thinker has learned a language capable of expressing them.) They conclude that thoughts are the source of intentionality.

I have put this alternative as bluntly as I have because I want to hammer away on the theme that the traditional puzzles about intentionality arise, in large measure, from the presupposition that because statements of the form "S means p" are often true, they must be capable of being gripped by such philosophical wrenches as "property", "relation", "attribute", "describe", etc. For given this presupposition one will either say (assuming that one doesn't fall into the trap of philosophical behaviorism) that in the sense in which to be a bachelor is to be an unmarried man, or to be an uncle of is to be the brother of a parent of,

> for a verbal performance to mean something is for it to be the expression of a thought which is about that something,

or one will say, as in effect you do, not in your seven sentences, to be sure, but in that "eighth sentence" which is your commentary on the other seven, that

> the being about something of thoughts and the meaning something of verbal performances are similar properties (both ways of being intentional) not, however, by virtue of anything like the above, but rather by virtue of being, if not the same property, then two properties which stand to one another much as the luminosity of the sun to the luminosity of the moon.

You see, it isn't so much that I disagree with your seven sentences, for I can use each of them separately, with varying degrees of discomfort, to say something which needs to be said. (I think we would both have reservations about C-3, but none that is relevant to our problem.) It is rather that I am unhappy about the force they acquire in the over-all framework in which you put them.

What is the second alternative left open by B-3? It is, needless to say, the one I have been trying to recommend. It enables me to say so many of the things you want to say, that I can't help feeling at times that there must be some happy formulation which, if only I could hit upon it, would convince you. At other times I realize that our failure to agree may spring from a more radical difference in our general philosophical outlooks than appears to exist. If so, I doubt very much that the trouble lies in the area of "synonymy", "analysis" and such fashionable perplexities. Unless I am very much mistaken, it lies in the area of "fact", "property", "describe" and their kindred. A discussion of "ought" would provide a test case, but I hesitate to start that here. I will, however, send you (without obligation, as merchants say) a copy of a forthcoming paper of mine on the subject.[21] It would be interesting to see how you react to it.

As for your remark that "[your] natural temptation would be to say that the business of the sentence ' "Hund" means dog in German' . . . is to tell us that German speaking people use this word 'Hund' to express their thoughts about dogs," I quite agree (a) that the sentence does tell us this, and (b) that to say that the business of the sentence is to tell us this is, as you imply, to espouse a certain philosophical interpretation of the sentence, and hence prejudge the question at issue between us. What catches my eye, however, is the fact that the philosophical interpretation which seems to be implicit in your "natural temptation" is none other than what I have called the "classical account," i.e., that for a verbal performance to mean something is for it to be the expression of a thought which is about that something. But this interpretation is incompatible with B-3, which you accept.

Now I grant, indeed insist, that there is a very intimate relation between " 'Hund' means dog in German" and "Statements involving the word 'Hund' made by German speaking people express thoughts about dogs." Although my piece of historical—prehistorical—fiction expresses my conviction that semantical sentences could play their characteristic role even if those who used them lacked the framework of thoughts, I would not for one moment wish to deny that as we use these sentences there is a legitimate sense in which "x makes meaningful assertions" logically implies "x has thoughts." An example from another area may illuminate this point. As people once used the word "water", "x is a piece of water" clearly did not imply "x consists of molecules of H_2O"; but as chemist Jones (1937-) uses the word "water", even in every-

Appendix

day life, does or does not "x is a piece of water" imply—in a sense of "imply" which it is quite legitimate to call "logical"—"x consists of molcules of H_2O"?

It might be thought that by saying that the framework of thoughts developed as a theory develops, with semantical discourse about overt verbal episodes as its model, I am making a purely historical point. One might be tempted to say that regardless of how there came to be such a thing as discourse about thoughts, discourse about thoughts now refer to thoughts as discourse about linguistic episodes refers to linguistic episodes and discourse about physical objects to physical objects. But the point I am making is both a historical and a logical one, nor can the two be separated as with a knife. Clearly the mere fact that

"Thought" refers to thoughts
"Sneeze" refers to sneezes
"Ought" refers to obligations

are all of them true, has not the slightest tendency to show that the 'logic' of "thought" is like that of "sneeze" or "ought". To say that the term "molecule" was introduced by means of 'postulates' and 'coordinating definitions' (so called) is to make, however clumsily, a logical point about the way in which this expression is used, and this use is quite other than that of expressions which refer to macro-observables, even though

"Molecule" refers to molecules

is every whit as true as the statements listed above.

Although I compare the framework of thoughts to that of theoretical entities, I qualify this comparison in (at least) the following two respects:

(1) I grant, as anyone must, that each of us has direct (and privileged) access to his thoughts in the sense that we can (on occasion) know what we think without inferring this from our overt behavior as we infer what the molecules in a gas are doing from the behavior of the gas as a macro-observable object. Broad epistemological considerations, however, expounded in "Empiricism and the Philosophy of Mind," lead me to conclude that this "direct access" is to be interpreted as an additional role which the language of thoughts (and the thoughts about thoughts which they express) has come to play, rather than as a matter of a replacement of an original 'theoretical' framework of thoughts by a framework in which they are on a par with public observables.

(2) In saying that the framework of thoughts developed with semantical discourse about overt linguistic episodes as its model (thoughts being 'inner speech'), I have distinguished between two roles played by the model:

(a) The semantical concepts of the model appear in the framework of thoughts as the basic categories of intentionality. The fact that the model is semantical rather than Rylean discourse about overt linguistic episodes accounts for the fact that intentionality is a necessary feature of thoughts, it being absurd to say of anything that it is a thought but lacks intentionality.

(b) The Rylean facts about linguistic expressions which, as I have put it, are implied, though not asserted by semantical statements about them are the model for the behavior of thoughts as episodes 'in the order of causes.'

This distinction between the two roles of the model is elaborated in my letter of September 19, and can be summed up by the formula that just as semantical statements about linguistic episodes do not describe, but imply a description, of these episodes, so statements about the 'content' or 'intentional object' of thoughts do not describe thoughts, though they imply a description of them.[22] It is the fact that these implied descriptions do not do more than draw an analogy between the way in which thoughts are connected with one another and with the world (in observation and conduct), and the way in which overt linguistic episodes are so connected—an analogy, however, which is qualified inter alia by the idea that overt linguistic epi-

536

sodes are the culmination of causal chains initiated by thoughts—it is this fact which makes it sensible to envisage the identification of thoughts in their descriptive character with neuro-physiological episodes in the central nervous system, in that sense of "identify" which we have in mind when we speak of the identification of chemical episodes with certain complex episodes involving nuclear particles.

Well, I don't know that we are any further along towards agreement than we were last August. I hope, however, that I have succeeded in clearing up some points about my interpretation of intentionality. And let me be the first to say that my present account, inadequate though it may be, is a substantial improvement over the gropings of my earlier papers. I can only plead that if they are looked at from the present vantage point, they seem to reach out for formulations which elude them.

Cordially,
WILFRID SELLARS

November 19, 1956

DEAR SELLARS:

I find very little to disagree with in your last letter (dated, I fear, October 19th). Most of what I wanted to say was in the points made in my previous letter, which you assent to. I think there is only one matter left.

I do concede your statement B-3, especially in the paraphrase you gave it in your last letter; that is, I concede that it is conceivable that people might make semantical statements about one another's verbal behavior before arriving at the conception that there are such things as thoughts; and I also concede that, given your account of analysis ("to say that X is to be analyzed in terms of Y entails that it would be incorrect to say of anyone that he had the concept of X but lacked the concept of Y") your statement A-12 follows. There is no point, so far as our present questions are concerned, in debating about the proper use of the technical term "analysis"; but I would note that, given this definition of "analysis", possibly we cannot say that Russell's definition of "cardinal number" is an analysis.

The only point I wish to make is this. The "paradox of analysis" reminds us that it is conceivable that people might have referred to certain things as "cubes" before they had arrived at the idea that there is anything having six sides. And, to borrow the example which Hempel borrowed from Neurath (see Feigl-Sellars, page 380),[2] it is conceivable that people might have referred to the fact that watches run well before they had arrived at the idea that there is a sun which bears certain relations of motion to the earth, etc., and I am inclined to feel that the sense in which I have conceded your statement B-3 is this "paradox-of-analysis" sense. If the people of your myth were to give just a little bit of thought to the semantical statements they make, wouldn't they then see that these semantical statements entail statements about the thoughts of the people whose language is being discussed?

With best wishes,
R. M. CHISHOLM

NOTES

[1] Roderick Chisholm, "Sentences about Believing," *Aristotelian Society Proceedings*, 56:125–148 (1955–1956). Reprinted above with omissions and additions.

[2] Roderick Chisholm, "A Note on Carnap's Meaning Analysis," *Philosophical Studies*, 6:87–89 (1955).

[3] The following paragraphs have been renumbered A-1, A-2, etc., in order to avoid confusion and permit ready reference. A similar procedure has been followed in the case of subsequent groups of numbered paragraphs or sentences.

[4] The nature and role of theories and models in behavioristic psychology is discussed in §§51–55 of "Empiricism and the Philosophy of Mind" (referred to, hereafter, as EPM).

Appendix

[5] ". . . once our fictitious ancestor, Jones, has developed the theory that overt verbal behavior is the expression of thoughts, and taught his compatriots to make use of the theory in interpreting each other's behavior, it is but a short step to the use of this language in self-description. Thus, when Tom, watching Dick, has behavioral evidence which warrants the use of the sentence (in the language of the theory) "Dick is thinking 'p'" (or "Dick is thinking that p"), Dick, using the same behavioral evidence, can say, in the language of the theory, "I am thinking 'p'" (or "I am thinking that p"). And it now turns out—need it have?—that Dick can be trained to give reasonably reliable self-descriptions, using the language of the theory, without having to observe his overt behavior. Jones brings this about, roughly, by applauding utterances by Dick of "I am thinking that p" when the behavioral evidence strongly supports the theoretical statement "Dick is thinking that p"; and by frowning on utterances of "I am thinking that p," when the evidence does not support this theoretical statement. Our ancestors begin to speak of the privileged access each of us has to his own thoughts. What began as a language with a purely theoretical use has gained a reporting role." EPM, p. 320.

[6] See the distinction between the *model* around which a theory is built, and the *'commentary' on the model* in EPM, §§ 51 and 57.

[7] See EPM, Part VI, "The Logic of Means," also §80 of my essay "Counterfactuals, Dispositions and the Causal Modalities," in this volume; see also below, pp. 525ff and pp. 530ff in this volume.

[8] See note 1 above.

[9] Rudolf Carnap, "Meaning and Synonymy in Natural Languages," *Philosophical Studies*, 6:33–47 (1955).

[10] See note 2 above.

[11] Wilfrid Sellars, "A Semantical Solution of the Mind-Body Problem," *Methodos*, 5:45–84 (1953); see also Wilfrid Sellars, "Mind, Meaning and Behavior," *Philosophical Studies*, 3:83–95 (1953).

[12] Wilfrid Sellars, "Empiricism and Abstract Entities," to appear in *The Philosophy of Rudolf Carnap*, edited by P. A. Schilpp (New York: Tudor, forthcoming), available in mimeograph form from the author.

[13] See note 12 above.

[14] ". . . once we give up the idea that we begin our sojourn in this world with any—even a vague, fragmentary, and undiscriminating—awareness of the logical space of particulars, kinds, facts, and resemblances, and recognize that even such 'simple' concepts as those of colors are the fruit of a long process of publicly reinforced responses to public objects (including verbal performances) in public situations, . . . we . . . *recognize that instead of coming to have a concept of something because we have already noticed that sort of thing, to have the ability to notice a sort of thing is already to have the concept of that sort of thing, and cannot account for it"* (EPM, p. 306).

[15] See EPM, p. 320, quoted above in note 5.

[16] P. 524 above.

[17] P. 525 above.

[18] In other words, one must distinguish two dimensions in the role played by semantical statements about overt linguistic performances as models for the concept of thoughts as episodes having aboutness or reference: (a) the dimension involving the semantical form itself, "S means p" being the model for "T is about p"; (b) the dimension in which the verbal-behavioral facts *implied* by semantical statements about overt linguistic performances are the model for the factual or descriptive character of mental episodes, their relationship *in the causal order* to one another and to overt behavior.

It is the *descriptive* structure of mental episodes which, as was written above, "we (reasonably) expect to interpret in terms of neurophysiological connections, as we have

538

succeeded in interpreting the 'atoms,' 'molecules,' etc. of early chemical theory in terms of contemporary physical theory." For a discussion of the logic of this 'interpretation' or 'fusion,' as it is sometimes called, see EPM, §§55, 58 and 40–41; also §§47–50 of my essay in this volume, particularly §49. For a reprise of the above analysis of the sense in which thoughts are really neurophysiological states of affairs, an analysis which defends the substance of the naturalistic-materialistic tradition while avoiding the mixing of categories characteristic of earlier formulations, see below, p. 536.

[19] P. 523 above.

[20] *Ibid.*

[21] "Imperatives, Intentions and the Logic of 'Ought'," *Methodos*, 8, 1956. See also §§77–78 of my essay in this volume.

[22] I now (March 1957) find it somewhat misleading (though not, as I am using these terms, incorrect) to say that statements as to what a person is thinking about *do not describe*, but, rather, *imply a description* of the person. This, however, is not because I reject any aspect of the above analysis, but because I am more conscious of the extent to which my use of the term "describe" is a *technical* use which departs, in certain respects, from ordinary usage. For the sort of thing I have in mind, see the discussion in §§78–79 of my essay in the present volume of the sense in which the world can 'in principle' be described without the use of either prescriptive or modal expressions. It is in a parallel sense that I would wish to maintain that the world can 'in principle' be described without mentioning either the *meaning* of expressions or the *aboutness* of thoughts.

[23] Herbert Feigl and Wilfrid Sellars (eds.), *Readings in Philosophical Analysis*. New York: Appleton-Century-Crofts, 1949.

Name Index

Name Index

Einstein, A., 327, 379n, 407, 483n
Elsasser, W. M., 376
Epstein, J., 392n

Fechner, T., 451
Feigl, H., 68, 130, 193n, 221, 222, 263n, 334n, 393n, 394n, 395n, 421, 425, 426, 427n, 430, 449, 453n, 507, 539n
Feyerabend, P. K., 393n, 430, 463
Flew, A., 172n, 483n
Foerster, H. von, 478n
Fox, S. W., 24
Frank, P., 483n
Frege, G., 418, 511, 520n
Freud, S., 82, 386, 388, 482
Freytag, W., 427n

Gaffron, M., 362
Galileo, G., 41, 207, 208
Gamow, G., 23
Gätschenberger, R., 446n, 447n, 483n
Gellhorn, E., 478n
Gellner, E. A., 172n
Gibson, J. J., 364
Ginsberg, A., 394n
Gold, T., 24
Goldschmidt, R., 24
Goodman, N., 204, 206, 227–242, 247, 248, 254, 269n, 392n, 426, 439
Graham, C. H., 367
Grünbaum, A., 393n, 484

Hampshire, S., 428n, 449n
Hare, R. M., 282n
Hartmann von, E., 426
Hayakawa, S. I., 27
Hebb, D. O., 478n, 480
Heider, F., 364
Hempel, C. G., 117, 118, 123, 124, 192, 193, 221, 222, 372, 376n, 393n, 414n, 427, 427n, 443, 483n
Henle, P., 414n
Hering, E., 413
Herrick, C. J., 478n
Hilbert, D., 121
Hobart, R. E., 382n, 389. See also Miller, D. S.
Hobbes, T., 382n
Holbach, Baron d', 371
Holt, E. B., 426, 520n
Hospers, J., 524
Hoyle, F., 24
Hull, C. L., 67, 68, 483n

Hume, D., 214, 215, 216, 217, 219, 220, 341, 352, 353, 371, 402, 426, 460, 464, 468
Husserl, E., 418
Huxley, T. H., 428

Jacobs, N., 389n, 427n
Jacoby, G., 446n
James, W., 407, 423n, 424n, 513, 518
Johnson, S., 115

Kaila, E., 201, 221, 414n, 483n
Kant, I., 307, 341, 353, 421, 451
Kaplan, A., 165n, 179, 260n, 483n
Kapp, R. O., 373, 377
Kaufmann, F., 389n, 427n
Keller, Helen, 433
Kemeny, J. G., 5, 14, 54, 376n
Kepler, J., 208
Kierkegaard, S., 499
Kneale, W. C., 167n, 208, 224, 267n, 289, 318, 327, 395n, 427n, 503
Koch, S., 364
Koffka, K., 380
Köhler, W., 363, 364, 380, 411, 413, 447n, 457n, 459, 468, 478n, 479, 483n
Kraft, V., 483n
Krech, D., 478n
Kronecker, L., 168n
Külpe, O., 426, 427n

Lashley, K. S., 363, 372, 479
Lean, M., 468n
Leibniz, G., 440, 463, 472
Lewin, K., 27, 68, 364, 483n
Lewis, C. I., 389n, 393n, 450n, 483n
Lewy, C., 392n
Lichtenberg, G. C., 334n
Lindzey, G., 394n
Locke, J., 224, 309, 382n
Lotze, H., 479
Lovejoy, A. O., 426, 427n
Lundberg, G., 498

MacCorquodale, K., 175, 394n
McCulloch, W. S., 19, 380, 457, 478n
Macdonald, M., 157n
McDougall, W., 373
Mach, E., 327, 371, 379n, 380n, 426, 468
MacKay, D. M., 423n
MacLeod, R. B., 364
Maeterlinck, M., 451
Mannheim, K., 18
Margenau, H., 414n

541

Name Index

Name Index

Subject Index

A priori, synthetic, 137, 421
Aboutness, 417, 507, 508, 530, 534, 538n18, 539n22: and behavior, 508; and mentalistic language, 508; of thoughts, 525
Acquaintance, 432, 433, 434, 435, 448, 450, 452–453, 462, 473, 476, 477, 478: and knowledge, 391, 393, 403, 404, 431, 435, 443, 446–450, 454, 457, 461, 474, 477; and concepts, 467
Act-psychology, 417
Ambiguity, 133: residual, 108
Analysis, 100–195, 529–537: content, 99; schools of, 99, 102; context, 99, 100, 100n2, 101n2, 160; extensional, 117; logical, 120, 141, 142, 375, 421–422; and definition, 139; paradox of, 154, 463, 537; formal, 168; statistical, 178; philosophical, 387, 396; conceptual, 452
Analytic propositions, 157–158. *See also Ex vi terminorum*
Analyticity, and synonymy, 90n29
Analytic-synthetic distinction, 137–138, 223n30
Atomism, 468n: and sense-data doctrine, 468
Axiom of Choice, 116
Axiomatic method, 89n12
Axioms, 78

Behavior, 20, 42, 476, 508, 509, 514, 527, 528, 530, 536, 538n18: molar, 67, 436, 437, 445, 447, 457; linguistic, 367, 405n, 508, 515, 527, 530, 538n5; rule-governed, 418; purposive, 419, 420, 480; and teleology, 474–475; explanation of, 481; unified micro-theory of, 507; and aboutness, 508; sign, 514; and thoughts, 522, 534, 536, 538n5; of physical objects, 526, 536
Behaviorism, 354, 368, 370, 380, 425, 429, 468n, 508, 521, 523: philosophical, 303, 347, 508, 535; logical, 373, 389, 399; crude, 393; neo-, 354; radical, 395, 429; linguistic, 424n; logical, 425, 429, 447, 476; methodological, 429
Believing, 522, 527: intentional character of, 521
Biology, 29n8: theories of, 89n12
Biophysics, 480
Brentano's thesis, 519ff

Calculus: propositional, 121; uninterpreted, 121
Causality, 58–59, 187, 194, 209, 223–224n40, 224n41, 225–248 passim, .248–307, 464: classical conception of, 88n7; discourse of, 188n72, 249, 253, 255, 257; Hume's theory of, 213, 215, 220, 285; classical entailment theories of, 289; principle of, 305, 306, 476–477; physical, 477. *See also* Modalities, causal
Common sense, philosophy of, 264
Concepts, 73, 167, 192, 193, 284, 374, 415, 433, 461–462, 464, 538n14: open, 52; explanatory, 70; theoretical, 78, 81, 82, 99, 188, 401, 424, 425, 431, 436, 444, 447–

Subject Index

448, 467, 481, 526; of physics, 90, 90n36, 465; cluster, 99, 175–180, 419; physical, 175n63, 371, 454, 456; formation of, 178, 450, 507; and theories, 179, 191; observational, 188; empirical, 197, 453; extensional, 218; framework of, 284n; "formal," 303; psychological, 371; mental, 377, 389, 406; behavioral, 389; and evidential bases, 401; of psychology, 426, 442, 509; of physicalism, 426; and raw feels, 431; neurophysiological, 442; spatio-temporal-causal, 451; phenomenal, 456, 457, 468n; psychoanalytic, 481, 482; and mentalistic vocabulary, 508; and overt behavior, 508; of mental episodes, 509; and meaning, 534; semantical, 536. See also Constructs; Dispositions; Entities; Language; Meaning

Conceptual system, 13, 28, 183, 225, 350, 351, 353, 375, 386, 408, 409, 421, 454, 456, 470, 474

Conditionals: counterfactual, 196–248, 269n, 309, 312, 324, 325, 325n, 326, 327, 329, 464; subjunctive, 202, 205, 214, 215, 217, 226, 236, 237, 245, 251, 254, 266, 272, 273, 297, 298, 322, 323, 326, 429; indirect confirmation of, 221n7; universal, 222n13; singular, 222n13; counter-identical, 323, 324. See also Hypotheticals; Implication

Confirmation, 208: degree of, 30n15; and truth, 200; paradox of, 221n5; direct, 221n7; indirect, 221n7; intersubjective, 385, 391, 400; of direct experience, 398–399; and meaning, 477. See also Evidence

Consciousness, 340, 341, 343, 348, 351, 352, 354, 370: states of, 332–353 passim; unity of, 353, 460; and ordinary language, 507; and behavior theory, 507; and molar psychophysics, 507; sensory, 507

Constructions, logical, 90n32, 371, 426, 456

Constructs: scientific (explanatory), 359; hypothetical, 91n51, 175, 385, 426, 447; theoretical, 434, 509. See also Concepts

Cosmology, 23, 24

Craig's Theorem, 76–80, 86, 92n59, 93n59, 93n61, 427

Cybernetics, and mind-body problem, 478–480

Data, 88n9, 334, 468: of direct experience, 392; phenomenal, 392, 428; private, 401, 402. See also Sense-data

Deduction, 45, 89n11, 197, 441n: and systematization, 38, 41, 75, 116, 117; and empirical science, 47, 89n12

Definition, 53, 61, 65–71, 74, 83, 89n11, 91n36, 92n55, 101n4, 114, 115, 122, 132, 134, 154, 161n49, 168, 172, 174n63, 175n63, 184, 281, 441n, 529–530: coordinating, 12; operational, 47, 50, 51, 198, 199, 212; explicit, 50, 52, 58, 59, 62, 66, 90n36, 91n38, 169, 191, 203, 210, 288, 404n; intensional, 54, 106; partial, 71; coordinative, 89n17, 405n; and science, 91n49, 106, 165; implicit, 99, 135, 168, 169, 405n; dictionary, 102, 103n6, 108, 113, 140, 141, 154, 155, 166; of class terms, 104; and description, 105, 169, 171; as substitution rules, 105–107, 124; and empirical truths, 110, 111–112; and language, 109, 111n8; ostensive, 113, 168, 404n, 405n; definition of, 113; contextual, 113, 135, 139, 168, 169, 170, 404n; recursive, 115, 136, 168, 170n58, 404n; and meaning, 115, 135, 405n; and law, 117, 147; and truth, 117, 137; extensional account of, 118, 198; in mathematics, 120, 168n57; as elimination rules, 121; ordinary sense of, 121; and translation, 133, 154; and object-language, 139; by postulate, 139, 167, 168; logical status of, 139, 165; in metalanguage, 139; stipulative, 140, 144, 146, 148, 150n39, 161n49; as rules, 149ff; borderline cases in, 162–163; conditional, 164ff, 404n; by example, 167n56, 169; lambda, 170n58; by correlative terms, 172; circularity in, 173; abbreviatory, 174; stipulative-ostensive, 404n; abstractive, 404n; of signs, 514–515; and intentionality, 517–518, 520n9

Description, 88n9, 127, 161, 165, 168, 188n72, 463, 511, 520n4, 524, 527, 528: definite, 124, 175n63, 177, 260n, 304; and definition, 158; theory of, 158, 161, 398, 478; meaning of, 161; and names, 162n50; language of, 282, 532; phenom-

545

Subject Index

incomplete, 99; statistical, 99; alternative, 184; as non-deductive, 192; analysis of, 192–195; in the behavioral sciences, 193; deductive model of, 193; in physical sciences, 193; probabilistic, 193, 385; in psychology, 194; in physics, 194; and prediction, 194n78, 384; and probability, 194; theoretical, 226, 263, 436, 526, 531; limitation of, 226; of behavior, 284n, 457, 481; logic of, 376n; methodology of, 376n; animistic, 383; retrodictive, 384; physical$_1$, 417, 422, 431; and description, 460; biopsychological, 475; physical$_2$, 431, 481; first-level, 482; neurophysiological, 482
Extension, of theoretical concepts, 467
Extensionalism, 217
Extra-sensory perception, 388

Falsification, 174n63, 320, 321
Formal mode, 322
Formalism, 167, 167n56
Free will, 389: problem of, 373, 382, 386
Functionalism, 167
Functors, 28, 91n38

Games, theory of, 150
General Systems Theory, 30n10, 480
Genetics, 20–22
Gestalt theory, 20, 354, 414: and isomorphism, 480; and biophysics, 480
Given, the, 391, 426, 460–461, 468: myth of, 521
Givenness, phenomenal, 419
Gresham's law, 17

Holism, and Gestalt philosophy, 414
Hypotheses, 29n2, 78, 317: cosmological, 31n36; empirical, 90n30; "higher level," 208, 209; psychophysiological, 482; and evidence, 503
Hypotheticals: general, 241, 242, 242n, 246–248, 252; complex, 245

Idealism, 301, 474
Identity, 440, 441, 444, 445, 447, 451, 456, 462: ψ-Φ, 46; of indiscernibles, 273, 440, 456, 463; personal, 330–353; meaning of, 398; in mathematics, 438; intensional, 439; in factual sciences, 439; extensional, 439, 440; analytic, 439, 441; empirical, 439, 467, 472, 477, 481; of universals, 440; kinds of, 440–441; theoretical, 447, 471, 477; psychophysiological, 463; logical, 471
Identity thesis, of mental and physical, 445, 446, 449, 457, 461, 463, 466, 470, 471–477, 484n
Implication, 223n24, 273: analytic, 196, 212; natural, 196, 197, 199, 200, 218, 220; material, 196, 197, 199, 212, 217, 219, 220–221n3, 224n48, 245; causal, 197, 212, 213, 214, 217, 218, 223n31, 223n32, 224n48, 251, 252; formal, 198; nomological, 212; probability, 214; extensional, 216, 217, 448; universal, 217; strict, 218, 224n48; paradoxes of, 197, 224n48; contextual, 254, 268, 269, 273, 280, 294, 296, 302; and meaning, 288. See also Conditionals
Indicators, 180n64
Induction, 271, 272, 278, 279, 286–288, 291–295, 298, 300, 304–306, 312, 313, 317, 324, 325, 328, 386: secondary, 290n; statistical, 290, 291, 293n, 295, 296, 300; problem of, 309, 436n; justification of, 314, 315
Inductive systematization, 40, 41
Inference, 251: deductive, 79; inductive, 79, 290n, 481; analysis of, 101n3; analogical, 481
Information theory, 28
Intelligence: concept of, 69; and purposive behavior, 412; and Φ_1 terms, 424

Subject Index

Intension, 282: and meaning, 467

Intention, 330, 349: expression of, 532; and prediction, 532

Intentionality, 373, 386–387, 413, 416–420, 445, 460, 507–539: Brentano's view of, 510ff; criteria of, 510–511; linguistic thesis of, 519; and definition, 520n9; categories of, 522, 530, 536; framework of, 530; source of, 533, 534; and thoughts, 534, 536

Interactionism, 371–389 passim, 400, 417, 428, 446, 474, 480, 481

Interpretative systems, 71–75, 92n56

Intervening variables, 48, 67, 175

Introjection, 455, 455n

Introspection, 42, 285n, 508, 527: and neurophysiological knowledge, 470

Isomorphism, 374, 456, 457, 461, 468, 470, 480

Kepler's laws, 37, 41

Knowledge, 220n1, 434: probable, 271, 272; intuitive, 432. *See also* Acquaintance, and knowledge; Description, knowledge by

Language, 82, 100, 182, 225, 312, 353, 409, 421, 470, 515, 519, 521, 525, 526, 527, 537: unity of, 4, 6; of logic, 46, 64, 251, 282; functions of, 71, 109; of science, 42, 43, 51, 57, 107, 168, 168n57, 174, 198, 225, 288, 302, 309, 374, 410, 436, 453; descriptive, stipulative use of, 74; reconstruction of, 101, 123, 468, 469; revision of, 109, 307; utility of, 111; and definition, 111n8; natural, 114, 141, 142, 191, 196, 523; artificial, 139, 189, 503; of rules, 148n38, 311; and use, 151, 303, 304, 389; disposition, 186; and logical modalities, 187, 251; and causal modalities, 187; causal, 188; applied, 189; extensional, 196, 203, 211, 214, 219, 222n17; prescriptive, 282, 527, 529, 531; and description, 282, 307, 532; and explanation, 307; ideally complete, 309; and inference rules, 329; structure of, 346, 348, 526; and experience, 367; mentalistic, 372, 507, 508; phenomenal, 372, 427, 429, 437, 442, 466, 467, 468n; private, 392–393, 402, 403, 404, 405n; and behavior, 411, 416, 418; physical, 425, 427, 448, 467, 481; of commonsense, 468; of behavior theory, 468n; unitary, 468, 469; and thoughts, 507–537 passim, 530, 533, 536, 538n18; of behavioristic, 508; of psychology, 508; intentional, 510–513, 515, 517; use of, 517, 520n8, 524, 527, 528, 530; construction of, 524; and meaning, 526; learning of, 527, 528; of justification, 527, 529; sign, 528; meaning of, 529, 530; discourse about, 530; of thoughts, 536; reporting role of, 538n5

   OBSERVATION, 42–93, 126, 126n24, 131, 166, 180, 182, 183, 184, 185n70, 186, 187, 188, 189, 192, 193, 263, 264, 372, 374, 377, 424, 425, 469

   THEORETICAL, 42–93, 125, 126, 131, 166, 167, 183, 185n70, 186, 188, 191, 192, 194, 263, 264, 359, 392, 394n, 424, 425, 436, 468n, 469, 538n5

   ORDINARY, 125, 167, 251, 254, 255, 256, 289, 302, 309, 328, 329, 366, 403, 411, 420, 421, 436, 456, 462, 508, 539n22: and scientific theories, 189; philosophy of, 264; and sensory consciousness, 507; and mentalistic terms, 508; and intentional sentences, 519. *See also* Concepts; Definition; Meaning

Laws, 29n2, 39, 41, 73, 84, 86, 88n6, 89n11, 90n23, 168, 170, 185, 188, 188n72, 192, 194, 203, 223n36, 224n46, 268, 270, 306, 318, 319, 321, 322, 324, 327, 328, 357, 374, 375, 376, 381n, 414, 415, 433, 440, 452, 473, 474, 478: unity of, 4; psychological, 19, 325, 355, 361, 499; general, 38, 40, 41, 45, 51, 57, 89n11, 178, 309, 310, 318; quantitative, 41; statistical, 41, 88n6, 214, 221n11, 299, 300, 381, 385; 441n; universal, 41, 88n7, 205, 291; containing theoretical terms, 45; as rules of inference, 93n70f, 309–329; bridge, 99, 193; nature of, 136n28, 301; correlation, 172, 428–430; and general statements, 186; formulation of, 186, 210; and observation, 192, 193; and conditionals, 202, 204; and evidence, 203; and universal propositions, 204; fundamental, 205; derived, 208; and explanation, 209; causal, 213, 214, 217, 221n11, 263, 292, 296; and lawlike statements, 222n, 299n; contrary-to-fact,

Subject Index

222n14; extensional interpretation of, 222n15; and counterfactuals, 233, 234, 241; and subjunctive conditionals, 236–237; as general hypotheticals, 248; and dispositions, 249; non-statistical, 263, 295; of logic, 318; and falsification, 320, 321; and deduction, 322; and structure dependence, 327, 328; indeterministic, 329; neurophysiological, 442

Learning, 19, 41, 528: Skinner's analysis of, 88n9; and intelligence, 419; theory of, 84, 93n67, 475

Logic, 29n1, 167n56, 329: propositional, 19; language of, 46, 64, 251, 282; deductive, 47, 133; truth-functional, 61; formal, 76, 167, 268; symbolic, 89n12, 91n41, 100, 170n58; and Craig's theorem, 93n61; non-formal, 121; and mathematics, 123n22; inductive, 133; of fact, 160; of fiction, 160; and psychology, 161n49; extensional, 167n56, 197, 198, 207, 209, 210, 214, 219, 224n44; modal, 245; traditional, 310; of explanation, 376n; concepts of, 524

Logical form, 167n56

Mach-Einstein program, 327
Mach's principle, 167, 379–380n
Material mode, 322
Materialism, 371, 383, 388, 429, 474
Mathematics, 29n1, 194n79: systems of, 89n12; Cantorian, 117; and logic, 123n22; formalization of, 168n57; discourse of, 287

Meaning, 90n25, 101n4–105, 113n11, 118, 174n63, 175, 175n63, 269, 287, 405n, 453, 469, 509, 516, 523, 526, 528, 529, 539n22: criterion of, 10, 93n67, 131, 377, 391, 392n, 393, 424n, 450, 477, 484n; and function, 100, 155; analysis of, 101n3, 164, 165; operational, 107; and definitions, 111; and rules, 114n12; and use, 142, 177, 525; pragmatic, 210; semantic, 210, 222n23; emotive pictorial, 220; and explicit definition, 288; concept of, 323; inner private, 345; and linguistic structure, 348; and behavior, 367; factual-empirical, 380; of scientific terms, 391; and verification, 393; conceptual, 466; and intension, 467; Frege's theory of, 511, 520n3; in natural language, 523; of thoughts, 524, 529, 530; and expression of thoughts, 526; and thoughts, 526, 535; and language, 530; and concepts, 534. See also Concepts; Definition; Language

Mechanics: Newtonian, 37, 38, 47, 48, 186, 381n; statistical, 441n
Memory, 436n
Mental states, 508, 509
Mentality: concept of, 411; criteria of, 415
Metaphysics, 464, 465: rationalistic, 305; Humean, 305; speculative, 370; panpsychistic, 446n; idealistic, 474; inductive, 474

Mind-body problem, 130, 370–497: Cartesian view of, 396; traditional, 507
Mind-body relation, 330–353: Cartesian view of, 331, 333, 336, 337, 339, 343
Minds, 370: of others, 349, 412n, 428; disembodied, 392n
Minnesota Center for Philosophy of Science, 102, 191, 223n33, 353n, 471n, 507
Modalities, 227, 277, 279, 283, 284, 296, 539n22: causal, 58–59, 90n24, 183, 185, 187, 194, 251, 272n, 278, 280, 302, 464; logical, 187, 251, 302; deontic, 302; sense, 474, 479

Models, 31n30, 31n32: mechanical, 31n31; and theories, 101, 538n6; and theoretical constructs, 509; nature of, 537n4
Monism, 396, 410, 437, 447n, 461, 474, 483: neutral, 371, 426, 446n; philosophical, 482, 483n

Monadology, of Leibniz, 472

Naturalism, 283
Necessity: nomological, 51; analysis of, 101n3; physical, 294; pragmatic, 327; natural, 328. See also Causality; Entailment; Ex vi terminorum; Laws

Subject Index

Neuroanatomy, 18
Neurochemistry, 18
Neurology, 19
Neurophysiology, 19, 31n24, 442, 445, 450, 455–456, 470, 478, 481
Nominalism, 86
Nomological net, 395, 433, 443, 444, 457, 465, 468, 469, 475: and rules of inference, 448
Norms, justification of, 400n
Numbers: theory of, 91n38; transfinite, 168n57, 190n73

Observables, 183, 185, 395, 508. See also Language, OBSERVATION
Ockham's razor, 386
Ontology, problem of, 264
Open texture, 260n
Operationism, 50, 166, 373, 395
Order, concept of, 31n38

Panpsychism, 446n, 451
Parallelism, 371, 376, 377, 380, 381, 382, 396, 428, 437, 446, 456, 472, 474, 475: scientific evidence for, 461; and identity doctrines, 463, 471, 472; language of, 479. See also Dualism; Isomorphism
Parapsychology, 388, 423n, 482
Parsimony, principle of, 386, 449, 461
Particulars: and universals, 456, 469; logical space of, 538n14
Pauli exclusion principle, 22
Perception, 19, 42, 331, 332, 341, 352, 362–364, 368, 397, 408, 431, 433, 434, 442, 443, 452, 468n: observable aspects of, 41; knowledge of, 361; and intentionality, 375; causal theory of, 382, 452; veridicality of, 407, 436n; and observation, 421; intentional acts in, 445; external, 462; sense, 462, 463
Phenomenalism, 303, 373, 425, 426, 427, 446n, 478: of Hume, 371; versus realism, 464; repudiation of, 464–465
Physical, definitions of, 421
Physical$_1$, 391, 422, 424, 428, 481: meaning of, 377, 454
Physical$_2$, 377, 391, 424, 481: defined, 377
Physicalism, 371, 426: of Carnap, 484n
Physics, 26, 28, 90n36, 91n49, 465, 524
Positivism, 264, 371, 373, 380, 426: and Vienna Circle, 393
Postdiction, 37, 38, 39, 40, 87n1. See also Retrodiction
Postulates, 12
Pragmatics, 523
Pragmatism, principle of, 424n. See also Truth, pragmatic theory of
Prediction, 37, 38, 39, 40, 42, 67, 87, 87n3, 88n6, 306, 317, 325, 326, 329, 375, 377, 379, 384, 385, 499, 500, 501, 502, 504, 505: in terms of observables, 45; and stipulative definition, 150n39; and explanation, 194n78; statistical, 384; physical$_1$, 417, 431, 436; physical$_2$, 431; of human behavior, 435; of mental states, 471; actuarial, 501; and intention, 532
Prescription, language of, 527
Presuppositions: logical, 160; pragmatic, 160; causal, 209; and counterfactuals, 235; metaphysical, of science, 401n
Privacy, 400, 401, 402: absolute, 509
Probability, 40, 166n54, 194n80, 221n11, 221n12, 293, 500, 501, 503: statistical, 39, 93n59, 194; logical, 88n4, 93n59; inductive, 88n4, 503, 504, 505; concept of, 185, 194, 195; of an hypothesis, 194; frequency concept of, 316; nature of, 503; and intentionality, 512

Subject Index

Protocol statements, 404
Psychical research, 482
Psychoanalysis, 394, 436, 461, 481, 482: and neurophysiological theories, 481–482
Psychokinesis, 423n
Psychologism, 418
Psychology, 8, 50, 91n49, 354–369, 370, 394n, 456, 481, 498–506, 508, 513: Gestalt, 20, 354, 480; generalizations in, 41; and logic, 161n49; theories of, 388; methods of, 507; behavioristic, 507, 508, 509, 523, 537n4; and intentional language, 510; experimental, 527. *See also* Behaviorism
Psychophysics, and sensory consciousness, 507
Psychophysiology, 458, 459, 469, 478, 480
Psychotherapy, 499, 505

Quantum theory, 91n36

Ramsey-sentences, 80, 81, 85, 86, 87, 93n68
Rationalism, classical, 288
Raw feels, 372, 375, 380, 390, 393, 399, 411, 412, 415, 416, 419, 427–429, 431, 432, 437, 445, 447, 454–458, 465, 468, 475, 477: as intersubjective (physical$_1$), 385; and emergence, 386; causal efficacy of, 428, 475; and neural processes, 445, 446, 448, 478; "private," 462
Realism, 393, 447n, 478, 514: semantic, 91n51; new, 264, 513, 514; critical, 426, 427n, 453, 483n; versus phenomenalism, 464
Reconstruction, 373, 468, 469
Reduction, 4ff, 29n5, 29n8, 29n10, 29–30n10, 118, 125, 126, 187, 188, 192, 465: epistemological, 3, 5; partial, 5; logical, 5; micro, 29n6, 30n13, 31n24
Reduction sentences, 52, 55, 58, 71, 72, 74, 83, 90n24, 90n30, 91n49, 210, 211, 221n4, 223n30: bilateral, 51, 165n52; and causal modalities, 90n24
Reductionism, 18, 371, 427: definability thesis of, 125, 128–130
Reference, 173: and evidence, 395
Relativity, 329n, 408, 441n
Res cogitans, 406
Res extensa, 406
Resonance, chemical, 22
Retrodiction, 87n1, 306, 329. *See also* Postdiction
Rules, 93n59, 99, 115n13, 136, 140n32, 148, 150, 180, 190n73: translation, 72, 135, 153, 155, 158, 162–165, 168–175, 183, 192; of inference, 87, 92n59, 289, 448; correspondence, 89n17, 167, 168, 193, 377, 394, 426, 467; of theory interpretation, 92n59; of logic, 92n59; substitution, 108, 111, 112, 115, 118, 122, 169; and meaning, 114n12, 146, 171, 177, 312; elimination, 120; semantic, 126n24, 164, 453, 467; and definitions, 120, 139–145; and games, 142–144; application, 164, 168, 174n63; and theories, 190; material, 309; formal, 309; vocabulary for, 311; and linguistic behavior, 405n; and behavior, 418; pragmatic, 453, 467; syntactical, 453, 467; ψ-Φ correlation, 475. *See also* Laws, bridge; Laws, as rules of inference

Science: "completed," 127, 128; metaphysical presuppositions of, 401n; method of, 482
Semantics, 82, 417–418, 523: discourse of, 526, 527, 530, 536
Sensation, 42, 330
Sense: impressions, 219; qualities, 401, 409, 410; modalities, 474, 479
Sense-data, 90n32: doctrine, 468. *See also* Data
Signs, 514–515
Simplicity, 5. *See also* Parsimony; Ockham's razor
Skolem paradox, 117

Subject Index

Sociology, 18
Solipsism, 469
Space: physical, 407–409, 459; phenomenal, 407–409, 459
States, and properties, 226
Steady state theory, 24, 25
Stroke-function, 120, 122
Structuralism, 450
Subconscious, 405, 406
Substance, 333, 409, 452: and states of consciousness, 333; metaphysical, 401
Synonymy, 113: and analyticity, 90n29
Systems: deductive, 46, 313; construction of, 92n59; formal, 116; logical, 134. See also Conceptual system

Teleology, 373: and mechanisms, 413; and behavior, 474–475
Theories, 29n2, 30n13, 30n14, 42, 81, 86, 93n60, 167, 183, 188, 189, 328, 415, 444, 449, 452, 464, 469, 472, 482, 508, 530, 539n18: cosmological, 25; micro-reducing, 31n30, 31n32; learning, 42; mathematical, 47; psychological, 49, 388; spatio-temporal continuous, 68; systematizing function of, 75; deductively formulated, 88n8; and empirical data, 89n11; biological, 89n12; formalization of, 92n59; interpreted, 93n67, 93n68; as inferential principles, 93n70; Skinner's definition of, 183n66; and unobservable entities, 190n73; intervening variable, 192; nature of, 263n, 537n4; construction of, 386, 449, 450, 507, 509; neurophysiological, 481; role of, 537n4; and model, 538n6. See also Language, theoretical
Thermodynamics, classical, 441n
Thing-kinds, 224n46, 255–261, 263–266, 451, 526: words for, 250, 252, 259, 260, 261, 266; micro-, 264; molar-, 264; identifying traits of, 264, 265; properties of, 264
Thing-language, 31n33, 371, 443
Thomism, neo-, 264
Thoughts, 284, 331, 332, 334n, 375, 381n, 402, 403, 405n, 412, 442, 445, 446, 509, 516, 521–528, 533–535, 537: framework of, 284n, 522, 530, 534–563; unconscious, 482; and language, 507–537 passim, 538n18; and behavior, 522, 536; and theoretical entities, 522; as inner speech, 522; and meaning, 526, 529, 535; expression of, 527, 529, 533–535, 538n5; as theoretical episodes, 527; meaning of, 530; aboutness of, 530, 539n22; as sources of intentionality, 533, 534; and verbal behavior, 534; language of, 536; content of, 536; description of, 536; logic of, 536; and intentionality, 536; discourse about, 536; and privileged access, 536, 538n5; and neurophysiological episodes, 537; and verbal behavior, 538n5
Time: phenomenal, 408; physical, 408
Token-reflexive terms, 449n
Truth: semantical theory of, 82; analytic, 136; definitional, 117, 137; and rules of use, 137; concepts of, 222n23; mathematical, 247; pragmatic theory of, 513–514, 518. See also Analytic Propositions; Ex vi terminorum
Truth-condition, 209, 223n27
Truth-functionality, 196
Turing-computability, 170n58
Type-token distinction, 137n29
Types, theory of, 371, 456, 478

Unconscious, 383n, 405, 406, 419, 420, 446, 461, 481, 482
Uniformity axiom, of Burks, 223n32
Unity of science, 3–29, 126
Universals, 439, 440, 463: and particulars, 456, 469

Vagueness, 111n8, 260n: intensional, 164

Subject Index

Verification, 62, 221n7: conditions of, 210; method of, 338; methodology of, 355; direct and indirect, 449n
Vienna Circle, and meaningfulness, 393
Vitalism, 379, 383, 447n

Weber-Fechner law, 19
Wiedemann-Franz law, 440

C